Culture in Practice

Culture in Practice

Selected Essays

Marshall Sahlins

ZONE BOOKS · NEW YORK

2000

© 2000 Marshall Sahlins
ZONE BOOKS
611 Broadway, Suite 608
New York, NY 10012

Printed in the United States of America.

Distributed by The MIT Press,
Cambridge, Massachusetts, and London, England

Library of Congress Cataloging-in-Publication Data

Sahlins, Marshall David, 1930–
    Culture in practice : selected essays / Marshall Sahlins.
        p.   cm.
    Includes bibliographical references.
    ISBN 0-942299-37-X (cloth).
    1. Culture. 2. Civilization. 3. Anthropology.
I. Title.
HM101.S168   1999
306 — dc21   99-11469
                                                    CIP

Contents

Acknowledgments

Peter Sahlins, Ramona Naddaff, and Meighan Gale put in heroic work to make this book possible. I am deeply grateful to them. More than I can say.

Introduction[*]

Written over the course of thirty years, the texts collected here represent a temporal succession of interests and topics, if not exactly a chronological sequence of publication. The studies of Part One, "Culture," appearing in the 1960s and 70s, are conceptual exercises on the nature of culture and comparative reflections on differences among cultures. Part Three, "Culture in Practice," consists of work done in the 1980s and 90s, usually more historical than the earlier essays and generally more grounded ethnographically. This movement from theory to history and ethnography — rising from the abstract to the concrete — is mediated by the essays of Part Two, "Practice," which are about the U.S. war in Vietnam and the American antiwar movement of the 1960s. The "political" essays of Part Two, largely accounts of personal experiences, not only mediate the movement toward cultural specificity but also help to account for it. Still, in all change there is continuity, a point I would argue as much for biography as for culture itself. Certain essays of the 1990s, especially the final one, "The Sadness of Sweetness" on the native cosmology of Western anthropology, return to earlier habits of conceptual high-flying.

There is another continuity, or at least a theme developing steadily through these texts, which has to do with the cultural integrity of the indigenous peoples. More and more, I am convinced,

[*] Several passages of this Introduction are repeated from my essay, "Two or Three Things That I Know About Culture," *Journal of the Royal Anthropological Institute* 5 (1999).

9

these peoples are "marginal" to history and modernity in nobody's eyes but our own. Indeed, at the point of the social action, the field on which indigenous peoples struggle to encompass what is happening to them in the terms of their own world system, theirs is the encompassing move on a peripheral culture of modernity. Just so, the essays of this book concern the cultural distinctiveness of the peoples, not only apart from or before Western imperialism but even as they endure the world-capitalist juggernaut.

Perhaps I can put the organization and movement of these collected studies into relief by an apparently far-fetched, yet curiously analogous, academic comparison. The analogy to Catherine Gallagher's reflections on the history of literary criticism since the 1960s (1997) is joined by a common interest in "forms of endangered specificity": a nostalgia for distinctive works of culture in either case, but in Gallagher's usage a reference to the integrity and autonomy of the literary text as once celebrated by the New Criticism — now also an endangered species. Indeed, the juxtaposition of endangered differences would be no great epistemological stretch if it is true, as Gallagher says, that the New Criticism's regard for the work in itself, for its noninterchangeability, was an aesthetic reaction to the domination of the market economy and the commodification of everything. In a broadly parallel way, the anthropological practices of relativism and historicism offered in the present book, above all the attention to the symbolic complexity of cultural orders, are motivated by the same general antitheses between Western utilitarianism and the specificity of other cultures. Manifold are the laments for works of art in the age of mechanical reproduction.

Yet what throws the anthropology represented here into relief is the way its evolving sense of cultural specificity crossed the path of humanist "cultural studies" that were going in the opposite direction. In the move from the New Criticism to poststructuralism, particular cultural works got dissolved in general discursive orders. Interesting that one can date this conceptual crisscross to the late 1960s and early 1970s, the time of the Vietnam War — hence its transitional role in the organization of this book.

10

The Vietnam War was a major intellectual watershed in the social sciences and humanities, at least in America; and particularly in the academy, it turned into the longest decade of the twentieth century. No doubt, it is too facile to say that the spectacle of the powerful United States beating up on the Vietnamese, or getting beaten up by the Vietnamese peasants, could affect cultural thought in similarly contrasting ways. One might be impressed either by the world domination or the local resistance, with cultural hegemony or indigenous autonomy — an alternative that continues to be the major axis of anthropological interest and argument right to the present moment. Perhaps because the humanities have always subsisted on inhumanity, as Jacques Barzun says, so many of that persuasion were disposed to fight the powers rather than to celebrate the cultures. Poststructuralism, postmodernism, and other afterological studies developed a sense of cultural determinism so oppressive, an idea of social order so totalizing, as to conjure up the "superorganic" notions of culture I had learned as a student in the 1950s from the writings of Alfred Kroeber and, especially, the teachings of Leslie White at the University of Michigan (Kroeber 1948, White 1949).

The village atheist of modern anthropology, a homegrown American radical, Leslie White (1900–1975) was noted for maverick theories of culture that somehow accommodated the irreconcilable combination of a positivist materialism and a foundationalist symbolism. Aimed at the discovery of thermodynamic laws of cultural evolution, White's positivism also entailed a metaphysics of cultural causation so total as to make its providential older cousin, the Invisible Hand of the market society, seem indeed like a reign of freedom. Culture, for White, was an independent, self-moving order, of which human action could only be the expression. Culture was determining, individual subjects determined. In relation to this superorganic cultural system, White once wrote, the individual is like a pilotless aircraft controlled from the ground by radio waves (1949:157).

How like the contemporary theory of "discourse" taking off in the humanities since the 1960s — and latterly invading a certain anthropology. As Foucault famously remarked, "it is a matter of

11

depriving the subject (or its substitute) of its role as originator, and of analyzing the subject as a variable and complex function of discourse" (Foucault 1984:118).[1] One could easily substitute White's "culture" for Foucault's "discourse" in this sentence without any apparent offense to the ideas of either. Indeed, a good many anthropologists have in recent years traded in their old models of "culture" for Foucauldian "discourse" — all the while disclaiming the "reified," "essentialized," and "totalized" character of the obsolete culture concept. They speak easily of discourse as "the process through which social reality comes into being," of how it selectively determines what can be said, perceived, or imagined (for example, Escobar 1995). "Discourse" is the new cultural superorganic — made even more draconian as the expression of a "power" that is everywhere, in all quotidian institutions and relations. I wonder if White and Kroeber had developed the sense of people being the moral and libidinous victims of the superorganic, they could have gotten away with it for a much longer time.

In a complementary act of moral highgrounding, too many anthropologists have also followed the advanced practitioners of cultural studies in condemning their discipline's traditional appreciation of cultural diversity as, in effect, a hegemonic act of differencing. The concept of culture is an instrument of discrimination — a functional idea, incidentally, that likewise supposes such "culture" is an all-powerful system of coercion. By so attending to cultural differences, the argument runs, anthropologists manage to "incarcerate" the peoples in their otherness, and thus conspire in the work of Western imperialism (Appadurai 1988, Abu-Lughod 1991, Young 1995). But, like all functionalizing arguments, this one bargains away (actual) content for (presumed) effect, what culture is for what it does, thus giving up what we know about it in order to understand it. The move forecloses any serious interest in the ways different peoples have meaningfully constructed their existence: just the issues developed in the later studies (Part Three) of this book. Leaving White's culturology, I got to wonder at cultures-in-themselves, and from that, the ways people indigenize their modernity and their history — the forms of their endangered specificity.

12

Yet that conceptual move was already built into the contradictions of my training. To speak of the ways in which people meaningfully construct their existence goes back to the other, symbolic side of Leslie White's anthropology. The symbol is "the origin and basis of human behavior," as White put it in the title of a well-known article; that was a position I was not then, nor have ever been since, prepared to give away. No ape, he used to say, could appreciate the difference between holy water and distilled water — since there isn't any, chemically. Nor does any other animal organize the avoidances and alliances of its reproductive strategies on meaningful grounds, as by historically contingent concepts of beauty and sexual morality. How would an ape know that a second cross-cousin was marriageable and a parallel cousin not? This ordering (and disordering) of the world in symbolic terms is the singular capacity of the human species. But it is not in itself a genetic capacity: witness the various human forms of life, the cultures.

It deserves notice that White was writing of the symbolic construction of the human condition at roughly the same time, and in the same general way, as a number of prominent intellectuals, among them, Susanne Langer, Kenneth Burke, and Ernst Cassirer. Langer and Cassirer, at least, he had read and appreciated. He was also one of the few anthropologists of his day (other than linguists) to engage the understandings of Ferdinand de Saussure and John Locke in the determination of the nature of human signifying. In Locke's *Essay Concerning Human Understanding* (1689), White would have found expositions of the notion that names — specifically "general names" and names of "complex ideas" — do not stand for the perceptible characteristic of things but ideas people hold of things; which explains how it is that people are able to classify ("sort") and relate the objects of experience in different ways — according to the "Fashions, Customs and Manners of the Country," as Locke put it. True, White was a convinced technological determinist. He insisted that people who have hand axes as their principal tools, hunters and gatherers, must have a correspondingly simple social order and limited (true) ideas of the cosmos. They could have no better ideas of the world than their technological practice revealed to them, nor any society

more complex than what was necessary to wield a simple technology. White liked to quote Marx to the effect that the hand mill
gave us society with a sovereign and the steam mill, industrial capitalism. Yet White also argued that this determining technology,
even so simple an instrument as a hand axe, was also an idea.
Fashioned according to the customs of the country, an axe was a
symbolic phenomenon, as much in regard to its mode of production as to its values and purposes as an object. It could be an object of property, for example, but that is not one of its properties
as an object. Thus, for White, symbolicity encompassed the technological determination of the symbolic.

White referred to Saussure — but not, except in profound an-
tipathy, to Franz Boas. Too bad: Boas's famous cultural epistemology, his observations on the selective cultural organization of
experience — the seeing eye as an organ of tradition — would have
made a fine complement to White's symbolic problematic, had
personalities and rivalries been otherwise. Certainly, in respect to
concepts of culture, White was much closer to the Germanic-
American anthropology of Boas than the specifically *social* anthropology of British and French derivation associated particularly
with Radcliffe-Brown (1881–1955). Settling in the United States
subsequent to his own intellectual formation, Boas (1858–1942)
became the dominant academic figure of American anthropology
in the first half of the twentieth century. Through him and his students, notably Ruth Benedict, the traditions of Herder, Dilthey,
and their like on the relativity and semanticity of cultures achieved
novel ethnographic realizations. In contrast, Radcliffe-Brown from
the 1930s was turning certain readings of Emile Durkheim — and,
beyond that, a certain social science positivism inherited from the
Enlightenment through Comte, J.S. Mill, and Herbert Spencer —
into the famous paradigm of structural-functionalism.

By comparison to American cultural anthropologists, however,
this British moiety of social anthropology had limited views of, or
uses for, "culture." It seems, rather, that culture was assimilated to
the received Anglo-French tradition of "civilization," as something of an ideological overlay on the more basic stuff of human
behavior and interaction. For structural functionalists, culture

14

was the ideational and representational complement of the real object of their anthropological science, which was "social structure" or "the system of social relations." In this view — which is still commonplace in the Western social sciences — culture is the expressive and customary means by which a social system is maintained.[2]

For social anthropologists in those halcyon days of positivism — that is, before the 1960s — the concept of culture had obvious epistemological deficiencies, even apart from its popularity in America. For one, cultural phenomena were merely contingent in relation to the systematic character of the social structures — of which culture, indeed, was merely the idiom. Christian men take off their hats when entering a house of god and Muslims wash their feet. The difference in customs is incidental to the expression of deference to the divine master of the house, which is their common raison d'être. Indeed, as customs, these acts are altogether distinct as well as historically contingent; whereas, the social relations they manifest are of a type and generalizable across societies. Thus, one can have a *science* of society but only a *history* of culture.[3]

To this "natural science of society," Radcliffe-Brown added some famous refinements of the body-mind dualism underlying the society-culture distinction (1940, 1957). Thinking (it seems) of the insubstantiality of ideas or traditions by contrast to the corpo-reality of acting persons, for him culture was "an abstraction." It was without empirical presence or effect, by comparison to the reality, observability, and efficacy of social relationships. Can you imagine two cultures coming together and producing a third, he asked, the way American anthropologists (and Bronislaw Malinowski) talk of "culture contact"? The idea that culture could move a person to action was as absurd to Radcliffe-Brown's thinking as holding a quadratic equation responsible for murder. Indeed, he had a point, if it was that people, not cultures, are the agents of social action; and perhaps also a more complex one, if it was that social action is no prescriptive or mechanical trope of the type cultural stimulus–individual response, the way White too often pretended.[4]

On the other hand, White could meet Radcliffe-Brown's objections on equally simple grounds — notably by an adaptation of Durkheimian arguments about the facticity of the social fact, to the effect that cultural forms, ideas, and objects are likewise realia of human experience, though not necessarily substances like physical things. So people may indeed commit murder or suicide because of their commitments to certain culturally specific moral sentiments. Nor are we dealing here with abstractions:

> Words are culture traits. Why call them abstractions any more than the bark of a dog or the quack of a duck?... Polygynous households are culture traits. But why call one husband and three wives an abstraction any more than one atomic nucleus and three electrons?... A wild horse is not an abstraction. Why call a domestic horse (a culture trait) one? (White 1949:96–97)

And of course, such "culture traits" were no less empirical than social forms. Indeed, one of them, the polygynous household, *is* a social form. So which is it, culture or society? What is the anthropological object, cultural order or social structure? Those were real ontological cockfights in the good old days.

The aftereffects can be traced in the studies of this book which, following White and Boas, are informed by a comprehensive sense of culture as the order of the symbolic, thus inclusive of Radcliffe-Brown & Co.'s system of social relations.[5] By this determination, the culture concept encompasses any and all forms of human practice, including the social relationships thereof, everything constituted and organized symbolically. The difference from Radcliffe-Brown's position is that the system of social relations, which for him was distinct from the so-called culture, is itself culture. Men, women, motherhood, criminals, gods, nations, hunting parties, and kings are symbolically construed persons, groups, or relations. The culture of a people — "a culture" — includes their social structures as well as their economy, their technology, their language, and their ideas. One might well ask what else an anthropologist could mean by "culture" or "a culture," were it not so common, however, for humanists and social scientists to remain unconverted from the original derivation of the Latin *cultura* as modes of cultivation or mentation (R. Williams 1983). For too many, "culture" still has this predominantly aesthetic or intellectual signification. Hence such ordinary expressions of the social science tongue as "the cultural aspects of nationalism," "cultural factors in economic development," "the culture of politics," "the interaction of culture and society," and the like. But again, since economy and polity, just as society, are constituted and orchestrated by meanings, since they are culture, such notions of "cultural factors" are ungrammatical in my book — as you shall see.

Given these views of culture, one can also see what kind of crisis the anthropological concept was experiencing in the 1960s, as the development of contradictory theoretical forces threatened not simply to pull it apart but to do away with it altogether. Endemic contradictions between the material and the symbolic in the Whitean model of culture made it vulnerable to criticism; but this was not the only expression of the problem. Translated into the going Marxist terms, White's problem was that the superstructure included the "economic basis." Indeed, something like that possibility was afflicting Marxist theory also, which set it to producing epicycles of reciprocal influences of ideology on the economy or other such Ptolemaic complications of the original. (This was the period of "the discovery of the true Marx," what Marx really said, or else of Marx Himself, "Himself" being the one whose theory actually covered all the apparent exceptions and was known solely to the author of the commentary demonstrating this, as opposed to the others who were acquainted with Marx but not Himself.) In my intellectual situation, the 1960s culture crisis pitting the material against the symbolic was exacerbated by the developing antithesis between domestic ideas of cultural ecology and the importation of French structuralism.

Lévi-Strauss's works were appearing in English translation: *Structural Anthropology* and *Totemism* in 1963, *Tristes Tropiques* in 1965, *The Savage Mind* in 1966. Of course, I was already preadapted to appreciate the broad and complex symbolic structures of culture they revealed. On the other hand, structuralism only helped to develop a climate of theoretical schismogenesis, an atmosphere of irreconcilable differences, since the cultural ecologists at Michigan and elsewhere with whom I also shared interests were in the process of doing away with culture altogether. For them, "culture" was just a name for species-specific behaviors, to be understood as and by their adaptive effects rather than their meaningful contents, hence no more worthy of being singled out as phenomena of a distinctive kind than the behaviors of any other animal species. Everything could be reduced to behavior, utilitarian behavior at that, and the symbol was lost.

Clearly, structuralism, as it specified the symbolic order of economic and ecological practice, was thus eccentric to much of utilitarian midwestern civilization as one knew it.[6] What fitted it naturally with my own predilections was that it transcended all infrastructure-superstructure distinctions by integrating both in common cultural logics. Relations of production were the complement, in a certain register, of symbolic categories of persons, meaningful orderings of landscapes, values of objects, and purposes of consumption which themselves were cosmological in scope. How would one understand the division of labor by sex in the Fiji Islands? Men and women worked not only in differentiated tasks but in distinctive areas of village, land, and sea according to an ontologic of persons and space that was reiterated through the culture: from legends of divinity and the structures of kingship to relations of exchange and the architecture of houses. These symbolic schemes defined the values and uses of things, yet they could not themselves be justified by an "objective" calculus of material rationality. Closer to home and utilitarian economics, neither could material rationality explain the value (including the price) that Americans put on steak or roast beef as compared to tongue or kidneys. True, in preparing a dinner for an important occasion, the rational choice would be to spend one's scarce pecuniary resources on steak, but all this proves is that not everything in economic rationality is economically rational. The essay *"La Pensée Bourgeoise"* included in this volume (Chapter Five) — as well as the book from which it was taken, *Culture and Practical Reason* (1976) — is in homage to the pervasiveness of rational-cultural logics of the concrete, that is, even among us and in the economic basis.

In a famous passage of *La Pensée sauvage* [*The Savage Mind*], Lévi-Strauss made something of the same point, with due homages to Marx: "Without questioning the undoubted primacy of infrastructures, I believe that there is always a mediator between *praxis* and practices, namely the conceptual scheme by the operation of which matter and form, neither with any independent existence, are realized as structures, that is as entities which are both empirical and intelligible" (1966:130). But if matter and form, having no independent existence, are realized as structures through the mediation of the cultural scheme — and presumably differently in different cultural schemes — what then remains of the "primacy of infrastructures"? I came away from all this with the idea that economic activity or the all-determining praxis was a particular functional expression of a more general cultural logic. The pervasiveness of the symbolic resolved some of the tension between utilitarian determinations of culture and cultural determinations of utility. It could even integrate the contradiction, insofar as (invoking Augustine) peoples differ by what they love — their differentiating utilities are symbolically ordered preferences.

Reaching as it did into relations of production, kinship and marriage rules, mythology, rituals, artistic motifs, determinations of use-values, and more, the depth and complexity of cultural codes that so fascinated structuralism had another, complementary effect (for me) on the going anthropological positivism of the 1950s and 60s. In any given place — in Fiji, in the Yukon Delta, in an Amazonian village — untold numbers of intellectuals for untold generations had been fashioning meaningful connections between various aspects of their lives into intricate relations and patterns, and who was I or any fly-by-night ethnographer to think he could understand it all by parachuting down on the people for a year or two? One had to question, as Clifford Geertz has put it recently, "the sheer possibility of anyone, insider or outsider, grasping so vast a thing as an entire way of life and finding the words to describe it" (1995:43). What now seemed particularly feckless was the theoretical operation of research-and-destroy — to continue the historically appropriate war metaphors — built into a cultural anthropology of natural science pretensions. I mean the 1950s and 60s anthropology of lawful generalizations, especially about cultural evolution. Where such scientific law is the objective and form of knowledge, any particular culture is just one instance more or less — a specimen of a class, of interest only in that capacity and not in itself or as such. The law is what is wanted, not the culture.

Boas had talked about this devaluation of the phenomenon in a famous article, "The Study of Geography," first published in 1887, a work that served as precursor to his anthropological perspectives (1968:639–47). The article drew a series of contrasts between the methods of the physical sciences and what Boas called *cosmography*: a multivalent distinction that invoked venerable oppositions of science and history, objectivity and subjectivity, and classicism and romanticism. Troubled by the analytic dismemberment of geography into its natural science components — geology, hydrology, climatology, geophysics, and so on — Boas regretted that this also meant the deconstruction of the geographical phenomenon as it was presented to experience, hence of any knowledge of geographical "facts" as such. This would be an obvious consequence for any geopolitically defined space: there could be no geography of Germany or the United States, for example. But, equally, the Rocky Mountains or the Mississippi River Valley would only be of passing and partial interest, interest only in certain of their aspects, if the concern were mountain formation or river drainage hydraulics. The Rockies become worthy of our attention only insofar as they are generically comparable to other mountain chains; whatever specifically made and distinguished them as the Rocky Mountains would be on that very account excluded. Scientific realism thus had a way of subsuming empirical phenomena in general classes, which also subtracted them as such from geography. Hence another of Boas's epistemological regrets: once the purpose of scientific generalization was achieved, the particular mountain range or river valley would be intellectually discounted. "The physicist," wrote Boas, "compares a series of similar facts from which he isolates the general phenomenon which is common to all of them. Henceforth the single facts become less important to him, as he lays stress on the general laws alone" (1966a [1896]:641). Still, there is the Rocky Mountains. One may be interested in knowing them because they are there. Nor could a cosmographer be satisfied with any explanation that did not account for them as they specifically are, in their characteristics as the Rockies rather than simply as mountains:

> Cosmography, as we may call this science, considers every phenomenon as worthy of being studied for its own sake. Its mere existence entitles it to a full share of our attention, and knowledge of its existence and evolution in space and time fully satisfies the student, without regard to the law which it corroborates or which may be deduced from it. (*Ibid.*:642)

Here is another "form of endangered specificity." Boas would rescue it by history and the cosmographic disposition anthropology came to know as cultural relativism. In anthropology, the one move and the other required the submission of the analyst, the knowing scientific subject, to the arrangement of the culture, to its own meaningful construction — as opposed to an analytic dismemberment into classes which loses the culture's specific characteristics. Relativism in this methodological sense, however, does not mean that any culture or custom is as good as any other, if not better; instead, it is the simple prescription that, in order to be intelligible, other people's practices and ideals must be placed in their own context, understood as positional values in a field of their own cultural relationships, rather than appreciated in terms of intellectual and moral judgments of our making. Relativism is the provisional suspension of one's own judgments in order to situate the practices at issue in the historical and cultural order that made them possible. Some of the articles of the present work address these moral (and political) perplexities, in particular, "The Discovery of the True Savage" (Chapter Twelve). Or again in "What is Anthropological Enlightenment" (Chapter Fifteen) we see what respect for endangered specificity followed from famous nineteenth-century attempts to classify cultures in progressive stages for the purpose of determining laws of their evolution. E.B. Tylor, in arguing the validity of such categorical procedures, could cite with approval Dr. Johnson's judicious dictum that "one set of savages is like another" (1903: vol. 1:6).

With too much generosity, Boas had accorded this kind of

21

"scientific" classification all the honors of "objectivity," while modestly and paradoxically devaluing the cosmographic attitude as "subjective" because it was rationalized by an experiential relation to the object of study. But, of course, he could as easily have turned these designations around, as in effect he did later when criticizing the likes of Tylor and Morgan for violating the distinctive empirical characteristics of the cultural object — that is, by putting it in a class of like objects (clan, totem, mask, representational art), though in fact the so-called totemism of Kwakiutl differed from that of Ojibway in meanings, properties, and origins. The category as such was a category mistake. Science in this regard was a kind of violence perpetrated on the cultural object rather than an objective-empirical respect. The paradox was already present in "The Study of Geography," when Boas distinguished the two forms of desire — two forms of masculine desire, some might say — respectively motivating science and cosmography. Contemplating the attractions of harmony, proportion, and order, science was founded on an "aesthetic impulse," a desire to render the world in beautiful systematicities. But the "affective impulse" of the cosmographer was something else, clearly more sexy intellectually, for unlike the law-searching and fact-dominating physicist, the cosmographer "holds to the phenomenon which is the object of his study, may it occupy a high or low rank in the system of physical sciences, and lovingly tries to penetrate its secrets until every feature is plain and clear. This occupation with the object of his affection affords him a delight not inferior to that which the physicist enjoys in his systematical arrangement of the world" ([1887] 1968:645).

For the sheer delight in the logical complexity of its connections, structuralism in the 1960s and 70s could likewise turn one's attention singularly to "the phenomenon which is the object of his study"; but protest against the Vietnam War could also help to transform a cultural physicist into a cosmographer. I already alluded to some of the obvious ways in which sympathy and even admiration for the Vietnamese struggle, coupled to moral and political disaffection with the American war, might undermine an anthropology of economic determinism and evolutionary development.[7] But it was not just the spectacle of the neolithic beating up on the industrial revolution — something of a cartoonish image I couldn't shake during a brief tour of Vietnam in 1965, which haunts "The Destruction of Conscience in Vietnam" (Chapter Eight) — not just that experience that deconstructed my scientific anthropology. It was being involved in the invention of a movement to stop the war which reflected curiously and contradictorily on what I had been doing intellectually. Leslie White always used to say that "a liberal was just a human neutron in the political process," somebody who ineffectively wanted a change that was no change — not to mention White's opinion, of which this was hardly the only expression, that individual action counted for naught in an all-determining culture. So what good could we do, beyond instantiating cultural-historical forces that were bigger than any and all of us?

Well, one thing was to invent the teach-in as a protest form, which was done at the University of Michigan in March 1965, launching an antiwar movement of national and even international proportions out of a concatenation of local circumstances and personalities which itself could not be determined from the larger structures it thus affected. The event was not only a cultural turning point but, for me, an anthropological parable. A group of twenty-five or so faculty, only a small number tenured, the greater number assistant professors and graduate student instructors, had decided to go on strike at a certain date against the University in protest against U.S. involvement in Vietnam. Instead of classes, we would hold discussions on the war. This kind of action was not totally unprecedented; on the contrary, it was the era of the Berkeley "Free Speech" movement, and rivalries among state universities in America being what they were, no doubt a measure of "riot envy" was in play. At Michigan, the local and higher powers that be, including the state legislature and the governor, as well as the press, the University authorities and a great many of the faculty came out in opposition to the strike action — some of the official opposition also backed with threats against the strikers or the University. A main argument of faculty who refused to support the action was that the University of

Michigan was not responsible for the Vietnam War, and the con-templated disruption of the institution was morally and politically misplaced. This argument carried some weight. Still, the instruc-tional purposes of the proposed strike turned out to be struc-turally important when the small group of tenured faculty, about five, met at the house of one of them to reflect on the deteriorat-ing political atmosphere. Who will examine the hearts of these men? No doubt, it was a mixture of worries — about themselves and their more vulnerable junior colleagues — that led them to raise various alternatives to the strike. But whatever and however impenetrable their motives, the logic of the different plan that came of their meeting was clear. Instead of holding classes outside the University, thus teaching out, we would "teach in," occupy the buildings all night and hold lectures, seminars, and workshops on the war. The assent in the room was instantaneous, immedi-ately the idea popped out, so many strategic virtues and political resonances did this simple symbolic inversion convey. (Structural inversions were in the intellectual air: this was the time of the first American publication of major works of Claude Lévi-Strauss.) A form of free speech of its own, devoted to momentous national issues, the teach-in was at least as good as, and different from, any of the current university politics. Rather than shirking our own responsibilities as teachers by not holding classes, we were multi-plying them by going on to teach through the night: making the university a source of greater enlightenment — a double entendre that seemed palpable during the event — instead of shutting it down. But of course, and most potently, "teach-in" drew heavily on the recent civil rights sit-in movement in the South, and hence more remotely, in this homeland of the UAW, on the tradition of labor protest and struggle. Moreover — as described below in "The Future of the National Teach-In: A History" (Chapter Six) — the teach-in was an idea whose time had come. When we called other schools to see if they would take up the protest, it was un-necessary even to explain it. It was enough to say "we're having a teach-in on Vietnam." "A teach-in on Vietnam?" was the common reply. "What a great idea."[8]

To have been a "participant observer" in that event was a privileged anthropological experience, if only because it could always be replayed afterward for insights, hindsights, and reality checks whenever Big Issues of culture and agency, structure and event came up academically. One evident lesson of the idea whose time had come — whose time came over and again when I worked on histories of other peoples — is that historical agency is a relationship to the cultural order: an embodiment of collective powers in individual persons, whether this instantiation is effected by the situational felicity of an action (as in the case of the teach-in) or constituted in the structural authority of the actor (such as Fijian or Hawaiian divine chiefs). In origin, the teach-in had been "a feather launched in a hurricane," as Sartre said of the social take-up of individual doings, here not necessarily a set of unintended consequences but one whose consequences at any rate were due to the society, not the intention. If the professor who invented it thus had a powerful influence, it was only because the act was empowered by the social-historical conjuncture. It is something like — though less enduring, only fifteen minutes — the way Alexander Graham Bell's fame grows in the social imaginary with the cumulative significance of telephonic communications. So agency was put on the agenda — not in distinction to structure, but in certain relations to it.

"The Return of the Event, Again" (Chapter Eleven) is concerned with the complementary structural position of agency: the historical efficacy of Fijian chiefs that comes from their constituted position in a social totality or, more precisely, from the embodiment of the collectivity in their particular persons, so that their individual actions, good or bad, smart or dumb, are necessarily universal events. What is most interesting, however, is that the totality they thus influenced did not as such determine their individuality. For the whole notion that individual agency depends on its cultural empowerment could well pass for nothing new — or, worse, for old-fashioned cultural determinism — were it not also noticed that the act in question had reasons for being of a different character than its collective dimensions. A function of local, biographical, and situational reasons, the teach-in cannot be accounted for by the politics of the Vietnam War, by public

25

opinion, by the condition of the nation, or by the general correlation of political forces. If it was sufficient to have an effect on the larger system, it was not systematically necessary that it happen.

I alluded to Sartre: his *Search for a Method* (1963) is another key text in the anthropology practiced in these studies, notably for the observations just made about agency and history. Sartre's argument passed by way of the critical insight that individuality had only a mediated relation to the totality, depending especially on the specific familial and psychological circumstances through which a person lived the larger structures and forces of the society. As against a certain "vulgar Marxism" that would reduce all human projects to class dispositions, he famously rejoined, "Valéry is a petit bourgeois individual, no doubt about it. But not every petit bourgeois individual is a Valéry" (1968:56). Just so, the social formation does not determine the individuality of the leaders it gives itself — even as it gives these leaders, and thus their individuality, determinate powers over its own destiny:

> We must go further and consider in each case the role of the individual in the historic event. For this role is not defined once and for all: it is the structure of the groups considered which determines it in each case. Thereby, without entirely eliminating contingency, we restore it to its limits and its rationality. The group bestows its power and its efficacy upon the individuals ... whose irreducible particularity is one way of living universality.... Or rather, this universality takes on the face, the body, and the voice of the leaders whom it has given itself; thus the event itself, while a collective apparatus, is more or less marked by individual signs; persons are reflected in it to the same extent that the conditions of the conflict and the structures of the group have permitted them to be personalized. (*Ibid.*:130)

Still, the most powerful lesson of the teach-in experience, encompassing this Sartrean personification of cultural universals, was the realization that it was sufficient to engender its general effects without really being necessary. In origin, the teach-in was a contingent, idiosyncratic event. As I say, its existence could not be specified by a growing opposition to the nation's presence in

Vietnam; and even if this opposition evoked the teach-in, other modes of protest could have expressed it, though probably with different social consequences and political outcomes. And yet — this is a huge metaphysical claim — it seems that all of culture is like that, composed of practices whose reasons are sufficient to their existence but never necessary. As a social organization of meaning, hence a meaningful organization of society, a cultural scheme knows a kind of freedom that the physical universe, bound by its material necessities, does not. Within the limits of biological viability, all that is culturally required is that things be sufficiently logical, intelligible, and communicable, that they make sense in a certain universe of meaning. But precisely, making meaningful sense involves an indeterminate number of possibilities: it is a far more liberal and creative process than any analytic or pragmatic rationality. Analogies, metonyms, synecdoches, connotation, permutation, inversion, proportion — tropes of every conceivable kind can be used to make sense of the resources of a given cultural scheme. It is this endemic possibility of "heteroglossia" — not an undifferentiated, shared culture but, as Bakhtin said, a complex relationship of shared differences — that explains how history can be culturally ordered without being culturally prescribed. If the anthropologist claims that a certain event — the teach-in, Captain Cook lying on the beach on Hawai'i — unfolds in a certain cultural logic, this is not (as is sometimes believed) a recuperation of an extinct species of cultural determinism. To say that a given sentence is grammatical is not to say that the grammar determined what was said. No more than to say that a certain act was logical, made cultural sense, means that the logic determined it were done, or that other acts would not also have been logically adequate and socially empowered. After all (to play doubly reflective anthropologist), the effects of the teach-in and the Vietnam War on ideas of culture were not the same for every anthropologist, not necessarily the same as those described in this text.

For myself, the rest was history — in a double sense. The turn toward history evident in Part Three of this book effectively began in 1970 and 1971, when I took up the archival record of nineteenth-

27

century Hawaiian land claims, though with the original intention of writing an ethnography of the Islands at contact. I had previously done ethnographic fieldwork in Fiji and had long been interested in Polynesia from a variety of points of view — evolutionary, political, economic, and ecological. But the problem of doing an historical ethnography, primarily in the archives rather than in the field, opened new dimensions of inquiry. Hawaiian land records led to other historical records, and to a growing realization that Hawaiian cultural schemes had significantly ordered this history, even as they were reordered in the course of it. In 1977, I began an analogous work on Fijian history which started in the Methodist archives in London and is still going on. Chapters Eleven and Twelve are results of that research. Of course, I do not claim that this historical turn was simply an empirical revelation. For one, I was stimulated in the 1970s by the historical work of anthropological colleagues at the University of Chicago, notably Barney Cohn and George Stocking. More generally, there was the legacy of political and intellectual events of the 1960s, which for me had twinned the specificity of cultures with their systematicity or structural order. I was already prepared to find the cultural structures in history. Yet the move also fit in with a growing respect for anthropological cosmography, hence for the history of structures. The cosmographer, as Boas said, cannot be content with a merely probabilistic knowledge, inasmuch as his interest itself is not generic but runs to the understanding of a particular and distinctive thing — Fiji in the mid-nineteenth century, for example, its wars and its kingdoms. For this, Boas said, only a true history will suffice, knowing "how it came to be."

As structured relationships of symbolic freedoms, cultures are relative and historical forms of life, each having a particular validity without some universal necessity. Hence the character of our cosmographic explications, their sufficiency without necessity, which consists in their being of the nature of logico-meaningful motivations of the practice in question. Physical things have causes, but human things reasons — symbolically constructed reasons even when they are physically caused. And this makes anthropology a science of another kind, different from the natural sciences, because its object and its method are the same kind of thing. If I say something like Fijian cannibalism is accountable by its logical motivations in Fijian culture, still the logic, *their* logic, is also something going on inside me. This again is not an original observation, only something I came to practice: the distinctive character of anthropological knowledge is that it involves a substantial unity of the knowing subject and that which is known.

Following a long tradition of human science that began perhaps with Vico, Lévi-Strauss once described the anthropological project as a transformation of the objectively remote to the subjectively familiar.[9] One is initially confronted with a practice, say again Fijian cannibalism, that is distant from our experience and perhaps even repugnant to our sensibilities. But the ethnographic texts may yet, by the nature of the mental operations they involve, operations of which we too are capable, provide an opening to intelligibility. A.M. Hocart relates the apology of a Fijian chief to the master builder of his sacred canoe that he could not reward the craftsman properly, as in the old days, with a "cooked man" or a "woman brought raw," for Christianity, he explained, "spoils our feasts" (1929:129). Confronted with this violation of our own dietary tabus, we can nevertheless grasp the operation of equivalence that links cooked men with raw women, even as we can metaphorically expand our native notions of exchange, appropriation, and consumption to what for Fijians are so describable. Raw women were of course virgins, not yet consumed, and numerous other practices put them in symmetrical opposition and interchangeability with cannibal victims. The warrior tribes (*bati*) of powerful chiefdoms, those who brought in human sacrifices cum cannibal feasts, were typically allied to the ruling chiefs through the marriages of their own leaders to the daughters of the former — cooked men for raw women. In many parts of Fiji, a fine war club, given to the warrior younger brother of a prospective bride was a customary betrothal gift — the club would bring a cannibal victim. The point of these equivalences is that raw women and cooked men have the same finality, if by different means, which is the reproduction of society through the appropriation of divinity.

The one secures the divine powers of reproduction for humanity through birth, the other by the provision of human sacrifice and commensality of a victim assimilated to the god. So in Fiji a man who has never killed, never brought a human sacrifice, is without reproductive power: he is condemned after death endlessly to pound a pile of excrement, negative food, through all eternity.

Is not anthropology thus dependent on a shared humanity with its interlocutors: a common symbolic capacity that allows the former to replicate in mind, as the meaningful logic of custom, what the latter express in practice? In a certain way, more or less imperfect of course, the anthropologist recapitulates the symbolic operations by which the phenomena of custom were produced. Method recapitulates truth, as I say, but here as identity, not in the manner of the natural sciences, as a human translation of a material process. Indeed, the more we know about physical objects the less familiar they become, the more remote they stand from any human experience. The molecular structure of the table on which I write is far removed from my sense of it — let alone, to speak of what is humanly communicable, my use of it or my purchase of it. Nor will I ever appreciate tableness, rockiness, or the like in the way I might know cannibalism. On the contrary, by the time one gets to the deeper nature of material things as discovered by quantum physics, it can only be described in the form of mathematical equations, so much does this understanding depart from our ordinary ways of perceiving and thinking objects.

The differences are Vichian. In a golden passage of *The New Science* (1725), Vico spelled out the conditions of the possibility of the new anthropological science by a foundational contrast between the epistemologies of culture and nature. Even societies of antiquity "so remote from ourselves" can become uniquely accessible to us because they were made by operations of the human mind; whereas, the things of nature we must know externally, as it were, since we did not create them. Of human doings we have understanding "through causes," why they are made as they are, but of nonhuman things only through attributes, by what they are. The true and the made are interchangeable (*verum et factum convertuntur*). As the famous text runs, we can acquire a unique truth of civil society since it "has certainly been made by men, and ... its principles are therefore to be found within the modifications of the human mind." Hence it is rather marvelous "that the philosophers should have lent all their energies to the study of the world of nature, which since God made it, He alone knows; and that they should have neglected the world of nations, or civil world, which, since men made it, men could come to know" (1984:par. 331; see also par. 349).

Accordingly, the very first principle of the new anthropological science would have to be "respect the specificity of the cultural object." Then this anthropology could realize its distinctive destiny as the Cosmography of Symbolic Forms.

NOTES

1. The sentence is from "What Is an Author?" Barthes's "The Death of the Author" has some analogous implications (1989). "Poststructuralist theories," M.H. Abrams writes, "whatever their disagreements, coincide in abstracting literary texts from the human world and relocating them in a nonhuman state — specifically in the play of language — as such, or else in the forces that operate within a discourse already-in-being" (1997:115).

2. In other works (M. Sahlins 1995, Chapter Sixteen below, M. Sahlins 1999), following on Elias (1978), I have noted the contrast of American cultural and British social anthropology in relation to well-known differences in Enlightenment (and counter-Enlightenment) philosophies, namely, between the Herderian *Kultur* as a distinctive mode of being and perceiving, a plural and pluralized notion by definition, and the *civilisation* of French philosophes, involving a universal progress of cultivation by means of an equally universal human reason.

3. "Culture provides the form, the 'dress' of the social situation. As far as I am concerned, the cultural situation is a given factor, it is a product and an accident of history. I do not know *why* Kachin women go hatless with bobbed hair before they are married, but assume a turban afterwards, any more than I know why English women put a ring on a particular finger to denote some change in social status; all I am interested in is that in this Kachin context the assumption of a turban by a woman does have this symbolic significance. It is a statement about the status of the woman" (Leach 1954:16).

Introduction to Part One

This first set of essays, which have to do largely with conceptualizations of culture (in general) and cultures (in particular), represent something like deep structures of my anthropological experience. Published from the mid-1960s to the mid-1970s, they amount to so many deployments of a received notion of culture as a distinctive phenomenon, as symbolic means and modes of the construction of human worlds. An opposition to reductionism necessarily informs these several studies, a conflict of meaningful logics with material and biological rationalities, or, more precisely, a set of arguments about how the latter are encompassed — that is, in cultural orders that have their own semiotic systematicity. Although not overtly political, such an anthropology is obviously not disengaged from its society. On the contrary, these essays, by confronting the native Western academic folklore with the scandals to its logic offered by other forms of life, reproduce the cultural dilemmas of virtually any anthropology.

Anyhow, to lighten up, we open in New York — off-Broadway. In the early 1960s, Robert Ardrey, a well-known playwright, wrote a series of works, beginning with *African Genesis*, on the biological sources of human cultural dispositions. Subtitled "A Personal Investigation into the Animal Origins and Nature of Man," *African Genesis* amounted to a passionate disquisition on the attempts of anthropologists and other well-meaning academics to cover up the terrible truth of innate human violence. As I explain in Chapter One, it seemed that the only appropriate anthropological response would be an off-Broadway review of the playwright's book — hence "African Nemesis." Aside from the structuralist inversion (*en dehors de la lettre*), the playlet is worth remarking for its arguments on the symbolic construction of experience as well as of cultural practice. It thus looks back to earlier anthropological work even as it also anticipates themes reprised in some of the latest essays reprinted here, notably "The Sadness of Sweetness" (Chapter Sixteen).

Chapter Four, "Colors and Cultures," originally published in 1976, also takes up the theme of culture-nature relations, but in the particularly challenging form posed by Berlin and Kay's *Basic Color Terms* (1969). By its experimental determination of the apparently universal loci (on Munsell color charts) of elementary color terms and their regular sequence of appearance in natural languages, Berlin and Kay's work gave evident support to the cause of "biological determinism" and thereby opened one of the most important discussions of modern anthropology. The discussion still goes on — though I tried to put an end to it with "Colors and Cultures." In fact "Colors and Cultures" is easily one of the best pieces I have done. Its widely ignored conclusion is that color terms take biological or perceptual constraints of reference insofar as they are engaged as signifiers in meaningful domains — as markers of clans or other social categories, for example, as indicators of social conditions such as sickness and health, in pragmatic codes such as stoplight signals. My point is that if a society is to invest meaning in the difference between, say, red and yellow, then it will go for maximal referential contrasts to these terms, bright and saturated red and yellow; it would not do for "red" to designate some sort of orange — in which yellow(ish) is perceptible. Hence the proposition: "It is not, then, that color terms have their meanings imposed by the constraints of human and physical nature; rather, they take on such constraints insofar as they are meaningful."

There is another part of that article, however, which is for me a most compelling truth about culture. It derives from the observation — which actually echoes a conundrum on colors as "primary ideas" posed by Locke in *An Essay Concerning Human Understanding* — that red-green colorblind people can go throughout their lives without knowing that their vision is different from other people's and without any serious difficulty functioning as others do. They call "red" what normal-sighted people call "red," "green" what the latter call "green"; they stop at red lights and go on green. The trick is that they have learned to make distinctions of brightness on their own spectrum (of blue-yellow) corresponding to other people's discriminations of hue. But, as the physiologist says, the important thing is not so much how the color differences are perceived — so long as they are perceived somehow — as what the colors mean. A somewhat eerie demonstration of Saussurean principle, this: *il n'y que de différences*. Yet what seems more enormous, a powerful comment on the nature of culture, is that people can participate fully and mutually in the same society, in the same universe of meaning, while having totally different (and untransmissible) experiences of the world. "Thinking by concepts," as Durkheim said, "is not merely seeing reality on its most general side, but it is projecting a light upon sensation which illuminates it, penetrates it and transforms it" ([1914] 1947:435). But then, as he also said, living socially, which is to say mastering our perceptions by their conceptual values, is a double act of renunciation — if in a double sense incomplete:

> [W]e cannot understand things without partially renouncing a feeling for their life, and we cannot feel that life without renouncing the understanding of it. Doubtless, we sometimes dream of a science that would adequately express all of reality, but this is an ideal that we can approach ceaselessly, not one that is possible for us to attain. ([1914] 1960:329)

Indeed, everything happens in our science as if the existential contradictions of category and experience were realized rather in an endless oscillation of structural and romantic (including postmodern) theoretical moments. In any event, the phenomenon of the color-competent person who is colorblind is a lesson in the cultural construction of nature.

The emphasis on cultural construction or symbolic order marking this set of essays has also another dimension: comparison.

By the differences one learns the properties. The articles "Poor Man, Rich Man" (Chapter Two), about political forms in Melanesia and Polynesia, and "The Original Affluent Society" (Chapter Three), on hunter-gatherers, are initiatives in a comparative genre. True, as the first of these texts admits, the method is one of "uncontrolled comparison." This helps to account for some of the criticism that the opposition between Polynesian office-power (of chiefs) and Melanesian personal power (of "big-men") has attracted — though the opposition is *not* between "ascribed" and "achieved" powers, as too many have supposed; one can also achieve office. Yet the most popular demurrals have been empiricist in tone, ranging from "there is no such thing as Melanesia" to ethnographic exceptions to the correlation of regions and political regimes. Under the latest theoretical dispensation, such positivist criticisms take on the added value of "anti-essentialism." This makes it worthwhile to ponder, for both "Poor Man, Rich Man" and "The Original Affluent Society," the question explicitly raised in the former as to whether I could have gotten away with it all by calling the cultural formations at issue "ideal types." A mild allergy to Max Weber (other than *The Protestant Ethic and the Spirit of Capitalism*) prevented that, but an even more interesting question is whether any knowledge — notably knowledge applicable to understanding particular societies, in a return movement, as it were — is to be gained by the systematizing or generalizing procedure. If there were only differences, which is to say variations without co-variations, there could be no knowledge. We would be in the position of the Heraclitean philosopher who in the end could do nothing but point.

But I learned a lot from Karl Polanyi (1886–1964) — who among other works wrote a book called *The Essence of Fascism*. One thing he once said to me was, "Have you ever seen a man with an injured or crippled hand try to lift a pencil off a table? He tries this way and that way, until he finds a way suitable to his own deformity. Our minds are like that," he continued, "when it comes to dealing with intellectual problems."[1] One of the sadder aspects of the current postmodernist, anti-essentialist mood is the way it seems to lobotomize some of our best graduate students, to stifle their imagination for fear of making some interesting structural connection or comparative generalization. The only safe essentialism left to them is that there is no order.

Polanyi's teaching is relevant to not only "The Original Affluent Society" but also the final article in Part One, "*La Pensée Bourgeoise*" (Chapter Five) — with evident homages as well to Lévi-Strauss.[2] Utilitarian theories of culture are critical foils in both these articles: explanations of culture by notions of economic or material maximization, which of course have been around a long time in the native Western social consciousness and have taken a variety of anthropological appearances. Most common in the 1960s and 70s were propositions to the effect that the cultural forms themselves — Hindu dietary tabus, Aztec cannibalism, New Guinea pig-exchange ceremonials, Northwest Coast potlatches — generated positive material benefits: benefits ranging from enhanced protein intake or maximizing resource use to maintaining population densities below the ecological carrying capacity. This rationality of custom was supposed to be its raison d'être. Speaking to the "objective" material values of cultural practices, such anthropological materialism is different from the economism or "rational choice theory" of neoclassical derivation, which poses its explanation as the mode of action of a universal economizing subject: the famous allocation of scarce means against alternative possible ends to derive the greatest satisfaction. In "The Sadness of Sweetness" (Chapter Sixteen), I try to show that the anthropological and economistic utilitarianisms have a common (Western) genealogy. But as an explanatory account of *culture*, of the specific attributes of cultural phenomena, rational choice economism is the weakest epistemologically and the least substantial — for the same reason that it is the most general and irrefutable. Neoclassical rationality is the absolute zero of cultural theories because it has to give itself the culture, assume as a priori the local system of meanings and values, in order to demonstrate people's rationality. Otherwise how would one know why it is rational for a Trobriander to save his yams for his sister's husband or a Kwakiutl chief to spend everything on a potlatch? As anthropology, rational economizing is tautology.

39

Hence the impetus of "*La Pensée Bourgeoise.*" It was an attempt to recuperate our own market mentality for culture and anthropology. As against the going opposition of "the West and the Rest," it claimed that the Western economy was organized by a "logic of the concrete," a system of the meaningful distinctions of the properties of things and persons, which in such regards was not distinct in nature or function from the *pensée sauvage* of nonliterate peoples.[3] Among the Americans, social persons and the objects of their existence, together with times, places, and occasions, are interrelated in vast cultural schemata that orchestrate use-value and desire — and thus underlie what passes in consciousness for economic rationality. Moreover, the symbolic values thus realized through pecuniary economizing do not in themselves constitute a scheme of material optimization — whether of energy, calories, proteins, population size, resource use, or any sort of natural-selective advantage. Many examples follow in the text. They amount to the observation that our vaunted economic rationality is based on another, symbolic logic of cultural value which is no less systematic than the former, for all that its system is not one of natural-material gain, collective or individual.

NOTES

1. A lot of people have learned a lot from Polanyi's *The Great Transformation.* Yet to shift the metaphor, he was one of J.S. Mill's "one-eyed men," one of the so-called systematic half-thinkers by whom "almost all rich veins of original and striking speculation have been opened." So the ideal-typical character of *The Great Transformation:*

> Ours is not a historical work; what we are searching for is not a convincing sequence of outstanding events, but an explanation of their trend in terms of human institutions. We shall be free to dwell on scenes of the past with the sole object of throwing light on matters of the present; we shall make detailed analyses of critical periods and almost completely disregard the connecting stretches of time; we shall encroach upon the field of several disciplines in the pursuit of this single aim. (1944:4)

2. While on the subject of influences and origins, I must acknowledge that "The Original Affluent Society" owes a lot to Elman Service, in whose classes I first heard the observation that the Arunta have a lot of "leisure."

3. So far as I know, the phrase "the West and the Rest" was coined for these dialectical purposes, first appearing in the chapter "*La Pensée Bourgeoise*" in my *Culture and Practical Reason* (Chapter Five below). However that may be, there is no doubt the work was paradoxically taxed for drawing this distinction, which it had rather hoped to overcome.

41

CHAPTER ONE

African Nemesis:

An Off-Broadway Review[*]

Foreword

Robert Ardrey, the author of *African Genesis*, is a playwright. But he's a thinking man's playwright. He has conducted, as he puts it, a personal investigation into the animal origins and animal nature of man. The investigation focuses on the social behavior of subhuman primates and other vertebrates — most notably, birds — and on the South African "man-ape" (Australopithecine) materials uncovered by Raymond Dart and his co-workers. Ardrey claims to have discovered not merely the true underlying nature of man but a large "unwitting combine" of influential scientists who refuse to acknowledge the evidence of this true nature. The true nature is made up of certain "cultural instincts" developed in the course of animal evolution and genetically transmitted in the human line. Most of the instincts are bad, and they are responsible for great troubles of the modern world. The combine, intellectually committed to the "romantic fallacy" that man is basically noble, unique among animals, and governed not so much by his animal nature as by his cultural circumstances, will not see this. So Ardrey has taken it upon himself to present the case to the public. He makes out his discovery to be a revolutionary doctrine, and with great flourish and considerable flair lets fly many barbs in the general direction of the "phalanx of modern thought" and the bastions of "scientific orthodoxy."

However different the subject, the book then belongs in the

* Originally published in *Kroeber Anthropological Society Papers* 30 (1964).

popular Kon Tiki genre: "it's agin the interests." It portrays a theory that sounds sensible but, for fuddy-duddy reasons, the professors-that-be generally ignore. Right away, Ardrey is an underdog. And to add to the appeal: simply by reading the book approvingly anyone can demonstrate that he is the intellectual equal — indeed, the superior — of the so-called scholars.

Obviously, it becomes difficult to enter the lists against Ardrey. Who wants to be accused of being a counterrevolutionary? Who *is* a counterrevolutionary? What an improbable position for an anthropological critic. To admit to intellectual conservatism is contrary to the spirit of any science, and not the least so to anthropology. In this context of conspiratorial allegation, how can an anthropologist convey the impression that the theory seems to him unsound? Well, if Ardrey, a dramatist, can pen a book about anthropology, an anthropologist can write his review in play form. That is what I have done.

The play speaks for itself. *Insofar as it speaks well it is because I have woven into it many of Ardrey's felicitous phrases.* It is only necessary to mention that the bracketed page numbers refer to some of Ardrey's more unusual statements, and the denouement of the drama is not Ardrey's book but my hope. So now your humble patience pray, gently to hear, kindly to judge:

Cast of Characters

ROBERT ARDENT:	Former dramatist. Now leader of a revolutionary movement to reveal the true animal nature of man.
EVE ARDENT:	His wife.
RAYMOND BLUNT:	Anatomist-paleontologist. Discoverer of Australopithecus, the nearest ancestor of man.
DR. L. FAUCET:	Noted anthropologist. Discoverer of the early hominid Zinjanthropus — under hazardous conditions due to the menace of prides of black-maned lions.
MARY FAUCET:	His wife, the real discoverer of Zinjanthropus.

ANYONE: Almost everyone.
KUNG: A Bushman shaman. (Only we know his real
name.)
MR. SHAPIRO: A Mr. Shapiro.

*Any resemblance between the characters of this play and persons living
or dead is purely incidental.*

PROLOGUE
Ardent and Eve on opposite ends of stage front.

ARDENT   Give order that these bodies
High on a stage be placed to view;
And let me speak to the yet unknowing world
How these things came about. So shall you hear
Of carnal, bloody, and unnatural acts;
Of accidental judgments, casual slaughters;
Of deaths put on by cunning and forced cause;

EVE   (*an interjected aside*) And, in this upshot, purposes
mistook
Fall'n on the inventors' heads —

ARDENT   All this can I truly deliver.

ACT I
*A cave near Johannesburg, late afternoon. A table and chair rear
center with typewriter on table. A pile of firewood front center, about
eight feet in front of table. Cave mouth, R; cave recess, L. Ardent,
standing on table, addressing Blunt, the Faucets, Eve, and Anyone.
Mary Faucet carrying large rifle.*

ARDENT   (*Dramatically*) A specter is haunting Europe — the mil-
lion-year-old specter of a killer ape whose home was
this very cave, the specter of man's carnivorous ancestor...his own murderous specter. All the powers
of orthodox science, all the orthodox producers and
consumers of the romantic fallacy, have entered into a
holy alliance to exorcise this specter: Marx and Freud,

45

Rousseau and Jefferson, the frightened anthropologists and their namby committed publics, the whole troop of howling monkeys that is man won't look in the goddam river of time to see reflected there their own hideous visage. (*Mocking*) Oh what a piece of work is man, they say: how noble in reason, in form and moving how express and admirable, in action how like an angel! The beauty of the world! The paragon of animals! (*Hardens*) Well, that is what he is, the paragon of animals: base to the core in instinct, in form and moving how like the beast of prey, in national action the consummate primate defending to a fool's death all the territory he can grab from others, the beauty of the mushroom cloud! Blunt, Faucet, Anyone — what is to be done? Murder will out, you thought, Blunt. Well you were wrong. So you cheerfully went up to the Livingstone conference to lay before the northern scientists the fossilized evidence from this cave. You put out in plain boxes the stupendous remnants of hominid carnage strewn here by our brutal Australopithecine father. Well, they ignored you! They took refuge behind the laughing hyena — hyenas did it, they said. (*Laughs bitterly*) And you, Faucet, you and Mary fighting off black-maned lions to dig in Tanganyika, to dig up the truth. I tell you this: they won't listen! Your specialist voices in obscure specialist journals have no echoes — even when you can get your stuff published. And they censor you. And they drown you in the milksop tears of the orthodox romantic prejudice. (*Exhorts*) I tell you this: You need drama! You need someone to put it all together, to forge a knife of prose that will rip the reactionary academics from groin to gorge. You need me! And we together will make our revolutionary truth known. Comrades, we are privy to a revolution in knowledge about man, about what he really is. South African workers in the caverns of man's origins, unite! Man has nothing to lose but the chains of his romantic illusion. Let us make him free with the truth. Let us break through the counterrevolutionary phalanx with a manifesto! And let us write it here — write here, right now! (*Anticlimax*) I have a publisher lined up — and catch this title, African Nemesis. (*Comes down from the table*)

ANYONE   Is Marx an enemy of the revolution? A counterrevolutionary?

ARDENT   Private property is an animal instinct, a territorial compulsion put into the genes of man a hundred million years before he was born. (*Contempt*) But to the romantics, man is a noble fellow. Circumstances, they say, brought him to this end. A unique fellow, they say, with a soul, or a will, or a culture. I say ... when Blunt found that bashed-in Australopithecine jaw, it said, said across millions of years of bloody history: man is a jabberwocky, a walkie-talkie, talking to disguise the fact that his talk means nothing. Man is an animal with the soul of a murderous, proprietary, status-seeking, in-group-loving predator! Ah, we have found the jaws that bite. Next to this, all else is talk. The instincts must burst through. They are the true legacy of a man. He owns them. They own him.

ANYONE   I'm with you. Marx, fancy that. The history of all hitherto-existing society is the animal history of animal struggles. Fancy that.

ARDENT   (*Motions Eve to table. She sits before typewriter. She types through scene, especially when Ardent speaks*) Light the fire for Eve to type by. Eve, you catch the spirit of the thing. I'll fix it up later.

FAUCET   (*Lighting fire, laughs good-humoredly*) Good job for the revolution that only man can make fire. (*Ardent glares at him and he stops laughing*)

ANYONE   Can I put out the fire when we're done?

BLUNT   No me, me —

FAUCET   I made it, and I —

ARDENT   Stop this Freudian romanticism. We'll all do it, all four
            of us. We'll take different sides. But let's go back to
            the *real* beginning, the animal beginning, the hun-
            dreds-of-million-years-old vertebrate beginning. Ter-
            ritory first, love of possession. Fish have it, birds have
            it, monkeys in the trees have it (Cole Porter 1938:2).
            It's in the genetic structure. The instinct to possess,
            the drive to gain, maintain, and defend the exclusive
            right to a piece of territory. Man's cultural instinct for
            Lebensraum. Small hope for any United Nations that
            won't recognize that. It's the basic condition of war,
            of crime, of the fact that humans have a general re-
            luctance to love their neighbors. Every man his own.
            Every tribe, every nation in territorial strife. An um-
            bilical bondage to a piece of ground that decrees xeno-
            phobic hatred of the others of his kind. Got that, Eve?
            (*Listens*) What's that? A scuffling in front of the cave.
            (*Sound alarm*) Counterrevolutionary scientific ortho-
            dox spies! Quiet everyone!

BLUNT   Ardent, I think you're getting a little paranoid.

ARDENT   In a world of man anything else would be insanity.
            Don't you ever have the feeling, Blunt, that paranoids
            are after you?

BLUNT   Don't worry, Ardent. I wrote up the report on this
            cave — no one could possibly find it.

FAUCET   (*Moves toward front of cave, R., startled, runs L. across
            stage and exit L., screaming in terror*) It's a pride of
            black-maned lions! Run for your lives!

*Mary Faucet advances boldly to cave mouth and fires high-powered
rifle twice.*

ARDENT   (*Emerging from behind table*) Get them, Mary old girl?

MARY   Got five lionesses and two cubs. I missed the male,
            though...he ran like hell.

ARDENT   It's hot in here. (*Removes shirt. Begins to pace around
            fire, with tempo of pacing gradually increasing through
            scene.*)

48

Faucet returns from stage left, dragging with him Kung, stone chisel and crude paintbrushes in hand.

FAUCET   Here's your counterrevolutionary, Ardent. He was painting a gazelle (schaft) back there on the walls of the cave. Human all right, but is it art?

ARDENT   (*To Kung*) What are you doing here?

KUNG   Hunting.

ARDENT   The hell you are, you're painting an animal back there.

KUNG   Someone has to do the hunting.

BLUNT   He means he's searching out game by imitative magic.

ARDENT   Why don't you hunt like a man?

KUNG   I enjoy it ... the arrow in the running beast, the red blood, the veldt. It *is* hunting. Besides I'm not very good at stalking. So I do the hunting. People give me some of the game sometimes.

ARDENT   Bushman, aren't you? You do this for band belong-you, people belong-you? Make-um magic?

KUNG   Sometimes for my band. But now I'm hunting for all the bands around here. Boys' initiation ceremony coming up. All the boys of all the bands and their people are coming in next week. We need a lot of game in our land to feed everyone. Big time. Good time.

ANYONE   What's your name, Bushman?
         No answer.

ARDENT   C'mon, tell us name belong-you.
         No answer.

BLUNT   He probably thinks you're going to take his name. He won't tell it to you. You might do something with his name, and he'll suffer.

ARDENT   (*Circling fire faster*) Leave him alone. A harmless people, and they suffer from it ... Let's go on with the manifesto. Where were we? ... territory, property ... yes and next ... Dominance! (*Excited again*) The status-seeker. Man's unquenchable thirst for rank. An end in itself too; make no mistake on that. A drive, a need, a compulsion to dominate that continues on

49

whether it's useful or useless. A basic desire for center stage. Try —

FAUCET But —

ARDENT (*Ignores interruption*) — to build an equalitarian society of men. Ha! Catch a falling star. How romantic. How delightful. Ha! Bushman, you got-em leader?

KUNG We mostly listen to Tomu. We like him — a good man. Talks well. Generous to a fault. It's sometimes up to me, though. I mean, if Tomu doesn't act right, we shamans see that he does. We know his real name, see. But no doubt you're right. Tomu must want badly to be the leader. Else why should he be so good?

Faucet begins to follow Ardent around fire. After a while, he takes off his shirt and carries it. Pen, matches, cigarettes, and other things periodically drop out of his shirt pocket. He reaches for them but often misses as he scurries to keep up with Ardent. Mary Faucet falls in after Faucet, picks up what he drops. Thus the two of them are stooping every once in a while as the dance goes on around the fire.

FAUCET But listen, this rugged individualism I can understand. Yet there is some cooperation, you know.

ARDENT Man is truly a social species, although when I say man here I don't embrace women (Linton 1932; after J. Miller 1698). Baboons too, and lots of lesser mammals. Necessary for survival, protection. Society is the animal's best friend, his defense, so sometimes he plays down his personal desire for the group. It's a kind of primal morality, a development of a double standard. Amity of the in-group, enmity toward the other groups. But listen to me, and don't get me wrong: it's a love born of hate, hate and fear of the outside. It multiplies hate by the factor of society. And in the end, the moral order depends on territory, and so it depends on hostility. Its consummate human product: xenophobic nationalism. Christ, take a look

50

at what's going on in Africa. Christ, we're in the midst of natural man exercising his natural social hate. *Aux arbres Citoyens!*

BLUNT   *(Excited, begins to follow Faucets in dance around fire. Takes off shirt from heat. Faucets stooping at more frequent intervals.)* Why don't you embrace women?

ARDENT   Complete anarchists. Men are the social animals. The male of the primate species is the defender of the horde, of its territory, of its fallen. Even dominance, the sheer struggle of it, breeds order. Man breeds social order, women only children. A specialized child-bearer. And take sex, who is really preoccupied with it? Who, the aggressor? What does order mean to women alongside child-bearing and the competitive struggle to latch on to the best-fixed male? You know why so many women are in psychoanalysis? Because we've been fool enough to give women social roles, votes, masculine jobs. They haven't the instincts for it [p. 165]. Can't clean up the mess that's inside.

Anyone takes off shirt and joins procession around fire, which moves into high gear. Only Kung stands aside, wide-eyed. Eve's typewriter beat becomes rhythmical: tap-tap-tap-tap, tap-tap-tap-tap, bell-carriage slide; tap-tap-tap-tap, tap-tap-tap-tap, bell-carriage slide.

BLUNT   The finishing touch, Ardent. Australopithecus. My cave here. My murderous, small predatory carnivore. My ancestor...our ancestor.

ARDENT   Yes, yes, the finishing touch, the jewel in man's crown of instincts — murder. All the primates are vegetarian. But what happened to man's line? Came out of the trees, stood up, lost his ripping canines and found his destiny — weapons. Weapons for defense, weapons for meat, weapons for survival. Cain! We are Cain's children, born with weapons in our hands. Oh, not in Asia and not in innocence is man born. In Africa his genesis, and he is nasty, brutish, and short. Man is a

51

predator with a natural instinct to kill with a weapon [p. 316]. No conditioning force has eradicated it, or can. All human history has had one supreme objective: the perfection of the weapon. United Nations, ha! We are cursed with an irrational, self-destroying, inexorable pursuit of death for death's sake.

FAUCET But look, Ardent. Zinjanthropus, you know, the one I ... uh, Mary and I found. No small carnivore predator. Hunted some smaller animals, maybe. Comes after Blunt's old thing. And he probably made those tools, those pebble tools that started the whole Stone Age sequence. How do you fit that in, I mean.

ARDENT (*Sneer*) Abel. A freak. A side-branch. Backward, inoffensive, lumbering ape-man. Chewing structure of a vegetarian ape. He lived at the bottom of a well, on treacle, and he was very ill. Obviously, then, he couldn't have been man's ancestor. Slain by Cain, who took his tools away from him [p. 282]. Simple. And that's it ... we've got it, the whole of it. (*Stops pacing around fire, whole procession brought up. Ardent is facing fire and audience. Others, save Kung, ranged on either side of him. The typewriter rhythm continues. Ardent shrieks*) African Nemesis!

ARDENT	CHORUS OF ALL
Man-is-evil	Man-is-evil
Mammalian-boll-weevil	Mammalian-boll-weevil
Was arboreal	Was arboreal
Became predatorial	Became predatorial
And carnivorial	And carnivorial
Also territorial	Also territorial
Status-seeker	Status-seeker
Property-keeper	Property-keeper
Instinct lies deeper	Instinct lies deeper
Here to stay	Here to stay
Won't go away	Won't go away
No matter what you say	No matter what you say
No matter what you say	No matter what you say

Ardent climbs on table. Firelight flickers on face. Spreads arms. Type-writer stops.

ARDENT   (*Frenzied*) Comrades, what to us is this quintessence
of evil? Let this be our watchword: Man delights not
me — no, nor women neither! To the publisher! (*He
rips the sheets out of typewriter. Leaps with a yell toward
cave mouth and exit R., grabbing Kung on way. The rest
follow running, yelling, save Eve, left alone, sitting at
table.*)

EVE   (*With compassion*) Oh, Ardent, you were a playwright
once — but now what Lenten entertainment the players shall receive from you.... And how do they expect
me to put out the fire?

Curtain

ACT II SCENE 1
*The sitting room of a flat in London. Table and chairs R. Door rear
center. Members of revolutionary band sitting around. Mary still
packs rifle. Ardent in dominant position, sitting on table with feet on
a chair.*

ARDENT   I'll never understand why the South African government deported us.

KUNG   Maybe the prime minister was jealous.

ARDENT   London's the place for our movement anyhow: the
workshop of Marx, the sanctuary of Freud. Most of
all, the very bastille of the romantic fallacy, the British
Museum: ivory tower of the world, guardian of the
fortress of man's ignorance of man. It's the drilling
ground of those snob north-of-the-equator anthropologists who turned their backs on Blunt at the Livingstone conference.... (*An idea*) And we're going to
storm it tonight! The manifesto wasn't enough, by
God. We need evidence. Evidence, evidence, evidence. That's their anthropological currency and we're
going to pay 'em in it. But it won't be easy, because I

happen to know they've taken it out of the Museum Library, hidden it from romantic eyes. Look, if people really knew how gibbons lived, how long do you think they'd beat their heads against the stone wall of love, how long could they cherish the hopeless hope that things can somehow turn out for humanity? For an hour today I combed through the Museum Library. Get this: not a single copy of Carpenter's monograph on the gibbon [pp. 36–37]. God knows what else they've sequestered. But I have a good idea where. Old Nose Washtree's office! Third floor of the museum. Come, my guerrilla band. To the Bastille!... (*They rise, except Kung*) You too, Bushman. You're one of... us now. And Christ, Mary, leave that blunderbuss here. Those were stone lions in front of the museum, take my word.

MARY Oh, all right. But may I at least take my pistol?

Curtain

Act II Scene 2

Nose Washtree's office, one hour later. A room lined with books, floor to ceiling. A door to hall L. Large desk with swivel chair R. Curtain opens to empty stage. Door yields under pressure and enter revolutionary band, led by Mary Faucet, waving pistol and motioning for quiet. She turns on light and closes door.

MARY We're safe now. I'll stand guard. (*Posts self at door*)

ANYONE Look at all these books. Wha' does he do with them?

ARDENT (*Rapidly crosses to desk, stands in front of it*) All right, everyone. Revolutionary discipline. We have to work fast. Eve, you take that bookcase there. (*At R., nearest door*) Faucet, you the next one, then Anyone, then Blunt, and I'll take care of this corner. (*Largest space. Kung, conspicuously left out, finally gravitates to one of the shelves. Ardent now ranges before books, reading shelf labels.*) European Paleolithic... North African Meso-

54

lithic...A huge compost heap of scientific orthodox-
ies. I hardly need impress upon you the revolutionary
importance of this mission, and now you see its difficulty. The evidence of man's nature must lie hidden
as a few slim needles in this great romantic haystack.
What are all these shelves? South American *ethnology?*
... *African ethnology? ... ethnology of the Pacific?*

FAUCET Ethnology is the study of peoples, the various conditions of mankind, primitive cultures, that sort of thing
—hundreds of them, Ardent.

ARDENT Paleozoic ethnology they never dreamed of. (*Sits at
desk with feet on it*) More things in heaven and earth,
oh academics —

EVE Look, I drew the *sanctum sanctorum* ... (*Puzzled*) So far
it is from his desk too. (*Reads titles*) Das Jean-Jacques
Rousseau Problem, The Social Contract. (*Takes out*
The Social Contract *and reads*) The strongest is never
strong enough to be always the master, unless he
transforms strength into right, and obedience into
duty. Hence the right of the strongest, which, though
to all seeming meant ironically, is really laid down as
a fundamental principle. But are we never to have an
explanation of this phrase? Force is a physical power,
and I fail to see what moral effect it can have. To yield
to force is an act of necessity, not of will—at the most
an act of prudence. In what sense can it be a duty?

KUNG (*Aside*) They don't make 'em like they used to.

ARDENT Duty and morals: the royal scepter and cloak of the
most dominant ape, the jabberwocky legitimization of
an animal compulsion to rule.

BLUNT (*Browsing shelves*) Muckraking. I say, that's what we're
doing too, you know. Lincoln Steffens —

ARDENT (*Excited*) Yes, yes, look into it, Blunt. Great revolutionary hero, Steffens. Laid bare the natural predatory
core of the city. The incomparable urban paleontolo-
gist, digging in an Australopithecine underworld of
organized crime, organized murder, organized power.

55

BLUNT   (*Reads*) I always like to put a story Wundt's assistant, Külpe, told us after a visit to the neighboring University of Jena to see the aged philosopher Erdmann, whose history of philosophy, in some ten volumes, we had all read and studied. They had a warm, friendly talk, the old scholar and the young scientist, all about the old philosophers and their systems. But when Külpe tried to draw him out on Wundt and the newer school, Erdmann shook his head, declaring that he could not understand the modern men. In my day, he explained, we used to ask the everlasting question: What is man? And you — nowadays you answer it, saying (*voice lowers*), he *was* an ape.

ARDENT   Ach! Nach einmal das Jean-Jacques Rousseau Problem!

FAUCET   Ah, here's a preliminary report from those fellows, Emlen and Schaller, the ones living with mountain gorillas —

ANYONE   No doubt, very happily.

FAUCET   It's buried in this obscure specialist journal, *Current Anthropology*. (*Takes off glasses and reads*) It has been possible for Schaller to observe many details of the behavior and social interactions of these animals. He has found a high level of social tolerance prevails among members of a troop —

ANYONE   (*Quickly interjected*) The primary morality of the in-group, the —

FAUCET   — and even between troops. (*Thoughtfully*) Several of the troops he has studied include more than one male, and he has never observed signs of aggressiveness among them. Isolated and peripheral males exist, as among other primates; and it is surprising that even these may be accepted into troops without (*voice lowers*) visible displays of antagonism. Neighboring troops have been watched as they peacefully mixed, socialized, and separated. Gorilla troops are apparently nomadic within vaguely defined spatial limits.

(*Whispers*) No traces of territorial behavior have been detected.

ARDENT   Don't let it bother you, old man. Pity the poor gorilla, the harmless Bushman of the higher primates. A dying species, an evolutionary failure. Committed to a forest that has disappeared from under him, he came out of the trees and became a stem eater. His oversized body, his tree-swinger's chest and arms: a mass of architectural incongruities about as meaningful to his present existence as an attic full of memories to a bankrupt nobleman. Doomed by ancient crises beyond control or memory, he knows it, knows it in the balance of instincts which govern his behavior. Vital instincts lose their hold. Primate compulsions fade like color from the skin of the dying. By day he seldom copulates, and by night ... by night he fouls his own nest [pp. 112–16]!

FAUCET   That's pretty, but is it science?

ARDENT   I detect in you, Faucet, a certain leakiness, a counter-revolutionary romantic tendency, a deviationist drift, a red shift. (*He notices Anyone, who has given up reading and is sitting on the floor*) What's the matter with you?

ANYONE   My lips get tired.

ARDENT   Counterrevolutionary devia — *Sh!* A noise in the hall! Mary! Mary!

FAUCET   (*Exasperated*) Not another goddamn black-maned lion, not another! Bushman, I told you to stop monkeying around with those paints.

KUNG   But it isn't monkeying.

MARY   (*Terrified*) Eeek! A mouse (*Runs into Faucet's arms. He comforts her. A general hubbub, from which emerges Kung's soothing voice.*)

KUNG   (*Reading*) We walked down the path to the wellhouse, attracted by the fragrance of the honeysuckle with which it was covered. Someone was drawing water and my teacher placed my hand under the spout. As the cool stream gushed over one hand she spelled into

57

the other the word water, first slowly, then rapidly. I stood still, my whole attention fixed upon the motion of her fingers. Suddenly I felt a misty consciousness as of something forgotten — a thrill of returning thought; and somehow the mystery of language was revealed to me. I knew then that w-a-t-e-r meant that wonderful cool something that was flowing over my hand. The living word awakened my soul, gave it light, hope, joy, set it free! ... a woman called Keller.

Eve has been absorbed in The Social Contract. *She beckons Mary. They sit on the floor, R. Eve speaks sotto voce to her and audience. Ardent engages Blunt in conversation, L., occasionally raising voice enough for all to hear. These outbursts come as counterpoint to Eve's voice.*

EVE   This must be *das Problem*. No noble savage here. (*Reads*) The passage from the state of nature to the civil state produces a very remarkable change in man, by substituting justice for instinct in his conduct, and giving his actions the morality they formerly lacked —

ARDENT   Civilization can never ultimately repress it —

EVE   Then only, when the voice of duty takes the place of physical impulses and the right of attitude, does man, who so far had considered only himself, find that he is forced to act on different principles, and to consult his reason before listening to his inclinations —

ARDENT   Conscience as a guiding force in the human drama is one of such small reliability that it assumes very nearly the role of a villain [p. 349] —

EVE   Although, in this state, he deprives himself of some of the advantages which he got from nature —

ARDENT   By nature, a murderer —

EVE   — he gains in return others so great, his faculties are so stimulated and developed, his ideas so extended, his feelings so ennobled, and his whole soul so uplifted, that, did not the abuses of this new condition often degrade him below that which he left —

ARDENT — the burning flesh of Jews —

EVE — he would be bound to bless continually the happy moment which took it from him forever, and, instead of a stupid and unimaginative animal, made him an intelligent being and ... a man (*She looks at Mary. Mary winks at her.*)

BLUNT (*Sotto voce to Ardent and audience. Interrupted contrapuntally by Eve, still reading to Mary.*) But the Eskimo still baffles me. A complete carnivore he is, and raw meat his dish. The greatest hunter of them all. The bloodthirsty ape in sealskin clothing. Yet look what Old Birket-Smith says here. Difficult for the average Eskimo to assert himself against others, he says —

EVE The social compact substitutes, for such inequalities as nature may have set up between men, an equality that is moral and legitimate. Men, who may be unequal in strength or intelligence, become every one equal by convention and legal right —

BLUNT And hunting grounds are the property of all and none, *res nullius*, he says, which not even the tribe can lay claim to. Something else — the Australian Aborigines. Sir Arthur Keith destroyed the Freudian fraud of the primal family by pointing out the Aborigine's larger-than-family society, and we'd go along with that, but you wouldn't want to talk about an Australian band's exclusive territoriality from what I read on these shelves —

EVE We must clearly distinguish possession, which is merely the effect of force or the right of the first occupier, from property, which can only be founded on a positive title.

ARDENT (*Loudly*) Dammit, these ethnology shelves are useless. What do the Eskimo and all the other timid, shy, cringing, gentle, gauzy, wistful Milquetoasts hiding out from mankind on the ice or in the jungle, what do they mean for pristine man? Precisely nothing, and far less that is than the strutting jackdaw. More harmless people,

59

suffering because of their timid dispositions. Who disputes the Eskimo his blubber, his long night, his home built of ice cubes? No one. By adapting himself to a way of life supremely unattractive to Sioux or Apache, a shy creature has insured his survival in perfect confidence that he will escape the notice of all but romantic anthropologists. All that has been actually demonstrated by this (*indicating bookshelves*) loosely disciplined but immensely popular raid into the outposts of man's nature has been that timid people tend to live at unfashionable addresses [pp. 149–50].

ANYONE   Right again, Ardent. And it goes for Sioux blubber too. They cried when they met people, it says here, in order to manifest the lively joy they felt in meeting them.

KUNG   Crying can have its own vocabulary.

ARDENT   (*Sneers*) Now a little child of nature shall lead us.

KUNG   It can happen to people — depends what they call the child... You know, the White shaman comes around and says to me — me, the magician from way back — I have something new, he says. The latest power, he says, the greatest magic. What? I say. The spell begins like this, he says: in the beginning was the Word. (*Bemused*) Oh, I tried hard not to laugh, not to his face. Oh, that's great stuff, I said, great stuff. Then he asked me to eat his god... and I gave him some of mine. And so I saw the White shaman was far behind the camp of his own people: they had known it all long ago... You know, there on the veldt are little white stones on the ground. Now baboons know about these stones, find them lying there. But it's just stones — hard, white, scratchy. To White man they're that too: the same touch, the same color as for the baboon. But then they're something the baboon never will understand — they're diamonds. And not only that — they're wealth: worth getting and giving. And not only that — they're power and they're good, or to some they're power and

60

they're hateful. A whole *world* of name-ideas. More important, more *real* than the touch of it, than the sight of it, than the smell of it. So the White men came to the veldt because of it. And they fought together because of it, and worked together because of it. White men who had been good became bad. Bushmen, who had been bad ... now they were good: come work for us, nice man, in our holes, they said. The Bushman still smelled as before the stones, as when they drove him out. Now they want us ... It depends a lot on names.

ARDENT (*Exasperated*) Names, names, names. I'm sick of names. The plaintive, inexhaustible primate voice, desperately trying to dupe inexorable vertebrate drives. It's the primeval gene that bursts my spleen, but names will never harm me! (*Flies angrily at shelf, flinging books helter-skelter*) Oh, just let me get my hands on something we can really use. Some real weapon! I'll forge a knife of prose that will rip those ... I'll kill the romantic fallacy. I'll murder — (*He finds a small pamphlet: Oakley's, Man the Tool-Maker. Shrieks in triumph. Laughs hysterically.*) Oh, what fools we've been! Taken in by a name — by the same damn device the romantics use to deceive themselves! See this Museum handbook: Man, the *Tool*-maker. (*Sarcastic laugh*) *Tool-maker.* Do you think the British Museum would ever, ever in a million years of orthodox folly, ever, ever publish a handbook called Man, the *Weapon*-maker [p. 205]? Look at these tools. (*Sneer*) Tools, ha! Cudgels! Weapons! (*Dramatically*) But to suggest that we find in the competition of weapons the most exhilarating human experience would be blasphemy. Would the museum dare to provoke in the House of Commons the question period of heroic proportions [p. 205]? And for a hundred responsible anthropologists gathered in a Rhodesian town to admit — to admit when Blunt put it to them — that Australopithecus

61

had systematically used weapons would be to invite a cultural definition of man as the creature who systematically makes them. Never! Never! Ha-ha-ha (*waves pamphlet*), but just you wait, Professor Higgins, just you wait. (*Menacingly*) No matter how eloquently you say it, no matter what you call it, a weapon by any other name will kill as neat! (*Leaps to desk, others gather round, except Kung, who slips out door and runs off.*) Comrades ... we have been tried and not found wanting ... This is our finest hour. We have tempered the sword of revolution in the very rosewater of the romantic brainwash. (*Exhorts*) And now I say to you, surrounded as we are by the pressing weight of what passes as evidence for those who choose to delude themselves, I say to you ... Man delights not me — no, nor women neither!

They exit, chanting, Ardent leading:

ARDENT	CHORUS
Man-is-evil	Man-is-evil
Mammalian-boll-weevil	Mammalian-boll-weevil
Was - arboreal	Was - arboreal
Became - predatorial	Became - predatorial
And - carnivorial	And - carnivorial
Also - territorial	Also - territorial
Sta-tus-seeker	Sta-tus-seeker
Property-keeper	Property-keeper
Instinct-lies-deeper	Instinct-lies-deeper
Here-to-stay	Here-to-stay
Won't-go-away	Won't-go-away
No matter-what-you-say	No matter-what-you-say
No matter-what-you-say	No matter-what-you-say

Faucet, lingering, sneaks back, hides a copy of Current Anthropology *in his jacket, and hurries out to join the rest. Curtain*

Act III

An apartment in lower Manhattan, late afternoon. One-room flat.
Door to hallway at rear. Door to bathroom L. Table and chairs R.
Other furniture. Ardent, Anyone, Eve, Blunt, and the Faucets draped
disconsolately about, Ardent sitting on table, feet on chair.

ARDENT I should have known better than to take that Bushman into the revolutionary movement.

ANYONE I still say the Bushman couldn't have known. He ran off before we set up the plan to change the labels on the Paleolithic tools — the cudgels, I mean — in the British Museum.

ARDENT So my gallant band, here we are. Deported victims of the primate British urge to defend a precious isle of ignorance against the shining sea-terrors of truth.

FAUCET What time is it?

ARDENT So little time...for it is the time of man, the time out of mind, the time of animal slime beyond all present memory, the time of vertebrate-hate-thy-neighbor, the time —

EVE It's five o'clock.

FAUCET Teatime. No wonder I feel so weary.

ARDENT What really governs the English — and their out-herod-ing colonials? Is it a protoplasmic urge to ingest? Oh no. A feudal-primate dominance order? Oh no. Big Ben. Ding-dong! Ding-dong! Ding-dong! Ding-dong! Ding-dong! Drink-tea! Drink-tea! Drink-tea! Drink-tea! Drink-tea!

FAUCET By God, Ardent, I've had enough! It tolls for thee. To impugn mankind is one thing, but to impugn Britons ...quite another!

BLUNT Quite!

MARY Hear! Hear!

ARDENT The territorial poison quite o'ercrows your spirit.

FAUCET Ardent, I've long had my doubts — and so have Mary and Blunt, I daresay — about your tactics, but now I question the issue, the whole flimsy revolutionary

63

at bay: its energy releases itself through another urge to make its play more terrifying and more irrational. When the Bolsheviks abolished private property, they decreed for themselves a reign of naked power, unleashed a dominance drive that made the English Industrial Revolution look like a Sunday-afternoon picnic on the Thames. The instincts lie deep. They line the human flesh. They are the chemistry of the genes. Cultural instincts, waiting their day. Like a desert river, vanished perhaps season after season, and then, then in a flick of a thunderstorm it comes ripping and raging out of the inscrutable earth. Yes, man builds his own realities. Do you know what it means to believe in the existence of things that don't exist? Self-delusion. All hail, man's unique capacity... self-delusion. And against it recollect the ease with which Adolf Hitler brought about in a generation of German youth his education for death [p. 203]. Was this the implanting of a learned response... or the release of an instinct? Defend one's own, *Lebensraum*, hate thy — (*Knock at door*) I'll get it. (*It's Shapiro, carrying a large challah and balancing a plate of gefilte fish*) You have the wrong apartment. We didn't order anything. Get out!

SHAPIRO   (*Politely*) Oh no, you'll excuse me, please, it's the right apartment, OK, Mr. Arbenz? You only today moved in?

ARDENT   Ardent, Ardent — get the name right. Yes, we moved in. We paid our rent. It's our apartment. So beat it!

SHAPIRO   Vell, you see, ve live down the hall. Shapiro, 2B. And Sarah for the veekend just happened to be making some gefilte fish. So she says to me, Hymie, why not take some fish to our new neighbors. It's Friday night, maybe they're Catlics? Get acquainted, she says, velcome them to the building. Mr. Arbenz, she says, he looks so pale, so bloodless, eat some good... Oh, but you'll excuse me. Please, if you're busy, vhy don't you just take the plate and the bread —

66

EVE   (*Coming to door*) Please won't you come in, Mr. Sha-piro? It's really so nice of you. (*Thank you, thank you, he says, and she and he manage somehow to get the food to the table*) So thoughtful —

SHAPIRO   Nothing really, absolutely, Mrs. Arbenz. You know, vhen Sarah and I moved in, Mrs. Cassidy, she used to live in this very apartment, she brought us some preserved pig's knuckles that first night. Such good people in this building, so considerate of the others. You know … anyhow, taste the gefilte fish, it's Sarah's best special dish.

EVE   (*Setting out food*) Here you are, Faucet. Teatime, old boy. C'mon Blunt, Mary, Anyone, Bushman. (*Aside to Ardent*) Robert, don't sulk. You'll make him feel bad.

Ardent comes to table and starts to cut challah.

SHAPIRO   You'll excuse me, Mr. Arbenz, for taking the liberty. Challah is a kind of bread tastes better it should be torn apart. Here … by the nubbles.

BLUNT   How barbarian!

MARY   (*Sarcastic*) The knife is so much more civilized.

SHAPIRO   Sure, sure, you're right, yes. Then I'll cut it for you. Ve too had problems with the pig's knuckles. Oi! (*Cuts finger, sucks blood*) It's nothing, nothing. Eat, eat. Like my mother used to say: eat, Hymie, eat … or I'll kill myself. (*Sets plate of fish and bread before Faucet*)

BLUNT   Faucet, you're pale as a ghost.

FAUCET   (*Running in screaming anguish to bathroom*) Yeeah! There's blood on the challah!

ANYONE   Did it release his animal instincts?

MARY   His lunch.

SHAPIRO   Vell, you should enjoy yourselves. Sarah said for me I should come right home if they're goyim … I mean if they're going to be busy. Come in anytime. Shapiro, 2B.

ARDENT   (*Going to door with him*) Yea, sure, sure … and to you the same. I mean, the same to you, you come over here. (*Slams door after Shapiro but then regrets it, so opens it quickly and shuts it again lightly*)

BLUNT I wouldn't eat that bloody challah. What's more, I'm fed up with this whole bloody revolution. It's about time, you knew, Ardent. The Faucets and I turned in that fool scheme of changing the museum labels on the Paleolithic tools. It is a science, you know. Just doesn't change like that. Not kosher, you might say.

ARDENT I was beginning to suspect it. The betrayal, I mean. Incurable romantics. I suspected you all along, all of you... Betrayed, betrayed. Who among us —

BLUNT Just a second before you produce a new drama, Ardent. Let me tell you just why I'm fed up. It's your mad theory of cultural instincts and compulsions. Vanished like a desert river and then springs up. Shall I grow a long canine soon, or part the hair of my tail behind? But never mind that. It's just too neat, that's the principal part of it. When we're good to our neighbors, it's the in-group amity of a social species, when we're bad, a primeval urge comes out. When there's no war, the instinct's just in hiding, and when there is war, it springs loose. Let a theory violate my beliefs. Let it even violate credulity. It doesn't matter to me. Nor am I afraid to go against the average opinions of geneticists, physiologists, paleontologists, anthropologists, Rousseau, Marx, Jefferson, or Queen Elizabeth. (Faucet: Come, come.) But I must fear to entertain a hypothesis if I can't imagine a situation in which it would fail to stand up. I must be able to conceive its failure. It's not a hypothesis if it can't be tested.

ARDENT (*Shouting*) Of course it's not a hypothesis. You know very well what it is, Blunt. Remember well what I put to you the day you first showed me the evidence of man's ancestral depravity. Dare you tell the world, I asked. Dare you tell a world on the brink of international disaster that man is an innate killer? We have

68

tried everything else, you said, why not try the truth for a change. It's no hypothesis, Blunt. (*Screams*) It's the truth! The Revolutionary Truth!

MARY   (*Calm*) No wonder it's proved so immune to evidence. The gorilla —

ANYONE   (*Sneers*) How does that so-called evidence compare? You know very well what the world is like ... the Bolshevik terror, racism, the Hungarian Revolution, the burning flesh of Jews, the hundred megatons ... I know it, and you know it.

MARY   Yes, of course you know it, Anyone. Let's go, gentlemen.

(*She takes Faucet by one arm, Kung by the other. They leave, followed by Blunt, who before he goes says*)

BLUNT   Goodbye, Eve. You too, Anyone. Ardent, a horde of gibbons guide thee to thy rest. You can forget the fiver you owe me.

(*Exit*)

ARDENT   Betrayed, betrayed ... the revolution betrayed. How ungrateful! I was doing it for them. What dogs. What worse-than-dogs. Would a dog betray? Never! ... (*A thought strikes him*) Never. You know, a dog couldn't. Only a man. (*Amazed*) By God! By God! By God!

EVE   Oh, Robert, Robert, oh, hast thou slain the Jabberwock? Come to my arms, my beamish boy! Oh frabjous day. Callooh, Callay!

ARDENT   (*Musing. He has seen the light.*) Remarkable animal... Only he betrays ... and only he is betrayed. (*Grins sheepishly at Eve. They embrace.*) Ah, Eve. In sickness and in health, in poverty or wealth, a smash or a flop, til death do us part ... the Eve to my Adam, the Damon to my Pythias, the Horatio to my Hamlet —

EVE   The Sancho to your Quixote.

ARDENT   And Anyone. Dear friend, Anyone. I could always count on you, couldn't I? You'd always believe in me, Anyone. (*Snaps out of it*) C'mon, it's six o'clock. I'm

69

hungry. I'm taking you both to dinner: a nice, bloody raw steak. On Blunt's fiver. Ha! And then...then to a show. West Side Story! (*Puts on Anyone's hat and Eve's coat*)

ANYONE Ardent, while you're in the mood, you know I would like to see the United Nations. I've never been in New York before.

ARDENT No, no, Anyone. Broadway. You'd never understand the East Side Story without the West Side Story. Never.

EVE Anyhow, the East Side Story'll have a longer run.

ARDENT Only because it makes war so well. No, the play's the thing. (*Takes both by the arm and shepherds them out the door, saying*) West Side Story. It's got everything [pp. 330–33]. Natural man. All the instincts right there. The whole damned animal legacy: the timeless struggle over territory, the gangs of primates, the rigid dominance order, the mutual protection of the horde, the collective hate of the others, and then...then... the unique contribution of man: the supreme dedication to the switchblade. Absolutely great. West Side Story. Life follows Art!

Curtain

CHAPTER TWO

Poor Man, Rich Man, Big-Man, Chief:

Political Types in

Melanesia and Polynesia*

With an eye to their own life goals, the native peoples of Pacific Islands unwittingly present to anthropologists a generous scientific gift: an extended series of experiments in cultural adaptation and evolutionary development.[1] They have compressed their institutions within the confines of infertile coral atolls, expanded them on volcanic islands, created with the means history gave them cultures adapted to the deserts of Australia, the mountains and warm coasts of New Guinea, the rainforests of the Solomon Islands. From the Australian Aborigines, whose hunting and gathering existence duplicates in outline the cultural life of the later Paleolithic, to the great chiefdoms of Hawaii, where society approached the formative levels of the old Fertile Crescent civilizations, almost every general phase in the progress of primitive culture is exemplified.

Where culture so experiments, anthropology finds its laboratories — makes its comparisons.[2]

In the southern and eastern Pacific two contrasting cultural provinces have long evoked anthropological interest: *Melanesia*, including New Guinea, the Bismarcks, Solomons, and island groups east to Fiji; and *Polynesia*, consisting in its main portion of the triangular constellation of lands between New Zealand, Easter Island, and the Hawaiian Islands. In and around Fiji, Melanesia and Polynesia intergrade culturally, but west and east of

* Originally published in *Comparative Studies in Society and History* 5.3 (April 1963). Reprinted with the permission of Cambridge University Press.

their intersection the two provinces pose broad contrasts in several sectors: in religion, art, kinship groupings, economics, political organization. The differences are the more notable for the underlying similarities from which they emerge. Melanesia and Polynesia are both agricultural regions in which many of the same crops — such as yams, taro, breadfruit, bananas, and coconuts — have long been cultivated by many similar techniques. Some recently presented linguistic and archaeological studies indeed suggest that Polynesian cultures originated from an eastern Melanesian hearth during the first millennium B.C.[3] Yet in anthropological annals the Polynesians were to become famous for elaborate forms of rank and chieftainship, whereas most Melanesian societies broke off advance on this front at more rudimentary levels.

It is obviously imprecise, however, to make out the political contrast in broad culture-area terms. Within Polynesia, certain of the islands (such as Hawaii, the Society Islands, and Tonga) developed unparalleled political momentum. And not all Melanesian polities, on the other side, were constrained and truncated in their evolution. In New Guinea and nearby areas of western Melanesia, small and loosely ordered political groupings are numerous, but in eastern Melanesia (New Caledonia and Fiji, for example), political approximations of the Polynesian condition become common. There is more of an upward west-to-east slope in political development in the southern Pacific than a steplike, quantum progression.[4] It is quite revealing, however, to compare the extremes of this continuum, the western Melanesian underdevelopment against the greater Polynesian chiefdoms. While such comparison does not exhaust the evolutionary variations, it fairly establishes the scope of overall political achievement in this Pacific phylum of cultures.

Measurable among several dimensions, the contrast between developed Polynesian and underdeveloped Melanesian polities is immediately striking for differences in scale. H. Ian Hogbin and Camilla Wedgwood concluded from a survey of Melanesian (mostly western Melanesian) societies that ordered, independent political bodies in the region typically include seventy to three

hundred persons; more recent work in the New Guinea Highlands suggests political groupings of up to a thousand, occasionally a few thousand people (Hogbin and Wedgwood 1952–53,
1953–54).[5] But in Polynesia, sovereignties of two thousand or
three thousand are run-of-the-mill, and the most advanced chiefdoms, as in Tonga or Hawaii, might claim ten thousand, even tens
of thousands.[6] Varying step by step with such differences in size of
the polity are differences in territorial extent: from a few square
miles in western Melanesia to tens or even hundreds of square
miles in Polynesia.

The Polynesian advance in political scale was supported by
advance over Melanesia in political structure. Melanesia presents
a great array of social-political forms: here political organization
is based on patrilineal descent groups, there on cognatic groups,
or men's clubhouses recruiting neighborhood memberships, on a
secret ceremonial society, or perhaps on some combination of
these structural principles. Yet a general plan can be discerned.
The characteristic western Melanesian "tribe," that is, the ethnic-
cultural entity, consists of many autonomous kinship-residential
groups. Amounting on the ground to a small village or a local
cluster of hamlets, each of these is a copy of the others in organization, each tends to be economically self-governing, and each is
the equal of the others in political status. The tribal plan is one of
politically unintegrated segments — segmental. But the political
geometry in Polynesia is pyramidal. Local groups of the order of
self-governing Melanesian communities appear in Polynesia as
subdivisions of a more inclusive political body. Smaller units are
integrated into larger through a system of intergroup ranking,
and the network of representative chiefs of the subdivisions
amounts to a coordinating political structure. So, instead of the
Melanesian scheme of small, separate, and equal political blocs,
the Polynesian polity is an extensive pyramid of groups capped by
the family and following of a paramount chief. (This Polynesian
political upshot is often, although not always, facilitated by the
development of ranked lineages. Called *conical clan* by Kirchhoff,
at one time *ramage* by Firth, and *status lineage* by Goldman, the
Polynesian ranked lineage is the same in principle as the so-called

73

obok system widely distributed in Central Asia, and it is at least analogous to the Scottish clan, the Chinese clan, certain Central African Bantu lineage systems, the house-groups of Northwest Coast Indians, perhaps even the "tribes" of the Israelites [Kirchhoff 1955, Firth 1957, I. Goldman 1957, Bacon 1958, Fried 1957]. Genealogical ranking is its distinctive feature: members of the same descent unit are ranked by genealogical distance from the common ancestor; lines of the same group become senior and cadet branches on this principle; related corporate lineages are relatively ranked, again by genealogical priority.)

Here is another criterion of Polynesian political advance: historical performance. Almost all of the native peoples of the South Pacific were brought up against intense European cultural pressure in the late eighteenth and the nineteenth century. Yet only the Hawaiians, Tahitians, Tongans, and to a lesser extent the Fijians successfully defended themselves by evolving countervailing, native-controlled states. Complete with public governments and public law, monarchs and taxes, ministers and minions, these nineteenth-century states are testimony to the native Polynesian political genius, to the level and the potential of indigenous political accomplishments.

Embedded within the grand differences in political scale, structure, and performance is a more personal contrast, one in quality of leadership. An historically particular type of leader figure, the "big-man," as he is often locally styled, appears in the underdeveloped settings of Melanesia. Another type, a chief properly so-called, is associated with the Polynesian advance.[7] Now, these are distinct sociological types, that is to say, differences in the powers, privileges, rights, duties, and obligations of Melanesian big-men and Polynesian chiefs are given by the divergent societal contexts in which they operate. Yet the institutional distinctions cannot help but be manifest also in differences in bearing and character, appearance and manner — in a word, personality. It may be a good way to begin the more rigorous sociological comparison of leadership with a more impressionistic sketch of the contrast in the human dimension. Here I find it useful to apply characterizations — or is it caricature? — from our own history to big-men and chiefs, however much injustice this does to the historically incomparable backgrounds of the Melanesians and Polynesians. The Melanesian big-man seems so thoroughly bourgeois, so reminiscent of the free-enterprising rugged individual of our own heritage. He combines with an ostensible interest in the general welfare a more profound measure of self-interested cunning and economic calculation. His gaze, as Veblen might have put it, is fixed unswervingly to the main chance. His every public action is designed to make a competitive and invidious comparison with others, to show a standing above the masses that is product of his own personal manufacture. The historical caricature of the Polynesian chief, however, is feudal rather than capitalist. His appearance, his bearing, is almost regal; very likely he just *is* a big man — "Can't you see he is a chief? See how big he is?" (Gifford 1929:124). In his every public action is a display of the refinements of breeding, in his manner always that noblesse oblige of true pedigree and an incontestable right of rule. With his standing not so much a personal achievement as a just social due, he can afford to be, and he is, every inch a chief.

In the several Melanesian tribes in which big-men have come under anthropological scrutiny, local cultural differences modify the expression of their personal powers.[8] But the indicative quality of big-man authority is everywhere the same: it is *personal* power. Big-men do not come to office; they do not succeed to, nor are they installed in, existing positions of leadership over political groups. The attainment of big-man status is, rather, the outcome of a series of acts which elevate a person above the common herd and attract about him a coterie of loyal, lesser men. It is not accurate to speak of "big-man" as a political title, for it is but an acknowledged standing in interpersonal relations — a "prince among men," so to speak, as opposed to "The Prince of Danes." In particular Melanesian tribes the phrase might be "man of importance" or "man of renown," "generous rich-man," or "center-man," as well as "big-man."

A kind of two-sidedness in authority is implied in this series of phrases, a division of the big-man's field of influence into two distinct sectors. "Center-man" particularly connotes a cluster of followers gathered about an influential pivot. It socially implies the division of the tribe into political in-groups dominated by outstanding personalities. To the in-group, the big-man presents this sort of picture:

> The place of the leader in the district group [in northern Malaita] is well summed up by his title, which might be translated as "centre-man." ... He was like a banyan, the natives explain, which, though the biggest and tallest in the forest, is still a tree like the rest. But, just because it exceeds all others, the banyan gives support to more lianas and creepers, provides more food for the birds, and gives better protection against sun and rain. (Hogbin 1943–44:258)

But "man of renown" connotes a broader tribal field in which a man is not so much a leader as he is some sort of hero. This is the side of the big-man facing outward from his own faction, his status among some or all of the other political clusters of the tribe. The political sphere of the big-man divides itself into a small internal sector composed of his personal satellites — rarely over eighty men — and a much larger external sector, the tribal galaxy consisting of many similar constellations.

As it crosses over from the internal into the external sector, a big-man's power undergoes qualitative change. Within his faction a Melanesian leader has true command ability, outside of it only fame and indirect influence. It is not that the center-man rules his faction by physical force, but his followers do feel obliged to obey him, and he can usually get what he wants by haranguing them — by public verbal suasion. The orbits of outsiders, however, are set by their own center-men. "Do it yourself. I'm not *your* fool" would be the characteristic response to an order issued by a center-man to an outsider among the Siuai (Oliver 1955:408).[9] This fragmentation of true authority presents special political difficulties, particularly in organizing large masses of people for the prosecution of such collective ends as warfare or ceremony. Big-men do instigate mass action, but only by establishing both extensive renown and special personal relations of compulsion or reciprocity with other center-men.

Politics is in the main personal politicking in these Melanesian societies, and the size of a leader's faction as well as the extent of his renown are normally set by competition with other ambitious men. Little or no authority is given by social ascription: leadership is a creation — a creation of followership. "Followers," as it is written of the Kapauku of New Guinea, "stand in various relations to the leader. Their obedience to the headman's decisions is caused by motivations which reflect their particular relations to the leader" (Pospisil 1958:81). So a man must be prepared to demonstrate that he possesses the kinds of skills that command respect — magical powers, gardening prowess, mastery of oratorical style, perhaps bravery in war and feud.[10] Typically decisive is the deployment of one's skills and efforts in a certain direction: toward amassing goods, most often pigs, shell monies, and vegetable foods and distributing them in ways which build a name for cavalier generosity, if not for compassion. A faction is developed by informal private assistance to people of a locale. Tribal rank and renown are developed by great public giveaways sponsored by the rising big-man, often on behalf of his faction as well as himself. In different Melanesian tribes, the renown-making public distribution may appear as one side of a delayed exchange of pigs between corporate kinship groups; a marital consideration given a bride's kinfolk; a set of feasts connected with the erection of a big-man's dwelling, or of a clubhouse for himself and his faction, or with the purchase of higher grades of rank in secret societies; the sponsorship of a religious ceremony; a payment of subsidies and blood compensations to military allies; or perhaps the giveaway is a ceremonial challenge bestowed on another leader in the attempt to outgive and thus outrank him (a potlatch).

The making of the faction, however, is the true making of the Melanesian big-man. It is essential to establish relations of loyalty and obligation on the part of a number of people such that their production can be mobilized for renown-building external distribution. The bigger the faction, the greater the renown; once momentum in external distribution has been generated, the opposite can also be true. Any ambitious man who can gather a following can launch a societal career. The rising big-man

77

necessarily depends initially on a small core of followers, principally his own household and his closest relatives. Upon these
people he can prevail economically: he capitalizes in the first instance on kinship dues and by finessing the relation of reciprocity
appropriate among close kinsmen. Often it becomes necessary at
an early phase to enlarge one's household. The rising leader goes
out of his way to incorporate within his family "strays" of various
sorts, people without familial support themselves, such as widows
and orphans. Additional wives are especially useful. With more
women gardening there will be more food for pigs and more
swineherds. A Kiwai Papuan picturesquely put to an anthropologist in pidgin the advantages, economic and political, of polygamy:
"Another woman go garden, another woman go take firewood,
another woman go catch fish, another woman cook him — husband
he sing out plenty people come kaikai [i.e., come to eat]" (Landtman 1927:168). Each new marriage, incidentally, creates for the
big-man an additional set of in-laws from whom he can exact economic favors. Finally, a leader's career sustains its upward climb
when he is able to link other men and their families to his faction,
harnessing their production to his ambition. This is done by calculated generosities, by placing others in gratitude and obligation
through helping them in some big way. A common technique is
payment of bridewealth on behalf of young men seeking wives.

The great Malinowski used a phrase in analyzing primitive
political economy that felicitously describes just what the big-
man is doing: amassing a "fund of power." A big-man is one who
can create and use social relations which give him leverage on others' production and the ability to siphon off an excess product —
or sometimes he can cut down their consumption in the interest
of the siphon. Now, although his attention may be given primarily
to short-term personal interests, from an objective standpoint
the leader acts to promote long-term societal interests. The fund
of power provisions activities that involve other groups of the
society at large. In the greater perspective of that society at large,
big-men are indispensable means of creating supralocal organization: in tribes normally fragmented into small independent
groups, big-men at least temporarily widen the sphere of cere-

mony, recreation and art, economic collaboration, of war too. Yet always this greater societal organization depends on the lesser factional organization, particularly on the ceilings on economic mobilization set by relations between center-men and followers. The limits and the weaknesses of the political order in general are the limits and the weaknesses of the factional in-groups.

And the personal quality of subordination to a center-man is a serious weakness in factional structure. A personal loyalty has to be made and continually reinforced; if there is discontent, it may well be severed. Merely to create a faction takes time and effort, and to hold it, still more effort. The potential rupture of personal links in the factional chain is at the heart of two broad evolutionary shortcomings of western Melanesian political orders. First, a comparative instability: shifting dispositions and magnetisms of ambitious men in a region may induce fluctuations in factions, perhaps some overlapping of them, and fluctuations also in the extent of different renowns. The death of a center-man can become a regional political trauma: the death undermines the personally cemented faction, the group dissolves in whole or in part, and the people regroup finally around rising pivotal big-men. Although particular tribal structures in places cushion the disorganization, the big-man political system is generally unstable over short terms: in its superstructure it is a flux of rising and falling leaders, in its substructure of enlarging and contracting factions. Second, the personal political bond contributes to the containment of evolutionary advance. The possibility of their desertion, it is clear, often inhibits a leader's ability forcibly to push up his followers' output, thereby placing constraints on higher political organization, but there is more to it than that. If it is to generate great momentum, a big-man's quest for the summits of renown is likely to bring out a contradiction in his relations to followers, so that he finds himself encouraging defection — or worse, an egalitarian rebellion — by encouraging production.

One side of the Melanesian contradiction is the initial economic reciprocity between a center-man and his followers. For his help they give their help, and for goods going out through his hands other goods (often from outside factions) flow back to his followers by the same path. The other side is that a cumulative buildup of renown forces center-men into economic extortion of the faction. Here it is important that not merely his own status but the standing and perhaps the military security of his people depend on the big-man's achievements in public distribution. Established at the head of a sizable faction, a center-man comes under increasing pressure to extract goods from his followers, to delay reciprocities owing them, and to deflect incoming goods back into external circulation. Success in competition with other big-men particularly undermines internal-factional reciprocities: such success is precisely measurable by the ability to give outsiders more than they can possibly reciprocate. In well-delineated big-man polities, we find leaders negating the reciprocal obligations upon which their following had been predicated. Substituting extraction for reciprocity, they must compel their people to "eat the leader's renown," as one Solomon Island group puts it, in return for productive efforts. Some center-men appear more able than others to dam the inevitable tide of discontent that mounts within their factions, perhaps because of charismatic personalities, perhaps because of the particular social organizations in which they operate.[11] But, paradoxically, the ultimate defense of the center-man's position is some slackening of his drive to enlarge the funds of power. The alternative is much worse. In the anthropological record there are not merely instances of big-man chicanery and of material deprivation of the faction in the interests of renown but some also of overloading of social relations with followers: the generation of antagonisms, defections, and in extreme cases the violent liquidation of the center-man.[12] Developing internal constraints, the Melanesian big-man political order brakes evolutionary advance at a certain level. It sets ceilings on the intensification of political authority, on the intensification of household production by political means, and on the diversion of household outputs in support of wider political organization. But in Polynesia these constraints were breached, and although Polynesian chiefdoms also found their developmental plateau, it was not before political evolution had been carried above the Melanesian ceilings. The fundamental defects of the Melanesian plan were overcome in Polynesia. The division between small internal and larger external political sectors, upon which all big-man politics hinged, was suppressed in Polynesia by the growth of an enclaving chiefdom-at-large. A chain of command subordinating lesser chiefs and groups to greater, on the basis of inherent societal rank, made local blocs or personal followings (such as were independent in Melanesia) merely dependent parts of the larger Polynesian chiefdom. So the nexus of the Polynesian chiefdom became an extensive set of offices, a pyramid of higher and lower chiefs holding sway over larger and smaller sections of the polity. Indeed the system of ranked and subdivided lineages (conical clan system), upon which the pyramid was characteristically established, might build up through several orders of inclusion and encompass the whole of an island or group of islands. While the island or the archipelago would normally be divided into several independent chiefdoms, high-order lineage connections between them, as well as kinship ties between their paramount chiefs, provided structural avenues for at least temporary expansion of political scale, for consolidation of great into even greater chiefdoms.[13]

The pivotal paramount chief as well as the chieftains controlling parts of a chiefdom were true office-holders and title-holders. They were not, like Melanesian big-men, fishers of men: they held positions of authority over permanent groups. The honorifics of Polynesian chiefs likewise referred not to a standing in interpersonal relations but to their leadership of political divisions — here "The Prince of Danes," *not* "the prince among men." In western Melanesia, the personal superiorities and inferiorities arising in the intercourse of particular men largely defined the political bodies. In Polynesia there emerged suprapersonal structures of leadership and followership, organizations that continued independently of the particular men who occupied positions in them for brief mortal spans.

And these Polynesian chiefs did not make their positions in society — they were installed in societal positions. In several of the islands, men did struggle to office against the will and stratagems of rival aspirants. But then they came *to* power. Power

81

resided in the office; it was not made by the demonstration of personal superiority. In other islands — Tahiti was famous for it — succession to chieftainship was tightly controlled by inherent rank. The chiefly lineage ruled by virtue of its genealogical connections with divinity, and chiefs were succeeded by first sons, who carried "in the blood" the attributes of leadership. The important comparative point is this: the qualities of command that had to reside in men in Melanesia, that had to be personally demonstrated in order to attract loyal followers, were in Polynesia socially assigned to office and rank. In Polynesia, people of high rank and office ipso facto were leaders, and by the same token the qualities of leadership were automatically lacking — theirs was not to question why — among the underlying population. Magical powers such as a Melanesian big-man might acquire to sustain his position, a Polynesian high chief inherited by divine descent as the *mana* that sanctified his rule and protected his person against the hands of the commonalty. The productive ability the big-man laboriously had to demonstrate was effortlessly given Polynesian chiefs as religious control over agricultural fertility, and upon the ceremonial implementation of it the rest of the people were conceived dependent. Where a Melanesian leader had to master the compelling oratorical style, Polynesian paramounts often had trained "talking chiefs" whose voice was the chiefly command.

In the Polynesian view, a chiefly personage was in the nature of things powerful. But this merely implies the objective observation that his power was of the group rather than of himself. His authority came from the organization, from an organized acquiescence in his privileges and organized means of sustaining them. A kind of paradox resides in evolutionary developments that detach the exercise of authority from the necessity to demonstrate personal superiority: organizational power actually extends the role of personal decision and conscious planning, gives it greater scope, impact, and effectiveness. The growth of a political system such as the Polynesian constitutes advance over Melanesian orders of interpersonal dominance in the human control of human affairs. Especially significant for society at large were privileges

82

accorded Polynesian chiefs which made them greater architects of funds of power than ever was any Melanesian big-man.

Masters of their people and "owners" in a titular sense of group resources, Polynesian chiefs had rights of call upon the labor and agricultural produce of households within their domains. Economic mobilization did not depend on, as it necessarily had for Melanesian big-men, the *de novo* creation by the leader of personal loyalties and economic obligations. A chief need not stoop to obligate this man or that man, need not by a series of individual acts of generosity induce others to support him, for economic leverage over a group was the inherent chiefly due. Consider the implications for the fund of power of the widespread chiefly privilege, related to titular "ownership" of land, of placing an interdiction, a tabu, on the harvest of some crop by way of reserving its use for a collective project. By means of the tabu the chief directs the course of production in a general way: households of his domain must turn to some other means of subsistence. He delivers a stimulus to household production: in the absence of the tabu further labors would not have been necessary. Most significantly, he has generated a politically utilizable agricultural surplus. A subsequent call on this surplus floats chieftainship as a going concern, capitalizes the fund of power. In certain islands, Polynesian chiefs controlled great storehouses that held the goods congealed by chiefly pressures on the commonalty. David Malo, one of the great native custodians of old Hawaiian lore, felicitously catches the political significance of the chiefly magazine in his well-known *Hawaiian Antiquities*:

> It was the practice for kings [that is, paramount chiefs of individual islands] to build store-houses in which to collect food, fish, tapas [bark cloth], malos [men's loincloths], pa-us [women's loin skirts], and all sorts of goods. These store-houses were designed by the Kalaimoku [the chief's principal executive] as a means of keeping the people contented, so they would not desert the king. They were like the baskets that were used to entrap the *hinalea* fish. The *hinalea* thought there was something good within the basket, and he hung round the outside of it. In the same way the people thought there

83

was food in the store-houses, and they kept their eyes on the king. As the rat will not desert the pantry ... where he thinks food is, so the people will not desert the king while they think there is food in his store-house. (1903:257–58)

Redistribution of the fund of power was the supreme art of Polynesian politics. By well-planned noblesse oblige the large domain of a paramount chief was held together, organized at times for massive projects, protected against other chiefdoms, even further enriched. Uses of the chiefly fund included lavish hospitality and entertainments for outside chiefs and for the chief's own people, and succor of individuals or the underlying population at large in times of scarcities — bread and circuses. Chiefs subsidized craft production, promoting in Polynesia a division of technical labor unparalleled in extent and expertise in most of the Pacific. They supported also great technical construction, as of irrigation complexes, the further returns to which swelled the chiefly fund. They initiated large-scale religious construction too, subsidized the great ceremonies, and organized logistical support for extensive military campaigns. Larger and more easily replenished than their western Melanesian counterparts, Polynesian funds of power permitted greater political regulation of a greater range of social activities on greater scale.

In the most advanced Polynesian chiefdoms, as in Hawaii and Tahiti, a significant part of the chiefly fund was deflected away from general redistribution toward the upkeep of the institution of chieftainship. The fund was siphoned for the support of a permanent administrative establishment. In some measure, goods and services contributed by the people precipitated out as the grand houses, assembly places, and temple platforms of chiefly precincts. In another measure, they were appropriated for the livelihood of circles of retainers, many of them close kinsmen of the chief, who clustered around the powerful paramounts. These were not all useless hangers-on. They were political cadres: supervisors of the stores, talking chiefs, ceremonial attendants, high priests who were intimately involved in political rule, envoys to transmit directives through the chiefdom. There were men in

84

these chiefly retinues — in Tahiti and perhaps Hawaii, specialized warrior corps — whose force could be directed internally as a buttress against fragmenting or rebellious elements of the chiefdom. A Tahitian or Hawaiian high chief had more compelling sanctions than the harangue. He controlled a ready physical force, an armed body of executioners, which gave him mastery particularly over the lesser people of the community. While it looks a lot like the big-man's faction again, the differences in functioning of the great Polynesian chief's retinue are more significant than the superficial similarities in appearance. The chief's coterie, for one thing, is economically dependent upon him rather than he upon them. And in deploying the cadres politically in various sections of the chiefdom, or against the lower orders, the great Polynesian chiefs sustained command where the Melanesian big-man, in his external sector, had at best renown.

This is not to say that the advanced Polynesian chiefdoms were free of internal defect, of potential or actual malfunctioning. The large political-military apparatus indicates something of the opposite. So does the recent work of Irving Goldman on the intensity of "status rivalry" in Polynesia (1955, 1957, 1960), especially when it is considered that much of the status rivalry in developed chiefdoms, as the Hawaiian, amounted to popular rebellion against chiefly despotism rather than mere contest for position within the ruling-stratum. This suggests that Polynesian chiefdoms, just as Melanesian big-man orders, generate along with evolutionary development countervailing anti-authority pressures, and that the weight of the latter may ultimately impede further development.

The Polynesian contradiction seems clear enough. On one side, chieftainship is never detached from kinship moorings and kinship economic ethics. Even the greatest Polynesian chiefs were conceived superior kinsmen to the masses, fathers of their people, and generosity was morally incumbent upon them. On the other side, the major Polynesian paramounts seemed inclined to "eat the power of the government too much," as the Tahitians put it, to divert an undue proportion of the general wealth toward the chiefly establishment.[14] The diversion could be accomplished by lowering the customary level of general redistribution, lessening the material returns of chieftainship to the community at large — tradition attributes the great rebellion of Mangarevan commoners to such cause (Buck 1938:70–77, 160, 165). Or the diversion might — and I suspect more commonly did — consist of greater and more forceful exactions from lesser chiefs and people, increasing returns to the chiefly apparatus without necessarily affecting the level of general redistribution. In either case, the well-developed chiefdom creates for itself the dampening paradox of stoking rebellion by funding its authority.[15]

In Hawaii and other islands cycles of political centralization and decentralization may be abstracted from traditional histories. That is, larger chiefdoms periodically fragmented into smaller and then were later reconstituted. Here would be more evidence of a tendency to overtax the political structure. But how to explain the emergence of a developmental stymie, of an inability to sustain political advance beyond a certain level? To point to a chiefly propensity to consume or a Polynesian propensity to rebel is not enough: such propensities are promoted by the very advance of chiefdoms. There is reason to hazard instead that Parkinson's notable law is behind it all: that progressive expansion in political scale entailed more-than-proportionate accretion in the ruling apparatus, unbalancing the flow of wealth in favor of the apparatus. The ensuing unrest then curbs the chiefly impositions, sometimes by reducing chiefdom scale to the nadir of the periodic cycle. Comparison of the requirements of administration in small and large Polynesian chiefdoms helps make the point.

A lesser chiefdom, confined, say, as in the Marquesas Islands to a narrow valley, could be almost personally ruled by a headman in frequent contact with the relatively small population. Melville's partly romanticized — also for its ethnographic details, partly cribbed — account in *Typee* makes this clear enough (or see Handy 1923 and Linton 1939). But the great Polynesian chiefs had to rule much larger, spatially dispersed, internally organized populations. Hawaii, an island over four thousand square miles with an aboriginal population approaching one hundred thousand, was at times a single chiefdom, at other times divided into two to six independent chiefdoms, and at all times each chiefdom was composed of large subdivisions under powerful subchiefs. Sometimes a chief-dom in the Hawaiian group extended beyond the confines of one of the islands, incorporating part of another through conquest. Now, such extensive chiefdoms would have to be coordinated; they would have to be centrally tapped for a fund of power, but-tressed against internal disruption, sometimes massed for distant, perhaps overseas, military engagements. All of this to be imple-mented by means of communication still at the level of word-of-mouth and means of transportation consisting of human bodies and canoes. (The extent of certain larger chieftainships, coupled with the limitations of communication and transportation, inci-dentally suggests another possible source of political unrest — that the burden of provisioning the governing apparatus would tend to fall disproportionately on groups within easiest access of the para-mount.[16]) A tendency for the developed chiefdom to proliferate in executive cadres, to grow top-heavy, seems in these circum-stances altogether functional, even though the ensuing drain on wealth proves the chiefdom's undoing. Functional also, and like-wise a material drain on the chiefdom at large, would be widen-ing distinctions between chiefs and people in style of life. Palatial housing, ornamentation and luxury, finery and ceremony — in brief, conspicuous consumption, however much it seems mere self-interest, always has a more decisive social significance. It creates those invidious distinctions between rulers and ruled so conducive to a passive — hence quite economical! — acceptance of authority. Throughout history, inherently more powerful political organizations than the Polynesian, with more assured logistics of rule, have turned to it — including in our time some ostensibly revolutionary and proletarian governments, despite every prerev-olutionary protestation of solidarity with the masses and equality for the classes.

In Polynesia, then, as in Melanesia, political evolution is even-tually short-circuited by an overload on the relations between leaders and their people. The Polynesian tragedy, however, was somewhat the opposite of the Melanesian. In Polynesia, the evo-lutionary ceiling was set by extraction from the population at large in favor of the chiefly faction, in Melanesia by extraction from the big-man's faction in favor of distribution to the population at large. Most important, the Polynesian ceiling was higher. Melanesian big-men and Polynesian chiefs not only reflect different varieties and levels of political evolution, they display in different degrees the capacity to generate and to sustain political progress.

Especially emerging from their juxtaposition is the more decisive impact of Polynesian chiefs on the economy, the chiefs' greater leverage on the output of the several households of society. The success of any primitive political organization is decided here, in the control that can be developed over household economies. For the household is not merely the principal productive unit in primitive societies; it is often quite capable of autonomous direction of its own production, and it is oriented toward production for its own, not societal, consumption. The greater potential of Polynesian chieftainship is precisely the greater pressure it could exert on household output, its capacity both to generate a surplus and to deploy it out of the household toward a broader division of labor, cooperative construction, and massive ceremonial and military action. Polynesian chiefs were the more effective means of societal collaboration on economic, political, indeed all cultural fronts. Perhaps we have been too long accustomed to perceive rank and rule from the standpoint of the individuals involved rather than from the perspective of the total society, as if the secret of the subordination of man to man lay in the personal satisfactions of power. And then the breakdowns, too, or the evolutionary limits, have been searched out in men, in "weak" kings or megalomaniacal dictators — always, "who is the matter?" An excursion into the field of primitive politics suggests the more fruitful conception that the gains of political developments accrue more decisively to society than to individuals, and the failings as well are of structure, not men.

NOTES

1. The present paper is preliminary to a wider and more detailed comparison of Melanesian and Polynesian polities and economies. I have merely abstracted here some of the more striking political differences in the two areas. The full study — which, incidentally, will include more documentation — has been promised the editors of the *Journal of the Polynesian Society*, and I intend to deliver it to them someday.

The comparative method so far followed in this research has involved reading the monographs and taking notes. I don't think I originated the method, but I would like to christen it "The Method of Uncontrolled Comparison." The description developed of two forms of leadership is a mental distillation from the method of uncontrolled comparison. The two forms are abstracted sociological types. Anyone conversant with the anthropological literature of the South Pacific knows there are important variants of the types, as well as exceptional political forms not fully treated here. All would agree that consideration of the variations and exceptions is necessary and desirable. Yet there is pleasure too, and some intellectual reward, in discovering the broad patterns. To (social-)scientifically justify my pleasure, I could have referred to the pictures drawn of Melanesian big-men and Polynesian chiefs as "models" or as "ideal types." If that is all that is needed to confer respectability on the paper, may the reader have it this way.

I hope all of this has been sufficiently disarming. Or need it also be said that the hypotheses are provisional, subject to further research, etc.?

2. Since Rivers's day, the Pacific has provided ethnographic stimulus to virtually every major ethnological school and interest. From such great landmarks as Rivers's *History of Melanesian Society*, Radcliffe-Brown's "Social Organization of the Australian Tribes," Malinowski's famous Trobriand studies, especially *Argonauts of the Western Pacific*, Firth's pathmaking *Primitive Economics of the New Zealand Maori* and his functionalist classic, *We, the Tikopia*, and Mead's *Coming of Age in Samoa*, one can almost read off the history of ethnological theory in the earlier twentieth century. In addition to continuing to provision all these concerns, the Pacific has been the site of much recent evolutionist work (see, for example, I. Goldman 1955, 1960; Goodenough 1957; M. Sahlins 1958; Vayda 1959). There are also the outstanding monographs on special subjects ranging from tropical agriculture (Conklin 1957, Freeman 1955) to millenarianism (Worsley 1957).

3. This question, however, is presently in debate. See Grace 1955, 1959; Dyen 1960; Suggs 1960; Golson 1961.

89

4. There are notable bumps in the geographical gradient — the Trobriand chieftainships off eastern New Guinea will come to mind. But the Trobriand political development is clearly exceptional for western Melanesia.

5. On New Guinea Highland political scale, see among others, Paula Brown 1960.

6. See the summary account in M. Sahlins 1958, esp. pp. 132–33.

7. The big-man pattern is very widespread in western Melanesia, although its complete distribution is not yet clear to me. Anthropological descriptions of big-man leadership vary from mere hints of its existence, as among the Orokaiva (F.E. Williams 1930), Lesu (Powdermaker 1933), or the interior peoples of northeastern Guadalcanal (Hogbin 1937–38a), to excellent, closely grained analyses, such as Oliver's account of the Siuai of Bougainville (1955). Big-man leadership has been more or less extensively described for the Manus of the Admiralty Islands (Mead 1934, 1937a); the To'ambaita of northern Malaita (Hogbin 1939, 1943–44); the Tangu of northeastern New Guinea (Burridge 1960); the Kapauku of Netherlands New Guinea (Pospisil 1958, 1958–59); the Kaoka of Guadalcanal (Hogbin 1933–34, 1937–38b); the Seniang District of Malekula (Deacon 1934); the Gawa' of the Huon Gulf area, New Guinea (Hogbin 1951); the Abelam (Kaberry 1940–41, 1941–42) and the Arapesh (Mead 1937a, 1938, 1947) of the Sepik District, New Guinea; the Elema, Orokolo Bay, New Guinea (F.E. Williams 1940); the Ngarawapum of the Markham Valley, New Guinea (Read 1946–47, 1949–50); the Kiwai of the Fly estuary, New Guinea (Landtman 1927); and a number of other societies, including, in New Guinea Highlands, the Kuma (Reay 1959), the Gahuka-Gama (Read 1952–53, 1959), the Kyaka (Bulmer 1960–61), and the Enga (Meggitt 1957, 1957–58). (For an overview of the structural position of New Guinea Highlands' leaders, see Barnes 1962.) A partial bibliography on Polynesian chieftainship can be found in M. Sahlins 1958. The outstanding ethnographic description of Polynesian chieftainship is, of course, Firth's for Tikopia (1950, 1957) — Tikopia, however, is not typical of the more advanced Polynesian chiefdoms with which we are principally concerned here.

8. Thus the enclavement of the big-man pattern within a segmented lineage organization in the New Guinea Highlands appears to limit the leader's political role and authority in comparison, say, with the Siuai. In the Highlands, intergroup relations are regulated in part by the segmented lineage structure; among the Siuai, intergroup relations depend more on contractual arrangements between big-men, which throws these figures more into prominence. (Notable in

90

this connection has been the greater viability of the Siuai big-man than the native Highlands leader in the face of colonial control.) Barnes's comparison of Highland social structure with the classic segmentary lineage systems of Africa suggests an inverse relation between the formality of the lineage system and the political significance of individual action (1962). Now, if instances such as the Siuai be tacked on to the comparison, the generalization may be further supported and extended: among societies of the tribal level (cf. M. Sahlins 1961, Service 1962), the greater the self-regulation of the political process through a lineage system, the less function that remains to big-men and the less significant their political authority.

9. Compare with the parallel statement for the Kaoka of Guadalcanal in Hogbin 1937–38b:305.

10. It is difficult to say just how important the military qualifications of leadership have been in Melanesia, since the ethnographic researches have typically been undertaken after pacification, sometimes long after. I may underestimate this factor. Compare Bromley 1960.

11. Indeed, it is the same people, the Siuai, who so explicitly discover themselves eating their leader's renown who also seem able to absorb a great deal of deprivation without violent reaction, at least until the leader's wave of fame has already crested (see Oliver 1955:362, 368, 387, 394).

12. "In the Paniai Lake region (of Netherlands New Guinea), the people go so far as to kill a selfish rich man because of his 'immorality.' His own sons or brothers are induced by the rest of the members of the community to dispatch the first deadly arrow. 'Aki to tonowi beu, inii idikima enadani kodo to niitou (you should not be the only rich man, we should all be the same, therefore you only stay equal with us)' was the reason given by the Paniai people for killing Mote Juwopija of Madi, a *tonowi* [Kapauku for 'big-man'] who was not generous enough" (Pospisil 1958:80, cf. 108–110). On another egalitarian conspiracy, see Hogbin 1951:145, and for other aspects of the Melanesian contradiction, note, for example, Hogbin 1939:81; Burridge 1960:18–19; and Reay 1959:110, 129–30.

13. Aside from the transitional developments in eastern Melanesia, several western Melanesian societies advanced to a structural position intermediate between underdeveloped Melanesian polities and Polynesian chiefdoms. In these western Melanesian protochiefdoms, an ascribed division of kinship groups (or segments thereof) into chiefly and nonchiefly ranks emerges — as in Sa'a (Ivens 1927), around Buka passage (Blackwood 1935), in Manam Island (Wedgwood 1933–34, 1958–59), Waropen (Held 1957), perhaps Mafulu

(Williamson 1912), and several others. The rank system does not go beyond the broad dual division of groups into chiefly and nonchiefly: no pyramid of ranked social-political divisions along Polynesian lines is developed. The political unit remains near the average size of the western Melanesian autonomous community. Sway over the kin groups of such a local body falls automatically to a chiefly unit, but chiefs do not hold office title with stipulated rights over corporate sections of society, and further extension of chiefly authority, if any, must be achieved. The Trobriands, which carry this line of chiefly development to its highest point, remain under the same limitations, although it was ordinarily possible for powerful chiefs to integrate settlements of the external sector within their domains (cf. Powell 1960).

14. The great Tahitian chiefs were traditionally enjoined not to eat the power of government too much, as well as to practice open-handedness toward the people (Handy 1930:41). Hawaiian high chiefs were given precisely the same advice by counselors (Malo 1951:255).

15. The Hawaiian traditions are very clear on the encouragement given rebellion by chiefly exactions — although one of our greatest sources of Hawaiian tradition, David Malo, provides the most sober caveat regarding this kind of evidence. "I do not suppose," he wrote in the preface to *Hawaiian Antiquities*, "the following history to be free from mistakes, in that material for it has come from oral traditions; consequently it is marred by errors of human judgment and does not approach the accuracy of the word of God."

Malo noted that "many kings have been put to death by the people because of their oppression of the makaainana (i.e., commoners)" (1951:258). He goes on to list several who "lost their lives on account of their cruel exactions," and follows the list with the statement: "It was for this reason that some of the ancient kings had a wholesome fear of the people." The propensity of Hawaiian high chiefs for undue appropriation from commoners is a point made over and over again by Malo (see 85, 87–88, 258, 267–68). In Fornander's reconstruction of Hawaiian history (from traditions and genealogies) internal rebellions are laid frequently, almost axiomatically, to chiefly extortion and niggardliness (1880: 40–41, 76–78, 88, 149–50, 270–71). In addition, Fornander at times links appropriation of wealth and ensuing rebellion to the provisioning of the chiefly establishment, as in the following passage:

> Scarcity of food, after a while, obliged Kalaniopuu (paramount chief of the island of Hawaii and half brother of Kamehameha I's father) to

92

remove his court (from the Kona district) into the Kohala district, where his headquarters were fixed at Kapaau. Here the same extravagant, laissez-faire, eat and be merry policy continued that had been commenced at Kona, and much grumbling and discontent began to manifest itself among the resident chiefs and cultivators of the land, the "Makaainana." Imakakaloa, a great chief in the Puna district, and Nuuampaahu, a chief of Naalehu in the Kau district, became the heads and rallying-points of the discontented. The former resided on his lands in Puna [in the southeast, across the island from Kohala in the northwest], and openly resisted the orders of Kalaniopuu and his extravagant demands for contributions of all kinds of property; the latter was in attendance with the court of Kalaniopuu in Kohala, but was strongly suspected of favouring the growing discontent. (*Ibid.* 1880:200)

Aside from the Mangarevan uprising mentioned in the text, there is some evidence for similar revolts in Tonga (Mariner 1827:80, B.H. Thomson 1894a: 294ff.) and in Tahiti (Henry 1928:195–96, 297).

16. On the difficulty of provisioning the Hawaiian paramount's large establishment, see the citation from Fornander (n. 15, above), and also Fornander 1880:100–101; Malo 1951:92–93, and passim. The Hawaiian great chiefs developed the practice of the circuit — like feudal monarchs — often leaving a train of penury behind as they moved in state from district to district of the chiefdom.

CHAPTER THREE

The Original Affluent Society*

If economics is the dismal science, the study of hunting-gathering economies must be its most advanced branch. Almost universally committed to the proposition that life was hard in the paleolithic, our textbooks compete to convey a sense of impending doom, leaving one to wonder not only how hunters managed to live but whether, after all, this was living? The specter of starvation stalks the stalker through these pages. His technical incompetence is said to enjoin continuous work just to survive, affording him neither respite nor surplus, hence not even the "leisure" to "build culture." Even so, for all his efforts, the hunter pulls the lowest grades in thermodynamics — less energy/capita/year than any other mode of production. And in treatises on economic development he is condemned to play the role of bad example: the so-called subsistence economy.

The traditional wisdom is always refractory. One is forced to oppose it polemically, to phrase the necessary revisions dialectically: in fact, this was, when you come to examine it, the original affluent society. Paradoxical, that phrasing leads to another useful and unexpected conclusion. By the common understanding, an affluent society is one in which all the people's material wants are easily satisfied. To assert that the hunters are affluent is to deny, then, that the human condition is an ordained tragedy, with man the prisoner at hard labor of a perpetual

* Originally published in *Stone Age Economics* (New York: Aldine de Gruyter, 1972). © 1972 Marshall Sahlins.

95

to the disadvantage of Esau, who was the elder son and cunning hunter but, in a famous scene, deprived of his birthright.

Current low opinions of the hunting-gathering economy need not be laid to neolithic ethnocentrism, however: bourgeois ethnocentrism will do as well. The existing business economy, at every turn an ideological trap from which anthropological economics must escape, will promote the same dim conclusions about the hunting life.

Is it so paradoxical to contend that hunters have affluent economies, their absolute poverty notwithstanding? Modern capitalist societies, however richly endowed, dedicate themselves to the proposition of scarcity. Inadequacy of economic means is the first principle of the world's wealthiest peoples. The apparent material status of the economy seems to be no clue to its accomplishments; something has to be said for the mode of economic organization (cf. Polanyi 1947, 1957, 1959; Dalton 1961).

The market-industrial system institutes scarcity, in a manner completely unparalleled and to a degree nowhere else approximated. Where production and distribution are arranged through the behavior of prices, and all livelihoods depend on getting and spending, insufficiency of material means becomes the explicit, calculable starting point of all economic activity.[2] The entrepreneur is confronted with alternative investments of a finite capital, the worker (hopefully) with alternative choices of remunerative employ, and the consumer... Consumption is a double tragedy: what begins in inadequacy will end in deprivation. Bringing together an international division of labor, the market makes available a dazzling array of products: all these Good Things within a man's reach — but never all within his grasp. Worse, in this game of consumer free choice, every acquisition is simultaneously a deprivation, for every purchase of something is a forgoing of something else, in general only marginally less desirable, and in some particulars more desirable, that could have been had instead. (The point is that if you buy one automobile, say, a Plymouth, you cannot also have the Ford — and I judge from current television commercials that the deprivations entailed would be more than just material.[3])

98

That sentence of "life at hard labor" was passed uniquely upon us. Scarcity is the judgment decreed by our economy — so also the axiom of our Economics: the application of scarce means against alternative ends to derive the most satisfaction possible under the circumstances. And it is precisely from this anxious vantage that we look back upon hunters. But if modern man, with all his technological advantages, still hasn't got the wherewithal, what chance has this naked savage with his puny bow and arrow? Having equipped the hunter with bourgeois impulses and paleolithic tools, we judge his situation hopeless in advance.[4]

Yet scarcity is not an intrinsic property of technical means; it is a relation between means and ends. We should entertain the empirical possibility that hunters are in business for their health, a finite objective, and that bow and arrow are adequate to that end.[5]

But still other ideas, these endemic in anthropological theory and ethnographic practice, have conspired to preclude any such understanding.

The anthropological disposition to exaggerate the economic inefficiency of hunters appears notably by way of invidious comparison with neolithic economies. Hunters, as Lowie put it blankly, "must work much harder in order to live than tillers and breeders" (1946:13). On this point, evolutionary anthropology in particular found it congenial, even necessary theoretically, to adopt the usual tone of reproach. Ethnologists and archaeologists had become neolithic revolutionaries, and in their enthusiasm for the Revolution spared nothing denouncing the Old (Stone Age) Regime. Including some very old scandal. It was not the first time philosophers would relegate the earliest stage of humanity to nature rather than to culture. ("A man who spends his whole life following animals just to kill them to eat, or moving from one berry patch to another, is really living just like an animal himself" [Braidwood 1957:122].) The hunters thus downgraded, anthropology was free to extol the Neolithic Great Leap Forward: a main technological advance that brought about a "general availability of leisure through release from purely food-getting pursuits" (Braidwood 1952:5; cf. F. Boas 1940:285).

In an influential essay titled "Energy and the Evolution of Culture," Leslie White explained that the neolithic generated a "great advance in cultural development...as a consequence of the great increase in the amount of energy harnessed and controlled per capita per year by means of the agricultural and pastoral arts" (1949:372). White further heightened the evolutionary contrast by specifying *human effort* as the principal energy source of paleolithic culture, as opposed to the *domesticated plant and animal resources* of neolithic culture. This determination of the energy sources at once permitted a precise low estimate of hunters' thermodynamic potential — that developed by the human body: "average power resources" of one twentieth horsepower per capita (*ibid.*:369) — even as, by eliminating human effort from the cultural enterprise of the neolithic, it appeared that people had been liberated by some labor-saving device (domesticated plants and animals). But White's problematic is obviously misconceived. The principal mechanical energy available to both paleolithic and neolithic culture is that supplied by human beings, as transformed in both cases from plant and animal sources, so that, with negligible exceptions (the occasional direct use of nonhuman power), the amount of energy harnessed per *capita* per year is the same in paleolithic and neolithic economies — and fairly constant in human history until the advent of the Industrial Revolution.[6]

Another specifically anthropological source of paleolithic discontent develops in the field itself, from the context of European observation of existing hunters and gatherers, such as the native Australians, the Bushmen, the Ona, or the Yahgan. This ethnographic context tends to distort our understanding of the hunting-gathering economy in two ways.

First, it provides singular opportunities for naiveté. The remote and exotic environments that have become the cultural theater of modern hunters have an effect on Europeans most unfavorable to the latter's assessment of the former's plight. Marginal as the Australian or Kalahari desert is to agriculture, or to everyday European experience, it is a source of wonder to the untutored observer "how anybody could live in a place like this." The inference that the natives manage only to eke out a bare existence is apt to be reinforced by their marvelously varied diets (cf. Herskovits 1958, quoted above). Ordinarily including objects deemed repulsive and inedible by Europeans, the local cuisine lends itself to the supposition that the people are starving to death. Such a conclusion, of course, is more likely met in earlier than in later accounts, and in the journals of explorers or missionaries than in the monographs of anthropologists; but precisely because the explorers' reports are older and closer to the aboriginal condition, one reserves for them a certain respect.

Such respect obviously has to be accorded with discretion. Greater attention should be paid to a man such as Sir George Grey (1841), whose expeditions in the 1830s included some of the poorer districts of western Australia, but whose unusually close attention to the local people obliged him to debunk his colleagues' communications on just this point of economic desperation. It is a mistake very commonly made, Grey wrote, to suppose that the native Australians "have small means of subsistence, or are at times greatly pressed for want of food." Many and "almost ludicrous" are the errors travelers have fallen into in this regard: "They lament in their journals that the unfortunate Aborigines should be reduced by famine to the miserable necessity of subsisting on certain sorts of food, which they have found near their huts; whereas, in many instances, the articles thus quoted by them are those which the natives most prize, and are really neither deficient in flavour nor nutritious qualities." To render palpable "the ignorance that has prevailed with regard to the habits and customs of this people when in their wild state," Grey provides one remarkable example, a citation from his fellow explorer Captain Sturt, who, upon encountering a group of Aboriginals engaged in gathering large quantities of mimosa gum, deduced that the "unfortunate creatures were reduced to the last extremity, and, being unable to procure any other nourishment, had been obliged to collect this mucilaginous gum." But, Sir George observes, the gum in question is a favorite article of food in the area, and when in season it affords the opportunity for large numbers of people to assemble and camp together, which otherwise they are unable to do. He concludes:

Generally speaking, the natives live well; in some districts there may be at particular seasons of the year a deficiency of food, but if such is the case, these tracts are, at those times, deserted. *It is, however, utterly impossible for a traveller or even for a strange native to judge whether a district affords an abundance of food, or the contrary. . . .* But in his own district a native is very differently situated; he knows exactly what it produces, the proper time at which the several articles are in season, and the readiest means of procuring them. According to these circumstances he regulates his visits to different portions of his hunting ground; *and I can only say that I have always found the greatest abundance in their huts.*[7] (1841, vol. 2:259–62 [emphasis added]; cf. Eyre 1845, vol. 2:244ff.)

In making this happy assessment, Sir George took special care to exclude the lumpenproletariat aboriginals living in and about European towns (cf. Eyre 1845, vol. 2:250, 254–55). The exception is instructive. It evokes a second source of ethnographic misconceptions: that the anthropology of hunters is largely an anachronistic study of ex-savages — an inquest into the corpse of one society, Grey once said, presided over by members of another.

The surviving food collectors, as a class, are displaced persons. They represent the paleolithic disenfranchised, occupying marginal haunts untypical of the mode of production: sanctuaries of an era, places so beyond the range of main centers of cultural advance as to be allowed some respite from the planetary march of cultural evolution, because they were characteristically poor beyond the interest and competence of more advanced economies. Leave aside the favorably situated food collectors, such as Northwest Coast Indians, about whose (comparative) well-being there is no dispute. The remaining hunters, barred from the better parts of the earth, first by agriculture, later by industrial economies, enjoy ecological opportunities something less than the later-paleolithic average.[8] Moreover, the disruption accomplished in the past two centuries of European imperialism has been especially severe, to the extent that many of the ethnographic notices that constitute the anthropologist's stock in trade are adulterated cultural goods. Even explorer and missionary accounts, apart from their ethnocentric misconstructions, may be speaking of afflicted economies (cf. Service 1962). The hunters of eastern Canada of whom we read in *The Jesuit Relations* were committed to the fur trade in the early seventeenth century (Jouvency 1710). The environments of others were selectively stripped by Europeans before reliable report could be made of indigenous production: the Eskimo we know no longer hunt whales, the Bushmen have been deprived of game, the Shoshoni's piñon has been timbered and his hunting grounds grazed out by cattle.[9] If such peoples are now described as poverty-stricken, their resources "meager and unreliable," is this an indication of the aboriginal condition — or of the colonial duress?

The enormous implications (and problems) for evolutionary interpretation raised by this global retreat have only recently begun to evoke notice (Lee and DeVore 1968). The point of present importance is this: rather than a fair test of hunters' productive capacities, their current circumstances pose something of a supreme test. All the more extraordinary, then, the following reports of their performance.

"A Kind of Material Plenty"
Considering the poverty in which hunters and gatherers live in theory, it comes as a surprise that Bushmen who live in the Kalahari enjoy "a kind of material plenty," at least in the realm of everyday useful things, apart from food and water:

> As the !Kung come into more contact with Europeans — and this is already happening — they will feel sharply the lack of our things and will need and want more. It makes them feel inferior to be without clothes when they stand among strangers who are clothed. But in their own life and with their own artifacts *they were comparatively free from material pressures.* Except for food and water (important exceptions!) of which the Nyae Nyae !Kung have a sufficiency — but barely so, judging from the fact that all are thin though not emaciated — they all had what they needed or could make what they needed, for every man can and does make the things that men make and every

woman the things that women make.... *They lived in a kind of material plenty* because they adapted the tools of their living to materials which lay in abundance around them and which were free for anyone to take (wood, reeds, bone for weapons and implements, fibers for cordage, grass for shelters), or to materials which were at least sufficient for the needs of the population.... The !Kung could always use more ostrich egg shells for beads to wear or trade with, but, as it is, enough are found for every woman to have a dozen or more shells for water containers — all she can carry — and a goodly number of bead ornaments. In their nomadic hunting-gathering life, travelling from one source of food to another through the seasons, always going back and forth between food and water, they carry their young children and their belongings. With plenty of most materials at hand to replace artifacts as required, the !Kung have not developed means of permanent storage and have not needed or wanted to encumber themselves with surpluses or duplicates. They do not even want to carry one of everything. They borrow what they do not own. With this ease, they have not hoarded, and the accumulation of objects has not become associated with status. (Marshall 1961:243–44 [emphasis added])

Analysis of hunter-gatherer production is usefully divided into two spheres, as Marshall has done. Food and water are certainly "important exceptions," best reserved for separate and extended treatment. For the rest, the nonsubsistence sector, what is here said of the Bushmen applies in general and in detail to hunters from the Kalahari to Labrador — or to Tierra del Fuego, where Gusinde reports of the Yahgan that their disinclination to own more than one copy of utensils frequently needed is "an indication of self-confidence." "Our Fuegians," he writes, "procure and make their implements with little effort" (1961:213).[10]

In the nonsubsistence sphere, the people's wants are generally easily satisfied. Such "material plenty" depends partly upon the ease of production, and that upon the simplicity of technology and democracy of property. Products are homespun: of stone, bone, wood, skin — materials such as "lay in abundance around them." As a rule, neither extraction of the raw material nor its working-up takes strenuous effort. Access to natural resources is typically direct — "free for anyone to take" — even as possession of the necessary tools is general and knowledge of the required skills common. The division of labor is likewise simple, predominantly a division of labor by sex. Add in the liberal customs of sharing, for which hunters are properly famous, and all the people can usually participate in the going prosperity, such as it is.

But, of course, "such as it is": this "prosperity" depends as well upon an objectively low standard of living. It is critical that the customary quota of consumables (as well as the number of consumers) be culturally set at a modest point. A few people are pleased to consider a few easily made things their good fortune: some meager pieces of clothing and rather fugitive housing in most climates;[11] plus a few ornaments, spare flints, and sundry other items such as the "pieces of quartz, which native doctors have extracted from their patients" (Grey 1841, vol. 2:266); and, finally, the skin bags in which the faithful wife carries all this, "the wealth of the Australian savage" (ibid.).

For most hunters, such affluence without abundance in the nonsubsistence sphere need not be long debated. A more interesting question is why they are content with so few possessions — for it is with them a policy, a "matter of principle," as Gusinde says (1961:2), and not a misfortune.

Want not, lack not. But are hunters so undemanding of material goods because they are themselves enslaved by a food quest "demanding maximum energy from a maximum number of people," so that no time or effort remains for the provision of other comforts? Some ethnographers testify, on the contrary, that the food quest is so successful that half the time the people seem not to know what to do with themselves. On the other hand, *movement* is a condition of this success — more movement in some cases than others, but always enough to rapidly depreciate the satisfactions of property. Of the hunter it is truly said that his wealth is a burden. In his condition of life, goods can become "grievously oppressive," as Gusinde observes, and the more so the longer they are carried around. Certain food collectors do have canoes and a few have dogsleds, but most must carry themselves all the comforts they possess, and so only possess what they can comfortably carry themselves. Or perhaps only what the women can carry: the men are often left free to react to the sudden opportunity of the chase or the sudden necessity of defense. As Owen Lattimore wrote in a not too different context, "the pure nomad is the poor nomad." Mobility and property are in contradiction.

That wealth quickly becomes more of an encumbrance than a good thing is apparent even to the outsider. Laurens van der Post was caught in the contradiction as he prepared to make farewells to his wild Bushmen friends:

> This matter of presents gave us many an anxious moment. We were humiliated by the realization of how little there was we could give to the Bushmen. Almost everything seemed likely to make life more difficult for them by adding to the litter and weight of their daily round. They themselves had practically no possessions: a loin strap, a skin blanket and a leather satchel. There was nothing that they could not assemble in one minute, wrap up in their blankets and carry on their shoulders for a journey of a thousand miles. They had no sense of possession. (1958:276)

A necessity so obvious to the casual visitor must be second nature to the people concerned. This modesty of material requirements is institutionalized: it becomes a positive cultural fact, expressed in a variety of economic arrangements. Lloyd Warner reports of the Murngin, for example, that portability is a decisive value in the local scheme of things. Small goods are, in general, better than big goods. In the final analysis, "the relative ease of transportation of the article" will prevail, so far as determining its disposition, over its relative scarcity or labor cost. For the "ultimate value," Warner writes, "is freedom of movement." And to this "desire to be free from the burdens and responsibilities of objects which would interfere with the society's itinerant existence," Warner attributes the Murngin's "undeveloped sense of property" and their "lack of interest in developing their technological equipment" (1964:136–37).

Here, then, is another economic "peculiarity" — I will not say

106

it is general, and perhaps it is explained as well by faulty toilet training as by a trained disinterest in material accumulation: some hunters, at least, display a notable tendency to be sloppy about their possessions. They have the kind of nonchalance that would be appropriate to a people who have mastered the problems of production, even as it is maddening to a European:

> They do not know how to take care of their belongings. No one dreams of putting them in order, folding them, drying or cleaning them, hanging them up, or putting them in a neat pile. If they are looking for some particular thing, they rummage carelessly through the hodgepodge of trifles in the little baskets. Larger objects that are piled up in a heap in the hut are dragged hither and yon with no regard for the damage that might be done them. The European observer has the impression that these [Yahgan] Indians place no value whatever on their utensils and that they have completely forgotten the effort it took to make them.[12] Actually, no one clings to his few goods and chattels which, as it is, are often and easily lost, but just as easily replaced.... The Indian does not even exercise care when he could conveniently do so. A European is likely to shake his head at the boundless indifference of these people who drag brandnew objects, precious clothing, fresh provisions, and valuable items through thick mud, or abandon them to their swift destruction by children and dogs.... Expensive things that are given them are treasured for a few hours, out of curiosity; after that they thoughtlessly let everything deteriorate in the mud and wet. The less they own, the more comfortable they can travel, and what is ruined they occasionally replace. Hence, they are completely indifferent to any material possessions. (Gusinde 1961:86–87)

The hunter, one is tempted to say, is "uneconomic man." At least as concerns nonsubsistence goods, he is the reverse of that standard caricature immortalized in any *General Principles of Economics*, page one. His wants are scarce and his means (in relation) plentiful. Consequently, he is "comparatively free from material pressures," has "no sense of possession," shows an "undeveloped sense of property," is "completely indifferent to any material possessions," manifests a "lack of interest" in developing his technological equipment.

In this relation of hunters to worldly goods there is a neat and important point. From the internal perspective of the economy, it seems wrong to say that wants are "restricted," desires "restrained," or even that the notion of wealth is "limited." Such phrasings imply in advance an Economic Man and a struggle of the hunter against his own worst nature, which is finally then subdued by a cultural vow of poverty. The words imply the renunciation of an acquisitiveness that in reality was never developed, a suppression of desires that were never broached. Economic Man is a bourgeois construction — as Marcel Mauss said, "not behind us, but before, like the moral man." It is not that hunters and gatherers have curbed their materialistic "impulses": they simply never made an institution of them. "Moreover, if it is a great blessing to be free from a great evil, our [Montagnais] Savages are happy; for the two tyrants who provide hell and torture for many of our Europeans, do not reign in their great forests, — I mean ambition and avarice ... as they are contented with a mere living, not one of them gives himself to the Devil to acquire wealth" (LeJeune 1897:231).

We are inclined to think of hunters and gatherers as *poor* because they don't have anything; perhaps better to think of them for that reason as *free*. "Their extremely limited material possessions relieve them of all cares with regard to daily necessities and permit them to enjoy life" (Gusinde 1961:1).

Subsistence

When Herskovits was writing his *Economic Anthropology* (1958), it was common anthropological practice to take the Bushmen or the native Australians as "a classic illustration of a people whose economic resources are of the scantiest," so precariously situated that "only the most intense application makes survival possible." Today, the "classic" understanding can be fairly reversed — on evidence largely from these two groups. A good case can be made that hunters and gatherers work less than we do; and, rather than a continuous travail, the food quest is intermittent, leisure abundant, and there is a greater amount of sleep in the daytime per capita per year than in any other condition of society.

Some of the substantiating evidence for Australia appears in early sources, but we are especially fortunate to have now the quantitative materials collected by the 1948 American-Australian Scientific Expedition to Arnhem Land. Published in 1960, these startling data must provoke some review of the Australian reportage going back for over a century, and perhaps revision of an even longer period of anthropological thought. The key research was a temporal study of hunting and gathering by McCarthy and McArthur (1960), coupled to McArthur's analysis of the nutritional outcome.

Figures 3.1 and 3.2 summarize the principal production studies. These were short-run observations taken during nonceremonial periods. The record for Fish Creek (fourteen days) is longer as well as more detailed than that for Hemple Bay (seven days). Only adults' work has been reported, so far as I can tell. The diagrams incorporate information on hunting, plant-collecting, preparing foods, and repairing weapons, as tabulated by the ethnographers. The people in both camps were free-ranging native Australians, living outside mission or other settlements during the period of study, although such was not necessarily their permanent or even their ordinary circumstance.[13]

One must have serious reservations about drawing general or historical inferences from the Arnhem Land data alone. Not only was the context less than pristine and the time of study too brief, but certain elements of the modern situation may have raised productivity above aboriginal levels: metal tools, for example, or the reduction of local pressure on food resources by depopulation. And our uncertainty seems rather doubled than neutralized by other current circumstances that, conversely, would lower economic efficiency: these semi-independent hunters, for instance, are probably not as skilled as their ancestors. For the moment, let us consider the Arnhem Land conclusions as experimental, potentially credible in the measure they are supported by other ethnographic or historic accounts.

The most obvious, immediate conclusion is that the people do not work hard. The average length of time per person per day put into the appropriation and preparation of food was four or five

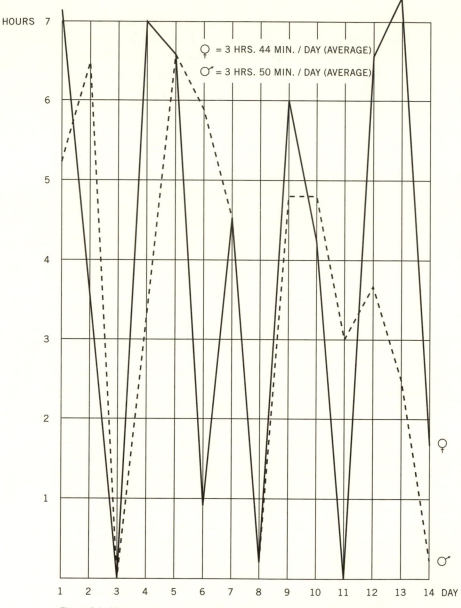

HOURS 7

♀ = 3 HRS. 44 MIN. / DAY (AVERAGE)

♂ = 3 HRS. 50 MIN. / DAY (AVERAGE)

1 2 3 4 5 6 7 8 9 10 11 12 13 14 DAY

Figure 3.1 Hours per day in food-connected activities: Fish Creek group (McCarthy and McArthur 1960).

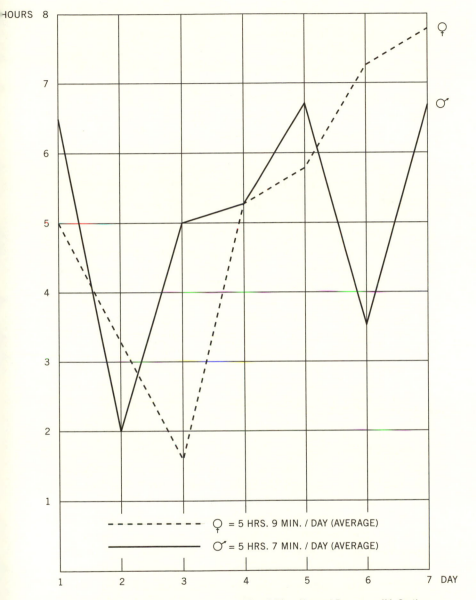

Figure 3.2 Hours per day in food-connected activities: Hempel Bay group (McCarthy and McArthur 1960).

hours. Moreover, they do not work continuously. The subsistence quest was highly intermittent. It would stop for the time being when the people had procured enough for the time being, which left them plenty of time to spare. Clearly, in subsistence as in other sectors of production, we have to do with an economy of specific, limited objectives. By hunting and gathering, these objectives are apt to be irregularly accomplished, so the work pattern becomes correspondingly erratic.

In the event, a third characteristic of hunting and gathering unimagined by the received wisdom: rather than straining to the limits of available labor and disposable resources, these Australians seem to *underuse* their objective economic possibilities.

> The quantity of food gathered in one day by any of these groups could in every instance have been increased. Although the search for food was, for the women, a job that went on day after day without relief [but see our Figures 3.1 and 3.2], they rested quite frequently and did not spend all the hours of daylight searching for and preparing food. The nature of the men's food-gathering was more sporadic, and if they had a good catch one day they frequently rested the next.... Perhaps unconsciously they weigh the benefit of greater supplies of food against the effort involved in collecting it, perhaps they judge what they consider to be enough, and when that is collected they stop (McArthur 1960:92).

It follows, fourth, that the economy was not physically demanding. The investigators' daily journal indicates that the people pace themselves; only once is a hunter described as "utterly exhausted" (McCarthy and McArthur 1960:150ff.). Neither did the Arnhem Landers themselves consider the task of subsistence onerous. "They certainly did not approach it as an unpleasant job to be got over as soon as possible, nor as a necessary evil to be postponed as long as possible" (McArthur 1960: 92).[14] In this connection, and also in relation to their underuse of economic resources, it is noteworthy that the Arnhem Land hunters seem not to have been content with a "bare existence." Like other Australians (cf. Worsley 1961:173), they become dissatisfied with an

112

unvarying diet; some of their time appears to have gone into the provision of diversity over and above mere sufficiency (McCarthy and McArthur 1960:192).

In any case, the dietary intake of the Arnhem Land hunters was adequate — according to the standards of the National Research Council of America. Mean daily consumption per capita at Hemple Bay was 2,160 calories (only a four-day period of observation), and at Fish Creek 2,130 calories (eleven days). Table 3.1 indicates the mean daily consumption of various nutrients, calculated by McArthur in percentages of the NRCA recommended dietary allowances.

Table 3.1 Mean daily consumption as percentage of recommended allowances (from McArthur 1960).

	Calories	Protein	Iron	Calcium	Ascorbic acid
Hemple Bay	116	444	80	128	394
Fish Creek	104	544	33	355	47

Finally, what does the Arnhem Land study say about the famous question of leisure? It seems that hunting and gathering can afford extraordinary relief from economic cares. The Fish Creek group maintained a virtually full-time craftsman, a man thirty-five or forty years old, whose true specialty however seems to have been loafing:

> He did not go out hunting at all with the men, but one day he netted fish most vigorously. He occasionally went into the bush to get wild bees' nests. *Wilira* was an expert craftsman who repaired the spears and spear-throwers, made smoking-pipes and drone-tubes, and hafted a stone axe (on request) in a skillful manner; apart from these occupations he spent most of his time talking, eating and sleeping. (*Ibid.* 1960:148)

Wilira was not altogether exceptional. Much of the time spared by the Arnhem Land hunters was literally spare time, consumed in rest and sleep (see Tables 3.2 and 3.3). The main alternative to work, changing off with it in a complementary way, was sleep:

> Apart from the time (mostly between definitive activities and during cooking periods) spent in general social intercourse, chatting, gossiping and so on, some hours of the daylight were also spent resting and sleeping. On the average, if the men were in camp, they usually slept after lunch from an hour to an hour and a half, or sometimes even more. Also after returning from fishing or hunting they usually had a sleep, either immediately they arrived or whilst game was being cooked. At Hemple Bay the men slept if they returned early in the day but not if they reached camp after 4.00 p.m. When in camp all day they slept at odd times and always after lunch. The women, when out collecting in the forest, appeared to rest more frequently than the men. If in camp all day, they also slept at odd times, sometimes for long periods. (*Ibid.* 1960:193)

The failure of Arnhem Landers to "build culture" is not strictly from want of time. It is from idle hands.

So much for the plight of hunters and gatherers in Arnhem Land. As for the Bushmen, economically likened to Australian hunters by Herskovits, two excellent recent reports by Richard Lee show their condition to be indeed the same (1968, 1969). Lee's research merits a special hearing not only because it concerns Bushmen but specifically the Dobe section of !Kung Bushmen, adjacent to the Nyae Nyae, about whose subsistence — in a context otherwise of "material plenty" — Marshall expressed important reservations. The Dobe occupy an area of Botswana where !Kung Bushmen have been living for at least a hundred years but have only just begun to suffer dislocation pressures (metal, however, has been available to the Dobe since 1880–1890). An intensive study was made of the subsistence production of a dry season camp with a population (forty-one people) near the mean of such settlements. The observations extended over four weeks during July and August 1964, a period of transition

Table 3.2 Daytime rest and sleep, Fish Creek group (data from McCarthy and McArthur 1960).

Day	Male Average	Female Average
1	2'15"	2'45"
2	1'30"	1'00"
3	Most of the day	
4	Intermittent	
5	Intermittent and most of late afternoon	
6	Most of the day	
7	Several hours	
8	2'0"	2'0"
9	50"	50"
10	Afternoon	
11	Afternoon	
12	Intermittent, afternoon	
13	——	——
14	3'15"	3'15"

Table 3.3 Daytime rest and sleep, Hemple Bay group (data from McCarthy and McArthur 1960).

Day	Male Average	Female Average
1	——	45"
2	Most of the day	2'45"
3	1'0"	——
4	Intermittent	Intermittent
5	——	1'30"
6	Intermittent	Intermittent
7	Intermittent	Intermittent

from more to less favorable seasons of the year, hence fairly representative, it seems, of average subsistence difficulties.

Despite a low annual rainfall (6–10 inches), Lee found in the Dobe area a "surprising abundance of vegetation." Food resources were "both varied and abundant," particularly the energy-rich mangetti nut — "so abundant that millions of the nuts rotted on the ground each year for want of picking" (all references in Lee 1969:59).[15] His reports on time spent in food-getting are remarkably close to the Arnhem Land observations. Table 3.4 summarizes Lee's data.

Table 3.4 Summary of Dobe Bushmen work diary (from Lee 1969).

Week	Mean Group size*	Man-days of consumption†	Man-days of work	Days of work/ week/adult	Index of subsistence effort‡
1 (6–12 July)	25.6 (23–29)	179	37	2.3	.21
2 (13–19 July)	28.3 (23–37)	198	22	1.2	.11
3 (20–26 July)	34.3 (29–40)	240	42	1.9	.18
4 (27 July–2 Aug.)	35.6 (32–40)	249	77	3.2	.31
4-week totals	30.9	866	178	2.2	.21
Adjusted totals§	31.8	668	156	2.5	.23

*Group size shown in average and range. There is considerable short-term population fluctuation in Bushmen camps.

† Includes both children and adults, to give a combined total of days of provisioning required/week.

‡ This index was constructed by Lee to illustrate the relation between consumption and the work required to produce it: S = W/C, where W = number of man-days of work, and C = man-days of consumption. Inverted, the formula would tell how many people could be supported by a day's work in subsistence.

§ Week 2 was excluded from the final calculations because the investigator contributed some food to the camp on two days.

The Bushman figures imply that one man's labor in hunting and gathering will support four or five people. Taken at face value, Bushman food-collecting is more efficient than French farming in the period up to World War II, when more than 20 percent of the population were engaged in feeding the rest. Confessedly, the comparison is misleading, but not as misleading as it is astonishing. In the total population of free-ranging Bushmen contacted by Lee, 61.3 percent (152 of 248) were effective food producers; the remainder were too young or too old to contribute importantly. In the particular camp under scrutiny, 65 percent were "effectives." Thus the ratio of food producers to the general population is actually 3:5 or 2:3. *But* these 65 percent of the people "worked 36 percent of the time, and 35 percent of the people did not work at all" (*ibid.*:67)!

For each adult worker, this comes to about two and one half days' labor per week. ("In other words, each productive individual supported herself or himself and dependents and still had 3½ to 5½ days available for other activities.") A "day's work" was about six hours; hence the Dobe workweek is approximately fifteen hours, or an average of two hours nine minutes per day. Even lower than the Arnhem Land norms, this figure however excludes cooking and the preparation of implements. All things considered, Bushmen subsistence labors are probably very close to those of native Australians.

Also like the Australians, the time Bushmen do not work in subsistence they pass in leisure or leisurely activity. One detects again that characteristic paleolithic rhythm of a day or two on, a day or two off — the latter passed desultorily in camp. Although food-collecting is the primary productive activity, Lee writes, "the majority of the people's time (four to five days per week) is spent in other pursuits, such as resting in camp or visiting other camps" (1969:74):

A woman gathers on one day enough food to feed her family for three days, and spends the rest of her time resting in camp, doing embroidery, visiting other camps, or entertaining visitors from other camps. For each day at home, kitchen routines, such as cooking, nut cracking, collecting firewood, and fetching water, occupy one to three hours of her time. This rhythm of steady work and steady leisure is maintained throughout the year. The hunters tend to work more frequently than the women, but their schedule is uneven. It is not unusual for a man to hunt avidly for a week and then do no hunting at all for two or three weeks. Since hunting is an unpredictable business and subject to magical control, hunters sometimes experience a run of bad luck and stop hunting for a month or longer. During these periods, visiting, entertaining, and especially dancing are the primary activities of men. (1968:37)

The daily per-capita subsistence yield for the Dobe Bushmen was 2,140 calories. However, taking into account body weight, normal activities, and the age-sex composition of the Dobe population, Lee estimates the people require only 1,975 calories per capita. Some of the surplus food probably went to the dogs, who ate what the people left over. "The conclusion can be drawn that the Bushmen do not lead a substandard existence on the edge of starvation as has been commonly supposed" (1969:73).

Taken in isolation, the Arnhem Land and Bushmen reports mount a disconcerting if not decisive attack on the entrenched theoretical position. Artificial in construction, the former study in particular is reasonably considered equivocal. But the testimony of the Arnhem Land expedition is echoed at many points by observations made elsewhere in Australia, as well as elsewhere in the hunting-gathering world. Much of the Australian evidence goes back to the nineteenth century, some of it to quite acute observers careful to make exception of the aboriginal come into relation with Europeans, for "his food supply is restricted, and... he is in many cases warned off from the waterholes which are the centers of his best hunting grounds" (Spencer and Gillen 1899:50).

The case is altogether clear for the well-watered areas of southeastern Australia. There the Aboriginals were favored with a supply of fish so abundant and easily procured that one squatter on the Victorian scene of the 1840s had to wonder "how that sage people managed to pass their time before my party came and taught them to smoke" (Curr 1965:109). Smoking at least solved the economic problem — nothing to do: "That accomplishment fairly acquired ... matters went on flowingly, their leisure hours being divided between putting the pipe to its legitimate purpose and begging my tobacco." Somewhat more seriously, the old squatter did attempt an estimate of the amount of time spent in hunting and gathering by the people of the then Port Phillip District. The women were away from the camp on gathering expeditions about six hours a day, "half of that time being loitered away in the shade or by the fire"; the men left for the hunt shortly after the women quit camp and returned around the same time (*ibid.*: 118). Curr found the food thus acquired of "indifferent quality" although "readily procured," the six hours a day "abundantly sufficing" for that purpose; indeed, the country "could have supported twice the number of Blacks we found in it" (*ibid.*: 120). Very similar comments were made by another old-timer, Clement Hodgkinson, writing of an analogous environment in northeastern New South Wales. A few minutes of fishing would provide enough to feed "the whole tribe" (1845:223; cf. Hiatt 1965: 103–104). "Indeed, throughout all the country along the eastern coast, the blacks have never suffered so much from scarcity of food as many commiserating writers have supposed" (Hodgkinson 1845:227).

But the people who occupied these more fertile sections of Australia, notably in the southeast, have not been incorporated into today's stereotype of an Aborigine — they were wiped out early.[16] The European's relation to such "Blackfellows" was one of conflict over the continent's riches; little time or inclination was spared from the process of destruction for the luxury of contemplation. In the event, ethnographic consciousness would only inherit the slim pickings: mainly interior groups, mainly desert people, mainly the Arunta. Not that the Arunta are all that bad off — ordinarily, "his life is by no means a miserable or a very hard one" (Spencer and Gillen 1899:7).[17] But the Central tribes should not be considered, in point of numbers or ecological adaptation, typical of native Australians (cf. Meggitt 1964). The following tableau of the indigenous economy provided by Edward John Eyre, who had traversed the south coast and penetrated the Flinders range as well as sojourned in the richer Murray district, has the right to be acknowledged at least as representative:

Throughout the greater portion of New Holland, where there do not happen to be European settlers, and invariably when fresh water can be permanently procured upon the surface, the native experiences no difficulty whatever in procuring food in abundance all the year round. It is true that the character of his diet varies with the changing seasons, and the formation of the country he inhabits; but it rarely happens that any season of the year, or any description of country does not yield him both animal and vegetable food.... Of these [chief] articles [of food], many are not only procurable in abundance, but in such vast quantities at the proper seasons, as to afford for a considerable length of time an ample means of subsistence to many hundreds of natives congregated at one place.... On many parts of the coast, and in the larger inland rivers, fish are obtained of a very fine description, and in great abundance. At Lake Victoria...I have seen six hundred natives encamped together, all of whom were living at the time upon fish procured from the lake, with the addition, perhaps, of the leaves of the mesembryanthemum. When I went amongst them I never perceived any scarcity in their camps.... At Moorunde, when the Murray annually inundates the flats, freshwater cray-fish make their way to the surface of the ground...in such vast numbers that I have seen four hundred natives live upon them for weeks together, whilst the numbers spoiled or thrown away would have sustained four hundred more.... An unlimited supply of fish is also procurable at the Murray about the beginning of December.... The number [of fish] procured...in a few hours is incredible.... Another very favourite article of food, and equally abundant at a particular season of the year, in the eastern portion of the continent, is a species of moth which the natives procure from the cavities and hollows of the mountains in certain localities.... The tops, leaves, and stalks of a kind of cress, gathered at the proper season of the year...furnish a favourite, and inexhaustible supply of food for an unlimited number of natives.... There are many other articles of food among the natives, equally abundant and valuable as those I have enumerated. (1845, vol. 2:250–54)

Both Eyre and Sir George Grey, whose sanguine view of the indigenous economy we have already noted ("I have always found the greatest abundance in their huts"), left specific assessments, in hours per day, of the Australians' subsistence labors. (This in Grey's case would include inhabitants of quite undesirable parts of western Australia.) The testimony of these gentlemen and explorers accords very closely with the Arnhem Land averages obtained by McCarthy and McArthur. "In all ordinary seasons," wrote Grey (that is, when the people are not confined to their huts by bad weather), "they can obtain, *in two or three hours*, a sufficient supply of food for the day, but their usual custom is to roam indolently from spot to spot, lazily collecting it as they wander along" (1841, vol. 2:263 [emphasis added]). Similarly, Eyre states, "In almost every part of the continent which I have visited, where the presence of Europeans, or their stock, has not limited, or destroyed their original means of subsistence, I have found that the natives could usually, *in three or four hours*, procure as much food as would last for the day, and that without fatigue or labour" (1845, vol. 2:254–55 [emphasis added]).

The same discontinuity of subsistence of labor reported by McArthur and McCarthy, the pattern of alternating search and sleep, is repeated, furthermore, in early and late observations from all over the continent (*ibid.*:253–54; Bulmer, cited in Smyth 1878, vol. 1:142; Mathew 1910:84; Spencer and Gillen 1899:32; Hiatt 1965:103–104). Basedow took it as the general custom of the Aboriginal: "When his affairs are working harmoniously, game secured, and water available, the aboriginal makes his life as easy as possible; and he might to the outsider even appear lazy" (1925:116).[18]

Meanwhile, back in Africa the Hadza have been long enjoying a comparable ease, with a burden of subsistence occupations no more strenuous in hours per day than the Bushmen or the Australian Aboriginals (Woodburn 1968). Living in an area of "exceptional abundance" of animals and regular supplies of vegetables (the vicinity of Lake Eyasi), Hadza men seem much more concerned with games of chance than with chances of game. During the long dry season especially, they pass the greater part of days on end in gambling, perhaps only to lose the metal-tipped arrows they need for big game hunting at other times. In any case, many men are "quite unprepared or unable to hunt big game even when they possess the necessary arrows." Only a small minority, Woodburn writes, are active hunters of large animals, and if women are generally more assiduous at their vegetable collecting, still it is at a leisurely pace and without prolonged labor (cf. *ibid.*:51; Woodburn 1966). Despite this nonchalance, and an only limited economic cooperation, Hadza "nonetheless obtain sufficient food without undue effort." Woodburn offers this "very rough approximation" of subsistence labor requirements: "Over the year as a whole probably an average of less than two hours a day is spent obtaining food" (Woodburn 1968:54).

Interesting that the Hadza, tutored by life and not by anthropology, reject the neolithic revolution in order to *keep* their leisure. Although surrounded by cultivators, they have until recently refused to take up agriculture themselves, "mainly on the grounds that this would involve too much hard work."[19] In this they are like the Bushmen, who respond to the neolithic question with another: "Why should we plant, when there are so many mongomongo nuts in the world?" (Lee 1968:33). Woodburn moreover did form the impression, although as yet unsubstantiated, that Hadza actually expend less energy, and probably less time, in obtaining subsistence than do neighboring cultivators of East Africa (1968:54).[20] To change continents but not contents, the fitful economic commitment of the South American hunter, too, could seem to the European outsider an incurable "natural disposition":

the Yamana are not capable of continuous, daily hard labor, much to the chagrin of European farmers and employers for whom they often work. Their work is more a matter of fits and starts, and in these occasional efforts they can develop considerable energy for a certain time. After that, however, they show a desire for an incalculably long rest period during which they lie about doing nothing, without showing great fatigue.... It is obvious that repeated irregularities of this kind make the European employer despair, but the Indian cannot help it. It is his natural disposition.[21] (Gusinde 1961:27)

The hunters' attitude toward farming introduces us, lastly, to a few particulars of the way they relate to the food quest. Once again we venture here into the internal realm of the economy, a realm sometimes subjective and always difficult to understand — where, moreover, hunters seem deliberately inclined to overtax our comprehension by customs so odd as to invite the extreme interpretation that either these people are fools or they really have nothing to worry about. The former would be a true logical deduction from the hunter's nonchalance, on the premise that his economic condition is truly exigent. On the other hand, if a livelihood is usually easily procured, if one can usually expect to succeed, then the people's seeming imprudence can no longer appear as such. Speaking to unique developments of the market economy, to its institutionalization of scarcity, Karl Polanyi said that our "animal dependence upon food has been bared and the naked fear of starvation permitted to run loose. Our humiliating enslavement to the material, which all human culture is designed to mitigate, was deliberately made more rigorous" (1947:115). But our problems are not theirs, the hunters and gatherers; rather, a pristine affluence colors their economic arrangements, a trust in the abundance of nature's resources rather than despair at the inadequacy of human means. My point is that otherwise curious heathen devices become understandable by the people's confidence, a confidence that is the reasonable human attribute of a generally successful economy.[22]

Consider the hunters' chronic movement from camp to camp. This nomadism, often taken by us as a sign of a certain harassment, is undertaken by them with a certain abandon. The Aboriginals of Victoria, Smyth recounts, are as a rule "lazy travellers. *They have no motive to induce them to hasten their movements. It is* generally late in the morning before they start on their journey, and there are many interruptions by the way" (1878, vol. 1:125 [emphasis added]). The good Père Biard in his "Relation" of 1616, after a glowing description of the foods available in their season to the Micmac ("Never had Solomon his mansion better regulated and provided with food"), goes on in the same tone:

In order to thoroughly enjoy this, their lot, our foresters start off to their different places with as much pleasure as if they were going on a stroll or an excursion; they do this easily through the skillful use and great convenience of canoes...so rapidly sculled that, without any effort, in good weather you can make thirty or forty leagues a day; nevertheless we scarcely see these Savages posting along at this rate, for their days are all nothing but pastime. They are never in a hurry. Quite different from us, who can never do anything without hurry and worry.... (1897:84–85)

Certainly, hunters quit camp because food resources have given out in the vicinity. But to see in this nomadism merely a flight from starvation only perceives the half of it; one ignores the possibility that the people's expectations of greener pastures elsewhere are not usually disappointed. Consequently, their wanderings, rather than anxious, take on all the qualities of a picnic outing on the Thames.

A more serious issue is presented by the frequent and exasperated observation of a certain "lack of foresight" among hunters and gatherers. Oriented forever in the present, without "the slightest thought of, or care for, what the morrow may bring" (Spencer and Gillen 1899:53), the hunter seems unwilling to husband supplies, incapable of a planned response to the doom surely awaiting him. He adopts instead a studied unconcern, which expresses itself in two complementary economic inclinations.

The first, prodigality: the propensity to eat right through all the food in the camp, even during objectively difficult times, "as if," LeJeune said of the Montagnais, "the game they were to hunt was shut up in a stable." Basedow wrote of native Australians, their motto "might be interpreted in words to the effect that while there is plenty for today never care about tomorrow. On this account an Aboriginal is inclined to make one feast of his supplies, in preference to a modest meal now and another by and by" (1925:116). LeJeune even saw his Montagnais carry such extravagance to the edge of disaster:

124

In the famine through which we passed, if my host took two, three, or four Beavers, immediately, whether it was day or night, they had a feast for all neighboring Savages. And if those people had captured something, they had one also at the same time; so that, on emerging from one feast, you went to another, and sometimes even to a third and a fourth. I told them that they did not manage well, and that it would be better to reserve these feasts for future days, and in doing this they would not be so pressed with hunger. They laughed at me. "Tomorrow" (they said) "we shall make another feast with what we shall capture." Yes, but more often they capture only cold and wind. (1897:281–83)

Sympathetic writers have tried to rationalize the apparent impracticality. Perhaps the people have been carried beyond reason by hunger: they are apt to gorge themselves on a kill because they have gone so long without meat — and for all they know they are likely to do so again soon. Or perhaps in making one feast of his supplies, a man is responding to binding social obligations, to important imperatives of sharing. LeJeune's experience would confirm either view, but it also suggests a third. Or rather, the Montagnais have their own explanation. They are not worried by what the morrow may bring because, as far as they are concerned, it will bring more of the same: "another feast." Whatever the value of other interpretations, such self-confidence must be brought to bear on the supported prodigality of hunters. More, it must have some objective basis, for if hunters and gatherers really favored gluttony over economic good sense, they would never have lived to become the prophets of this new religion.

A second and complementary inclination is merely prodigality's negative side: the failure to put by food surpluses, to develop food storage. For many hunters and gatherers, it appears, food storage cannot be proved technically impossible, nor is it certain that the people are unaware of the possibility (cf. Woodburn 1968:53). One must investigate instead what in the situation precludes the attempt. Gusinde asked this question, and for the Yahgan found the answer in the selfsame justifiable optimism. Storage would be "superfluous" because throughout the entire year and with almost limitless generosity the sea puts all kinds of animals at the disposal of the man who hunts and the woman who gathers. Storm or accident will deprive a family of these things for no more than a few days. Generally no one need reckon with the danger of hunger, and everyone almost anywhere finds an abundance of what he needs. Why then should anyone worry about food for the future! ... Basically our Fuegians know that they need not fear for the future, hence they do not pile up supplies. Year in and year out they can look forward to the next day, free of care.... (1961:336, 339)

Gusinde's explanation is probably good as far as it goes, but probably incomplete. A more complex and subtle economic calculus seems in play — realized however by a social arithmetic exceedingly simple. The advantages of food storage should be considered against the diminishing returns to collection within the compass of a confined locale. An uncontrollable tendency to lower the local carrying capacity is for hunters *au fond des choses*: a basic condition of their production and main cause of their movement. The potential drawback of storage is exactly that it engages the contradiction between wealth and mobility. It would anchor the camp to an area soon depleted of natural food supplies. Thus immobilized by their accumulated stocks, the people may suffer by comparison with a little hunting and gathering elsewhere, where nature has, so to speak, done considerable storage of her own — of foods possibly more desirable in diversity as well as amount than men can put by. But this fine calculation — in any event probably symbolically impossible (cf. Codere 1968) — would be worked out in a much simpler binary opposition, set in social terms such as "love" and "hate." For as Richard Lee observes (1969:75), the technically neutral activity of food accumulation or storage is morally something else again, "hoarding." The efficient hunter who would accumulate supplies succeeds at the cost of his own esteem, or else he gives them away at the cost of his (superfluous) effort. As it works out, an attempt to stock up food may only reduce the overall output of a hunting band, for the have-nots will content themselves with staying in camp and

126

living off the wherewithal amassed by the more prudent. Food storage, then, may be technically feasible, yet economically undesirable, and socially unachievable.

If food storage remains limited among hunters, their economic confidence, born of the ordinary times when all the people's wants are easily satisfied, becomes a permanent condition, carrying them laughing through periods that would try even a Jesuit's soul and worry him so that — as the Indians warn — he could become sick:

> I saw them, in their hardships and in their labors, suffer with cheerfulness.... I found myself, with them, threatened with great suffering; they said to me, "We shall be sometimes two days, sometimes three, without eating, for lack of food; take courage, *Chihiné*, let thy soul be strong to endure suffering and hardship; keep thyself from being sad, otherwise thou wilt be sick; see how we do not cease to laugh, although we have little to eat." (LeJeune 1897:283; cf. R. Needham 1954:230)

Rethinking Hunters and Gatherers

> Constantly under pressure of want, and yet, by travelling, easily able to supply their wants, their lives lack neither excitement or pleasure. (Smyth 1878, vol. 1:123)

Clearly, the hunting-gathering economy has to be revaluated, both as to its true accomplishments and its true limitations. The procedural fault of the received wisdom was to read from the material circumstances to the economic structure, deducing the absolute difficulty of such a life from its absolute poverty. But always the cultural design improvises dialectics on its relationship to nature. Without escaping the ecological constraints, culture would negate them, so that at once the system shows the impress of natural conditions and the originality of a social response — in their poverty, abundance.

What are the real handicaps of the hunting-gathering praxis? Not "low productivity of labor," if existing examples mean anything; but the economy is seriously afflicted by the *imminence of diminishing returns*. Beginning in subsistence and spreading from there to every sector, an initial success seems only to develop the probability that further efforts will yield smaller benefits. This describes the typical curve of food-getting within a particular locale. A modest number of people usually sooner than later reduce the food resources within convenient range of camp. Thereafter, they may stay on only by absorbing an increase in real costs or a decline in real returns: rise in costs if the people choose to search farther and farther afield, decline in returns if they are satisfied to live on the shorter supplies or inferior foods in easier reach. The solution, of course, is to go somewhere else. Thus the first and decisive contingency of hunting-gathering: it requires movement to maintain production on advantageous terms.

But this movement, more or less frequent in different circumstances, more or less distant, merely transposes to other spheres of production the same diminishing returns of which it is born. The manufacture of tools, clothing, utensils, or ornaments, however easily done, becomes senseless when these begin to be more of a burden than a comfort. Utility falls quickly at the margin of portability. The construction of substantial houses likewise becomes absurd if they must soon be abandoned. Hence the hunter's very ascetic conceptions of material welfare: an interest only in minimal equipment (if that), a valuation of smaller things over bigger, a disinterest in acquiring two or more of most goods, and the like. Ecological pressure assumes a rare form of concreteness when it has to be shouldered. If the gross product is trimmed down in comparison with other economies, it is not the hunter's productivity that is at fault but his mobility.

Almost the same thing can be said of the demographic constraints of hunting-gathering. The same policy of *débarassment* is in play on the level of people, describable in similar terms and ascribable to similar causes. The terms are, cold-bloodedly: diminishing returns at the margin of portability, minimum necessary equipment, elimination of duplicates, and so forth—that is to say, infanticide, senilicide, sexual continence for the duration of the nursing period, and so on, practices for which many food-collecting peoples are well known. The presumption that such devices are due to an inability to support more people is probably true — if "support" is understood in the sense of carrying them rather than feeding them. The people eliminated, as hunters sometimes sadly tell, are precisely those who cannot effectively transport themselves, who would hinder the movement of family and camp. Hunters may be obliged to handle people and goods in parallel ways, the draconian population policy an expression of the same ecology as the ascetic economy. More, these tactics of demographic restraint again form part of a larger policy for counteracting diminishing returns in subsistence. A local group becomes vulnerable to diminishing returns — so to a greater velocity of movement, or else to fission — in proportion to its size (other things equal). Insofar as the people would keep the advantage in local production, and maintain a certain physical and social stability, their Malthusian practices are just cruelly consistent. Modern hunters and gatherers, working their notably inferior environments, pass most of the year in very small groups widely spaced out. But rather than the sign of underproduction, the wages of poverty, this demographic pattern is better understood as the cost of living well.

Hunting and gathering has all the strengths of its weaknesses. Periodic movement and restraint in wealth and population are at once imperatives of the economic practice and creative adaptations, the kinds of necessities of which virtues are made. Precisely in such a framework, affluence becomes possible. Mobility and moderation put hunters' ends within range of their technical means. An undeveloped mode of production is thus rendered highly effective. The hunter's life is not as difficult as it looks from the outside. In some ways, the economy reflects dire ecology; but it is also a complete inversion.

Reports on hunters and gatherers of the ethnological present — specifically on those in marginal environments — suggest a mean of three to five hours per adult worker per day in food production. Hunters keep banker's hours, notably less than modern industrial workers (unionized), who would surely settle for a workweek of between twenty-one and thirty-five hours. An interesting comparison is also posed by recent studies of labor costs among agriculturalists of neolithic type. For example, the average adult Hanunóo, man or woman, spends twelve hundred hours per year in swidden cultivation (Conklin 1957:151), which is to say, a mean of three hours twenty minutes per day. Yet this figure does not include food-gathering, animal-raising, cooking, and other direct subsistence efforts of these Philippine tribesmen. Comparable data are beginning to appear in reports on other primitive agriculturalists from many parts of the world. The conclusion is put conservatively when put negatively: hunters and gatherers need not work longer getting food than do primitive cultivators. Extrapolating from ethnography to prehistory, one may say as much for the neolithic as John Stuart Mill said of all laborsaving devices, that never was one invented that saved anyone a minute's labor. The neolithic saw no particular improvement over the paleolithic in the amount of time required per capita for the production of subsistence; probably, with the advent of agriculture, people had to work harder.

There is nothing either to the convention that hunters and gatherers can enjoy little leisure from tasks of sheer survival. By this, the evolutionary inadequacies of the paleolithic are customarily explained, while for the provision of leisure the neolithic is roundly congratulated. But the traditional formulas might be truer if reversed: the amount of work (per capita) increases with the evolution of culture, and the amount of leisure decreases. Hunters' subsistence labors are characteristically intermittent, a day on and a day off, and modern hunters at least tend to employ their time off in such activities as daytime sleep. In the tropical habitats occupied by many of these existing hunters, plant-collecting is more reliable than hunting itself. Therefore, the women, who do the collecting, work rather more regularly than the men and provide the greater part of the food supply. Man's work is often done. On the other hand, it is likely to be highly erratic, unpredictably required; if men lack leisure, it is then in the Enlightenment sense rather than the literal. When Condorcet attributed the hunter's unprogressive condition to want of "the leisure in which he can indulge in thought and enrich his understanding with new combinations of ideas," he also recognized that the economy was a "necessary cycle of extreme activity and total idleness." Apparently what the hunter needed was the *assured* leisure of an aristocratic philosophe.

Hunters and gatherers maintain a sanguine view of their economic state despite the hardships they sometimes know. It may be that they sometimes know hardships because of the sanguine views they maintain of their economic state. Perhaps their confidence only encourages prodigality to the extent the camp falls casualty to the first untoward circumstance. In alleging this is an affluent economy, therefore, I do not deny that certain hunters have moments of difficulty. Some do find it "almost inconceivable" for a man to die of hunger, or even to fail to satisfy his hunger for more than a day or two (Woodburn 1968:52). But others, especially certain very peripheral hunters spread out in small groups across an environment of extremes, are exposed periodically to the kind of inclemency that interdicts travel or access to game. They suffer — although perhaps only fractionally, the shortage affecting particular immobilized families rather than the society as a whole (cf. Gusinde 1961:306–307).

Still, granting this vulnerability, and allowing the most poorly situated modern hunters into comparison, it would be difficult to prove that privation is distinctly characteristic of the hunter-gatherers. Food shortage is not the indicative property of this mode of production as opposed to others; it does not mark off hunters and gatherers as a class or a general evolutionary stage. Lowie asks:

> But what of the herders on a simple plane whose maintenance is periodically jeopardized by plagues — who, like some Lapp bands of the nineteenth century, were obliged to fall back on fishing? What of the primitive peasants who clear and till without compensation of the soil, exhaust one plot and pass on to the next, and are threatened with famine at every drought? Are they any more in control of misfortune caused by natural conditions than the hunter-gatherer? (1938:286)

Above all, what about the world today? One third to one half of humanity are said to go to bed hungry every night. In the Old

131

Stone Age, the fraction must have been much smaller. *This* is the era of hunger unprecedented. Now, in the time of the greatest technical power, is starvation an institution. Reverse another venerable formula: the amount of hunger increases relatively and absolutely with the evolution of culture.

This paradox is my whole point. Hunters and gatherers have by force of circumstances an objectively low standard of living. But taken as their *objective*, and given their adequate means of production, all the people's material wants usually can be easily satisfied. The evolution of economy has known, then, two contradictory movements: enriching but at the same time impoverishing, appropriating in relation to nature but expropriating in relation to man. The progressive aspect is, of course, technological. It has been celebrated in many ways: as an increase in the amount of need-serving goods and services, an increase in the amount of energy harnessed to the service of culture, an increase in productivity, an increase in division of labor, and increased freedom from environmental control. Taken in a certain sense, the last is especially useful for understanding the earliest stages of technical advance. Agriculture not only raised society above the distribution of natural food resources, it allowed neolithic communities to maintain high degrees of social order where the requirements of human existence were absent from the natural order. Enough food could be harvested in some seasons to sustain the people while no food would grow at all; the consequent stability of social life was critical for its material enlargement. Culture went on then from triumph to triumph, in a kind of progressive contravention of the biological law of the minimum, until it proved it could support human life in outer space — where even gravity and oxygen were naturally lacking.

Other men were dying of hunger in the marketplaces of Asia. It has been an evolution of structures as well as technologies, and in that respect like the mythical road where for every step the traveler advances his destination recedes by two. The structures have been political as well as economic, of power as well as property. They developed first within societies, increasingly now between societies. No doubt, these structures have been functional, necessary organizations of the technical development; but within the communities they have thus helped to enrich they would discriminate in the distribution of wealth and differentiate in the style of life. The world's most primitive people have few possessions *but they are not poor.* Poverty is not a certain small amount of goods, nor is it just a relation between means and ends; above all, it is a relation between people. Poverty is a social status. As such, it is the invention of civilization. It has grown with civilization, at once as an invidious distinction between classes and, more important, as a tributary relation — that can render agrarian peasants more susceptible to natural catastrophes than any winter camp of Alaskan Eskimo.

All the preceding discussion takes the liberty of reading modern hunters historically, as an evolutionary baseline. This liberty should not be lightly granted. Are marginal hunters such as the Bushmen of the Kalahari any more representative of the paleolithic condition than the Indians of California or the Northwest Coast? Perhaps not. Perhaps also Bushmen of the Kalahari are not even representative of marginal hunters. The great majority of surviving hunter-gatherers lead a life curiously decapitated and extremely lazy by comparison with the other few. The other few are very different. The Murngin, for example: "The first impression that any stranger must receive in a fully functioning group in Eastern Arnhem Land is of industry.... And he must be impressed with the fact that with the exception of very young children... there is no idleness" (D.F. Thomson 1949a:33–34). There is nothing to indicate that the problems of livelihood are more difficult for these people than for other hunters (cf. D.F. Thomson 1949b). The incentives of their unusual industry lie elsewhere — in "an elaborate and exacting ceremonial life," specifically in an elaborate ceremonial exchange cycle that bestows prestige on craftsmanship and trade (D.F. Thomson 1949a:26, 28, 34ff., 87, passim). Most other hunters have no such concerns. Their existence is comparatively colorless, fixed singularly on eating with gusto and digesting at leisure. The cultural orientation is not Dionysian or Apollonian but "gastric," as Julian Steward said of the Shoshoni. Then again it may be Dionysian, that is, bacchanalian: "Eating

133

among the Savages is like drinking among the drunkards of Europe. Those dry and ever-thirsty souls would willingly end their lives in a tub of malmsey, and the Savages in a pot full of meat; those over there talk only of drinking, and these here only of eating" (LeJeune 1897:249).

It is as if the superstructures of these societies had been eroded, leaving only the bare subsistence rock, and since production itself is readily accomplished, the people have plenty of time to perch there and talk about it. I must raise the possibility that the ethnography of hunters and gatherers is largely a record of incomplete cultures. Fragile cycles of ritual and exchange may have disappeared without trace, lost in the earliest stages of colonialism, when the intergroup relations they mediated were attacked and confounded. If so, the "original" affluent society will have to be rethought again for its originality, and the evolutionary schemes once more revised. Still, this much history can always be rescued from existing hunters: the "economic problem" is easily solvable by paleolithic techniques. But then, it was not until culture neared the height of its material achievements that it erected a shrine to the Unattainable: *Infinite Needs.*

NOTES

1. At least to the time Lucretius was writing (Harris 1968:26–27).

2. On the historically particular requisites of such calculation, see Codere 1968, esp. 574–75.

3. For the complementary institutionalization of "scarcity" in the conditions of capitalist production, see Gorz 1967:37–38.

4. It deserves mention that contemporary European Marxist theory is often in accord with bourgeois economics on the poverty of the primitive: cf. Bukharin 1967; Mandel 1962, vol. 1; and the economic history manual used at Lumumba University (listed in bibliography as Anonymous, n.d.).

5. Service, for a very long time almost alone among ethnologists, stood out against the traditional view of the penury of hunters. The present paper owes great inspiration to his remarks on the leisure of the Arunta (1963:9) as well as to personal conversations with him.

6. The evident fault of White's evolutionary law is the use of "per capita"

134

measures. Neolithic societies in the main harness a *greater total amount of energy* than pre-agricultural communities, because of the greater number of energy-delivering humans sustained by domestication. This overall rise in the social product, however, is not necessarily effected by an increased productivity of labor — which, in White's view, also accompanied the neolithic revolution. Ethnological data now in hand raise the possibility that simple agricultural regimes are not more efficient thermodynamically than hunting and gathering — that is, in energy yield per unit of human labor. In the same vein, some archaeology in recent years has tended to privilege stability of settlement over productivity of labor in explanation of the neolithic advance (cf. Braidwood and Wiley 1962).

7. For a similar comment, referring to missionary misinterpretation of curing by blood consumption in eastern Australia, see Hodgkinson 1845:227.

8. Conditions of primitive hunting peoples must not be judged, as Carl Sauer notes, "from their modern survivors, now restricted to the most meagre regions of the earth, such as the interior of Australia, the American Great Basin, and the Arctic tundra and taiga. The areas of early occupation were abounding in food" (quoted in Clark and Haswell 1964:23).

9. Through the prism of acculturation one glimpses what hunting and gathering might have been like in a decent environment from Alexander Henry's account of his bountiful sojourn as a Chippewa in northern Michigan. See Quimby 1962.

10. Turnbull similarly notes of Congo Pygmies: "The materials for the making of shelter, clothing, and all other necessary items of material culture are all at hand at a moment's notice." And he has no reservations either about subsistence: "Throughout the year, without fail, there is an abundant supply of game and vegetable foods" (1965:18).

11. Certain food collectors not lately known for their architectural achievements seem to have built more substantial dwellings before being put on the run by Europeans. See Smyth 1878, vol. 1:125–28.

12. But recall Gusinde's comment: "Our Fuegians procure and make their implements with little effort" (1961:213).

13. Fish Creek was an inland camp in western Arnhem Land consisting of six adult males and three adult females. Hemple Bay was a coastal occupation on Groote Eylandt; there were four adult males, four adult females, and five juveniles and infants in the camp. Fish Creek was investigated at the end of the dry season, when the supply of vegetable foods was low; kangaroo hunting was

rewarding, although the animals became increasingly wary under steady stalking. At Hemple Bay, vegetable foods were plentiful; the fishing was variable but on the whole good by comparison with other coastal camps visited by the expedition. The resource base at Hemple Bay was richer than at Fish Creek. The greater time put into food-getting at Hemple Bay may reflect, then, the support of five children. On the other hand, the Fish Creek group did maintain a virtually full-time specialist, and part of the difference in hours worked may represent a normal coastal-inland variation. In inland hunting, good things often come in large packages; hence, one day's work may yield two day's sustenance. A fishing-gathering regime perhaps produces smaller if steadier returns, enjoining somewhat longer and more regular efforts.

14. At least some Australians, the Yir-Yiront, make no linguistic differentiation between work and play (Sharp 1958:6).

15. This appreciation of local resources is all the more remarkable considering that Lee's ethnographic work was done in the second and third years of "one of the most severe droughts in South Africa's history" (1968:39, 1969:73n).

16. As were the Tasmanians, of whom Bonwick wrote: "The Aborigines were never in want of food; though Mrs. Somerville has ventured to say of them in her 'Physical Geography' that they were 'truly miserable in a country where the means of existence were so scanty.' Dr. Jeannent, once Protector, writes: 'They must have been superabundantly supplied, and have required little exertion or industry to support themselves'" (1870:14).

17. This by way of contrast to other tribes deeper in the Central Australian Desert, and specifically under "ordinary circumstances," not the times of long-continued drought when "he has to suffer privation" (Spencer and Gillen 1899:7).

18. Basedow goes on to excuse the people's idleness on the grounds of overeating, then to excuse the overeating on the grounds of the periods of hunger natives suffer, which he further explains by the droughts Australia is heir to, the effects of which have been exacerbated by the White man's exploitation of the country.

19. This phrase appears in a paper by Woodburn distributed to the Wenner-Gren symposium "Man the Hunter," although it is only elliptically repeated in the published account (1968:55). I hope I do not commit an indiscretion or an inaccuracy citing it here.

20. "Agriculture is in fact the first example of servile labor in the history of man. According to biblical tradition, the first criminal, Cain, is a farmer" (Lafargue, 1909 [1883]:11n).

136

It is notable too that the agricultural neighbors of both Bushmen and Hadza are quick to resort to the more dependable hunting-gathering life come drought and threat of famine (Woodburn 1968:54, Lee 1968:39–40).

21. This common distaste for prolonged labor manifested by recently primitive peoples under European employ, a distaste not restricted to ex-hunters, might have alerted anthropology to the fact that the traditional economy had known only modest objectives, so within reach as to allow an extraordinary disengagement, considerable "relief from the mere problem of getting a living."

The hunting economy may also be commonly underrated for its presumed inability to support specialist production: cf. Sharp 1934–35:37; Radcliffe-Brown 1948:43; Spencer 1959:155, 196, 251; Lothrup 1928:71; Steward 1938:44. If there is not specialization, at any rate it is clearly for lack of a "market," not for lack of time.

22. At the same time that the bourgeois ideology of scarcity was let loose, with the inevitable effect of downgrading an earlier culture, it searched and found in nature the ideal model to follow if man (or at least the workingman) was ever to better his unhappy lot: the ant, the industrious ant. In this the ideology may have been as mistaken as in its view of hunters. The following appeared in the *Ann Arbor News*, 27 January 1971, under the heading "Two Scientists Claim Ants a Little Lazy":

> Palm Springs, Calif. (AP) — "Ants aren't all they are reported [reputed?] to be," say Drs. George and Jeanette Wheeler.
>
> The husband-wife researchers have devoted years to studying the creatures, heroes of fables on industriousness.
>
> "Whenever we view an anthill we get the impression of a tremendous amount of activity, but that is merely because there are so many ants and they all look alike," the Wheelers concluded.
>
> "The individual ants spend a great deal of time just loafing. And, worse than that, the worker ants, who are all females, spend a lot of time primping."

STAGE   I   II   III   IV   V   VI   VII

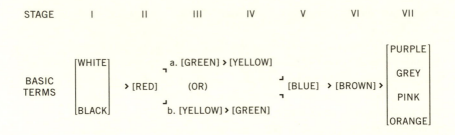

Figure 4.1 Progressive sequence of basic color terms in natural languages (Berlin and Kay 1969).

CHAPTER FOUR

Colors and Cultures[*]

It seems no exaggeration to claim for Berlin and Kay's *Basic Color Terms* (1969) a place among the most remarkable discoveries of anthropological science.[1] If exaggeration there be, it would consist in attributing the results to the authors alone, without reference to the development of the methods by Lenneberg and Roberts (1956) or the anticipation of the conclusions in the early researches of Magnus and Rivers — the debt to all of whom Berlin and Kay generously acknowledge.

Within a few short years, knowledge of the Berlin-Kay results has been widely diffused and intensely debated. For the purposes of the present commentary, it will be sufficient to mention briefly the three findings of most general and fundamental import: First, that despite the proven ability of human subjects to discriminate thousands of color percepts, natural languages manifest only a very limited number of "basic color terms," such as are applicable to a wide variety of objects; the number ranges from two to eleven, corresponding to English "black," "white," "red," "green," "yellow," "blue," "brown," "gray," "purple," "orange," and "pink." Second, these terms show a regular, cumulative order of appearance cross-culturally, such that natural languages can be arranged in a progressive sequence of color determinations, all those of any given stage discriminating the same basic hues (Figure 4.1). Finally, the empirical referents of the basic terms on a spectrum of colors are very similar from society to society: the most repre-

*Originally published in *Semiotica* 16.1 (1976). © Mouton de Gruyter.

sentative or focal "red," for example, is virtually the same for informants of different cultures, the agreement of average focal identifications between societies being generally greater than the range of experimental variation within a single society.

It is not necessary to suppose that the discoveries of *Basic Color Terms* are secure from further refinement or changes in detail. But on the evidence and in their essentials, the conclusions do seem to be beyond the reach of the empiricist controversy they have occasioned — and beyond the misguided fears of an entrenched cultural relativism that, it is already possible to foresee, can only emerge from the encounter confirmed and enriched. Relativism will simply have to come to grips with the cross-cultural regularities of color categorization, though the unexpected findings challenge such basic doctrines as the arbitrary nature of the sign or, even more fundamentally, the sui generis character of culture. It is not a question of salvaging a linguistic relativity of the kind usually attributed to Sapir and Whorf. Still less of defending the received wisdom that each society is at liberty to segment the spectrum by its own lights, as it were, to impose its own particular discontinuities upon the continuum of color experience. Rather, in the face of the universals determined in *Basic Color Terms*, the decisive issue for relativism becomes synonymous with the autonomy of cultural activity as a symbolic valuation of natural fact. At stake is the understanding that each social group orders the objectivity of its experience as the precipitate of a differential and meaningful logic, and so makes of human perception an historic conception. It is the essential problematic that the objectivity of objects is itself a cultural determination, dependent on the assignment of significance to certain "real" differences, while others are ignored (cf. F. Boas [1911] 1966b; Saussure [1915] 1966; Lévi-Strauss 1966; Douglas 1966, 1973a). On the basis of this segmentation or *découpage*, the "real" is systematically constituted, that is, in a given cultural mode. As Cassirer explains:

> "Objective" representation — this is what I would like to explain — is not the point of departure for the process of language formation, but, rather, the end to which it leads; not a *terminus a quo* but a *ter-*

minus ad quem. Language does not enter into a world of already-realized objective perceptions merely to add exterior and arbitrary signs to individual objects; it is itself a mediator par excellence, the most important and valuable instrument for the construction and conquest of a true world of objects. (1933:23)

In this brief article, I will defend these conventional ideas, not as against Berlin and Kay's results but with their help. I argue that these results are consequent on the social use of color not merely to signify objective differences of nature but *in the first place* to communicate significant distinctions of culture. Colors are, in practice, semiotic codes. Everywhere, both as terms and concrete properties, colors are engaged as signs in vast schemes of social relations: meaningful structures by which persons and groups, objects and occasions, are differentiated and combined in cultural orders. My thesis is that because colors subserve this *cultural significance*, only certain color percepts are appropriately singled out as "basic," namely, those which by their distinctive features and relations can function as signifiers in informational systems. For a crude example, if "yellow" is to be opposed semantically to "red," the latter is not likely to be concretely identified as a form of orange (that is, on pain of evident contradiction between conceptual and perceptual relations). *It is not, then, that color terms have their meanings imposed by the constraints of human and physical nature; rather, they take on such constraints insofar as they are meaningful.*

Accordingly, it is practicable to concede the strongest possible case to the naturalistic interpretation, for the same biological facts of color discrimination are not merely accommodated by a semiotic theory, they are demanded by it. Evidence for a universal set of contrasts and combinations on the natural level, especially taken in conjunction with their differential realization in cultural systems, becomes testimony of a semiotic project, not unlike the diverse phonemic elaborations of a limited number of distinctive sound features by means of which perceptual distinctions are engaged as the support for conceptual constructions. Besides, the salience and generality of contrasts on the natural plane should help account for the progressive sequence we are now presented with on the cultural. Berlin and Kay themselves refrain from offering any grounds for their linguistic findings in perceptual psychology or physiology.[2] Yet consider, for example, the light/dark distinction comprising the starting point (Stage I) of the series set forth in *Basic Color Terms* (hereafter *BCT*). This happens to be perceptually the most general of all "color" experiences, based on the most elementary physiological response to luminous flux — a contrast at once inclusive of hue and independent of it, as even persons completely colorblind are able to perceive differences in this form. Apart from induction effects, the lightness/darkness distinction (or in direct light sources especially, "brightness" or "luminosity") works on a simple sensitivity response — a "signaler" of achromatic light presence as opposed to the discriminatory contrast mechanisms ("modulators") of hue perception. The first stage in the evolution of basic categories, determined by *BCT*, thus corresponds to the most comprehensive "color" contrast the human eye can make, applicable panchromatically to all visible objects and lights (cf. Linksz 1952:72ff., 1964; Hurvich and Jameson 1957; Padgham and Saunders 1975; Boynton 1971; Burnham, Hanes, and Bartleson 1963).

Parenthetically, a simple sensitivity to light is also older in the history of life than hue discrimination; it can thus be said that cultural ontogeny here recapitulates evolutionary phylogeny. In the terms Trubetskoy proposes for phonological oppositions, the luminosity response is on the physiological level "privative," a presence/absence mechanism; whereas the oppositions of hue discrimination are "equipollent" ([1939] 1968). On the perceptual level, however, the contrasts are more complex, as will be seen. It is important to reiterate that the light/dark distinction, although focused in white/black, is panchromatic. There is indeed a relative difference in lightness effect by wavelength of the source, amounting to a parabolic "luminosity curve" with its peak in the yellow region — so that, on an equal energy spectrum, the yellows will appear brighter (and less saturated) than hues of long and short wavelengths (reds and violets). The brightness of a self-luminous source is also dependent, of course, on the absolute intensity. In the case of object color, brightness depends on reflectance as well, which gives a sensation of whiteness and lightness to surfaces. The light/dark curve across the spectrum obtained by E.R. Heider (1972) for the Stage I Dani system is probably due to the differential reflectance of the Munsell red chips, which apparently give them in fact a greater brightness than greens or blues of the same low "values." (Red-and-green color blinds, when asked in casual trials to divide the light from the dark colors on the Berlin-Kay chart, likewise start low in the red range and move quickly up in the yellows [J. Pokorny, personal communication].)

In the next stage (II) of the *BCT* series, a distinction of hue, represented by "red," is combined with the existing light/dark system. Why "red"? Once more, it is possible to adduce biological grounds. Red is to the human eye the most salient of color experiences. At normal light levels, red stands out in relation to all other hues by virtue of a reciprocal heightening effect between saturation and brightness. On the one hand, red will appear brighter or more luminous than other colors at the same level of saturation — an effect (the Helmholtz-Kohlrausch effect) that holds at all but the highest saturations, where blue and purple surpass red in brightness (cf. Padgham and Saunders 1975:135–37). This salience is given added perceptual significance by the fact that red appears to achieve a relatively high saturation over a greater variety of wavelength combinations than other colors. On the other hand and conversely, reds are perceived as purer or more saturated than other hues of the same brightness (Purdy 1930–31). But red not only "stands out," it stands closer — a direct spatial effect known as "chromatic aberration," which brings red surfaces subjectively nearer to the observer than objects of other hues at an equal distance (cf. Bidwell 1899:100ff.; Southall 1937: 234). Red, simply, has the most color; hence its focal position in the contrast of hue to achromicity (lightness/darkness) at Stage II.

The advancing, attracting, or penetrating quality of red (as opposed especially to pale greens and blues) is commonly known to phenomenologists, as well as aestheticians and psychologists (cf. Merleau-Ponty 1962; Sargent 1923; Ellis 1900; Graves 1951;

Birren 1956, 1961; Spengler [1918] 1956; Bartley 1958). Chromatic aberration is usually attributed, physiologically, to differences in focal points of different wavelength, such that they are brought in or projected back for retinal focusing. As for saturation, blue ranks after red in capacity to maintain a relatively strong chroma level over a range of spectral combinations, followed by green, then yellow. As a rule, in object colors (as distinguished from the printed Munsell chips), red also achieves the highest absolute levels of saturation, along with blues and violets, these hues having the lowest coefficient of achromatic light response (see Hurvich and Jameson 1957; Burnham, Hanes, and Bartleson 1963; among others). In this connection, I should like to enter an objection to the use of "saturation" as an independent variable in perceptual tests — an objection that, admittedly, is supported mainly by invocation of the emperor's clothes principle. Although it is evident that saturation enters into sensation as a function of definite physical properties of the radiant flux, it seems equally obvious that it does not do so independently, that is, as a distinctive response variable correlated with one specific physiological channel. (This is already implied by the simultaneous variation of brightness and saturation in such phenomena as the Helmholtz-Kohlrausch effect, for which Padgham and Saunders suggest the explanation that, apparently, "luminance information [brightness] is transmitted to the brain along the non-opponent [degree of luminosity] channels, whereas the colour information is sent as colour difference opponent signals. It seems probable that when saturated colours are observed, the colour difference signals are very strong, and that perception of luminosity is involved in the brain from information received not only from the non-opponent channels but from the colour difference mechanisms" [1975:137].) In any case, *in a single percept*, it is impossible to differentiate the relative saturation of a color from its brightness value, as both may sensibly appear as a whitening or darkening of the hue. It is possible to train subjects (or oneself) to make the distinction between brightness and saturation in Munsell chips, for example, by holding the value constant and varying the chroma, or vice versa. But this discrimination is not a fact of naive experience. It may thus very well be that the so-called psychological color solid, constructed of the three equivalent dimensional coordinates of hue, brightness, and saturation, is an egregious error: a purportedly "etic" grid which rests essentially, if paradoxically, on an "emic" determination of light as physical properties, and stems rather from the physical apparatus of color science than from the experience of human color vision. Anyone who has had to make the distinction between saturation and brightness for himself, or teach it to others, can testify that it occasions no end of confusion — which, moreover, will not be easily resolved by the textbooks where "desaturation" is variously defined as the whiteness, paleness, dullness, darkness, grayness, shade, tint, impurity, or neutrality (at the same value) of the color. This confusion of the texts is itself testimony to an "ambiguity" of the folk categories — ambiguous, however, only so long as one continues to privilege the "reality" of physical descriptions over perceptual experience; "bright" and "brilliant" are especially applied indeterminately to highly luminous or highly saturated colors. ("The term luminosity is not normally used when dealing with surfaces, lightness being the preferred term. *Brightness, brilliance* and *value* also occur frequently. *Bright, brilliant, vivid* and *clear* are often used to describe highly saturated colours especially for objects of high reflectance" [*ibid.* 103].) Moreover, there are comparable problems in the tridimensional system with respect to hue and brightness, inasmuch as people's judgments of equal brightness are "very unreliable" if the light sources are different in wavelength — although such judgments are reliable in the reverse case (Cornsweet 1970:235–36). It seems to me that anthropology as well as other fields would be better served by a color-testing system constructed in closer accord with perceptual and physiological realities than those now in common use.

In *BCT* Stages III–V, red is joined by green, yellow, and blue to form a system of two complementary pairs whose privileged position in the evolutionary sequence again makes eminent natural sense. Da Vinci had long ago called red, green, yellow, and blue (along with black and white) the "simple" colors, just as modern psychology considers them "primary" color experiences

— or even more to the cross-cultural point, as the "primitives" or *Urfarben*.

On the level of perception (which is, of course, a different matter from mixing pigments), only these four colors are seen as unique, the percepts unalloyed with any other hue, even as all other colors, including the "basics" of later *BCT* stages, are perceived as some combination of two noncomplementary "primitives." Thus, purple appears as a mixture of red and blue, orange of red and yellow, and so forth. Unique yellow, green, blue, and red correspond to spectral loci of approximately 578nm, 505nm, 475nm, and the complement of 495nm, respectively. These *Urfarben* are not only perceptually elementary, but they alone remain constant in hue over variations in luminance; whereas other colors shift perceptibly toward one of their primitive components as they change in intensity (the Bezold-Brücke phenomenon). It might be noted that brown, although physically analyzable as a dark yellow or dark red-yellow, appears to be an exception to the rule of compounded perception: like the *Urfarben*, it seems to be experientially unmixed (Padgham and Saunders 1975:143). Correspondingly, brown occupies a special position in the *BCT* sequence, marking Stage VI, which comes after the four elementary hues but before the several compound colors of Stage VII. The latter — purple, pink, and orange — emerge in no fixed order. Gray is also placed by Berlin and Kay in Stage VII, but, on the evidence cited, its position seems uncertain ethnographically, and it may evolve earlier. But then, as an intermediate of the "black" and "white" already present in Stage I, gray is not under the same ordering constraint (from simple to mixed) as the other hues of Stage VII, which would have to wait until Stage V before their own constituents were available.

As complementary pairs of red and green, yellow and blue, the *Urfarben* moreover display certain relations of opposition and correlation: classic patterns of negation and evocation, well known both to the logic of perception and the structure of conception. Green is never consubstantial with red, nor yellow with blue: complementaries cannot be seen together in the same time and space; yet each demands its opposite in such familiar effects as spatial induction and successive afterimage. Thus, it becomes understandable why green should appear culturally in temporal proximity with red, as blue with yellow. Finally, the evolutionary priority of the four primitives, in conjunction with black and white, makes a neat connection on the physiological plane with the Hering "opponent process" theory of color vision — a theory that has recently received support from electrophysiological study. In modern form, the Hering theory states that the neural processing of color sensation — as distinct from retinal photoreception — is organized as a triadic complex of binary contrastive processes: red-green, blue-yellow, and black-white. Impulses are fired to the brain from each of these processes in an oppositional manner, through cells that respond to one of the complementary hues but exclude the other; for example, the red-green process is activated as +R-G or +G-R, according to the wavelength composition of the sensation. Hence, not only does the *BCT* series here find physiological support, but, also, so does Lévi-Strauss in his observation that binary coding is a structural mode already known to the body (1972). We should not be surprised to find it manifested by the mind, thus to reappear as a fundamental principle of "objectified thought" (that is, cultural order).

Authorities differ on whether the black/white response functions on the same neural mechanisms as the two pairs of primaries (red/green, blue/yellow). With regard to the latter, it is further pertinent to their early appearance in natural languages that they act in coupled and inverse manner under variations in intensity (the Bezold-Brücke effect, noted above) and changes in stimulus size. Again, the complementary pairs of *Urfarben* are linked in pathologies of color vision, i.e., as red-and-green or yellow-and-blue syndromes of color blindness. (On these and other perceptual and physiological qualities of the "primitives" noted above, see Hering [1920] 1964; Linksz 1964; Hurvich 1960; Hurvich and Jameson 1957; Padgham and Saunders 1975; Pokorny and Smith 1972; Purdy 1931; Boynton 1971; Burnham, Hanes, and Bartleson 1963; Bornstein 1973; Cornsweet 1970; Durbin 1972.)

In sum, we can conclude that the emergence of basic color terms in natural languages follows a natural-perceptual logic. This logic is compounded of several broad evolutionary trends, most notably: (1) from general to specific, that is, distinction of light-ness/darkness to discriminations of hue; (2) from more to less salient, for example, red before other hues; and (3) from simple to complex, that is, from the unique to the mixed hues. Now, given also the common, average anthropological opinion that whatever is universal in human culture must find its explanation in human nature, it is difficult to escape the conclusion that the basic color categories are basically natural categories. Even a linguist can find in the *BCT* results the suggestion that "the realm of semantics is based on species-specific biomorphological structures and that particular biological structures underlie what linguists generally call semantics" (Durbin 1972:269). Yet the problem is precisely what is here being called *semantics*. And it is surprising nonetheless to find anthropology conspiring with a certain cognitive psychology to collapse the problem of meaning into the act of pointing, that is, the act of naming objective differ-ences present to the senses. It is curious also that the entire dis-cussion of color categories, both before *BCT* and since, has chosen to relegate the true ethnographic existence of color terms and percepts — their actual cultural significance as codes of social, economic, and ritual value — to a secondary place of connotation. Instead, it is simply assumed that an empirical test of spectral ref-erents is a determination of the essential meaning of color words. A priori we have understood the classification of color as the representation of experience, supposing the terms to intend and denote, in the first instance, the immanent properties of sensa-tion.[3] It then becomes inevitable that Saussurean notions of the arbitrariness of the sign would be compromised by the results of the research — inasmuch as they had already been compromised in the premises. And, as Saussure himself foresaw, when language is thus taken for a mere nomenclature rather than a differential sys-tem of meaningful values, cognition will be reduced to recogni-tion, concept to percept, sign to signal — and in the end, culture to nature.

Phrased in another discourse, the semantic nominalism of the color test procedure comes to a confusion of "meaning" with "reference" (Quine 1963). As for the definition by ostension of any such object-attribute as color in a social situation, one could well ask, with Wittgenstein,

> ...what does "pointing to the shape," "pointing to the colour" consist in? Point to a piece of paper. — And now point to its shape — now to its colour — now to its number (that sounds queer). — How did you do it? — You will say that you "meant" a different thing each time you pointed. And if I ask how that is done, you will say you concentrated your attention on the colour, the shape, etc. But I ask again: how is *that* done? ([1958] n.d.:16)

One might have been alerted, on the other hand, by the logical paradox inherent in Berlin and Kay's differentiation of "basic" from "secondary" color terms according to the freedom of the former from specific objective reference. Insofar as the basic terms are monolexemic and the "secondary" ones complex, the distinction may be morphologically justified. But insofar as the so-called basic terms are uniquely independent of the object, they are of a higher logical type: thus not a discourse of particular experience but a metalanguage by which such experience is classified. It should be considered that, except in the form of certain self-luminous sources, color is never a simple fact of naive experience. As an object-property, it has no more intrinsic claim to our attention than do shape, size, weight, texture, and many other coexisting attributes.[4] Hence basic color terms amount to the abstraction of perceptible features according to an arbitrary criterion of significance — which is then capable of achieving for society such miracles unknown to arithmetic as the conjoining of two apples, three cherries, and a pint of blood. Color in culture is indeed just this process of relating, not of recognizing. It cannot be, as Mauss says in a brilliant discussion of sympathetic magic, that the conceptual coupling of objects by similarities or differences in color is sequitur to the act of perception. For, "far from there being any association between the two objects due to their colour, we are dealing, on the contrary, with a formal convention, almost a law, whereby, out of a whole series of possible characteristics, colour is chosen to establish a relationship between two things" (Mauss [1902–1903] 1972:77; cf. Sperber 1975 on the arbitrariness of motivated relationships). "Basic" color terms testify to a selective ordering of experience: that kind of intervention in natural-perceptual fact whose presence is the certain indication of a cultural project.

To suppose color terms merely name differences suggested by the visible spectrum, their function being to articulate realities necessarily and already known as such, is something like the idea — to which Schneider (1968, 1972) has taken valid exception — that genealogical relations comprise a de facto grid of "kinship types," inevitably taken in this significance by all societies, which differ merely in the way they classify (cope with) such universal facts of "relationship." The point, however, in color as in kinship, is that the terms stand in meaningful relations with other terms, and it is by the relations between terms within the global system that the character of objective reference is sedimented. Moreover, the concrete attributes thus singled out by the semantic differentiation of terms then function also as *signifiers* of social relations, not simply as the *signifieds* of the terms. In the event, it is not even necessary that those who participate in a given natural order have the same substantive experience of the object, so long as they are capable of making some kind of sensory distinction at the semiotically pertinent boundaries. Hence the cultural facility of color blinds, functioning on differences in brightness — in a world that everyone else sees as differentiated by hue.

> Red-and-green color-blind people talk of reds and greens and all shades of it [*sic*] using the same words most of us assign to objects of a certain color. They think and talk and act in terms of "object color" and "color constancy" as do the rest of us. They call leaves green, roses red. Variations in saturation and brilliance of their yellow gives [*sic*] them an amazing variety of impressions. While we learn to rely on differences of hue, their minds get trained in evaluating brilliance.... Most of the red-and-green blind do not know of their defect and think we see things in the same shades they do. They have no reason for sensing any conflict. If there is an argument, they

find *us* fussy, not *themselves* defective. They heard us call the leaves green and whatever shade leaves have for them, they call it green. People of average intelligence never stop to analyze their sensations. *They are much too busy looking for what these sensations mean* (Linksz 1952:119 [last emphasis added]).

Another way of discussing the insufficiency of the naturalist interpretation is to note that by its commitment to empirical tests of color discrimination, it allows itself to be subsumed in a pre-anthropological, pre-symbolic epistemology of subject-object relations. Identifying "semantic category" as the verbal response to physical stimuli, naturalism would confine the problem of meaning within the endemic Western antinomy of a worldless subject confronting a thoughtless object: antique dualism of mind and matter, between the poles of which 2,500 years of philosophy have succeeded in plausibly drawing the line of reality at every conceivable position from the idealism of Bishop Berkeley to the materialism of Vladimir Ilych. One of the apparent virtues of *BCT* is that it can be enlisted in a certain scientific resolution of the opposition — although at the expense of an anthropological consciousness of the symbolic. Only a century ago, James Clerk Maxwell could write:

> In the eye we have on one hand light falling on this wonderful structure, and on the other we have the sensation of sight. We cannot compare these two things. The whole of metaphysics lies like a great gulf between them. ([1872] 1970:82)

Yet today it seems that science has succeeded in bridging the gulf, passing safely over the metaphysical chasms of an age-old philosophy. Of course, no one can claim to have filled the space between sight and "light"; the qualitative difference subsists. But it is possible to say that human color sensations stand in specific correspondence to real differences in the world, the incomparability between stimulus and response reconciled by neurophysiological processes which here play the role of a kind of Kantian operator — yet not transcendentally, or beyond experience, as the

151

neurological organization is itself the product of natural selection (cf. Durbin 1972, Bornstein 1973). Given the universals of *BCT*, it follows that thought, too, shines with this borrowed light. The physical effect seems extendable now to cognition and culture, which apparently can do no more than translate into their own modalities the imperatives of a natural order. Ironic, then, that the modern concept of culture should have been formulated out of Boas's discontent with just this mechanistic idea of subject-object relations (see Stocking 1968:133ff. and 1974). Doubly, triply, infinitely ironic, as it all began with the very same problem of color: with the difficulties Boas encountered, during his doctoral research on the color of seawater, in judging the relative intensities of lights that differed slightly in hue. Boas was to pass on from physics to Fechnerian psychophysics, then to geography, linguistics, and ethnology, but only to rediscover at each step the selfsame discontinuity between the subjective and the objective. Quantitative differences in the stimulus did not evoke a corresponding gradation of response. Hence, the organic could not be said to follow directly from the inorganic, the mind from the world nor, ultimately, culture from nature. Rather, the incommensurability in each case could only be comprehended by the existence of an interposed and third term, appropriate in form to the phenomenal level at issue. In the psychological experiments, this would consist of a mental operation, contingent on the present situation and past experience of the subject, which transforms perception into apperception. On the ethnological plane, it would be the collective tradition, or *Völkergedanken*, which informs the subjective apperception by an historic conception. The set of understandings men entertain of themselves and the objects of their existence — this was the novel, specifically anthropological contribution to the venerable dualism of mind and matter: a *tertium quid*, culture, not merely mediating the human relation to the world by a logic of significance but constituting by that scheme the objective and subjective terms of the relationship. For Boas, as Benedict put it, the seeing eye was the organ of tradition.

152

How, then, to reconcile these two undeniable yet opposed under-standings: that color distinctions are naturally based, albeit that natural distinctions are culturally constituted? The dilemma can only be solved, it seems to me, by reading from the cultural meaning of color to the empirical test of discrimination, rather than the other way around. We must give just due to this third term, *culture*, existing alongside subject and object, stimulus and response, and mediating between them by the construction of objectivity as significance. Moreover, a semiotic theory of color universals must take for "significance" exactly what colors do mean in human societies. They do not mean Munsell chips. Is it necessary to document that colors signify the differences between life and death, noble and common, pure and impure? That they distinguish moieties and clans, directions of the compass, and the exchange values of two otherwise similar strings of beads? I stress again that to adopt this point of semantic departure is not to ignore the biological facts of color naming; it is only to assign these facts their proper theoretical place. Information, as Bateson often says, is a difference that makes a difference. No less than any other code, a system of color meanings must be grounded in a corresponding set of distinctive perceptual properties. Hence the natural correlates of color words: they comprise the minimal *distinctive features* on the object plane — of lightness/darkness, hue/neutrality, uniqueness/admixture, and the like — by which differ-ences in meaning are signaled.

This semiotic function of colors helps to explain an important result of *BCT* — one that Berlin and Kay leave uninterpreted: the strong cross-cultural regularities in the foci of basic color cate-gories, as determined in Munsell coordinates. Here one must dis-allow as in a way misleading the authors' claim that saturation is not a distinctive feature of color categories, especially as concerns the *Urfarben*. For, given the identification of hue, saturation is *the* distinctive property of its focus — hence is the hue in its essential quality. Although, in the construction of their chart, Berlin and Kay chose the maximum chroma for each brightness value, it can-not be said that saturation was thereby held constant, since these chroma maxima vary in absolute level according to hue and value.

The *BCT* test spectrum accordingly shows a great range of saturation differences (from Munsell chromas of 2 to 16, in fact). And most important, these differences were decisive in informants' selections of category foci, which typically fall around the "home value" of the hue — that is, the brightness value at which that particular hue attains its greatest saturation (for example, Munsell value 4/ for "red," 5/ for "green," 8/ for "yellow"; cf. Evans 1948). This experimental result, I submit, is most consistent with the semiotic interpretation, for another way of describing it is to say that hues are socially relevant in their *most distinctive perceptible form*, where they are least subject to shading or tinting. And this because they mean something as such, and as distinct from black and white.

Yet the color code is more than an aggregate of distinctive features. A set of distinctive features will compose certain *perceptual relations*, and these in turn a specific totality, or *structure*, of a given type. By perceptual relations I mean the several types of contrast, complementarity, and compatibility evident in ordinary color experience. Such relations are, on the one hand, ends of a natural process; yet, on the other, they are means of a semiotic project, and, so considered, they permit a reading of the *BCT* sequence as something more than a progressive cumulation of individual elements. Berlin and Kay set out their findings as an evolutionary sequence from simple to complex, each stage typically defined by the emergence of a new basic term and percept. Seen in the semiotic vantage, however, what actually develops at each stage is not a new term or perceptual substance but a new perceptual relation. *The units of evolutionary differentiation are not terms but relations between terms.*

Hence, what is found at the very beginning of the sequence, as the most elementary set, is a contrast of two categories. From a purely progressivist vantage, there is no evident reason why the simplest color system should consist of two terms rather than one (cf. Berlin and Kay 1969:15). This circumstance only becomes reasonable when it is acknowledged that we are confronted not with the cumulative recognition of spectral differences in semantic categories but with the meaningful differentiation of social

154

categories in spectral terms. Therefore, contrast is, from the beginning and throughout, a necessary condition of color terminology and color discrimination, the most rudimentary code projecting the most general empirical distinction that can be made (light/dark). The elementary dualism of Stage I is, of course, preserved in more developed systems and always available for cultural use. (The use of the light/dark contrast is truly widespread in human societies, perhaps universally significant, and usually symbolic of fundamental oppositions of the social life — pure and impure, life and death, sacred and profane, male and female, and so on.[5]) Crosscut and differentiated by other perceptual contrasts, however, the initial dualism is transformed at later stages into more complex structures of ternary, quaternary, and higher order, and of diverse logical type.

For example, the triad of red-white-black at BCT Stage II. This is the substantive perceptual result of the crossing of the basic dark/light dualism by a second contrast of hue/neutrality (see above on red as "the most color"). A distinction between these types of variation is easily made experientially, since neutrals vary only in one dimension, lightness, whereas hues differ in this respect as well as in color. But precisely as red also varies in lightness/darkness, the triad of Stage II is not a simple order of three equivalent terms but a mediated opposition, that is, of black and white by red. Red is particularly suited to this role because of its ability to maintain saturation over a wide range of brightness values, although reaching its strongest form at relatively low values. Therefore, red is especially like black in opposition to white, but occasionally like white in opposition to black. Where the complete triad is in cultural use, then, one can expect — as in all such cases of mediation — that certain meaningful values of red will themselves be opposed in moral sign, positive and negative. Furthermore, two additional dyads will be included in the structural set, red versus white and red versus black — the latter, due to the low brightness value of saturated red, probably the stronger or more marked opposition. In a classic work on Ndembu symbolism, V. Turner (1967) describes a red-white-black trilogy of ritual values having many of these relations semantically, that is, just those we discover perceptually. Turner goes on to document the widespread occurrence of the red-white-black triad in ritual systems, and to suggest an iconic and expressive interpretation of the symbolism different from the perspective adopted here.

In Stages IIIa and IIIb of *BCT*, the triad of Stage II is transformed into a four-part system. In IIIa, recall, green appears alongside red on the dimension of color; in IIIb, it is yellow instead of green. The consequent elementary structure is formally the same in both cases: a diagrammatic set, A:B::C:D, matching two contrasting pairs by an analogous opposition. In Stage IIIa, the chromatic side has been factored by a complementary opposition, red/green, which is similar in induction effects to the achromatic black/white contrast. In IIIb, as focal yellow is a light value and red strongest at dark values, the colors reproduce on the side of hue the same distinction as characterizes the achromatic pair. (The actual color ethnography of such quaternary systems remains to be done. That it would prove fruitful is suggested by the ubiquity of diagrammatic relations on such semiotic levels as kinship — cf. Lévi-Strauss 1963a, Bourdieu 1971, M. Sahlins 1976b.) Restricting ourselves to the hues, one encounters in Stage V of *BCT* a more complex kind of four-part system. In effect, I have already described this structure in discussing the Hering opponent-process theory of color vision and its phenomenal correlates. The four hues are the *Urfarben*: red, green, yellow, and blue. Each is opposed to its own complement experientially: red cannot coexist with green in the same percept, nor yellow with blue. But each demands its complement by simultaneous contrast in adjacent space, or successive afterimage. Each of the four "primitives," accordingly, can mix visually with only two of the remaining three. From such possible combinations of two *Urfarben*, all other hues are perceptibly composed. This structure of visual exclusion and compatibility among the *Urfarben* might be diagrammed as in Figure 4.2.

In another essay (1976b), I have suggested that the semantic relations of these colors in English — as may be gauged from the *Oxford English Dictionary* and dictionaries of common usage —

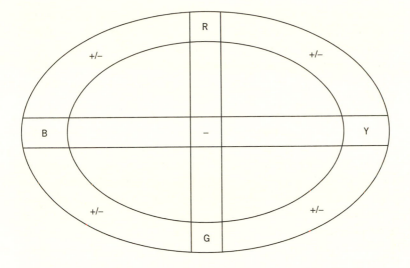

Figure 4.2 Perceptual structure of the *Urfarben*.

have the same general structures as their perceptual system. In several domains — politics, human bodily or mental states, religion, and so on -- red, for instance, is like yellow in opposition to green (and blue) or like blue in opposition to yellow (and green). Note that the stoplight triad would be one derivation of these relations; indeed, it seems to reappear in a number of cultural contexts. As a flag of quarantine, yellow is, like red, a sign of danger; yet, specifically, the danger signaled by yellow is illness, which aligns it also with "sickly" or "bilious green" in contrast to "rosy red." Or, to take another permutation: as compared with the positive sexuality of red (both male and female), green and yellow are forms of relative impotency, yet themselves at the opposite poles of immaturity and maturity — fresh, inexperienced youth (greenhorn), and a ripe old age whose course has been run ("My way of life / Is fall'n into the sere, the yellow leaf"). Note, of course, the correlated domains of sex and vegetation, which may be rounded out with "ripe red." In all such semantic relations, the complementary *Urfarben* seem to have directly opposed meanings, as would be predicted from the perceptual model. Blue is always different from yellow, for example: depressed ("the blues") where yellow is gay, loyal ("true blue") where yellow is cowardly, and the like. Blue has a similar meaning to yellow about once in a blue moon.

The *Urfarben*, of course, represent only a subsystem of *BCT* Stage V, and my intention here, as in the notices of other stages, has not been to provide a complete account of the several structures, their permutations, and symbolizations. A lot more could easily be said, including some wild thought: ethnologists will not have failed to observe, for instance, that the structure of visual compatibilities and exclusions among these four "primitives" is the same as a system of marital exchanges among four groups divided into exogamous moieties (as Arunta). The purpose, however, was rather to suggest investigation than encourage speculation. It seems to me that *BCT* opens up very exciting prospects for an ethnography of color whose general aim, quite beyond the determination of the empirical correlates of semantic categories, might consist especially in the correlation of the semiotic and perceptual structures of color. For colors, too, are good to think (with).

It should be stressed that these perceptual structures are in themselves devoid of meaning, merely formal *combinatoires* of opposition and correlation. As such they are only the raw materials of cultural production, remaining latently available and incompletely realized until a meaningful content is attributed to the elements of the cultural set. Objectifying itself, then, in a system of colors, a human group accomplishes the essential cultural act of making a conceptual order out of a natural order. But such a code must be socially accessible: the success of the cultural project depends on the collective appropriation of objective features and relations that are generally present to the senses. Hence the biological correlates and cross-cultural regularities of basic color schemes.

As the perceptual structure of color has no meaning in itself, the content emanating from the culture rather than the color, this process of symbolic formation does not violate Saussurean principles of arbitrariness. However, if the perceptual set has no meaning, still it consists of marked contrasts of sensation, and it follows that for *any given culture* the choice of color meanings will not appear arbitrary but conditioned or motivated. In a universal sense, the iconicity is itself arbitrary, as it is relative to a specific cultural order and consists of a selection among all possible contrasts of color and social features in the interest of a particular relationship between them. But then, from within the system, the choice will seem motivated by analogy between color sensations and cultural relations — which may well have a common metaphoric base in the semantics of space (cf. Friedrich 1970, M. Sahlins, 1976b). Consider, for example, that red is an experientially "advancing" color, as compared with the receding blues or whites. Given Western notions of sexuality, it will then hardly seem aleatory that red is harlotry as opposed to the prudery of blue or the purity of white (cf. Spengler [1918] 1956:256). This kind of ethnographic inevitability probably helps to account for the popularity of iconic understandings of symbolic generation.

In interpreting color categories as the social appropriation of natural processes, I raise a central and contested issue of cultural theory. For this phrase, "social appropriation of natural processes," entails a certain reading of the famous structuralist invocation of "universal laws that regulate the unconscious activities of the mind" (Lévi-Strauss 1963a:59). No need on our part to clear Lévi-Strauss of the "biological reductionism" such statements have seemed to suggest. The burden of his own recent argument is that *no particular custom* will ever be accounted for by the nature of the human mind, for the double reason that in its cultural specificity it stands to mind as a difference does to a constant, and as a practice to a matrix (Lévi-Strauss 1966:130, 1971a, 1972). One may thus understand his appeal to *l'esprit humain* as an attempt not to short-circuit the symbolic, but to draw the full consequences of its ubiquity. The argument would seem simply to be that inasmuch as the human world is symbolically constituted, any similarities in the operations by which different groups construct or transform their cultural design can be attributed to the

159

way the mind itself is constructed. By the same essential condition — that is, symboling — "similarities" here cannot intend the content of that design, only the mode of ordering. It is never a question of specific meanings, which each group works out by its own lights, but the way that meanings are systematically related, which in such forms as "binary opposition" may be observed to be general. Consequently, it is never a question, either, of biological reductionism. In *L'Homme nu*, Lévi-Strauss explains that the human nature he invokes consists not of an assemblage of substantial and fixed structures "but the matrices from which structures belonging to the same ensemble are engendered" (1971a:561). He characterizes the reductionist enterprise as an attempt to explain a given type of order by referring to a content that is not of the same nature but acts upon it from the outside. But such is not the structuralist's procedure:

> An authentic structuralism, on the contrary, seeks above all to understand [*saisir*] the intrinsic properties of certain types of orders. *These properties express nothing which is outside of themselves.* But if one is compelled to refer them to something external, it shall be necessary to turn towards the cerebral organization, conceived as a network of which the most diverse ideologies, translating this or that property in terms of a particular structure, reveal in their own fashion the modes of interconnection. (*Ibid.* [emphasis added])

Perhaps, then, the problem of reductionism has resided mainly in a mode of discourse which, by giving mind all the powers of "law" and "limitation," has seemed to place culture in the position of submission and dependence. The whole vocabulary of "underlying" laws accords the mind all force of constraint, to which the cultural can only respond, as if the first was the active partner of the relation and the second passive. The interesting implication of a semiotic theory of color categories, however, is that the mind-culture relation is more adequately conceived the other way around. The structures of the mind here appear not as the imperatives of culture but as its implements. They constitute a set of organizational means and possibilities at the disposition of the human cultural enterprise, which remains at liberty variously to engage them or not and also variously to invest them with meaningful content. How else to account for the presence in culture of universal structures that are nevertheless not universally present? And at another level, how else to deal, other than mystically, with such contradictions in terms as "collective consciousness," "collective representation," or "objectified thought," which attribute to an entity that is social a function patently individual? To answer all questions of this kind, it will be necessary to situate the human mental equipment as the instrument of culture instead of the determinant. Then, like Hegel's cunning of Reason, the wisdom of the cultural process would consist in putting to the service of its own intentions natural systems which have their own reasons.

NOTES

1. I should like to thank Drs. Joel Pokorny and Vivienne Smith for generous technical help on problems of color perception. Any errors, as well as outrageous opinions on these matters, in this paper are entirely my own.

2. *Faute de mieux*, I am obliged to make the case myself, within the range of my limited comprehension of the general texts, and without any claim to expertise in these matters. The same sort of apology must serve for the entire project of this essay, which I have felt impelled to undertake only because the central issues raised by *Basic Color Terms*, as it seemed to me, were not being considered in debates over the book. Again I can only claim the rankest amateur status with regard to the matters of linguistic and structuralist theory which, nonetheless, I am forced to discuss. I have waited a long time for someone more qualified to enter the lists, but so far in vain.

3. "Color categorization is the cultural classification of certain physical stimuli following their sensory reception and physical processing" (Conklin 1973:938; cf. Lenneberg and Roberts 1956).

4. There is indeed experimental evidence that shape is a more salient object-property than color for the very young and most age groups; besides, shape-constancy seems to be substantially greater in perception than color constancy (Arnheim 1974:335). Consider the difficulties Conklin had in eliciting color identifications from the Hanunóo in the absence of any general term for "color": "Except for leading questions (naming some visual-quality attribute as a

161

possibility), only circumlocutions such as *kabitay tida nu pagbantayun?* 'How is it to look at?' are possible. If this results in description of spatial organization or form, the inquiry may be narrowed by the specification *bukun kay ?anyu?* 'not in the shape (or form)'" (1955:341n).

5. "With fine weather, and therefore with individual and social well-being, the Andamanese associate brightness and whiteness (for which they have only one word) and any bright or light colour. The association of light and dark with euphoric and dysphoric conditions respectively has a psychological basis, for it seems to be universal in human nature" (Radcliffe-Brown [1922] 1948:316).

CHAPTER FIVE

La Pensée Bourgeoise:

Western Society as Culture*

> The field of political economy, constructed exclusively
> on the two values of exchange and use, falls to pieces
> and must be entirely reanalyzed in the form of a
> GENERALIZED POLITICAL ECONOMY, which
> will imply the production of symbolic exchange-value
> [valeur d'echange/signe] as the same thing and in the
> same movement as the production of material goods
> and of economic exchange-value. The analysis of the
> production of symbols and culture is not thus posed as
> external, ulterior, or "superstructural" in relation to
> material production; it is posed as a revolution of
> political economy itself, generalized by the theoretical
> and practical intervention of symbolic exchange-value.
> (Baudrillard 1972:130 [trans. M.S.])

Historical materialism is truly a self-awareness of bourgeois society — yet an awareness, it would seem, within the terms of that society. In treating production as a natural-pragmatic process of need satisfaction, it risks an alliance with bourgeois economics in the work of raising the alienation of persons and things to a higher cognitive power. The two would join in concealing the meaningful system in the praxis by the practical explanation of the system. If that concealment is allowed, or smuggled in as

---

* Originally published in *Culture and Practical Reason* (Chicago: University of Chicago Press, 1976).

premise, everything would happen in a Marxist anthropology as it does in the orthodox economics, as if the analyst were duped by the same commodity fetishism that fascinates the participants in the process. In conceiving the creation and movement of goods solely from their pecuniary quantities (exchange-value), one ignores the cultural code of concrete properties governing "utility" and so remains unable to account for what is in fact produced. The explanation is satisfied to re-create the self-deception of the society to which it is addressed, where the logical system of objects and social relations proceeds along an unconscious plane, manifested only through market decisions based on price, leaving the impression that production is merely the precipitate of an enlightened rationality. The structure of the economy appears as the objectivized consequence of practical behavior, rather than a social organization of things, by the institutional means of the market, but according to a cultural design of persons and goods.

Utilitarianism, however, is the way the Western economy — indeed the entire society — is experienced: the way it is lived by the participating subject, thought by the economist. From all vantages, the process seems one of material maximization: the famous allocation of scarce means among alternative ends to obtain the greatest possible satisfaction — or, as Veblen put it, getting something for nothing at the cost of whom it may concern. On the productive side, material advantage takes the form of added pecuniary value. For the consumer, it is more vaguely understood as the return in "utility" to monetary disbursements; but even here the appeal of the product consists in its purported functional superiority to all available alternatives (cf. Baudrillard 1968). The latest model automobile — or refrigerator, style of clothing, or brand of toothpaste — is by some novel feature or other more convenient, better adapted to "modern living," more comfortable, more healthful, sexier, longer lasting, or better tasting than any competing product.[1] In the native conception, the economy is an arena of pragmatic action. And society is the formal outcome. The main relations of class and politics, as well as the conceptions men entertain of nature and of themselves, are generated by this rational pursuit of material happiness. As it were, cultural order is

sedimented out of the interplay of men and groups severally acting on the objective logic of their material situations:

> Till jarring interests of themselves create
> The according music of a well-mixed state....
> Thus God and Nature linked the general frame,
> And bade Self-love and Social be the same.
> (Alexander Pope, *Essay on Man*)

Such is the mode of appearance of our bourgeois society, and its
common, average social science wisdom. On the other hand, it is
also common anthropological knowledge that the "rational" and
"objective" scheme of any given human group is never the only
one possible. Even in very similar material conditions, cultural
orders and finalities may be quite dissimilar. For the material conditions, if always indispensable, are potentially "objective" and
"necessary" in many different ways — according to the cultural
selection by which they become effective "forces." Of course, in
one sense nature is forever supreme: no society can live on miracles, thinking to exist by playing her false. None can fail to provide
for the biological continuity of the population in determining it
culturally — can neglect to provide shelter in producing houses, or
nourishment in distinguishing the edible from the inedible. Yet
men do not merely "survive": they survive in a definite way. They
reproduce themselves as certain kinds of men and women, social
classes and groups, not as biological organisms or aggregates
of organisms ("populations"). True, that in so producing a cultural existence, society must remain within the limits of physical-
natural necessity. But this has been considered axiomatic at least
since Franz Boas, and not even the most biological of cultural
ecologies can claim any more: "limits of viability" are the mode of
the practical intervention of nature in culture (cf. Rapapport 1967).
Within these limits, any group has the possibility of a great range
of "rational" economic intentions, not even to mention the options of production strategy that can be conceived from the diversity of existing techniques, the example of neighboring societies,
or the negation of either.

165

Practical reason is an indeterminate explanation of cultural form; to do any better, it would have to assume what it purports to explain — the cultural form. But allow me a justifiable "nervousness." Insofar as this applies to historical materialism, it is Marx who here criticizes Marx, if through the medium of a later anthropology. The point of these objections had already been anticipated in Marx's understanding of production as devoted not simply to the reproduction of the producers but also to the social relations under which it is carried out. The principle is, moreover, interior to Marx's work in an even more general form. I repeat a seminal passage of *The German Ideology*: "This mode of production must not be considered simply as being the reproduction of physical existence of individuals. Rather it is a definite form of activity of these individuals, a definite form of expressing their life, a definite *mode of life* on their part" (Marx and Engels 1965:32). Thus it was Marx who taught that men never produce absolutely, that is, as biological beings in a universe of physical necessity: they produce objects for given social subjects, in the course of reproducing subjects by social objects.

Not even capitalism, despite its ostensible organization by and for pragmatic advantage, can escape this cultural constitution of an apparently objective praxis. For, as Marx also taught, all production, even where it is governed by the commodity-form, by exchange-value, remains the production of use-values. Without consumption, the object does not complete itself as a product: a house left unoccupied is no house. Yet use-value cannot be specifically understood on the natural level of "needs" and "wants" — precisely because men do not merely produce "housing" or "shelter": they produce dwellings of definite sorts, as a peasant's hut or a nobleman's castle. This determination of use-values, of a particular type of house as a particular type of home, represents a continuous process of social life in which men reciprocally define objects in terms of themselves and themselves in terms of objects.

Production, therefore, is something more and other than a practical logic of material effectiveness. It is a cultural intention. The material process of physical existence is organized as a meaningful process of social being — which is for men, since they are always culturally defined in determinate ways, the only mode of their existence. If it was Saussure who foresaw the development of a general semiology devoted to "the role played by signs in social life," it was Marx who provided the mise-en-scène. Situating society in history, and production in society, Marx framed the problematic of an anthropological science yet unborn. For the question he proposed to it contains its own answer, inasmuch as the question is the definition of symbol itself. How can we account for an existence of persons and things that cannot be recognized in the physical nature of either?

We have seen that Marx nevertheless reserved the symbolic quality to the object in its commodity-form (fetishism). Assuming that use-values transparently serve human needs — that is, by virtue of their evident properties — he gave away the meaningful relations between men and objects essential to the comprehension of production in any historical form. He left the question without an answer: "About the *system of needs* and the *system of labours* — at what point is this to be dealt with?"

In order to frame an answer, to give a cultural account of production, it is critical to note that the social meaning of an object that makes it useful to a certain category of persons is no more apparent from its physical properties than is the value it may be assigned in exchange. Use-value is not less symbolic or less arbitrary than commodity-value. "Utility" is not a quality of the object but a significance of the objective qualities. The reason Americans deem dogs inedible and cattle "food" is no more perceptible to the senses than is the price of meat. Likewise, what stamps trousers as masculine and skirts as feminine has no necessary connection with their physical properties or the relations arising therefrom. It is by their correlations in a symbolic system that pants are produced for men and skirts for women, rather than by the nature of the object per se or its capacity to satisfy a material need — just as it is by the cultural values of men and women that the former normally undertake this production and the latter do not. No object, no thing, has being or movement in human society except by the significance men can give it.[2]

Production is a functional moment of a cultural structure.

167

This understood, the rationality of the market and of bourgeois society is put in another light. The famous logic of maximization is only the manifest appearance of another Reason, for the most part unnoticed and of an entirely different kind. We too have our forebears. It is not as if we had no culture: no symbolic code of objects — in relation to which the mechanism of supply-demand-price, ostensibly in command, is in reality the servant.

Consider, for example, just what Americans do produce in satisfying basic "needs" for food and clothing.[3]

Food Preference and Tabu in American Domestic Animals

The aim of these remarks on American uses of common domestic animals will be modest — merely to suggest the presence of a cultural reason in our food habits, some of the meaningful connections in the categorical distinctions of edibility among horses, dogs, pigs, and cattle. Yet the point is not only of consuming interest; the productive relation of American society to its own and the world environment is organized by specific valuations of edibility and inedibility, themselves qualitative and in no way justifiable by biological, ecological, or economic advantage. The functional consequences extend from agricultural "adaptation" to international trade and world political relations. The exploitation of the American environment, the mode of relation to the landscape, depends on the model of a meal that includes a central meat element with the peripheral support of carbohydrates and vegetables — while the centrality of the meat, which is also a notion of its "strength," evokes the masculine pole of a sexual code of food which must go back to the Indo-European identification of cattle or increasable wealth with virility.[4] The indispensability of meat as "strength," and of steak as the epitome of virile meats, remains a basic condition of American diet (note the training table of athletic teams, in football especially). Hence also a corresponding structure of agricultural production of feed grains, and in turn a specific articulation to world markets — all of which would change overnight if we ate dogs. By comparison with this meaningful calculus of food preferences, supply, demand, and price offer the interest of institutional means of a system that does not include production costs in its own principles of hierarchy. The "opportunity costs" of our economic rationality are a secondary formation, an expression of relationships already given by another kind of thought, figured a posteriori within the constraints of a logic of meaningful order. The tabu on horses and dogs thus renders unthinkable the consumption of a set of animals whose production is practically feasible and which are nutritionally not to be despised. Surely it must be practicable to raise some horses and dogs for food in combination with pigs and cattle. There is even an enormous industry for raising horses as food for dogs. But then, America is the land of the sacred dog.

A traditional Plains Indian or a Hawaiian (not to mention a Hindu) might be staggered to see how we permit dogs to flourish under the strictest interdictions on their consumption. They roam the streets of major American cities at will, taking their masters about on leashes and depositing their excrements at pleasure on curbs and sidewalks. A whole system of sanitation procedures has to be employed to get rid of the mess — which in the native thought, and despite the respect owed the dogs themselves, is considered "pollution." (Nevertheless, a pedestrian excursion on the streets of New York makes the hazards of a midwestern cow pasture seem like an idyllic walk in the country.) Within the houses and apartments, dogs climb upon chairs designed for humans, sleep in people's beds, and sit at table after their own fashion awaiting their share of the family meal. All this in the calm assurance that they themselves will never be sacrificed to necessity or deity, nor eaten even in the case of accidental death. As for horses, Americans have some reason to suspect they are edible. It is rumored that Frenchmen eat them; but the mention of it is usually enough to evoke the totemic sentiment that the French are to Americans as "frogs" are to people.

In a crisis, the contradictions of the system reveal themselves. During the meteoric inflation of food prices in the spring of 1973, American capitalism did not fall apart — quite the contrary; but the cleavages in the food system did surface. Responsible government officials suggested that the people might be well advised to buy the cheaper cuts of meat such as kidneys, heart, or entrails —

after all, they are just as nutritious as hamburger. To Americans, this particular suggestion made Marie Antoinette seem a model of compassion (see Figure 5.1). The reason for the disgust seems to go to the same logic as greeted certain unsavory attempts to substitute horse meat for beef during the same period. The following item is reprinted in its entirety from the *Honolulu Advertiser* of 15 April 1973:

PROTEST BY HORSE LOVERS

WESTBROOK, CONN. (UPI) — About 25 persons on horseback and on foot paraded outside Carlson's Mart yesterday to protest the store's selling horsemeat as a cheap substitute for beef.

"I think the slaughter of horses for human consumption in this country is disgraceful," said protest organizer Richard Gallagher. "We are not at a stage yet in the United States where we are forced to kill horses for meat."

"Horses are to be loved and ridden," Gallagher said. "In other words, horses are shown affection, where cattle that are raised for beef... they've never had someone pet them or brush them, or anything like that. To buy someone's horse up and slaughter it, that, I just don't see it."

The market began selling horsemeat — as "equine round," "horsemeat porterhouse" and "horseburger" — on Tuesday, and owner Kenneth Carlson said about 20,000 pounds were sold in the first week.

Most butchers who sell horsemeat have purchased "real old, useless horses" which would otherwise be sold "for dogfood and stuff like that," Gallagher said. But "now they're picking up the young horses. We can't buy these horses now, because the killers are outbidding us."

The principal reason postulated in the American meat system is the relation of the species to human society. "Horses are shown affection, where cattle that are raised for beef ... they've never had someone pet them or brush them, or anything like that."[5] Let us take up in more detail the domesticated series cattle-pigs-horses-dogs. All of these are in some measure integrated in American society, but clearly in different statuses, which correspond to

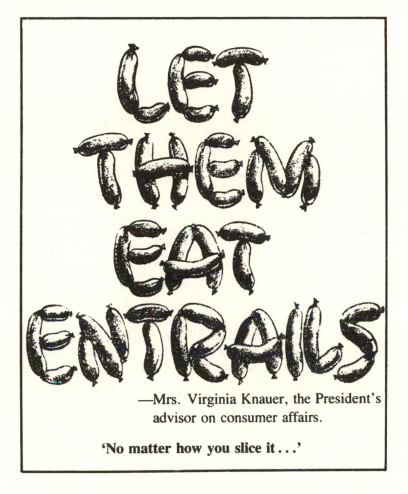

Figure 5.1 From the *Honolulu Advertiser*, 2 March 1973.

degrees of edibility. The series is divisible, first, into the two classes of edible (cattle-pigs) and inedible (horses-dogs), but then again, within each class, into higher and less preferable categories of food (beef versus pork) and more and less rigorous categories of tabu (dogs versus horses). The entire set appears to be differentiated by participation as subject or object in the company of men. Moreover, the same logic attends the differentiations of the edible animal into "meat" and the internal "organs" or "innards." To adopt the conventional incantations of structuralism, "everything happens as if" the food system is inflected throughout by a principle of metonymy, such that taken as a whole it composes a sustained metaphor on cannibalism.

Dogs and horses participate in American society in the capacity of subjects. They have proper personal names, and, indeed, we are in the habit of conversing with them as we do not talk to pigs and cattle.[6] Dogs and horses are thus deemed inedible, for, as the Red Queen said, "it isn't etiquette to cut anybody you've been introduced to." But as domestic cohabitants, dogs are closer to men than are horses, and their consumption is more unthinkable: they are "one of the family." Traditionally, horses stand in a more menial, working relationship to people; if dogs are as kinsmen, horses are as servants and nonkin. Hence, the consumption of horses is at least conceivable, if not general, whereas the notion of eating dogs understandably evokes some of the revulsion of the incest tabu.[7] On the other hand, the edible animals such as pigs and cattle generally have the status of objects to human subjects, living their own lives apart, neither the direct complement nor the working instrument of human activities. Usually, then, they are anonymous, or if they do have names, as some milk cows do, these are mainly terms of reference in the conversations of men. Yet, as barnyard animals and scavengers of human food, pigs are contiguous with human society, more so than cattle (cf. Leach 1964:50–51). Correspondingly, cut for cut, pork is a less prestigious meat than beef. Beef is the viand of higher social standing and greater social occasion. A roast of pork does not have the solemnity of prime rib of beef, nor does any part of the pig match the standing of steak.

Edibility is inversely related to humanity. The same holds in the preferences and common designations applied to edible portions of the animal. Americans frame a categorical distinction between the "inner" and "outer" parts which represents to them the same principle of relation to humanity, metaphorically extended. The organic nature of the flesh (muscle and fat) is at once disguised and its preferability indicated by the general term "meat," and again by particular conventions such as "roast," "steak," "chops," or "chuck"; whereas the internal organs are frankly known as such (or as "innards"), and more specifically as "heart," "tongue," "kidney," and so on — except as they are euphemistically transformed by the process of preparation into such products as "sweetbreads."[8] The internal and external parts, in other words, are respectively assimilated to and distinguished from parts of the human body — on the same model as we conceive our "innermost selves" as our "true selves" — and the two categories are accordingly ranked as more or less fit for human consumption. The distinction between "inner" and "outer" thus duplicates within the animal the differentiation drawn between edible and tabu species, the whole making up a single logic on two planes with the consistent implication of a prohibition on cannibalism.

It is this symbolic logic which organizes demand. The social value of steak or roast, as compared with tripe or tongue, is what underlies the difference in economic value. From the nutritional point of view, such a notion of "better" and "inferior" cuts would be difficult to defend. Moreover, steak remains the most expensive meat even though its absolute supply is much greater than that of tongue; there is much more steak to the cow than there is tongue. But more, the symbolic scheme of edibility joins with that organizing the relations of production to precipitate, through income distribution and demand, an entire totemic order, uniting in a parallel series of differences the status of persons and what they eat. The poorer people buy the cheaper cuts, cheaper because they are socially inferior meats. But poverty is in the first place ethnically and racially encoded. Blacks and Whites enter differentially into the American labor market, their participation ordered by an invidious distinction of relative "civilization." Black is in American society as the savage among us, objective nature in culture itself. Yet then, by virtue of the ensuing distribution of income, the "inferiority" of Blacks is realized also as a culinary defilement. "Soul food" may be made a virtue; but only as the negation of a general logic in which cultural degradation is confirmed by dietary preferences akin to cannibalism, even as this metaphorical attribute of the food is confirmed by the status of those who prefer it.

I would not invoke "the so-called totemism" merely in casual analogy to the *pensée sauvage*. True, Lévi-Strauss writes as if totemism had retreated in our society to a few marginal resorts or occasional practices (1963a, 1966). And fair enough — in the sense that the "totemic operator," articulating differences in the cultural series to differences in natural species, is no longer a main architecture of the cultural system. But one must wonder whether it has not been replaced by species and varieties of manufactured objects, which like totemic categories have the power of making even the demarcation of their individual owners a procedure of social classification. (My late colleague Milton Singer suggested that what Freud said of national differentiation might well be generalized to capitalism, that it is narcissism in respect of minor differences.) And yet more fundamental, do not the totemic and product-operators share a common basis in the cultural code of natural features, the significance assigned to contrasts in shape, line, color, and other object properties presented by nature? The "development" that is effected by the *pensée bourgeoise* may consist mainly in the capacity to duplicate and combine such variations at will, and within society itself. But in that event, capitalist production stands as an exponential expansion of the same kind of thought, with exchange and consumption as means of its communication.

As Baudrillard writes in this connection, consumption itself is an exchange (of meanings), a discourse — to which practical virtues, "utilities" are attached only post facto:

> As it is true of the communication of speech, so it is likewise true of goods and products: consumption is exchange. A consumer is never

174

isolated, any more than a speaker. It is in this sense that we must have a total revolution in the analysis of consumption. In the same way as there is no language simply because of an individual need to speak, but first of all language — not as an absolute, autonomous system but as a contemporary structure of the exchange of meaning, to which is articulated the individual interaction of speech — in the same sense neither is there consumption because of an objective need to consume, a final intention of the subject toward the object. There is a social production, in a system of exchange, of differentiated materials, of a code of meanings and constituted values. The functionality of goods comes afterward, adjusting itself to, rationalizing and at the same time repressing these fundamental structural mechanisms.[9] (1972:76–77 [trans. M.S.])

The modern totemism is not contradicted by a market rationality. On the contrary, it is promoted precisely to the extent that exchange-value and consumption depend on decisions of "utility." Such decisions turn upon the social significance of concrete contrasts among products. It is by their meaningful differences from other goods that objects are rendered exchangeable: they thus become use-values to certain persons, who are correspondingly differentiated from other subjects. At the same time, as a modular construction of concrete elements combined by human invention, manufactured goods uniquely lend themselves to this type of discourse. Fashioning the product, man does not merely alienate his labor, congealed thus in objective form, but by the physical modifications he effects, he sediments a thought. The object stands as a human concept outside itself, as man speaking to man through the medium of things. And the systematic variation in objective features is capable of serving, even better than the differences between natural species, as the medium of a vast and dynamic scheme of thought: because in manufactured objects many differences can be varied at once, and by a godlike manipulation — and the greater the technical control, the more precise and diversified this manipulation — and because each difference thus developed by human intervention with a view toward "utility" must have a significance and not just those features, existing

175

within nature for their own reasons, which lend themselves to cultural notice. The bourgeois totemism, in other words, is potentially more elaborate than any "wild" (*sauvage*) variety, not that it has been liberated from a natural-material basis, but precisely because nature has been domesticated. "Animals produce only themselves," as Marx taught, "while men reproduce the whole of nature."[10]

Yet if it is not mere existence which men produce but a "definite *mode of life* on their part," it follows that this reproduction of the whole of nature constitutes an objectification of the whole of culture. By the systematic arrangement of meaningful differences assigned the concrete, the cultural order is realized also as an order of goods. The goods stand as an object code for the signification and valuation of persons and occasions, functions, and situations. Operating on a specific logic of correspondence between material and social contrasts, production is thus the reproduction of the culture in a system of objects.

One is led naturally to exploit the double meanings in such terms as "fashion" and "fabricate": I take the American clothing system as the principal example.

Notes on the American Clothing System
Considered as a whole, the system of American clothing amounts to a very complex scheme of cultural categories and the relations between them, a veritable map — it does not exaggerate to say — of the cultural universe.[11] The first task will be to suggest that the scheme operates on a kind of general syntax: a set of rules for declining and combining classes of the clothing-form so as to formulate the cultural categories. In a study of *mode* as advertised in several French magazines, Roland Barthes discriminated for women's dress alone some sixty foci of signification. Each site or dimension comprised a range of meaningful contrasts: some by mere presence or absence, as of gloves; some as diversified as the indefinite series of colors (1967:114ff.).[12] It is evident that with a proper syntax, rules of combination, a formidable series of propositions could be developed, constituting so many statements of the relations between persons and situations in the cultural sys-

tem. It is equally evident that I could not hope to do more than suggest the presence of this grammar, without pretense at having analyzed it.

There are in costume several levels of semantic production. The outfit as a whole makes a statement, developed out of the particular arrangement of garment parts and by contrast to other total outfits. Again, there is a logic of the parts, whose meanings are developed differentially by comparison at this level, in a Saussurean way — as, for example, the value of women's slacks is simultaneously determined by opposition to other garments of that locus, such as skirts or men's pants, as well as by contrast to other examples of the same class (slacks) that differ in color, pattern, or whatever. My concern in discussing this syntax will be more with what is conveyed than with an account of the entire set of rules. It will be enough to indicate that it provides a systematic basis for the cultural discourse "fashioned" upon it:

> "Most people wear some sign, and don't know what it's saying. Choose your sign according to your audience," Malloy said ... "a good dark suit, white shirt and conservative tie are a young man's best wardrobe friends, if he's applying for a white collar job in a big range of business and professional categories. They're authority symbols. It's that simple," he said. ("Fashion Column," *Chicago Daily News*, 11 Jan. 1974)

But there is another problem, somewhat more difficult. I should like to move down a level to the constituent units composing the discourse: to demonstrate here how particular social meanings are related to elementary physical contrasts in the clothing object. It will be a movement also of rapprochement with totemic thought. For the principle is very much the same: a series of concrete differences among objects of the same class to which correspond distinctions along some dimension of social order — as the difference between blue collar and white is one between manual labor and bureaucratic; the relative saturation or brightness of hue discriminates fall from spring; or, "A sweet disorder in the dress / Kindles in clothes a wantonness" (Herrick). By such means the set of manufactured objects is able to comprehend the entire cultural order of a society it would at once dress and address. (Two words whose derivation from a common root — as Tylor said of "kindred" and "kindness" — expresses in the happiest way one of the most fundamental principles of social life.)

The overall objective in all this, I should stress, is some contribution toward a cultural account of production. It is to this end that I explore the code of object-properties and their meaningful combinations. The emphasis on the code implies also that we shall not be concerned at present with how individuals dress. This is not simply a decision for *langue* over *parole*. How people dress is a far more complicated semiotic problem than can be attempted here, including as it does the particular consciousness or self-conceptions of the subject in a specific meaningful "context of the situation." Again, I touch too briefly on the related question of the manipulation of the fashion code within the clothing industry. However, if all such limitations, which have a common reference to the system in action, render this account regrettably incomplete, they do have the advantage of focusing upon the position it is necessary to establish in advance, and without which all further analysis of action risks relapse into a vulgar pragmatics: that production is the realization of a symbolic scheme.

Notice what is produced in the clothing system. By various objective features an item of apparel becomes appropriate for men or women, for night or day, for "around the house" or "in public," for adult or adolescent. What is produced is, first, classes of time and place which index situations or activities; and, second, classes of status to which all persons are ascribed. These might be called "notional coordinates" of clothing, in the sense that they mark basic notions of time, place, and person as constituted in the cultural order. Hence, what is reproduced in clothing is this classificatory scheme. Yet not simply that — not simply the boundaries, divisions, and subdivisions of, say, age-grades or social classes. By a specific symbolism of clothing differences, what is produced are the meaningful differences between these categories. In manufacturing apparel of distinct cut, outline, or color for women as opposed to men, we reproduce the distinction between femininity and masculinity as known to this society. This is what is going on in the pragmatic-material process of production.

More specifically, what is going on is a differentiation of the cultural space as between town and country, and within the town between downtown and neighborhood — and then again, a contrast between all of these, as collectively making up a public sphere, and the domestic-familial domain. When a woman goes shopping, she normally "dresses up" a domestic costume, at least by the addition of peripheral display of elements such as jewelry; and the more so if she is shopping downtown rather than "in the neighborhood." Conversely, when a man returns home from "a hard day at the office," he dresses down a public style in a way consistent with the "familiarity" of the domestic sphere.[13] At the other extreme are the higher distinctions of national space: for example, the West Coast and East Coast, of which the marked subclasses are California and the Northeast (cf. Rosencranz 1972: 263–64).

We also substantialize in clothing the basic cultural valuations of time — diurnal, hebdomodal, and seasonal. We have evening clothes and daytime clothes, "little afternoon dresses" and nighttime dress (pajamas). Each references the nature of the activities ordered by those times, in the way that weekday apparel is to Sunday "best" as the secular is to the sacred. The marked seasonal variations are spring and fall, the colors of these seasons usually conceived to parallel the vegetation cycle. (Outdoor color per se, however, seems to be inverted for summer and winter dress: spectral green and red mark the winter solstice — Christmas — whereas white is traditionally appropriate between Memorial Day — 30 May — and Labor Day.)

A similar treatment could be made of the class, the sex, and the age-grade of clothing. All these social categories have determinate markers, characteristic variations on the object level. In the common ideology of producers and consumers, this consubstantiality of subject and object is predicated on an identity of essences, such that the silk is "womanly" as women are "silky." "Fine as silk," "soft as silk," the cloth opposes itself on one side to the masculinity of wool and on the other to the inferiority of cotton (cf. Dichter 1959:104ff.).[14] But this Veblenesque correlation

179

of the height of luxury with the height of femininity is likely transposed by race, as for American Blacks the male seems to be the marked sex whereas Whites decorate the female.[15] Yet in turn, the correlation between Black male and White female elegance along such dimensions as texture will be differentially inflected by class, insofar as race and class overlap, and it is a commonplace of the homegrown sociology that muted color and minor contrast are upper-class Establishment whereas brilliant color and major contrast are "mass" (Birren 1956). On the other hand, the silken sobriety of the upper-class White woman is exchanged in her daughter's clothes for the textures of youth: which brings us back full circle to wool by the common discrimination of youth and male from the adult female on the attributes of activity/passivity (ceremonial).[16]

Gender and age-grade serve to illustrate another property of the grammar: certain mechanisms of opening the set to make it more complex without, however, a revision in principle. Even in expansion, the system seems to adhere to Sapir's dictum that fashion is custom in the guise of a departure from custom. New species and subspecies are permuted, for example, by a combinatory synthesis of existing oppositions. In designer's categories, the received distinction between infants and schoolchildren has latterly been segmented into "infants," "toddlers," "preschoolers," and "schoolchildren"; adolescents are likewise not what they used to be, but "preteens," "subteens," and "teens" (Rosencranz 1972:203). In the same way, various categories of homosexuality can be evolved by particular combinations of male and female apparel, to the extent that we now have six more or less clearly distinguishable sartorial sexes. But at the line between adolescent and adult, a second type of permutation is currently in evidence: the adaptation of an existing distinction from elsewhere in the system, a kind of metaphorical transfer, to signify a change of content in a traditional opposition. The received idea of an "adolescent revolution" doubtless predisposed the change, but since the Vietnam War the conflict with the constituted — that is, adult — authorities has been specifically idiomized politically, and so in apparel by the contrast, adolescent/adult::worker/capitalist, with youth appropriating the blue jeans and work shirts of society's underclass. Perhaps nothing could better prove the absence of practical utility in clothing, since work is one of the last things youth has in mind. But the example serves as well to reveal the singular quality of capitalist society: not that it fails to work on a symbolic code, but that the code works as an open set, responsive to events it both orchestrates and assimilates to produce expanded versions of itself.

Parenthetically: This view of production as the substantialization of a cultural logic should prohibit us from speaking naively of the generation of demand by supply, as though the social product were the conspiracy of a few "decision-makers" able to impose an ideology of fashion through the deceits of advertising. In Marx's phrase, "The educator himself needs educating." It is not as if the producers' *parole* becomes our *langue*. Nor need one indulge in the converse mystification of capitalist production as a response to consumers' wants: "We always try to adapt," says the head of public relations for the company that has profited most from the recent expansion of blue jeans sales.[17] But who then is dominant, the producer or the consumer? It should be possible to transcend all such subjective representations for an institutional description of capitalist production as a cultural process. Clearly, this production is organized to exploit all possible social differentiation by a motivated differentiation of goods. It proceeds according to a meaningful logic of the concrete, of the significance of objective differences, thus developing appropriate signs of emergent social distinctions. Such might well describe the specialization of age differences in clothing, or the metaphoric transfer of blue jeans — especially if it is noted that the iconic integration of social and object distinctions is a dialectic process. The product that reaches its destined market constitutes an objectification of a social category, and so helps to constitute the latter in society; as, in turn, the differentiation of the category develops further social declensions of the goods system. Capitalism is no sheer rationality: it is a definite form of cultural order, or a cultural order acting in a particular form. End of parenthesis.

I turn to another type of variation in costume, this corresponding to the division of labor broadly considered, to suggest the presence of systematic rules for social categorization of the clothing form. First, however, we must establish the classification on the social level. In his discussion of the *monde* in the *mode,* Barthes distinguishes two alternate ways in which the social significance of costume is conceived (1967:249ff.). These are, in effect, two modalities of social discourse, the active and the passive: doing and being, *faire* and *être,* activity and identity. Adapting the distinction to present purposes, one might say that the first has to do with functions: it indexes costume according to the type of activity, such as sport or manual labor. The second relates to occupational status — the characteristic habit of the industrial worker, the farmer, the waitress, the doctor, the soldier. Again, in the following very general and oversimplified table of functions (Figure 5.2), I abbreviate a considerable argument, and more than one assumption:

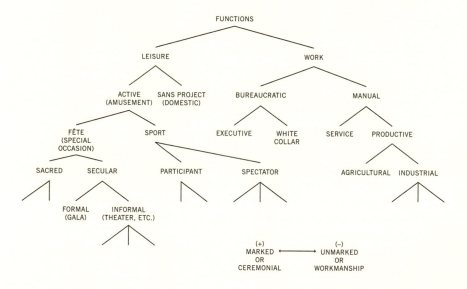

Figure 5.2 Schema of functions signified in American clothing.

The main assumption is the validity of Veblen's distinction of ceremony and workmanship in American categories of activity and clothing. The key to the entire table is this principle. In each opposition, the marked or ceremonial function is placed to the left, the unmarked and workmanlike to the right, the whole then a set of differentiations of the master distinction between work and leisure (cf. Veblen [1899] 1934). If this assumption is allowed as more or less ethnographically correct, and the consequences likewise worked out through the classes and subclasses in a faithful way, two remarkable regularities in the system of clothing are presented to view. The first might be called the "rule of ceremonial correspondence": it refers to the analogous differentiation of costume in any two functional classes similarly ordered on the opposition of ceremony and workmanship. Consider, for example, the "dress clothes" affected by men on "special occasions" (*fêtes*), culminating perhaps in formal tuxedo for very ritualized affairs (for example, marriages, galas) or, slightly less formally, the highly styled dark suit. Notice then that these outfits specifically resemble the "conservative" suits worn by business executives, in a way corresponding to their respective differences from sportive wear in the area of amusement and white-collar dress in the domain of work. The latter two — by their relative "informality," permissible color schemes, and so forth — again resemble each other; indeed, to the extent that a younger office worker may be discriminated from the higher corporate executives precisely by his "sports jacket." Yet exactly the same differences characterize, in a general way, the opposition between the more formal costumes of amusement and the relative undress permitted when "doing nothing; just sitting around the house" (*sans projet*). Or, again, it is the difference between the blue jeans or overalls of an industrial worker and the more stylized uniforms of waitresses, deliverymen, and other service workers. This particular opposition also reappears on the leisure side in the sporting outfits of hunting or skiing, which are like uniforms even as they are differentiated from the "casual clothes" of the spectator.[18] It is thus a rule of analogy in the oppositions of ceremony/workmanship, at whatever level they may appear in the system. The terms of any opposition correspond to the terms of any other, such that the marked (cere-monial) costumes of any two classes resemble each other by an analogous differentiation from the unmarked (workmanlike) cos-tumes of their respective classes. Or, more formally:

(1) $M_x/\overline{M}_x \cong M_y/\overline{M}_y$ — which says that the opposition (/) of

marked ($\overline{M}$) and unmarked (M) in any given class (x) corresponds

($\cong$) to $M/\overline{M}$ in any other class (y).

Besides the similarities in the differences, there are also differ-ences in the similarities — a tuxedo is still more "stylized" than a business suit, as domestic clothes (especially for night) are more "undressed" and "casual" than work clothes — which leads to a second rule: "the rule of ceremonial exaggeration." The rule is that, on one hand, the marked costume in a more ceremonial opposition is itself more ceremonial than its counterpart in some workmanlike opposition: as the uniforms of active sport are more colorful and cut with more flair than the uniform of the waitress or the milkman. On the other hand, the unmarked costume of the ceremonial opposition is even less workmanlike than its coun-terpart on the more workmanlike side: as the spectator's outfit is more "casual" than the industrial worker's. The same might be said of the opposition of *fête* and sport within the category "amusement," as compared with executive and clerical in the cat-egory of managerial work, even as the last pair is at once more ceremonial (the executive suit) and less workmanlike (white col-lar) than, again, the service versus industrial worker. The rule, therefore, is that the opposition stipulated within a workmanlike class is exaggerated by the corresponding opposition in a more ceremonial class. The exaggeration occurs in both directions: the ceremonial outfit is more ceremonial at its marked pole, less workmanlike at its unmarked pole. Formally:

(2) $M_x^1 > M_y^2 :: M_x^1 < M_y^2$, where the superscripts (1, 2, 3 ... n)

184

represent a factor of workmanlike function and > and < represent relative formality.

Or, by diagram (Figure 5.3):

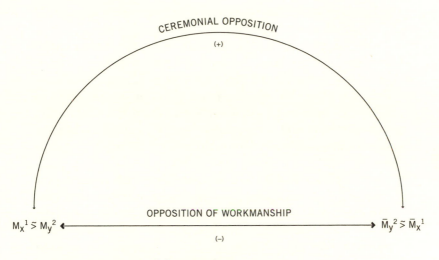

$$M_x{}^1 \gtrless M_y{}^2 \qquad\qquad \bar{M}_y{}^2 \gtrless \bar{M}_x{}^1$$

Figure 5.3 Rule of ceremonial exaggeration.

I spare the reader a corresponding discussion of the modality of "being," which, as it responds to a proliferating specialization of occupation, is even more protean than the system of functions.[19] But it seems legitimate to pause at this juncture to explain what claims are being made for exercises of the sort just indulged in. The overall aim is to respond to a question initially posed by Marx, but so far as I know without answer in his or any other Economics: What kind of theoretical account can be given for production as a *mode of life*? I propose here an example of the beginning of such a cultural account — example, because it is concerned only with the system of clothing in modern America; beginning, because it has been concerned so far mostly with the general syntax, social classes of the clothing object, and certain rules of its social declension. But it is necessary to be still more cautious. The claim made for the rules of ceremonial correspondence is only that they suggest such a syntax. To have any higher pretensions, the discussion would have to stipulate the kinds of clothing features to which the rules apply — features of color, color contrast, line and outline, type and congruence of garment pieces, kinds of accessories, qualities of texture — and the modes of their combination. The full scope of the project is very large; this is only an example of the suggestion of a beginning.

In the same spirit, I would discuss the symbolic process on the lowest level of constituent elements and their specific meanings. What I have in mind is the determination of minimal distinctive contrasts in object features, as in line, color, or texture, that signify differences in social meaning. Not to claim here, either, any novelty in the attempt, or any superiority by virtue of an apparent systematics to the observations many others have made:

> So far as I know, overalls are a garment native to this country...the standard or classical garment at very least...of the southern rural American working man: they are his uniform, the badge and proclamation of his peasantry.... The basis: what they are: can best be seen when they are still new; before they have lost (or gained) shape and color and texture; and before the white seams of their structure have lost their brilliance....
>
> In the strapping across the kidneys they again resemble work harness, and in their crossed straps and tin buttons.
>
> And in the functional pocketing of their bib, a harness modified to the convenience of a used animal of such high intelligence that he has use for tools....
>
> A new suit of overalls has among its beauties those of a blueprint: and they are a map of a working man.
>
> The shirts too; squarely cut, and strongly seamed; with big square pockets and with metal buttons: the cloth stiff, the sweat cold when it is new, the collar large in newness and standing out in angles under the ears. (Agee 1941:265–67)

It is these elementary meaningful units — the squareness of the pockets, the stiffness of the cloth, the crossed straps — that the present discussion intends. There is, at a higher level, a lexicon of the producible units: types of cloth such as silk or wool, kinds of upper garment such as shirts and blouses: products as such, entering integrally into the total outfit and usually contributing several conceptions to the whole. But these are already complex constructions whose meaningful import is predicated on constituent details of the form. In a work that ridicules the conceit that our clothes are in any sense "modern" or "civilized," Rudolfsky writes:

> Any piece of fabric can be charged with sexuality by simply working it into a precise shape. The resulting form might determine the actual sex....
>
> The overlap of a blouse, a jacket or a coat determines the sex of the article. By buttoning a garment on the right side, it becomes suitable for men only and definitely unsuitable for women. Whatever the quaint explanations of folklore are, the right side of the body has always been male, the left side female; this orientation survived despite its irrationality. (1947:126–27)

One might easily adduce a number of similar elementary features that differentiate the gender of clothes. Men's sleeves, for instance, are characteristically more tailored than women's and extend the full length of the arm by comparison with three-quarter (or less) lengths that expose the lower extremity — contrasts exactly repeated on the lower limbs in trousers and skirts.[20] The masculine fabric is relatively coarse and stiff, usually heavier, the feminine soft and fine; apart from the neutral white, masculine colors are darker, feminine light or pastel. The line in men's clothing is square, with angles and corners; women's dress emphasizes the curved, the rounded, the flowing, and the fluffy. Such elements of line, texture, and the like are the minimal constituents, the objective contrasts that convey social meaning.

I refrain from calling them "vestemes," but if necessary they might be deemed ECUs — for "elementary constituent units" and as a pun on McLuhan's dictum that "conformity to a fashion literally gives currency to a style." I propose to consider just three classes of elementary units: texture, line, and color.

187

Texture first, mainly to illustrate that significance is developed from binary contrasts of signifiers. Texture operates semantically on a number of objective oppositions — heavy/light, rough/smooth, hard/soft — several of them simultaneously pertinent to any given cloth. Marilyn Horn, in a text subtitled "An Interdisciplinary Study of Clothing," compiles a fair list of textural dyads, supposing each pair the two poles of a graded continuum of variation (1968:245). I myself would be pressed to discriminate between several of the pairs, but one must incline to Horn as expert and informant. In any event, the cloth may be:

dull	shiny
rough	smooth
uneven	flat
grainy	slippery
coarse	fine
bulky	gossamer
heavy	light
compact	porous
bristly	downy
crisp	limp
stiff	pliable
hard	soft
rigid	spongy
inelastic	stretchy
warm	cool
scoopy	waxy

The presumption is that such objective differences are at once observable and socially significant (see note 14). Any piece of cloth is a particular combination, then, of several textural qualities. Insofar as each quality bears some meaning, in contradistinction to its objective opposite, the texture communicates a parataxic set of propositions concerning age, sex, activity, class, time, place, and the other dimensions of cultural order.

The structural lines figuring in the cut or patterns of costume make up an analogous class of meaningful contrasts. Significance seems to be correlated with at least three characteristics of line: direction, form, and rhythm. *Direction* refers to orientation in relation to a ground: thus, vertical and horizontal and the mediating oblique, the last again divisible into left (downward left to right) and right (upward left to right) (Figure 5.4).

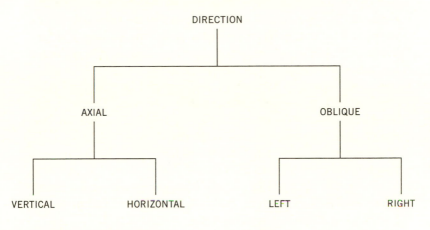

Figure 5.4 Direction in line.

Notice that it is already a small paradigm of the cultural constitution of meaning that an oblique line proceeding downward from right to left is considered by Europeans to slant "up," whereas a line downward from the left slants "down." The distinction "up"/"down" is perfectly arbitrary, if sometimes implicitly accepted experimentally (for example, Poffenberger and Barrows 1924). Supposing the lines are "read" from left to right, the distinction renders them the potential objectification of any ranked social relation similarly conceived in terms of "up" and "down," "higher" and "lower."[21] The second dimension of line, *form,* refers to its properties as straight or curved, with a mediate angular or zigzag. *Rhythm* is the periodicity of the curve or angle — an indefinite series usually idiomized as movement or velocity from the "slow" or "undulating" to the "rapidly oscillating" but which may also include a significant variation in amplitude.

With the aid of some vintage psychology and aesthetic commentary on the meaning of line, it is possible to present cultural valuations for certain contrasts of line. The experimental psychology can only be suggestive: typically designed to elicit the expressive or affective value of lines, the procedure tests the relation to the individual subject rather than that between objective and social representations as such. Nevertheless, the responses of mood at least indirectly imply cultural interpretations. For further reflection, I append therefore an early example of experiment on "the feeling-value of line," the Poffenberger and Barrows study just cited, reporting percentage responses of five hundred educated subjects to a set of eighteen different lines. The lines differed in form as curved or angular; no straight lines were included. For rhythm, both periodicity and amplitude were simultaneously operating, while direction comprised only the horizontal and the two obliques. There was no vertical orientation. The subjects were asked to assign values to the lines presented from a list of thirteen adjectives, such as "sad," "quiet," "lazy." The principal results are summarized in Table 5.1.

Results of this kind are enhanced by another type of information, such as is provided by trained aestheticians, whose descriptions of the significance of the concrete often achieve specifically cultural dimensions. In a fascinating text, *The Art of Color and Design* (1951), Maitland Graves, for example, provides several comments of the following sort on line: "The slightly curved or undulating line is loose and flexible. Because of harmonic transition in the change of direction, it has flowing continuity." The "slow, lazy movement," he goes on to say, is "passive," "gentle," "soft," "voluptuous," and "feminine" (202). The straight line, in contrast: "suggests rigidity and precision. It is positive, direct, tense, stiff, uncompromising, harsh, hard, unyielding." One might then add — perhaps without taking undue advantage of the prerogative of informant — that the straight line is, by comparison, masculine. Graves makes an analogous comparison of the vertical and the horizontal, with such additional connotations as strength and authority. Here everything depends on the relation to a ground, and as Graves describes it, most naively, to *the ground*. The horizontal line: "is in harmony

190

Table 5.1 Feelings and Their Appropriate Lines

	FORM		RHYTHM			DIRECTION			
	Curve	Angle	Slow	Medium	Fast	Horizontal	Up	Down	
1. Sad	86.3	14.3	86.8	6.9	6.9	12.1	4.2	84.3	Slow descending curve
2. Quiet	97.2	3.0	81.5	7.2	8.5	90.2	5.8	4.2	Slow horizontal curve
3. Lazy	74.0	26.1	72.3	19.9	7.9	38.7	9.9	51.5	Slow descending curve
4. Merry	79.7	20.4	11.5	54.4	34.2	16.4	79.5	4.2	Medium rising angle
5. Agitating	17.4	82.8	4.5	39.1	56.6	23.1	68.8	8.3	Rapid rising angle
6. Furious	10.7	89.2	9.7	44.0	46.2	16.4	62.8	20.7	Rapid or medium rising angle
7. Dead	53.0	46.2	70.3	6.3	22.6	46.6	2.2	50.4	Slow horizontal or descending curve or angle
8. Playful	76.0	23.7	9.8	51.8	38.1	28.2	65.0	6.5	Medium rising curve
9. Weak	69.2	30.6	53.6	14.0	32.2	31.6	8.0	60.2	Slow descending curve
10. Gentle	89.6	10.3	51.7	22.2	26.0	73.7	15.5	10.7	Slow horizontal curve
11. Harsh	7.1	92.9	11.8	62.5	25.7	40.1	30.6	29.3	Medium horizontal curve
12. Serious	35.5	64.2	50.5	28.2	21.0	64.4	19.1	16.2	Slow horizontal angle
13. Powerful	15.3	85.4	27.8	52.7	19.9	37.9	55.5	7.0	Medium rising angle

with the pull of gravity, that is, at rest. It is quiet, passive, calm, it suggests repose.... The vertical is suggestive of poise, balance, and of strong, firm support. Vertical lines ... are severe and austere; they symbolize uprightness, honesty or integrity, dignity, aspiration and exaltation" (210).

Now, how does one get from the object feature of the ECU (for example, straight/curved) to its cultural significance (masculine/feminine)? One must beware of the simple naturalistic trap. The meaning is not a self-evident icon, immanent in the sign; the mental process is something more than an association of resemblances present to the senses. It is hardly enough to remark that men are, on average, straighter than women — even if the fact that plenty of men are rounder than plenty of women could somehow be disregarded. The problem is infinitely more interesting and subtle and, when one reflects upon it, altogether incorrectly posed in the initial question. *So far as production is concerned,* it is unnecessary to "get to" the cultural gender from the geometric form, as to the signified from the signifier, because from the beginning, as it were, each of these is alternately the meaning of the other. In the society as constituted, "rounded" and "soft" are as much the definition of women as "feminine" is the definition of the line. Gender and line: each is the signification of the other, and each stands to the other as the physical sign whose meaning is being determined. From this point of view, the difference between men and women is also "objective," a distinction of the concrete-perceptual type, in relation to which such object notions as "straight" and "curved," "hard" and "soft," "rigid" and "yielding" play the role of the concept. As we understand the difference in line to be a distinction of sex, so we understand the distinction of sex in terms of line.

But more, a second moment of reflection on the language suggests that as much can be said for a great number of social distinctions: they are characteristically idiomized in geometric terms. Our social world is presented as an enormous object world — and vice versa. Death is a "decline" to the "end" of immobility and prostration; hence, in the Poffenberger experiment, the line of "slow" horizontal or "descending" curve is "dead." But likewise, status is a "standing" among men, understood in the terms of "higher" and "lower," as a command is something before which we "incline" or "yield." Some people are "upright"; others are "crooked," or at least "devious" — some are even "deviants." Some are "strong," others are "weak." Certain are "forceful"; "force" also is an attribute of constituted authority. We speak "directly" or "indirectly." We act "rigidly" or "flexibly." We have "near" kinsmen and "distant" kinsmen, on some of whom we may "lean" while others we "support." It would be easy to go on indefinitely, but I shall cut the discussion "short" to make the "point." The point is that the social world is commonly figured by the so-called objective, which precisely as it is figurative here functions as the idea. Consequently, when it comes to the manufacture of a product, of a clothing set that objectifies the proportion straight/

192

curved::masculine/feminine, no greater privilege has to be given to the attribution of gender to shape than of shape to gender. The correspondence already exists in full before and outside that moment when "any piece of fabric can be charged with sexuality by simply working it into a precise shape" (Rudolfsky). Merely a particular realization of that correspondence, the cloth is a total social fact, at once material and conceptual, which seamlessly interweaves the spatial meaning of sex with the sexual meaning of space.

Production, then, is the practice of a much more pervasive logic of the concrete, which logic is itself produced as a symbolic appropriation of nature. It is not merely species that are "good to think." Lévi-Strauss's famous dictum is applicable to all kinds of naturally occurring things and relations. The whole of nature is the potential object of the symbolic praxis. The difference between vertical and horizontal line may carry with it a commonly experienced "resistance" and "submission" to a well-known "force." Hence the suitability of a contrast provided by nature to a distinction present in culture — for instance, between authority and subordination. Nor need we be deceived by the apparent objectivity of the sign, which is only the result of a dialectical process in which the natural fact was first seized culturally in order to be reapplied naturally. Nature rigidly separated from man, as Marx said, does not exist for man: the notions of "force," "resistance," and the like are already valuations, relative cultural representations of the natural process. Contrary to our received perspectives, this sort of metaphor does not really proceed from the concrete to the abstract, from nature to culture. Such would suppose that language's power of classification mysteriously fails at the moment of "real" experience, that it can merely then give forth a new name, which is to say degenerate into a signal. We can be sure that "force" was a spiritual relation before it became an objective fact; and, correspondingly, the material appropriation of nature we call "production" is a sequitur to its symbolic appropriation.

Saussurean principle, therefore, is not violated, whatever the apparent resemblances between object-sign and cultural referent. More than a reflection, the sign is a conception of objective differences. Arbitrariness thus retains a double historical guarantee. Which features of nature are harnessed by culture to its own intentions remains a relative determination: that particular contrast of line to represent gender is not the only one possible. Conversely, the specific content of any particular contrast on the object level is not given with the difference: whether the upright line is to represent honesty, masculinity, or authority, and if authority, what kind — none of this can be said apart from a determinate cultural system. Yet, at the same time, the historical appropriation of concrete contrasts must carry into the order of culture at least two conditions of nature if it is to function as social discourse. First, the selection of a given material opposition — as straight/curved::masculine/feminine — must be true: the penalty of a contradiction between the perceptible object contrasts and the relationships signified is meaninglessness and, ultimately, silence. In use, the sign is relatively motivated, if according to a certain cultural scheme. And second, then, the condition of perceptible resemblance, itself relative and indeterminate (as merely a condition of noncontradiction), argues the encompassment within the symbolic system of specific natural structures — those of perception itself. This is an activity of appropriation and exploitation, the employment of sensible contrasts and relations as a semiotic code....

In its economic dimension, the project consists of the reproduction of society in a system of objects, not merely useful but meaningful, whose utility indeed consists of a significance. The clothing system in particular replicates for Western society the functions of the so-called totemism. A sumptuary materialization of the principal coordinates of person and occasion, it becomes a vast scheme of communication — such as to serve as a language of everyday life among those who may well have no prior intercourse of acquaintance.[22] "Mere appearance" must be one of the most important forms of symbolic statement in Western civilization, for it is by appearances that civilization turns the basic contradiction of its construction into a miracle of existence: a cohesive society of perfect strangers. But in the event, its cohesion

194

depends on a *coherence* of a specific kind — on the possibility of apprehending others, their social condition, and thereby their relation to oneself "on first glance." This dependence on seeing helps to explain, on the one hand, why the symbolic dimensions have nevertheless not been obvious. The code works on an unconscious level, the conception built into perception itself. It is precisely the type of thought generally known as "savage" — thought that "does not distinguish the moment of observation and that of interpretation any more than, on observing them, one first registers the interlocutor's signs and then tries to understand them; when he speaks, the signs expressed carry with them their meanings" (Lévi-Strauss 1966:223). On the other hand, this dependence on the glance suggests the presence in the economic and social life of a logic completely foreign to the conventional "rationality," for rationality is time elapsed, a comparison — at least another glance beyond, and a weighing of the alternatives. The relation between logics is that the first, the symbolic, defines and ranks the alternatives by the "choice" among which rationality, oblivious of its own cultural basis, is pleased to consider itself as constituting.

NOTES

1. Of course, we know at some level that these claims are fraudulent, but this knowledge is only further evidence of the same principle, namely, the ordering power of gain. Having penetrated the secrets of advertising, taken away all substance and sense, what else is left but the gainful motive underneath all social form? Now, by the very abstractness and nakedness in which we discover it, its power is confirmed — even more so by the illusion that we have been able to determine it behind the mask of false claims.

2. In one respect, that of being less bound to a specific situation, use-value is more arbitrary than exchange-value, although in stricter association with concrete properties of the object. Marx was surely correct in understanding the commodity-value as a differential meaning established in the discourse of things, that is, standing as the concept (*le signifié*) of a given object only by relations developed in the commercial discourse and not by reference to concrete properties. In the latter respect, commodity-value is the more abstract. In order to

enter into these determining relations, however, the object must be a use-value, that is, have a conventional meaning assigned to its objective properties, such as to give it "utility" to certain persons. Since this meaning is a differential *valuation* of the properties, it cannot be grasped by the senses; but it is always connected to the sensible — hence use-value is the more concrete value. On the other hand, the utility-meaning can be invoked outside any specific action, being taken as the meaning of the object as such. But exchange-value is determinable only from the economic interaction of commodities, and differently in each such situation. It is bound to and stipulated within the discourse of commodities; outside the context of exchange, the object resumes the status of a use-value. Viewed thus, use-value is the more arbitrary; exchange-value is a pragmatic "shifter."

3. The discussion that follows is but a marginal gloss on the larger analysis of notions of edibility and relations to domestic animals launched by Douglas (1966, 1971), Leach (1964), and Lévi-Strauss (1966). See also Barthes (1961), R. Valeri (1971), and, on certain correspondences between social and zoological categories, Bulmer (1967) and Tambiah (1969). The intent here is not so much to contribute to the semiotic analysis as to stress the economic implications.

4. Cf. Benveniste (1969, vol. 1) on Indo-European *pasu vīra* for example: "it is as an element of mobile wealth that one must take the avestic *vīra* or *pasu vīra*. One designates by that term the ensemble of movable private property, men as well as animals" (49). Or see the extensive discussion of the Latin *pecu, pecunia,* and *peculium* (55ff.).

5. "Supposing an individual accustomed to eating dogs should enquire among us for the reason why we do not eat dogs, we could only reply that it is not customary; and he would be justified in saying that dogs are tabooed among us, just as much as we are justified in speaking of taboos among primitive people. If we were hard pressed for reasons, we should probably base our aversion to eating dogs or horses on the seeming impropriety of eating animals that live with us as our friends" (Boas [1938] 1965: 207).

6. French and American naming practices appear to differ here. Lévi-Strauss's observations on the names the French give animals (1966:204ff.) apply only fractionally to American custom. A brief ethnographic inquiry is enough to show that the latter is quite complex in this regard. The general rule, however, is that named/unnamed: inedible/edible. The names of both dogs and horses (excluding racehorses) are sometimes "like stage names, forming a series parallel to the names people bear in ordinary life, or, in other words, metaphorical

names" (*ibid.*:205) — for example, Duke, King, Scout, Trigger. More often, however, the names used in English are descriptive terms, likewise metamorphical but taken from the chain of discourse — Smokey, Paint, Blue, Snoopy, Spot, and so on. The French reserve such names for cattle. Our cattle are generally unnamed, except for milk cows, which often have two-syllable human names (Bessie, Ruby, Patty, Rena — these were collected from informants). Work horses — as distinguished from riding horses — also had human names. Differences between related societies in these regards, as Lévi-Strauss (1966) points out, represent different cultural *découpages* or superpositions of the animal on the human series.

7. Leach develops this point in his important paper on English animal categories as fitting into a systematic set of correspondences between relations to people and relations to animals according to degrees of distance from self (1964:42–47 and appendix). Leach claims the scheme has wide validity, although not universality; of course, it would require some permutation for peoples who (for example) eat domestic dogs. The Hawaiians treat dogs destined for eating with great compassion, "and not infrequently, condescend to treat them with Poi [pounded taro] from their mouths" (Dampier 1971:50). Dogs destined for eating, however, are never allowed to touch meat (Corney [1821] 1896:117). It is not clear whether they are eaten by the family who raised them or, like Melanesian pigs, similarly coddled in the household, reserved for prestations to others.

8. The meat taxonomy is, of course, much more complex than these common appellations. Steak, for instance, has a whole vocabulary of its own, in which some organic reference occurs, although usually not the terms applied to the human body (sirloin, T-bone, and so on). Calves' liver is an exception to this entire discussion, the reasons for which I do not know.

9. Moreover, there is to this notion of communication a fundamental base, set down by Rousseau in his running debate with Hobbes:

> But when it should prove true that this war of each against all of unlimited and indomitable covetousness shall have developed in all men to the point supposed by our sophist, still it would not produce that universal which Hobbes ventures to trace the odious *tableau*. This unchecked desire to appropriate all things is incompatible with that of destroying all fellow beings; and having killed everyone the victor would have only the misfortune of being alone in the world, and could enjoy nothing even as he had everything. Wealth in itself: What good does it do if it cannot be

197

communicated; and what would it serve a man to possess the entire universe, if he were its only inhabitant? (1964, vol. 3:601)

10. As Baudrillard put it, "Objects are neither flora nor fauna. Yet they give the impression of a proliferating vegetation, a jungle, where the new savage man of modern times has trouble finding the reflexes of civilization. This fauna and flora that man has produced and that return to encircle and invest him ... we must try to describe ... never forgetting that in their splendor and profusion, they are *the product of human activity* and are dominated not by natural ecological laws but by the law of the value of exchange" (Baudrillard 1970:19–20).

11. Fashion in clothing is, of course, frequently commented upon by social scientists and is occasionally given empirical investigation (Barthes 1967, Richardson and Kroeber 1940, Simmel 1904, G.P. Stone 1959). But there is a much richer literature upon which one may draw for ethnographic purposes: the direct reflections of participants in the process. Our discussion makes use of the writings of such as admen, market researchers, designers, buyers, fashion editors, and critics, as well as of textbooks by teachers of home economics, design, and aesthetics. Moreover, the discussion does not deny itself the advantage of observation and self-reflection in the one situation where the ethnographer finally realizes the privileged position of the participant-observer, namely, in his own village. I do not claim to have exhausted any of these resources — very far from it. For a treatment of costume analogous to that attempted here — which, however, came to my attention after this chapter had gone to press — see Bogatyrev (1971).

12. Although Barthes was exclusively concerned with the rhetoric of fashion as written (*le vêtement écrit*) rather than with the symbolic system of the clothing object as such, much of his discussion is pertinent to the present effort, and I have drawn heavily upon it.

13. Cf. Crawley's "principle of adaptation to state": "Dress expresses every social movement, as well as every social grade. It also expresses family, municipal, provincial, regional, tribal, and national character. At the same time it gives full play to the individual. A complete psychology of the subject would analyze all such cases with reference to the principle of adaptation" (1931:172). Some of the objective changes that accompany the fundamental proportion of public/private::impersonal/familial are conjured up by the stereotypic image of the good bourgeois returning home from "a hard day at the office": a banal scene in which the social passage is signified by the man successively removing his hat, kissing his wife, taking off his jacket, stripping away his tie (exaggerated ges-

ture), opening his shirt collar (deep breath), sinking into his favorite armchair, donning the slippers fetched by a well-trained child, spouse, or dog — and breathing a sigh of relief. A whole set of statements about the contrast between kinship and the "larger world" is going on. In G.P. Stone's sociological study of clothing in Vansburg, Michigan, it was observed that about 70 percent of manual and white-collar workers arrive at work in what they consider their work clothes, and about 60 percent change when they go home. More than 90 percent of their wives changed clothing before going shopping, and about 75 percent did so again upon returning home (1959:109–10). Lynes sometime ago noticed that on weekends, since the (suburban) home has become an arena of do-it-yourself, the white-collar class has affected "workclothes" (for example, blue jeans) in the domestic sphere — except for the "backyard barbeque," which is distinguished by bright and dashing holiday wear, "symbols of revolt against the conformity imposed on men by the daily routine of business" (1957:69).

14. Varieties of cotton are again differentiated by sex according to heaviness and stiffness; so the common four-class paradigm in materials:

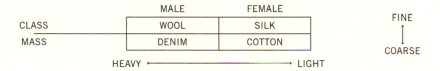

In a book on advertising technique, Stephen Baker (1961, unpaginated) presents pictures of the same woman draped in four different fabrics. He comments: "Fabrics have sexual connotations. Wool is the least feminine of the four materials.... It makes a women appear businesslike, urban, sophisticated. Linen has a mixed image. If it is white, the fabric strongly suggests purity. It is more feminine than wool but has little seductive power. Linen is associated with clean, wholesome fun. The delicacy (and lightness) of lace makes it very much a woman's fabric. Rich in pattern, lace exudes an air of elegance, aloofness, yet soft femininity. Silk is the most sensuous of all materials. It shines and reflects the play of light. It is very soft and clings to a woman's body. This characteristic makes silk (or satin) bring out the seductive qualities of the wearer."

15. Cf. Schwartz 1958 on clothing among African Americans. One observation of this empirical study that seems quite generalizable is that "the least significant motive underlying the selection and wearing of certain items of clothing is protection from the elements" (27).

16. An empirical study of favored costumes of upper-class college and mid-dle-aged women developed contrasts of the following type (N. Taylor, cited in Rosencranz 1972:214–15):

	Young college women	Middle-aged women
Garment	Dark gray wool dress and coat; scarf of gray, black, and red paisley	Black silk ottoman suit
Shoes	Black brogans	Black silk pumps with bow
Hose	"Hint" of gray	Black sheer
Handbag	Black calf	Black silk
Bracelet	Silver with pearls	Gold
Pin	——	Diamond sunburst
Ring	Pearl	Pearl and diamond

From the above information and preceding discussion one could probably make a few guesses about production: for example, that (other things being equal, and they are many) the amount of black silk produced is correlated with the number of middle-aged, upper-class White females in the population — which is itself a product of the total organization of society (notably including production). The proposition is at once banal and totally un-self-evident. It is hardly in the nature of things that silk has some affinity with White middle-aged women, although it is in *the culture of the things*.

17. Not to deny that such may be the genuine mode of appearance to the participants in the process: "'I don't think I ever figured it would come to this,' says Haas, who along with his brother Peter, the (Levi-Strauss) company president, was responsible for molding Levi's into its present structure. 'Basically, what we've tried to do is to serve society's needs.'"

"'The consumer still determines what he wants,'" says Bud Johns, the company's public relations director. 'We always try to adapt'" ("Blue Jeans: Uniform for a Casual World," *Chicago Tribune*, 5 May 1975).

18. Or consider the following example of stylization in relation to ceremonial hierarchy noted by Jacinski in one factory: "Suntan trousers and shirts but no ties for inspectors; slacks and sport shirts for lead men; slacks, white shirts, and ties for assistant foremen; and the same, plus a jacket, for the foreman" (quoted in M.S. Ryan 1966:66).

19. On occupational differentiation of clothing, see, for example, M.S. Ryan 1966:62 and Horn 1968. One of G.P. Stone's Vansburg informants commented as follows on the changes wrought by recent agricultural specialization:

> A few years ago you could tell any farmer. They used to wear denim over-alls all the time. Now they have diversified farming, so the clothes have changed, too. Well, some still wear denims. Those in the dairy business have uniforms. Those in the poultry business have white uniforms. Those in beef wear women's skirts and corduroy pants — out in the field, they have to wear something heavier. It's altogether different than it was thirty years ago. (1959:120–21)

20. As has often been remarked, there is an asymmetry in the gender of almost all objects, including clothing: it is feminine things that are marked and exclusive; male objects, even such things as razors or electric shavers, are often used by women or appear in feminine versions. On the gender of objects, see Levy 1968 and Baker 1961.

21. This cultural construction of a line as "going upward to the right," which a Japanese would conceive just the reverse way, is a small but interesting indication that action, including language, proceeds in a world already symbolized and interacting nondiscursively with the conventional code of action.

22. "With briefest visual perception, a complex mental process is aroused, resulting within very short time, 30 seconds perhaps, in judgment of the sex, age, size, nationality, profession and social caste of the stranger together with some estimate of his temperament, his ascendance, friendliness, neatness; and even his trustworthiness" (G. Allport, cited in Horn 1968:109; cf. Linton 1936:416).

PART TWO

Practice

Introduction to Part Two

An unexpected thing happened on the way to the Academy: the war in Vietnam. I have already described the perturbations it occasioned in the anthropology represented here, and these effects may be appreciated by a comparison of the essays in Part One and Part Three. The works of the present section give some immediate sense of the impact of the event.

The first, "The Future of the National Teach-In: A History," was commissioned by the *New York Times Magazine* after the national teach-in of May 1965 in Washington. However, the *Times* refused the article, I believe because it didn't say enough about the future — so it is printed here for the first time. (I sympathize a lot with Durkheim's remark, noted in these essays in another context — that of the always-imminent disappearance of indigenous cultures — that a science of the future has no subject matter.) Above all else, what the article reflects is the hands-on experience of organizing the national teach-in. For a week before the event, Arnold Kauffman, a philosopher from the University of Michigan, and I, two relatively short and rotund professors, set up the teach-in from a room in Washington's Mayfair Hotel which eventually had three phones constantly ringing off the hook with calls from virtually every major press, radio, and television office, domestic and foreign, in the city, not to mention the negotiations over speakers and formats with the White House or the numerous inquiries from congressional aides. We learned a lot, thanks to some generous advice from certain members of the media — how to write a press release, for example. Arnie, who died untimely in an airplane crash not long after, was a great philosopher of political liberalism; and that also shows in what we were learning, and in this piece. What I tried to describe was a movement in the antiwar movement from protest to politics-in-the-system, or at least to the adoption of populist-democratic opposition tactics. This tendency of the antiwar politics was later to be defused by the demagogy, and sometimes overshadowed by the violence, that emerged in the late 1960s. Although I am not generally a conspiracy theorist, I do believe attempts were made to infiltrate and discredit the movement by government agent provocateurs. However that may be, a clear and simple law of revolution was already apparent at the time of the first teach-ins: namely, that subversion of the system is not initiated by the eventual revolutionaries but by the powers that be. As in the Vietnam War, the rulers are the ones who undermine the received values and established political processes. By the same token, it is from deep traditional values that the opposition draws its outrage — and, in defense of them, takes to the streets.

The penultimate article, "The Destruction of Conscience in Vietnam" (Chapter Eight), is actually a sequel to the National Teach-In. The day after the event, many of the organizers and participants gathered to plan further activities, and in the course of that meeting I was deputed to go to Vietnam, in part to show the antiwar flag but mainly on a kind of fact-finding mission. (I was also appointed to establish a liaison among the university groups involved in organizing or broadcasting the teach-in. Later, when the files of the Chicago Police "Red Squad" were opened, it was ominously revealed that I had "set up a network" as well as given a speech against the war at the University of Chicago. The same files also disclosed, apropos of Nikita Khrushchev's visit to the United States, that he "was reputed to be a Communist.") The eventfulness of this brief visit to Vietnam, as described in the article, was due to two chance (?) encounters. First, the man who sat down next to me on the flight from Hawaii to Tokyo was an officer in the U.S. Information Service in Saigon. Second was the meeting with the two American antiguerrilla guerrilla-warriors or "advisers" in the Mekong Delta, which led to the patrol at the Cambodian border and the existential interview on torture.

The patrol turned out to be a condition of the possibility of the interview. As "advisers," the Americans had left the leadership of the operation to Vietnamese, who put us through two somewhat risky maneuvers. For one, the platoon had split into two parties that had to rendezvous by walkie-talkie after the fruitless ambush at the border: two groups of highly armed and nervous men wandering around in the dark, either one of which could have easily been Vietcong (we were in "black pajamas"). Then, our leaders led us back to camp single-file through an extensive rice paddy, at times sufficiently visible by moonlight for us to be easy targets from the nearby clumps of coconut trees. I believe that the revelatory character of the conversation on torture that followed in the early hours of the morning was facilitated by the sheer relief that we had returned without incident. (The interview, incidentally, achieved fifteen minutes of fame: it appeared in the *Nation* and a British antinuclear paper; the entire article was printed in *Dissent* and a volume of *Best Magazine Articles: 1967* published by the *New York Times*.)

The remaining two articles are fairly self-explanatory except for their occasions. Chapter Seven, "The Peace Offensive and the Ky Regime," was an address delivered in early March 1966 at a trade union conference in Detroit on Vietnam and U.S. foreign policy sponsored by the UAW. It concerns one of the disingenuous peace campaigns mounted by the Johnson administration between 1965 and 1968. The second, "The Established Order: Do Not Fold, Spindle, or Mutilate" (Chapter Nine), addressed a corollary political issue, Project Camelot, a social science exercise in "counterinsurgency prophylaxis" (or spying) in Latin America sponsored by the U.S. Department of Defense. Project Camelot evoked a reaction from the American Anthropological Association: a session of the November 1965 national meeting — where this article was originally presented — was devoted to it. In 1967, the article was published in *The Rise and Fall of Project Camelot*, edited by Irving Louis Horowitz.

CHAPTER SIX

The Future of the National Teach-In:

A History[*]

No one could have guessed what a Big Thing was to come from
our meeting in March. Anyone who foretold the event had to be
a dabbler in political science fiction. Even so, it was an obscure
and improbable group of Martians who met that night, little more
than a handful of teachers and scholars, most of us young (in our
thirties), mostly social scientists, gathered in a modest home on
a side street of Ann Arbor — a small university city made up exclusively of side streets. And we were resolved on an improbable
act of obscure meaning: to cancel classes 24 March 1965 and hold
lectures instead on Vietnam, in exasperated protest of the government's policy and its drift toward greater war. By 24 March we
had decided to "teach in," all night, instead of "teaching out." By
15 May, after a chain reaction of "teach-ins" on campuses across
the country and the formation of an "Inter-university Committee
for a Public Hearing on Vietnam," we had challenged the government to a question period of historic proportions. At an all-
day National Teach-In in Washington, DC, the Vietnam policy —
developed for a decade in private councils beyond reach of public debate — was defended by administration spokesmen and selected academic supporters against the contentions of an informed
opposition.

Perhaps it *was* science fiction. It defied first laws of physics and
politics: the response of the government and people on 15 May

[*] Previously commissioned and unpublished by the *New York Times Magazine*,
1965.

was all out of proportion to the weak impulse of the Ides of March that had set it off. An eleventh-hour call of other duties on National Security Advisor McGeorge Bundy unfortunately diluted the confrontation. Still, the official policy was opened to public review. An important segment of the country came to express critical opinions of it; a larger and more important part listened and learned something. Four thousand people tensely followed the proceedings in Washington. On 122 campuses in 35 states, students and faculty were tuned in by telephone hookup to the afternoon policy debate. Radio stations in major eastern and midwestern cities carried all or part of the day's discussion. The principal television networks put on live or taped "specials" coast to coast. In New York, Boston, and Washington, educational stations telecast the entire event, from nine in the morning to twelve-thirty the next morning. In the week following, National Educational Television would distribute a one-hour digest to 92 affiliated stations.

And those who had not heard or seen it could read all about it — on the front pages. Over two hundred reporters covered the Teach-In, including foreign press. On 17 May, the *New York Times* printed two pages of excerpts from the day's program. For days afterward, the Teach-In reverberated in editorial columns of the nation's newspapers, though not always in tones of clear praise, nor without ominous overtones of red-baiting. (The hometown *Ann Arbor News*, incidentally, was predictably dull and out of sorts.) For some time to come, the events of 15 May would be elegantly discussed in the nation's monthlies.

Clearly, the National Teach-In has a brilliant future behind it. Now it faces a question period from its own supporters and the country at large, on an agenda that transcends Vietnam. Can a National Teach-In carry on, to become a continuing forum for the debate of national policy? Some hopes have been stirred in the universities, the press, and the citizenry — that the administration will acknowledge a responsibility to give candid accounts of past actions and present difficulties; that a conversation between informed dissent and main power can take place, to the enlightenment of the whole nation; that the people shall not be alienated from large decision-making and subject merely to the television of accomplished fact. It is no accident that these hopes are voiced in the wake of the National Teach-In. It has proved the social function of the teach-in movement to develop and express them and, by action, to raise them to the level of political demand.

In its own evolution, the teach-in movement turned from a confrontation with the system to a confrontation within the system, from an argument with the established order to an argument with the Establishment. (I refer specifically to the experience of the University of Michigan group; developments on other campuses took their own course, not necessarily parallel, although insofar as support was committed to the National Teach-In the later phases became similar.) What began as a call to existential withdrawal became a series of calls to the White House — to negotiate the terms of debate. Step by step, the protest was temporized — from walk-out to teach-in, teach-in to public hearing — until it became *dissent*; and "dissent in a democratic forum," as a publicity release of the Inter-university Committee was to remark, "is the highest form of cooperation." Running concurrently with this change from civil disobedience to civic disputation, and in reciprocal relations with it, were two further developments: a broadening of university participation and public interest, and a broadening criticism of U.S. policy.

Each new accommodation to traditional democratic dissent brought a geometric increase in the number of dissenters. (Close scrutiny would probably show that the proportion of well-known, senior faculty also increased dramatically.) Forty-nine Michigan faculty supported the initial call to cancel classes; 250 supported the teach-in of 24 March. By the time of the National Teach-In, active participation on every campus had cut across a wider section of the university community than had ever involved itself in public affairs. The relation between faculty and student activism quickly passed beyond alliance. The two stimulated each other: just as faculty commitment increased in response to the dedication of students, so the ranks of engaged students were swelled by the curious discovery that their teachers were human beings, willing to turn their academic passions and learning to

211

something going on in the world — which suggested something was seriously wrong.

The teach-ins effected a genuine relaxation of the academic bureaucracy against which the students had been protesting, and which they saw as one of many institutions in America organized to alienate themselves and others. Beyond that, the teach-ins were a genuine intellectual experience, for many the first they ever had on campus, perhaps because for the first time *both* teachers and students were discussing, seriously and with respect for each other's opinions, something both were deeply interested in understanding.

As the ripple of protest swelled to a wave of dissent, the criticism of Vietnam policy was broadening and changing emphasis. Partly this could reflect the continuing process of self-education going on in the teach-in movement. Argument was pushing into the larger background of Vietnam. More was said of the simpleminded demonology of the Cold War; of the preference expressed by American policy for the Intelligence of the CIA over an intelligent understanding of the postcolonial world; of the failure to make the connection between the American tradition and the hopes of harassed peoples for national independence and economic progress. In the last weeks before the National Teach-In, however, criticism evolved most rapidly on another level. Clearly this was because the teach-in movement had entered into a definite social relation — a relation of loyal opposition — with the administration. Now, apart from the nature of American actions in Vietnam, issue was taken with the *way* policy was made, behind closed Executive doors, without debate; and the way consensus was demanded, on grounds of Higher Authority, or, if need be, of patriotism. The administration, in official documents and statements of its spokesmen, had not set any records for credibility — for consistency of argument, candid presentation of fact, soundness of interpretation, or accuracy of prediction. It was a weak basis for insisting on confidence — and further military adventures. Indeed, it could be argued that further adventures were now deemed necessary precisely because the government had deceived itself and the people about what was going on in Vietnam.

Yet more telling, politically, and more than academic in form, were the arguments thus opened – arguments from democracy. The people had a right to know, the administration an obligation to give frank account. Surely, the *conduct* of foreign affairs is delegated to the Executive, but this does not give it leave to determine the *content* of policy without regard for democratic procedures. The administration did not have leave to foreclose debate in Congress, nor to consider some military appropriation upon which it insisted a substitute for the constitutional prerogative of Congress to declare war. It did not have leave to adopt policies on Vietnam against which it had campaigned and won a national election six months before. Nor ought it petulantly dismiss serious critics, nor inform the people of military acts committed in America's name in the form of extended television commercials. These arguments from democracy, although present from the beginning of the teach-in movement, became central to the National Teach-In.

A list of distinguished academic people – Robert Hutchins, David Riesman, Robert Merton, and, originally, eighty more, ultimately eighteen hundred more – agreed to sponsor the National Teach-In, not as the endorsement of any particular solution to the Vietnam situation but specifically on the proposition that "questions of war and people should be open to responsible public debate." Anyone there 15 May would have sensed the people assembled in Washington felt a right to this discussion. And anyone would have sensed the feelings of personal outrage – common even to many who supported the government position – when it was announced Mr. Bundy would not appear. Two days later, Republican senator Winston Prouty of Vermont, a man totally out of sympathy with academic critics of the administration, rose on the Senate floor to deplore Mr. Bundy's failure to show and the manner in which he had conveyed regrets. The senator then went on: "Let there be no mistake about it, Mr. President. The American people have a right to know. They have a right to hear our national policies attacked and defended." Coming from the duly constituted forum of people's representatives, the statement is somewhat embarrassing – but the sentiments are all right.

To comment coldly about the "correlation of forces," the teaching community revealed some unappreciated political strength, including a strategic press support, while the administration showed some unsuspected softness.

Academics do have a measure of political capital — aside from the fact that the nation's children are confined to their tender mercies, and all the fear that inspires the moment a professor takes a novel moral stand. The university community is a sizable population. It has certain local and national "connections," as for instance in the Democratic Party. An editorial in the *Nation*, commenting on the Teach-In, remarked: "Professors and students now know that they have a political role to play, that their views count, that to be an intellectual is no mean estate." Perhaps the greatest leverage of the intellectuals resides just in this: as the government increasingly finds the competence of academics indispensable, it puts them precisely in the bargaining position of a *political* estate, the fifth estate. Not only are hard scientists concerned. The army is right now attempting to enlist American anthropological field-workers in the development of counterinsurgency techniques — a contamination of the discipline, especially of the anthropologist's fundamental relation of confidence with the people he studies, that is going to be sorely resented and strongly resisted.

Meanwhile, the administration suffers the weaknesses of its growing strength. Against the background of a democratic tradition, the Executive's assumption of total decision on foreign policy creates a political vacuum it is hard put to fill by an engineered consensus. Historic balances and forums of dissent have been rendered moribund. Yet the enlargement of Executive power has not been accompanied by a corresponding capacity to finesse the populace; nor have critical avenues of information been blocked. The administration remains vulnerable to demands for an accounting, and it strains credulity at some risk.

Consider that some of the same problem the administration is having with the universities over Vietnam it has already had in Vietnam with reporters who insisted on "calling them as they saw them." Those who dismiss out of hand the long-range possibilities of teach-ins might ponder this experienced comment of John

Mecklin's: "American reporters in Vietnam achieved an influence in the making of U.S. foreign policy that had been equalled in modern times only by the role of the New York newspapers in precipitating the Spanish-American war more than half a century earlier. There was a significant difference. In the earlier case it was deliberate.... In Vietnam, a major American policy was wrecked, in part, by unadorned reporting of what was going on." It is notable, as a friend said of the National Teach-In, that the press — part of it — turned out to be our hidden ally. But then there was something in common: a concern for what was really going on, for freedom of inquiry and that the people be informed.

One ought to allow — even in discussions of Realpolitik — for a proper amount of idealism all around. The people in the administration are not Strangeloves; they are looking for ways out, and I suspect they welcomed the Teach-In for more than the purpose of draining off the annoying noise on campus. This curious suspicion first came over me the week before the Teach-In, while answering phones in the Washington office of the Inter-university Committee. We got a number of calls that week from State Department people asking for tickets for themselves, friends, and family. (The State Department and White House, on their request, had been given blocks of tickets to dispose of as they wished.) The demand for tickets from legislative assistants, incidentally, was very heavy.

One could reasonably speculate that an effect of the Teach-In was to clear some air in Washington. Part of the legacy of the China lobby and McCarthy era is well known: the flow of informed, outstanding scholars to government service was seriously curtailed. About another effect one can only guess: a lingering disinclination to raise certain issues, discuss certain possibilities, to the extent that internal dialogue in policy bureaus is constrained, options are reduced, and some people perhaps even forced to compromise their judgment, their intelligence, and their morality. If these speculations hold, then the Teach-In will have been useful in a subtle way. Clearly, though it may have been the most comprehensive debate of the decade on Vietnam, it could of its nature solve nothing, least of all call off the war then and there. But the opposition, by making an intelligent case for alternative interpretations and strategies, might just have put these on the "agenda" of the corridors of power, and made legitimate some conceptions of the world that had been tabu. Even if the options thus opened are not now adopted — there is the next time, and the next issue, and the next country. Perhaps the Teach-In, as in the good academic tradition, managed to communicate the knowledge and the freedom to do better. Perhaps, too, it had some such public effect, which would further free the hand of public servants. A Teach-In probably cannot alter policy of the moment, which is inevitably most responsive to its own past. What it may affect is the set and drift, the direction national policy will take.

This potentiality is relevant to two fairly contradictory criticisms one hears of the National Teach-In: first, that it can deal only with immediate crises, such as an intensification of war in Vietnam, instead of addressing underlying general causes — nationalism, underdevelopment, what to do about China; second, that in this era of the fateful snap decision, it does little good to dredge up past mistakes or talk about what's the matter generally. The first criticism is ostensibly true: teach-ins, especially a national teach-in, have to convene on specific current difficulties. But this overlooks the congenital impulse of scholars to *interpret* the specific case, which immediately engages the larger context and the general causes. And, if the previous speculations are any good, it is from this larger context, and upon it, that the Teach-In eventually takes effect. As against the second criticism, it is important to consider what is implied by a sudden decision to take dangerous and forceful action at some outpost of world trouble. It means we had failed to understand what was going on and to construct a policy against the untoward eventuality; so that events decisive for a people, a hemisphere, or the world now catch us by surprise and push us to drastic remedial measures. In brief, our policy had been wrong, ignorant, and counterproductive. Surely the objective of foreign policy should be not to make these quick decisions but, rather, not to have to make them. The Teach-In might be evaluated by its contribution to that objective.

It is a misconception to see the National Teach-In as the

216

consummate final product of the teach-in movement. As in any evolutionary process, there are many lines of development. Awakened to their powers and responsibilities, the universities have evolved a whole family of political actions. The teach-in is only one, very adaptable genus of the family; the National Teach-In one species of the genus.

In turn, future National Teach-Ins, if they are to have meaning and effect, will be born of discontent on the nation's campuses. The National Teach-In has a special historic function. It is a way of transmitting to the government and people critical, studied opinions of national policy; of opening to intensive review courses of national action that have escaped democratic debate; of permitting a large segment of the country to examine the complexities of national circumstance, to learn, and (hopefully) to affect the national response — in short, one way to revive the homespun democracy that everyone thought in this age impossible to recapture.

CHAPTER SEVEN

The Peace Offensive and the

Ky Regime[*]

I want to cast some aspersions on the government of South Vietnam. Critics of the war often point to the contradiction between our announced defense of "freedom" and the tyranny of this regime, whose present premier has publicly expressed his admiration for Adolf Hitler, but the criticism does not go deep enough, neither into the character of the decadent system we now support nor into the power it has captured over our own policy decisions. For example, our so-called peace offensive of last December and January [1965–1966]. It was undermined by the South Vietnamese government. More accurately, an honest overture of peace to the National Liberation Front (the "Vietcong") would have undermined the South Vietnamese government, whose existence depends entirely on a state of war and continuous transfusions of American blood and money. Had we recognized the Front, as Senator Kennedy was later to suggest, the Ky government would have fallen before you could even say "Geneva," let alone get there from here. We would have been left holding a seven-card bust, which is no way to sit at a bargaining table. In other words, we could not make peace in January because we were tied up with such a bad cause.

I am suggesting that the peace offensive had many levels of reality. The diplomatic flying circus — featuring Arthur Goldberg talking with the "Holy Father," Soapy Williams in darkest Africa, McGeorge Bundy, and other peculiar acts, such as Averill Harriman

*Originally published in *Labor Today* 5.2 (1966).

making erratic attempts to beard Marshal Tito in the mountains of Yugoslavia — this flimflam was superficial in many respects. What could it accomplish? We negotiated with thirty-four neutral countries, avoided the one enemy, and concluded from that we would have to spend 15 percent of the national budget killing people whose existence we refuse to acknowledge. But then, barely concealed by our efforts to open unconditional discussions were certain minimal specifications of peace upon which we insisted in advance. Even during the offensive, high-ranking U.S. officials publicly pledged to uphold these conditions, come whatever. And these "certain conditions" amounted to a demand for surrender. To North Vietnam we held out the prospect of a partitioned country: we would give up the idea of bombing if they would give up the idea of Vietnam. To the Front we offered the possibility of dissolving itself: we would not recognize the Vietcong as a political entity, nor deal directly with them, nor tolerate their inclusion in a postwar government. So our terms came down to the suggestion that our enemies "reason together" with us, anytime, anyplace, on how they were to give up the causes for which they were fighting — and also, in the case of the NLF, how they were to negotiate themselves out of existence.

And one other absurdity of the American peace overture needs special mention: our sudden infatuation with free elections in Vietnam — which certainly would be commendable, if it were believable. Everyone knows that the United States encouraged Diem to sabotage the unification elections scheduled for 1956 by the Geneva Agreements. Perhaps not so well known, America-Diem again refused North Vietnamese requests for pre-election consultations in July 1957, March 1958, July 1959, and July 1960. But most important, our inspired call for free elections must be weighed against another American pronouncement, a pronouncement that explains our existence in Vietnam and tells us why so many people must die: that if the communists are not stopped here, if a people's war can bring them to power, there will be no stopping them anywhere — not in Thailand, Cambodia, Indonesia, the Philippines, Australia, or New Zealand — and we shall have to fight them on the beaches, in the streets, and in the houses — of Honolulu. Then how on earth can we even mention free elections? Is the National Liberation Front to be disqualified? Surely the model of democracy we propose here is not the legislature of the state of Georgia! In the middle of the peace offensive, the U.S. Mission in Saigon warned Washington there was no organized political force in South Vietnam except the National Liberation Front (A.P., 19 Jan. [1966]) — therefore, we had better not recognize the Front as a legitimate political force. But even if we could be more optimistic about the outcome of free elections, would we dare stake all of Southeast Asia, with Waikiki Beach thrown in, on the voting behavior of Vietnamese peasants? If it is true that we seek free elections, then it is a lie that communist (NLF) control of South Vietnam would doom Southeast Asia and threaten our security. But if it is true that communist control would be disastrous, then it is a lie that we seek free elections. You cannot have it both ways.

Final Blow

The dismal view on peace taken in January by the U.S.-Vietnam Mission happened to be released to the American press in the midst of serious events in Saigon, events that delivered the final blow to the peace offensive. The offensive had given Premier Ky a very bad month. It had the same effect on American officialdom in South Vietnam. Fully aware of the political vacuum in the country, and of the investment and hopes riding on Ky's government, the U.S. Mission knew that Ky's collapse would be curtains. But this is exactly what could be predicted in the event of a genuine American bid for peace. In fact, it *was* prophetically predicted last August by General Maxwell Taylor. "The army," Taylor said, "bear in mind, the army — is the power in South Viet Nam. The generals are completely committed. They've burnt their bridges behind them. They would never tolerate a government that was caught surreptitiously or overtly negotiating with Hanoi or with the Viet Cong." By 15 January, Taylor's prediction had been dramatically verified. The South Vietnamese government visibly shook. The pressure came from the apparent sincerity of our peace offensive, and the planned coup from certain officers who had everything to lose by it. On 16 January, the *New York*

221

Times reported troop movements into Saigon, "amid rumors of a possible power play against Premier Ky's government by generals fearing a sell-out to the Viet Cong in the diplomatic campaign to end the war." Four days later, the Ky government arrested ten to fifty officers alleged to have been involved; these plotters, according to the *Times* (20 Jan.), had been rebuffed in attempts to get support from U.S. officials "who want above almost all else to see the present government maintain stability."

Nasty Choice

The collapse of the peace offensive was no simple case of tail wagging dog. Here is a better description: By manufacturing the offensive, Washington put itself in a quandary, and then had to make a nasty choice — between the National Liberation Front (that is, recognition of it) and the existing South Vietnamese government, which was no less than the choice between peace and war. Nor was this a true dilemma, because the relationship between these alternatives made selection of one of them inevitable. Any concession to the Front — or, for that matter, to Hanoi — would have destroyed the Ky government right then, and thus put America in an untenable negotiating position. To push the peace line was therefore suicidal: America chose the Ky regime and its desperate belligerence. One dark implication is that the decision on further escalation has already been taken. But more than that follows. The peace offensive forced American policy, brought it to a crisis, and gave it a decisive turn. It threw us in, irretrievably, with the government of Vice Marshal Nguyen Cao Ky. Suddenly, and quite clumsily, we, too, had burned our bridges, lost our options, and were marooned with the existing cabal of generals. What had been an engagement, subject always to the constancy of the betrothed, turned into a shotgun wedding, 'til death do us part — with a three-day honeymoon in February at the Royal Hawaiian Hotel. And at the end of that honeymoon, the premier of Vietnam had the effrontery to flaunt his interesting condition in public, to say now right to the face of American reporters what in January could only be whispered distressingly, that he would "never" recognize or negotiate with the Vietcong.

Corruption

Ky also took the opportunity of that press conference to make an impromptu speech on how clean he was. "I don't even have a sec-ondhand American car," he said. Maybe not — but what became of his stripped-down American plane? I quote Malcolm Browne, the time, late 1964: "I am sitting in a hotel room at the charming mountain resort of Dalat, about 150 miles northeast of Saigon. A few miles down the mountain, at the Dalat airport, an American built T28 fighter with no guns or rockets is parked. This fighter, a two-seater, is the property of the dashing Air Commander Ky." Of course, the issue is not Ky, but the mare's nest of corruption, exploitation, and intrigue over which he presides. The constraints under which Ky operates you can read all about in any good American newspaper. For instance, Raymond Coffey in the *Nation*:

> Several weeks ago the U.S. mission pulled its aid representative out of Binh Tuy Province on the basis of evidence that the province chief, a Lt. Col. Pham Dinh Chi, had diverted to his own uses a substantial amount of U.S. money. The aid men had also reportedly been threat-ened with death if they exposed the situation. Ky hemmed and hawed for weeks under U.S. pressures to oust Chi. Finally he did — but only to give him another post in the defense ministry where the pickings may be even better. (17 Jan. 1966)

As I say, the scandal of South Vietnam is an open secret that any-one is free to pick up in the American press. I don't have time to rake up all this muck, but let me piece it together in a composite picture.

The Ruling Class

The freedom we defend in South Vietnam is in the hands of an inbred class of landed gentry, merchants, and contractors. These several thousand rich families live in the towns and cities and hold the countryside in chattel. The rich are, by function and kinship, interlocked with the military administration, itself rarely re-cruited from the Delta and almost never from the peasantry. Pivo-tal positions in the government, down to the district level, are

223

staffed by army officers. In this respect, the administration is the direct heir of the last French colonial regime; the nationality has been changed, but the structure and attitudes remain the same. The ruling class has a monopoly on higher education — yet it remains ignorant of the delta and the mountains, and counterposed economically and culturally to the people.

Actually, the war sets up a two-way hydraulic system for maintaining the Vietnamese upper class: squeezing the local poor and draining the American rich — activities that can be combined to promote one continuous profitable flow. The elite thrive on land rents, administrative extortion of the countryside, marketing an increasingly scarce food supply in the cities, embezzlement of American funds, hijacking and reselling U.S. aid goods, real-estate speculation around American bases, delivery of Vietnamese labor for war-related American construction, a variety of other contracting for Americans, and servicing a growing U.S. army with prostitutes, liquor, and other prerequisites of rest and recreation. Since many peasants have been put out of reach by the war, ruling-class predation turns increasingly toward the American boondoggle, combined with a related exploitation of urban workers and lower civil servants. (Associated with this shift, certain elements of the old rentier class seem to be losing power to mercantilist bourgeoisie with strong connections in the military administration — which controls the disposition of American aid.) In return for benefits received, the Vietnamese upper class undertakes to play the bulwark against communism and to deliver certain quotas of men to the Good Fight, though not so much its own sons. But its main interest in the whole process is its own safety and comfort. The profits of the rich are exported for safekeeping in foreign banks or for purchase of foreign luxuries — not secondhand American cars but the new Mercedes that choke the streets of Saigon. The runaway black market has testified to these worshipful uses of the almighty dollar.

Indifference to People
The attitude of the ruling group toward the underlying Vietnamese people is indifference or worse: "It seems to me," said

Malcolm Browne, "that of the thousands of Vietnamese officials I have known, I can think of none that does not more or less hold the people in contempt." This attitude can change to falsely solicitous when Americans are watching — but then, Americans are conceived quite gullible and overly sentimental. Members of the ruling class, however, are intensely suspicious of each other. The one thing on which they can agree is to combine against any of their number who threatens a serious interest in peace or reform — as opposed to a verbal interest. Thus, normal politics in Vietnam consists of intrigue and repression of the opposition through exile or coup, and the premier speaks wistfully to Western reporters of the effectiveness of Adolf Hitler.

Americans say, "We are helping the Vietnamese to help themselves," and that's exactly what they're doing — helping themselves. As a result, for all our anticolonial protestations, we perpetuate a colonial condition in the country, the same structure of dominant foreigners and profiteering local collaborators that the French had established. We are thoroughly compromised in Vietnam, and it no longer matters what we say, what we intend, or how much candy we pass out. As a Vietnamese friend put it to one reporter, "You don't have to be a communist to hate the Americans." The president says we seek no wider war, no territory, no bases, no economic advantages. I believe him — but how could anyone in Vietnam? We are supporting with our blood and treasure a group of people who do seek every one of these things: a wider war, territorial control, lucrative American bases to defend them, all to their lasting profit. And now, by virtue of the peace offensive, we have combined our fate with the particular faction of Premier Ky.

America's Dien Bien Phu
I think we will live to regret this marriage. Nguyen Cao Ky is America's Dien Bien Phu. We had been looking anxiously at the map, at Da Nang, Pleiku, and Ankhe, concerned not to make the same mistake as the French had in investing an indefensible position with the flower of her armies. And we were relieved to decide it couldn't happen again, that all our main bases were secure

and their supply lines guaranteed. It was a delusion. The American Dien Bien Phu cannot be located on a map: it is not a place but something much less substantial, the existing government of South Vietnam. Like the French commitment to Dien Bien Phu, the American commitment to Nguyen Cao Ky is a desperate attempt to improve an uncertain bargaining position in the shadow of an impending Geneva conference. Like Dien Bien Phu, it is an offensive overextension of the civilian ministers' strategy, which was to hold the line until negotiations. Like Dien Bien Phu, the Ky government is a fortified hedgehog erected in the middle of the countryside but not a part of it and morally isolated from it. Like Dien Bien Phu — commanded by a cavalry officer, though there was no room to maneuver — the command of a people's government is here given to a fighter pilot, though this is no place to strafe. Like Dien Bien Phu, the defense depends heavily on conscripted colonial battalions, who in the heat of battle can be expected to throw away their arms and hide in the riverbank. Like Dien Bien Phu, supporting this embattled regime will mean an accelerated waste of our national wealth: in the final hours, the supply parachutes will litter the battlefield, draped over the barbed wire, their cargos beyond reach and beyond use, or else fallen into enemy hands. Like Dien Bien Phu, we miscalculate the enemy. Deceived by our own fears, we accept the estimates of our Vietnamese commander, who holds his opponent in contempt and thinks of him as a mere assassin, failing to understand that the cause he champions can achieve miracles of supply and firepower. Like Dien Bien Phu, we lock ourselves into an indefensible valley, with no way out, and yield the heights to the enemy.

Some of you, as critics of the war, may be comforted by this forecast. I do not mean to comfort you. The defeat would not be *theirs*, that of the hardheaded surrealists in Washington, it would be *ours*, and such a sacrifice of our kinsmen and humiliation of our country can never be cause for comfort. Worse, it is some cause for fear. In the last hours of Dien Bien Phu, if you will recall, there was a desperate move within the highest circles of the American government to send U.S. airpower to the rescue of the French garrison. Not as well remembered, because not as well known,

226

the form of this "Operation Vulture" (as it was called) seriously contemplated atomic bombing of the Viet Minh positions. This when all we had at stake was some material equipment, but neither our men nor our prestige. And at that time we still had a halfway decent respect for the opinions of mankind, notably of our British allies, whose scorn finally put an end to our adventurism. The context of the second Dien Bien Phu will be entirely different. Who will deter us this time? If the opposition is not in the American people and a few beleaguered members of Congress, *if it is not in this room, it is nowhere at all.*

Chapter Eight

The Destruction of Conscience

in Vietnam*

Tea in Ambush
Villages in the Mekong Delta are laid out mainly along the canals and rivers. *Village* may be the wrong term. The houses stand side by side, strung out for hundreds of yards along a road or path paralleling the water course. Besides, one community virtually runs into the next; so that the line of settlement extends sometimes for miles, punctuated periodically by a short stretch of forest, a pagoda, or a focal marketplace town.

It is often said of South Vietnam that the day belongs to the government, the night to the "Vietcong." Perhaps it is better said of An Phu District that the day belongs to the Neolithic, the night to the Cold War of the mid-twentieth century. Driving that day to the South Vietnamese Popular Force outpost at Khánh An, I was in Samoa or New Guinea again: the thatch-roof houses on stilts in endless procession along the road; the shaded front verandas overlooking decorative tropical shrubs; the big clay pots in the yard and mats spread out for sunning; the solid fishing boats drawn up on the shore; here and there a woman placidly tending kids or a man mending nets — hardly anything to suggest a civil war, an invasion, and least of all a social revolution other than the neolithic one that brought man from the mobile hunting condition and allowed him to settle down and accumulate a modicum of simple wherewithal. These people, I thought, are historically out of it. Probably they have had little conception of it for centuries,

* Originally published in *Dissent* (Jan.–Feb. 1966).

and that mainly in the form of a more or less alien landlord or tax collector, a monk, and the few goods from elsewhere they got at market. They have been more subjects than participants in the cultural evolution of the archaic civilizations of Southeast Asia, of the state but not in it, a petty agricultural existence that civilization has rested upon but not incorporated. The Neolithic is here joined as a tributary to the Bronze and Colonial Age, yet preserves its character; so the state is an historic medley of incongruent and opposed nations — the one urban, wealthy, sophisticated, and latterly comprador, the other seeking to perpetuate against exaction "the idiocy of rural life."

But at night, in this war, the two historic epochs join in a ballet which, when it is not a dance of death, is a moment of high comedy. Our Popular Force, platoon strength in black peasant clothes, took stealthily to the road for an ambush position at a river crossing several kilometers from camp. There was something of a moon: one could make out the man several yards ahead and perhaps the man ahead of him, and then one or two others in the parallel line on the opposite side of the road. Somewhere in the middle were two American advisers. Somewhere ahead was a scout with a walkie-talkie; toward the rear was another. We went quietly, watchfully, a little afraid, hunched forward with carbines at the ready. A few hundred cautious steps, then you stop at a signal from the man ahead, crouch down, look for something, go down on one knee. Then off again on the all-clear. Thus we moved, armed black phantoms. Toward what? Last night the platoon had been ambushed just near here. You could never tell.

Certainly not from the incongruent setting. We were carrying guns in the midst of life, where the people live: house by house, family by family, casually going on with it, all along the road we took so seriously. Our antics seemed to make a difference only to the dogs, and then the racket they raised made even our silence ridiculous. (I understood then that whoever controls "the hearts and minds" of the dogs will win the war.) Still, their howls brought no response from the houses. The people stayed just so, arranged around their hurricane lamps in peasant set piece: a sequence of lighted dioramas in a darkened museum, before which passed beings of such papier-mâché purpose and expression as to raise the question of who was the imitation of humanity. Sometimes an old woman would peer out and say something to us. She was kibitzing the war. For the most part, the family went about its domestic business: an old man working over some tools, a grandmother fussing with crying grandchildren, younger men and boys talking and laughing softly, a woman singing; in one house a transistor radio blaring Vietnamese music at a spellbound family — and all their neighbors hundreds of yards around. Life went on, and why not? The Neolithic (transistorized) was the human occupation; while the black gang with carbines and recoilless rifles and walkie-talkies and Americans seemed as meaningful to this existence as the court ceremony of the Inca emperor.

Around here — in this "loyal" area — it's not a civil war, I thought; nor a revolution, nor an invasion from the North. It's the latest thing in warfare — a medieval war. The feudal barons with their kept knights ravage through the countryside to engage in mortal combat for forty days. The peasants go back and forth between the lines, unconcerned except to see that they don't get ravaged or to sell a few things to either or both sides. The peace will certainly affect them, but is it their war — as war?

Last night the platoon had gone through a similar performance. They settled carefully into an ambush position at the river. Waiting tensely, one of the American advisers was startled by an arm softly placed over his shoulder. Fortunately, before he could react the thin voice of an old village woman penetrated his senses. It was Mother Courage. "You boys want some tea?" she asked, with plaintive ingratiation. "Go 'way," he said, "we're waiting for someone."

I had got to this district, An Phu, by courtesy of the U.S. Information Service (now part of the Joint U.S. Public Affairs Office). It was rather a model village tour: an area of Hoa Hao, a Buddhist reform group now solidly (for the time being) with the South Vietnamese government. But An Phu may have been a perfect model, complete with all the flaws of its political virtues. The Hoa Hao allegiance is probably more practical than principled and based fundamentally on "to thine own self be true." Subject for years to opposition and oppression, the Hoa Hao have fought everybody: the Viet Minh, the Diem regime, the Vietcong. Today they accept the Realpolitik — and the weapons and good payoff — of the American presence, decisive in this province where there are no "Arvin" (Army of Vietnam) regulars. It seemed to me quite clear from conversations with the Hoa Hao commander that it was the Americans with whom they were now allied, not the government to whom they were loyal.

The late intensification of this war between Good and Evil seems to bring no decision between them so much as it throws into relief a submerged third term of incommensurate value — life. Recalcitrant under pressure, life insists on manifesting itself in all manner of ways — refugees in the cities, revolts in the mountains, desertions in the army, or perhaps just a studied indifference at An Phu. The involvement of the peasant must always have been uncertain and incomplete, *particularly on the government side*. It is difficult to see how the peasant can be "on" the side — "for" the cause — of a world from which he has been structurally excluded. Historically, peasants have their *own* side: their family, their fields, their village. Saigon surely offers little alternative to this allegiance. It is allegiance to oneself as a human being, to what one knows as the right human condition. Outsiders must appear as only more or less damaging — or beneficial — to this condition. Foreign warriors in the land may open a new, complicated calculus of alternatives. Even so, what appears to us as a choice of sides may present itself to the peasant as a tactical choice of masters — with a meaning culturally incomparable to the American who is "for" America, or even the Republican Party.

Piastres de Resistance
At the Saigon airport I handed over the immigration form to the Vietnamese officer. In the space next to "Purpose of your visit" I had written "tourist." On 5 August, 1965, it was an irrelevant purpose. But was it any more irrelevant than the things other Americans were doing in Vietnam?

Actually, I am an anthropologist and an academic critic of the

war. Neither is a qualification, in the view of administration supporters, to speak on Vietnam: one ought to have been there. I
always thought it a weak retort, if only because the critics were as
a rule better informed than the tropisimatic adherents of official
policy; for another thing, because the record compiled by Americans who had been in Vietnam making and implementing mistakes suggested they had no understanding of Vietnam or of their
own existence there. To have been in Vietnam makes one not an
expert but perhaps something of a fool or a victim.

Nevertheless, as an anthropologist if not as a critic, I had to
accept the argument: one should go into the field. I spent six days
in Vietnam: mostly in Saigon, one day in Chau Doc Province (An
Phu District), and half a day at III Corps Headquarters, Bien Hoa.
Much of the time I passed with U.S. Information Service people,
to whom I had offered the proposition that they try to convince
me they were right. They accepted — "only in America!" — and
put me in touch with others, civilian and military (though not
with the gung-ho types I asked to see), and with the war (such as
it was) in An Phu. These six days did not make me an expert —
and I hope not a fool or a victim.

It is difficult to become an expert anyhow on things that aren't
what they seem. Every day I saw something or learned something
that made the country appear irrelevant to what was happening to
it. After all, we are fighting Chinese there. There are no Chinese
there. So *Vietnamese* die by way of demonstration. War is the continuation of Madison Avenue by new means; death becomes an
advertisement — and "we mean what we say." The single most important and general condition of the American war in Vietnam is
its irrelevance. But to kill irrelevantly is a contradiction in terms.
All the compromises and the self-deceptions of Americans, and
all the brutalization, originate in this contradiction.

But the most obvious incongruity is that we are defending the
"freedom" of South Vietnam. The absurdity of the statement is
not fully manifest by the existing government. To speak of the
government disguises the issue of the class of "brave and determined people" we are involved with, of who are our natural allies,
who our enemies. It confronts you as you drive into Saigon. The

rich men's big houses are protected by great iron gates and barbed wire deployed along the tops of thick walls. At the American Embassy and other U.S. establishments the same architectural motif is repeated — with variations as minor in social meaning as the differences between the Mercedes and the Mercuries that jostle aside pedicabs in the crowded streets. Together with a large number of Saigon friends who are doing well while we are thus doing good, we are under siege.

The defense of freedom in a lately colonial country takes on elements of a class war. I met a few of our lesser collaborators; also a former enemy:

> The district chief at An Phu was established, with servants, in a well-guarded headquarters; the exterior decor was barbed wire again, and a guard detachment of Regional Forces. A mandarin, proclaimed by the long nail of his little finger; a captain in the army, graduate of a French secondary school. His father was a businessman and a landowner who left an estate of some 60 hectares in Long Xuyen Province. He apparently is joint heir with his brothers and maintains a home in the provincial seat. The estate, he said, is occupied by sixty tenant farmers. Officials at this level and above are appointed from Saigon.
>
> Mr. B. works for the Voice of America as a researcher and occasional broadcaster. Born in Saigon, his father was a clerk in a French company. Mr. B. was educated in a French college and then embarked on a lifelong career of collaboration with foreigners. He worked before the war and through 1944 as a clerk for a French lawyer. In 1945 he was employed by Mitsui (Japanese). During the French-Indochina War he worked for local newspapers and a French periodical. Now, for the Americans.
>
> Mr. L., a radio broadcaster for VOA for the past eight years, was born in Haiphong and came south after the peace of 1954 because he "could not live with the Communists." During the French-Indochina War he had deserted from the Viet Minh and gone over to the French army, where he served as an interpreter. Mr. L. interviews VC defectors and refugees from VC areas for broadcast materials. He related some interesting cases: a VC regular who defected because he saw a

comrade killed for reading a government leaflet; a farmer who fled from Long An Province because he saw his relative, a rich farmer, killed by the VC for refusing to pay taxes; a VC captain, "an intellectual," who defected because, as he told Mr. L., "the communists only served one class!"

"What class was that?" I asked.

"The poor," said Mr. L. — the captain was angry because "intellectuals" were not treated well.

I later discussed this conversation with an American employee of USIS. He warned me that there are Vietcong everywhere in Saigon!

I, myself, interviewed only one VC defector, an instructor of anticommunist revolutionary cadres at Khánh An (Chau Doc Province). He was from a Central Vietnamese middle-peasant family. As a Viet Minh, he had lied to the authorities about his background, saying he was of poor-peasant origin. He was terrified by the North Vietnamese land reform of 1955–1956, when middle peasants were axed. He said he decided then to get out as soon as he could. Infiltrated South in 1963, he immediately defected.

I asked all these people at the end of the interview if they would like to question me. They put it in different ways, but everyone expressed concern that the Americans might lose patience and withdraw.

Critics of the war point to the contradiction between our announced defense of "freedom" and the character of the South Vietnamese government. The criticism does not go deep enough. It is not a question of what government but of what ruling class, what *power,* we are supporting — and creating — against "communist aggression." It becomes in general a question of what type of society we offer as an alternative. A massive amount of American money is poured into Vietnam. Part of this money corrupts, breeding prostitutes and vendors of "feelthy pictures"; the larger share is simply corrupted and a Vietnamese elite becomes the latest beneficiary of American affluence. The colonial comprador outlives colonialism. He enters into symbiosis with the Cold War. Marshal Ky says the land speculators who drive up prices around the American development at Cam Ranh Bay will be punished.

The black marketeers and other profiteers will be punished. But under what constraints does the government of Vietnam operate? Large Chinese merchants have a major influence on the government, a senior USOM (U.S. Operations Mission, the AID [Agency for International Development] program) officer told me, an influence that increases in direct proportion to their wealth. He said too that the contracting business was the going swindle. The still-uncontrolled black market is testimony to a large flow of U.S. dollars out of the country, for safe deposit in foreign banks and the import of prohibited luxury goods.

Meanwhile, back at the village —

The scene that day at An Phu was reminiscent of the colonial payday described by Aubrey Menon in *The Prevalence of Witches*, with overtones as degrading and cynical. Through the good offices of the local U.S. Special Forces Detachment, ten selected families of a hamlet several kilometers from the base were ceremoniously to receive food doles and the children of the hamlet school to get new school kits (though there weren't enough of these to go around). The goods had come down through USOM. Everyone was waiting around when I arrived — it turned out they were waiting for me; it made the most propaganda of a limited supply. The American commanding officer and some noncoms were there, and the commanding officer of the Vietnamese Regional Forces with his bodyguards. A little hollow near the school made do as a ceremonial ground. We stood back on a rise above: it was not an American function; "we're only advisers here." The masters of ceremonies were a VIS (Vietnamese Information Service) officer, a Vietnamese nutritionist, and the hamlet chief. They were down in the hollow with a portable loudspeaker system shouting to the assembled forty people who were standing several feet from them. Ten heaps of food lay in two rows on the ground. The VIS officer spoke first. He made it clear to the people what the food meant: as one of the recipients told me later, now they would turn in any Vietcong they saw. The nutritionist spoke briefly — too briefly, I thought, considering the exotic character of the foods. Then the hamlet chief proceeded to dole out the food heaps, calling each family by name and insisting the family representative — many

236

were widows — come over and stand next to his or her food pile. Everyone was so conscious of us on the hill, especially the shy women being given food.

These families had been selected by the hamlet chief and a local committee. I don't doubt they were deserving — the man I talked to was a landless peasant, unrelated (he said) to the hamlet chief — it's just that they deserved better. The ten families had been selected from a community of two thousand people. According to the sergeant in charge of it, this food program had begun about nine months ago. A settlement of two thousand people could expect to be visited with food packages about every two to three months, although this hamlet had been given food only once before, if that. And what was the benefit of years of American expenditure in Vietnam? Each family received 100 lbs. cornmeal, 5 lbs. bulgar wheat, 5 lbs. maple syrup, 6–7 lbs. powdered milk, and 1 gallon of cooking oil. The Vietnamese eat rice and prefer it — with corn only on occasion.

The motivation and dedication of American AID people is beyond question and not at issue. Many, I understand, work tirelessly under dangerous conditions to bring a modicum of betterment to the countryside. Likewise the small Special Forces detachment I saw at An Phu was committed to a program of medical and economic aid for the people — the Peace Corps of the War Corps. But these slim measures of good intention have to be put in the balance against the huge, unplanned subsidization of decadence in the cities to determine a final reading on the American presence. It is not simply that much more goes to bad causes than to good. Hijacked American dollars in the cities capitalize a whole social system, and one in which just this unequal distribution of wealth is proper, a constituted condition. The compradors of Saigon are counterposed economically and ideologically to the people and the resources of the country. The fate of the people, therefore, is not mitigated by small aid in the countryside: it is sealed by big robbery in the city.

Saigon, one cynical American said to me, is full of Kennedy idealists who have discovered the facts of life. I thought it a good *mot* as far as it went, but incomplete. He might have added that crossing Kennedy idealism with the facts of life produces a curious political hybrid: a hardheaded surrealist. I spoke with several of the tribe, middle to senior officers mainly, in their air-conditioned sanctuaries at the Embassy, USOM, USIS. I wanted to know how they related, morally at least, to the Saigon cats growing fat on American aid whose interests rather contrast with the dying people. I was reproached for my naiveté: "every Eastern country is full of graft and corruption; it's just like that and always has been" (and therefore always will be?). One or two said that conditions were improving because the present government included dynamic young leaders who took the people's well-being to heart. The most general sentiment was that if the government could somehow be stabilized, the problem of "corruption" would somehow be solved. I had come up against standard American innocence of society: "who is the matter" — as if it were just personalities and not a political structure of economic interest; that the accumulation of wealth is a mere question of "graft" and "corruption" rather than an economic formation of society, a matter of excess rather than a constituted relation to the national economy and the underlying population; that, despite the circumstances, a government could be established on some basis other than the prevailing distribution of wealth and power, apart from its constraints, and become more the executive committee of the people than of the comprador.

The last is anyhow ruled out by the "advisory" role of American personnel (civilian as well as military) in Vietnam. In the decisive sense, it is an American war: it is Vietnam's tragedy to have been chosen the battleground for America's stand against the forces of evil. Technically, however, we are just "advisors." I had always thought this was put out for international and home consumption, to make the American intervention palatable for whoever might be inclined to swallow it — but I misunderstood. The "advisory" capacity is taken very seriously by Americans within the country, especially by civilian officials, and it has internal functions much more meaningful than the international propaganda effect. At one level, it is a concession to Vietnamese national feeling; and Americans have a complementary need to believe and practice it. As a denial of any colonial status or intentions, it provides for Americans an acceptable meaning of their existence in the country. Beyond that, it serves as a convenient institutional means of personal dissociation from the sufferings of Vietnam, sufferings largely inflicted by the American presence — which is one's own presence. To be an adviser is to be involved yet free of the place, to indulge a sense of duty yet disdain responsibility; so it becomes a prefabricated barrier erected wherever and whenever the ugliness intrudes into consciousness, a denial that one is implicated by what may be going on. It is a moral anesthetic. (And I venture to say that the necessity for moral anesthesia is one reason there are so many versions of truth, why it is so difficult to determine just what is going on in Vietnam.)

At the institutional level, which is perhaps the critical level, the function of the "advisory" role must be judged from its effects. The effect at every order of organization from hamlet to nation is to interpose obstacles to American direction of Vietnamese affairs, and so give free play to indigenous forces and interests — especially self-interests. Thus even as America generates powerful economic and political force in Vietnam, it turns around to deny itself the leverage. The free-floating resources are appropriated instead by local collaborators for construction of their own version of Vietnamese society. We give them the advice to do good and the power to do as they please. We say we are "helping they're doing — helping themselves.

The "advisory" capacity is a new chapter in the relations between the West and the underdeveloped world. It is a Cold War epilogue of nineteenth-century colonialism. For all our anti-colonial protestations we perpetuate a colonial condition in the country.

A serious argument against American withdrawal is the blood-bath that would ensue in South Vietnam when the NLF gains control. But against this one might consider the bloodbath without foreseeable end going on now, and the ruling class of South Vietnam to whose tender mercies we would confine the peasant. The escalation of war may be narrowing the alternatives for the people to an end with misery or a misery without end.

Refugees are streaming en masse into government camps — where they live, newspapers say, in unspeakable conditions. Many Americans I met in Vietnam are convinced the Vietcong have been lately violating their own principles, stepping up economic pressure and terror in the countryside, for their very success has bred control and logistic problems. Washington officials have said that Vietcong terror is the simple explanation. I asked one of the Vietnamese who interviews refugees for Voice of America — principally, however, on agricultural matters — why, in his opinion, the peasants come over to the government. His prompt answer was the "bombing"; the people, he said, want security for their lives and peace for their work. An American VOA employee present at the interview insisted I get the meaning of "bombing" straight. On my request for elucidation the Vietnamese said "bombing and fighting," the fire from both sides. Then he went on to relate that provincial officials who have accompanied him in talks with peasants have several times "asked" him to erase complaints about "bombing" from the tapes. The refugees are supposed to say they have fled from Vietcong terror to a happy life under the government, he said. The provincial officials indicated that the "bombing" need not be broadcast. (Charles Mohr writes in the *New York Times* of 5 September [1965]: "Already more than 5 per cent of the population has fled into refugee camps. Although it is popular among Washington officials to say that the refugees are fleeing from Vietcong terrorism, some officials on the scene are quite willing to concede or even to volunteer that the majority are fleeing from the insecurity of the countryside and that air strikes are the largest single cause of that insecurity.")

I had a number of experiences of this kind, times when I heard a Vietnamese or an American in the presence of another American of official position report something compromising to American ideals, policy, or the Washington line on Vietnam. The incident must be repeated often, as a circumstance of the American presence in Vietnam. On the occasions I could observe it, I was interested in the reaction of the American who was thus suddenly confronted with damning information on which he would have to make some reckoning — like the American VOA employee confronted with censorship. If not exactly a moment of truth, the American's response gives subtle intelligence of the critical battle of this war — of how much of America, of what America has meant to us, can be consumed in Vietnam. The Americans I have seen in this predicament were good men and intelligent; but they blanked out, every one of them. Intellectually, they refused to come to terms with it. Morally, they passed. Some said nothing. Some spoke of Vietcong crimes, as if to justify our own or our South Vietnamese agents'. Some glossed over the reported incident as exceptional, as not happening most of the time. And some shrugged, referred to the feudal-oriental character of the country, then asked what one could do since "we're only advisers here." It is, I repeat, an important point. If we are whored by our commitment, if we must lose ourselves in Vietnam, we lose the war — whatever the military outcome.

The contradictions of Vietnam may thus reflect themselves in the everyday behavior of Americans. Among military personnel, of course, such translations of big structural events into terms of ordinary existence will take other forms. Still, the American military adviser who turns his back on the torture of Vietcong prisoners by South Vietnamese soldiers is the khaki counterpart of the VOA civilian who closes his mind to compromising information. But these seem advanced stages of moral decay, people now dangerously close to a final plunge into brutalization. Unless one is so disposed in advance, it may take a certain initial disillusionment with Vietnam to reach this point, a disillusionment that undermines local meanings of the war, leaving one either with the Cold War conviction that it is necessary to stop this Chinese-inspired aggression, Vietnam notwithstanding, or else without any conviction at all. I had a glimpse of this earlier phase among American combat troops at Bien Hoa, most of whom were comparatively new arrivals and had seen comparatively limited action. It was enough exposure: Vietnam was incubating in them. Yet one or two resisted the infection:

241

They were eight army enlisted men — at least some were draftees — with whom their commanding officer (knowing I was "a professor against the war") had generously given me ninety minutes' privacy. And there was also a ninth: an officer of junior rank who came up to the jeep around which we stood, listened to what we said, and asked then if he could have a word with me because there were a few things I ought to "get straight."

Seven of the men did not at all question their purpose in Vietnam. We had to "stop the communists from taking over here," or else "they'd go on to Hawaii." At the same time, several had experienced the recalcitrance of Vietnam, its disengagement from what was supposed to be its own life-and-death struggle, and they were disturbed by it. A Black private brought it up — by his own compulsion, for the discussion was open just then — and others seemed to agree. He didn't see "the people here" getting with the war. They hold bicycle races in the village while he is on a field problem. He wondered angrily why they did nothing while we fought "their war," fought to make them "free from communism." As for the South Vietnamese soldiers (and this is I think a very common complaint), they aren't worth a damn: poorly trained and undisciplined, they talk and smoke on patrol and cannot work as a unit.

Every war and every army has its complaints. But Vietnam could foster a new type of American military dissenter, an anti-ideologist, a man whose life has been interrupted when it did not seem threatened and yet, come upon the distant scene of emergency, sees there a people not so much involved in a fight for their lives against communist expansion as a flight from their deaths — perhaps at American hands. I asked these men what they thought of the statement of Lt. ———, who had refused assignment to a Special Forces outpost and expressed the sentiment that the war "wasn't worth a single American life." All disagreed — except one. To that moment silent, he spoke now unabashedly: "All the people and all the ground in Vietnam are not worth a single American life." He believed this, he explained, because he has a high regard for human life, American and Vietnamese; and many people are being needlessly killed because of the ideological views of a few Americans, the president and those around him. They say we are here to defend South Vietnam against

242

communist aggression, which is a threat to ourselves, but for himself he does not believe it. The commitment to Vietnam is all out of proportion to the importance of Vietnam. He waxed Lippmannesque: "If we start here, we'll soon be all over the world doing the same thing. It's not worth it to America." He was a soldier in a light brigade: "The people here have been fighting guerrilla war for twenty years; I don't know anything about that kind of warfare." I asked him which he would choose if it came to a question of American involvement or NLF control. He would pull out — "because I'm selfish — I don't think the communist control of Vietnam will concern me in my lifetime."

The men left and I remained with the young officer who wanted me to get matters straight. He was not new to the war but almost through with it, twenty-nine days to go, and now there were several things he had to say about it. He spoke from notes he had just made, and I repeat his points here. I am obliged to insist that I do not present his views as facts of war, as necessarily true in specific content. But they are unequivocal truth of another kind — they are an American experience of Vietnam:

1. The officer had it from "an informed source in a position to know" that Arvin desertion rates jump from 25 to 40 percent whenever American troops came into an area. He was seriously concerned. It meant to him that Arvin has no inclination to fight; that, neither brave nor determined, they "would rather have us do the work for them."

2. He has heard on good authority — "though it is not confirmed and must be" — that on occasion Arvin units fire upon U.S. units in battle, in order to make the situation look worse and encourage a greater U.S. involvement. "I want to know," he said, "if this is reported to the American people, and if it is reported to the president, and if not, why not? And if it is, what are we going to do about it? Or does it just stay in MAC-V [Military Assistance Command, Vietnam]?" In his opinion such actions as these would have the effect, desired by Vietnamese, of relieving their military participation and increasing direct aid to the local economy through military and other assistance — aid that would find its way to local vested interests.

243

3. When we were preparing to build up a landing base in [a certain coastal] area, why did we have to negotiate with private land-owners for space at so many piastres per acre? This is war; we are defending them. He is sure we didn't pay rent to the French in World War II for the privilege of fighting for French freedom. Nor was this compensation for hardships caused to civilians. Leasing land, he said, is distinguishable from compensations. [Note that the officer did mention a particular area, but I am unable to pinpoint his transliteration of the Vietnamese. The *New York Times* reported what seems to be an analogous incident on 15 September 1965: the U.S. "acquired" 30 square miles near Ankhe from the Vietnamese government for the newly arrived First Cavalry Division.]

4. I had talked with the others about civilian casualties. In that connection, he said, "a lot of officers if given the opportunity would bomb the shit out of all the villages around here. A great many have the urge and the mentality." He had "so many times heard it said, 'let's drop the load on that village.'" He has not seen it yet, however, and thinks it probably never will happen because the brigade commander wouldn't have it. But it is a definite streak in an interesting number of officers — "and," he added, "just what the VC would want."

5. He seemed to know my own position, and since I had talked with the other men about the criticism of the war in the States, he wanted to insist that "the criticism of the war is extremely healthy. It concerns me that many military men are critical of the critics and want to deny them the constitutional right to dissent." He is "upset" by the career officers who speak only of "beatniks" and whose response is "those guys ought to be brought out here and sent on patrol to get shot!" The career officers fear criticism because they are put in jeopardy by it. "If we were less militant, they would lose their jobs and have to return to civilian life, where they are not fit for anything." He wondered, in this regard, to what extent the situation in Vietnam is accurately reported insofar as the facts are purveyed through the military.

As we walked slowly together toward the commanding officer's tent, he said I could draw my own conclusions from all this. I responded with the obvious: "You mean to say that the war is being escalated because of the South Vietnamese desire to be relieved and make a fast buck, complemented by the mentality of the American military?" He made no objection. In parting he remarked that if Vietnam wants peace, and if peace means VC control, he for one is willing to accept it. If the VC are elected in a free election, he said in response to my question, he must go along with it — "for God's sake, it's the only honorable thing to do." And he added then: "If they want peace at any price, not to be shot at, the freedom to raise a few crops; let them have it. These are common wants of everyone, aren't they?"

Losing the Hearts and Minds of Americans in Vietnam

"China" is indispensable to the existence of Americans in Vietnam.

The fixation has its own internal, Vietnamese dialectic; but it begins from external conditions, from the Washington Cold War policy and its confrontations with world events. An outsider can attempt only a superficial and partial analysis of the Washington line and very little on its fundamental causes. Clearly, it proceeds from an injunction of sacred ancestral ideology, the Dulles demonology, which defined the struggle against the forces of evil. The evil is the "International Communist Conspiracy," known also in its emanation of "Aggressive Communism" and appearing in Vietnam as "Chinese Expansionism." America, medicine man to the world, is impelled to Vietnam to exorcise the evil spirits. But it was not a simple process of divination that led to this move. The policy for Vietnam seems to have developed from the intersection of the demonology with at least two important events, the Cuban missile crisis and the détente with Russia, which have impressed themselves firmly and in certain ways on political consciousness. The missile crisis is understood to have spiked Russia's guns for the foreseeable future. The détente is taken in evidence that when a communist revolution generates an economic stake in the world, and when the revolutionary generation with its heady ideas of world uprising dies off, a communist power ceases to be aggressive and instead evolves an interest in the status quo. Transferred to China, these understandings dictate a policy of buying time for the revolution — that economic development and generational replacement might exhaust its fervor — and, in the meantime, during all that period in which it is dangerous, cordoning the revolution by a strong military stand and preventing its export. Vietnam is the Asian analogue of the missile crisis — therefore, a critical tactic. The "domino theory," moreover, becomes unsuppressible. Its function is to explain the American action, and as the only reasonable explanation of *that fact* it becomes immune to contradiction by any other fact of life in Southeast Asia.

Such seems to be the hardheaded surrealism. In Vietnam, however, the strategy does not present even so rational an appearance. It has to be discussed in more primitive terms. For one thing, the key decision-makers are not there; one sees only partial intimations of the grand design among the few who can seriously reflect on it, and among Americans in general only a vulgar *idée fixe* about the Red Menace. Besides, the strategy here is refracted through the ugly circumstances of Vietnam, which reshape it into something of an obsession: stopping the Chinese threat is the kind of end that will sanction adoption of any means — even, as I shall tell, Chinese means. We are losing the hearts and minds of Americans in Vietnam. Joining battle with the evil spirits by ritual techniques of bloodletting, we get covered all over with blood ourselves and become ourselves dark forces in the land. It is a classic mythical denouement. Between the medicine man and the spirit of disease there is a close relation to begin with: a set of shared assumptions about the nature of illness, its infliction, and its cure. And, as they struggle for supremacy over the inert body, only shaman and spirit can seem real to each other. The body becomes immaterial, something merely that each attempts to possess and manipulate to defeat the other. The horrifying quality is that the evil spirit is a construction of the medicine man, and though his operation prove a brilliant success the patient may die from it. In the end, the medicine man is indistinguishable from an evil spirit.

Americans in Vietnam hold it as a basic expression of purpose that there we oppose Chinese communist expansion. I encountered it among men of fighting ranks and among their officers,

246

among staff members of U.S. civilian agencies and among their senior officials. It is the expert opinion of those we employ as political experts. (Vietnamese collaborators, I found, are apt to put it most directly, almost as if the NLF was Chinese.) The confrontation with China has the character of an unquestionable premise of our involvement. Politically aware Americans find it possible to believe it the higher wisdom, even though they are unable to trace the chain of NLF command beyond Hanoi. Everyone knows that communist China is expansionist. Everyone knows, too, that we are faced in Vietnam with communist subversion, which if not contained here will have to be faced again, closer to home. That we are fighting China follows with the force of a categorical syllogism.

Perhaps it is the higher wisdom; still, it gives Vietnam a certain air of insanity. Paranoids are after us. The death of Vietnamese is unrelated to their lives. Do we mean to indicate by these deaths that the Chinese must stop threatening us? Then we are involved in killing people to show other people that they should stop threatening us. Or do we mean to show the Chinese they must stop threatening the Vietnamese? Then we are killing people to show other people that they should stop threatening the people we are killing. The "Chinese threat" obscures in advance the nature of the enemy. We cannot know who he is or what he wants. So we destroy in advance the possibility of deciding if he is really our enemy. The counterpart on the political level is the total failure of American policy to support, or even to recognize, nationalism and its human aspirations. Not recognizing it, we succeed in destroying it. Opposing it, we drive it into self-defeating dependence upon major communist powers — and thus in the end obtain the confrontation we sought from the beginning. In my experience, nationalism is simply not discussed by Americans in Saigon. Vietnamese nationalism is a dead issue, buried and covered over by communist aggression.

But there is a reason for the madness. Without it one could go insane. Even if "the threat of Chinese expansion" did not exist in Washington, it would be necessary to invent it in Vietnam. The objective conditions make it impossible to sustain any other image of the American presence. The lack of freedom mocks our "defense of freedom." The military dictatorship mocks our "defense of democracy." The indifference of the people mocks their "brave struggle against subversion." The thought that these people have been suffering war for twenty-five years must be repressed. And shall we admit our responsibility for the misery of Vietnam? How shall we face the innocent victims of our weapons? Conscience must be destroyed: it has to end at the barrel of the gun, it cannot extend to the bullet. So all peripheral rationales fade into the background. It becomes a war of transcendent purpose, and in such a war all efforts on the side of Good are virtuous, and all deaths unfortunate necessity. The end justifies the means.

I stood one morning outside the Psychological Warfare office at III Corps Headquarters, Bien Hoa. Clearly I was an alien: a civilian and an academic dissenter. The bare courtesy of the reception I had just had inside did not trouble to conceal it. Now a young officer came out of the building. With a curious politeness he handed me a newspaper, saying that "a compatriot" of his (but not of mine?) wanted to present it to me and I should especially consider the inside spread of pictures on pages 4 and 5. The paper was the *Observer*, a weekly published for U.S. forces in Vietnam. The officer was a little surprised when I asked if he could spare any other issues. He did not understand my motives, that I wanted to know what the *Observer* seeks to teach those who read it. But that general point is not important. The important point is a specific one, dictated by the man who anonymously gave me a present: the inside two pages of the 3 July [1965] edition. It meant something critical to him, and he wanted me to be convinced by it.

The two-page banner read: "'A New Glorious Exploit,' Broadcasts Communist Radio." Underneath were seven blood-soaked pictures of the My Canh restaurant bombing in Saigon of 25 June. Most of the photographs, such as the one captioned "Evacuating Innocent Child," showed Americans coming to the aid of shocked and bleeding victims, many of them Vietnamese.

Should we share our "compatriot's" understanding of the moral? He might indulge himself in the hate of evil killers at the expense of

248

indifference to human pain and death. But no judgment of these pictures should be made in the absence of memory. The American soldiers who see the *Observer* have already seen certain other pictures. They have looked upon the slaughter of villages, contemplated the civilian victims of American bombs and shells — perhaps not just in photographs. If they are then outraged at the My Canh, it is a cynical lie. They distinguish between "good" and "bad" innocent victims. Human agony has no meaning; the meaning is external, a judgment of those who inflict, not of those who suffer. The outrage at suffering is indifference to suffering. The soldier outraged at this deception of Vietnamese misery has been prepared to commit it.

Advanced anticommunism trades places with the enemy. It becomes opposite-communism, and "opposites" are things alike in every respect save one. The final stages of American dissolution in Vietnam will be marked by imitation of the enemy's techniques. I have heard it foreshadowed in the talk of Saigon officialdom: *discipline*, a senior American civilian officer told me, is what the South Vietnamese government needs; *power*, he said, is the only thing the Chinese can understand; *history*, he said, will prove us right. In a remote provincial outpost I found two Americans who had appropriated as their own draconian Chinese methods of interrogation and indoctrination ("motivation" is the American newspeak). The forced destruction of people's beliefs is no longer properly described as something "they" do. Torturously exacted confession and conversion are no longer things we fight against: these are now part of our own arsenal, weapons of our own struggle.

The two Americans were leaders of a "motivation" team working among Vietnamese Popular Forces. The team included four Vietnamese instructor-cadres, two of these ex-Vietcong. The dominant of the two Americans was a field representative of a civilian agency; he was assisted by a Special Forces officer. Both were highly qualified, competent in Vietnamese language and custom, and dedicated to Vietnam and their vision of its future. Their program was anticommunist revolution: they were training Popular Forces as revolutionary cadres. The texts were classic communist handbooks on revolutionary warfare, books these

Americans studied and clearly admired; it does not go too far to say they were disciples, or at least revisionist disciples, of Mao Zedong, Ho Chi Minh, and Che Guevara. The revolutionary "techniques" were copied in fine detail. (I was given a pledge card that the Americans issued to Vietnamese trainees; it listed "The Four Principles and Eight Rules" of cadre behavior, apparently an amendation of "The Three Rules and the Eight Remarks" Mao developed for partisan warfare against the Japanese.) The Americans insisted, however, on one departure from communist attitudes: alongside self-criticism they encourage the troops to question their instructors and formulate their own views. The indoctrination team moves from outpost to outpost, living in with the troops while "motivating" them.

I lived in with them for a night and a good part of a day. They briefed me and allowed me to see the work for myself. But it is not of this guerrilla program that I write. It is of a discussion I had with the Americans about torture and the transformation of Viet-cong prisoners to anticommunism. The two Americans allowed they had some experience with it, and some ideas of how it is properly done. I recorded most of that discussion and will excerpt parts of it verbatim. But first allow me to develop the context.

The interrogation methods the Americans described are copied from those used most effectively by the Chinese, as they themselves explained. (Of course, there are precedents — for example, the Inquisition.) The treatment seems a compressed and abbreviated version of the procedures used on American POWs during the Korean War. The interrogator has at most four or five days before he must send the prisoner on. Physical torture is precluded. A special type of "mental torture" (their term) is instead inflicted. But it aims not merely at eliciting military information. The prisoner's disclosures are at the same time a betrayal of his cause and a confession of his errors, a renunciation of belief. The betrayal is the first phase of a "cure" of communism — the American civilian kept likening the process to the rehabilitation of alcoholics. If the technique really is effective, and the Americans claim it is, I think it must be because of some rather special qualities of revolutionary warfare and warriors. It has to be understood that a Vietcong prisoner comes in with certain comprehensions and expectations that are deeply entwined with his revolutionary ("communist") commitment. A guerrilla movement depends decisively on secrecy. Its members are visible daily to the enemy but must be unknown to him; they maintain a hinterland conspiracy of silence; a single traitor wrecks the organization of a whole village, perhaps a district. The guerrilla thus understands that secrecy is a first principle of the revolution. But, by the same token, intelligence becomes a first principle of the counterrevolution. The prisoner, therefore, expects to be tortured for information and ultimately killed if he remains steadfast. He meets his interrogators prepared to resist the worst: it is a test of his revolutionary soul.

But by a carefully calculated approach, the interrogator can from the beginning disappoint the prisoner's expectations, disarm and confuse him. Instead of being tortured, the guerrilla finds himself in the company of an "enemy" who nevertheless treats him with respect, even befriends him, feeds him, makes him comfortable — which is to say, profoundly uncomfortable. The relation the interrogator seeks to effect is one between them as against the world. For even as he binds the prisoner's wounds, he systematically invokes the threat of "the others" — that there are these others (Arvin regulars) around who want at the prisoner and have "more basic ideas" of how to interrogate him. (The Chinese in Korea invoked the North Koreans in the same way when dealing with American POWs.) The interrogator is protecting the prisoner, shielding him against the "big, ugly outside world." Thus, the bond between prisoner and interrogator is forged, the captive caught in a deepening dependence upon his captor. At some point, the latter feels he might press for reciprocity. The guerrilla yields some minor information. Yet emotionally it is not slight: it is a fundamental betrayal of himself, his comrades, and his cause. Still, he is told the information is nothing, not enough, that he will have to do better or the others will move in on him. The trap has been closed. The interrogator is now the only one in the world with whom the prisoner has anything in common. Behind are the people he has sold out, ahead those who would kill him —

251

and only the interrogator can help him. The revolutionary is likely to break completely. It is a moment of extreme anguish — "the lowest point in his life in terms of human meaning and existence" (the American civilian said). Yet again, in a disorganized and probably unintentional parody of Chinese techniques, the prisoner learns his confession is still not good enough: he cannot unite with his captors; he must have further "processing" at a rehabilitation center. So I understand the procedure.

Something must be said as well of those who described it to me. First — and it is a thing seriously to consider — these two Americans are not strangers, not people who have been metamorphosed by some satanic forces to a point beyond our understanding or recognition. Met on a college campus or in a business office, they would not attract unusual attention. Their attitudes toward Vietnam are indeed more scholarly than demonic. They want to involve themselves in the country. They profess with sincerity their respect for the people — so much that they actively wish them a better fate. For the first several hours of my visit, we had only sparred in a rather formal way. It was not until they saw me sit cross-legged on the floor of a Vietnamese house, and with them eat Vietnamese food with Vietnamese people, that they, these two Americans, accepted *me*. They did not give the impression of evil. On the contrary, they presented the appearance of good.

And now consider this interview, what they said and what they revealed of themselves.

The main protagonist — identified here as "Mr. X" — describes himself as an "agnostic atheist," but clearly he believes in the Devil if not in God. In fact, his is a holy work: to exorcise the communist devils possessing Vietcong. He undertakes the prisoner's "conversion" for the prisoner's own good: he is "helping" the man, saving him. I ask, "How do you offset the damage to yourself?" "Your belief," he answers.

Why do these Americans so intensely need to crack down the prisoner, to convince him he is wrong, they right? Is it because they need to convince themselves? The officer ("Captain Y") says that if you don't try to break the prisoner, you're admitting he's right. And Mr. X makes a curious slip: he speaks of an "emotional *inter*dependence" between the prisoner and the interrogator, where he means to discuss the dependence of the prisoner upon the interrogator. I sense these men are identified with the prisoner, that they have themselves under the knife, that the prisoner's conversion will validate their own integrity. And so inevitably they fall into a hopeless contradiction. For if their own righteousness is at test in the prisoner's response, then they need too to fail. The prisoner's successful resistance is the interrogators' greatest satisfaction: his strength proves their strength, his will their will, his conviction their conviction. There is no question of Mr. X's admiration of the prisoner who will not be broken. "Tremendous," he says, "just tremendous." Then he lies when I ask if he admires this man. And at the end he lies the ultimate lie of Americans in Vietnam. Notwithstanding that he had just described a specific prisoner who would not yield, he denies he was ever involved in such an interrogation: "because we're advisers — in every sense."

> MR. X: At this time [the prisoner] kind of feels an emotional dependence upon you because for two days you've been protecting him from the big, outside ugly world that he doesn't understand: feeding him good chow, talking with him, calling him a [*can-bo?*] of the NLF, not the derogatory term of Vietcong . . . Then you indicate that this nice treatment that he's had so far [has] not been disinterested good treatment, that we expect his cooperation. This again reintroduces the whole issue of the big, ugly outside world. What's going to happen to him now? Well, he might tell you a couple of things, beginning with rather innocuous things. Well, you can imply that you knew that already, what you're really after are better things and this might rather [uncalm?] him. Then you might say, "Jeez, that scrape you got on your shoulder . . . it obviously needs attention; we'll have to give you some penicillin." And while you're giving him the penicillin, you're telling him that, "You know, there are these other types of people who just . . ."
>
> [. . .]
>
> MR. X: Actually again, this is the technique that Captain [Y] . . . and myself have been trying to promote in an advisory relationship.

253

Again, it's a technique that's been used most effectively by the Chinese, in which you've pulled the man out of his familiar environment: he's dependent... upon you for his continual well-being. And even though the prisoner may [resist?], it's kind of an emotional interdependence that's created, and what you try and do is [use?] this emotional interdependence in such a way that he comes to the point where he *must* tell you what he knows.

SAHLINS: It's in effect brainwashing — is that the point of this?

MR. X: No, what it is, is breaking him down. But... once you've broken him down, it comes to the point where he wakes up in a sweat one morning and tells you, "All right." Then he tells you the names of the two people in his cell; or, he gives you the location of the camp that he just recently came from. Then you're through with him, in practical terms. You've got what you needed to continue operating. But at this point, if you really believe in anything yourself, what you've got to do is give him something to hope for before you send him back for further processing. Because you have just brought this individual to the *lowest point in his life* in terms of human meaning and existence. So at that point, that's when you've got to stress that, "Well now we're releasing you for further processing. But for you, what you've just told us is the beginning of a positive affirmation. We just can't process you right into our unit now; because you don't know what we stand for and what we're fighting for, but we hope that someday you will be joining us." See, we don't have time to get any brainwashing. The Chinese can do that because they have POWs for months and months and months. If we get a guy, we've got him for two to five days, and then he's out of our hands. In that two to five days, we've got to get the information we need. But we will not get the information we need by physical torture. We've got to get it by an emotional and mental torture. And you can do that because that's what they're least adequately prepared for. It's what Americans are least adequately prepared for when they find themselves in the other side's hands.

[...]

SAHLINS: What kind of control do you have over Arvin types of interrogation [i.e., physical torture]?

MR. X: Well again, that's an advisory function. And what you're try-

254

ing to do is — this is just a traditional, feudal Asian society, Mainland-style — and what you're trying to do is change the course of warfare in Asia. To some extent this has been done: the Chinese People's Liberation Army; it's happened probably in the Japanese army, the Japanese Self-Defense and Home Defense Armies. But until the end of World War II, we always thought of the Japanese army as a real cruel, vindictive bunch of cutthroats. Well, it turned out in post–World War II analysis that the Bataan Death March was something that they handled to the best of their ability, given the available transport and the way that they would have handled their own prisoners. They just moved them, and they moved them as fast as they could. People who couldn't keep up the pace in some cases were helped and in some other cases — just according to the individual guard — were bashed and thrown aside. Vietnamese to our eyes seem rather cruel sometimes to prisoners, but they're not doing this with any ideological vengeance. They're doing that because that's just been the bent of warfare in Mainland Asia for a thousand years, and what we have got to try to do is sophisticate it, and tell them, "Look, that's just not the way." It's a slow process; we're attempting a reformation of a whole society.

SAHLINS: What practical is being done to discourage this kind of thing?

MR. X: Well, guidance on the spot —

CAPTAIN D (SAHLINS'S ESCORT): It's up to the individual advisers —

MR. X: The individual adviser giving guidance on the spot.

CAPTAIN D: Sometimes it's successful, sometimes not —

CAPTAIN Y: In most cases, it's not.

SAHLINS: From what you say about mental torture, you wouldn't make any distinction in the morality of either kind [i.e., physical versus mental torture]?

MR. X: Hell, no! I don't make any distinction in morality at all: torture is torture, and when you fuck around with a guy's mind and his whole basic raison d'être, you're *really* hurting him — especially when he's prepared mentally, spiritually, for the physical torture.

SAHLINS: Then the attempt to discourage Vietnamese water torture … is just because the other type [mental torture] doesn't offend American sensibilities as much?

255

MR. X: No, it's not because of that. Because we don't concern our-selves here with American sensibilities. We concern ourselves with what will work.

CAPTAIN Y: It's relatively ineffective.

MR. X: It's ineffective. It may sound hard-boiled to say that we don't concern ourselves with American sensibilities — but we don't. We're concerning ourselves with Vietnamese sensibilities.

SAHLINS: What about the sensibilities of the Americans who are involved...the person who's torturing?

MR. X: To most of the Americans, to most of the simpleminded Americans who get involved in Vietnam — that's all the *boobus Amer-icanus* that H.L. Mencken spoke about — undoubtedly they think that the mental and emotional torture we're talking about is the least objectionable, because they've never really paused to seriously reflect about it themselves; or perhaps they did not go through the experience of being a POW in the Korean conflict themselves. And they can probably tell you, "Oh, Jesus, I'd try and stop that physical torture, because I know it's just wrong" — you know. But we think that we're looking into it a little more deeply, and we see that the mental and spiritual torture that we bring a man through to the point where he voluntarily gives you the information is pretty rough stuff to get involved in too. But it works.

SAHLINS: How do you offset the damage to yourself?

MR. X: Your belief. Your belief: you have to sincerely believe that in the long run you're helping this man. It's like an AA cure. If you're just breaking the guy down for the sake of getting a poor helpless alcoholic who's hipped on NLF propaganda to admit that he was wrong and give you the information, then you're going to send him out in the street a crushed derelict, then there's something wrong with you. But you have to really believe, as we do — although we get discouraged sometimes by our [Vietnamese] counterparts — you have to really believe that you're *helping* this guy to something better.

SAHLINS: Conversion from communism is involved in the torture.

MR. X: Conversion from anything to anything involves a certain degree of self-torture. We just accelerated the process because we need that fucking information.

SAHLINS: This is better for him?

256

MR. X: He's alive, and you can still help him . . .

[. . .]

MR. X: Most Americans, unfortunately, don't bother to think deeply about the stuff they get involved in and they make superficial judgments: "Well, it's wrong to torture this guy physically because we're all part of the same [background]" —

CAPTAIN Y: If you ask you'll get probably 80 percent of the people [U.S. military] will say, "Well, I didn't get involved in it. When they capture them, when they capture the Vietnamese communists, I just turn my back and go and have a cigarette."

MR. X: They take a drink from their canteen and light up a cigarette. And that's discouraging . . . I'd rather get — not get involved in it, not in the actual physical torture myself — but I'd rather be right there and see it done, and then laugh like a horse when it doesn't work and they don't get the information. And then in the long run you're affecting the situation when you just laugh at this guy and say: "Look, you think he's gonna break? So you cut up his stomach a little bit and his insides fell out . . . He got the last laugh on you, because he didn't talk a bit." And maybe it'll make the guy think, you know, and ten times later, after ten more people have faded out because he physically tortured them, maybe he'll say: "Okay, wise American adviser, what would you do?" . . . We have a moral responsibility, it seems to me, once we've stepped into this country to involve ourselves in the complete fabric of the country, and to understand it, and then try and help the Vietnamese to look at some different alternatives . . . We should be acting as a catalyst, as a thinking catalyst in Vietnam. But you cannot be a catalyst unless you know the entire fabric of the thing. And lighting up a cigarette when they bring a prisoner in for questioning is, well, that's an immoral —

CAPTAIN Y: It's just like saying, "It doesn't happen."

MR. X: That's just about the height of immorality, I think. To think that you can just absolve yourself. That's saying that every man *is* an island; or at least when it is comfortable, when it's comfortable for me to be an island unto myself, then I am; and the bell's tolling for that poor fucker under the knife, not me. That's real bad. And again, it's a simpleminded approach.

[. . .]

[Mr. X had mentioned that one of the rules imparted to the cadres in training was "be kind to prisoners." I asked if that wasn't a rule he disobeyed.]

MR. X: Well, if the final result of it is — it's a cruel process — but the result of bringing him closer to you, of conversion — it's a tortuous process of conversion — but the result is a kind one ... If you believe in your program, this is what you do . . .

SAHLINS: Do you believe in breaking people down so they agree with your program? And breaking them down justifies the end?

MR. X: No ... That's why we would not take a guy who's been broken directly into our unit at this time . . .

SAHLINS: Either you will rehabilitate him by converting him to your belief or you're going to leave him a mental wreck ... Can your ends be so God-given as to give you this right among humanity to do this?

MR. X: I don't know. I don't really believe anybody's hands are God-given. I'm an agnostic atheist.

SAHLINS: No, your ends. I'm not asking you for religious beliefs. What I'm asking is, do you believe you have the right to impose by this method —

MR. X: I think I've got the right to try. Nobody's got the right to succeed — guaranteed. But everybody's got the right to promote and proselytize what they believe.

[...]

CAPTAIN Y: If we do not break this guy, if we do not attempt to change his ideas, then in essence what have we done? We've said that basically he's right!

SAHLINS: No, that isn't so. One agrees to disagree as a matter of principle in a democratic system.

MR. X: Oh wait, this is [where] we begin ... I've had some tremendous conversations with these guys, and we begin by agreeing to disagree. But you can soon get this guy so flustered and so shaken up that before he knows it, he's agreeing with you — because his assumptions to begin with were rather vulnerable.

SAHLINS: But that isn't the issue here. The issue here is whether you will impose your will by this technique, which is —

MR. X: We don't know what our will is yet.

SAHLINS: You will impose your ideas by this technique —

MR. X: What ideas?

[...]

SAHLINS: ...I asked the question, how do you justify the effect upon yourself of acting in this way? And you said you're doing the guy a service. Now, I'm asking you, do you believe you have the right to impose your will on somebody, impose what you believe —

MR. X: We are not imposing our will. We are not imposing will. Even after you've broken him and gotten the information, he's still a free agent.

[...]

MR. X: Not impose will — if he fails to accept...an alternative. And not *our* alternative; there are a number of alternatives. Because in essence that's what we're trying to show him.

[...]

SAHLINS: You don't accept that [i.e., that there is only one way of doing things and nobody can dispute it], but you accept the other premise that there are many ways...So, as a matter of fact, by this process you either transform him from that belief into one of a range of acceptable beliefs, or you will leave him a mental wreck —

MR. X: But we don't leave him this way. We have brought him to a point where he realizes that the faith he placed in his previous system was essentially not powerful. He has volunteered the information. At this point he's got to find a new way. He's got to have a way out of his dilemma, and the people at the training centers should be skillful enough to point out to him a number of alternatives.

SAHLINS: We come back to the question: whether you have the right — by these techniques, which are external to him — to deny him [the] belief that he came in with in his hand and only accept a set of alternatives which you propose?

[...]

MR. X: Listen, I've met guys...We had a guy in Phu Yen Province in the summer of '63 who was the Propaganda Director for the NLF in that province; and boy, we just worked ourselves literally ragged in four days trying to bring that guy to the point where he'd tell us a few things, and he was tremendous — just tremendous. Didn't tell us a thing.

SAHLINS: You admire this guy?

259

MR. X: Tremendous — tremendous.

SAHLINS: So you admire more a person who will not acquiesce to the thing that you say is right than one who does?

MR. X: No, not true. I didn't say that at all. I admire a guy who will tortuously admit — if he really believes — that, "Oh Jesus, I never thought about that before. Those guys [NLF] they told me something else; and you're really doing something else." A guy like that who will examine his previously arrived conclusions and change his mind, I admire that —

SAHLINS: That's very admirable, but it doesn't describe the process you went through, which was to leave him in a situation where either he takes his set of alternatives which you give him or he is a mental wreck.

MR. X: Remember, this was an act of *affirmation* on his part, where he yields the information voluntarily. But it's only a beginning; it's only a beginning; and it's not fair to leave him at the point where he's just made the beginning.

[…]

MR. X: It's just like an alcoholic. An alcoholic can attend the meetings and he can see everybody else get embarrassed; and if he doesn't want to join them he can just back out again. But once a guy begins to join this little society of alcoholics —

CAPTAIN Y: These cadres we have [as instructors] — these ex-VCs, ex-NLF, ex Viet Minh — they all in some way or another gave up something in their own mind when they turned, came to the government.

[…]

MR. X: … what we're trying to show these guys when we're interrogating them, through this tortuous process, is that you're not better [off] under the NLF. "Your whole series of assumptions has got to be reexamined here, and we're here to help you reexamine them. And, Jesus, there's some guys here have got some more basic ideas of how they'd like to examine you, but we're just holding these guys off… and we'll take good care of you." That's the kind of a dirty trick — [but] when you've only got four days…

SAHLINS: Have you done this with Vietcong?

MR. X: We don't do anything because we're advisers — in every sense.

CHAPTER NINE

The Established Order:

Do Not Fold, Spindle, or Mutilate*

We all know what the right to investigate freely, to think freely, and to write freely means to our field and ourselves and what the loss of these would mean. Mr. Chairman, I am concerned that our involvement in Cold War activities such as Project Camelot does jeopardize these freedoms. Of course, I speak for myself; but the sentiments are not entirely my own. I have had a chance to discuss these matters with colleagues from several universities. Without presuming to represent them, I am trying here to formulate concerns many have expressed.

The following, Mr. Chairman, constitute grounds for apprehension:

First, the scale and character of government interest in Strategic Social Science. In the nature of things, this is seen only through a glass darkly. We do know the six million dollars allotted to Camelot was merely for a "feasibility" study (three and one half years). An ultimate investment of several times that per annum was contemplated — one ex–Camelot scholar told me the talk was of fifty million a year. Meanwhile *Problem* Camelot goes on, with the aid of some anthropologists, in Africa as well as Latin America, New Guinea as well as Southeast Asia. And on the home front, intelligence agencies erect concealed bases of support: sundry "front" foundations or "pass-throughs" created with covert

*Delivered first at the November 1965 Meeting of the American Anthropological Association in Denver, Colorado. Published in Irving Louis Horowitz, ed., *The Rise and Fall of Project Camelot* (Cambridge, MA: MIT Press, 1967).

government funds. These funds dispense "grants" for certain "academic" research and travel. There are grounds to suspect the CIA fronts are camouflaged by names closely approximating those of listed and legitimate private foundations.

Second, Mr. Chairman, there is a serious possibility that such tactics will become our tactics. It is already a minimum demand of internal vigilance that everyone investigate the source of funds he is offered for foreign-area research, conferences on fieldwork needs, or the like. I understand that, in at least one instance, anthropologists have been invited by colleagues to attend a conference subsidized by the Defense Department without, however, being informed in advance of this sponsorship. Here is an example of the corrosion of integrity that must accompany an enlistment of scholars in a gendarmerie relation to the Third World. Subversion of the mutual trust between field-worker and informant is the predictable next step. The relativism we hold necessary to ethnography can be replaced by cynicism, and the quest for objective knowledge of other peoples replaced by a probe for their political weaknesses.

Third, the State Department announces it will create a board of review for government-sponsored external research, with the aim of blocking investigations not in the nation's best interests. This is a clear threat to free inquiry. I realize the purpose of the broadly worded presidential directive was to prevent repetitions of Camelot. But directives outlive the intentions of those who issue them and ought to reckon with those who implement them; so, directives wrong in principle must be opposed on principle. Nor is the theory of good people administering bad laws a proper philosophy of American democracy.

Fourth, as it is, we cannot get into half the world; as scholars-in-armor we would soon not be on speaking terms with the other half.

I refer to the call to this meeting:

Some field work already in progress in various parts of the world, particularly in Latin America, has already suffered adversely, being forced to curtail or even suspend operations. Reports have been received and verified about the investigation and embarrassment by their governments of foreign scholars who have been actively helping United States social scientists. This, in turn, rapidly erodes the resources of goodwill upon which we can draw and militates against the conduct of adequately staffed and assisted field work.

The *New York Times* foresaw just this predicament in September 1964, in commenting on the disclosure by a congressional subcommittee of a CIA front foundation: "What evidence," the *Times* asked, "can American professors or field workers present to prove they are not engaged in underground activities when it is known that the CIA is using its money to subsidize existing foundations, or is creating fictitious ones?"

This harassment falls on everyone, just or unjust: independent scholar or academic Cold Warrior, foreign intellectuals as well as the Americans with whom they work. In some sense, it is not our fault. It is not our fault that America appears to many people an interventionist and counterrevolutionary power. And it is not our fault that American agents, whose relations to progressive movements seem instinctively hostile, operate under cover in the Third World. But the least we can do is protect the anthropologist's relation to the Third World, which is a scholarly relation. Fieldwork under contract to the U.S. Army is no way to protect that relation.

Perhaps it was Camelot's greatest irony that it forgot to program itself into the project. As a tactic of fomenting Latin American unrest and anti–North American sentiment, Camelot would be the envy of any communist conspiracy. We have heard of the self-fulfilling prophecy; here was the self-fulfilling research proposal.

Fifth, strategic research raises serious issues of classification and clearance. Scientifically, the relevant concerns are the right freely to communicate one's experiences to colleagues at home and abroad and the right to participate in research according to one's merit and promise — without regard to the FBI's understanding of patriotism. Here we should take into account a distinction much favored by the Camelot scientists: that it *is* research,

263

not intelligence. Participating scholars conceived the project to be a fine opportunity to develop knowledge useful, even critical, to social science. It was a chance, too, to advance the frontiers of research technique. The project design of 1 April 1965 indeed opens new vistas on the study of revolution and counterrevolution, such as "operations research techniques, manual and machine simulation, machine content analysis, and new types of analysis of survey data" — which is perhaps why one friend, an unautomated anthropologist of decided views, suggested that the most heartening thing about Camelot was its intellectual prognosis.

For Project Camelot, the Defense Department gave assurance that findings would not be classified and clearance would not be necessary. In fact, there are no ironclad guarantees. The government has the power; in this respect, the scholar is in very unequal relation to Defense, State, or the CIA. And what will the ruling be on Project Kula-Ring, Operation Leopard-Skin Chief, and other future scientific investigations of the CIA or the Defense Department? Moreover, it is difficult to conceive that classification would not have eventually occurred in Camelot. A working paper of 5 December 1964 stipulates as the most significant criterion for inclusion in the study the relevance of the country to U.S. foreign policy interests. The program for historical studies (1 April) asks investigators to probe official corruption, the strength of insurgent parties, and the measures taken to cut off external aid to insurgents; to determine the effectiveness of the established government's intelligence service; to give approximate numbers of forces available for counterinsurgency; to say whether the regime fomented foreign wars or "black" coups to suppress internal unrest; to determine whether the government permitted communist infiltration of itself or radical movements; to name names, note groups, and identify leaders. All sorts of questions such as these were deemed important in the preliminary archival studies. Suppose the answers proved important and informed the fieldworker's checklists. Can you now suppose these field reports would be published?

(In connection with the assurances about classification, I understand that when Camelot was summarily canceled the Defense

Department asked participants not to discuss the project publicly, and this request was respected. That Defense's request was
prompted by the international repercussions of Camelot's premature disclosure is better understood as an augury than a mitigating
circumstance, and as a reflection on the character of the project.)

Sixth, the idea that Strategic Social Science will liberalize
strategy as it advances science seems to me a snare and a delusion.

I form the impression that good and conscientious Camelot
scientists thought they might put something over on the Defense
Department. They were going to get in some good research,
whatever the U.S. Army's objectives. Besides, if somebody's going
to do this sort of thing, better it be sensible and humane people.
Here was a chance to educate the military to foreign realities, an
opportunity to reconstruct American attitudes and policies. And
with this hope went the perception that the Defense Department
is divisible into "good guys" and "bad guys"; and the former,
although a minority, managed to get this "software" research
through and ought to be encouraged.

I think this all unnecessarily naive, a failure to analyze the structure of the Establishment, the relation of the sword to the pen,
the strengths of the Cold War demonology, and the present for-
eign-political position of this country. The quixotic scholar enters
the agreement in the belief that knowledge breeds power; his military counterpart, in the assurance that power breeds knowledge.
The level of innocence is best documented by ethnography, although the point appears also in Camelot documents. I asked a
Camelot psychologist, who was pleased to expound this distinction between black knights and white knights, what was the content of the progressives' program. He said, in the first place, that
enlightened Pentagon officers see the military of Latin America —
acting in concert with the U.S. Army — as the best available vehicle for reform: they are organized, efficient, intelligent, and have
the social machinery. That is what he said. So help me.

Seventh, the Cold War researcher is potentially a servant of
power, placed in a sycophantic relation to the state unbefitting
science or citizenship. The scholar sells his services to a military,
intelligence, or foreign policy client, who has certain plans for the

product. Although formal clearance requirements may be suspended, it is only artless to claim there is no informal selection of academic personnel on the basis of agreement in Cold War principle — if not tactic — or no penalty to outspoken public criticism. Academicians who have demonstrated creative support are at least differentially favored for higher appointments in the existing scheme of things; those who cannot agree run some risk of being shut out, unless they shut up. If this is important research, carried out as it may be under institutional contract, the government agency is in a position to make one's commitment to prevailing policy a condition of professional opportunity and success. On the other side, one's freedom as a citizen to dissent is constrained, on pain of antagonizing the employers-that-be. This fate can be predicted even for those first engaged by the agency on research of their own choosing, "basic research": they are equally retainers, mortgaged to past and future favors. Clearly, neither science nor democracy can function in such an atmosphere.

The science and government question is delicate, complicated, and perennial. But now that it has come to us, perhaps we can add an understanding of the sociology in it that betrays all good intentions. Even the military or intelligence agency may have good intentions about academic independence; yet informal screening and watchful discretion will go on. For the agreement between Cold War scholar and government bureau is largely self-policing. "Cameloticians" themselves understood the principle and wrote it into their project. In the checklist for case studies appears a section titled "Government Control of Scientific Institutions." It aims to assess the power of the established regime and the loyalties it could command in a crisis. There is a subhead called "Scientists." It asks only this: "What percentage of scientists work for Government and for private organizations? Of those who work for private organizations, such as universities, what percentage supplement their income through Government contracts, extra jobs, consultations?"

Eighth, the scientific status of Cold War research is equivocal. Camelot documents bear out Senator Fulbright's suspicions: "Implicit in Camelot," he said, "as in the concept of 'counterinsurgency' is an assumption that revolutionary movements are dangerous to the interest of the United States and that the United States must be prepared to assist, if not actually to participate in, measures to repress them." Consider this example of a "scientific" question from the project design: "Was the Government guilty of excessive toleration of alienated, insurgent, or potentially insurgent groups?"

But most clearly in its characterizations of revolutionary unrest does Camelot reveal its basic valuations. I am not speaking of personal biases or construing anything about motivations. It seems a better — and sufficient — interpretation that what had been for some time a cultural common-law marriage between scientific functionalism and the natural interest of a leading world power in the status quo became under the aegis of Project Camelot an explicit and legitimate union. In any event, revolutionary movements are described in Camelot documents as "antisystem activities," indications of "severe disintegration," varieties of "destabilizing processes," threats to "legitimate control of the means of coercion within the society," facilitated by "administrative errors." Movements for radical change are in Camelot's view a disease, and a society so infected is sick. Here was a program for diagnosing social illness, a study in "epidemiology," called just that by a senior researcher. Another consistently refers to revolutionary movements as "social pathology," though disclaiming in a footnote that they are necessarily to be avoided. A third conceives the growth of demands for change as "contagion." "Did the government," he proposes to determine, "couple limited and managed reforms with repressive measures to prevent the contagion and spread of social unrest?" Of course, waiting on call is the doctor, the U.S. Army, fully prepared for its self-appointed "important mission in the positive and constructive aspects of nation-building." The indicated treatment is "insurgency prophylaxis."

If Camelot had been given a title more appropriate to its "scientific" character, it might have been "The Established Order: Do Not Fold, Spindle, or Mutilate." But aside from President Kennedy's fondness for the musical comedy, "Camelot" was apparently for the army happily symbolic of the knight in shining armor come to slay the dragon of disorder — and so gain half the kingdom. Social scientists, however, might have reflected on the deeper medieval connotation: their recruitment as the scholastics of Cold War theology.

Every citizen has the right to engage in counterinsurgency research and practice. But, in my opinion, none of us has leave, as scholar or citizen, to so delude himself and others about the scientific legitimacy and disinterested objectivity of this work. Here certain distinctions must be made. Just because the subject of research is intellectually important, it does not mean that the research proposal is important, or even any good. And just because the people involved in a bureaucratic operation are honest and conscientious — as every Camelot scholar I know is — does not mean that what they are engaged in has these qualities. This last sad fact all recent history teaches us.

Mr. Chairman, I have tried to formulate colleagues' opinions I have heard and which I share. For each and all the reasons stated, I object to any further engagement in strategic research by American anthropologists working under contract to defense, foreign policy, or intelligence agencies of the U.S. government. I happen to believe it is no good for the country or the peoples among whom we have lived. I am convinced it is no good for our discipline or our mortal selves. I frame no resolutions, however, because I am undecided on the value of doing so. It would be an advantage to make clear to our government and the world that we are autonomous scientists concerned in our studies with a rational inquiry into man and his works. As against this, tedious debate and discussions of wording would probably not enhance solidarity nor produce a resolution of moral strength. More critical, we have no sanctions and cannot legislate ethics, and perhaps we should not try. For the moment, I favor the principle of letting each man learn to live with himself.

PART THREE

Culture in Practice

Introduction to Part Three

Written in the 1980s and 90s, this final set of essays represents a double engagement of culture with history. First are the studies in the genre of historical ethnography, investigations of early modern Pacific island cultures especially. They attempt to "ground truth," as it were, big issues of the relations between cultural order and temporal change: relations between structure and event, between agency and society, and, most generally, between the anthropological and historical disciplines. A second group of essays concerns contemporary issues of cultural order among the peoples subjected to the hegemonic forces of a globalizing capitalism. The argument is that many indigenous cultures still live — notwithstanding the "sentimental pessimism" of dependency, modernization, and globalization theories. Indeed, the various indigenizations of modernity undertaken by people who have escaped the death sentence imposed by world capitalism now offer a whole new manifold of cultural variations for a renewed comparative anthropology.

"Individual Experience and Cultural Order" (Chapter Ten) and "The Return of the Event, Again" (Chapter Eleven) are useful for understanding the kind of cultural history I have been writing in some larger monographs as well as studies included here (M. Sahlins 1981, 1985a, 1992, 1995). Together they illustrate the main points of an historiography that aims to synthesize the relationships of cultural order with the particularities — or, from the viewpoint of a certain structuralism, the contingencies — of agency and situation. "Individual Experience" makes the necessary first move of distinguishing the values of cultural phenomena in collective social fields from their values as diversely lived by particular subjects. The concept of "mother" as constituted by relationships to "father," "aunt," "child," etc., is different from what "mother" means to me in particular, as a consequence of my life experiences. The first concerns categories in relation to each other, thus intersubjectively or in the society as such, where the second has to do specifically with cultural concepts in relation to the persons pragmatically using them. That meanings in the latter case will necessarily vary with the biography and social condition of the persons concerned has been known at least since John Locke. Analyzed by Meillet, the variability has lately become more familiar in such guises as "the linguistic division of labor" (Putnam), "polyphony" (Clifford), and "heteroglossia" (Bakhtin). Of course, when it became political and postmodern to celebrate such "contested categories," it was supposed that the differential relationships of subjects to concepts was a novel discovery. Coupled to the nominalist nonsequitur that there could be no such essentialist thing as cultural categories — and inferentially no coherent relationships between them — this discovery of a diversity that was unsystematic (or not worth systematizing) would at least allow us to be done worrying about culture and history: for a variation that is not regularly connected to anything is amenable to no form of human explication, except possibly pointing.

The notion of a "structure of the conjuncture" was meant to rescue history for intelligibility by an analysis of the dynamics of cultural order. At issue most explicitly in "The Return of the Event, Again," it is there described as "the way the cultural categories are actualized in a specific context through the interested action of the historic agents and the pragmatics of their interaction." The structure of the conjuncture is a way of thinking about how cultural categories, variously implemented by diverse parties to an historical action, are *in the event* worked out contextually, in the sociology and politics of their interaction. It is a framework for discussing the referential mediation of structural values by social practice.[1] Further worked out in the article in question, the concept of a conjunctural structure or structures also proves valu-

272

able for exploring the possibilities of agency and contingency in the making of history.

Briefly, the argument is something as follows. By various structural means, ranging from the ascribed powers of heroic status (Fijian chiefs) to the contextual felicity of a strategic action (invention of the teach-in), the historic course of larger social totalities may be inscribed in the doings and relationships of particular individuals — though not in their individuality, which caveat is critical. Recall the Sartrean phrasing: "The group bestows its power and efficacy upon the individuals whose irreducible particularity is one way of living universality; or rather, this universality takes on the face, the body and the voice of the leaders it has given itself" (1963:130). Note that the empowerment of persons is itself a structural determination. In virtue of the sacred uterine nephew relationship (*vasu*), the security of entire Fijian kingdoms has hinged on succession struggles among the sons by different mothers of the ruler of a dominant state. If the intensity of the ensuing fratricidal strife reflected this instantiation of the fate of several kingdoms in the relations of particular kinsmen, still the larger political order itself did not determine either the character or effectiveness of the persons who thus incarnated them — nor, a fortiori, could it determine the outcome of their struggles. Descending to persons and structures of lower order, universality is subjected to biography, not to mention the myriad contingencies of time and place. An error of judgment can thus become a collective disaster, or personal cunning translate into political hegemony, yet neither do these totalized effects — the return of action to system — account for the specificities that produced them. Such are the theoretical schemes embodied in the essays here on Fijian history.

"The Discovery of the True Savage" (Chapter Twelve) also raises another issue, which is further developed in the following essays as it is carried through successively more contemporary histories. It is about agency in another sense — the way indigenous peoples appropriate the forces and relations of an encroaching Western capitalism in their own cultural schemes; which is also to say, in their own projects of "development," according to their historical ideas of good things. The "True Savage" — which concerns the heroic status accorded by Fijians to a Swedish beachcomber of the early nineteenth century, Charlie Savage — makes this very point about the integration of Europeans as well as muskets in the organization and ambitions of the expanding kingdom of Bau. Indeed, the ritual and practical uses of muskets make it clear that they entered into Fijian wars, rather than that Fijians entered into wars of musketry. Moreover, I try to provide documentary support for the position of certain Fijian intellectuals to the effect that the trade in sperm-whale teeth rather than guns was the reason behind the increasing scale of warfare and ambition in this period. Given the effective values of whale teeth in the local scheme of things, the more whale teeth available, the more power there was in the Fiji Islands.

The study "Cosmologies of Capitalism: The Trans-Pacific Sector of 'The World System'" (Chapter Thirteen) expands this thesis through the Pacific by a comparative look at the ways three societies in particular, imperial China, Hawaii, and native Americans of the Northwest Coast (primarily Kwakiutl), responded differentially to the British-Canton trade of the late eighteenth and early nineteenth centuries in which they were all engaged. The contrasts in demand patterns were striking. The Chinese refused virtually all British commodities — thus writing off the Industrial Revolution — while showing an appetite for silver coin as importunate as the British interest in Chinese teas. The Hawaiians had no misgivings about the virtues of the Western traders' goods — especially the constantly changing fashionable goods of personal lux, by means of which the chiefs differentiated their otherwise comparable genealogical claims to foreign (cum divine) powers. The Kwakiutl chiefs, however, went in for standardized imports, ultimately Hudson's Bay blankets, by the distribution of which they could calibrate their essentially distinct ancestral powers. Each people thus developed their relations to capitalism through their own cosmological conceptions, a point I also try to extend to the curious tea habit of the British natives, which set this whole network of cultural distinctions in motion.

The two essays "Goodbye to *Tristes Tropes*" (Chapter Fourteen) and "What Is Anthropological Enlightenment?" (Chapter Fifteen) trace such historical motions into the present struggles of indigenous peoples to organize culturally what is happening to them. The articles speak to an "indigenization of modernity" that develops in tandem with and opposition to the globalizing culture of capitalism. Here is a new planetary structure of human culture — a world "Culture of cultures" — ushering in unforeseen modes of historical production. The effects are not exactly what was envisioned by modernization and dependency theories, even less by their logical precursor "despondency theory." Rather, such new things as the worldwide self-consciousness of culture and the formation of transnational migratory communities have sponsored unprecedented modern (and postmodern) processes of cultural diversification. Another effect could be unprecedented kinds of anthropology. Anthropologists, for too long lamenting the passing of the old-time "aboriginal" cultures, and too obsessed with capitalist hegemony to notice the cultural integrity of its victims, have thus been too slow to appreciate theoretically the new spectrum of cultural variations history has presented them.

Part of the difficulty may be the cosmology of their own culture, to which the anthropological consciousness of others could be overly indebted. Such is the argument of the final essay included in this collection, "The Sadness of Sweetness; or, The Native Anthropology of Western Cosmology" (Chapter Sixteen). Following Sidney Mintz's famous analysis of the role of sugar in the formation of modern Euro-American cultures (1985), this work amounts to an archaeological excursion into the pleasure-pain principle on which we have philosophically and practically modeled ourselves. It finds the lineaments of the biologism, realism, and providentialism which still haunt our anthropology, as well as the utilitarianism, in inherited Western ideas of humanity, nature, and society. The essay thus caps the apparently misguided optimism of the previous essays on the indigenization of modernity with the analogous hope that even anthropologists can develop themselves in some measure free of Western culture.

NOTE

1. In this respect, the idea of "the structure of the conjuncture" was not meant to apply simply to the relations of "culture contact," as seems too widely believed, nor was it supposed that the notion could only be useful in such contexts, as also has been said. On the contrary, the claim from the beginning was this: "The general statements I derive about historical processes do not require conditions of intercultural contact. They suppose only a world on which people act differentially and according to their respective situations as social beings, conditions that are as common to action within a given society as they are to the interaction of distinct societies" (M. Sahlins 1981:vii). Perhaps "The Return of the Event, Again" (Chapter Eleven) helps make this point.

276

Chapter Ten

Individual Experience and

Cultural Order[*]

I am going to resurrect an issue that anthropologists these days hate to think about, even though as students of culture they have a main responsibility for discussing it. I mean the problem of "cultural determinism," or the relation between individual action and cultural order. True, an older generation with some strong ideas on the subject has now died off and a younger one having other preoccupations taken its place; and, while such is the normal definition of progress in the social sciences, we are not really free to forget the problems that plagued the ancestors. The issue was important; and, besides, we have been speaking it all this time while pretending not to know it. What I propose to do is to reflect (in a much too schematic way) on the implications of current interests in symbolism and structuralism for the received idea that culture is sui generis, a so-called superorganic object independent of the human subjects who enact it.

Utilitarian Individualism and Cultural Determinism
It must be recalled that the concept of the superorganic developed in anthropology — and also, with the Durkheimian "social fact," in sociology — by opposition to the complete theory of culture already present in Western society and consciousness — present, indeed, as the way this society takes consciousness of itself. I

---

* Originally published in William Kruskal, ed., *The Social Sciences: Their Nature and Uses* (Chicago: University of Chicago Press, 1982). © 1982 The University of Chicago Press.

refer to the mainstream idea of an "economic man" whose rational choices precipitate, as if by an Invisible Hand, not only the
well-being of the Nation but its very social forms. Marxism perhaps excepted, this utilitarian individualism is the only coherent
analysis of culture the West has produced. Our colleagues in the
University of Chicago Economics Department are brilliantly engaged in quantitative demonstrations of it, but even on the basis
of naive experience we can be sure in advance of their success.
For since the development of the self-regulating market, we have
had this certain, if peculiar, knowledge of ourselves as businesslike social beings, bent on maximizing life's benefits and minimiz-
ing its costs. "Utility dominates the study of culture," as A.M.
Hocart said, "because it dominates the culture that studies."

Rendering all kinds of goods and services commensurable in
their capacity as monetary values, the market society did not merely disguise to itself the meaningful differences between things. To
an anthropologist, the historical peculiarity is that the kinds of acts
he recognizes in a tribal context as instances of "social organization," "politics," "kinship," "art," even "religion," appear, when he
returns from the field, as so many quests for "utilities." For in the
context of a total market, no matter what the nature of such acts
taken in themselves, our relationship to them is decisively economic. Whether one chooses to go to a baseball game or to a
concert, vacation in Hawaii, or buy the Oxford English Dictionary, all such actions and options must first be translated into
their apparent common denominator of "pleasures" or "satisfactions," among which we prudently allocate our limited pecuniary
means. In the translation, then, their distinctive social content is
lost, with the result that from the natives' point of view all of culture seems constituted by (and as) the businesslike economizing
of autonomous individuals. I have to admit that many Western
anthropologists have been tempted to reproduce this indigenous
folklore in their own studies, as a consciousness also of the others.
For when a society makes a fetish of the commodity, its anthropology is disposed to make a commodity out of the fetish.

Bourgeois life turns culture into the hidden a priori of a calculus of pragmatic action. The symbolic order is subsumed in hier-

archies of means and ends, as motives and interests located within the subject and realized by a process of rational choice also natural to him/her. Culture thus become a presupposition, we are left unaware of other logics inscribed in our intentions. I refer not merely to the difficulties of making other judgments of a Weberian sort on rational action; for example, that the collective disutilities of a system of private transport are not envisioned in the way that buying and driving a car, as a project of economizing, appears in personal experience. More significant yet is the qualitatively different logic of symbolic value that enters into action as an unreflected premise.

For instance, what is the ground of our preference for outer "meats" of food animals rather than the "innards," whose déclassé status is distinctly signified by names the same as human organs ("heart," "kidneys," "lungs")? Or why do we tabu as food certain nutritious creatures, such as dogs and horses, whom we instead take into human society in the capacity of subjects, bestowing on them proper names and the status of interlocutors in human conversation? As was discussed above in Chapter Five, the fact is that we act economically on a sustained set of anticannibalistic metaphors that have nothing to do with practical values — *except to determine them.* Or again, steak is a masculine food, thus most appropriate to the training table of the Chicago Bears, in opposition to the femininity of salads (especially tomatoes). But since all such distinctions are merely unstated premises of actions we know as the maximization of "utility," even as we can see that social arrangements are sedimented by them, mainstream social science hastens to make its own the Benthamite principle that "society is a fictitious body, the sum of the individual members who compose it." Society is no more than the contracts rational men and women enter into in the pursuit of their several private interests.

Yet as Nietzsche remarked, "Man does not seek happiness; only Englishmen do that." Anthropology has been forced to reconcile its own cultural presuppositions with the experience of other natives. In the event, the indigenous Western concepts were turned inside out. The response to individualism was to alienate man from his own activity and creativity, transferring these instead to a kind of supersubject, Culture, which for its part was accorded all powers of movement and determination. Admittedly this "culture" had no phenomenal existence apart from human beings, but it had autonomous characteristics and functions, and men could do no more than express its internal constitution and dynamics. The naive consciousness of capitalist society was thus exchanged for its historic Unhappy Consciousness.

A.L. Kroeber and L.A. White were the main American prophets of the Superorganic Being. Saddled, however, with a new series of contradictions—a nonsubstantial yet active being, a collectivity with the characteristics of an individual organism, and a mind subsisting independently of human subjects—anthropologists were forced to invent highly metaphorical descriptions of this "culture," and of its relationships to people. For White, the individual finally became a particle in the magnetic field of his culture, or else a pilotless airplane controlled by radio waves:

> The human organism lives and moves within an ethical magnetic field, so to speak. Certain social forces, culturally defined, impinge on the organism and move it this way and that, toward the good, away from the bad. The organism experiences these forces though he may mistake their source. He calls this experience conscience. His behavior is analogous to a pilotless aircraft controlled by radio. The plane is directed this way and that by impulses external to it. These impulses are received by a mechanism and are then transmitted to motors, rudders, etc. This receiving and behavior-controlling mechanism is analogous to conscience. (White 1949:157)

To sum up: Utilitarianism concealed culture within a faulty human epistemology, while the "superorganic" dissolved humanity in a fantastic cultural ontology. One is inclined to wish a plague on both their houses. But not before exhausting certain anthropological observations, such as the absence of any necessary relation between what people do and the reasons they may have for doing it.

Intention and Convention

Eskimo are famous for customs of gift-giving. "Gifts make slaves," they sometimes explain, "as whips make dogs." By contrast, a people famous for belligerence may have equally paradoxical motives for fighting. "They fought, they beat each other," writes a longtime resident among the Yanomamö of Brazil. "I don't know why; they said it was in order to be more peaceful and to be friends." There seems to be no adequate relation between the character of conventional practices, such as giving gifts or making war, and the intentions that predicate them, whether these intentions be described in social terms (for example, gaining status) or as subjective dispositions (for example, belligerence). The cross-cultural argument, moreover, can be supported from our own social experience. Psychoanalysis as well as common experience documents that an aggressive intent can be realized in an act of sex or on a field of football, by being excessively polite to someone, ignoring him or insulting him, by presenting a lecture or writing a book review ("that'll teach 'em"). Any given intention may correspond to an indefinite set of cultural practices and vice versa, since the intention is connected to the convention by a relative and contextual scheme of significance.

But if the connection is arbitrary, it is not for all that aleatory, inasmuch as it is motivated within the cultural order. This would be true even if the act had unprecedented social effects. Say that gift-giving established a novel form of social advancement: it would still find some logical motivation — it would "make sense" — in the culture as constituted. The disparity between conventions and intentions thus becomes a strong argument for culture as sui generis. It seems incorrect to deny that individual action is culturally determined, since this is all it can be.

The same dismal prospect appears implied by intrinsic features of symbolic consciousness and discourse. Nothing is socially known or communicated except as it is encompassed in the existing cultural order. From the first moment, experience undergoes a kind of structural co-optation: the incorporation of the percept within a concept of which the perceiver is not the author. This is Durkheim's famous "sociological epistemology." Likewise,

281

Walker Percy remarks, "It is not enough to say that one is conscious *of* something; one is also conscious of something as *being something*." Perception is instantaneously a *re*-cognition, a matching of the percept with some received social category — "There goes a bird." Human or symbolic consciousness thus consists of acts of classification involving the subsumption of an individual perception within a social conception. Hence, as percept belongs to concept in the way that an instance belongs to its class, so does experience belong to culture.

Moreover, we know — at least since Saussure and Cassirer — that the cultural category by which experience is appropriated is for its part referentially arbitrary. It does not follow directly from the world but from a set of principled relationships between categories. The contrast in French between the terms "fleuve" and "rivière" entails a different segmentation of fluvial objects than the usual English glosses "river" and "stream," inasmuch as the French distinction does not turn on relative size but on whether or not the water flows into an ocean. There is no necessary starting point for any such cultural scheme in "reality," as Stuart Hampshire writes — while noting that many philosophers have believed there is (1983). Rather, the particular conceptual scheme or "language game" constitutes the possibilities of worldly reference for the people of a given society, even as that scheme is constructed on principled distinctions among signs which, in relation to objects, are never the only possible distinctions. It follows that there is no such thing as an immaculate perception.

The argument from symbolic discourse has the same apparent implication. Insofar as a sentence asserts, it does so by seating a specific identification within a cultural class. A sentence is minimally a grammatical subject and a predicate — "There goes a bird." The grammatical subject identifies something in particular — "[it] there." But the predicate describes it in the terms of (relative) generals — "bird," "going": once more a class whose criteria are values of the prevailing cultural scheme.

On the other hand, it is well known that in speaking the individual puts the entire cultural scheme at his own personal disposition. The famous "shifters" of discourse — the pronouns "I" and "you," adverbs of time and place ("now" and "then," "here" and "there"), tenses of the verb, and so on — contextualize all abstract categories by the speaker's reference to himself and his particular situation. Speech invents a Cartesian world, developed outward from the true and certain knowledge of the "I." In practice, the individual is the Archimedean point of the cultural universe: for on the coordinates of his standpoint, hence of his interests, all of culture is transcendentally laid out, and all meanings, which without him are merely virtual or possible, become actual, referential, and intentional.

Yet here linguistics joins up with certain clear and distinct ideas of social psychology, sociology, and anthropology: the common finding that "I is another" (*Je est un autre*). Such was the point of George Herbert Mead's sustained demonstration that the self becomes known as an object by assuming the attitude of another toward one's own act or gesture — an identification with the other that alone permits reflection upon the self and to which language is indispensable. For Mead, as for Schütz, this "interchangeability of standpoints" is essential both to the origin of the self and the origin of human society. For Rousseau, it was the origin of human society itself: uniquely endowed with the sentiment of *pitié* which places him in the position of the one who suffers, man begins by experiencing himself as identical to his fellows. But that too, as Benveniste teaches, is the true character of the apparently egocentric symbolic discourse.

For the "I" of speech necessarily predicates a "you," and vice versa, even as the two are always reversible. No matter how egocentrically the world is laid out in speech, "I" am never alone in it. In dialogue, "I" and "you" exchange places: referential standpoints are necessarily reversed — shall we not say? — between *us*. This interchangeability is indispensable to interpretation and communication, since without it I could not know that your "here" is my "there." It must follow that the "you" to whom I speak, and who becomes "I" in speaking to me, is in some fundamental sense like me, namely, in the capacity of social person.

The consequences, as Benveniste says, spread out in all directions. We can understand why Lévi-Strauss founds the passage

283

from nature to culture on reciprocity as the decisive (that is, objectified) form of overcoming the opposition of self and other. Since reciprocity in this parallels the essential characteristics of symbolic discourse, we might even credit his explanation by inherent principles of the human mind. But more consequential for present purposes are inherent qualities of human society. If there are other "I"s whose standpoints I make my own, it becomes uniquely possible for humans to constitute social universals, categories, and groups that extend indefinitely in space and time. Somewhat enigmatically, Sartre says that a city derives its reality from "the ubiquity of its absence. It is present in each one of its streets *insofar* as it is always elsewhere." The enigmas dissolve when it is recognized that the existence of other "I"s, become "us," generalizes the representation from a diversity of perspectives and so determines a collective entity. Nor would Durkheim's "collective consciousness" and "collective representations" then appear so fantastic.

The interchangeability of opposed standpoints is decisive for the development of all such objectified social entities that are likewise ubiquitous in their absence — "lineages," "governments," "nations," "humanity" — including their normative attributes. These categories cannot be merely nominal, because even if there are only individuals they are conscious of themselves as "species beings." I have heard a Fijian elder narrate the doings of his clan over eight generations in the first-person pronoun. Upon such symbolic reification rests all that we call "tradition," "norm," "morality" — in brief, "a culture."

Never present as such to individual experience, the institutions of society thus become capable of ordering subjective interests and actions — that is, by virtue of a common membership with "the generalized other." Nor will my purposes be completely idiosyncratic: even when opposed to some other they are formulated on a common cultural logic. Yet this further allusion to Mead reminds us that different values of the social logic, some more particularistic, some more universal, intersect in the person. The individual is a social being, but we must never forget that he is an individual social being, with a biography not the same as that of anyone else. Here is someone to whom "attention must be paid." For, to adopt Mead's vocabulary, if there is a "me" that incorporates the attitude of some group at some level of generality, there is also an "I" that retains a potential freedom of reaction to the "generalized other." This means that life in society is not an automatic genuflection before the superorganic being but, rather, a continuous rearrangement of its categories in the projects of personal being. In the final section of this paper, I will describe this dialectic, which is nothing less than structural transformation, as a symbolic process.

Dialectics of Structure and Action

The word "interest" derives from a Latin impersonal verbal construction meaning "it makes a difference." An interest in something is the difference it makes for someone. Happy etymology, since it runs parallel to the Saussurean definition of conceptual value. The sign is determined as a concept by its differential relation to other signs. The meaning of "blue" is fixed by the co-presence of other terms, such as "green"; if, as is true in many natural languages, there were no "green," the term "blue" would have greater conceptual and referential extension (above, Chapter Four). The same goes for God the Father, a dollar bill, motherhood, or filet mignon: each has a conceptual sense according to its differential place in the total scheme of such symbolic objects. On the other hand, the symbolic object represents a differential interest to various subjects according to its place in their life schemes. "Interest" and "sense" are two sides of the same thing, the sign, as related respectively to persons and to other signs. Yet my interest in something is not the same as its sense.

Saussure's discussion of linguistic value helps make the point, as it is framed on an analogy to economic value. The value of a five-franc piece is determined by the dissimilar objects with which it can be exchanged, such as so much bread or milk, and by other units of currency with which it can be contrastively compared — one franc, ten francs. By these relationships the significance of five francs in the society is constituted. Yet this general and abstract sense is not the value of five francs *to me*. To me, it appears as a specific interest or instrumental value, and whether I buy milk or bread with it, give it away, or put it in the bank, all depends on my particular circumstances and objectives. As implemented by the subject, the conventional value acquires an intentional value, and the conceptual sense an actionable reference.

I am suggesting that the classic distinction between language and speech be expanded into an argument about culture in general — that culture likewise has a dual mode of existence. It appears both in human projects and intersubjectively as a structure or system. Intentionally arranged by the subject, it is also conventionally constituted in the society. But, as a symbolic process, it is differently organized in these two dimensions.

Following Ricoeur's remarks on language, immediately we see that culture-as-lived has a different kind of phenomenal existence than culture-as-constituted. The sign enjoys an actual being, *in praesentia*, only as it is inscribed in human action. As a scheme of relationships between symbolic categories, the "system" is merely virtual. It exists *in absentia*, in the way that the English language, as distinct from people's actual utterances, exists perfectly or as a whole only in the community as a whole. We can say that, as lived, the symbolic fact is a phenomenal "token," whose "type" is its mode of existence in culture-as-constituted. Besides, in culture-as-constituted the sign has an abstract sense, merely signifying, by virtue of all possible relations with other signs, all its possible uses; it is thus "stimulus-free," not bound to any particular worldly referent. But people live in the world as well as by signs, or better, they live in the world by signs, and in action they index the conceptual sense by reference to the objects of their existence. In naive and evidently universal human experience, signs are the names of things "out there." What I am trying to say in a too fancy way was better put by an Indian recounting his experiences with the Canadian government in Ottawa: "An ordinary Indian can never see the 'government.' He is sent from one office to another, is introduced to this man and that, each of whom sometimes claims to be the 'boss,' but he never sees the real government, who keeps himself hidden."

Like Sartre's city, then, the Canadian government is the distant

echo of a Kantian "community." Community is a temporally dis-
junctive judgment, as of a whole having many parts, which are
thus comprehended as mutually determining: "as coordinated
with, not subordinated to one another, not in one direction only
as a series, but reciprocally as in an aggregate." Likewise culture-
as-constituted is a mutual determination of significant forms, and
as the significance of any given form depends on the co-presence
of the others — as God the Father is defined by God the Son, and
vice versa — the "system" is indeed systemic on the condition that
it is synchronic. Structure is a state; but action unfolds as a temporal process. And in intentional action the logic of relationship
between signs lies precisely in their orientation: sequentially and
consequentially, as means and ends of people's purposes. Moreover, I (the others) are constantly putting these signs in various
and contingent relationships. Today I decide to humiliate someone by giving him a gift he cannot repay; no, better perhaps to call
him the name he deserves; or then again, I could review his book.
In structure, the sign is fixed by differential relationships to other
signs; in action, it is variously combined with other signs in impli-
cational relationships.

I have said that the sign is substantialized in action by reference to the world. But, as every such context by which the sign
is substantially defined is unique, so then is every individual's
expression of the culture-as-constituted. Moreover, in their several projects people effect contingent relationships between signs
which are not necessarily those ordained in the culture-as-constituted. Recall Mead's observations on the possible slippage between intentional values and conventional values, figured as a
distinction between the "I" and the "me." Now, it seems incorrect
to deny that people can change their culture, because, as Mead
concluded, that's all they ever do.

The two dimensions of culture are indeed mutually irreducible, but we are now in a position to show that they are dialectically interpenetrable. First, however, some ground rules. The
possibility that a personal arrangement of symbolic forms will
have structural effect clearly depends on many conditions of the
culture-as-constituted: the improvisations that can be logically

287

motivated, as by analogy, metaphor, or the like; the institutional freedom to do so; the position of the actor in a social hierarchy that gives his action structural weight, makes it more or less consequential for others. All such conditions vary from society to society and may be empirically ascertained; but they are not here matters of theoretical principle. Here I am concerned solely with the ways — if you want, the mechanisms — by which structure and project interact as a symbolic process. I identify two such ways: the functional displacement of sign relationships in personal action, and the practical revaluation of signs in the famous "context of the situation."

Action begins and ends in structure, begins from the biography of the individual as a social being to end by the absorption of his action in a cultural practico-inert, the system-as-constituted. But if, in the interim, signs are functionally displaced, set into novel relationships with one another, then by definition the structure is transformed; and in this interim the condition of the culture-as-constituted may actually amplify the consequences of an individual's action. When, during the Vietnam War, some young professor in a large midwestern university thought to adapt the tactics of the civil rights movement to the campus by inventing the "teach-in" on the model of the "sit-in," it politicized the academy in an unprecedented way — not envisioned, for example, by the already-established "free speech" movement (see above, p. 23). It even became appropriate for middle-class students in eastern universities to abandon their Ivy League costumes for what Tom Wolfe calls "prole gear," especially blue jeans and work shirts (see above, Chapter Five). The students metaphorized their changed relations to an adult bourgeois world they had once anticipated inheriting by masquerading in the symbols of society's underclasses. In the upshot, the contrast between youth and adult in the middle classes, before modeled on the distinction between junior and senior executives (the Ivy League style), was transformed into a drama of labor and capital (prole gear). During the 1970s, the effects were largely dissipated by "the system," but things haven't been quite the same since — at least in the universities and the clothing business. The garment industry was once the cutting edge (so to speak) of union militancy, but there is now much more Marx in the university. The university before was the bastion of the established structure, but there is now much more Levi Strauss in the garment industry.

The pragmatic revaluation of signs has to do with their determination in a particular worldly context, process specific to culture in the dimension of action. Signs are notoriously "polysemic" as conceptual values; they have multiple meanings. But as human interests they acquire determinate representations, amounting to some inflection of the conceptual sense. And because the "objective" world to which they are applied has its own refractory characteristics and dynamics, the signs, and by derivation the people who live by them, may then be categorically redefined. I give an exotic example of such meaningful relations between praxis and structure, though I believe the process is commonplace.

When great numbers of ordinary Hawaiian women flocked aboard Captain Cook's ships in 1779 demanding sexual relations with the too-willing British seamen, they were acting on traditional considerations. To sire a child by a god or chief — for such the British were — was all the women wanted. Then, as Hawaiians say, "the bones of the grandparents will live": the kinship connection traced through the half-chiefly child will be the source of many benefits. As it turned out, the common women thus put themselves in opposition to their own chiefs, who, likewise acting on the traditional code, sought to engross all trade with the foreigners, since it represented a *mana* uniquely consistent with their own.

Although the women had made no material stipulations on their paramours, the British seamen knew how to repay the services done them — indeed, defined the women's acts as "services" or "prostitution" by giving them gifts. These gifts, moreover, included iron tools for the kinsmen — fathers, brothers, or husbands — who had gladly brought the women aboard: precisely the goods in which chiefs had interest and to which they demanded a privileged access. Thus was initiated a collective interest between commoner men and women that set them against the Hawaiian powers that be.

In particular, the commoners were set against the tabu system orchestrated by chiefs and priests. And this in a double way. For one, commoner women were consistently tempted, as well as encouraged by the British, to violate the tabus by which the chiefs controlled relations with Cook's ships. Second, the women were less inclined to observe the domestic tabus that separated them from their own men, such as eating with them, and of certain foods reserved as sacrifices to ancestral and greater gods. The men alone could eat these things, because relative to women they had tabu status, which made them kinds of domestic chiefs. But onboard the ships, women tasted the forbidden fruits as well as tabu pork, and in the company of men — the British seamen.

To appropriate Bateson's bon mot: *plus c'est la même chose, plus ça change.* Chiefs, men, and women were all following their traditional self-conceptions and interests. Yet, in this particular pragmatic situation, the entailed definitions of social and ritual categories were revalued and relationships between them transformed. The effects of practice, returning then to structure, would have subsequent meaningful impact on the historic course. Eating with the British men, the Hawaiian women polluted them. The English in general lost their divine status, and a cultural separation set in that was not supposed in the initial interpretation of the foreigners as Hawaiian gods. Moreover, when certain chiefs finally decided in 1819 to abolish the tabu system by eating with women — an apparently spectacular "cultural revolution," as anthropologists have called it, undertaken before the first Christian missionary set foot on the Islands — they were merely ratifying an accomplished fact. The chiefs found many commoners ready to join them, since people had been doing the same for decades.

As I say, the paradigm here suggested does not really require such unusual circumstances. The deployment of received cultural understandings to specific worldly contexts always harbors the possibility that things will never again be the same — precisely because the "objective" things, as well as the social persons, thus represented in the terms of a conventional reason also have their own reasons. The world is under no obligation to correspond to the categories by which it is thought — even if, as Durkheim said, it can only exist for people in the way that it is thought. Thus, in the dialectic of culture-as-constituted and culture-as-lived, we also discover some possibility of reconciling the most profound antinomy of social science theory, that between structure and practice: reconciling them, that is, in the only way presently justifiable — as a symbolic process.

CHAPTER ELEVEN

The Return of the Event, Again

With Reflections on the Beginnings of the Great Fijian War of 1843–1855 Between the Kingdoms of Bau and Rewa[*]

The general aim of this paper is to say something not too banal about the nature of historical events and their relations to cultural orders. It is difficult not to be banal because one can hardly do more than say explicitly what good historians have been doing for a long time. There are two things, however, that make the attempt seem worthwhile. One is the history I deal with, the early modern history of the Fiji Islands. Culturally exotic from the perspective of most academic history, Fiji may nevertheless be a revelatory case, if the unusual structural features then make it easier for us to see their play in the course of events. (At the same time, to keep certain issues comparable, the events I focus on fall into a classic historiographic category: the contingent incidents that set off a great war.) The second reason why this effort at an anthropological history is perhaps worthwhile is the lingering presence, in the disciplines of anthropology and history both, of an exaggerated opposition between "structure" and "event." This antithesis has had too long a run. Probably it is already vestigial in scholarly practice, although in abstract talk it still seems to be the current word. And there is still a problem with practice.

The problem with practice, at least in classic narrative history, is that it rarely gives an account of itself. As one philosopher complains, "no historian spends sleepless nights over the question, 'What is an historical event?'" (Gruner 1969:141).[1] Apart from

* Originally published in Aletta Biersack, ed., *Clio in Oceania: Toward a Historical Anthropology* (Washington, DC: Smithsonian Institution Press, 1991).

the metaphysical elusiveness of historical "causality," this reticence may be because explanation is built into the form itself, the narrative being "one thing because of another" (cf. Ricoeur 1984). Ruth Benedict says somewhere that if deep-sea fish could speak the last thing they would name is water. On the other hand, historians who do not live in the narrative element, notably those who move with the Annales school, must have spent a lot of waking hours puzzling over events in order to invent all those ways of putting them down. I refer, of course, to those who have followed Lucien Febvre and Fernand Braudel in devaluing "evenemential history" — to domesticate the phrase, *enfin*.[2]

The terms of this dismissal of the event make it irreconcilable with "structure" and therefore with a supposedly better history that deals with the latter or at least with "series," phenomena comparable and quantifiable over time (cf. Furet 1982). Braudel's metaphorical turns are well known. Events are merely surface disturbances, foam on the great tides of history. They shine like fireflies whose feeble glow still leaves the surrounding world in darkness; or else like flames that can scarcely be perceived but whose "delusive smoke" fills the minds of the onlookers (Braudel 1980:3, 10–11, 27, etc.).[3] The language is almost equaled in the early structural-anthropological wound literature, with its descriptions of the logical disfigurements inflicted by history on archaic systems of classification. The big difference is that, in the anthropological versions, the contingent events were the flood tides of history, leaving the disassembled jetsam of once-coherent cultural schemes floating in time's wake (Lévi-Strauss 1966; 1963a:101ff.). But this was only an inversion of the same structure. More important, for a certain anthropology, as for a certain history, it seemed that "event" and "structure" could not occupy the same epistemological space. The event was conceived as antistructural, the structure as nullifying the event.

The antithesis could not last; it is giving way to synthesis. The exile of the event was only temporary, partly because (in good Hegelian fashion) it was taking refuge all the time in its opposite. Unless it is totally immobile, a history of the long run has rather the form of a narrative history — in slow motion. "Can the historian detest the event," Ricoeur asks in making this point, "without detesting himself?" (1980:11). Then in France came "the Events" — of 1968. Within a few years two important articles appeared under the same title, "The Return of the Event," one by a historian (Nora 1974), one by a sociologist (Morin 1972a).[4] It was not simply a return to the event. It was a call for the synthesis of event and system. Said Morin: "System and event, should they not in the end be considered together?" (*ibid.*:19).[5]

I would like to associate this essay with the project of synthesis — first by briefly rehearsing the received antithesis of "structure" and "event," to see where the problems lie.

Structure and Event

Reviewing some sympathetic reviews of *The Mediterranean*, Hexter remarks on the sense they all convey of Braudel's inability to achieve a satisfactory liaison between the structural levels — structures of the long run, as imposed geographically, or conjunctural phenomena such as economic cycles — and the more conventional political history of the third part (1979:134ff.). The book "does not solve the historiographical problem that it poses: how to deal with the perennial historiographic difficulty of linking the durable phenomena of history with those that involve rapid change" (*ibid.*:137) — perhaps because the book also re-creates the problem. Once *structure* and *event* are defined in mutually exclusive ways, the one cannot be made intelligible in the terms of the other; all King Philip's men will not be able to put them together again. How shall we reconcile structures that are logical and durable with events that are emotional and ephemeral? The first somehow belong in the order of the real and the efficacious, whereas the apparent potency of events is only illusory. "To the smoke of events," Ricoeur comments, "is opposed the rock of endurance" (1984:105). Indeed, the table of oppositions that could be constructed from Annales texts would be worthy almost of the cosmological dualisms of certain Amazonian peoples. Structure is to event as the social to the individual, the essential to the accidental, the recurrent to the idiosyncratic, the invisible to the visible, the lawful to the aleatory, the quotidian to the extraordinary, the silent to the audible, the anonymous to the authored, the normal to the traumatic, the comparable to the unique, and so on (Braudel 1972:4, 21; 1980:passim; Le Goff 1988c; Nora 1974; Furet 1982; cf. Ricoeur 1980, 1984; L. Stone 1981).

Sometimes the ontological oppositions are backed up by ideological contradictions. Contradictions arise out of the scrambling for the moral high ground in politics and attitudes toward "positivism."[6] Evenemential history is condemned as "merely political." Concerned singularly with the doings of the elite, as if they were the sole movers and shakers, this kind of history carries within itself a hierarchical idea of society — with its cult of power, its idealization of the state, and its implication of a future, as of a past, incarnated by the directors. Whereas the structural histories, in privileging mass, general, and institutional phenomena, can pretend to be populist, at least by comparison (Burguière 1988). This is to say that evenemential history is "merely political" but structural history is truly political. Ironic that in an age where nothing can escape being "political," where everything that is said has a value in terms of "power," which is supposed to be its "meaning" — witness this very criticism of evenemential history — it is ironic, then, that it should be criticized as "merely political." The paradoxes are matched by the suspicions that Annales history may reserve for the experiences of the people. Taken too seriously, their lives and hopes could imperil an historical understanding, just as much as the narrow ideas of Philip II himself:

> We must learn to distrust this history with its still burning passions, as it was felt, described and lived by contemporaries whose lives were as short and as short-sighted as ours. It has the dimensions of their anger, dreams, or illusions. In the sixteenth century, after the true Renaissance, came the Renaissance of the poor, the humble, eager to write, to talk of themselves and of others. This precious mass of paper distorts, filling up the lost hours and assuming a false importance.[7] (Braudel 1972:21)

Moral high-grounding in methodology consists in adopting the stance toward natural science explanations currently fashion-

able in the human sciences. Here it seems that some new historians have been caught by the changing of the avant-garde: they
would now stick evenemential history with the unpopular pretensions of "scientism" — by a certain slide in the older criticism
of its "positivism" (Burguière 1988:139–40; cf. Ricoeur 1980:9).[8]
Originally, however, the structuralist position claimed to be the
scientific one, in invidious contrast to mere chronicles of haphaz-
ard events. Most of the familiar antinomies of structure and event
go back to turn-of-the-century social science. They are to be found
in François Simiand's (1903) article "Méthode historique et science sociale," often invoked as a theoretical charter by Annales
historians. But Simiand denounced the event in the name of a
generalizing social science, which an obsession with the unique
and the individual would render impossible. Today, the same concern for the event, taken as a form of atomistic empiricism — the
event is to history as the atom to physics or the cell to biology —
this concern makes evenemential history the bastion of an old-
fashioned science. *Autres temps, autres moeurs.*

On the other hand, as taken up in the Durkheim group of
which Simiand was a member, his arguments about the unintelli-
gibility of the contingent enjoyed a long success in structural
anthropologies — notably in Radcliffe-Brown's "natural science of
society," a project for developing comparative and lawful statements about social relations, which seemed to require that one
ignore the historical accidents of their expression.[9] The important
comparative point was not that some donned their hats and some
doffed their hats in a house of god but that, either way, one showed
respect. Considered as the account merely of the accidents, historical knowledge was as unessential in principle as it was, for
nonliterate peoples, unattainable in practice. Or again, by another
line of development, Durkheimian ideas were crossed with Saussurean to produce the radical opposition of structure and history
we have noted in the early French structural anthropology. As an
analysis of pure values in which the significance of any sign depended solely on its differential relations to coexisting signs, the
linguistics of Saussure had made simultaneity a condition of its
scientific possibility (Saussure [1915] 1966; cf. M. Sahlins 1981:

297

3–6). Language (*la langue*) could be a systematic object if and only if its concepts were synchronically determined. From this vantage, history appears as an imposition from outside in the form of contingent and dislocating events, a sense of discontinuity amplified by Saussure's treatment of diachrony as the intersection of phonetic change and syntactic relations. Transposed then into continental anthropology, "structure" and "history" became contending forces on the field of society, locked in a "constant struggle," a "repeated battle," between order and disorder. Here is structure always valiantly but never altogether successfully trying to repair the damages to its ancient harmonies inflicted by untoward events (cf. Lévi-Strauss 1966:155, 157, 232, etc.).[10]

Paradoxically, however, from the same structuralisms that would make "system" and "event" into contraries, that have the one precluding the other, from these structuralisms it follows that there is no event without system. For the definition of a "something-happened" as an event, as well as its specific historic consequences, must depend on the structure in place. All it takes to see this is a little goodwill. If, as Saussure says, there is no "inner bond" between the nature of a phonetic change and the effect it may have on the system (1966:87), it follows that the evenemential character of the change, as opposed simply to its phonetic properties, is the work of the system. The same kind of thing is implied by Lévi-Strauss's dictum that "there is always a mediator between *praxis* and practices, namely the conceptual scheme by the operation of which matter and form, neither with any independent existence, are realized as structures, that is as entities which are both empirical and intelligible" (1966:130). It does not seem to stretch this idea too far to make it out as a description of the constitution of historical events by cultural structures. For it speaks to the transformation of sui generis happenings, having their own properties and reasons, to the order of culture in which these properties acquire a determinate mode of existence. And the implication of the one and the other, Saussure and Lévi-Strauss, is that events become such by the meaningful integration of material circumstances:

The event is at once produced and received by the community in which it happens and to understand its existence and modalities it is necessary to know the cognitive and symbolic system of this community.... It is not a question of some extreme relativism, according to which events would be purely ideal or symbolic, but rather of seriously taking the symbolic into account: one cannot separate something in the event that would be "what really, materially happened" from something else that would be the meaning the actors and spectators attributed to it; the two are indissociable. (Molino 1986:264)

No event without system. Consider the radical case of exogenous events, phenomena that erupt in a given society from nature or another society, such as an earthquake or Captain Cook sailing into some Hawaiian bay. What kind of event this may be, what historic significance it has, cannot be predicated simply from the "objective properties" of the happening. The specific historical effects turn on the way those properties are taken up in the culture in question, a way that is never the only one possible. I am rehearsing here some ideas more fully expressed elsewhere, with the aim of developing further an anthropological concept of the historical event (M. Sahlins 1981, 1985a; 1988). For that matter, I am merely putting into another context Evans-Pritchard's reflections on why the Azande, who know very well that it is a natural disposition of elephants to trample people's gardens, nevertheless when it happens will hold some neighbor or affine responsible and accuse him of witchcraft (1937). Evans-Pritchard said the response was intelligible, one placed the blame on a personal enemy, for although it might be a property of elephants to trample gardens, it is not a property of elephants to trample *your* garden. To which one might add, neither is it a property of elephants to trample *property.* Once introduced into the human domain, given a definite cultural value, the natural phenomenon will assume some particular effect, as orchestrated by the relations of the particular cultural scheme. The natural properties of the phenomenon are clearly necessary conditions for the effect, but they do not account for its historical form. There is no adequate relation between an elephant trampling a garden and an accusation of witchcraft: the latter does not follow logically from the former — except by way of Azande culture.

In the same way, the Thessalians held that Poseidon made the gorge through which the Peneus River runs; and so would anyone, Herodotus says, who believed Poseidon was responsible for earthquakes (*Hist.*:7.129). The famous Lisbon earthquake of 1757 had a different theological significance. But if these Iberian tremors shook the philosophes' panglossian confidence in Divine Providence, is this because they differed from the shocks of Poseidon by their intensity on the Richter scale? Of course the cultural effects of earthquakes are not confined to mental perturbations. The scale of the social catastrophe likewise varies according to the structures in place, as was literally true of Mexico City in 1985:

> While many buildings, both large and small, performed well during the earthquake, 5,728 buildings in the city were damaged.... The report noted that a high percentage of damage occurred in buildings 6 to 17 stories high. It said the natural period of motion — the time to complete a vibration — of such buildings was amplified by the ground motion of the drained lake bed on which Mexico City lies. Those buildings and the earth's movement had periods of motion that were roughly equal, about two seconds, resulting in serious damage. Taller and shorter buildings were less likely to be affected, the study found. (*New York Times*, 27 Sept. 1987)

Then again, an upheaval of exactly the same force in the same place would have had other consequences when it was inhabited by Chichamec hunters and gatherers. "Does the physical ever affect the social," Marc Bloch asked, "unless its operations have been prepared, abetted, and given scope by factors which themselves have already derived from man?" (1953:24).

Notice that the too-simple dualism of "event" and "structure" is causing conceptual problems. What is generally called "event" is itself complex: at once a sui generis phenomenon with its own force, shape, and causes, and the significance these qualities acquire in the cultural context, significance in the double sense of

300

meaning and importance. In fact, this is an argument in three terms — happenings, structures, and events — in which the event is the relation between the other two (M. Sahlins 1985a:xiv, 153).[11] And while events emanating from natural or foreign causes can show this complexity *en clair*, endogenous events, developing within a given historical order, are constructed in the same general way. They likewise involve a work of cultural signification, which can be similarly described as the appropriation of local phenomena that have their own reasons *in* and *as* an existing cultural-historical scheme. Let us simply substitute *incident* for *happening* in the above argument about exogenous events: an endogenous event is a relation between an incident and a structure. And again, the same kind of incident arising in different societies will have different historical consequences — think of Chinese, French, and American student protests of recent decades. The historical significance of a given incident — its determinations and effects as "event" — depends on the cultural context.

We shall be dealing here with such internally generated events, events that developed out of incidents involving certain Fijian chiefs into the greatest war the islands had ever seen. Yet, from the perspective of the larger structure or the system of relations between the kingdoms whose destinies were put at stake, the decisive actions and subjective dispositions of these chiefs were at least relatively autonomous. They were not simply expressions or (in Bourdieu's term) "executions" of the larger system. Indeed, in common historiographic practice what makes an act or incident an event is precisely its contrast to the going order of things, its disruption of that order.

Here at least is a broad area of agreement among historians, philosophers, anthropologists, sociologists: the event is "a difference," as Paul Veyne says, "something that stands out against a background of uniformity ... a thing we could not know *a priori*" (1984:5). It is a difference and it makes a difference. The event is a *"coupure"* (Bastide 1980:822) — and not merely an "epistemological break" this time; for we know the event by the change that ensues in the existing order (cf. Teggart 1960:18, Morin 1972a:18, Jayawardena 1987:41, Gruner 1969, Moles 1972:90). "Once the

301

event is produced, nothing is any more as before" (Molino 1986: 55). All the scholars I have cited and many others would consent to distinguish events from actions or happenings that repeat themselves, from reproduction of the order. Not every action is an historical event. In a physical sense, of course, every human act qualifies as an event — but this is not physics. A human action is a meaningful value, having existence and effect that cannot be determined from its physical-empirical properties. Let us recall famous examples: the difference between a wink and a blink or between moving from point A to point B and "going home." And although they may be equally physical happenings, actions are not all alike historically, insofar as they have greater or less effect on a state of affairs. "History is historical," Ricoeur puts it, "because there are unparalleled actions which count and others which do not count; men who carry weight and others who do not; a lost battle, a leader who dies too soon ... the result being a changed destiny" (1965:90; cf. Veyne 1984:31). In the general category of human actions, historical events are a subclass only, consisting of those actions that change the order of things.[12]

We see how endogenous events resemble the exogenous since both arise in circumstances eccentric to the structural schemes they affect. By inference from recent reflections of historians, one might say that events articulate phenomena of different levels or registers, such as the individual and the social, actions and institutions, the short term and the long term, the local and the global (Nora 1974, Vovelle 1988, Pomian 1988; cf. Gallie 1968, Ricoeur 1984:131, 193). Alternatively, social scientists speak of the intersection of different systems or subsystems: Edgar Morin, for example, for whom modifying events are those "which result from meetings or interactions between a principle of order or an organized system, on one side, and on the other, another principle of order or organized system, or any sort of perturbation" (1972a:17). Such interacting systems may be independent of one another — as culture and nature (earthquakes again) — or they may be only relatively autonomous — as individual talents and class relations (cf. Sartre 1968). But what then marks all these ways of conceiving the event are the discontinuities in the properties and the determinants of the phenomena so articulated. Hence the Big Question: How are these incommensurables related to produce the historical process? How can a momentary incident, for example, resume and carry forth a whole historical trajectory of the relations between nations? How can these social totalities be reduced to individualities, thus allowing personal fates to shape the collective destinies? Such are fundamental enigmas of the event.

The problem is precisely that the one cannot be reduced to the other, the structure to the event nor vice versa, and yet each is somehow determining the other. The structures and relations of higher order whose history this may be — the warring kingdoms in our Fijian examples — their characteristics as such do not specify the unique circumstances or individual biographies through which their history is worked out. If the destiny of the totality is subjected to the dispositions of the individual, still there is no adequate relation in either direction between the politics and the persons in the sense that neither can satisfactorily motivate the description of the other. Sartre said it was true that Valéry was a petit-bourgeois intellectual, but not every petit-bourgeois intellectual is a Valéry (1968). Or in the terms of another discourse: neither the nominalist argument that there are only individuals nor the realist respect for the coercive powers of the cultural order turns out to be a good historical explanation. To paraphrase Ricoeur, history unfolds as a synthesis of the heterogeneous (1984:216).

Just so in the history we are about to consider, the fates of Fijian kingdoms are integrated in the ambitions and disputes of certain ruling chiefs, a story that will hinge moreover on critical escapades of adultery and the roaming of a fat pig through a particular village at a particular time. Here is a history of war with all the inevitabilities of Cleopatra's nose and the geese that saved Rome. One could even speak of a dialectic of the heterogeneous. A higher order of structure — the relations between kingdoms — momentarily devolves upon certain circumstantial relations between particular chiefs, to be reconfigured in the terms and dynamics of this lower level, where it is besides subject to various accidents including those of personality, to emerge finally from the "structure of the conjuncture" in the changed state of an all-out war. The event develops as a reciprocal movement between higher and lower orders, a translation of each into the register of the other. Clearly, this is a work of signification. The metamorphoses are tropes. The equation between the action of a person and the fate of a group, for instance, is a logic of synecdoche — the claim of the chief to embody his people. Or again, in the Fijian system, adultery with a chief's wife is a metaphor of usurpation. But if history is thus a kind of poetics, it is again structurally grounded. Without certain logical relations in the cultural order such tropes would neither be formulable nor intelligible. The key problem will be to find the structural motivations of the transpositions.

Finally, our Fijian history will reveal another kind of "synthesis of the heterogeneous." It concerns what historians call the intersection of different causal series in the event, the coincidence of different chains of determination. Without denying this element of "chance," the argument here will be that something more than "intersection" is involved in the historical relations between series. These series are themselves put into relations by the thinking subjects in whom they intersect so as to form complex structures which then may have synergetic effects. In the incidents about to be described, hostilities between rival kingdoms get linked into a fraternal struggle for succession to one of the kingships, so that, in prosecuting his personal ambitions in the latter field, a certain prince exacerbates the oppositions of the former. Effecting a correlation between different conflicts, the incident adds the interests of the one to the energies of the other. Such structures of synergy, revealing the invisible significances of an event that "testifies less to what it is than to what it sets off" (Nora 1974:299–300), thereby help us to understand the disproportions so commonly observed between the incident and the consequent — historiographic hallmark of the event, which is another formulation of its enigmas.

The Incidents

The cryptic entry for 11 January 1841 in the diary of the Methodist missionary Thomas Jaggar reads, "Q. driven away & other
chiefs." Normally stationed upriver at Rewa (Lomanikoro), Jaggar
happened to be visiting the town of Suva on the Viti Levu coast
and so was able to record a fateful insult suffered by the high
Rewa chief Ratu Qaraniqio, by all accounts the first in a series of
events that issued in the great war of 1843–1855 between the
kingdoms of Rewa and Bau.[13] Since the efficacy of such events
consists in what they led to — as reciprocally the magnitude of the
sequel gives them notoriety in historical memory — a word should
be said about the organization and dimensions of the war.

In the mid-nineteenth century, Bau and Rewa were the most
powerful states in the Fiji Islands (Map 11.1).[14] Although the war
they fought engaged allies from far and wide and seemed to have
the rule of all Fiji at stake, the main arena of battle was the popu-
lous Rewa Delta that lay between them (Map 11.2). The Bau confederacy was centered on the small islet of that name just off the
coast to the northeast. Encircled by stone-lined jetties sheltering
large oceangoing canoes, with much of its twenty-three acres
covered by the houses of some three thousand inhabitants, Bau
was not much more than an offshore naval base on the flank of the
fertile Rewa Delta. Yet, for at least a century, its great fleets of
warriors had been terrorizing Fiji from one end to the other: from
the Lau Islands in the east to the west coast of Viti Levu, with
notable forays also along the north and south coasts of Vanua
Levu and through the channels of the Rewa Delta. The terror
had successfully spread Bau's political writ. By the beginning of
the war, the Bau confederacy could be reckoned as including the
islands of the central Koro Sea (Lomaiviti), several lands in and
around the northern and eastern sides of the delta, the neighboring island of Viwa, certain important warrior peoples called
Waimaro in the northeast of Viti Levu, as well as outlying places
such as Suva and Nausori. The foods, wealth, and men of these
subordinate lands, transported in Bau's famous canoe fleets, were
put to the service of her increasingly hegemonic ambitions. Unlike
the other main eastern Fijian states, but more like the mountain

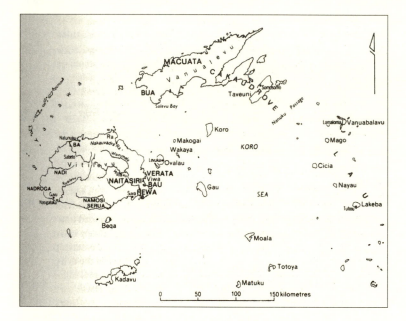

Map 11.1 Fiji Islands.

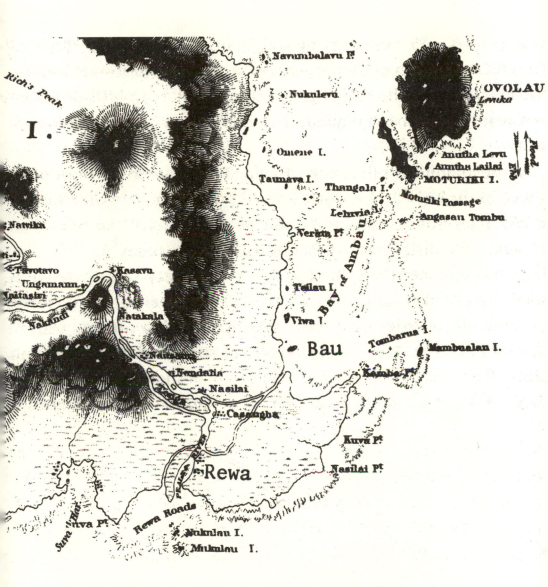

Map 11.2 Detail of Southeast Viti Levu, from "Chart of the Viti Group or Feejee Islands" (Wilkes 1844).

lands, Bau was indeed led by warrior-kings, those of the title Vunivalu, "Root of War" (or "God of War"), men for whom violence was a condition of their being — according to Fijian conceptions, it ran in their blood. Such a man was Tānoa, the war king of Bau who initiated the conflict with Rewa, as also his famous son Cakobau, who actively plotted and led it (cf. Scarr 1970).[15]

In double contrast to Bau, Rewa was a kingdom of established status and of agricultural rather than maritime orientation. Its ruling sacerdotal king, the Roko Tui Dreketi, descended in the collateral line from the ancient rulers of Verata on the east coast of Viti Levu, and Verata was the homeland of high nobility in eastern Fiji. The Rewa confederacy was concentrated in the delta, in low-lying swampy lands well known for the production of the giant "horse taro" (*via kana* [Fijian]; *Crystosperma chamissionis*). Connected by causeways and river channels, the numerous villages of the confederacy were strongly fortified. Their surrounding moats, earthworks, and timber palisades made them virtually impregnable. Most of these Rewa villages were within five to ten kilometers of the Rewa capital (Lomanikoro), a town also of about three thousand inhabitants in the mid-nineteenth century (Parry 1977).

To compare little things with great ones, this Polynesian War, like the Peloponnesian War, thus joined a major land power in prolonged struggle with a major sea power, each at the head of a considerable league of allied states — although, in the Fijian case, the sea power won out. Bau won, but not before the bloodiest and most destructive war Fiji had ever known, in the opinion of the Wesleyan missionaries who were witnesses to its sufferings. In scale, duration, and casualties it was probably the greatest war ever fought by any island people of this ocean. And it all began when the Rewa chief Ratu Qaraniqio attempted to requisition a pig — an act he could justify as a kinship right — in Suva, a Bauan village of no great account.

There is a large area of agreement in the principal documents about what happened in Suva that day in January 1841, as well as about the attacks on Suva by Rewa that followed. The primary sources are also in accord about the significance of these incidents in setting off the long war between Bau and Rewa, or at least these incidents plus one other: the flight of the ranking wife of Tānoa, the Bau war king, to Rewa in 1843, together with certain secondary wives, all of whom were distributed among the chiefs of Rewa.

I should note that the sources I am relying on are of several kinds:

First, reports of missionaries at or near the scene of the events, at or near the time they occurred. These are principally the letters and journals of John Hunt and Thomas Jaggar (J. Hunt, "Fiji Journals"; Jaggar, Diaries; Methodist Missionary Society [hereafter MMS], In-Letters).

Second, accounts of other Europeans living elsewhere in Fiji during the period, including missionaries such as James Calvert (Williams and Calvert 1859, vol. 2; Calvert, Journals) and Joseph Waterhouse ([1866] 1978) as well as people associated with the bêche de mer trade such as Mary Wallis ([1851] 1983). Not all these sources are independent: Wallis got a lot from Hunt, and other missionaries from Hunt and Jaggar both.

Third, Fijian oral traditions of the war recorded several decades later in the vernacular (Anonymous 1891; Toganivalu, "Ai Tukutuku kei Bau"; NLC/TR, Tailevu South) or in English (Hocart, Fijian Field Notes [hereafter FFN], 2507–513, 2564–71; Wall 1919). Toganivalu appears to get his information from the anonymous account in *Na Mata* (Anonymous 1891) and may be responsible in turn for the Bau Lands Commission history (NLC/TR, Tailevu South). In general, the Fijian traditions — including those collected by Hocart and Wall from Suva people — are consistent with the earlier European chronicles, but much more detailed and interesting.

Ratu Qaraniqio — hereafter Ratu Qara — the Rewa chief driven off by the Suvans, was the younger brother of Kania, the ruling king (Figure 11.1; Roko Tui Dreketi).[16] Often contending with his royal brother, whose principal wife he had recently slept with, Ratu Qara was the greatest fighter among the Rewa chiefs: a "man of war" (*tamata ni valu*), as the Rewans said, whose bellicose

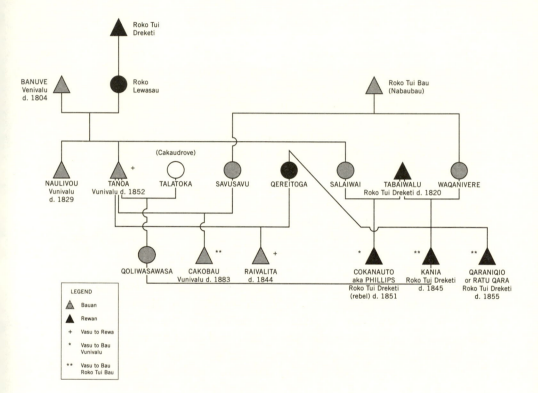

Figure 11.1 Relations of Bau and Rewa ruling families.

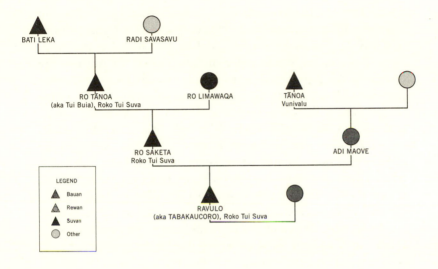

Figure 11.2 Suva ruling line. After Hocart FN 2509–10; Wall 1919; Cargill (1977:179).

disposition was clearly related to his political ambition.[17] What happened to him at Suva in 1841 goes something like this: Accompanied by a retinue of other chiefs and followers, he was making his way homeward from a journey to Nadrogâ in southwestern Viti Levu. It is said the Rewans were at first feasted by the Suva people and only afterward did Ratu Qara spy the large pig wandering about the village and demand it be seized. (Such is the historical fame of this pig that its name, "Tamavua," has come down to us, along with its description as a prize red porker, *vuaka damu*.) Inasmuch as Suva was a Bauan land, Ratu Qara's demand was not arbitrary but within his rights as a uterine nephew (*vasu*) of the Roko Tui Bau, the sacerdotal king of Bau. On the other hand, Ravulo, the young ruler of Suva (Roko Tui Suva) — the owner of the pig according to some — was likewise a uterine nephew to Bau (*vasu ki Bau*), but to the paramount king Tânoa (Figure 11.2). Ravulo resented and resisted the Rewa chief's attempt to take the pig. There followed a fracas in which clubs and spears were used, and some Rewans were injured. According to Suva tradition, the one Rewa fatality occurred late that night when a Suva scouting party fell on Ratu Qara's people encamped at Laucala Bay. Tradition also has it that Ratu Qara was personally insulted when, escaping from the fight, he climbed up the mast of his canoe, whence a comb fell from his head, which was picked up and broken by a Suva warrior — an insult, this, because of the association with the chief's head, to which the Suvans added the injury of offering him a piece of firewood and daring him to come down and burn down their village (Hocart FFN:2507–508; Wall 1919; Jaggar, Diaries:25 June 1842; MMS, In-Letters, Hunt:6 Nov. 1846; J. Hunt, Journals:following 19 Oct. 1845; Waterhouse [1866] 1978:110–12; Wallis [1851] 1983:162ff.).

In months to come, Ratu Qara would have revenge by destroying Suva, thus parlaying the quarrel over the porker to a major crisis in the relations between the kingdoms of Rewa and Bau. But even by itself, the affair of the pig may have contributed to a deterioration in these relations. Months before Suva was actually attacked, Jaggar was reporting from Rewa that all sailing between that place and Bau was prohibited (Diaries:7 Feb. 1842). Some days later came the more ominous note in his journal of, "rumour of war with Bau being near" (*ibid.*:15 Feb. 1842). The rumor was premature. However, twice in the next fourteen months Ratu Qara mounted major assaults on Suva, the second resulting in a massacre.

The first time the Rewans were beaten off, despite the fact that they mobilized fighting men from all over the delta. Hocart's informants (seventy years after the event) listed many of the traditional lands of the Rewa confederacy in the attacking force (Noco, Dreketi, Toga, Burebasaga, Vutia, Naselai, Nakelo, and Tokatoka; Hocart FFN:2508, 2564). This late tradition might seem elaborated were it not for Jaggar's contemporary notice of an army of "perhaps 2000" leaving Rewa to attack Suva on 23 June 1842 (Diaries). Jaggar was still there two days later to record the return of the embarrassed Rewan host. Unable to penetrate the enemy town, they had suffered five dead and some wounded. Suva had been too well fortified, too well supplied with ammunition — and too well resolved to defend itself:

> The Suva people said to the chiefs [of Rewa], "We shall not run away or be driven away, for where shall we run to? — to the reef? We are not fish but men, this is our land, and if we die we will die in our town. We have but one burial ground and it is this, our town."[18] (*Ibid.*:25 June 1842)

The sequel reveals something Fijian about whose war it was anyhow. Chagrined at the defeat, Ratu Qara was anxious to return to the attack immediately, but, says Jaggar, "he does not seem to be seconded or encouraged by any" (*ibid.*). It took the Rewa chief almost a year to regroup the Rewan forces.[19] Just as the cause of the conflict appears as an insult to the chief's person, so the effective interests in the war were the interests of ruling chiefs.

Another incident during the lull between the battles of Suva affords further insights into the aristocratic politics of war. This was in August 1842. The Rewa first king, Roko Tui Dreketi, asked formal permission of his brother-in-law, the Bau war king Tânoa, to attack the Naitasiri people, who were remotely allied to Bau (*vanua vakaBau*). Such was the customary "chiefly practice" (*tovo vakaturaga*). In this instance, Tānoa refused to sanction the attack and it never came off (*ibid.*:21 Aug. 1842); but the scrupulousness of the Rewa king, his observance of the properties, makes a nice contrast to the behavior of his younger brother Ratu Qara. The contrast expresses the broad Fijian opposition between constituted authority and the pretensions of violence, which these brothers would demonstrate several times over in the events that followed. Ratu Qara had already ignored chiefly custom by not asking leave of the Bau rulers to attack Suva — thus defying the extension of their power in the lower delta.

Arriving at Suva on the morning of 7 April 1843, Jaggar's missionary colleague John Hunt found the town had been reduced to ashes by a large Rewan force the day before (MMS, In-Letters, J. Hunt:12 June 1843). The negotiations and rituals required to mount an attack of this scale may help account for the many months it took to bring it off. In addition to recognized lands of the Rewan confederacy, tradition has it that the attacking army was bolstered by warriors from Soloira and Viria to the north, by former allies of Suva from the south coast who had been seduced by Ratu Qara's "gifts and promises," and by a cannon from *L'Aimable Joséphine* — a French ship taken off Bau in 1834 manned by Charlie Pickering, a White friend of the Rewa chiefs (Wall 1919; Hocart, FFN:2508–509). The cannon had no particular effect — or at least nowhere near the effect of a conspiracy between the Rewans and the Lomaivuna people, who were in Suva at the time attending a feast and turned upon their hosts at a decisive moment. They are supposed to have opened the fortifications to the besieging army. The survivors of the ensuing slaughter fled upland and inland to an old village site. A day or two later they sent a whale tooth of submission (*i soro*) asking for safe passage for the women and children (*nai katikati*). The request was granted. But the Suva noncombatants were set upon as they were making their way to safety — a violation of the surrender rituals that at least one commentator believed unprecedented in Fijian warfare (Wall 1919). The total casualties suffered by the Suvans were also unusually heavy; estimates vary from four hundred killed in the retreat alone (*ibid.*) to Jaggar's figure, probably more reliable, of one hundred dead in all (MMS, In-Letters, Jaggar:29 May 1843). In the same context, Jaggar tells of a new "rumour of war between Rewa and Bau, because of the destruction of Suva by the Rewa people" (*ibid.*).

Within two or three years, while the war was raging full out, the opinion that it had originated in the destruction of Suva was settling into the status of an historical tradition. Jaggar's report of this opinion, however, is marked by the italics of his own skepticism: "Tānoa, who is carrying on this war, is exceedingly attached to the Chief of Suva, whose town the Rewa people destroyed, and on which account *it is said* the war was commenced" (MMS, In-Letters, Jaggar:5 July 1845; cf. Hocart, FFN:2509–510). Still, contemporary documents confirm that Tānoa and his son Cakobau were furious about the attacks on Suva, the more so since the Rewans embellished their defiance of Bau with other little treacheries (MMS, In-Letters, Jaggar:29 May 1843; Williams and Calvert 1859, vol. 2:175). It seems that the Rewans sent their envoy to Bau — a formal title, Mata ki Bau, held by the Navolau clan — to report officially the destruction of the town to Tānoa, while assuring him that the women and children had been spared. The envoy was himself deceived and embarrassed by the subsequent news of the slaughter of the Suva innocents. According to traditions current to the present day, this was the reason for his betrayal of Rewa (Lomanikoro) to the besieging Bau army in December 1845. But we are not there yet. In fact, Bau did not open the war with Rewa until late November 1843, nearly eight months after the destruction of Suva that was presumably the cause of war.[20] Suva was indeed a cause, but not sufficient to move the Bau king.

Reverend Hunt recalled Tānoa's hesitations, even though the Suva massacre had made "a deep impression on Bau":

> I remember having a conversation with Tānoa on the subject about this time, and he assured me that something further must be done by Rewa before hostilities would commence. He observed with his characteristic calmness: They have destroyed one town, but never

mind, let them destroy another, and then we will fight. (Journals: following 19 Oct. 1845)

Likewise, according to wide report, Cakobau, who was already acting as war king for his father, left Bau for Lakeba (Lau) at this time in order to avoid opening hostilities with Rewa (*ibid.*; cf. Williams and Calvert 1859, vol. 2:175–76). Hunt's colleagues Thomas Williams and James Calvert duly record the arrival of the Bau fleet at Lakeba on 21 May 1843, "to receive the homage and riches of [the Lau paramount] Tuinayau and his people" (T. Williams 1931, vol. 1:162–63). Here let it be noted that Lau, which was tributary to Bau, was a great source of Fijian wealth, especially of the maritime goods the Bauans could use in Viti Levu to reward their fighting allies and "turn" the allies of their enemies to their own cause. In view of the strategy Cakobau later employed in the Rewa Delta, which was to undermine the towns of the Rewa confederacy by a combination of force and bribery until the Rewa capital Lomanikoro was bereft of all support, this voyage to Lau could be interpreted as something more than a political respite.[21]

All the same, there were good reasons why the Bau warrior-rulers should show customary forebearance (*vosota ga*) with Rewa. Himself a *vasu*, or privileged uterine nephew of the royal house of Rewa, even as his wife was the sister of the Rewa ruler, Tānoa represented the party of Rewa within Bau (see Figure 11.1). In 1832, Tānoa had been deposed as war king and sent into exile by a faction that included certain paternal half-brothers (whose mother was from the island of Nairai) and the clan of the former war kings of Bau — rebels who could give as the reason for their usurpation the favoritism that Tānoa had openly and secretly shown for Rewa, especially in the distribution of wealth (Wilkes 1845, vol. 3:63–64; Cross, Extracts of the Journal:3 May 1838; Eagleston, "Ups and Downs," pt. 1:439). The rebels held power until 1837, using it to launch several attacks on Rewa towns, whereas Tānoa himself took refuge in Rewa (after Cakaudrove), whence he was carried in triumph back to Bau after his son Cakobau had routed his enemies.[22] In sum, the relations subsisting between the Bau war king and his kinsman the Rewa ruler Kania were running against an outbreak of hostilities between them.

Reverend Hunt picked up another reason for Bau's unwillingness to avenge Suva:

> A Bau chief told me the people of Bau do not wish to fight as they shall gain nothing by it. If they fight at Somosomo [Cakaudrove] or Lakemba [Lau] they obtain riches, but Rewa being another kingdom [like Bau] they have nothing to expect from them. So covetousness has a lot to do with Fijian wars. (Journals:13 Nov. 1843)

Nevertheless, for weeks Hunt had been noting the palpable tension and the preparations for war in Bau (Lyth, Letters [Hunt to Lyth]: 21 Oct. 1843, 9 Nov. 1843). And within the month the Bauans — or, more precisely, the ruling house of warrior-kings — had found good reason to declare total war on Rewa. Moreover, for the next twelve years Cakobau had good enough reason to keep it going: indeed, covetousness of a kind, though rather a lust for domination (*libido dominandi*) in the Augustinian sense. Soon after the war began, Hunt was reporting that "the idea of universal domination of the Fiji islands" was growing in Bau (following 19 Oct. 1845).

This is one of those historical moments that are easily imagined otherwise (cf. Aron 1981). Desultory war had been going on with Rewa for decades — or at least a kind of warfare that, if not exactly desultory, was always terminable in a relatively short time and short too of total victory and defeat. But now something occurred that not only exacerbated the tensions over Suva but completely ruptured the kinship of Bau and Rewa ruling families and led to war in the worst form known to Fiji: a "war of the chiefs...in which the leading chiefs on either side [that is, on one side or the other] must be killed before it can terminate" (Hunt, Journals:following 19 Oct. 1845). We need not be too cynical, then, about Cakobau's vaulting ambition of "universal domination," supposing it was the true cause of the all-out war on Rewa. The converse is equally plausible: total war fueled the chief's total ambitions, made them conceivable, whereas the war itself developed from an all-out insult. The turn toward a war of chiefs came when Tānoa's principal wife, Qereitoga, accused of adultery in Bau, fled along with several secondary wives to refuge with her brother Kania, first king of Rewa. We do not know with whom Qereitoga contracted this (reputed) liaison, or why; there is only reason to suspect that she took the initiative, as her own son by Tānoa, Raivalita, was losing ground as potential successor to his half-brother Cakobau. The sequel to her flight was even more significant: Qereitoga and her co-wives were redistributed among Rewan notables (*ibid.*; MMS, In-Letters, Hunt:6 Nov. 1846; Williams and Calvert 1859, vol. 2:175–76; Waterhouse [1866] 1978: 110–12; Wallis [1851] 1983:165–66). The claim of John Hunt — our principal source in the matter — that the Rewan appropriation of the women "was contrary to all customs of Fiji" may be misleading inasmuch as the seduction of royal women was a recurrent sign of usurpation. Hence the sequitur in the Hunt text: "this was too gross an insult" for Tānoa.

Indeed, insult as it may have been, the sacerdotal king of Rewa was generally more measured in his conduct than these warrior-kings of Bau, whose functions took them beyond the boundaries and proprieties of their fellow men (M. Sahlins 1987). When Bau sent a message taking leave of Rewa, breaking off all relations, the Rewans answered by offering to atone ceremonially (*i soro*) for their wrongs. The Rewa move was appropriate and normal according to custom; but it was too late, observed Reverend Hunt. Tānoa and Cakobau

> had passed the Rubicon, and the malignant perseverance of the father, the ambitious perseverance of the son, to say nothing of the abilities and resources of each, rendered it quite unlikely that anything less than the blotting out of Rewa from the list of independent states in Fiji could satisfy them. Such was the origin and commencement of this destructive war. (Journals:following 19 Oct. 1845)

Interpretations

As is true of more famous wars, the causes of this Polynesian war did not lie so much in the particular incidents that set it off as in the larger and longer situation, the global relations of hostility already existing between Bau and the great Fijian states of noble lineage, Rewa notably. In the same way, the truce between Athens and Sparta had been broken by a series of local disputes, disputes in which their interests clashed, "but the real reason for the war," Thucydides said, "is most likely to be disguised by such an argument. What made the war inevitable was the growth of Athenian power and the fear which this caused in Sparta" (*Peloponnesian War* I.23). For a long time, Bau likewise had been expanding against the established Fijian kingdoms. If the Rewa rulers insisted on provoking the Bau war king, if they chose to make a demonstration of their own might by reducing Suva, which was after all a Bauan town in their own backyard, was it not in reaction to the historic growth of Bauan power? Fear of Bau, yes, but also envy, exasperation, and contempt for these parvenu kings whose treacherous methods were fair testimony to their dubious ancestry.

The growth of Bauan power had been going on longer than the introduction of muskets into Fijian wars in 1808 by the notorious Charlie Savage, to whom Westerners beginning with the early Methodist missionaries have been too quick to attribute Bau's successes (cf. France 1969:21; Campbell 1980). This is not the place to document the antiquity of Bau's expansion; perhaps it will be enough to note that years before Savage, Bau was controlling the main islands of the Koro Sea (Lomaiviti) and large Bauan armies were fighting along the coast of Vanua Levu. Sometime in the latter half of the eighteenth century, one such army, complemented by warriors from northeast Viti Levu (Nakorotuba), had successfully stormed the inland fortress of Kedekede at Lakeba, Lau. Indeed, in the list of Fijian place names collected by Captain Cook from Tongans in 1777 — perhaps the earliest European notice of Fijian politics — only two are mentioned from the area in and around the main island of Viti Levu: Bau and Rewa.[23] Notably not mentioned is Verata. The ancient hearth of Fijian aristocracy, including the ruling clan of Rewa, Verata once enjoyed a hegemony of a certain kind over much of eastern Fiji. The kind in question was legitimate descent, in contrast to hegemony by conquest. Verata people still say theirs was a "government of [the] blood" (*matanitū ni dra*), owing to the descent of their sacred

319

king (Rātū) in the senior line of high Fijian nobility, by contrast
to Bauans who know only a "government of force" (*matanitū ni
kaukauwa*) or a "government of war" (*matanitū ni valu*). We shall
see that Bau royalty was the issue of a misalliance of a woman of
the Verata noble stock — thus a bastard sister's son (*vasu*). The
genealogical irregularity is the counterpart of a customary political conduct that likewise transcends the established norms. Bau
is famous for treachery: *vere vakaBau*, "conspiracy à la Bau," is a
proverbial phrase in Fiji.

The war between Bau and Rewa was thus generations old before it began. The great Fijian kingdoms "have shown no disposition to submit to Bau rule," observed an American trader in 1832,
"consequently war with them is going on and has been for years"
(Eagleston, "Ups and Downs," pt. 1:385). If war was still immi-
nent in 1843, a Thucydidean view of its causes would seem appropriate: that it could not be sufficiently explained by the relatively
minor events that unleashed it. And although the like has been
said of many great wars since the Peloponnesian, it is not always
recognized that neither would the general correlation of the social forces explain the events. Nothing so specific as history follows from the state of hostilities prevailing between Bau and
Rewa. It does not follow that in January 1841, Ratu Qara would
be insulted in Suva on his way home from Nadrogā; that he would
persist in seeking revenge; that in April 1843 Suva would be betrayed by Lomaivuna visitors to a besieging Rewa army; that soon
after, the wife of the Bau war king would commit adultery, flee to
Rewa, and take up another liaison there. Conversely, it is not self-
evident from the nature or sequence of these events why they had
such remarkable consequences. The effect on the larger relations
between states was distinctive as well as decisive: a "war of chiefs,"
war to the end, unlike all the previous wars.[24] System and event
seem indissolubly joined in the kind of double indeterminacy
remarked earlier. Each is responsible for the existence of the
other, yet neither can account for the characteristics of the other;
thus, to say that the situation was ripe for war does not do away
with the event. On the contrary, it opens an issue of even greater
scope than at first appears, because the whole historic course of

the war — not just its beginnings, but every strategic movement and engagement — will likewise turn on the contingencies of person and action. Clearly, we need to know how the higher-order relations, as of Bau and Rewa, are relayed into practice, in a way that allows the actions of certain persons, such as Ratu Qara and Tânoa, to represent the larger system — and thereby to configure its destiny.

It may help to have some names. Let us call these relays between the larger system and action *mediations*. Mediations would be the covering term for both the reductions from system to action or *instantiation* and the amplifications from action to system or *totalization*. Instantiation refers to the embodiment of generals in particulars, as of social groups or categories in specific persons, places, objects, or acts.[25] Totalization is the converse movement by which specific beings, objects, or acts achieve systematic significance, as by constituting relations between groups. Mediations are clearly complex processes, processes involving the engagement of compelling social relations — as the powers of Fijian chiefs — which are at the same time significant cultural meanings. But this is getting too abstract; let us look at some of the mediations by which the apparently trivial incidents at Suva turned into the worst Fijian war.

Social-Historical Individuals

The appropriation of a pig at Suva in 1841 could have been an unremarkable incident, the normal exercise of the uterine nephew (*vasu*) privilege, not even an "event" by the definition adopted here, were it not that the persons concerned represented certain lands whose historic relations were entailed in this otherwise mundane act. The instantiation of the land in and as the chief is of course a meaning formation, but it is not an abstract play of signs. It is also well described as "power." The heroic capacity of Ratu Qara to signify Rewa and so incarnate its fate is built into the structures of the people's domination. The chief's power, then, does not simply reflect something outside itself, as a dividend on the control of real-coercive force, but it is itself this symbolic magnification of the person.

People so endowed with the power to embody a larger social order become *social-historical individuals*. The paraphrase is intended to resemble Hegel's world-historical individuals in part only. By *world-historical individuals* Hegel meant the "best men" (though not women) of their times: those whose own goals — perhaps only obliquely, through the cunning of reason — corresponded best to the progressive-dialectic movement of the World Spirit, which movement they made manifest. We can retain the notion of persons whose own acts unfold a collective history, but not because they incarnate an inevitable march of the Idea; rather, because they personify the clan or the land and because their acts, universalized through the acquiescence of the historic group, then signify its dispositions. Of course, everybody's actions signify, are meaningful. But what distinguishes social-historical individuals is that their acts transcend self-reference — by far and in a twofold way. Their acts engage social totalities, in the first place by virtue of structures of hierarchy in which as chiefs they encompass the others. This is logical as well as sociological: the chief represents the logical class of which the people are members (Dumont 1970). Second, then, the acts of the chief acquire a sense equally social, in the Polynesian case a sense that is always political and cosmological in import, though the intention may be substantially personal. If Tānoa responds to the loss of his wives — of which, incidentally, he had plenty more — by a declaration of total war, it is because the liaisons they contracted showed contempt of the aging king's powers of fertility and, thereby, his claim on the sovereignty. And notice that this movement from instantiation to totalization is also a sequence from metonymy to metaphor, as the acts of the person who stands for the historic group become icons of concepts that pertain to the totality as such, to structures of that higher level.

Hence a final contrast to the Hegelian world-historical individual: where the project of the latter is the realization of a necessary and progressive historical course, here history may appear as a contingent realization of an individual project. True, Fijian chiefs are social beings: they make up a more or less uniform sociological class, with inclinations often alike, and their actions are

322

generally skilled or knowledgeable (in Giddens's sense [1976, 1984]). All of this implies that how they act is often a predictable working-out of the social categories and forces. Yet nothing guarantees that the king is the best of men, or even much of one. And though his status may multiply his intelligence by supplying it with the power of society — thus making him a genius — it could also amplify every defect, pettiness of disposition, or weakness of spirit into a historical debacle. At decisive moments the collective fate is at the mercy of the individual psyche. Which is probably why the course of true history never did run smoothly.

To include the existence of others in one's own person: this classic concept of hierarchy is curiously reminiscent of Polynesian ideas of *mana*. Speaking of Maori, Johansen suggests that *mana* can be thought of as a kind of "fellowship," implying a life-power of the chief that extends to and activates others, whether people or objects (1954:85ff., V. Valeri 1985:95ff.). Thus the sometime dangers of the chief's *mana* as a life more powerful than one's own, which could invade and cancel one's own. Not to claim that Fijian concepts of chiefly *mana* are identical to the Maori; but they are in this respect similar and share the common implication that the chief lives the life of the group. He is the principle of the group's existence, a kind of living ancestor, and, accordingly, its history is his own. He recounts this history in the first-person singular. Consider the following argument between the sacred ruler of Verata (Na Rātū) and a Bauan representing the war king (Vunivalu) at a government hearing on fishing rights in 1947, each challenging the other's version of eighteenth- and nineteenth-century history:

> The Rātū of Verata (responding to question by the Bau representative [*mata*]): "I never heard of our meeting at Naivonini in 1750.... I don't know any Tunitoga [Bau herald] named Sainisakalo that you say I killed at the beach at Walu [late 1830s].... I don't know when you burned Natavatolo [this was 1839; Cross, Diary:30 Oct. 1839].... I know of no such set of 10 whale teeth that you say were offered on my behalf by Nagalu to Ratu Cakobau and Ratu Mara [probably in the 1850s]. I only know we are true kinsmen, myself and both these chiefs [Cakobau and Ratu Mara]." ("Veitarogi ni Qoliqoli":243–44)

The Bau *mata* (responding to questions of the Verata ruler): "From long ago until 1750 you were the owner of all the reefs we are disputing here, but I seized them from you in 1750 when I defeated you in our war at Naivonini.... I know that I destroyed you [literally, "clubbed you," *mokuti iko*] the third time I took your town.... I never heard that you were able to take or destroy a single land in all of Fiji. You never captured a single place in Fiji because of your weakness: the reason you have never made war on another state is not [as you say] because you are the first born [i.e., the senior line of Fijian ruling aristocracies; see above]. (*Ibid.*:284–88)

Elsewhere I have discussed the "heroic" organization of the Fijians and societies of the like (1985a:35ff.). Here it is necessary only to stress that the heroic system involves a certain mode of historical production, a kind of historical practice. One aspect of this practice — of which these uses of the "heroic I" give such clear testimony — is the sense of history as incorporated in the chiefly person and expressed in his current action. It follows that not everything in the event is evenemential. The presence of the chief brings forth political relations of ancient memory, carries them into the organization of current experience and actions. This is an instance of the transposition of registers, here temporal, that characterizes important events: a long trajectory of the relations between states is brought to bear in a given incident and a single instant. When Ratu Qara of Rewa is refused a pig in Suva, this is no mere injury to a great noble's amour propre: it evokes the whole course of deteriorating relations between Rewa and Bau (to whom Suva gives allegiance and whence no doubt it gets its cheekiness). All of a sudden, in a village marginal to both and of no vital economic importance to either, the issue between two great kingdoms is joined. Surging out of the depths comes all that notorious history of the growth of Bauan power and the fear it inspires in Rewa. The event, as Pierre Nora says, is "the site of social projections and latent conflicts and the most important of events is that which invokes the most archaic heritage" (1974: 303).

Embodying and making history, ruling chiefs thus practice

socially the capacities they are given cosmologically, for in the great kingdoms the holders of the highest titles are "human gods" (*kalou tamata*).[26] History thus appears as the continuation of the creation by human means, and making society as the sublunar version of making the cosmos. In Bau, Cakaudrove, and, in all probability, the other major states — for Rewa we have no information on this — the sacred king ritually re-creates the social world every day. Until kava is ceremonially offered to him in the early morning, no noise or work is permitted in the village: human society is suspended. A loud cry reverberating through the community indicates the king has drunk the offering, which moreover he shares with — dedicates to — the unseen gods. Thereupon, the life of the people may begin (Lyth, Tongan and Feejeean Reminiscences [hereafter TFR], vol. 1:61–63; Wilkes 1845, vol. 3:157–58; Lester 1941–42:113–14).

Following Hocart, the Fijian state (*matanitū*) can be described as a ritual policy, organized as a system of worship of the king (Hocart 1950, 1969, 1970). The several clans (*mataqali*) of the kingdom are defined by the specialized services they perform for the divine ruler — fishers, heralds, priests, warriors — even as the word for such service (*veiqaravi*) also means "to worship." Hence the principle of heroic generalization we have seen at work in events, the structural extension of the king's acts and concerns to the people in general. The marriages of Fijian rulers are not domestic affairs merely but political alliances, their kinship prestations turn into massive exchanges of local products, and their personal disputes — the wars of states. "As for the common people," the historian comments, "the chief's cause was their cause" (Derrick 1950:78). Reverend Hunt explains how, early in the Bau-Rewa war, nearly half the Rewans readily defected to the enemy: "one of their own chiefs [Cokânauto] having joined Bau made the disgrace connected with joining that place but trifling, as whichever party they fought for they were fighting for their own chief" (Journal:following 19 Oct. 1845). Something similar might be said of the whole war, insofar as it developed from the incidents that have been recounted:

325

The most important [of the new wars of conquest of the nineteenth century] — the Bau-Rewa War of 1843–1855, for example — grew out of family feuds or the quarrels of blood relations in a few leading families. The common people fought to avenge the wrongs, real or fancied, of their high chiefs; sons of one father were to be found on opposite sides. (Derrick 1950:48, cf. 83)

Making history this way is a function of the system of hierarchy, but by the principles of that system it is not the exclusive privilege of the king. The titled heads of clans and villages have similar powers in the space given by affairs of their own people. But, more important, in any such constituted group, inasmuch as the chief's being includes the whole, so reciprocally the other people participate in his person and thus retain the right, in proportion to their rank, to represent him. In any ceremonial prestation — which is also to say any important negotiation because the affair will have to be marked by the ritual offering of kava (*i sevu-sevu*) — if the chief is absent, his place is taken by the person next senior. The latter is accorded the chiefly title in the exchange of honors. This principle of substitution is important, as it implies the presence of the collective whenever high-ranking people, such as Ratu Qara of Rewa, are involved.

When Ratu Qara was denied a pig in Suva, it was an offense as well against his royal brother the Roko Tui Dreketi and the revenge accordingly engaged the whole Rewan confederacy. Yet, at the same time, this devolution of powers to the younger brother submitted the affairs of Rewa to certain personal ambitions that magnified the collective-political consequences — for the quarrel with Suva was then articulated with the fierce rivalry over the kingship, the history of parricide, fratricide, intrigue, and betrayal, for which the Rewa ruling house was already too well known (Lyth, TFR, vol. 1:126–28; Wilkes 1845, vol. 3:131ff.; Waterhouse [1866] 1978:42). Ratu Qara's attempt to seduce a wife of his brother the king was a prolongation of these battles royal: an apparently mild thrust, yet the most terrible carnage had been set off by a similar episode of adultery a generation back. Ratu Qara's other evident passion — for violence — may be understood in the same connection. A well-spent youth spreading terror and mayhem was a qualification for succession, especially recommended for younger brothers or the sons of junior wives. (In Bau, the careers of both Tānoa and his son Cakobau would illustrate the point.) Well into the 1830s and 1840s, the several brothers of the Rewa king, Kania, were outdoing him and each other in feats of atrocity, as in their respective punitive expeditions to the islands of Beqa and Kadavu, not to neglect their conspiracies against one another. If the response of Ratu Qara to the refusal of a pig at Suva seems out of proportion — I mean his persistent ambition to annihilate the place — it was in part due to the insertion of the affair in other heroic projects. This is also to say that the larger historic relations of Rewa, Suva, and Bau were implicated in other structures, importing to these relations new dimensions of hatred and violence. The instantiation of larger systems in chiefly individuals brought the former into a field of interpersonal conflict, itself marked by an intensity worthy of the greater glory at stake — the kingship.

We shall meet this kind of structural palimpsest again, where relations of one sphere are inscribed on those of another. Of course, it is merely another way of describing what historians customarily remark about events, that they stand at the intersection of different casual series. Yet there is more here than "intersection," a meeting. There is a *synthesis* of heterogeneities, with the effect of a *structural synergy*. The combination of relations from different fields — here relations between states and between brothers contending for kingship — thus transforms local incidents into global crises.

Sovereignty, Marriage, and the Uterine Nephew (Vasu)
Insofar as the destiny of kingdoms is displaced onto certain social-historical individuals, their acts assume meanings of proportionate universality. Ratu Qara's quarrel at Suva and Tānoa's marital misfortunes metaphorically figured the general balance of forces among Fijian kingdoms. These were structural connotations, grounded in the Fijian scheme of sovereignty, involving the famous privileges of the *vasu*, the sacred uterine nephew (cf. M. Sahlins 1983, 1985a:ch. 3).

327

The ruling line in the great Fijian kingdoms typically comes from elsewhere. "The chiefs came from overseas," a Lauan said to Hocart; "it is so in all countries of Fiji" (Hocart 1929:129). An immigrant prince who leaves his homeland because of some contention, and whose character and circumstances suggest violence, even cannibalism, this stranger founds a dynasty by marrying a ranking woman (or women) of the indigenous people, a union that domesticates him and sets up an ordered and productive society. As the indigenous people are known as "the owners" (*i taukei*) and "the land" (*na vanua*), the constituting union has the qualities of a Frazerian sacred marriage. It is the union of the king (the sea) with the land, from the issue of which — the ruling line — the society will continue to enjoy fertility and tranquillity (*sautū*). The Cakaudrove people go so far as explicitly to articulate a Frazerian theory, for when the sacred king (Tui Cakau) is installed, he is said to marry the land:

> After the new Tui Cakau has drunk the installation cup of *yaqona* [kava], a member of the [former rulers] Mataikoro ties the *vesa i sole mana* on his upper right arm. As it is being tied the Mataikoro *turaga* [chief] calls out that he is marrying the Tui Cakau to the *vanua* [land] Cakaudrove (*vakamautaka kina na vanua kei na turaga Tui Cakau*). When a people gave themselves and their land to a paramount, it was said that they married, or betrothed, him to their land (*musuka vua na vanua*).[27] (Sayes 1982:204–205)

Marriage to the land sublimates the powers of the stranger-king. (Indeed, it remains the function of the chieftains of the indigenous people, the "mature ones" [or "elders," *matua*], to control the proverbial anger of the king.) The king's cannibal disposition is directed outward, turning royal violence into reproductive benefits through the provision of sacrificial victims to the gods of the land. The ruling king has charge of the sacrificial and fertility ritual. The sovereign powers of violence devolve upon an active, second king, such as I have here called the war king. "War is his part," Fijians say. Traditionally the war king is the successor in the lineage of the indigenous rulers. And since his victims are of the

nature of the stranger-king — in the best case, famous enemy warriors and chiefs — this warfare is a recursive form of the legendary
events that founded the dynasty: in war, the terrible stranger, captured and made an offering to the god and sacred food to the
people, has been metamorphosed into the prosperity of the land.
Again, the installation rites of the ruling king have the same general structure, as they entail his symbolic death as an outsider
and his rebirth as a domestic god. Indeed, in formal speech the
ruler, as the issue of the indigenous woman, is the "child chief"
(*gone turaga*). More precisely, by virtue of the initial sacred marriage, the chiefly line is sister's son to the land, the sacred uterine
nephew (*vasu*).

Here is a Lauan version of the theory of sovereignty, as recently told to the anthropologist Steven Hooper:

> When there is a place [*vanua*] and they have their chief, or customary
> leader, if a greater chief comes along he will lead them. The thing
> that will be done — the chief will marry a woman of the land. In their
> marriage, when they have issue, he/she [*o koya*] will be chief in the
> land. Formerly the ladies [*marama*], the first-born ladies, were the
> ones who married the chief. . . . If a lady is married to a chief who has
> arrived, gardening land will be given to the chief. . . . It is possible for
> the chief of the land to give all the gardening land to the chief who
> has come by sea. His child [land chief's daughter] is given . . . the lady
> of this land comes and resides with the chief. Every thing is his. The
> first fruits can be done — then will come the first fruits of the earth
> to the chief and the lady, because their child, when their child is
> born, will be the great chief in this land. Because the mother [is]
> the land, the father [is] the chief (*Baleta a jinana: a vanua, a tamana:
> a turaga*). They are mutually facing, bound together. So the things
> which come from the sea, the chief will bring, the valuables of the
> chief. (1982:153)

We come to a point most pertinent to the Bau-Rewa war. As
the king is the male element in the reproduction of the land, so
his control of women is an essential icon of the sovereignty itself.
When a defeated land formally submits (*i soro*) to its conqueror, it

presents to the latter a basket of earth symbolic of the land and a daughter or daughters of its ruling chief — still another version of the dynastic founding myth. In the same connection, the ruling nobility were renowned for their sexual and marital exploits. Manifest sign of the chief's reproductive powers, testimony in the human mode of a divine creativity, the number of "wives" of great kings ran to many score — difficult in fact to number because they included many secondary consorts (*vada*), whose status graded into simple domestics, as well as ceremonially married women of high rank (*marama*) (MMS, In-Letters, J. Hunt: 30 Dec. 1839; John Jackson 1967:421; cf. B.H. Thomson 1908:235). The chief's power to commandeer women was balanced by a certain noblesse oblige; he was ready to distribute the favors of the lesser wives, for example, in hospitality to visiting notables (Lyth, "Reminiscences":81; Lyth, "Daybook":1 July 1851; J. Hunt, Journals:19 Feb. 1844). Illicit intercourse with the ruler's wife, however, was another matter. If the mother is the land, the father the chief, as the Lauan says, if the privileged right to woman is the sign of cosmic cum sovereign powers, then a liaison with the royal wife is lèse majesté: it is the negation of the king's rule and a claim to replace him, of which the early missionaries record more than one example (Lyth, "Journal":18 Oct. 1841; J. Hunt, Journals:11 Jan. 1841, 8 Feb. 1842, 8 Apr. 1844). He who takes the king's wife is a political rival and potential assassin. In Fijian terms, the outrage is literally an act of war: "War!" (*Ai Valu!*) is the cry raised at its discovery. So it was understood by Namosimalua, ruler of Viwa:

> About three hours after we had gone to bed last night, we were alarmed by the powerful voice of the chief crying, "Hold fast, hold fast. A war, a war." He then with a still louder voice called to some people of Bou [Bau] who were fishing near our shore [N.B.: The Bau fishers are famous warriors, especially the Lasakau; and the Viwa chief was a close ally of Bau]. I soon ascertained that some man had been lying with one of the chief's wives, and this he considered as an indication that the party concerned were about to take his life, and that war would immediately ensue, hence he called the men who were fishing to assist him. (Cross, Diary:9 Mar. 1840)

330

We can appreciate the force of the insult to the Bau war king Tânoa entailed in the distribution of his consorts, including his principal wife, by the brother of the latter, the Rewa king. Recall that it had been necessary to overcome Tânoa's own maternal relationship and long-standing loyalty to Rewa in order to rouse Bau to war. In this light, the Bau ruler's loss was doubly meaningful: the negation of the gift of the woman from Rewa, thus breaking off the marital reciprocities, as well as an attack on the aging Tânoa's sexual-sovereign powers. Not good timing on Rewa's part: "Old Snuff," as the Whites called Tânoa, was always darkening his beard, calling for young girls, and otherwise worrying about his declining sexual powers (as if haunted by the footsteps of a rival stalking the sacred grove at Nemi).

The political metaphors draw their effect from the relationship between the uterine nephew (*vasu*) and his mother's people, which we encounter over and over again in this history. At this point, we need to know more about it.

The quotidian ethnography of the *vasu* relation is perhaps well known already. The sister's son has a special claim on the movable wealth of his mother's brother: claim that may be exercised without leave, simply by appropriation, but more commonly takes the form of a request (*kerekere*) that can hardly be denied. These privileges of the *vasu* are socially generalized in proportion to his paternal rank and to the status of the family of his mother. A man of standing in Bau who is uterine nephew to the ruler of Cakaudrove (Tui Cakau) is a "great *vasu*" (*vasu levu*) or a "noble *vasu*" (*vasu turaga*) in Cakaudrove as a whole; his powers extend throughout the domain of his royal mother's brother. We see why Fijians say that the internal *vasu* (*vasu i taukei*), maternally connected to an ancient ruling line of his own kingdom, is the greatest man of the realm (Hocart 1929:234; note the analogy to the founding of the dynasty). Moreover, the privileges of the foreign great *vasu* are subject to another condition — the power of his own kingdom relative to that of his maternal kin. A Bauan noble *vasu* is a regular terror in Lau, but not vice versa.[28] The ruling chief of a lesser land whose mother is from Bauan nobility — such was the relation of the Suva paramount to Tânoa's family — is an honored

331

man (*turaga dokai*) in Bau, but he does not act there in a high-handed way. Whereas Ratu Qara of Rewa was *vasu* to the sacred king of Bau (Roko Tui Bau), hence insofar as Suva was connected to Bau, he could do what he wished in Suva. Seize the pig of a Suva chief, for example.

Hocart always insisted on the sacred force of the *vasu* rights. His field notes include Fijian texts that describe the system of cross-relations in terms such as "gods" (*kalou*) and ritual tabus (FFN: 2575). "Much more [is] involved in the cross-cousin system than the classification of relatives," he concluded: "there is a whole theology" (1970b:237). Accordingly, the *vasu*'s claims on the goods of ceremonial exchanges (*solevu*) are paradigmatic: he has the right to carry off the stuff formally presented to his mother's brother. Yet as all such prestations are offered to the god or gods of the recipient, the nephew's privilege is appropriately described as the right to seize the sacrifice. He replaces the god, the one who consumes the sacrifice. The *vasu* is the human, visible form of the god of his maternal relatives. Hence is the king, as *vasu* to the people, their human god (*kalou tamata*). Conversely, the great god (*kalou vu*) may be styled the *vasu* of the land (Hocart 1912:445). And insofar as all the things that come to the ruling town — cannibal victims, ceremonial valuables, first fruits of the crops — insofar as all are offered to the great god, they fall to the "child chief" who represents him in this world.

Fijians are also sensitive to the agonistic dimensions of their theory of sovereignty. Offspring in the paternal line of a dangerous foreigner, the chiefly sister's son forcibly seizes the offering and substitutes himself for the indigenous gods — he is a usurper. Hocart remarked on the antagonism in the rituals of the *vasu* system: upon taking the sacrifice, the uterine nephew is beaten by his cross-cousins, the sons of his mother's brother — but they cannot take back the property (Hocart 1952:142, 205; 1923; FFN: 2777). Something similar is found in ordinary kinship practice. The normal patterns of relationship encode a little drama, unfolding over the generations, in which the dénouement of the sacred respect for the sister's son is the prescribed exchange of humorous insults between cross-cousins — thus from deference to joking, which is also from the exchange of goods to "the exchange of bads" (Graeber 1987). Mother's brother and sister's son are tabu to each other, their conduct marked by a reserve that is the sign of their mutual respect; but a man and his male cross-cousins are required to abuse each other, notably in sexual matters, banter that they are also bound to take in good spirit.

We need not be surprised, then, at the resentment attending the historic practice of *vasu* rights by ambitious chiefs. The hostile reaction evoked by Ratu Qara's seizure of the Suva chief's pig is one only of many such episodes (cf. Gordon-Cumming 1882:165; MMS, In-Letters, Calvert:6 July 1861; Wilkes 1845, vol. 3:77). In the early years of the Colony, one of the members of the Council of Chiefs, complaining of the way Whites were taking Fijian women and recruiting Fijian men, observed that "the evil caused by the white men, who despise us and our laws, is a great and increasing one. They are said to be 'Vasus to heaven'" (Council of Chiefs 1875:14).

In like fashion, certain standing relations of rivalry between Fijian states were based on the *vasu* custom. Known as *veitabani* or relations of "side-to-side," the rivalries came into effect between lands descended of a brother and sister respectively, hence of an exogamous marriage of the ancestors. Generalized cross-cousins, then, the states were hereditary rivals whose members were prepared to verbally flail each other on meeting and to come to blows at the slightest pretext. Bau stood in this side-to-side relation with both Verata and Rewa. As we have seen, the Bau kings were in origin *vasu* to these aristocratic lands, descended of an irregular union between the older sister of the Verata and Rewa ancestors and a local chieftain of no particular nobility (Figure 11.3). Bau's growing power and the fear this inspired in Rewa were encoded in the same terms as the particular incidents that ignited the showdown between them. The enmities at the personal level and the hostilities at the kingdom level were icons the one of the other.

Not all *vasu* relations between kingdoms, however, were so long-standing. Fijians also knew how to organize and reorganize current situations in these terms. Such were their marital politics.

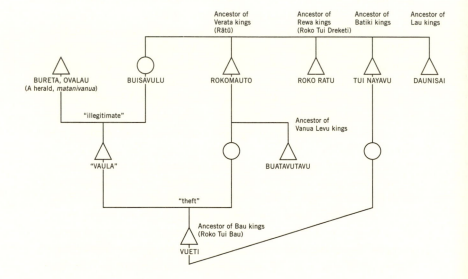

Figure 11.3 Relations of Fijian sacred kingships.

The marriages of noble women (*marama*), marriages that would give rise to sisters' sons in other clans and lands, amounted to a key arena of political practice.[29] In contrast to founding unions of royalty with indigenous women, these political alliances were more often with the ruling houses of outside places. Several tactics were employed, of which two are relevant to the events at issue here: the import of ranking women from foreign lands by the polygynous rulers of major states such as Bau; and the export of the daughters of these rulers to dependent lands such as Suva. In different ways, these alliances will then bring to bear the strategic position and powers of one state on the internal politics of another — that is, in the person of a sister's son of the one who is a prince and potential successor in the other. Here is another structural ground — coordinate to the Fijian system of hierarchy — of the social-historical individual.

The war king Tânoa, for example, had nine royal wives (*marama*), all but two from lands outside Bau, including great states such as Rewa and Cakaudrove and dependencies such as the islands of Koro and Nairai. In the years just before the war, his Rewa wife (Adi Qereitoga) was evidently recognized as the official consort (Radini Levuka), though there is some evidence that earlier the Cakaudrove woman (Adi Talatoka) held the honor. No doubt, there is a story hinging on political interest behind this change, as there would be for all Tânoa's marriages. Indeed, the sequence of the Bau king's unions would make a shorthand chronicle of the recent geopolitical history of eastern Fiji. And the struggles for power and the succession that ensued in Bau among the sons of these wives, *vasu* to their respective maternal peoples, well and truly shaped the further political history of the region. The exogamous marriages of the king articulated the respective fates of whole lands with the careers of their sister's sons in powerful Bau — as reciprocally the success of the royal *vasu* in Bau might depend on pressures mounted by his mother's brother's land.[30] We can now understand why the fratricidal struggles in Fijian ruling families, notably the strife between paternal half-brothers, so readily transcend the bonds and sentiments of their kinship; and also why royal wives, respectively advancing the interests of their own sons

335

and brothers, become key players in these tragedies. Yet the ambitions of these chiefs are not personal only. They represent in their persons an entire regional correlation of forces. The outcome of their heroic conspiracies and cruelties could change the fortunes of entire kingdoms. Here is a conjunction of structures that can indeed give synergetic impulse and effect to individual action.

The specific set of *vasu* relations among Bau princes was a factor in the declaration of all-out war with Rewa, at least as a condition of possibility. Fijians understood this, for among the information they passed to Reverend Hunt was a story of how Cakobau, alone of Tānoa's sons, answered his call to exact revenge for the loss of his wives to the Rewans (Journals:following 19 Oct. 1845). As an account of Cakobau's ascension to the war king functions, the story is misleading because Cakobau had been so acting for years. The sense is otherwise: the disenfranchisement of the sons Tānoa sired by his Rewa and Cakaudrove wives, despite the titled status of these women as official consorts. But as we know, Cakobau was by contrast *vasu* of the people (*vasu i taukei*), his mother being the daughter of the ritual king (Roko Tui Bau). Unlike his half-brothers, Cakobau need have no loyalty to, nor dependence upon, the enemies of Bau. So when Tānoa responded to the appropriation of his women by the declaration of a war of extermination, he could safely entrust the war to Cakobau, who was at once the most gifted of all his sons and the most single-minded. Not long after the conflict began, Raivalita, Tānoa's son by Qereitoga, suspected of a conspiracy with the Rewan enemy, was assassinated on the orders of his father and his half-brother, Cakobau (Wallis [1851] 1983:102–105). In the same vein, when Cakobau successfully attacked Rewa and dispatched Kania the king, he is reputed to have said: "Treachery is your custom, you sisters' sons [*vasu*] of Bau everywhere. If another one of you incites a rebellion, you will be eaten by Uvi ni Siga [my war club]" (Toganivalu, "Ai Tukutuku kei Bau").

Finally, the *vasu* relation was in play in still another way. If Tānoa was already angered by Rewans for the attack on Suva, it should be remembered that the Suva ruler Ravulo was Tānoa's daughter's son — so a *vasu* to Bau (see Figure 11.2). Bau did not itself produce many valuables (*i yau*) for exchange, but it did have a lot of noble women, or at least women of important clans — for this purpose one need not be very fussy — who could be accorded to ranking men of lesser lands. This was a major means of Bauan expansion, a classic kind of "conspiracy à la Bau" (*vere vakaBau*). It functioned politically in a double way: the gift of the woman ensured the loyalty of the wife-taking chief, perhaps even canceling the latter's allegiance to another place such as Rewa; also the Bauan wife could ennoble and empower the local chief, bringing to him the backing of her people — support from Bau, which could prove decisive in contests with his own rivals for rule of the land. The Bau kings were notorious for their ability to interfere this way in succession struggles of other places. They would decide the issue between contending brothers or houses by betrothing a woman to one of them, thus promising (in the person of her son) a local paramount who is sacred nephew to Bau. Fijian traditions commonly attribute the very constitution of government (*mata-nitū*) in lesser lands such as Suva to the acquisition of royal women from nearby greater kingdoms.[31] According to the Suva view of their history, they used to live in relatively unorganized (dispersed) fashion and marry with Rewa, until the ancient land people of Suva brought a noble woman from Bau, chose a man of the chiefly clan to marry her, and made him ruler of Suva. Thereupon the Suva polity was reorganized. The people were collected together under their chief and a new high god — from Bau. Here is Hocart's summary of Suva people's accounts:

> They are now in the [colonial] province of Rewa; but they claim they were not subject to Rewa of old, but independent. When they became uterine nephew to Bau they turned to that state. This is how it happened. They used to live dispersed, in Vatuwaqa...in Naulu-vatu...in Solia. At that time they intermarried with Rewa. Then the elders of Nadonumai, the clan of the Lord of the Green (Tui Rara) ["land people," *i taukei*], agreed to go to Bau to fetch a lady. They chose a man of the clan of Roko Tui Suva to marry her and be lord over them. Then they all lived in Solia to wait upon the lady of Bau. They gave up intermarrying with Rewa. The lady came with a god

(*tevoro*), Cagawalu. Those who brought her, the envoys to Bau, are his priests. That is how the nobles of Suva increased.... Bau and Suva have gods in common. (Heart of Fiji:374b–c; cf. Wall 1919)

These understandings of the *vasu* relations in hand, we are able to determine certain other historic structures evoked particularly by the incidents at Suva.

Traces

The incidents summon up historical relations — "trace structures," I have called them elsewhere (1985a:66n) — which become dynamic factors in the situation. By the same token, these historical relations are put at stake in what is happening. A brief present thus becomes the resolution of a long past. But this present is not simply or necessarily the continuation of a given historical trajectory. Subject to the contingencies and other structures of the event, the old relations take a new turn.

Suva itself assumed a specific historic value in the relations of Bau and Rewa. Because of the shifting marital arrangements of Suva's ruling chiefs, the whole menacing rise of Bauan power surfaced in the local contretemps with Ratu Qara of Rewa. Ravulo, the Suva chief who battled Ratu Qara over the pig, was a *vasu* to Bau, as we know; whereas, his father and predecessor was *vasu* to Rewa (see Figure 11.2). The pig incident thus comes as a sequitur to the shift in the marital alliances of the Suva ruling line from Rewa to Bau. To so change wife-taking is to change political allegiances. Suva oral tradition is not so explicit: it maintains, rather, that Suva was independent before the marriage of Ravulo's father with Tānoa's daughter, which then made it Bauan land (*vanua vakaBau*). But this tradition was recorded when Suva was located in the colonial province of Rewa. Suvans would have a continuing interest in denying their ancient subordination to Lomanikoro — an interest that indeed continues the classic political maneuver they were engaged in during the early nineteenth century.[32]

The classic maneuver is reflected in the geopolitical situation of Suva as a Bauan land in the immediate vicinity of Rewa (see Map 11.2). Thus have lesser Fijian states sought to escape domination by their larger neighbors, that is, by placing themselves under the protection of the latter's powerful enemies. In this way, the smaller land is able to avoid exploitation by the neighboring kingdom, while its distance from the kingdom to which it does submit precludes any systematic payments of tribute such as providing subsistence to the ruling town. The effect is the mosaic pattern of political affiliation that marks the landscape of eastern Fiji, testifying especially to the latter-day evolution of Bauan power. Nausori and the large land of Naitasiri are other Bauan outliers in the Rewa River drainage. In the northeast of Viti Levu are similar detached Bau lands that were once part of the Verata confederacy: the most famous defectors were great warrior peoples of the interior known as Waimaro; former fighting allies (*bati*) of Verata, they became a feared Bau army (Dri Tabua). So far as I am aware, Colman Wall was the first to recognize this distinctive Fijian geopolitics — precisely in regard to Suva and the origins of the Bau-Rewa war. In any fight between these two great kingdoms, Wall wrote,

> Suva and Serua would side with Bau, while Namosi that lay between them would side with Rewa, for the simple reason that the smaller states preferred an alliance with a powerful but distant kingdom to one closer at hand, as while it could help them when needed, they ran little risk of being absorbed by it. (Wall 1919)

The allegiances of these peripheral lands to great confederacies sometimes changed and were always uncertain. Subject to shifts in the regional balance of forces, the alliances were then recognized through tactical negotiations that left their traces notably in the history of the marriages of local rulers with noble women from powerful kingdoms. This must be why it was said that Tânoa of Bau had a special regard for his grandson Ravulo, the ruler of Suva, and why he was so vexed at the attacks on the town by Ratu Qara (cf. MMS, In-Letters, Jaggar:5 July 1845). By the same token, the insult offered to Ratu Qara in Suva summarized Bau's encroachment upon Rewa and the danger thus posed to the established order in Fiji.

339

The Suva affair, moreover, elicited other structural traces that likewise exaggerated the historical consequences. For the trouble between Ratu Qara and the Suva paramount Ravulo was actually a confrontation between *two* sacred nephews of Bau, who were, however, *vasu* to the two opposed royal lines of the Roko Tui Bau (sacerdotal king) and the Vunivalu (war king). Ratu Qara's mother was a daughter of the house currently detaining the sacred kingship.[33] That house had taken the title, and the support of the numerous clans and villages appended to it, in the earlier nineteenth century after the war kings had killed the reigning Roko Tui Bau and deposed his lineage. In every subsequent civil dispute in Bau, however, the two kings continued to be on different sides. And while it was generally acknowledged that the war kings since Tānoa's father or grandfather had become supreme, reversing the traditional ranking in the diarchy, the sacerdotal king still received the first cup in kava ceremonies and otherwise continued to play the ritual part of the "human god" (*kalou tamata*). Paradoxically, the war king needed the sacred king in order to confer legitimacy on the powers he had usurped. And wherever the Roko Tui Bau's writ ran, there Ratu Qara, as sacred nephew, could please himself with the people's property. Fijian sources, Bauan included, explicitly understand Ratu Qara's requisition of the pig in Suva as his *vasu* right (Anonymous 1891:8; Toganivalu, "Ai Tukutuku kei Bau"). But, then, since Ravulo of Suva was *vasu* to Tānoa, his contention with Ratu Qara of Rewa was a displaced form of the ancient conflict within Bau between the ritual and warrior kings.

Here is another synergetic interaction in the event, a system of correlated antagonisms, making a kind of chiasmic structure, such that the outbreak of hostilities in one opposition would be magnified by the force of the other (Figure 11.4). It is a double "schismogenesis," with built-in dynamics of "deviation amplification." For on the principle that the enemies of one's enemies are one's friends — and the corollary that the friends of one's enemies are one's enemies — by stimulating any one rivalry in the system, the whole set of solidarities and hostilities will come into action. In the event, the showdown in Suva acquires a signif-

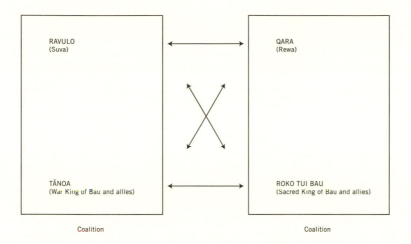

Figure 11.4 Chiasmic structure of the conjuncture.

icance for Tânoa, again invisible in its characteristics as an empirical happening, that evokes a reaction proportionate to what has
thus been put at issue — his own rule in Bau, as well as Bau's rule
in Fiji.

Conclusions: Dimensions of the Event
In other studies, I have in effect described the evenemential process as a "structure of the conjuncture," meaning the way the cultural categories are actualized in a specific context through the
interested action of the historic agents and the pragmatics of
their interaction (1981; 1985a:xiv, 125ff., 152, etc.). The present
essay is a development of the concept as it applies notably to
internal events. From the concrete discussion of the origins of
the Polynesian war, we can abstract some salient dimensions of
the event-in-general.

The event unfolds as a conjunction of different structural
planes respectively marked by phenomena of a different order. It
entails a dialogue between the larger relations and forces that

constitute the historical object, such as the Fijian kingdoms whose history is at issue, and the local interactions through which this history runs its course. The synthesis requires complementary processes of mediation: the devolution of the global forces to the terms of the local action and, conversely, the expansion of local actions to global significance. It is thus half-true that the event is a unique realization of a general structure; the other half is the realization of the unique event as a new general order.

Three moments may be distinguished in this dialectic of the event. First a moment of *instantiation* wherein the larger cultural categories of the history are represented by particular persons, objects, and acts, in the manner that Fijian lands are embodied in their ruling chiefs. With as much structural warrant as Louis XIV, the Fijian sacred king could say, "*l'état, c'est moi,*" for whatever happened to him happened to the kingdom. Not only are collectives thus embodied in certain persons, but the course of social history may likewise be epitomized by certain acts of these people. The second moment is the denouement of the incarnated forces and relations, the incidents proper, being what the persons so empowered as main historical agents actually do and suffer. What they do and suffer, of course, is not simply the expression of the larger categories they are putting in play, since as persons they are subject to circumstances and interests that are not foreseen in the categories. The third moment, then, is the *totalization* of the consequences of what happened, or the return of the act to the system by the attribution of general meanings to particular incidents. The chief lost his wife to another — this was an attempt on the sovereignty; and a pig was taken by a Rewa chief in Suva — this was defiance of the historic expansion of Bau. But it should be cautioned that in specifying these three "moments," one makes an analysis of the event that is not necessarily its sequence; the temporal relations are usually more complex.[34]

The dialectic of the event is symbolically constituted, the symbolism drawing on general structures of the cultural order, whence its intelligibility and efficacy. Instantiating a group in a person or a history in an episode, as also universalizing a chief's anger as an affair of state — these entail various kinds of meta-

342

phors and metonyms. Yet, even when improvised, the play of tropes is never completely free. It is logically motivated in and engages existing cultural schemes, such as the Fijian cosmology of chiefship or theology of kinship.

I stress a point already noted: the three moments of the dialectic are also marked by structural discontinuities. Otherwise it would not be an event but the working-out merely of the cultural order. What makes the event is a dynamics of the incident that alters the larger relations figuring there — that is, in the persons of the social-historical actors and their social-historical doings. And what makes the alteration of larger relations is the fact that in this lower-order incident, all kinds of considerations apart from the larger forces these actors instantiate, other forces of which they may be unaware, motivate them. Other beings and objects, with their own projects or causes and their own modes of action, affect them. Thus the famous "contingencies" of the event, with the effect of an "aleatory transition from one structure to another" (Le Roy Ladurie 1979:114). These other series, however, are not in themselves contingent. They are so only in relation to the object of historical study; in themselves, they may be quite systematic.[35] Here is a place, then, for psychohistory. For if by instantiation the totality devolves upon the person, and in the denouement the destiny of the first is submitted to the activity of the second, then society is decided by biography and — Durkheim and White forgive us — culture by psychology.

In the denouement, the intersection of structures is itself structured. The global order enters into relations with diverse local orders. These are not just juxtapositions of, say, political forces and certain kinship connections. Since their intersection is through persons (thinking and feeling subjects), the different structures are in action put into definite relationships. *The structures interact in the medium of people's projects.* According to the nature and manner of the interaction, local structures can restrain, intensify, orient, and otherwise direct the development of larger historical forces. The main agent of a history of imperial expansion, the Bau war king Tânoa comes up against his royal maternal kin in the confrontation with Rewa. By virtue of the conduct

appropriate to the uterine nephew (*vasu*), this link between kinship and kingdom established through Tānoa has an inhibiting
effect on the military conduct of Bau. It took a series of untoward
incidents to set off the destructive war with Rewa, culminating
in the flight of Tānoa's Rewa wife to her homeland — a symbolic
cancelation, this, of the kinship restraints on Bau's aggression.
Whereas other structures of the conjuncture engaging Bau-Rewa
relations in considerations of different orders had synergetic
effects on the development of the conflict between them. One
conflict is linked to another, the way Ratu Qara's quarrel with
Suva and Bau was joined to his contention for power with his
older brother, the Rewa king. So while his interest in the Rewa
kingship would be served by exploits of violence against Suva, the
effect was to worsen the tenuous relations between Rewa and
Bau — as it turned out, to the peril of the Rewa kingship. In the
same general way the enmity of Rewa and Suva — by the *vasu* connections of their respective ruling chiefs — is displaced onto the
frictions of the Bau dual kingship, which then allows Tānoa to
strengthen his position in Bau by retaliating against Rewa.

These complex structures of the conjuncture are of different
types, which would be well worth analyzing for their corresponding evenemential effects. But it would take another long paper.

Coda

Let me finish by referring to Georges Duby's great work *The Legend of Bouvines* ([1973] 1990), which has been a source of inspiration and instruction in the writing of this paper, though I have not
much mentioned it. But as the present paper was written while
Fiji was suffering the effects of a military coup, there is a passage
in Duby's text about the difference between the medieval trials of
sovereignty by battle and the methods of the modern-day tinhorn
totalitarians that seems a fitting close to this reflection on the
doings of Fijian chiefs of yore:

> We can well see why the last traces of the event are disappearing in
> front of our very eyes.... Our age chases battles out of its memory
> and justly so. And how could it remember there was once a time

344

when the heads of state thought of measuring themselves one to one, putting their power in the hands of God? In our days, indeed, we seldom see power put itself at the mercy of the fate of combat or seek its legitimacy in victory. The opposite is rather the case: the renown, true or false, of dubious success is used as a pretext by captains, great or small, to take power by force. When they hold it, they avoid venturing. The war they wage is shadowy. It shuns open combat; it uses other means, more insidious, more efficacious — means which definitely aim to destroy. (*Ibid.*: 178–79)

NOTES

1. The absence of reflection among historians on the nature of historical events has troubled more than one philosopher: "Curiously this question seems to have become of very little interest to historians, although what is at stake is fundamental: what makes an event, an historical event?" (Molino 1986:265).

2. "The Annales school loathed the trio formed by political history, narrative history, and chronicle or episode [*évènementielle*] history. All this, for them, was mere pseudo-history, history on the cheap, a superficial affair which preferred the shadow to the substance" (Le Goff 1972:340).

3. Hexter characterizes all this as Braudel's views on "the idiocy of the *évènementielle*" (1979:100). On the antiquity of the oceanic metaphors, see Moretti (1986: 187–88).

4. Not to neglect important studies of specific events that appeared about the same time, as Le Roy Ladurie's comments on the Chouan uprising (1972) and Duby's great work on the battle of Bouvines ([1973] 1990). In the same period, Le Goff published the article "Is Politics Still the Backbone of History?" (1972) — the answer being a qualified *yes*.

5. "The great anthropologico-historical problem is to conceive history as a combination of auto-generative processes and hetero-generative processes (in which noise, event, accident contribute decisively to the evolution)" (Morin 1972a:13; cf. Morin 1972b).

6. Moretti observes that "one should not ignore the polemical exaggerations and the objections of '*politique culturelle*' present in most of the texts given to a [critical] 'discourse on the event'" (1986:190).

7. To an outsider, it looks as if there are indeed structures of the long run, at

345

least in historiography. One is reminded of Thucydides' dismissal of the marvelous reasons people gave for their actions in place of the deeper rationality he put into their mouths (in the famous speeches before the assembly). But as the Fijian said to the New Ethnographer, "That's enough talking about you; let's talk about me."

8. Lucien Febvre's original strictures on the evenemential historians' notions of elementary self-constituted "facts" had nothing to do with logical positivism — and still less with the positivism of Auguste Comte, of whom it can be said the Annales historians are modern heirs (Carbonell 1976:401ff.). The present sense of reproach in the term "positivism" comes from its common use to refer to the methods of the natural sciences, and the bad odor now attached to the use of such methods in history and other human sciences (cf. Collingwood 1946).

9. I have in my possession a University of Chicago Libraries "Borrowers Card" (of a kind no longer used and now officially discarded) for the library's copy of Simiand's *Le Salaire: L'Evolution sociale et la monnaie*. It was borrowed on 18 July 1933 by "A.R.-Brown."

10. Although Lévi-Strauss has latterly taken to reconciling history and structure, for Saussure the opposition was a "radical antinomy": "One consequence of the radical antinomy between the evolutionary and the static fact is that all notions associated with one or the other are to the same extent mutually irreducible.... The synchronic and diachronic 'phenomena,' for example, have nothing in common.... One is a relation between simultaneous elements, the other the substitution of one element for another in time, an event" (Saussure 1966:91).

11. Moreover, the word *structures* is also an evident oversimplification. We shall see that what is characteristic of the event, or of the incident as event, is the connections it makes between different orders of structure (Sewell 1989) — alternatively, one could follow Sewell in speaking of different structures — in the culture of a given society.

12. I am aware of the looseness of the formulation of events as acts or incidents that change rather than simply implement structures. *Structure* here can mean anything from the state of relations between historic groups (as peace and war between nations) to institutional and categorical systems, depending on the choice of the historical object. There are also practical difficulties in distinguishing acts that reproduce an existing cultural order from those that alter it, insofar as every intelligible act is at once novel and continuous with the order (cf. M. Sahlins 1985a). Cultural orders are event-systems, as they reproduce themselves

by means of a world they do not themselves produce (Morin 1972a, 1972b). All this raises problems of the kinds and magnitudes of change necessary to qualify as "event." I deal with certain of these issues concretely only, in the following sections of the paper, leaving further consideration of the abstract problems to haunt me another time.

13. The Fijian name of the ruling town of Rewa is "Lomanikoro," although it has been called "Rewa" by Europeans since the early nineteenth century. I will continue the latter usage so long as the context makes the reference clear; otherwise I use "Lomanikoro." Notice of a few peculiarities of standard Fijian orthography will help in the pronunciation: *b* and *d* are prenasalized; *q* is near the "ng" sound in the English *finger*; *g* is the "ng" in *singer*; *c* is English "th."

14. I adopt the following conventions in translating Fijian political terms:

"State" or "kingdom" for the Fijian *matanitū*, a term nowadays usually glossed as "government."

"Land" for *vanua*, the core of a state, a set of clans with a common history of migration and settlement, acknowledging a common ruler.

"Clan" for *mataqali*, a localized group, most of common patrilineal descent, having a status (*tūtū*) and specialized office — such as priest, herald, carpenter — in the kingdom. A village usually has several such clans.

"Fighting allies" for *bati* and "subject people" for *qali*: these are lands or states in their own right confederated with a given kingdom, the *bati* originally by negotiation and the *qali* traditionally by conquest. However, these lands, insofar as each is a "land of itself" (*vanua vakai koya*), are apt to speak of themselves as independent, especially the *bati*.

What I call "confederacy" has no specific Fijian term nor any determinate boundaries. It consists of a kingdom with its allied and subject lands, the latter being designated as lands of the dominant kingdom — for example, Tokatoka (*a bati*) is a "Rewan land" (*vanua vakaRewa*). However, the sense of the term *Rewan lands* or *Bauan lands* surpasses the actual political relations of the confederacy, for distant states traditionally connected to Rewa or Bau may be likewise so designated. For example, Nadrogā was of old a Rewan land, Lau a Bauan land, and so forth. Descriptions of the Bau and Rewa polities may be found in Waterhouse 1978 (1866), Toganivalu 1912, and B.H. Thomson 1908. Waterhouse gives some general account of the Bau-Rewa war, as do Williams and Calvert 1859, vol. 2, Wallis 1983 (1851), Derrick 1950, Clunie 1977, Tippett 1973, Routledge 1985, and M. Sahlins 1987, among published sources. For a brief discussion of the unpublished sources see M. Sahlins 1987:326.

347

15. I hereafter translate Vunivalu as "war king." In the usual eastern Fijian hierarchy, this title is subordinate to the Roko Tui title, here glossed as "sacerdotal king" — though not in Bau, where the rank of the two kings had been historically reversed (cf. M. Sahlins 1987). The title of the Rewa ruling king was Roko Tui Dreketi; here the Vunivalu was the second king. I do not want to make a big theoretical point by calling these rulers kings; it is mainly a convenient way of distinguishing the paramount from other *turaga* or "chiefs" (by the usual gloss).

16. "Ratu" is a Bauan honorific; the Rewan would be "Ro" or "Roko." However, Qaraniqio appears in contemporary missionary and later Fijian documents as "Ratu Qaraniqio" or "Ratu Qara," perhaps in testimony to his connection to the Roko Tui Bau through his mother. His other names include Dakuwaqa and Lagivala (Longfellow). Kania was also known as Bānuve.

17. As we shall see, Ratu Qara's liaison with his brother's wife was also the sign of his designs on the kingship. As a result of the quarrel with his brother that followed, Ratu Qara fled to Bau in late 1839 or early 1840. For what it is worth, one should note that contemporary European observers believed that an ensuing attempt of the Bau chief Cakobau to put things aright between the Rewa brothers by taking an atonement (*i soro*) to Kania on behalf of Ratu Qara contributed to the outbreak of the war. The offering from Bau was refused; and when Ratu Qara soon after returned to Rewa and was reconciled with his brother without Bau help, Cakobau is supposed to have been miffed (Wallis [1851] 1983:163). This never seemed an important incident to me, except as it may have contributed a bit to the erosion of the Tānoa-Kania solidarity, which was necessary for hostilities to begin but was much more significantly affected by the flight of Tānoa's wife Qereitoga to Rewa.

18. The Roko Tui Suva, Ravulo, is said to have single-handedly held off the Rewans at one of the town gates with a musket (Hocart, FFN:2508). It should be noted that the Suvans were well prepared, as the assault had been rumored for weeks in advance (Jaggar, Diaries:2 Apr. 1842); according to the tradition, they were also forewarned by a Lami woman (Hocart FFN:2508 and 2564).

19. Even so, during a critical moment of the second assault, the Rewans were ready to back off until Ratu Qara rallied them. "You fly," the Suva tradition has him saying to the Rewan forces, "I shall go home to Rewa and die there; and you may get another chief" (Hocart FFN:2565). See the remarks at pp. 321–27 on the identification of the people's cause with the chief's cause.

20. In two separate accounts collected by Hocart from Suva and Suvavou people, the well-known story of Bau's destruction of Rewa (in December 1845),

when the Roko Tui Dreketi met his death, is connected as sequitur to Rewa's destruction of Suva (in April 1843; cf. Hocart, FFN:2507ff. and 2564ff.).

21. Before Cakobau's visit, on 1 February 1843 a fleet left Lakeba carrying "property" to Bau, evidently a regular tribute. Included were: an "immense" new canoe, fifteen large packages of tapa cloth, some fifty tapa cloth mosquito screens, seven large bales of sinnet, ten whale teeth, and "the favorite daughter of the King" of Lau, the latter destined for Tānoa, who "is old enough to be her great-grandfather" (T. Williams 1931, vol. 1:145–46). When the Bau fleet arrived at Lakeba in May, it brought a relatively modest prestation for the Lau chief: two spears, more than thirty clubs, twenty whale teeth, one large kava root, and several hundred fathoms of Kadavu tapa cloth (ibid.:164). Apart from another large canoe and other things given Cakobau in May, the Bau party must have received an incomparably greater return; we know not how much because Calvert and Williams left in August, before the departure of the Bauans, whose leaving would have been the occasion for substantial offerings of property by the Lau people.

22. The concourse of the famous Lasakau fisher-warriors of Bau was decisive in the restoration of Tānoa; they had been won over by Cakobau, among other ways by the promise of a large number of canoes, which afterward were delivered through the Roko Tui Dreketi of Rewa, having been made by carpenters of Kadavu subject to Rewa (Cross, Diary:15 Sept. 1838).

23. Bau and Rewa are "Kopaoo" and "Kolaiva" in Cook and King 1784, vol. 1:368–69. I am indebted to Paul Geraghty for this information and the identifications of Cook's versions of Tongan pronunciations of Fijian names. Other early sources on the extent of Bau power include Lockerby 1925; Turpin, Diary; Dumont d'Urville 1832–34, vol. 4:698ff.; Mariner 1827.

24. Nora thus calls attention to the "nonevenemential" nature of the event, the large structural effects it carries: "The event is evidence less for what it translates than for what it reveals, less for what it is than for what it sets off" (1974:300–301).

25. Like Sartre's (1963) notion of "mediation," which was a stimulus to the present discussion, this process of instantiation is not a simple or direct reflection of larger groups such as social classes in individual acts. We shall see that the distinctiveness of the event develops from the imperfect reproduction of the larger system at the lower level, due to the intersection of other, local systems.

26. "The Roko Tui Bau was our 'human god.' He was the chief of the priests who attended the Vatanitawake [the principal temple of Bau]" (CSO–MP 5947/

349

1917, testimony of Aisea Komaitai; cf. NLC/TR, Tailevu North). The same is said of the sacerdotal king of Cakaudrove: "In Thakaudrove only the chief (*turaga*) is believed in (*vakabau*); he is a human god (*e kalou tamata*)" (Hocart 1952:93; cf. 1970a:61; 1912:447; 1915). "The chiefs are the gods of Fiji" (Rabuku 1911:156; cf. Williams and Calvert 1859, vol. 1:183; Wallis [1851] 1983:241; Waterhouse [1866] 1978:338).

27. For some reason the Fijian is Bauan rather than the Cakaudrove dialect. The *vesa i sole mana* tied on the Tui Cakau's arm is "the arm band of binding *mana*." The last phrase of the text should be translated "betroth the land to him." The word for "betroth" here, *musuka*, is notably used for the giving of chiefly women in marriage (Capell 1973:151).

28. The famous example is Ratu Mara Kapaiwai of Bau, first cousin of Cakobau, who was a great and feared *vasu* to Lau on the credentials of a woman of a former ruling line of Lau (Mataqali Cekena), who surrendered after battle to Ratu Mara's father's father (the Vunivalu, Bānuve).

29. In major kingdoms the arrangement of betrothals of chiefly children — with an eye singular to the fortunes of the ruling house — was a primary function of the chief's herald, a chieftain of the land who generally acted as the ruler's man of affairs as well as ceremonial attendant. In the traditional system this would be the "inside-face-of-the-land" (*matanivanua e vale*), such as the Tunitoga of Bau, herald of the Vunivalu.

30. Shortly before the Bau-Rewa war a cousin of Tānoa, Komainaua, *vasu* to Cakaudrove, succeeded in stirring up the latter to military action against Bau, in all probability with a view toward an appropriation of power in Bau by Komainaua. In the same way, during the war, Tānoa rewarded his Rewa *vasu* Cokanauto, who defected to the Bau side, by installing him as ruler of Rewa, Roko Tui Dreketi.

31. Hocart cites a Fijian explanation of the term *matanitū* ("state" or "government") that appeared in *Na Mata* in 1906: "In the old days, men used to seek their chiefs; they used to betroth ladies from various lands in which there was a noble line to marry into their own line so that her children might be noble and their land become a *matanitū* land thereafter" (Heart of Fiji:328; cf. Hocart 1970b:105–106).

32. The statement in Wilkes (1845, vol. 3:206) to the effect that in 1840 the Suvans were "subjects of the king of Rewa" is an error. Wilkes indicates he was relaying information reported by a surveying party under the command of Lt. Emmons. But the relevant passage of Emmons's journal reads "subjects of the

king of Bow," where Wilkes writes "subjects of the king of Rewa" (Emmons, Journals:19 May 1842). Wilkes always has to be watched.

33. This was the house of Nabaubau. In fact, the holder of the title Roko Tui Bau since the early nineteenth century descended from a member of the war king's clan (Tui Kaba) who was married into Nabaubau; he took the title in the absence of male heirs. No doubt the genealogical ambiguity was to the liking of the war kings. But the sacerdotal kingship itself would separate its holder from the war kings, since the title depended economically and politically on a different set of supporting clans and villages — who had not much use for the war king.

34. One can easily envision instances in other histories, instances of martyrdom, for example, in which the act as it were creates the instantiation and at the same time the totalization. But the same example would suggest the value of analytically separating the three moments of the event.

35. Compare Le Roy Ladurie's discussion of the Black Death, which was a catastrophic event in Europe and at the same time a systematic consequence of planetary history and epidemiology (1979:112–13). But because the epidemic was systematic on a higher, planetary level, it was no less an event in France.

Chapter Twelve

The Discovery of the True Savage[*]

This, then, is my sort of historian ... in his writings a
foreigner, without city or country; living under his own
law only, subject to no king, nor caring what any man
will like or dislike, but laying out the matter as it is.
— Lucian, *How to Write History* 41

Perhaps no one would be quicker to take issue with Lucian (or
with me) than Greg Dening, since few scholars have explored the
dialectic between our present and other peoples' pasts more than
he, and perhaps no one has made the project of "laying out the
matter as it is" seem more chimerical. But then, who else has
written such a good history as *Mr. Bligh's Bad Language*, and how
did he do that? Could the fact — it *is* an historical "fact" — that he
had his training and Ph.D. in anthropology have something to do
with it? So he must have known that "laying out the matter as it
is" is the historical issue of understanding people's cultural constructions of events, not of determining "facts" in the physicalist
sense of objective happenings. Given an appreciation of the cultural organization of experience, history is no more condemned
to go round in hermeneutic circles than is its twin discipline of
anthropology.

* Originally published in Donna Merwick, ed., *Dangerous Liaisons: Essays in
Honour of Greg Dening* (Parkville: University of Melbourne, 1994).

Historiographic Politics

Still, it has to be admitted that an anthropology that defines itself as "cultural critique" too often dissolves into a "pseudo-politics of interpretation" (Graff 1983). Floating free of its cultural and historical referents, of the anthropological matter it is supposedly about, it demands to be judged by its supposed moral virtues or presumed political effects. Everything resolves into a kind of lit-crit functionalism, the moral-political implications of the text being all one needs to know for rejection or conviction. It is as if the truth of other societies necessarily consists of our own right-mindedness. Concrete arguments or alternative points of view can thus be intellectually dismissed as "politically unacceptable." This was actually said of certain relativizing tendencies in a recent issue of the vanguard journal *Cultural Anthropology*. Again, a summary comment in a book of essays on Melanesian history warns that Clifford Geertz's *Negara* and my own Polynesian studies, by attempting to understand history in terms of "culture" or "structure," introduce "dangerous" notions into the understanding of others — essentializing notions that falsely endow a people with eternal cultural qualities or overvalue hegemonic ideologies by neglecting "the politically fractured and contested character of culture." "Dangerous"? Hopefully the day is not far off when such statements will be perceived as patently lunatic. But in the meantime, the best anthropological argument is the moral high ground. To know what other peoples are, it is enough to take the proper attitudes on racism, sexism, or colonialism.

Yet what kind of anthropology is "colonizing" or "decolonizing" turns out to be historically problematic, a judgment itself subject to time and the conjuncture. Given the secular shifts in the politics of interpretation, an argument can change radically in moral-political value without changing in intellectual content.[1] Consider the opposing interpretations that may be, and have been, functionally attached to the proposition that European colonials were the determining agents of early modern Pacific history. Originally, this was advanced as an imperialist position, and more recently it was criticized as such, on one and the same

354

grounds — that it deprives the indigenous peoples of any historical autonomy. Yet for a long time in between the same argument was championed by critics of imperialism, because it spoke of the arrogant domination of the peoples by White men.

Something like this oscillation has marked the long debate in Fijian historiography over the role of Europeans and muskets in the formation of the great nineteenth-century kingdoms such as Bau, Rewa, and Cakaudrove (see Map 12.1). The Charlie Savage tradition is archetypal.[2] Savage was a (presumably) Swedish sailor cast away in the wreck of the brig *Eliza* off Nairai island in 1808. Soon after, he settled in Bau as the leader of a gang of twenty or so foreigners who fought in the service of the great warrior king Naulivou. After a number of important victories on behalf of the Bau ruler, Savage was killed in a battle at Wailea, Vanua Levu, in 1813. For a long time, writers of Fijian history — including missionaries and colonial officials — have credited Savage with making Bau the dominant kingdom in the Islands.

But the political context of this opinion has changed over the past 150 years, and so have its apparent historic virtues. If the earlier, colonizing theory was that Savage and his ilk were responsible for it all, on the grounds that Fijians alone were incapable of such political accomplishments, the decolonizing response was that Savage and his ilk were responsible for it all, introducing an unparalleled violence that made victims of the people and their institutions. Nowadays, however, statements of this kind are often considered politically embarrassing for the way they dispossess Fijians of cultural integrity as well as historical agency. Hence the postcolonial proposition to the effect that Savage and his ilk had nothing to do with it.

Allow me to illustrate with some representative examples. First, a colonialist interpretation, as expressed by the early Methodist missionary John Hunt. For the most part a good observer of Fijian life, Hunt was in the Islands from 1838 until his death in 1848. Relatively early on, he wrote a history of Fiji (extracts of which appear in the papers of his colleague, R.B. Lyth).[3] Here Hunt develops a series of arguments in support of the conjecture that before Western contact Fiji "consisted of a number of

355

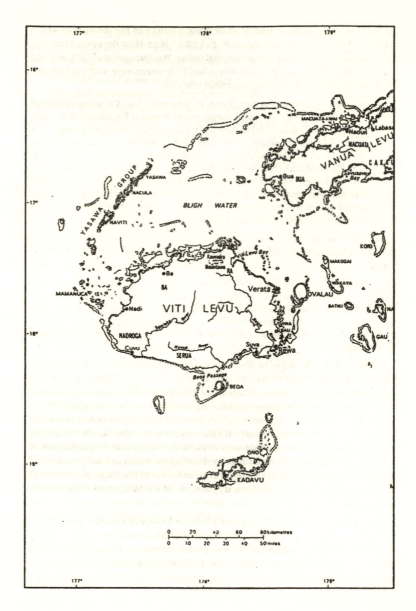

356

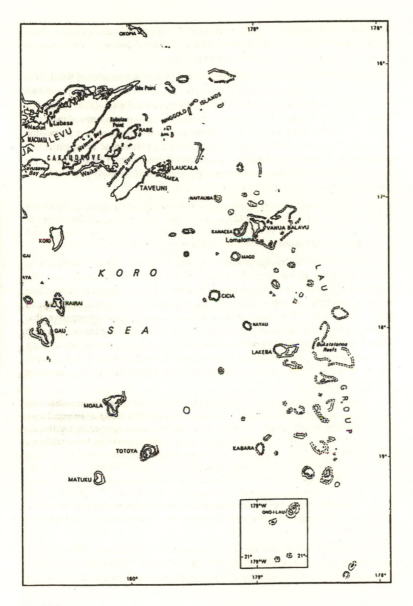

Map 12.1

357

Independent States which had little intercourse with each other."
For Hunt, the final and clinching argument was that

> we know by what means Bau, Rewa & Somosomo [that is, Cakau-
> drove] attained their superiority over the rest of Feejee, viz. by
> means of Englishmen & it is very probable that Lakeba [Lau] became
> what it is by its connexion with Tonga. It is remarkable that the
> people on the coast of the large land of Thakaudrovi [that is, Vanua
> Levu], & most probably of Viti Levu, who have had but little inter-
> course with Europeans are more independent of one another, & are
> continually at war with each other. I should think this is more like
> the original state of Feejee, than any other part can now present.
> The idea of Conquest & extensive dominion was I think introduced
> into Feejee by Europeans. I think the natives are too great cowards to
> think of such things themselves. (Lyth, Tongan and Feejeean Remi-
> niscences [hereafter TFR] vol. 1:42–43)

In a letter written in 1848 to Captain Henry Worth (HMS *Calypso*), Hunt elaborated this put-down of the Fijians by attention to
the historical role of Charlie Savage:

> Charley Savage did a great deal in teaching them to extend their
> territory, and to bring people who were conquered into entire
> subjection.... He became a great chief in Bau, greatly extended the
> influence of that now potent place, and has a name in these islands
> equal to that of Napoleon in civilized countries.... Since then Bau
> has been rising, so that now it is the first place in the Group in every
> respect.[4]

There will be occasion to discuss the transmission of the Charlie Savage tradition; suffice it now to note its later expression by
Basil Thomson, colonial official and ethnologist, who had a genius
for taking most historical arguments at least as far as their logical
conclusions. In Thomson's view, this single White man and his
one musket were enough to reorganize the political system of the
Fiji Islands. Savage, he wrote, "armed with the only musket in the
islands, raised Bau from the position of a second-rate native tribe

to the mistress of the greater part of the group" (1894b:238). Thus magnifying Savage by reducing the status and achievements of the Bauans, the interpretation reproduces colonialism in the mode of intellectual caricature, a transfer of the power and historicity of the indigenous society to the heroic European intruder.[5]

Yet without changing its explanatory form of European causes– Fijian effects, the same argument can reappear at the opposite political pole, provided only that it is taken as the domination of the indigenous people by the capitalist World System. Fijians are thus left to suffer the fatal impact of external forces they do not create or control, forces they are compelled merely to express. Marked by unparalleled violence — the exacerbation of warfare and cannibalism — local history now becomes a melancholy reflex of global history. Its course is transformed and corrupted by Western expansion.

So European trade "spurred the rise" of small states in a number of South Seas islands, Eric Wolf writes, when local chiefs "found themselves equipped with greatly enhanced military potential" in the form of muskets (1982:209). (What does this mean, "found themselves"?) Fiji then comes in for a curious symmetrical inversion of Thomson's just-so story of the White Savage with his exclusive possession of European firearms, involving an historical exaggeration of complementary proportions. Rather than Charlie Savage, Wolf credits the rise of Bau to the famous warrior king Cakobau, by virtue of a supposed monopoly of European muskets — which he in fact never had:

> Five thousand guns were introduced into Fiji between 1828 and 1835, and probably an equal number between 1842 and 1850, in the wake of the sea cucumber [bêche de mer] trade. This wealth in guns prompted the rise of the polity of Bau, when a chief called Cakobau was able to monopolize the importation of firearms.[6] (*Ibid.*:259)

In fact, Bau was the leading power in Fiji well before the rule of Cakobau, who effectively acted as war king (Vunivalu) of the island in the 1840s and 1850s. Acknowledgment of this indigenous development has become more fashionable recently, since the late

1960s, as the writing of Fijian history increasingly takes a postcolonial turn (see, for example, Routledge 1985:36–38). For whatever the political values, positive or negative, that had been attached
to beachcombers and muskets during the long fascination with
European power, they now seem one and all ethnocentric: an
overvaluation of the Western presence that could only be achieved
by rendering the Fijian cultural genius invisible. Comes then the
counterassertion to the effect that Fijians did it all by themselves:

> Firearms arrived, along with about 20 British and American beach-
> combers, by 1810, who made it their role to maintain the arms while
> acting as intermediaries with the trading vessels.... Their marks-
> manship was employed by the Bauans particularly ... and no doubt
> Savage, the most famous marksman, helped reduce a town or two
> before the Wailea men drowned him at the foot of Dillon's Rock in
> 1813. But firearms alone did not establish Bau's political fortunes....
> The club was not quickly superceded. Political preeminence should
> have gone to Bau, centre of the sandalwood trade, if firearms had
> been the key.... All through the first half of the nineteenth century,
> even when more foreign imports were introduced by sandalwood's
> successor trade, bêche-de-mer, Fijian politics followed its own rules.
> (Scarr 1984:11–12; cf. France 1969:21)

Ian Campbell (1980) made a particularly interesting postcolonial case by demystifying the apparent allegory in the traditions of
Charlie Savage. Campbell's thesis was something like Vico's "discovery of the true Homer," a Homer who was not an historical
person but "an idea or an heroic character of Greek men, insofar
as they told their histories in song." This is why many Greek cities
claimed Homer as a citizen, said Vico, for "the Greek peoples
were themselves Homer." In the same general way, Charlie Savage
was perceived as the self-representation of European glory, according to Campbell. He became the symbol of a certain colonial
outlook — now outmoded:

> To the writers of Fijian history this story [of Charlie Savage] has been
> an allegory for the historical impact of Western civilisation on Fiji.

360

He became in retrospect a medium of, and symbol for, both social change and political transformation. It is alleged that he fostered scepticism of Fijian mores; that his military and political activity made Bau the political centre of Fiji, and therefore the principal centre of European attention. Bau's eventual failure to govern Fiji made it possible for some to see Savage as the ultimate cause of Britain's annexation of Fiji in 1874. This role, the European as *deus ex machina* in Pacific history, has been repeatedly challenged by modern scholarship, so that whereas in the past Savage could symbolise European potency and penetration, he is now due to become a symbol of no more than an outmoded colonial outlook.[7] (*Ibid.*:144–45)

Perhaps so. Perhaps in pretending to write about others we only speak about ourselves. The histories we compose are after all *our* history. In so many ways, from selection of topics through notions of significance and causation, they respond to our present purposes. Are we not then forced to conclude that these histories are probably untrue — if I may be allowed such a quaint expression? For the cultural values and relations of other times and places, the events they organized and the persons responsible for them, none of these were fashioned to answer to whatever has been troubling us lately. Those people did not live either for us or as us — nor (to paraphrase Herder) did they suffer and die just to manure our European academic fields. Hence even the postcolonial deconstruction of Charlie Savage as an icon of European imperialism, the interpretation that now gains widespread approval, can only be sustained by ignoring certain historical facts — again, if I may be allowed such a nostalgic expression as "historical facts." One forgets that Fijians were at least as responsible as Europeans for the historical traditions of "Jale Saveti" (Charlie Savage) — indeed, they were primarily responsible (Routledge 1985:47, Thomas 1991:115). The narrative was Fijian before and more than it was European. Hence the critical issue is not our purposes but theirs: What made Jale a significant event in Fijian history?

The exit from historical narcissism passes by way of an anthropological sense of culture — and the corollary Vichian principle of *verum factum*. The past need not be a victim of the present, insofar as it can be granted its own cultural order. Even if history is constructed according to our purposes, are anthropological purposes then irrelevant? What about the purpose of finding out how other people have constructed themselves, according to their own interests, values, and purposes? Not "what actually happened" in a simpleminded positivist sense, of course, but *wie es eigentlich konstruiert wurde*. It is a cruel postmodernist fate that demands the anthropological historian recognize the counterhegemonic multiplicity of views in any society — the famous conflicting voices of the ethnographic situation, the polyphony or heteroglossia — while his own historiographic voice is presumed to be the unmediated expression of a totalized system of power.[8] The pseudo-politics of interpretation is the last refuge of the idea that the individual is the tool of his culture — which again proves that people who do not know their own functionalism are destined to repeat it.

Nor need we suppose that history is impossible, then, on the same grounds that ethnography is. I mean the argument that we are the prisoners of received categories, that exotic values are unfathomable because we already have ours. A crude linguistic relativism is this, which presumes that the capacity to manipulate meaning is suspended once one speaks a language. Yet a heterology or science of the other, as Certeau says, begins just where the character of another society "resists Occidental specifications." It begins with the scandals that other peoples offer to our categories, our logic, and our common sense:

> in the text of the ethnographic project oriented initially toward reduction and preservation, are irreducible details (sounds, "words," singularities) insinuated as faults in the discourse of comprehension, so that the travel narrative presents the kind of organization that Freud posited in ordinary language: a system in which indices of an unconscious, that other of conscience, emerge in lapses or witticisms. The history of voyages would especially lend itself to his analysis by tolerating or privileging as an "event" that which makes an exception to the interpretive codes. (Certeau 1991:223)

362

Consider the assertion of certain Fijian intellectuals writing in the first decades of the century to the effect that trade with Europeans for whale teeth, not muskets, was the true reason for the rise of the kingdom of Bau. Or again, missionary reports from Fijian battlefields that clubs were preferred to muskets for dispatching an enemy even after firearms became available. "Faults in the discourse of comprehension," such statements will only make historical sense when we have exchanged the native Western folklore of power for Fijian structures and values.

Muskets and the Power of Bau

"The rise of pocket-Napoleons," wrote J.C. Beaglehole, "was implicit in the first sight of a musket on an island shore" (1955: clxxii). A version of the "fatal impact" theory, these words of the famous New Zealand historian embody an axiomatic Western notion of the relation between force and authority — no doubt also shared by Napoleon — which has given rise to more than one scholarly exaggeration of the role of European muskets in the development of Pacific island kings and kingdoms.[9] Not to say that muskets were without military-political effects. But for Fiji, to understand these effects, it is necessary to appreciate that until the establishment of the Colony in 1874, or at least the battle of Kaba in 1855 involving an alliance of Bau and the Tongan Islands against the Rewa kingdom, until well into the nineteenth century, then, it was muskets that entered into Fijian wars rather than Fijians into musketry wars.

Fergus Clunie's brilliant monograph *Fijian Weapons and Warfare* is the authoritative text on the role of the musket in Fijian history (1977). Clunie documents that muskets were rare until the bêche de mer trade of the late 1820s, when their availability rose dramatically and many came into the hands of ordinary Fijians. During the earlier, sandalwood commerce of 1804–1814, few or no European firearms were put into circulation, and those involved in Fijian wars were wielded by foreign sailors and beachcombers, the likes of Charlie Savage. With the exception of a few high-ranking chiefs, foreign mercenaries continued to be the main possessors of guns during the trade doldrums of 1814 to

1828, between the sandalwood and bêche de mer periods. Yet as Clunie shows, it was precisely during the first three decades of the nineteenth century, when guns were rare, that they were most consequential militarily and politically. After 1830, as muskets became widely and evenly distributed, their effects on political fortunes and formations diminished. In such respects, the historical significance of the musket was inversely related to the available firepower.

This is not exactly the connection between musketry and polity that Beaglehole and others had in mind (see also Maude 1968:156). What they had in mind was a direct relation between mechanical force and political authority, rather like the Maoist idea that "power grows out of the barrel of a gun." The underlying historical theory is a positive physics of power, power as created by conquest and maintained by coercion. Power consists essentially in physical compulsion: it comes down to an advantage over others in the capacity to inflict bodily harm.[10] Hence the symmetrical and inverse speculations on the relations between firearms and Fijian politics we have already noticed, both of them based on Western common sense and neither historically supportable: that the appearance of the musket inevitably gives rise to "pocket-Napoleons" with monopolistic visions of rule; and that the rise of pocket-Napoleons such as Cakobau must have been due to a monopoly control of muskets.

R. Gerard Ward's study of the Fijian bêche de mer trade has been the most influential statement of the constitution of state power by firepower. Ward also called attention to the considerable labor requirements of the trade, but the guns were politically critical, especially to Bau:

> The freeing of labor from other tasks, brought about by the introduction of metal tools, and the new firepower provided by muskets, gave a means and incentive for increased warfare during the first half of the century.... In the wider political scene, the forces of Mbau [Bau] greatly increased their firepower during the bêche-de-mer period as Mbau had close relations with many of the coastal groups in the main production areas. This was to be an important factor

enabling Thakombau [Cakobau] to establish Mbau as the dominant political unit in the 1850s.[11] (1972:110–11)

Guns were more significant than labor to Ward's argument, since Bau's role in bêche de mer production was minimal, particularly in Cakobau's time. On the other hand, the casual observation that Bau was able to control the musket supply because it had "close relations with many of the coastal groups in the main production areas" amounts to a *petitio principii*. It indicates that Bau was already the leading power in Fiji when the bêche de mer boom began, around 1828–1829, which is how Bau came to control that trade. Bau had no great bêche de mer resources within its own territory, and such as existed in the reefs around the Rewa delta had been fairly fished out by 1831 (Cary [1887] 1987:55, 60; Eagleston, "Ups and Downs," 293–94). The principal sea cucumber reefs in Fiji were off the northern coasts of Viti Levu and Vanua Levu, far from the Bau homeland (Eagleston, "Ups and Downs," 219; Lawry 1850:130; Ward 1972; Wilkes 1845:218–19; Williams and Calvert 1859, vol. 1:73). Nor, for that matter, were most of the other major *matanitū* or states of nineteenth-century Fiji particularly well endowed for this trade: not Rewa, Verata, Cakaudrove, Naitasiri, Nadroga, or Lau (see Map 12.1). Bau's access to the bêche de mer areas was indirect and symptomatic of her already existing dominance: a predatory or tributary relation, achieved by leaning on the parties directly involved, both European and Fijian.

Occasionally, the Bauans used strongarm tactics, intervening with armed parties in distant areas. More regularly, they operated through their allies of Viwa island, whose chiefs traditionally had influence in the bêche de mer areas and were dispatched with European vessels to arrange the organization of labor with the local authorities. Besides, until the middle 1850s, the "Levuka men," the White residents of Levuka (Ovalau) who acted as intermediaries in the trade — they were interpreters and pilots, and ran tenders for the merchantmen — were also functioning within the Bauan political order. Their leader since the mid-1820s, David Whippy, held the official title of Mata ki Bau, "Liaison to Bau." (In the Fijian system, such *mataki* titles usually reflected interlineage kinship ties and entailed loyalties that in crises might be privileged over local solidarities.) Given this clout of the Bau rulers, visiting shipping made a point of stopping at the island and offering the ruling chiefs generous presents, not to mention flattering gun salutes and other courtesies, in order to facilitate the trade. "All these things," said the missionary John Hunt, speaking of Cakobau, "tend to inflate the Bau chief with pride" (to Lyth and Calvert, 4 Jan. 1845, in Lyth, Letters).[12]

But the Bau war kings (Vunivalu) had been taking pride in their political accomplishments for some time. The form, extent, and hegemonic ambitions of the Bau kingdom were already in place during the time of Naulivou, Cakobau's father's brother, who was Vunivalu from about 1802 to 1829. Observers early and late have considered Naulivou's reign the zenith of Bauan power (Clunie 1984:42–86, Derrick 1950:58, Routledge 1985:43, Waterhouse 1866:30). By 1827, Naulivou would be perceived by Western visitors as "the king of the Fiji Islands"—a dignity accorded him *before* the heyday of bêche de mer and while wars were still being fought with "arrows, clubs, spears and a few guns and bayonets" (Gaimard quoted in Dumont d'Urville 1832–34, vol. 4:700, 704; cf. Endicott, "Journal," 24 Nov. 1830).

An episode in Dumont d'Urville's visit of 1827 epitomizes Bau's status at the time. Indeed, Bau's preeminence was written all over the bearing, the being, and the experience of the high chief Tubuanakoro, brother's son to Naulivou (Figure 12.1), who was taken on board the *Astrolabe* at Lakeba, the capital of the Lau Islands. Two important Tongans and a ranking Lau chief were also in this party. At the time, the French were searching for the ill-fated La Pérouse, and Tubuanakoro was searching for tributes, a function he exercised "in a great number of islands of the Fiji archipelago" on behalf of Naulivou (Dumont d'Urville 1832–34: 698). During the week he sailed with the French, Tubuanakoro won their unqualified admiration for his dignity and intelligence. In contrast to the other chiefs, who manifested some panic when Dumont d'Urville decided to disembark them in Cakaudrove territory, Tubuanakoro was not only indifferent to the prospect but

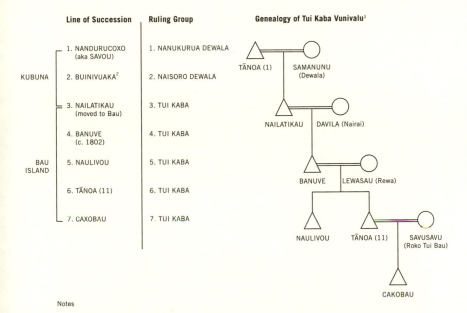

Line of Succession	Ruling Group	Genealogy of Tui Kaba Vunivalu[3]
1. NANDURUCOXO (aka SAVOU)	1. NANUKURUA DEWALA	
2. BUINIVUAKA[2]	2. NAISORO DEWALA	
3. NAILATIKAU (moved to Bau)	3. TUI KABA	
4. BANUVE (c. 1802)	4. TUI KABA	
5. NAULIVOU	5. TUI KABA	
6. TĀNOA (11)	6. TUI KABA	
7. CAXOBAU	7. TUI KABA	

KUBUNA

BAU ISLAND

TĀNOA (1)   SAMANUNU (Dewala)

NAILATIKAU   DAVILA (Nairai)

BANUVE   LEWASAU (Rewa)

NAULIVOU   TĀNOA (11)   SAVUSAVU (Roko Tui Bau)

CAKOBAU

Notes

1. Principal Sources: NLC/TR, Bau (three versions); Evans Collection; Wainiu, Etuate; Toganivalu, "Ai Tukuluku kei Bau."

2. This Buinivuaka appears only in the Bau land records (NLC/TR), third version, and in certain private genealogies. Buinivuaka is more usually an alternative name for Nailatikau. However, the minority version is used here, as it is more consistent with purer data.

3. In most versions, the Tui Kaba genealogy is integrated by descent into the genealogy of its predecessors Buinivuaka and Nadurocoko (Dewala), making Nailatikau the son of one of the latter two. The distinct Tui Kaba genealogy described here may be found in NLC/TR Bau (third version) and is consistent with traditions of the Kaba peninsula (private sources). On alternate unitary and binary versions of the consulation of Fijian politics, see M. Sahlins, "Foreword" in Schrempp 1992.

Figure 12.1 Succession of Bau war kings (*Vunivalu*).[1]

undertook to reassure the others by promising he would protect them on shore. Meanwhile, the Bau chief was gaining respect for his intelligence by the lessons he gave the French in the geography of Fiji, "nearly all the islands of which he had visited himself" (*ibid.*). He was, in the words of the naturalist Gaimard, "the Don Luis de Torrès of this archipelago." Tubuanakoro proceeded to furnish Gaimard with a list of sixty-three inhabited islands — from the Yasawas in the northwest to Lau in the southeast — together with population figures for each that were, with a few exceptions, consistent with later surveys and censuses. On these matters he was deferred to by the ranking Lau chief, who said that Tubuanakoro "was the Fijian most appropriate to furnish information of this nature" (*ibid.*:708). The Lau chief and his fellows were well pleased when Dumont d'Urville, unable to make Taveuni, proposed to land them at Moala instead, since Tubuanakoro also had a brother there acting as "tribute collector" for Bau. Quite possibly, this other brother was the young Cakobau (Anonymous, 1891:13).

Bau's rise to supremacy among Fijian states (*matanitū*) began well before Dumont d'Urville's passage; for that matter, it was well under way before any White man set foot in the Islands, Charlie Savage included (France 1969:21). Exactly when this expansion began, however, is presently unknown. The prehistory of it is unknown because Fijian genealogies, dynastic and other, characteristically cut off some six or seven generations before the time of their recounting. Moreover, earlier events, if memorable on strategic grounds, are then cumulated with the deeds of later heroic figures. There is good reason to believe that something of the like has happened in the chronicles of the Vunivalu or war king Naulivou, who in certain traditions is given too much credit for Bau's successes. It is said that during his tenure as war king, the sacred king of Bau (Roko Tui Bau) was driven off and then killed, a usurpation that gave the Vunivalu title supremacy in the Bauan diarchy. Yet we shall adduce some reasons to believe this reversal of the dual kingship occurred earlier. More important for the moment, Naulivou — as aided by Charlie Savage — is supposed to have been the architect of Bau's displacement of the aristocratic kingdom of Verata, until then the dominant kingdom of Fiji (see Map 12.1). Centered on the Viti Levu coast north of Bau, Verata had held a legendary sway over the greater part of Fiji. (I say "legendary" because it was more a matter of genealogical priority than of functional polity.[13]) But Naulivou's alleged conquests notwithstanding, some rather direct evidence of Bau's usurpation of Verata's position actually antedates his reign — as well as any European presence in Fiji, which begins about 1800.

I mean the list of Fijian place names collected in Tonga by William Anderson during Captain Cook's visit of 1777 (Cook and King 1784, vol. 1:368–69). Published in the form of English transliterations of Tongan transliterations of Fijian, these names included only two from the area in and around Viti Levu, namely Bau ("Kopaoo") and Rewa ("Kolaiva").[14] Indeed, Viti Levu itself was known as "Ambau" (Bau) to the London Missionary Society (LMS) missionaries laid up on the Macuata coast in 1809–1810; likewise, it was "Ambow" in the Arrowsmith Chart of 1814, the first semireasonable published map of Fiji (Im Thurn and Wharton 1925: 151 and map).[15] Vanua Levu was generally known as "Tackanova" (from the Tongan) or somesuch in early maps, referring to its most powerful kingdom, Cakaudrove. In all probability, the same principle was entailed in the identification of Viti Levu with Bau.

Notices of Bau in many local traditions of central Fiji, particularly those collected in Lands Commission inquiries from the late 1880s into the 1930s, likewise indicate that the kingdom was on the ascendancy before Naulivou and Jale Saveti, let alone before the musket appeared in Fijian wars. Some narratives take the Bauan expansion back to an earlier dynasty of war kings (Vunivalu), to a heroic figure known as Nadurucoko (see Figure 12.1). Leader of the Nanukurua people, a different lot from Naulivou's clan (Tui Kaba), Nadurucoko reigned before the Bau chiefly groups migrated to the island — an event conventionally dated to 1760 by those with misplaced confidence in chronological speculations from Fijian genealogies. In the time of these old war kings, the polity was centered in Kubuna, on the mainland opposite Bau (Kubuna is still the ceremonial title of the Bau matanitū). But even as early as this, Kubuna's writ ran as far as certain islands of the Koro Sea, including Nairai and Koro, places that were formerly subject (*qali*) to Verata (see Map 12.1).

Nairai traditions of the establishment of a Bauan (or Kubuna) presence are instructive: they speak to a kind of prepotency not usually envisioned in Western political philosophy, a mode of domination that will have to be examined in order to understand the historic impact of Charlie Savage and his gang. Local people relate that the island's paramount title, Tui Nairai, passed to a person of the clan of Nadurucoko, the Kubuna war king, by a characteristic maneuver for seeking protection from a powerful and belligerent land (NLC/EB/L; NLC/TR, Nairai, 1–4; Lomaiviti, vol. 2:3–4). The indigenous Nairai people (*i taukei*) went to Kubuna "to ask for a chief" (*kere turaga*). Several Kubuna ranking men were accorded them, one of whom secured the supreme Nairai chiefship, which thus secured Nairai as a "Bauan land" (*vanua vaka-Bau*). Such is a process that in later memory may also appear as a triumph of Bauan arms, which in a Fijian sense it was. As regards Charlie Savage's role in such "conquests," in this particular instance Bau's domination helps to explain the historic role of Jale more than vice versa, for it provides reason for why the *Eliza* crew wound up in Bau after the brig was wrecked off Nairai.

It is probably not necessary, and it would certainly be tedious, to go into all the evidences of Bau's political reach before 1800.[16] Tedium would attend the recitation of the many conflicting accounts, with their respective chronological implications. Perhaps it will be enough to notice those local traditions which, despite the Fijian historiographic tendency to devolve long-standing relationships upon late-appearing heroes such as Naulivou and Cakobau, nevertheless acknowledge a supremacy of Bau that goes behind these war kings of recent memory. The successes attributed to the war kings Buinivuaka and Bānuve as well as Nadurucoko, and to the ancestor of Bau sacerdotal kings, Vueti, would all have occurred without benefit of White men (see Figure 12.1). Under these rulers, Bau's authority extended into important islands of the Koro Sea: into Koro island and Nairai, as mentioned, but also Ovalau, Moturiki, Batiki, Viwa, and Gau. Many villages of the Viti Levu coast and the Rewa delta are alleged to have been within the Bau orbit in the pre-Naulivou period, including Kaba, Kiuva, Dravo, Mokani, Naisogovau, Buretū, Oveâ, Namara, Namata, and the Qalivakabau (Namuka, Natila, Nakoroivau). Again, according to some traditions, former fighting allies (*bati*) of Verata in northeastern Viti Levu had already defected to Bau in pre-European times, most notably Nâmâlata and Sawakasa.[17] Under Bânuve, Naulivou's immediate predecessor as Vunivalu, the warriors of Nâmâlata and Sawakasa were mobilized for a battle in Lakeba, Lau. This was the forerunner of a more famous expedition in Bânuve's reign, involving the Nakorotubu people of the Viti Levu coast on the Bau side, which successfully attacked the fortress of Kedekede in Lakeba. During Bânuve's rule also, fleets of Bau war canoes made raids to the northeast as far as Vanua Levu and around the southern and western shores of Viti Levu as far as Nadi.[18]

I do not say that the domination of Bau was an accomplished fact by the time Europeans arrived in Fiji or that Verata had been totally eclipsed. My point is that around 1800, when foreigners became a significant presence, they inserted themselves into a long-term political process, a secular trend marked by the rise of Bau at the expense of established *matanitū* that had been ongoing for many decades, arguably a century or more. Neither Charlie Savage nor any other White man was the author of this development. This is not to say that foreign mercenaries played no part in it; they did — in its final stages. What is claimed here is that the part they played must be understood from the Fijian political situation, from its specific cultural forms and ongoing course, rather than as the sui generis effect of the force they mustered.

On the other hand, the thesis that the muskets brought in by the bêche de mer trade of the 1830s and 1840s were responsible for the major political developments of nineteenth-century Fiji has very little going for it. The war kings of Bau did not need European weapons to set them thinking of dominating the Fiji Islands. Muskets are said by modern students of Western imperialism to have made Cakobau; yet in 1840, or about the time Cakobau was taking over Bau, the number of muskets on the Bua and Macuata coasts of Vanua Levu was greater than anywhere else

371

in Fiji (Derrick 1950:47). (The Bua polity, as many have noted, was the principal beneficiary of the early sandalwood trade as well as a center of bêche de mer commerce; yet it never became more than a power of the second or third order in Fiji.) Muskets were not responsible for wars in Fiji, let alone for states; they were not even the preferred weapons of Fijians, let alone the decisive weapons.

Fergus Clunie has masterfully analyzed the limitations of reliance on muskets, especially the early muzzle-loading muskets, in Fijian battles (1977). To rehearse summarily some of the principal drawbacks: the time required to reload exposes the gunner to a rush and attack by hand weapons; in the humid tropics muskets are subject to misfire due to damp powder, not to mention the worn flints and the unconventional charges Fijians were wont to use; muskets are highly inaccurate at ranges above one hundred meters, or much closer for individual targets; Fijians lacked serious training in care and management of firearms, as well as in marksmanship, though it is claimed they were quick enough to dodge the bullet in the interval between the flash and the discharge; fortifications were quickly modified to offset the use of muskets.[19] As Dorothy Shineberg sums up an analogous discussion: "Few writers concerned with the Pacific Islands appear to have been as conscious of the limitations of early fire-arms as those who had to use them" (1971:78).

The Cultural Politics of Muskets, Clubs, and Whale Teeth

The great Cakobau's reputed dependence on muskets notwithstanding, he dreamed of calling them all in and going back to fighting with clubs and spears — which was safer, so far as he personally was concerned. "When we fought with clubs and spears," he explained to a missionary, "I could go right up to the enemy's [war] fence, and, being a great chief, no one would think of killing me, but from these muskets the shots come whizzing out, and they never ask whether you are a great chief or a common man" (in Watsford 1900:58–59). Cakobau failed to return to the good old days. But one is reminded of the remarkable success of the Tokugawa shoguns in banishing Western firearms from the Japanese arsenal for over two hundred years, although in the sixteenth century they had been as common on the battlefield as they were in Europe (Perrin 1979). The analogy seems close, insofar as the shoguns' interdiction would have the effect of protecting the samurai class and its bushido ethic as well as themselves. A similar antithesis between Western arms and aristocratic custom is involved in several problematic notices of the employment of guns in nineteenth-century Fiji. These and related "faults in the discourse of comprehension" having to do with the political potency of various historic weapons and wealth goods are worthy of further reflection. They will turn out to be pertinent to a deciphering of the Charlie Savage enigma.

The historical relations between firearms, clubs, whale teeth, and warfare are briefly summarized as follows. Due to the bêche de mer trade, muskets became common after 1830. Yet, as late as 1870, the indigenous clubs and spears were still "the most numerous weapons on the battlefield" (Clunie 1977:81). A considerable flurry of warfare had followed on the increase of muskets, notably the great Bau-Rewa war of 1843–1855. This was the second period of intensive warfare in the century. Fighting was at least as intense in the two decades before 1824, which was also before Fijians had significant access to guns. The earlier period was correlated rather with the acquisition of whale teeth in unprecedented quantities, which came through the sandalwood trade of 1804–1814 — and with the likes of Jale Saveti.

To consider first the relative values of muskets and war clubs as technologies of power: The differential role of these weapons in Fijian history did not depend so much on technical effectiveness as on the social relationships of death they entailed. Rendering the act of killing impersonal, the musket would efface the relationships between men on the battlefield. And as Cakobau complained, the untoward consequence for men such as he, chiefs of established authority and warriors of great fame, was the erosion of a certain immunity from attack they had enjoyed in traditional warfare. The missionary Thomas Williams records the reasons for such deference:

373

Warrior Chiefs often owe their escape in battle to their inferiors — even when enemies — dreading to strike them. This fear partly arises from Chiefs being confounded with deities, and partly from the certainty of their death being avenged on the man who slew them. (Williams and Calvert 1859, vol. 1:30)

Thomas Jaggar reported an actual occurrence of this disposition in the course of a Rewa attack on an insubordinate town: "24 [Oct. 1840] [Rewa] Gone against Noco today. Food destroyed.... Noco did not fire on Rewa Chiefs lest any be killed. Rewa men walked about without fire" (1988:57). So the missionaries could even conclude that the mass introduction of muskets had resulted in a *decline* of warfare:

> The introduction of fire-arms has tended to diminish war. The fact that bullets are so promiscuous in their work, striking a Chief as well as commoner men, makes people less disposed than ever to come to fighting, while their faith in the diviner qualities of their commanders is much shaken.[20] (Williams and Calvert 1859, vol. 1:41)

Contemporary observers, including such insiders as Cakobau, had ideas about the relationship between musketry and hierarchy that were the reverse of those presumed by later historians when speaking of the political effects of the musket in Fiji. The musket rather undermined chiefly authority than improved it: "their faith in the diviner quality of their commanders is much shaken" — something like the alleged democratic effects of the introduction of firearms in feudal Europe. A technology unable to recognize divinity, the musket was perceived as a threat to established chiefship — but, I hasten to emphasize, "established chiefship," such as the titles due to genealogical seniority. For what the deeds of Charlie Savage and company will show is that the vulnerability of such personages inscribed their fate in dialectics of power that could produce heroes of an unprecedented cosmic grandeur.

The indeterminacy of the victim of musketry, moreover, was matched by the anonymity of the killer, at least in mass action. This helps to explain why the war club remained the weapon of choice for killing an enemy — this plus the fact that the victim became a sacrificial offering of the highest kind, a value that in turn redounded on the manslayer and his club, endowing both with a certain spirituality:

> It is generally accepted that the heavy, two-handed war club was the most prestigious of Fijian weapons, and had a special aura or even spirit of its own. To club an enemy brought more honour to a warrior than killing with another weapon (even if the enemy had been felled first with shot or spear, he or she needed to be clubbed to qualify as a really reputable kill). (Clunie 1983:106–107)

Alan Tippett likewise observed that even in those places and times that saw the greatest concentration of firearms, "the leading warriors still fought with clubs, and the desire of every young warrior was not to kill with a gun but with a club, that he might become a *Koroi*, a *Visa* or perhaps a *Waqa*" (1968:76). These terms refer to a series of warrior titles through which one presumably progressed according to the number of enemies one had killed. (Today the most common manslayer title, *koroi*, denotes a university degree.) Bestowed in elaborate ceremonies (*veibuli koroi*) that made the warrior a "short[-time] chief" (*turaga lekaleka*), the distinction also put the slayer in a special relationship with one or another ruling chief, whose own name or title, affixed to the military honor, thereupon became the warrior's usual sobriquet. For example, Koroinavunivalu, which may be glossed as "Fortress of the Vunivalu" — this was Jale Saveti's title, affiliating him with the war king Naulivou. The successful warrior went through these investiture rituals bearing his club, until a certain moment when a man in the crowd would take it from him and give him another weapon in its stead, a process that could be repeated a number of times. Everything happened as if war clubs acquired extraordinary power in passing through the manslayer's hands — the power represented in his own social elevation — which is also to say that the club functioned as an objective medium of transactions in divinity.

This epiphanal value of the ironwood war club was an expression of its role as the privileged instrument of human sacrifice.

375

The offering and consumption of the enemy brought divine benefits of life and prosperity (*sautū*) to the land. Other customary uses of the war club were related to these reproductive virtues. In olden times, a great warrior's club was enshrined in the temple — as in modern times it may be secured in a descendant's seaman's chest — as the embodiment or vehicle of the god (*waqawaqa*). Dead men were laid out with a fine war club and a whale tooth, the souls of which objects enabled their own souls to pass to Bulu, the afterworld that was the continuing source of human and natural fertility. (The club would be used to defeat Soul Destroyer, the spirit who barred the path; the whale tooth [*vatu ni balawa*, "stone of the pandanus"], thrown against a certain pandanus tree, ensured that the wife of the deceased would be strangled to accompany him — thus forming a reproductive couple in Bulu.) Again, the disposition of in-laws (or what is the same, male cross-cousins) to exchange famous weapons over long distances, noted for Vanua Levu by Buell Quain, is another logical complement, as the weapons would thus parallel or reciprocate the movement of women in marriage (1948:174). In brief, the successful warrior is a hero of social reproduction and his war club becomes the revered objectification of his accomplishments. And, given the hierarchical organization of Fijian wars, which were generally of chiefly origin and purpose — and in which the underlying people had mainly a "deferential interest" — there were few enough other popular reasons for fighting besides personal distinction.[21]

By contrast to these specifically manly virtues of war clubs, muskets could be perceived as womanly — or so Buell Quain was told, since the musket "required no strength, no bravery," it "was considered effeminate" (*ibid.*:44n). But the opinion thus metaphorically expressed, recorded long after Fijian warriors were forced to give up their firearms, should not be taken as a blanket devaluation of the muskets that the ancestors of Quain's interlocutors had eagerly sought and highly prized. What the statement does signify is the relative prestige of the war club, and more generally that here again the musket entered into the Fijian system, which is to say *as a club*, rather than that the Fijian system was reorganized by musketry. Thus, in certain rituals, the musket could serve as a complement or alternative to the war club. This did *not* include the high privilege of dispatching the victim nor, then, the initial place of the club in the investiture of the manslayer. But muskets might be among the weapons that then passed through the hero's hands, and they might be found suspended in temples or laid alongside the deceased in mortuary ceremonies. Muskets were thus indigenized, as Clunie remarks: "It was in bludgeon-dominated ritual that guns came into their own as Fijian artefacts, carrying out functions never envisioned by their distant designers" (1983:108). Even in battle, something of the same Fijianization was happening. Serendipitously reminiscent in form of certain indigenous war clubs — since called "gun-stock clubs" in the popular and museum literature, though they antedated European guns — the musket, when its ammunition was spent, was reversed by Fijian fighters and used like a bludgeon to lay to on the enemy. Fijians preferred the gun butt to the bayonet, which was a surprisingly poor item of European trade (*ibid.*:107). May we not conclude from this cultural subordination and assimilation of the musket to the war club, practically as well as ritually, that the mass firepower of the 1830s and 1840s did not engender new concepts of power? In some respects, rather, Cakobau's fantasy of neutralizing muskets had become the historical reality.

Unlike the effects of the earlier trade with Europeans for sperm-whale teeth (*tabua*), the large-scale importation of guns did not even bring about a proportionate increase of power. The influx of whale teeth in the first two decades of the nineteenth century had opened new horizons of intrigue, violence, and domination for those chiefs who best knew how to get them and use them. Here was a real increase in the medium of power, made available notably by the sandalwood trade. Although not everyone was structurally and conjuncturally in a position to take advantage of it, Bau and certain other states could. According to the Fijian historian Ratu Deve Toganivalu, this accession of *tabua* was the basis of their supremacy in the nineteenth century:

At the time Naulivou [1802–1829] and Tānoa [1829–1852] were Vunivalu [war kings] at Bau, many whale teeth were bought for

377

bêche-de-mer, and this indeed was the reason for Bau's rise to power, as many whale teeth were taken to various lands to raise war. The same for the *matanitū* of Rewa, Cakaudrove, Bua and Macuata: the origin of the power of their kings were the whalers and traders who brought whale teeth to exchange for bêche-de-mer and sandalwood. (Toganivalu, "Ai Tukutuku kei Bau")

Ratu Deve's argument is motivated by the social powers of whale teeth in the Fijian scheme — creative and destructive powers coming from beyond society, not unlike those of the god. But as objects of exchange, whale teeth are also human-structuring powers; they function in the active or performative mode and in response to contingent circumstances. Of old, they were presented to allies or would-be allies to enlist them in war, to allies of one's enemies to cause them to defect, and again to warriors in return for enemy bodies brought for sacrifice and consumption. Given as betrothal gifts and carried by the bride to the husband's house, whale teeth were reciprocal prestations of the noble form of marriage. They thus made political alliances between clans (*mataqali*) and lands (*vanua*), that is, as marital alliances of ruling chiefs. God-houses and chiefs' houses were built by whale teeth, the expert and collective labor being thus engaged and compensated. Accorded to those who cared for the newborn chiefly child and those who cared for the body of a deceased ruler, *tabua* made the chief appear and again transformed him into an ancestor — which is to say that, in this respect as in others, whale teeth affected the life-giving passages between visible and invisible modes of divinity. Their use in contracts of assassination of rival or rebel chiefs was a darker form of the same transactional logic. So Hocart would derive the name of the whale tooth, *tabua*, from *tabu*, "sacred" or "consecrated." The *tabua*, he argued, "began its career as one of the many materials used to contain the god; a little of it was given away in exchange for quantities of stuff because a few ounces of divinity were worth pounds of gross matter" (1970:101).[22]

The way this power gets realized in social order is something as follows. Transactions of whale teeth concern ruling chiefs of clans and lands. But for their part, the chiefs encompass and incarnate the existence of their people, such that their personal histories, what they do and what they suffer, become collective destinies (cf. Chapter Eleven). In the event, whale teeth have totalizing powers: they organize and reorganize the higher levels of society. Thus, the value of large and venerable whale teeth, *tabua* whose well-used, polished, and reddened appearance signified the fate of kings and kingdoms — the alliances made and unmade, the wealth created and gods propitiated, the gifts of chiefs' daughters and cannibal victims, the wars and successions, the submissions and assassinations. It follows that *the more whale teeth in circulation, the more power in existence in the Fiji Islands.*

But power, again, of a certain kind: active and historical, performative and transformative. Fijian whale teeth were not objects such as Australian *tchurunga* or the stone monuments of Belau, not enduring testimonies to the existing order, signs of its immortality. Nor did they have proper names or anything that would thus memorialize the relationships they had constructed. Their anonymity reflected a certain political fluidity. *Tabua* represented and realized the pragmatics of the Fijian order rather than its inscribed forms — in the same way, we shall see, as Bau did relative to Verata and Charlie Savage relative to chiefs of the blood.

Hence the politics of intrigue, bloodshed, and o'ercrowing ambition that followed upon the sandalwood trade of the early nineteenth century. In the unprecedented violence that ensued, Bau under Naulivou was able to bring the former allies and dominions of Verata irrevocably under its control. Rewa likewise secured its hold in the large southern islands of Beqa and Kadavu. Many years later, Paddy O'Connell, a long-lived beachcomber who played something of the same role in Rewa's success as Charlie Savage did in Bau, reflected on those bad old days:

> Nothing I can say can give you a clear statement of what Fijian politics were like at the time. I do not think that at any time before or since was there so much bloodshed as there was in the twenty years ending 1825. The cause of so much fighting, I could never fathom; probably the possession of white men with new and far more fearful

methods of destruction led chiefs to be more ambitious, [though] not more venturesome, as the whites were usually placed in the van when any fighting was to be done. (Quoted in Turpin, Diary, 129)

In all probability, the proximate cause of the fighting that eluded old Paddy was the one suggested by Ratu Deve Toganivalu: "Many whale teeth were taken ... to raise war." Clunie likewise links the cycles of warfare in the early nineteenth century to the periodic influx of *tabua*:

> The sandalwood trade lasted only ten years, but by that time had concentrated a wholesale supply of *tabua* in the hands of the chiefs of a few maritime chiefdoms, most notably Bau, freeing them to conduct intrigue and diplomacy and to campaign on a hitherto unprecedented scale. A dearth of supply over the following decade began to be made good after the mid 1820s, with the onset of the bêche-de-mer trade.... Again these thousands of diplomatically essential *tabua* were concentrated in the hands of a few increasingly powerful maritime chiefdoms, contributing greatly to their growth. (1986:177)

The leviathan helped make the Leviathan, in conjunction with the foreigners who likewise drifted ashore. But not all Fijian kingdoms were able to take advantage of these new means of power — which were also means of new power. There was something special about Bau.

Charlie Savage and the Structure of Bau
There were all kinds of affinities between Charlie Savage and Bau, including, it seems, a complementarity of character between him and Naulivou, the Vunivalu. For all the nasty things that have been said about Jale Saveti, he was clearly smart, tough, and loyal — even as Naulivou, a man of intrigue and ruthlessness, knew how to generously reward those who benefitted him. Yet beyond that there was a structural match: a correspondence between the foreigners — both in their being outsiders and in the excessive way they could fight — and the distinctive organization of Bau — manifest in the belligerent character of their warrior rulers and their

grandiose projects of domination. While the mercenaries may have had avaricious projects of their own (as we shall soon see), their assembling on Bau, to the number of twenty or thirty in Charlie's time, was sustained by a determinate policy on Naulivou's part. In 1835, Warren Osborn heard tell of it:

> Oolibou [Naulivou] was a man of strong mind & soon perceived that he should have a great increase [of] power if he could collect these whites together & induce them to live with him. He accordingly held out such inducements to them that about 30 some collected in Bowe [Bau], one of them named Savage by his superior courage & wisdom raised himself to the command, with the whites assistance, he soon conquered most of the smaller Fegee tribes. Brata [Verata] was too well fortified and resisted all his attacks though he managed to take from them all their principal places. ("Journal," 386)

The foreigners at Bau were a motley group of shipwrecked, discharged, and deserted seamen of various nationalities. Some nine to twelve who participated in the ambush at Wailea, where Savage got his, are identified by Peter Dillon, including two Chinese, a Lascar, a Tahitian, a Tongan carpenter, a German, a Swede (Charlie), and the rest Irish or Brits (1829, vol. 1:25). (Eight beachcombers died in this ambush; at least five had been living at Bau.[24]) Dillon is also the contemporary source of the report that many of the foreigners had been tempted to jump ship at Fiji by the rumors of treasure to be had at Bau or Nairai. When the *Eliza* was wrecked near Nairai in 1808, it was carrying, besides Charlie Savage, something like $30,000 or $34,000 in silver coin (Lockerby, cited in Im Thurn and Wharton 1925:15; Patterson, cited in *ibid*.:96; Walters 1974). Approximately half of this was recovered by or for the captain, but the rest has never been satisfactorily accounted for, though a good bit apparently was taken by Savage (and/or Naulivou) to Bau. This could have been one of Naulivou's "inducements" to foreigners, as mentioned by Osborn. In any event, the money was a means by which the mercenaries were armed: "Some of those men, with the few dollars then procured, bought fire-arms and gunpowder [from passing sandalwood vessels], with which they rendered important assistance to the king of the neighbouring island of Bow" (Dillon 1829, vol. 1:4).

Savage was the acknowledged leader of Bau's foreigners, respected as such by them and by Bauans. Although some other foreign mercenaries are named in Dillon's chronicle and a few in Fijian oral traditions, Charlie is exclusively designated and credited by all when it comes to recounting great deeds ranging from the introduction of firearms to the creation of the Bau polity. His preeminence in life and legend owed much to his knowledge of Fijian (Patterson, cited in Im Thurn and Wharton 1925:99). He alone of the *Eliza* crew could speak it, and this facility probably got them safely to Bau and helped to sustain his position in the mercenary community.[25] Everything indicates that Savage had been in Fiji before, probably for some months in 1807 on a clandestine sandalwood voyage in the brig *Harrington* (Clunie, personal communication). The *Eliza* had taken on Savage and another man at Tonga, the two (falsely) claiming they were survivors of the *Port au Prince* massacre. Savage originally came out to Australia in 1804 as a free immigrant, and his seafaring career was apparently more honorable than many have supposed.[26] Or than his association with the gang of beachcombers at Bau might imply, as they have gone down in history as a generally bad lot: "demons in human form" (Derrick, quoted in Walters 1974:64), "their morals were those of the poultry yard" (Derrick 1950:45). Apart from fights among themselves in which some may have been killed, the foreigners sustained losses in quarrels with Bau people (B.H. Thomson 1908:29, Cargill 1855:249, Tatawaqa 1913). Dillon reported three were killed in such a fray with Bauans (1829, vol. 1:3, 4–5). This may correspond to the tradition recorded by Warren Osborn concerning a fight between the foreigners and Bau's own Fijian mercenaries, the Lasakau people. The fracas began with the Whites' attempt to prevent a cannibal feast and resulted in several deaths on both sides. "The other Bowe clans," Osborn noted, "did not interfere but encouraged the Whites who in the end beat the Laskow & made them beg pardon to them" ("Journal," 386).[27] Yet all this only partially rubbed off on the historical character given to Charlie, which is much more ambivalent or at least runs the gamut from pretty vile to fairly noble.[28] The missionary Jaggar, of whom something else might have been expected, said that "Whatever qualificat[ns] Charlie might possess as a warrior, he appears to [have] loved peace, & determ[d] to avoid quarrels with whites as much as possible" ("History of Fiji"). On the other hand, Fijians, precisely by virtue of Jale's extraordinary prowess as a warrior, never doubted Savage's nobility or hesitated to accord him the honors of an indigenous chief.

There was a specific correspondence between the derring-do of Charlie Savage and the character of Bauan hegemony. Bau was distinguished by certain transformations of the classic Fijian order: forms of kingship, hierarchy, and clanship which privileged warfare as a vocation and force as a value. While, for their part, Savage and his comrades not only afforded Bau a violence beyond all previous measure but, as foreigners, could give violence an unprecedented legitimacy. So the question is why the Bau war kings, better than any other Fijian ruling chiefs, were able to appropriate the wildness of the White man?

This is in significant part a structural question, a relationship between the forms and forces of imperialism and indigenous Fijian modes of domination. In the persons of Charlie and his gang, Western imperialism entered into an ongoing contest between alternative Fijian schemes of authority and power. The long struggle between Bau and Verata represented an endemic opposition between usurpation and the established order, between the rule of strength (*kaukauwa*) and an inherent nobility (*kena kawa*, by descent). To this day, Fijians say Bau is a "government of war" (*matanitū ni valu*) or a "government of force" (*matanitū ni kaukauwa*), by contrast to aristocratic Verata, which is a "kingdom of [the] blood" (*matanitū ni drā*). Again "conspiracy à la Bau" (*vere vakaBau*) is a proverbial expression, modified in recent times to "*politiki* à la Bau" (*politiki vakaBau*). But the quasi-mythical sway Verata once held over much of Fiji was based on ancestral right: on the seniority of its own rulers in the genealogical pantheon of Fijian kings (see Figure 11.3). Indeed, much of the social and natural landscape of eastern Fiji was created by the peregrinations of the Verata ancestor Rokomauto and his family.

Places were named from the incidents and personages of these journeys, and they became Veratan lands (*vanua vaka Verata*) because the sacred ancestors set foot on them and founded their ruling dynasties.

A recurrent scheme of usurpation of the god by his sister's son, the well-known Fijian *vasu*, runs through this famous genealogy (see Chapter Eleven). It is the representation in a certain code of the temporal dimension of the structural order that was alluded to in connection with the advent of whale teeth and White men. So the Verata ancestor Rokomauto displaces his maternal uncle, the original creator god Degei, and likewise becomes a source of human and natural generation.[29] Then Bau, in turn, plays the part of the parvenu uterine nephew in the aristocratic genealogy, otherwise patrilineal in form, of Rokomauto and his brothers. As we have seen (Chapter Eleven), the Fijian *vasu* replaces the god of his mother's people or represents the god in a visible, living form. Ritually he steals the sacrifice destined for the god of his mother's brothers; politically he captures their realm and becomes their man-god (*kalou tamata*). In the instance of Bau, this usurpation is doubly significant, since the Bau royals are the offspring of successive misalliances: descended of warriors of unknown provenience who spirit away chiefly women by force or guile (see Figure 11.3). Such is notoriously "Bau's work" (*nona cakacaka*), its ancestral vocation of violation and conspiracy, which was also its historical modus operandi. Reflecting on certain examples of Bauan politics, Wilkes considered it "not at all surprising that the chiefs and people of Ambau should be so much detested by the inhabitants of the group" (1845, vol. 3:149).

Singularly organized for violence, Bau was an antistructural force. The Bau polity was marked by certain reversals of the order found in Rewa, Verata, Lau, and other coastal kingships, permutations of the usual Fijian system that gave the Bauans a definite military advantage to go with their like inclination. First, Bau was distinguished by its subordination of land-based agriculture to maritime raid and trade. Here alone, the indigenous people (*i taukei*) who comprised the principal subjects of the

384

polity were not "land people" (*kai vanua*) of an essentially peaceable disposition. The "owning clans" of Bau were sailors and sea warriors — the Kai Butoni and Kai Levuka — who were, moreover, dispersed over the islands of the Koro Sea as far as Lau and Taveuni, while still retaining their Bauan status and still at the disposition of the Bau war king. Most of the residents of Bau island were likewise sea warriors, notably the Lasakau clans, who reveled in their wide reputation of "dangerous men" (*tamata rerevaka*). Bau was organized for raising hell all over Fiji.

"We shall fight until we die," the famous ruler Cakobau said to the missionary; "we will teach our children to fight, and our children's children will fight" (quoted in Waterhouse [1866] 1978: 86). Spoken like a true Vunivalu, "Root of War" or "God of War," whose ascendancy in relation to the sacerdotal king, the Roko Tui Bau, was another reversal of the classical Fijian system. In the usual Fijian diarchy, the war king, whose main functions are beyond the land — the one who transcends boundaries and the constituted order — this war king is second to the ritual paramount, the sacerdotal king who "sits in the center of the (ruling) village" and is the condition of the continuity, order, and cohesion of the land. But at least twice in traditional memory the Roko Tui Bau had been assassinated, the second time in a conflict with the clan of the Vunivalu around the beginning of the nineteenth century or the end of the eighteenth. As the Roko Tui Bau was the lord of wealth and fertility, and the Vunivalu of people and battle, the submission of the first to the second was also the encompassment of economy in projects of victory. Singularly in Bau, the ideology of war was placed at the center of society.[30]

Although both the colonial and the anticolonial historiography would make Charlie Savage the author of Bau's military ambitions, he was not apparently involved in the overthrow of the old regime and the ascendancy of the war king. By almost all accounts, the assassinations of the Roko Tui Bau were internal Bauan affairs. According to different versions, the second regicide took place at the time of the Vunivalu Bānuve or else in Naulivou's reign; but even in the latter instance Charlie Savage does not figure in the narration (Anonymous 1891; Koto, Ko Viti; Toganivalu, "Ai Tukutuku

385

kei Bau"; NLC/Final Reports 1959; NLC/TR Bau). Indirectly, though, Savage probably had a significant effect on the balance of power in the Bau dual kingship, not only by his association with the war king (Naulivou) but through the relationship between the long struggle with Verata and the relative authority of the two rulers. In the usual Fijian diarchy, all dependencies of the kingdom — all outlying villages and affiliated lands (*vanua*) — are divided between the two kings, subjected respectively to one or the other, typically on the basis of ancestral kinship. But the dependencies secured by Bau in war, notably the Verata lands that "turned to Bau," seem to have accrued to the Vunivalu rather than the Roko Tui Bau. The internal usurpation was in a dialectical relation with the accumulation of external powers — a process that in the nineteenth century became a clear trend toward centralization. This is where Jale comes in. The Fijian historian Seteriki Koto recounts the tradition of Savage's participation in a battle against Verata, the shock of which is said to have detached certain fighting allies from the latter and brought them over to Bau — and specifically to the Vunivalu:

> Ratu Naulivou again advised war with Verata and two White men joined in: Savage and another named Matai who was a long time in Bau, apparently a seaman from the ship [*Argo*] wrecked at Bukatatanoa reef in Lau about 1800. Charlie Savage and Matai took their guns to the attack which immediately set the Veratans into a massive flight, as it was the first time they had seen guns and they believed they were fighting with an army of spirits [*mataivalu ni tevoro*]. When the army returned to Bau, some of the fighting allies of Verata [*vanua bati ki* Verata] were assigned to the Vunivalu as they had gone over to him. This was the beginning of the downfall of Verata, although they still maintained a manly defiance [*sa yalo toka ga vakatagane*] and refused to surrender [*i soro*]. As for Naulivou, in the time he led Bau he did not rest from roaming about and smiting the various lands in order to make them come over to him. (Ko Viti, 106)

These words of Seteriki Koto give insight into the structural strategies of Fijian "conquests," even as they testify to a certain kind of efficacy that Whites lent to the ambitions of the Bau war king. Yet Charlie Savage and his bunch proved valuable to Bau in other ways as well: in the specific and uninhibited ways they killed, or what might be called the structural tactics of battle, and in the cosmological legitimacy they as foreigners bestowed on the rule of force or a "government of war" (*matanitū ni valu*). The successive examination of these three topics — the structural strategies of conquest, the structural tactics of battle, and the cosmological legitimacy of force — will allow us finally to discover the true Charlie Savage, meaning the significance he had for Fijian history.

The several dimensions of Charlie's historicity are related, as all revolve around the specifically Bauan ambition of giving political value and effect to sheer force. In an analogous context, Rousseau complained that the Hobbesian formula of Might makes Right was insufficient, since it left unanswered the more critical question of what makes submission a duty? "Were I considering force alone and the effects of force, I should say: 'So long as a people is constrained to obey, and does in fact obey, it does well. So soon as it can shake off its yoke, and succeeds in doing so, it does better'" ([1762] 1964, vol. 3:351–52). Just so, in the Bauan strategy of conquest, force is called upon to do double duty, only one aspect being the pragmatic function of constraining — or more commonly, inducing — people to obey. Such was achieved by repeatedly pounding on Verata and creating a general reputation for violence; it led to people all over Fiji changing sides, "turning" to Bau. At the same time, though, these victories led to an acknowledgment of Bauan superiority on the part of aristocratic Verata, thus conferring a warrant of domination that constraint alone did not afford and without which its effects did not endure. Verata's acquiescence could make submission (to Bau) a duty.[31]

The pragmatics of changing the correlation of alliances by inducing defections from the enemy depends on certain structural features of Fijian politics. Here it is critical that the many Fijian chiefdoms, large and small, are, as they say, "lands of themselves" (*vanua vakai koya*). The notion of "independence" does not fully capture the sense, since what is ultimately entailed is a distinction of divinities and thereby the final impossibility of dissolving the differences between these lands in a social and political unity. Having their own gods and, what is effectively the same, their own paramounts, one land was not easily or ever completely brought under the rule of another. This remains a political problem to the present day, in the modern Fijian nation, and it would be difficult to find a traditional chiefdom that did not claim to be a "land of itself" even though it might "listen to" Bau, Rewa, or some other great power. On the other hand, by the same constituted condition of autonomy, a given land could often maneuver, change sides, petition for protection, or otherwise accept a certain heteronomous status, at least provisionally, in response to changing realpolitical circumstances. Here again is an open, temporal, historical dimension of the Fijian system — on which Bau notoriously worked by force and intrigue. Force and intrigue were, of course, complementary, and it is pertinent that Naulivou was known as much for the latter as for the former. It was said of him, "*Drau vakadrau na nona vere*" — "a hundred times a hundred were his plots." In the event, what is called "conquest" in the Fijian historical literature was some exponential product of actual victory as lands other than the defeated rushed to submit to the victors. Conquest was the amplification of victory by reputation, consummated then by negotiation: the way that Nairai island, in an incident mentioned earlier, petitioned the rising power of Kubuna (Bau) for a chief (*kere turaga*) and thus passed out of the Verata orbit. Or again, in the tradition recounted by Seteriki Koto, the way the defeat of Verata in which Charlie Savage distinguished himself as a holy terror moved Verata's allies to come over to the Bau Vunivalu. We need to take cognizance of such "conquests," or else the discrepancy between the historical reputation of Charlie Savage and his documentable accomplishments would seem just another one of those scandals to the Western scholarly imagination.

All accounts of Charlie's conquests to the contrary, whether European or Fijian, the actual number of his remembered victories are few, three or four, and in not one case was the defeated group then encompassed in the Bau dominions. Basil Thomson made the extravagant claim that Savage subdued for Bau "all the coast villages as far as the frontiers of Rewa" (1908:28); but of the three places he mentions by name in an analogous passage (1894b: 312), two (Buretu and Kiuva) had been Bauan lands before Savage and for other reasons, while the third (Tokatoka) never was Bauan, except for a period in the late 1840s. The well-documented Savage attacks on Viti Levu were these: first, Verata (Toganivalu, "Ai Tukutuku kei Bau"; Koto, Ko Viti; NLC/TR Bau; Waterhouse [1866] 1978:27; B.H. Thomson 1894b:303–304; Wall 1911; Derrick 1950:44–45) — or, in one version, this was a fight with the Verata sea warriors (Macoi people) at Macoi Point (Tatawaqa 1913:47) — second, Nakelo in the Rewa delta (*ibid.*:32, 46; B.H. Thomson 1894:308–311; Wall 1911; Derrick 1950:45); and third, Kasavu, a fair way up the Rewa river toward Naitasiri (Wilkes 1845, vol. 3:123; Cargill 1855:249; Cargill 1977:165; Jaggar 1988:113; Waterhouse [1866] 1978:30). Traditionally a fighting ally (*bati*) of Rewa, Nakelo remained so after this defeat, just as Kasavu, though decimated, remained a *bati* of Verata. As for Verata, it was never conquered, however often defeated by Bau. A fourth battle in which Savage was engaged, in Lau on behalf of the Lakeba paramount, again added no territory to Bau — and probably no luster to Charlie's reputation since, according to one version, he was captured by Tongans (Fison, Miscellaneous Papers, letter, 5 Jan. 1868; cf. Jaggar 1988:110).[32]

On the other hand, the triumphs of Jale Saveti were noisy and spectacular, and are said to have culminated in general massacres. Taken together with a close reading of Naulivou's "conquests," as these are related in the Fijian and earlier European chronicles, everything suggests that during and after Savage's advent the Bau war king was capitalizing on a now-outrageous reputation to bring other places under his control — or else to renew their subordination — by a variety of means. Such is the implication of the way David Whippy, the old Fiji hand, described Naulivou's successes to Wilkes in 1840:

> Taking advantage of all the means he now possessed [namely, muskets, Savage, and the other foreigners], to extend his power and reduce that of Verata, he finally succeeded, *either by fighting or intrigue*, in cutting off all its dependencies, leaving the chief of Verata

only his own town to rule over. (Wilkes 1845, vol. 3:62 [emphasis added]; cf. Osborn, "Journal," 386)

Or consider this notice by Ratu Deve Toganivalu:

Naulivou had been Vunivalu about six years when he undertook a campaign against Verata and destroyed most of their towns. Many tribes that had been subject to Verata now came and declared allegiance to Bau and have since been loyal subjects to the Bau kingdom. ("Ai Tukutuku kei Bau")

But Fiji was not conquered in a day. Nearly half a century later the same Bauan strategy of aggrandizement by inflicting humiliation on Verata was still going on. In 1850, Cakobau — effectively the Vunivalu of Bau, though his father, Tânoa, was still alive — organized a massive attack on Verata by many of the latter's ancient allies (*bati*). When his motives were questioned by the missionary James Calvert, he craftily replied that the war was not his but Verata's enemies'. Besides, he wished to please these peoples because he would need them for his own battles in the Rewa delta (Notebooks and Miscellaneous Papers, Vewa Record, 24 May 1858). In the event, the Bauan-led army did not succeed in storming Verata's defenses, but by negotiation Cakobau did achieve a certain victory. The Verata chiefs agreed to evacuate the town so it could be burned to the ground by the Bau forces. A customary chivalric arrangement (*vakaturaga*), the destruction amounted to a recognition of Cakobau's authority by the Verata rulers — while at the same time, in doing so, they reaffirmed their own inherent supremacy. All this, including the ambiguities of supremacy, was also part of the long-term structures of "conquest."

Even after Britain took over Fiji, these jousts between Bau and Verata continued — in and as competition for chiefships, lands, and rents in the system of indirect rule. For that matter, Britain could serve as Bau's example. Did not the British owe their own empire to violence? So a chief of the Bau war king clan argued in a memorandum claiming ground rents all over Fiji. Britain was proof, said Etuate Wainiu, that "force [*kaukauwa*] alone rules this world" (Wainiu, Papers). But the long-term Fijian problem was precisely that force was not a sanction of rule, unless and until it was recognized by what it would subdue, the virtue and authority of noble lineage.

This opposition (and negotiation) between pragmatic force and inherited rank was reproduced at all levels of the Fijian order: between major powers such as Bau and Rewa; between the rulers of dual kingships such as the Vunivalu of Bau and the Roko Tui Bau; between clans (*mataqali*) contending for high titles in the land (*vanua*); and between persons contending for the title of the clan. At all levels, however, the contention was asymmetrical and ineradicable. It was asymmetrical because of the a priori supremacy and legitimacy of lineage. No usurpation could be sustained without recognition by the deposed superior people. In Fiji — unlike the analogous contests in Tonga and Hawaii discussed by V. Valeri (1990) — the reversal of hierarchy was not resolvable, that is, as a definitive replacement of one ruling line by another. Fijian politics are marked by the enduring coexistence of the usurper and the "true chief" in a relationship of envy and resentment. The rule of the usurper is confirmed by the concurrence or at least the passivity of the superior chief, but all such acquiescence to force continues to signify the priority of lineage. So Bau would again and again be obliged to hammer Verata into submission — and thus affirm Verata's superiority — from sometime before the coming of the White man until well into the colonial era.

And from early on, the battle tactics of Charlie Savage and his like structurally fit in with the opposition of Bauan force to established lineage, not only in a general way but in the particular contempt the foreigners showed for the lives of enemy chiefs. This exemption of non-Fijians from the tabus and circumspections of chiefship — which is to say, their disrespect for the "diviner qualities" of Fijian rulers — has long been incorporated in Fijian custom as a regular practice in domains other than warfare. Clunie points out that Tongans often served as chiefs' hairdressers and handlers of chiefly corpses, since the dangers of such contact did not faze them; the Cakaudrove paramounts would use Tongan sailors and canoes so that when they visited Bau they would not

391

have to perform certain customary rites of debasement (Clunie, personal communication). Hence the popularity of Tongan, and later European, mercenaries, as they were unconcerned by the sanctity that gave ruling chiefs protection against Fijian warriors. Not that Savage and other beachcombers were ignorant or indifferent to the divine aura of enemy chiefs and famous war heroes (qāqā). On the contrary, they singled out enemy leaders as targets, since the divinity of these figures vastly multiplied the tactical effects of their demise. Savage's tactics were thus homologous with Bauan politics. The former translated into battle and action the ancestral project of the latter — the overthrow of the received order by main force.

For when a leading chief or warrior fell to Savage's musket, his people were thrown into disarray, which opened the way to their massacre by Bauan warriors operating with traditional weapons in the foreigner's train (M. Sahlins 1985a:40ff.). Fijians were wont to celebrate Jale Saveti's marksmanship, which they perhaps exaggerated in proportion to such extraordinary results. However, there is reason to believe Savage was equipped with a rifle, a gun whose rifled barrel made it much more accurate than the common smoothbore musket (Cargill 1977:165; Jaggar 1988:110; Clunie, personal communication). In one battle, at Nakelo, Jale is supposed to have had a kind of arrow-proof blind built, or else a high platform overlooking the war fence, from which he fired and took down a chief (B.H. Thomson 1894b:309). Some dozen years after Savage's death, William Cary — whose main informants were Naulivou and certain resident Whites — recounted the story of Charlie's first battle for Bau:

> He had not been here long before war was declared against one of the neighboring towns, and an army was raised to go against them. Charlie applied to the king [Naulivou] for permission to go with them and use his muskets, and after much persuasion was allowed to do so. When the attack commenced, Charlie singled out one of the enemy's chiefs and as he [the chief] raised his spear to dart he [Charlie] levelled at him and shot him dead. The natives, hearing the report of the musket and seeing their chief fall, immediately fled

in the greatest confusion, the Ambow [Bau] people following and killing all who came within their reach. They plundered the town, set fire to it, and marched home in triumph without the loss of a man. ([1887] 1987:30–31)

Cary, incidentally, saw the like with his own eyes when he accompanied David Whippy — a "pocket Savage," in Clunie's phrase — and a party of Levuka warriors in an attack in Cakaudrove:

David, dressed like a native [to avoid being singled out himself], led one party. He got shelter behind a stump, singled out one of their chief warriors, fired and shot him through the head. As soon as their chief fell the enemy fled for the woods and mountains. Then we rushed forward, broke down their bamboo fence and entered the village.... We killed all who had not made their escape, plundered the town and set it on fire, then marched back to Navarto singing songs of victory. (*Ibid.*:53)

Clunie has collected a number of like incidents (1977:90ff.), including one involving Savage's contemporary Paddy O'Connell, serving the Rewa chiefs in a battle at Kadavu. As the oral tradition runs:

Nabea [probably Vabea] was once taken by Rewa by stratagem. Rewa sent to Nakasaleka to send some messengers to Ono and tell the Nabea people that they were coming to fight them and that when they heard the sound of the...bamboo pipes they better give in or else the white devil would strike them. Rewa came out and beset the town. Paddy O'Connor [O'Connell] was with them. They made a stage for him a vesi [ironwood] tree commanding a view down into the town. On this they placed O'Connor and then sounding the bamboo pipes. O'Connor fired and shot the chief coming out of his house. He shot a second and the people soro'd (i.e. surrendered). (Swayne, quoted in *ibid.*:92)

In attacking chiefs, Savage and his kind went beyond the usual limits of Fijian violence, while functioning in the normal line of

393

Bauan violation. Outsiders, they were capable of sacrileges that the Bau war king knew well how to exploit. So Naulivou could overturn what Clunie perceives as

> the stalemate inherent in formal chiefly warfare through the sacrilegious and brilliant deployment of Charles Savage and a spearhead of several dozen beachcombers armed with muskets and rifles. These foreign mercenaries, in worldly contrast to the tradition-bound Fijian warriors they fought for and against, cared naught for the divinity of chiefs, and less for their sacred immunity in battle, potting them first on principle. This tactic, more perhaps than their flintlock guns, gave them disproportionate shocking power, and Naulivou a clear cut military decision. (1984:51–52)

The "disproportionate shocking power," the discrepancy between the toll of a few musket shots and the ensuing catastrophe, is an equation that can only be balanced by the structural values of the chiefs who fell to the foreigners' fire. If the musket became a dreaded weapon in the hands of Charlie Savage and his companions, it was by virtue of a determinate organization of the Fijian cultural order. The consequences of the few guns in play were magnified by a classic system of hierarchy: a system in which the life of the chief embodied the existence of his people — and his death was, accordingly, a cosmic disaster (Hocart 1970, M. Sahlins 1985a:41–44). The death of the king was the end of order and the death of all, spontaneously on the battlefield as it was symbolically in royal rituals. One good shot, then, and it's all over.

Are we then entitled to turn around the old historical wisdom about the politically creative effects of European firearms in Fijian wars? It was not so much muskets that made Fijian chiefship powerful as it was chiefship that made muskets powerful. There was no direct or mechanical relationship between force and its military-political effects. It was not the sheer amount of harm, the casualties Bau could inflict that made it powerful, but the socio-meaningful significance of certain selected victims. And if, as the missionary says, the people's "faith in the diviner qualities of their commanders is much shaken" when the latter fall to gunfire

394

(Williams and Calvert 1859, vol. 1:41), should we not conclude that muskets were inimical to authority in Fiji?

True, but they were not inimical to the authority of the King of the White man's violence, Naulivou. All that these paradoxes indicate is the dialectical movement in Fijian history between force and lineage, now tipped in favor of force by the concurrence of Savage & Co. And even here, the White men offered something to the cause of violence which violence alone could not convey: it was a greater sanction of sovereign authority than anything that was contained and transmitted in a merely Fijian ancestry. This is a third and final structural support of Charlie Savage's historic efficacy, the cosmic authority that allows force to pass, in relation to lineage, as a transcendental value.

The glorification of Charlie Savage, during his lifetime and afterward, was a Fijian work and not simply the allegorical self-representation of European imperialism. Still, we can retain something of Ian Campbell's Vichian perspective on the true Savage, provided Jale is understood as a sign of the specifically Fijian imperialism of Bau. Noting that Western historians tend to overlook the fact that Charlie Savage stories are most often told by Fijians themselves, Nicholas Thomas acutely observes that if Fijians then overvalue his significance as an historical individual, they must have some stake in the mystification. Thomas remarks on the parallels to the interest of Fijian chiefs in Tongan warriors. He argues, I believe correctly, that the Savage narrative "would not have been repeated if it lacked political and cultural salience: there must have been some interest in linking conquest to the presence of foreign warriors and a king's retinue and the use of guns" (1991: 115–16). It remains only to specify this interest, namely, as the transformation of physical force into sovereign right.

Western-imperialist tales of Charlie Savage are not even particularly exaggerated by comparison to the Fijian since, apart from the celebration of his military exploits, it was a matter of significance to Fijians that he was a great man in the White man's world. Lorimer Fison certainly put himself in a bad and unbelievable light when he asked the ancient ruler of Lau (Tui Nayau), Ta-liai Tupou, who was alive in Charlie Savage's time, just who this

395

foreign character had been and where he came from.[33] It was a matter of astonishment to the old chief that Fison did not know that Jale was the son of Saint George the dragon slayer:

> "Why do you ask?" cried the old King, eyeing me with great astonishment, and some suspicion. "Why do you ask? for you know him. A great chief was Charley in your land; and yet you ask 'Who was he, and whence did he come?'!! Look you, I know the truth thereof, for he told it me, even he himself. Because of his father it was; for in the days when Charley was a child, a great and fearful beast used to devour your people, so that the souls of your chiefs became as water, and they knew not what to do, because of this dreadful monster, which was eating the land. Therefore did your King promise great wealth and honour to him who should kill the beast, the eater of your people. And the father of Charley, even he, fought with it and killed it, delivering the land; wherefore was he made a great chief, a mighty lord, and much wealth also was given to him.... 'Lies,' do you say? Lies! What words perchance are these? Lies indeed, when feasts are still made for him in your land even to this day, because of the deeds of his father!" (Miscellaneous Papers, 5 Jan. 1868)

By contrast, for the Lau chief's missionary interlocutor, Charlie Savage was "a miserable wretch" and his fellow beachcombers the worst sort of scoundrels: "some of them were savager than savages,... the dismal horror of whose lives may not be told to women's ears" (*ibid.*). But then, some such disparity between Charlie's European and Fijian reputations was present from the beginning, among those who had known him. His contemporaries Peter Dillon and William Patterson say nothing remarkable about Savage's military or political accomplishments. Chevalier Dillon's description is at best complementary to Fijian accounts in portraying Charlie as all too sure of his mastery of Fijian people, custom, and language — hubris that led directly to his death at Wailea (1829, vol. 1:8ff.). Almost none of Savage's companions at Bau, incidentally, lasted long enough to pass his story on to the bêche de mer traders and early missionaries, who were the first Westerners who did make much of his role in Bauan history. Only

Paddy O'Connell and the more obscure Thomas Riley might have done so; or they might have formed a relay to David Whippy, who arrived in the Islands in December 1824 and for decades after was a major source of local information for other White men.[34] Even so, Fijians were certainly major retailers of the Savage traditions to the missionaries and other European chroniclers. Among these Fijian sources was the Rewa chief — and sister's son (*vasu*) to the Bau war kings — Cokānauto, a principal informant to Thomas Jaggar, John Eagleston, and Lt. Wilkes. Moreover, Savage had a star witness in Naulivou, the Vunivalu himself, who was the first to acknowledge that he owed everything, all his conquests, to Jale. In 1825, Naulivou told the Salem man William Cary that "Charlie stopped a good many years with him, was a great warrior and conquered all the islands" ([1887] 1987:30). From what has been said here about the "conquest," the claim may be somewhat extravagant; yet, in thus speaking generously about Jale Saveti, the Bau ruler was in no way diminishing his own accomplishments. On the contrary, Naulivou was clearly taking pride in the very extravagance of the claim that to him belonged the power that rules this world.

Nor did Naulivou fail to honor Jale with high esteem and chiefly status during the foreign warrior's lifetime. Early on, Savage acquired the manslayer title (*koroi*) that associated him directly with Naulivou: Koroinavunivalu, "Fortress of the Vunivalu" (Tatawaqa 1913:47, B.H. Thomson 1908:108). In turn, a certain Bauan warrior later earned the title Koroijale, "Fortress of Charlie," in itself a warrant of Savage's chiefly standing.[35] Indeed, everything supports the tradition recounted by Emosi Tatawaqa that Savage, or rather "Koroinavunivalu, was reckoned and accepted as a chief by birth, a native chief in Bau" (*ka sa wilika talega ka vakabauti tiko ko Koroinavunivalu mevaka e dua na turaga sucu se turaga i taukei mai Bau*) (1913:47). Jale's house (Naitauyawalu) placed him in a section of the war king clan (Naikasakasa of Tui Kaba ira), together with the descendants of former ruling lineages. His wives again testified to his Fijian rank: not merely by their number, which grew quickly in the retelling to one hundred or more, but by the fact that one was Naulivou's own daughter (by a Lomaloma

wife) and another a daughter or a member of the immediate lineage of the Roko Tui Bau, the sacerdotal king (Cargill 1855: 249;
Tatawaqa 1913; Wilkes 1845, vol. 3:62; Jaggar, Diaries).[36] So
Charlie was a Fijian great man, not just a figment of the Western-
imperialist imagination.[37]

What was going on in Fiji was like the complex Western appropriation of the wild man's powers described by Taussig for Indian-
White relations in Colombia (1987) — except that here it was the
indigenous imperialists who would encompass the fearful powers
of the White Savage. Jale Saveti's repute in Fijian eyes, the stories
of his prowess, grew to enormous proportions. John Erskine, who
was in Fiji in 1849, testifies that Savage's name "is still spoken of
with terror by his foes and admiration by his friends, who relate
incredible tales of his warlike exploits" ([1853] 1967:197). Jaggar
relates that "Any chief thought [him]self great if [he] cd. persuade
us that [he] had Savage's musket in [his] possession" (Jaggar, Diaries:
Appendix; Osborn, "Journal," 311). Thomas Williams records a
conversation in 1844 about the "(in)famous Charley and his companions" with the Cakaudrove chief Ratu Lewenilovo: "Some of
his narrations were fearfully bloody. Whilst delivering them his
eye lighted up, and his whole countenance assumed at times an all
but fiend-like aspect" (1931, vol. 1:240–41).[38] Much later, in 1911,
Colman Wall testified that though "Savage's death was in September, 1813, nearly 100 years ago ... his name and fame are still celebrated in native song and story, [where] he towers above all his
compeers of the island beaches." And should we not take seriously
— I mean as evidence of how it was really constructed — the numerous reports that Fijians under attack by these foreigners and their
outrageous weapons thought themselves up against spiritual forces:
"believing," as old Taliai Tupou told Fison, "that the gods had
come out against them with thunder and lightning" (Miscellaneous Papers, 5 Jan. 1868). For decades after Savage, White men
who were able to repair Fijian muskets were asked if they were not
"spirits" (kalou). Perhaps most pertinent was Naulivou's questioning of William Cary to this effect, when Cary had fixed the Bau
chief's firearms:

"Are you a spirit?" I told him no, that I was flesh and blood the same as himself. "Well," said he, "if you are the same as me, what makes you so white?"[39] ([1887] 1987:52)

Of the Fijians in those days it might be said that nothing foreign was merely human to them. The *vulagi*, the stranger, was a kind of divine guest, as Hocart observed; the term could be glossed as "heavenly god" or "heavenly ancestor" ([1952] 1973:82; alternatively, "heavenly source"). For the notion of spirit (*kalou*) itself had a spatial dimension — a being from the beyond, outside the bounds. So if Naulivou was content to credit his success to Jale, and if the tales of Jale's ancestry and prowess took on celestial proportions, was not this just the Fijian point? I mean the point thus being made about Bau's supremacy, that force had a universal legitimacy.

Coda: A Comparative Polynesian Note

Savage and his gang were not the first or the last foreign toughs to play a destabilizing role in Fijian wars. Having certain of the same qualities as outsiders, untroubled by the local tabus and proprieties, Tongans, as we know, had been engaged in Fijian battles for some time before. But more, the importation of Tongan rituals and trappings of high chiefship in the maritime polities of Fiji suggests that this whole process of transcendent legitimation was not invented in the nineteenth century. It seems, rather, a recurrent structural disposition, a Fijian resolution of the dialectical opposition of force and lineage.

The great chiefs of eastern Fiji have for a long time cloaked themselves in Tongan guises, which is also to say in cosmic forms of prestige. The Tui title of Fijian paramounts is apparently Tongan in origin (Tongan *Tu'i*). The body ornaments of these chiefs were likewise Tongan, in some cases fashioned by imported Tongan craftsmen (Clunie 1986). The chiefly kava ritual (*yaqona vakaturaga*) and its paraphernalia are supposed to be derived from Tonga — supposed, that is, by Fijians themselves. Before the whaling ships, Tongans were the main source of whale teeth (*tabua*). Perhaps the most prestigious lineage of Fijian chiefs (from Kubunavanua) is said to have migrated latterly by way of Tonga. All this, it seems, is a way of endowing Fijian power with universal virtues.

Yet the same celestializing move, lending the divine authority of the foreign to local ambitions of sovereignty, is known all over Polynesia. From Hawaii and Tahiti to New Zealand, it has attended analogous struggles between chiefs of the blood and warrior rivals, senior lines and cadet branches, and — in the most general and paradigmatic versions — the usurpations of gods by men, giving the latter possession of the land. In a recent study of Maori cosmogonic myth, Gregory Schrempp makes a stunning analysis of the structural dynamics (1992) — the same that was destined to be involved in the career of more than one Polynesian conquering king of the early nineteenth century. For, like the mythical hero Tū, the ancestor of warrior man in Te Rangikaheke's famous text, the self-affirmation of the Polynesian historical kings involved the inclusion of others through a demonstration of courage on a universal stage.

Indeed, by his courageous action on a higher plane, Tū's status in the Maori myth changes from younger brother to older brother: the triumph of force over lineage — which by preserving the latter in principle is also their synthesis. Tū was able to subsume his older brothers, the origins of foods and natural creatures, because he alone stood up to the fierce squalls, whirlwinds, and hurricanes loosed on the earth by another sibling, Tâwhiri. Excuse me for thus rehearsing the well-known story of "The Sons of the Sky (Rangi)"; I abbreviate to the essentials we need here. Tâwhiri was the only one of the brothers to join the Sky Father (Rangi) when the others forcefully separated their heavenly parent from the Earth Mother (Papa). Tâwhiri's violent storms were the retaliation on the brothers for this crime, this usurping separation (they now lived on Earth Mother). Origin of winds and ally of the Sky, a being who is himself everywhere, universal, Tâwhiri drives his brothers hither and yon. Their dispersal constitutes the further separations and oppositions that comprise (earthly) nature: separation of the trees, birds, and other forest denizens who are the offspring of Tâne; of the fish of the sea and reptiles who fled to the land, all children of the ocean, Tangaroa; of the sweet potato and other cultivated foods, the progeny of Rongo; and of the fern and other wild foods descended from Haumia. The differentiation of the world arose in strife. But because Tū alone battled Tāwhiri to a standstill, because "Tū alone was brave" when his brothers scattered before Tāwhiri, he now turned upon them in revenge and consumed them. As well as rendering the brothers common (*noa*) and junior to him, this act of consumption differentiated Tū by his inclusion of them. The brothers (that is, nature) also came under Tū 's control, which is to say man's control, for he assigned the incantations (*karakia*) by which he could govern their reproduction. Politically, the cosmogony finishes as hierarchy in the Dumontian sense, except that here bravery replaces purity as the principle of encompassment.

In this way, as Schrempp remarks in a golden passage, bravery is able to dominate as a value, not just as a physical force. Expressed on a cosmological scale, in an arena beyond that of earthly lineage, victory becomes an external measure of superiority. Maori say that bravery is "a sign of nobility" (*he tohu rangatira*). So it achieves a "reversal of hierarchy," indeed a "centric" resolution of the classic Polynesian dualism (V. Valeri's terms), something that force alone cannot do (Rousseau's terms). To cite Schrempp at length:

> The question can be raised whether a hierarchy established fully from within — rather than through measurement against an external scale — would be other than a formulation of power (as opposed to value). What is particularly interesting about this Arawa episode in terms of Dumont's argument [distinguishing a hierarchy of purity from "empirical" power] lies not in the fact that it pictures an instance of a formulation going outside of the inner-worldly practice of power in order to construct hierarchy. Rather, what is interesting is that, within a formulation in which ability to demonstrate forcefulness in inner-worldly practice does figure in the establishing of hierarchy, it nevertheless seeks to constitute that practice cosmologically. Because man *in* practice, *but initially on a cosmological plane*, demonstrates himself to be braver and more steadfast in purpose

than his earthly brothers, man's subsequent inner-worldly demonstration assumes the character of a cosmic act carried out in terms of
a scheme of cosmic value. (1992:83)

Tū alone was brave and so was able to encompass and incorporate his brothers. In the same way, as if they were enacting historical metaphors of such mythical realities, a series of Polynesian
conquerors of the early nineteenth century were prepared to associate themselves with an advancing European presence — not only
pragmatically but subjectively, and in order to give their own arriv-
iste rule an unprecedented validity. For the most part famous warriors, these were the "pocket-Napoleons," so called in colonialist
jargon, men such as Hongi Hika of New Zealand, Kamehameha
of Hawaii, Iotete of the Marquesas, the Pomares of Tahiti, King
George Tupou of Tonga, and Naulivou of Fiji. The historical transformations they worked in politico-cosmogonic myths, replacing
celestial sanctions of sovereignty by foreign, could be logically
motivated by the connections between the heavens, the gods, and
overseas lands in traditional Polynesian schemes. But just as their
own rule involved new totalizations of power — the unification
of ancestrally distinct groups by force and to an unprecedented
extent — so they would make this inclusive domination a value by
measuring themselves on an external scale. They formed relationships with what was, in the novel cosmography of the early nineteenth century, the new encompassing power. The irony of the
put-down of these Polynesian heroes as pocket-Napoleons was
that more than one of them was interested to incorporate Bonaparte in his own imperium: for as it was actually constructed in
Pacific history, Napoleon was the Kamehameha of Europe.

Many of the island conquerors achieved power in the Napoleonic era or not long after. They were fascinated by the French
emperor and often pressed passing European visitors for news of
him. It was reported of Pomare II, after his conversion to Christianity (which itself seems relevant to this discussion):

The form of their religion is changed and their habits in some measure, which altogether is an improvement, but they are still Tahyteans.

Pohmare left off drinking Kava, but he afterwards took to European liquours; and it was his delight to sit for evenings together, along with his chiefs, over a bowl of grog, talking about Bounaparte, Captain Cook, King George, and foreign events.[40]

Then again, Napoleon was a Tongan. Or so say the Tongans — to Lorimer Fison, the great connoisseur of the European-hero genre of the Polynesian legendary corpus who had it from the lips of one Vave of Kolonga (1904:135). Vave set the context for understanding Napoleon by speaking of the glories of the Tongan nobility — "the root of greatness," he said — and the fame of Tongan warriors: "From our stock has sprung the race of warriors — men whose names are known — some whose mighty deeds have been done among our own people, and others who have lived and fought among foreign nations. Thus Napoleoni was a son of Tonga" (ibid.). Napoleoni's mother, Vave explained, was a tall and fair American who became pregnant while on a visit to Tonga during the whaling days and then returned to Merikei to bear her son. Sometime later the men of Faranise came to Merikei to beg for help against their nemesis Uelingtoni, for their high priest had foreseen that here they would find the child of a red father to lead them against their enemies. Employing a combination of broad Tongan humor and traditional motifs, the narrator then describes the search for the hero. First the Faranise men were tricked by an American youth who led them to a house in the forest — "for you must know that in Merikei the husbandmen are not permitted to dwell within the town" — where the one they sought turned out to be a calf whose father was red. Their next effort is successful, but the child they find, Napoleoni, has been dumb and immobile since birth. Only when the Faranise disclose their mission does he for the first time rise and speak, revealing thus that he is strong and tall: taller than the tallest of the strangers. So was King George Tupou, it might be noted; while the sudden metamorphosis from an abnormal passivity to herculean action is a common Polynesian theme, a device for revealing the superhuman qualities of the hero. The rousing of the warrior from the stable condition of the autonomous sacred chief is also iconic of the reversal of

403

hierarchy under discussion here. With that the narrator proceeds to make a long story short: "I could tell you of his mighty deeds," he says, "how he chased Uelingtoni from land to land, till he caught him at Uatalu [Waterloo], and banished him to a desert island, where he died." But Vave's point was more particularly the truth about Napoleoni's birth because the Faranise hide it. They say Napoleoni was born on an island, "the dwelling place of their royal clan"; but they lie about which island he is derived from — it was Tonga.

Clearly, Polynesian chiefs could see in the great men of Europe — very commonly Cook and King George (III) as well as Bonaparte — an ideal of themselves and a story of their own times. Their interest in Napoleon was locally and structurally motivated. Of course, they understood the sheer tactical advantage of fashioning an alliance with Europeans, whence came firearms and the military help of such as Charlie Savage. But there was more to the chiefs' relationships to Europeans, one could even say their "acculturation," than a desire to *faire plaisir aux Blancs* with a view toward enlisting the Westerners' military support. For their connection with Europeans and things European went as far as their own subjectivities as well as their own sovereignties. Nicholas Thomas recounts of Iotete, conquering chief of Vaitaha, that "he was strongly oriented towards links with Europeans." Keen to associate himself with the early missionary William Pascoe Crook and a sandalwood trader named Sibrell, Iotete told the latter "he is an *Englishman* and Vaitaha is Pikitani (or Britain) where we may do as we please" (Thomas 1991:145).

I have elsewhere discussed how Hawaiians took on the names and identities of the European great, including King George, Bonaparte, Billy Pitt, John Adams, and others (below, Chapter Thirteen). Also how Kamehameha incorporated the dead Captain Cook into his own sovereignty, how he flew the Union Jack at his residence and from his canoe even before he put his island under King George, whom he considered and addressed by correspondence as his brother (M. Sahlins 1981:28ff., 1990:26–56, 1992). "The King of Owhyhee [Hawaii] always enquires when a vessel comes in how George is," reported an American visitor in 1798

(Townsend 1888:74). A few years earlier, during the Vancouver visit, Kamehameha posted a man to one of the ship's galleys to learn how to cook, and when the expedition was leaving he made more than one request of the British for domestic furnishings and culinary implements. Commented master's mate Thomas Manby: "And now that he was in possession of the requisites for the table, a tolerable Cook and every kind of implement for culinary purposes, the Monarch boasted with pride and satisfaction that he should now live like King George" (1929:46). And why not, since, as Manby learned from a high priest, the ruling line of Hawaii could be traced to White men who had come to the Islands a few generations previously? "From these visitors it is recorded that the present branch of Royalty are descended" (ibid.:45). If we have learned nothing else, we now know how to understand such traditions.

But the last word should go to Greg Dening. For he effectively said it all in discussing the incorporation of the British ensign left by Wallis on the beach at Matavai into the famous *maro ura*, the red-feather girdle of Tahitian royalty. A palladium of rule, the royal British loincloth became the prize of bitter struggles for hegemony among Tahitian ruling chiefs. Yet there is no evidence that the Tahitians were thus making a sign of deference to the English. Rather, Dening suggests, "they saw it as a sign of overarching sovereignty that was outside and above local politics but was imbued with all their metaphors" (1992:280).

NOTES

I am most grateful to Fergus Clunie, who generously provided me with two long discussions of his excellent work on the early history of Charlie Savage.

1. Graff warns of this possibility:

> History suggests that the same theory is often used for different and sometimes sharply antithetical political effects. There is left Hegelianism and right Hegelianism, left and right Christianity, and even left and right deconstruction.... It appears, then, that theories — again, rather like the

principles of ballistics or nuclear fission — are politically *ambidextrous*; they can be appropriated by the Right, Left, or Center, and, indeed, they come to be fought over by these factions once they reach a certain point of acceptance in a scholarly community. This is not to say that such theories are politically neutral — they invariably have *some* political consequence — but *what that consequence is* in a specific instance can't be deduced a priori from the theory itself. (1983:602–603)

2. Campbell (1980) is the most comprehensive published study of the matter. The reader is referred to Campbell for a genealogy and summaries of the main historiographic traditions. Leaving aside their differences on details of Savage's career, these traditions are remarkably consistent in attributing the political rise of Bau to the intervention of White men. Campbell's own criticism of the documents is one of the earliest postcolonial devaluations of this tradition. Another important work on Savage is Walters's study of the *Eliza* wreck (1974).

3. Many of the same phrases occur in different historical sketches of Fiji written by the early Methodist missionaries, up to and including certain notices in Williams and Calvert's *Fiji and the Fijians* (1859). One of the earliest, if not the first, instances of these repeated remarks may be found in Jaggar's papers, and either he or Cross may have originally penned them. But as I have not had the opportunity to check out this problem in the relevant archives, I cannot swear who was the original author of the passage on Bauan history and Charlie Savage cited here.

4. J. Hunt to Worth, n.d., 1848, in Calvert, Personal Papers and Correspondence. Cf. Worth 1852–53:366.

5. B.H. Thomson completed his story of Savage's single musket with a speculative account of how he kept his unique position among the other Whites at Bau: "Savage cleverly kept his fellow-Europeans in the background without arousing their enmity. He alone carried the musket; he alone could speak the language fluently, and to him the other whites thought they owed the good-will of the natives" (1908:28).

6. Wolf's assertion of a Bauan monopoly of muskets through control of the bêche de mer trade is a misreading of Ward 1972:91–123. We shall return to the relation between the musket trade and the formation of Fijian states. Arguing positively for an anthropology of history, I have not stressed the usual negative epistemological criticisms of the current pseudo-politics of interpretation, though these remain as valid as they are habitually ignored. Among them, that

there is no necessary relation between the social or personal motivations of a proposition and its explanatory value. Or that — to paraphrase a Weberian comment on explanations by utilitarian function — just because an idea has political implications does not mean that it was politically determined.

7. Campbell's allegorical interpretation of Savage was prefigured by Wall, writing in 1911: "In fact the story of Charlie Savage as we know it is most likely a compound of the story of many wrecks, and of many castaways, all centered on one individual."

8. On the systematicity of heteroglossia or conflicting voices, see Chapter Fourteen below.

9. For general criticisms of this view, see Shineberg 1967:170–75, 1971: 61–82; Howe 1974:21–38; and Clunie 1977.

10. The pleasure and pain of the body is the ultimate Western referent of power, whether in the Hobbesian and Enlightenment sense of the power to do oneself good or the Nietzschean and Marxian sense of the power to do others harm. Thus Foucault — but also the failure of Western concepts of power to describe (let alone explicate) schemes such as Fijian chiefship. See also Chapter Sixteen below.

11. A footnote adds that in the late 1820s only about 100 muskets were noted in a Bau army of 4,000 men; whereas in 1846, Cakobau led a Bau force that included at least 484 muskets.

12. Bau's fortunes had waned temporarily from 1832 to 1837, during the exile of Cakobau's father, the war king Tānoa, and its hold on foreign commerce slackened. Thus, during this critical period of the bêche de mer trade Bau was suffering severe shortages of powder and shot (Eagleston, "Ups and Downs," 365; Knights, Journal, 19 May 1833). This confirms that Bau's relation to the trade, which anyhow was never anything like a monopoly, depended on its political dominance as much or more than vice versa. Other relevant primary sources on Bau's tributary connection to the bêche de mer trade include: Calvert, Journals, 12 May 1855; Lyth, "Journal," 29 Aug. 1846, 29 Apr. 1851; Eagleston, "Ups and Downs," passim; Wallis 1851:243, 256–57, 328, 330, 343; Cheever, Journal, various dates Jan. 1845, 25 Feb. 1845; Archer, Journal, 29 Apr. – 1 May 1846; Hartwell (attrib.), 15–19 Dec. 1844, 19 Aug. 1845; and Wilkes 1844, vol. 3: 60, 190–91. In any event, the historical effects sometimes attributed to the bêche de mer trade seem disproportionate to its extent. In 1848, near the end of the bêche de mer heyday, Reverend Hunt summarized the recent commerce of the islands for the benefit of Captain Worth of HMS *Calypso*: "during the last eight

years about two cargoes of Beche de mar have been taken from the islands annually. Considerable Tortoise-shell has also been collected and a few cargoes of oil.
A few small vessels have taken curiosities, provisions, etc., and lately there has
been occasionally a whaler seeking refreshment, but the character of the natives,
the difficult navigation, and the general ignorance of Masters of vessels, etc.
respecting the islands present a great barrier to commerce" (Hunt to Worth, in
Calvert, Papers).

13. For a different depiction of Verata's hegemony in central Fiji, including
part of Vanua Levu, see Sayes 1984:3–20.

14. As previously noted, Paul Geraghty deciphered the Fijian names through
their Tongan and English transliterations. Other identifiable Fijian names in
Cook's list are Tubou (Kotoobooo), Moce (Komotto), Moala (Komarra), Vuna
(Kotoona), Cakaudrove (Takounouve), and perhaps Vuya (Kovooeea). Geraghty
will shortly be publishing his analysis of Anderson's place name lists in an article, "Linguistic Evidence for the Tongan Empire."

15. Note that Arrowsmith shows Verata [Verat] as a separate small island
(Lockerby 1925:151). Mariner's references to Vanua Levu as "Pau," repeated on
the occasion of his own visit there in 1810, are apparently derived from the hill
fort of "Nabau" in the Savusavu area, a favored resort of Mariner's Tongan informant "Cow Mooala" (Clunie, personal communication; Mariner 1827, vol. 1:
257n, 267, 270; vol. 2:75–77).

16. In a critique of the "accepted history" that had Charlie Savage single-
handedly taking Naulivou to victory and Bau to a "position of influence"
throughout Fiji, Peter France suggests such readings may be "merely further
examples of the ethnocentricity of the white man in reconstructing the past"
(1969:21). On several lines of evidence – including certain of those pursued here
– he argues that Bau's rise began before Savage arrived in Fiji.

17. The calculated tendency of allies and subordinate villages in the vicinity
of dominant lands to defect to more distant, powerful states is discussed in
Chapter Eleven of this volume. The effect is a geopolitical mosaic rather than a
system of territorially integrated confederacies. The Bau *matanitu* was of this
sort, with outlying allies such as Namālata and Sawakasa, and affiliated villages
such as Suva and Nausori, though the former pair are in the region of Verata and
the latter in the vicinity of Rewa.

18. As indicated, a good number of the places said to be "Bau lands" (*vanua
vakaBau*) in the pre-Naulivou (and pre-Savage) period are, in other versions,
reputed to have come under Bau in Naulivou's reign. These statements are not

necessarily contradictory, as will be seen in the discussion of Fijian "conquests." Versions of the traditions of the several villages or lands mentioned in the preceding paragraph may be found under the place name (and usually the ranking *yavusa*) in the General Reports (Tukutuku Raraba) of the Native Lands Commission (NLC/TR) for Tailevu South, Tailevu North, and the several Lomaiviti islands; and in the NLC Evidence Books (NLC/EB) for these areas, including the registers of Maxwell (1915–16) and Thomson (1893). See also Etuate Wainui's grandiose discussion of the Bau dominions in Wainui Papers (n.d.:88ff.). On Bau's raids during Bānuve's time, including the fights at Kedekede in Lakeba, see NLC/TR, Tailevu South, Bau, Tailevu North, Namālata; Koto, Ko Viti; Anonymous 1980:5; Turpin, Diary, MS 1; Reid 1990. It might be added that, in the view of certain Bauan ruling chiefs as asserted at the turn of the nineteenth century — no doubt with an interest in rents — Bau's domination of certain critical places in the Koro Sea had existed from time immemorial. The Bauans thus claimed control of Moturiki, part of Ovalau (the Qalivakabau), Koro, Nairai, Batiki, and part of Gau, distinguishing this control from conquest: "All these islands have been subject to Bau from the time the world was formed.... It would be a different thing if they were taken in war as slaves" (S. Veiwili et al., to the Secretary of State for the Colonies, 14 May 1909, in CSO-MP 7259/1910, 27, 29).

19. The early missionaries were often contemptuous of Fijian musketry. John Hunt retailed the story that "the natives put powder into the gun in proportion to the size of the person they intend to kill. If he be a large man they put in a large charging, and if a small one a small charging. They then fire without taking any aim" ("Fiji Journals of Rev. John Hunt," 18 Aug. 1840). Or again, John Watsford: "I once met a hundred or more men going away to war, each carrying his musket. I asked them to present arms and fire. Being willing to oblige me, they did so, and I noticed that when they pulled the trigger the muzzles of the muskets rose so considerably that very little damage could be done to anyone by the volley" (1900:53). As late as 1875, reports of Fijian effectiveness with firearms remained the same: see Von Hügel 1990:226.

20. See also Jaggar, Diaries, 15 Nov. 1839. It is possible that missionary reports of a reduction of warfare reflect conditions of the late 1820s to the beginning of the 1840s, when there was a relative decline in fighting despite the massive importation of firearms, by comparison to the intensive pregun warfare of circa 1805–1825.

21. A lot of evidence could be cited of the shallowness of the ordinary warrior's personal commitment to battle and its dependence on chiefly commitments

— including the disarray that sets in when an important chief is killed. The missionaries described this as "cowardice," and some thought it helped explain why wars became less severe when firearms were introduced. Alternatively, it could be understood as a limited ability to take casualties, related to the hierarchical order and structural cleavages in the organization of Fijian warfare. Contrasts in this regard appear even among historically related peoples, as proven by the conduct of Tongans at the battle of Kaba in 1855. The Tongans, under King George Tupou, had come to the aid of Cakobau in a critical showdown against rebel Bauans and certain other foes of long standing. In the attack on Kaba, the Tongans were able to press on and take the town despite losses that would have discouraged a Fijian force. The missionary James Calvert commented that the Kaba people "resisted nobly and would have repulsed any Feejeean army, which would not have sacrificed their men and proceeded vigorously to the attack" (Journals, 7 Apr. 1855). The defeated adversary of Cakobau, Ratu Mara, speaking to one of the native teachers, is supposed to have said of this astonishing behavior: "Ay, Aquila, your spirit is still in you, because you have not seen them. The man is a fool who fights with Tongans, I fired on them twenty or thirty times; but all we could do was of no avail. They rushed on impetuously. They are gods, and not men" (MMS, In-Letters).

22. One should note that Fijians did not hunt the sperm whale, the source of *tabua*, though the animal existed in local waters (Wilkes 1845, vol. 3:194). Whale teeth thus remained suprasocial, beyond ordinary human control; and insofar as a sacrificial offering partakes of the divinity of its destinaire, Hocart's views of the sacredness of whale teeth are supported by Fijian practice. Even in transactions among men, *tabua* are archetypally presented by inferiors to superiors in the mode of sacrifice. They are characteristically accompanied by a petition for life, and acknowledged by the superior with a bequest of life — *Mo dou bula*, "May you live."

23. "Old Paddy's" account, although transmitted thirdhand (through "Brown Boots" Brown to Turpin) is supported by retrospective views of Fijians as recorded by the early missionaries. According to newly Christianized Fijians, in the early part of the century war and cannibalism "received a new impulse, and raged with a new vigour, a vigour unknown to former generations" (Lawry 1850:43–44). Walters, however, has criticized this observation — while arguing that the effects of Savage & Co. have been exaggerated — on grounds that the converts said it just to please the missionaries (1974:63n).

24. Of the beachcombers killed at Wailea, it is not clear from Dillon's text

that three of them (Graham, Dun, and Packard) were actually living at Bau rather than elsewhere in the Islands.

25. An alternate tradition involves an episode that, if true, would speak to the continuing importance of Verata in Savage's time, for it holds that some or all of his shipmates were taken to Verata and only later went to Bau with Charlie's connivance. See, for example, Tatawaqa 1913:31, Wall 1911. Derrick accepts this story (1950:45). There is no way of telling if it is accurate or perhaps refers to some other Whites, not of the *Eliza*, who were living in Verata and made their way to Bau in the general assemblage of mercenaries taking place at the time.

26. This again on the authority of Fergus Clunie, who has done considerable research on Savage's background and career.

27. Jaggar — or, rather, his Fijian informant — seems to be the earliest source recounting another fight that broke out when the foreigners attempted to appropriate yams collected in Bau for a feast. All the Whites were killed except three — "Make," "Vakete," and Savage — and those who were at Viwa or sailing about; the Bau chief, Koroiradilevuka, was wounded (Jaggar 1988:111).

28. Compare Wilkes 1845, vol. 3:186, and *The Cyclopedia of Fiji* ([1907] 1984:72–73).

29. Born in the form of a snake, Degei's own appearance, Rokomauto (the *vasu*) then assumed a human chiefly form and repeated, in the southeastern Viti Levu heartland, the creative activities of his maternal uncle. Rokomauto plays the part of the usurping sea-king or god relative to indigenous (*i taukei*) Degei, whose home is in the mountains of northeastern Viti Levu — in Fijian directional terms "below" relative to the Verata god's "above." Where Rokomauto trailed his royal loincloth on the ground behind, the coast became sandy beach. Where he raised it up, he left a rocky shore. Villages of eastern Viti Levu are named from parts of Rokomauto's body: Kumi ("Beard"), Daku ("Back"). (See Lyth TFR:97ff.) Similarly, much of Vanua Levu was named and ordered by the journeys of Rokomauto's son Buatavutava and his entourage.

30. The reversal of hierarchy in the Bau diarchy, putting the war king over the ritual king, is matched by a reversal of the classic Fijian traditions of the founding of the polity. Almost everywhere in maritime Fiji, the war king (Vunivalu) is the descendant of the original rulers, thus head of "the land," who was replaced by an immigrant stranger-king, the ancestor of the now-preeminent ritual kings (Roko Tui). In Bau, it is the other way around: the ritual kings were the original rulers, and two successive dynasties of war kings came after (Nadurucoko and

Tui Kaba). The war kings migrated from the interior of Viti Levu (rather than by sea) and married women of the Roko Tui Bau people (a sign of usurpation).

31. What might be interpreted as a curious confirmation of Verata's continuing ideological preeminence occurs in the list of island kings compiled by Gaimard of the Dumont d'Urville expedition in 1827 from the lips of the Bau chief Tubuanakoro. Recall that Tubuanakoro's activity and other evidence had led the French to name Naulivou of Bau the "King of Fiji." For Viti Levu itself, however, Tubuanakoro named "Nasobosoba" as the king — a name connected to Verata, but not the name or title of the ruler. Naisobasoba is the name of the principal temple in Verata. See Dumont d'Urville 1832–34:709.

32. One wonders if this had not occurred during Savage's first stay in Fiji, in 1807, and if he was not taken prisoner to Tonga — whence he boarded the *Eliza* in 1808. If so, the report that he was a survivor of the *Port au Prince* taken by the Tongans could have been an understandable mistake on Patterson's part (in Im Thurn and Wharton 1925:95), rather than a fabrication of Charlie's.

33. Fison's interview with Taliai Tupou took place in 1867 or 1868. When the old chief died in 1874, according to Reid: "The oldest inhabitants could not recall having seen him as a young man, and his origins were lost in the mists of the eighteenth century when his father Rasolo had come over from Nayau and established the family as ruling dynasty in Lakeba" (1990:65–66). Fison records that the Bau chiefs used to lend out Jale Saveti to other chiefs in return for canoes and other wealth, and that Taliai Tupou had once so availed himself of Jale's services to take the island of Nayau (Miscellaneous Papers, 5 Jan. 1868).

34. Some twelve foreigners resident in the Islands dropped out of Fijian history as a result of the 1813 Wailea fracas alone, either killed or fled (Dillon 1829, vol. 1:25–26). A number of others had already died in skirmishes in Bau. As the sandalwood trade ceased at this time (1813 or 1814) and a lull in foreign commerce set in until the bêche de mer era of the late 1820s, the number of resident foreigners likewise declined radically.

35. This man, Koroijale, was one of the henchmen of Tānoa in 1832. He is said to have earned his title at the revenge taken by Bau on Wailea for the defeat in which Savage was killed. This attack by Bau is variously dated as a year later than the Wailea battle, thus 1814, or at the installation of Tānoa as Vunivalu of Bau, around 1829 or 1830. See B.H. Thomson 1908:31; Wilkes 1845, vol. 3:217; Waterhouse [1866] 1978:28; Tatawaqa 1913:48.

36. One of Savage's own daughters would become a consort of the Rewa paramount (Roko Tui Dreketi). According to some traditions, his sons were all

done away with by the Bau people, a story that may or may not be so and is of equally uncertain meaning — as beyond the self-evident, it could signify a fear they would grow up to be a threat to established chiefs.

37. Fergus Clunie writes:

> While *Jale* clearly does not appeal to latter day *pakeha* saints ... who look upon his mythology as closely akin to heresy, documentary evidence establishes beyond doubt that *Jale* was indeed a celebrated Fijian military hero, one foreigner who really fitted into the Fijian scheme of things: a *vulagi* [foreigner] who exhibited admirable virtues of a type profoundly appreciated by the Fijians of his day.... It is clear that his Fijian contemporaries admired him, *admiration* being the essence of all early accounts derived from the Fijians of his day. I'm inclined to think that he was the beau ideal of a *vulagi* from a Fijian viewpoint. A true child of thunder. (Personal communication)

38. The identification of this "famous Charley" as Charles Pickering (a Levuku man of the 1840s and 1850s) by Williams's editor G.C. Henderson is plainly mistaken (Williams 1931, vol. 1:240n). The passage in Williams's journal begins: "R.L.L. [Ratu Lewenilovo] opened out this evening respecting the conduct of the first European captains with whom he was acquainted, and also respecting the (in)famous Charley and his companions."

39. Hocart thought "there is no doubt that when muskets were dubbed 'kalou bows' (*ndakai kalou*) the natives really thought they were made by spirits or were spirits themselves" (1912:446).

40. From an article titled "Missions" in the *South-Asian Register*, cited in Gunson 1969:82.

CHAPTER THIRTEEN

Cosmologies of Capitalism:
The Trans-Pacific Sector of
"The World System"*

Develop-Man Economics

On 20 November 1839, the Reverend John Williams of the London Missionary Society was killed shortly after landing at Dillon's Bay, Eromanga, one of the New Hebrides islands (now Vanuata). Already famous as "the Apostle of Polynesia," Williams was abruptly translated to martyrdom by certain Melanesians, purportedly in blind revenge for outrages earlier inflicted on them by White sandalwood traders — or so runs the pious description of the event which, like calling it "murder" or them "savages," characteristically inscribes the actions of islanders in the notions of Westerners. The historiographic tradition of such incidents has since improved, but not to the extent of ridding itself of the Christian virtue of understanding the Melanesians on the grounds that it was not them who cast the first stone. As if they could have no reasons or violence of their own devising. Never mind that the indigenous meaning of Williams's death — in its ceremonial details strangely reminiscent of the fall of Captain Cook at Hawaii — never mind that the local meaning seems to have been nothing less than deicide.[1] In almost all the European accounts of these events, the islanders have nothing to do but to react to the determining presence of the foreigner.[2]

Of course, I invoke the missionary's fate in a metaphoric way: in order to join the anthropological chorus of protest against the

* Originally published in *Proceedings of the British Academy* 74 (1988). © The British Academy, 1989.

idea that the global expansion of Western capitalism, or the World System so called, has made the colonized and "peripheral" peoples the passive objects of their own history and not its authors, and through tributary economic relations has turned their cultures likewise into adulterated goods. In *Europe and the People Without History*, Eric Wolf is compelled to argue that attention must be paid to these people, that they are in fact historical beings, somebody more than the "victims and silent witnesses" of their own subjugation (1982:x). Wolf was moved to say so because, in the headier days of World System theory, it had seemed that there was nothing left for anthropology to do but the global ethnography of capitalism. Anthropology would be manifest destiny. Other societies were regarded as no longer possessing their own "laws of motion"; nor was there any "structure" or "system" to them, except as given by Western-capitalist domination.[3] Yet such ideas, are they not the academic form of the same domination? As though the West, having materially invaded the lives of others, would now intellectually deny them any cultural integrity. World System theory becomes the superstructural expression of the very imperialism it despises — the self-consciousness of the World System itself.

Yet why is it that in Wolf's magisterial book the same kind of thing happens? One searches here in vain for a sustained analysis of how local peoples attempt to organize what is afflicting them in their own cultural terms. Wolf invites us to see the Mundurucú and the Meo as historic agents, but what he actually shows is how they "were drawn into the larger system to suffer its impact and become *its* agents" (1982:23 [emphasis added]). An evident problem is Wolf's nostalgia for the Marxist-utilist theory favored by many world systematists. I mean the idea of culture as a reflex of the "mode of production," a set of social appearances taken on by material forces that somehow possess their own instrumental rationality and necessity.[4] From this comes the contradiction that neutralizes all the anthropological good intentions. On the one hand, Wolf argues for the people's active historic role, which must mean the way they shape the material circumstances laid on them according to their own conceptions; while, on the other hand, he advocates a cultural theory that supposes the people's conceptions are a function of their material circumstances.

But we need to take more seriously Marx's understanding of production as the appropriation of nature within and through a determinate form of society. It follows that a mode of production itself will specify no cultural order — unless and until its own order as production is culturally specified. Production, Marx wrote, is the reproduction of "a definite mode of life" (Marx and Engels 1965:32). A system of production is the relative form of an absolute necessity, a particular historical way of meeting human requirements. Hence the people's cultural assumption of external conditions that they do not create and cannot escape is the very principle of their historic action. Constructed in relation to the forces of nature — and typically also in relation to pressures of other societies — every cultural scheme known to history has been the product of just this pragmatic predicament. Not to suggest, then, that we ignore the modern juggernaut, only that its historical course be viewed as a cultural process. Western capitalism has loosed on the world enormous forces of production, coercion, and destruction. Yet precisely because they cannot be resisted, the relations and goods of the larger system also take on meaningful places in local schemes of things. In the event, the historical changes in local society are also continuous with the superseded cultural scheme, even as the new state of affairs acquires a cultural coherence of a distinct kind. So we shall have to examine how indigenous peoples struggle to integrate their experience of the world system in something that is logically and ontologically more inclusive: their own system of the world.

The problem is how to avoid the usual reduction of the intercultural encounter to a kind of physics on one side or a teleology on the other. I mean the common perception of the global economy simply and mechanically as material forces, and the corollary descriptions of local histories as unrelieved chronicles of cultural corruption. True, within a century of Captain Cook's "discovery" of the Sandwich Islands, American entrepreneurs were seizing the land and making the Hawaiians into a rural proletariat. But not true that the course of Hawaiian history since 1778 was governed by this outcome, or that it consisted merely in the replacement of Polynesian by bourgeois relations. The Islands, on the contrary, had seen a significant period of indigenous development, when the ruling chiefs appropriated Western commodities to their own hegemonic projects — which is also to say, to traditional conceptions of their own divinity. In 1810, the islands were for the first time unified, in a kingdom under Kamehameha I. If, thereafter, Hawaii succumbed to imperialist pressures, it was precisely because the effects of foreign commerce were amplified by its encompassment in a Polynesian competition for celestial powers. This happens over and over in modern world history: the capitalist forces are realized in other forms and finalities, in exotic cultural logics far removed from the native European commodity fetishism (cf. Simmons 1988).[5] Hence, the World System is not a physics of proportionate relationships between economic "impacts" and cultural "reactions." The specific effects of the global-material forces depend on the various ways they are mediated in local cultural schemes.

Rather than a planetary physics, this is a *history* of world capitalism — which, moreover, in a double fashion will testify to the authenticity of other modes of existence. First by the fact that modern global order has been decisively shaped by the so-called peripheral peoples, by the diverse ways they have culturally articulated what was happening to them. Second, and despite the terrible losses that have been suffered, the diversity is not dead. It persists in the wake of Western domination. Indeed, respectable scholars now argue that modern world history since *c.* 1860 has been marked by the simultaneous development of global integration and local differentiation.[6] For a long time, anthropologists and historians were taken in by a certain mystique of Western domination: the conceit that the world expansion of capitalism brings all other cultural history to an end. It would be wiser, as John Kelly suggests, to add the concept of "post-Westernism" to the current postmodernist vogue for postisms (1988).[7]

But I mean to focus here on an earlier stage, from the mid-eighteenth to the mid-nineteenth century, with a view toward illustrating how the peoples of the Pacific islands and the adjacent

418

Asian and American mainlands reciprocally shaped the "impact" of capitalism and thereby the course of world history. In part, the title "Cosmologies of Capitalism" comes from the observation that often in the islands, in a sort of Neolithic homage to the Industrial Revolution, Western goods and even persons have been incorporated as indigenous powers. European commodities here appear as signs of divine benefits and mythic bestowals, negotiated in ceremonial exchanges and displays that are also customary sacrifices.[8] Hence the local interests in certain European goods that, by a motivated logic of the concrete, could be assimilated to indigenous ideas of social "valuables" or sacred kinds. In contrast to relatively limited markets in means of production or short-term booms in muskets and other means of destruction, European traders in the Pacific often found this demand for luxe insatiable (Fisher 1977, M. Sahlins 1992, Salisbury 1962, Shineberg 1967).

Notice that from the viewpoint of the indigenous people, the exploitation by the world system may well be an enrichment of the local system. Even as there is net transfer of labor power to the metropole through unequal exchange rates, the hinterland peoples are acquiring more goods of extraordinary social value with less effort than ever they could in the days of the ancestors. There follow the greatest feasts, exchanges, and sing-sings that ever happened (cf. Gregory 1982, Lederman 1986a, A. Strathern 1979). And as this means the greatest accumulation of divine benefits cum human social powers, the whole process is a *development* in the cultural terms of the people concerned.

It is not "backwardness" — except from a Western-bourgeois perspective. Nor is it just "conservatism." Surely, there is a cultural *continuity*. But continuity is not the same thing as immobility; indeed, *the strongest continuity may consist in the logic of the cultural change.* "Neo-traditional development" might be the appropriate term, given the evident paradoxes in harnessing custom to commerce; but I prefer the improvised neo-Melanesian I overheard at the University of the South Pacific, where the insertion of the English "development" in a pidgin sentence came out sounding (to me) like "develop-man." From the point of view of what the people consider worthy of human beings, this is indeed *develop-man*. It is a cultural self-realization on a material scale and in material forms never before known, yet not for all that the simple penetration of capitalist-market relations. Of course, the dependence on the world economy, which has its own reasons and progress, can render the local develop-man vulnerable over the longer run. But again, destiny is not history. Nor is it always tragedy. Anthropologists tell of some spectacular forms of indigenous cultural change turning into modes of political resistance — in the name of a cultural persistence.[9]

So in response to various develop-man impulses, Western merchants searching the Pacific for exchange-value were forced to accede to local demands for prestige-value. But this was ultimately because of certain Chinese prestige values, to which the whole of world commerce was held hostage. Ever since the opening of direct trade with the West in the earlier sixteenth century, the Chinese had been vastly unimpressed with European manufactures, even with the latter-day wonders of the Industrial Revolution, and were taking little but precious silver in return for their own goods. During the eighteenth century, moreover, this Chinese allergy to Western commodities was coupled to a rapidly growing craving for tea in Britain and its English-speaking colonies, which resulted in a flood of silver toward the Orient — with reverberating effects on the mines of Potosí and thus on the African slave trade.[10] As is well known, Britain was able to overcome the unfavorable trade balance it contracted from its tea habit only by inflicting an even greater addiction on the Chinese in the form of opium imported from India — an illegal traffic backed up in 1839 by an infamous war. Having few such resources to push nor much silver, the Americans and Australians roamed the Pacific for products acceptable to China. Hence the maritime fur trade of Northwest America (in which the Americans followed the British) and the commerce in sandalwood and trepang in South Sea islands. Shineberg notes that although the Australians "were fond of expiating on the superstitious nature of the Chinese who would buy sandalwood at high prices to burn before their altars," considering their own balance of trade, "the colonial tea-drinking habit was no less quaint" (1967:6). Add in the tobacco and the luxury

420

goods the islanders were content to receive for their part in all this, and the Pacific trade proves, as Shineberg says, "that human frailty knows no race" (1967:151).

Stated more positively and anthropologically, this is also the most general argument of this chapter. The general idea is that the world system is the rational expression of relative cultural logics, that is, in the terms of exchange-value. A system of cultural differences organized as a division of labor, it is a global market in human frailties, where they all can be gainfully transacted in a common pecuniary medium. Just as Galileo thought that mathematics was the language of the physical world, so the bourgeoisie have been pleased to believe that the cultural universe is reducible to a discourse of price — despite the fact that other peoples would resist the one idea and the other by populating their existence with other considerations. Fetishism, then, is the custom of the capitalist world economy, since precisely it translates these real-historic cosmologies and ontologies, these various relations of persons and systems of objects, into the terms of a cost-benefit analysis: a simple chrematistic pidgin language by means of which we are also able to acquire social-science understandings at bargain rates. Of course, the capacity to reduce social properties to market values is exactly what allows capitalism to master the cultural order. Yet at least sometimes the same capacity makes the world capitalism the slave to local concepts of status, means of labor control, and preferences in goods which it has no will to obliterate, inasmuch as it would not be profitable. A history of the world system, therefore, must discover the culture mystified in the capitalism. As a famous historical theater of Western exploration, the Pacific seems a good place to start.

China Trade

> Nous ne plierons jamais cette nation
> à nos goûts & à nos idées.
>
> — Cibot (1782a:267)

In September 1793, George Lord Viscount Macartney, the envoy of the Western Ocean barbarian ruler George III, having come to present tributes to the Celestial Emperor and to be "turned toward civilization" by the imperial virtue — or in his own view, Ambassador Plenipotentiary and Extraordinary of his Britannic Majesty, instructed to establish diplomatic relations with China with a view toward liberalizing the Canton trade while opening new markets for British manufactures, some fine examples of which he was carrying as presents to the Ch'ien-lung Emperor on the occasion of his eighty-third birthday — in September 1793, then, Macartney received the imperial reply to his King's message. Addressed to a subject lord, this famous edict reads in part:

> We, by the Grace of Heaven, Emperor, instruct the King of England to take note of our charge.
>
> Although your country, O King, lies in the far oceans, yet inclining your heart towards civilization you have specially sent an envoy respectfully to present a state message, and sailing the seas he has come to our Court to kotow and to present congratulations for the Imperial birthday, and also to present local products, thereby showing your sincerity.
>
> We have perused the text of your state message and the wording expresses your earnestness. From it your sincere humility and obedience can clearly be seen....
>
> The Celestial Empire, ruling all within the four seas [that is, the world], simply concentrates on carrying out the affairs of Government properly, and does not value rare and precious things.... In fact, the virtue and power of the celestial Dynasty has penetrated afar to the myriad kingdoms, which have come to render homage, and so all kinds of precious things from "over mountain and sea" have been collected here, things which your chief envoy and others have seen for themselves. Nonetheless we have never valued ingenious articles, nor do we have the slightest need for your country's manufactures.[11] (Cranmer-Byng 1962:337, 340)

It has been said of the Ch'ien-lung edict (by no less than Bertrand Russell) that China cannot be understood until this document has ceased to seem absurd (Cranmer-Byng 1957–58:182). I would not claim to dispel the strangeness; on the contrary, I begin by generalizing it.

The Ch'ien-lung Emperor was not the first or the last ruler of the Celestial Kingdom to dismiss Western things. In 1816, his successor, in refusing to see another English ambassador (Lord Amherst), expressed the same imperial indifference: "My dynasty attaches no value to products from abroad; your nation's cunningly wrought and strange wares do not appeal to me in the least" (Malone 1934:173). Nor was the disinterest in European goods a sentiment of Manchu emperors only. It had been going on since the previous dynasty, the Ming, upwards of three hundred years, and as concerns the British ever since 1699, when the Honorable East India Company established itself at Canton. From the beginning, the company was embarrassed for want of any English goods to put into the trade.[12] Besides, the traffic was increasingly controlled and harassed by Chinese regulations. By the mid-eighteenth century it had settled into the classic arrangements of an insulated "port-of-trade" (cf. Polanyi et al. 1957). British shipping was limited to Canton, where the company's supercargoes were required to treat exclusively with licensed Chinese merchants — who passed along the numerous duties and extortions of lower and higher imperial officials as irksome charges on the terms of exchange. The Westerners were also quarantined socially and not greatly appreciated culturally. Dermigny summarizes the situation of European merchants at Canton:

> Relegated to their 300 meters of quay, a simple *guichet* on the flank of this enormous China through which passed silver and merchandise only, but by no means language or ideas, they [the Europeans] remained nearly completely marginal to a civilization which they gave up all hope of understanding. To the contempt manifested for them as Barbarians they would respond with a redoubled contempt for the barbarian country that China was in their eyes.[13] (1964, vol. 2:512)

Still, the English had put up with it to get silks, nankeens, and porcelains, and then more and more because of tea. By the middle of the eighteenth century, tea-drinking in Britain had diffused to all social classes and become, as Lord Macartney said, not simply "an indispensable luxury" like other chinoiserie, but "an indispensable necessity of life" (Cranmer-Byng 1962:212). Were England to be suddenly deprived of tea, observed the secretary of the Macartney mission, Sir George Staunton, the effect would be a national "calamity" (1799, vol. 1:12). Yet, historically speaking, tea had appeared in Britain only yesterday, around 1650 (Milburn 1813, vol. 2:527ff.; Repplier 1932; Ukers 1935). The first tea brought in by the East India Company amounted to 143 pounds, 8 ounces, in 1669. By the 1740s, however, the company's annual imports were running over two million pounds, and by 1800 over twenty million pounds (Morse 1966, Pritchard 1929).[14] So if the Chinese Emperor's status as the Son of Heaven was entailed in his contempt for foreign-barbarian manufactures, on the British side, in their own cosmic scheme, "tea was...the god to which everything else was sacrificed" (Pritchard 1936:163).

Notably sacrificed were the famous British woolens, offered up on the Canton market at significant losses in order to finance the purchase of teas. (This must be the origin of the [New York] garment industry joke to the effect that they made up their losses in volume — the tea, of course, bringing superprofits in Britain.) During the last decade of the eighteenth century, the dumping of woolens increased substantially, which helped to reduce silver expenditures (Pritchard 1929:155). In 1820, the directors of the company reported they had sustained a net loss of £1,685,103 on British products over the past twenty-three years, due to "forcing the trade beyond the demand" (Morse 1966, vol. 1:75).[15] By now, the Industrial Revolution was well under way, and apart from the woolens manufacturers, the producers and merchants of steel and iron goods, of ships and marine equipment, and of cotton textiles were all clamoring for the opening of new markets — especially the cotton kings, after the freeing of the Arkwright patent in 1785 caused a crisis of overproduction. The clamor was one good reason why the government decided on the Macartney mission — which cost the East India Company another £78,000. Yet no more after the mission than before were the Chinese merchants willing to take risks on these sundry British goods.[16] The one thing always acceptable was silver coin. On the Westerners' part, however, this continuous drain of treasure was not at all to their mercantilist liking.

Until the early nineteenth century, or for nearly three centuries, China was the tomb of European silver — from which none ever returned. Over 150 million in Spanish dollars (*reals*) thus disappeared into the Celestial Kingdom during the eighteenth century alone. Soon, the British (although not the Americans and other Westerners) would be clear of this problem, due not only to woolen imports but especially to the private "Country Trade" in Indian opium and raw cotton, operating under license from the East India Company. Credit procedures allowed the Company to put the Canton returns of the Country Trade to its own account. Still, during the 250 years before the First Opium War (1839–1842) an estimated 350 millions (*reals*) in silver bullion were exported by Western merchants into China (Mancall 1984:100). And although Europe's Asian trade was thus clearly complementary to its American trade — whence came the silver that bought the tea that John Bull drank — Wallerstein finds the whole affair "strange indeed," considering Europe's "passionate hoarding of bullion," and proposes to exclude it from the capitalist world system, apparently because it was organized on Asian terms (1974/1980: 330; but see Axtell 1982:89–90).

These terms were evident not only in the Ch'ien-lung Emperor's reply to George III but in nearly every incident of the Macartney mission, which is why I focus attention on it.[17] Sent to "negotiate" a treaty, as he conceived between equal sovereigns of independent states, Lord Macartney came face-to-face — at that by special grace, as he should have been face-to-ground — with the Unique Man whose benevolent rule was the sole means of order in the human world. His Lordship, who wanted to impress the Chinese court with the powers of his own civilization, represented as the extension of the virtues of his own king, was received by the Supreme Lord whose own virtue (*te*) was the condition of the possibility of any civilization whatsoever. With such universal power there could be no question of treating or negotiating, only of submitting or "coming to be transformed." This means, transformed to culture from the undifferentiated and

425

disordered state of barbarism that the English shared, in such outer realms as Europe, with the wildest monstrosities of nature. Through his sacrificial offices and the example of his sage behavior, through the virtue of his person as diffused by the conduct of his officials, the Son of Heaven uniquely mediated between humanity and the transcendent celestial source of earthly welfare. His were classical powers of hierarchy — inclusive politically, as they were total culturally.[18]

In the ancient imperial tradition, the founder of the dynasty, recipient of a renewed Mandate of Heaven, promulgates a new calendar, new weights and measures, and a new musical scale. He thus institutes human time and space, economy and harmony — all as the extension of the imperial person: "'His voice was the standard of sounds,'" a famous Han historian writes of the legendary founder of the Hsia dynasty, "'his body was the standard of measures of length.' He could thus determine the Numbers which serve to regulate Time and Space, as well as the Music which creates the universal harmony" (Granet 1930:16). The first Manchu emperor did not hesitate to employ a Jesuit astronomer to formulate the dynasty's calendrical system (Fu 1966, vol. 1:3–4; Spence 1980:3ff). Nor did he or his successors neglect to harmonize the occupations of mankind with the Heavenly passage of the seasons: by the correct sacrifices, of course, but also by the exclusive distribution on New Year's Day of the annual calendar — counterfeit of which was a penal offense and falsification a capital crime.[19] Such gifts of time were among the benefits barbarians could receive in return for submitting tributes, along with the seals to affix to their own dated edicts, patents of office, and noble ranks in the Chinese system, valuable presents from the emperor, and often the right to trade for Chinese goods.[20]

Trade fits into the tribute system, normally as the sequitur, since the "tribute system" in its most general sense referred to the material mode of integration into civilization. Barbarians' tributes were signs of the force of attraction of the imperial virtue, objectifications of the Emperor's civilizing powers. "The kings of former times," relates an official Ming document, "cultivated their own refinement and virtue in order to subdue persons at a distance, whereupon the barbarians (of the east and north) came to Court to have audience" (quoted in Fairbank 1942:132). Thus the following perception of the Carolingian empire, from a Ch'ing period account:

> During the middle of the T'ang Dynasty [A.D. 618–906], Charlemagne, a wise and learned man, gifted with civil and military talents, became Emperor of the Germans and the French. His fame and virtue spread far afield, and all the barbarians submitted to him. (Quoted in Schurmann and Schell 1967:123)

The tributes of the barbarians were obligatorily special products of their own country. Hence, in certain symbolic respects, the more bizarre they were the better: as signifying at once the inclusiveness of the imperial virtue, its capacity to encompass a universal diversity, and the Emperor's ability to order the fluctuations of the world beyond the Chinese pale by the control of its monsters and its wonders (cf. Mancall 1984:16). Consider this flowery encomium penned in 1419 by a Confucian literatus in celebration of the arrival of a tributary giraffe, that is, a "unicorn" (ch'i-lin):

> When the virtue of the Imperial Ruler above reaches the Great Purity, below reaches the Great Stillness, and in between reaches the Myriad Spirits, then a ch'i-lin [giraffe] appears.... It is also said: when the virtue of the Ruler penetrates into the dark waters of chaos and his transforming influence reaches out to all living beings, then a ch'i-lin appears. (Quoted in Walker 1956:24)

Rendered principally at the winter solstice and the Emperor's birthday, the barbarians' tributes were in this way connected with world rebirths, securing for them the material benefits of the Ruler's intercession with Heaven. Prosperity was entailed also in the valuable presents received by the tribute emissary from the Emperor, showing that the latter knew how to "cherish men who come from afar." Again, trade was part of the same set of conceptions: officially regarded as a "boon" granted to the barbarians, as

427

Fairbank explains, "the necessary means of their sharing in the bounty of China" (1942:139). So Lord Macartney's intention to liberalize trade by offering birthday presents to the Emperor was not unintelligible to the Chinese, or at least it lent itself to a working misunderstanding.[21] Nor would such conceptions imply Chinese disinterest in trade or preclude its functional uses in politics or profits. In the long history of the Chinese frontiers, most famously in the north, commerce was often an instrument of policy — whether encouraged as part of a forward policy of expansion, or permitted in an effort to neutralize a barbarian threat (cf. Lattimore 1940, Fairbank and Têng 1941).

As I say, such structures appear as events in the chronicles of the Macartney mission. But I can only just refer, for example, to His Lordship's refusal to ko-tow before the Emperor, of which perhaps too much has already been made in an Orientalist vein (cf. Pritchard 1943). Enough to note that Macartney, insisting that one should distinguish between the homage of tributary princes and the respects of "a great and independent sovereign" such as his own, proposed that he would go through with the ko-tow if a Chinese official of equal rank would do the same before a portrait of George III (Cranmer-Byng 1962:100, 119, and passim). This proposal, said the Imperial Court documents, "showed ignorance" (Cranmer-Byng 1957–58:156–58). Again, there is Macartney's repeated desire to get down to the business of negotiating, once the embassy had been ceremoniously received by the Emperor and the gifts exchanged. The desire was never fulfilled because, so far as the Chinese were concerned, the business was already finished — the ceremonies *were* the business (Cranmer-Byng 1962:137, 148; cf. Hevia 1986). Here it seems relevant to note that during the first fifty years of the East India Company's existence in China, it had not a single (Western) employee who could speak Chinese (Pritchard 1929:39). The so-called astronomer of the Macartney mission, Dr. Dinwiddie, complained repeatedly about the inability of the English to understand what was going on. "With what countenance will Lord Macartney return to Europe after his shameful treatment?" he asks. "No apology will satisfy. We go home — are asked what we have done. Our answer — we could not speak to the people" (quoted in Proudfoot 1868:87, cf. 71).[22]

However, Lord Macartney was aware that the banners flying on the fleet of Chinese river junks carrying him toward Peking read "The English Ambassador bringing tribute to the Emperor of China." He knew, but he diplomatically chose to ignore it, as a tactic in the sustained counterargument the British were also making in the language of goods. As they understood, the so-called tributes were "specimens of the best British manufacture, and all the late inventions for adding to the conveniences and comforts of social life," carefully selected to answer to "the double purpose of gratifying those to whom they were presented, and exciting a more general demand for the purchase of similar articles" (Staunton 1799, vol. 2:23).[23] So in the several incidents where the distinction was explicitly drawn between "presents" (what the British were calling them) and "tributes" (what the Chinese called them), one could never guess what the cunning Occidentals were really thinking. Their "presents" were really *samples* of their wares; even beyond that they were *examples* of industrial ingenuity, designed to signify the "superiority" of British civilization and the majesty of George III. Including instruments for scientific experiments, a globe with the tracks of Captain Cook's discoveries, handsome carriages and sword blades that could cut through iron without losing their edge, these presents, as Sir George Staunton put it, had been carefully chosen to "denote" the progress of Western science and to "convey information" to the Emperor (*ibid.*:243). "It was meant to surprise the Chinese with the power, learning and ingenuity of the British people," says Dinwiddie, "for which purpose a splendid assortment of astronomical and scientific apparatus were among the presents to his Celestial Majesty"; this included a planetarium that had taken thirty years to make "and was allowed to be the most wonderful piece of mechanism ever emanating from human hands" (quoted in Proudfoot 1868:26). To the British, then, their presents were self-evident signs of an industrial logic of the concrete — the signs of "our preeminence" (Cranmer-Byng 1962:191). They were supposed to communicate a whole political, intellectual, and moral culture (Hevia 1986:135ff.). Yet if ever anyone carried coals to Newcastle, it was British people carrying signs of civilization to the Chinese.

In his journal, Macartney is repeatedly indignant at the mandarins' refusal to be mortified. But from the mandarins' perspective, if the "presents" were indeed "tributes" expressing the barbarians' sincere desire to turn to civilization, manifestly they could not be superior to things Chinese. At best, they were what they should be: rare and strange exotica from an outer world where categories were crossed, blurred, inverted, and confused. So were the British "presents" interpreted, Staunton learned, on the streets of Peking:

> Among the stories that caught, at this moment, the imagination of the people, the arrival of the Embassy was said to furnish no inconsiderable share. The presents brought by it to the Emperor, were asserted to include whatever was rare in other countries, or not known before to the Chinese. Of the animals that were brought, it was gravely mentioned, that there was an elephant the size of a monkey, and as fierce as a lion, and a cock that fed on charcoal. Everything was supposed to vary from what had been seen in Pekin before, and to possess qualities different from what had been there experienced in the same substances.[24] (Staunton 1799, vol. 2:21; cf. Cranmer-Byng 1962:114, Proudfoot 1868:51)

In a wonderful Orientalist text written some half century later, the English sinologist Thomas Meadows explains that Chinese people, beholding such a technical marvel as an English ship, simply do not get the message that the country in which it was produced "*must*" be inhabited by an energetic and rich population "free to enjoy the fruits of its own labour," that it "*must*" have a powerful government and good laws "and be altogether in a high state of civilization" (1847:235; Meadows sounds like a modern functionalist archaeologist, though not more mistaken). The Chinese will allow, he adds, that the English can do some extraordinary things, but so do elephants and other wild beasts. Indeed, Dinwiddie recorded just this kind of contemporary reaction to the Macartney mission, including the Chinese failure to appreciate the native Western theory of the systematic relation between technology and civilization:

> Their prejudices are invincible. Ask them whether the contrivers and makers of such curious and elegant machinery must not be men of understanding, and superior persons. They answer — "These are curious things, but what are their use? Do the Europeans understand the art of Government as equally polished?" (quoted in Proudfoot 1868:50)

All this helps explain Lord Macartney's failure to induce a general demand for British goods — why, for example, he did not get the Chinese to throw away their chopsticks, as he was convinced they would when he demonstrated the "conveniency" of Sheffield knives, forks, and spoons (Cranmer-Byng 1962:225–26).[25]

As it happened, when the Emperor told Lord Macartney he had no need of Britain's ingenious devices, he was not lying. He had them all, and in greater magnificence than ever Macartney could offer, though he kept them notably in his outlying hunting parks and summer palaces, Jehol beyond the Great Wall, where he received the English ambassador, and the "Garden of Perfect Brilliance," Yuan Ming Yuan, also outside Peking. If here the Emperor displayed his universality, his inclusion of the barbarians, it was at a distance from the Chinese harmonies that contrastively set off the capital and the Middle Kingdom as a whole. This symbolic contrast, I mean to show, is a key to the imperial trade policies.[26]

At Jehol, where the Emperor hunted, were stored untold riches from the lands of barbarians — who were likewise hunted and collected. In numerous pavilions decorated with scenes of the Emperor's progresses and imperial feats of the chase (in which he was "always seen at full gallop shooting wild beasts with arrows"; Staunton 1799, vol. 2:82), Lord Macartney was able to see for himself:

> every kind of European toys and sing-songs; with spheres, orreries, clocks, and musical automatons of such exquisite workmanship, and

in such profusion, that our presents must shrink from the comparison and "hide their diminished heads." And yet I am told that the
fine things we have seen are far exceeded by others of the same kind
in the apartments of the ladies and in the European repository at
Yuan-ming Yuan. (Cranmer-Byng 1962:125–26)

The English never did see the "European repository": the impres-
sive set of palaces in the Italianate baroque at Yuan Ming Yuan,
designed for the Emperor by Jesuit missionaries and cluttered
with all sorts of European wealth. A French missionary who had
viewed these palaces found it "incredible how rich this sovereign
is in curiosities and magnificent objects of all kinds from the
Occident" (quoted in Malone 1934:160).[27] Yet the foreign treasures were only part of an assemblage that aimed to make the
imperial retreats complete with every imaginable creation of
nature as well as of humanity. As Granet says, even things that
no collector could find nevertheless figured there, sculpted or
drawn: it was a universal collection of "evocative singularities"
(1968:274). Such diversity was directly linked to the ruler's
power. Indeed, if the Chi'en-lung Emperor made Jehol a museum
of his prowess, it was in the tradition of the original conqueror,
Ch'in Shih Huang-ti (reign: 221–210 B.C.), who, "in order to
enjoy all his victories at once and in detail," had as many palaces
built in his grandiose gardens as he had destroyed in foreign prin-
cipalities, each edifice reproducing the residence of a defeated
ruler (Cibot 1782b; cf. Yang and Yang 1974:168).

The synthesis of diversity and conquest made these imperial
retreats perfect microcosms: they represented the whole world as
the work of the Emperor and within his power. "All the beasts of
the air, of the water, of the earth thronged in his fish ponds and
his parks. No species was wanting in his botanic gardens; the
waves of his lakes could be seen breaking against the distant lands
in which could be recognized the mysterious Isles of the immor-
tals" (Granet 1930:394). Written of the great Emperor Wu of
Han, the description summarizes just as well Lord Macartney's
wide-eyed account of the East Garden of the Ch'ien-lung Emper-
or at Jehol (Cranmer-Byng 1962:124ff.; cf. Malone 1934).[28] For

the Manchu emperor, one would only need to add the condensed collections of human life: the villages and monasteries, libraries and temples, as well as peasant fields of every crop. The libraries housed exhaustive collections of knowledge, the results of a search initiated by the Emperor in 1771 for the most rare and valuable books of the realm (Guy 1987). Yet, merely by contemplating his garden, the sage king could cultivate his powers of rule, since in such a setting meditation amounted to the absorption of the universe.[29] At Yuan Ming Yuan, there was even a miniature walled town with streets, squares, temples, marketplaces, shops, and civic buildings (Figure 13.1). If at Versailles Marie Antoinette played the shepherdess in pastoral idylls, at Yuan Ming Yuan the Empress, women of court, and the Emperor dressed up as city-dwellers to join a throng of eunuchs, themselves impersonating merchants, artisans, peddlars, porters, soldiers, and even pick-pockets, in scenes that reproduced "all the hurly-burly, the comings and goings, and even the swindling of the big cities" (Attiret [1743] 1843:790).

The Jesuit painter Attiret, to whom we owe this eighteenth-century description, goes on to contrast the apparent disarray of the summer gardens with the balanced arrangements of the imperial palace at Peking. The "beautiful order" of the latter he likens to our Western notions of symmetry and uniformity, where nothing is without parallels, nothing displaced, but everything responds exactly to what is *en face* and counterposed to it (Figure 13.2). In Yuan Ming Yuan, however, there reigns a "beautiful disorder," which could even be called an "anti-symmetry." Chinese sources confirm that the apparent disorder — while avoiding submission to "a symmetry even more tiresome than it is cold and monotonous" — is again meant to imitate nature (Cibot 1782b:318). The linked connotations of natural heterogeneity and imperial power are resumed by Attiret's observation that not one of the pastoral pavilions resembled another; instead, "one would say that each is made according to the ideas and model of some foreign country" (1843:791). Extending even to the smallest architectural details, the diversity repeatedly evokes from the Jesuit artist the sense of a human mastery of a universal plenitude: "Not until I came here

433

Figure 13.1 She Wei Ch'eng in Yuan Ming Yuan. Street flanked by shops leading toward a gate in the background. From Síren (1949); original painting by T'ang Tai and Shên Yuan, Bibliothèque Nationale, Paris.

had I seen doors and windows with such a variety of form and figure: round, oval, square, polygons of all kinds; or in the form of fans, flowers, vases, birds, beasts, fishes — in short, in every regular or irregular shape" (*ibid.*:792). Yet it is remarkable, comments Granet, that when the Chinese have welcomed "legends or techniques, *jongleries* or ideas tinged with exoticism, they have never admitted these in the house." Since ancient times an elegant system of classification has reigned over such domestic habitations, a balanced order of things Chinese. Whereas in the parks reserved "to their hunts, their *fêtes*, their games," the rulers receive "everything that is brought to them: ideas or gods, exotic or new, astrologers, poets and clowns" (Granet 1968:295–96).[30] And, one might add, English lords and their curious gifts, such as the fine carriages Macartney brought, which were never used but instead consigned to an undignified place in one of the rococo palaces at Yuan Ming Yuan (Barrow 1805:145, Swinhoe 1861:331).[31]

The point I want to make is that these imperial gardens and hunting lodges signified a cultural politics, encompassing an economics that was likewise inclusive and exclusive and could thus adapt appropriately to the practical situation. The opposition between the emperor's countryside and the imperial city recapitulated a whole cosmography of civilization — sometimes called "the inner-outer separation" (Wang 1968) — which the Chinese have represented also in other ways. Joseph Needham reproduces an ancient Chinese plan of the world, laid out as a series of inclusive squares surrounding a central royal domain (Figure 13.3). Extending outward from the royal center, the epitome of a structured order, are barbarian zones of decreasing civilization and pacification, ending in the far reaches of a "cultureless savagery" (1959:502). By setting China apart while at the same time making it the central source of world order, this theory of civilization lends itself equally to projects of imperial expansion and cultural withdrawal, to hegemonic inclusions or xenophobic exclusions, according to the contingencies of the situation.

This may well be a normal dynastic cycle, including the pendulation between a forward economic policy and a period of xenophobic retreat, coinciding with a territorial expansion that

435

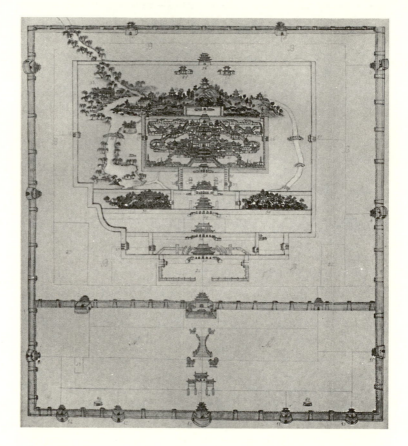

Figure 13.2 Imperial City, Peking, from the album (v. IV) of the original Dutch manuscript of A.E. van Braam, *Memoriaal wegens de ambassade der Nederlandsche Oost-
Indische Compagnie voor den Kyzer van China in de jaren 1794/95*, as reproduced in
Jan Julius Lodewijk Duyvendak, "The Last Dutch Embassy to the Chinese Court
(1794–1795)," *T'oung Pao Archives* 34 (1938).

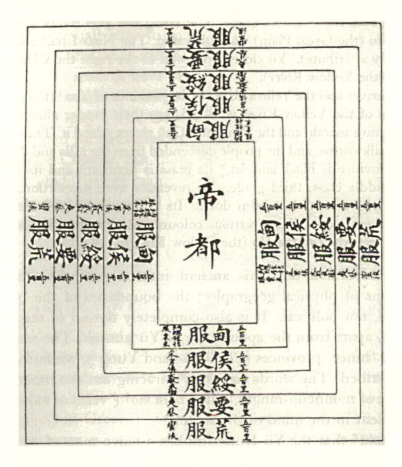

Figure 13.3 Traditional conception of the radiation of Chinese civilization (J. Needham 1959:502). Proceeding outward from the metropolitan center, Needham writes, "we have, in concentric rectangles, (a) the royal domains, (b) the lands of the tributary feudal princes and lords, (c) the 'zone of pacification,' i.e., the marshes, where the Chinese civilization was in the course of adoption, (d) the zone of allied barbarians, (e) the zone of cultureless savagery."

437

ultimately reveals the limits and weaknesses of the Chinese imperium. The dynastic conquests in ascendant phases would encourage just those processes Lattimore identifies as sources of decline, notably the development of gentry power and mercantile wealth (1940). Diverting revenues from the central government and imposing ruin on the peasantry, the rise of these private powers issues in a crisis of the imperial regime. The government proves less and less able to cope with the twinned menaces of domestic uprising and barbarian incursion that now appear, the unwanted offspring of its own successes. Hence the close correlation between the achievement of world empire and the inauguration of a political economy of exclusion, by contrast to an earlier, inclusive relation to the barbarian periphery when the new dynasty was proving its claim to the Mandate of Heaven.

Sinologists have made this argument for the Ming period (Fletcher 1968) as well as for the Ch'ing dynasty at issue here (Dermigny 1964, vol. 2:468ff., esp. 487–95). The spectacular expansion of Ming under the Yung-lo Emperor (reign: 1403–1434) is well known, especially the great voyages of the eunuch admiral Chêng-ho which ran China's writ from East Africa to the East Indies. In huge armadas, with personnel running into the tens of thousands, Chêng-ho sailed as far as the Persian Gulf and African coast, "collecting vassals like souvenirs" (Cameron 1970:124; Lo 1958; Needham 1971:487ff.; Fairbank 1942:40–41; Dermigny 1964, vol. 1:300ff.). By contrast, the later Ming saw a radical decline in foreign tributary embassies, together with an imperial disinterest in foreign trade — just when the Europeans came in (Fairbank and Têng 1941).[32] A similar withdrawal had marked the later T'ang dynasty (post–eighth century), when strict trade restrictions were imposed in the name of the ethical integrity of the Middle Kingdom. Yet a century before, Chinese noblemen dressed à la Turque were camping out in felt tents on the streets of Peking. In the earlier "fullness of T'ang," a passion for the exotic in every shape and form — from green-eyed Inner Asian dancing girls to the sandalwood of India or the spices of the Moluccas — had gripped all classes of Chinese society (Schafer 1963).[33] Still, this kind of oscillation, as Joseph Fletcher observes

438

of the comparable Ming cycle, entailed no change in the Chinese theory of empire. The inclusive and exclusive policies were alternative practical modalities of the same concept of hierarchy. In later Ming, Fletcher writes, the emperors

> began to fulfill their mandate more passively. More and more, China stood aloof, disdained trade, and viewed the acceptance of Central Asian tribute as a concession; nevertheless, it would be a distortion to regard the early Ming explorations simply as the events of an isolated episode. That the Ming tried to draw the world closer during the early history of the dynasty and not afterwards reflects the Ming's early strength and its later weakness. It does not reflect a change of doctrine or an abdication of the emperor's world supremacy. The early initiative and later withdrawal occurred within the context of the same institutions and imperial claims. The foreign expeditions and diplomatic concessions of the Hung-wu and Yung-lo periods represent Ming values in a period of strength, while the antiforeignism and anticommercialism of the later Ming are their expression in a period of weakness. (Fletcher 1968:215; cf. Dermigny 1964, vol. 1:296)

We see how inadequate is the idea of Chinese "self-sufficiency" which Western scholars have been repeating tautologically and for too long to explain Ming and Ch'ing indifference to European commodities (Cranmer-Byng 1962:12, Fairbank 1942:139, Greenberg 1951:5). Even in the earlier Ch'ing there had been more than traces of a revived commercial cycle, complemented by the interest of the long-ruling K'ang Hsi Emperor (reign: 1662–1722) in European arts and sciences (Mancall 1984:60–63, 84ff.; Spence 1975; Pritchard 1929:104ff.; Wills 1979). But now there were new factors in play, including the Manchu failure to control a developing private trade in the southeast, in which also were engaged barbarian forces of an unprecedented kind (cf. Fu 1966: 122–23, Fairbank and Têng 1941). Outside the orbit of Chinese civilization, these Western forces were eccentric to its tempos. Unlike the traditional frontier peoples and vassals, the Europeans could never be controlled or bought off (cf. Lattimore 1940).

Indeed, their demands on China generally augmented over time, according to their own entrepreneurial rhythms. The Manchu dynasts found Western silver quite useful for their own world system projects. But during the rule of the Ch'ien-lung Emperor, precisely at the greatest extent of Manchu conquests and the height of the imperial powers, the Son of Heaven preferred to satisfy his interest in things foreign through the contemplation of his own gardens. From what he saw there, he could always be sure of his world-constituting virtue.

The Sandwich Islands

While the Celestial Emperor had no need of British manufactures, the kings and would-be kings of the Sandwich Islands, by reason of their own heavenly status, could not get enough. Nor was their avidity confined to European material goods, which they considered generally superior to their own; they wanted the identity of the European great, whose names and habits they adopted as signs of their own dignity. By 1793, the same year the Ch'ien-lung Emperor commended the tributary English king for showing him the proper reverence, the three most powerful Hawaiian rulers had been pleased to name their sons and heirs "King George" (Bell 1929 I[5]):64).[34] An agent of the American Fur company describes the Honolulu sporting scene in 1812:

> At the race course I observed Billy Pitt, George Washington and Billy Cobbet walking together in the most familiar manner, and apparently engaged in confidential conversation; while in the center of another group, Charley Fox, Thomas Jefferson, James Madison, Bonnepart and Tom Paine were seen on equally friendly terms with each other. (Cox 1832:144)

Within the decade the Hawaiian "Billy Pitt," aka Kalanimoku, will indeed be "Prime Minister" of a unified Sandwich Islands kingdom, with his classificatory brothers "Cox" Ke'eaumoku and "John Adams" Kuakini respectively ruling as the governors of Maui and Hawaii Island.

Clearly, these foreigners by whom Hawaiian ruling chiefs took consciousness of themselves were not unruly barbarians from the margins of the earth. Rather, they came from the sky beyond the horizon: from the mythical Kahiki, the celestial and overseas homelands of gods, sacred chiefs, and cultural good things. Like the royal ancestors who brought thence foods, rites, tabus — the means of human life and the distinctions of social order — the White men or *Haole* were perceived as bearers of powers civilizing and divine (cf. M. Sahlins 1981, 1985a, 1992). Well into the nineteenth century, the history of the Islands was shaped by this correlation between foreign and Polynesian powers that be.

From the time of Cook, who was searching a northwest passage to the Orient, Westerners had come to Hawaii because of the China trade. But nearly everything in the intercultural encounter was the opposite to their Chinese experience. Macartney had refused to ko-tow to the Chinese Emperor, as it would impugn the dignity of his own King; whereas, when Cook first stepped ashore at Kaua'i Island, the Hawaiians promptly prostrated before him, as they did for those high chiefs they called *akua*, "gods" (Malo 1951:54). And if the great Hawaiian chiefs competed to distinguish themselves by taking on European identities, it was because, unlike the Celestial Emperor, the Unique Man, they confronted each other as perpetual rivals who in their own divinity were virtual doubles (cf. V. Valeri 1972, 1981; M. Sahlins 1985b).

Traditionally, Hawaiian ruling chiefs had vied for ancestry and tabu status by strategic marriages with noble women and violent sacrifices of royal adversaries. Such exploits could represent in social practice the theory of sovereignty encoded in myth and enacted in annual rite: theory of usurpation by the upstart warrior, who is archetypally a stranger and whose victory over the god or king of ancient lineage involves also the seizure of his predecessor's sacred wife. The realm of the political, then, appears as a practical version of the cosmological: a transposition of the Polynesian scheme of the appropriation of the bearing earth (= the sacred wife) from the god (= the reigning king) by and for human kind (= the usurper-warrior). But as thus transposed to practice, the competition for divine honors becomes permanent and indecisive. By virtue of a long history of strategic intermarriages,

441

contending chiefs are all able to trace their lineage one way or another (that is, bilaterally) to the same godly sources. Genealogy turns into an argument rather than an entitlement; and a kind of entropy appears in the system of rank, a tendency to move toward an undifferentiated state, for by some line of descent or another an ambitious chief could pretend to seniority over political rivals who on similar grounds supposed themselves superior to him. In traditional times, a chief rich in lands and followers could always hope to turn such assets into a legitimate claim of distinction. Thus the role assumed by the late eighteenth-century visitations of Kahiki: in analogous ways, the chiefs searched distinction in the relations and goods of Western commerce. The whole of this history seems epitomized by an incident of 1793, when the soon-conqueror of archipelago Kamehameha formally greeted the British commander Vancouver while clad in a fine Chinese dressing gown he considered "the most valuable garment in his wardrobe," as his predecessor (Kalaniopu'u) had received it as a present from Captain Cook (Manby 1929:40).[35]

However, the report of certain Americans alongside English and Frenchmen among the *tout* Honolulu of 1812 reflects an important shift in the international order of the trans-Pacific commerce. By the turn of the nineteenth century, Yankee entrepreneurs had captured the Northwest Coast–Canton fur trade, the possibilities of which were originally disclosed by Cook's third voyage and initially exploited by British shipping.[36] Cut off from the British West Indies after the Revolution, the merchants of the fledgling United States had turned to the markets of the Far East. The problem was that they had precious little silver to offer for Chinese goods. "To find something saleable in Canton was the riddle of the China trade," Samuel Eliot Morison observes, but "Boston and Salem solved it" (1961:46).[37] Morison perhaps exaggerates, inasmuch as Pacific sea otter pelts and other fine furs never yielded the Americans more than about one sixth of the funds they needed to pay for China goods (Pitkin 1835:245ff.). The rest had to be covered in specie, such as they got from the neutral carrying trade in Europe during the French Revolutionary and Napoleonic wars.[38] This continuing silver drain gave American traders an equally persistent interest in products of Pacific islanders that could fit the categories of Chinese consumers.

Thus the search for sandalwood, such as the Chinese had been importing from India and the Indies since the T'ang dynasty for use in noble architecture and fine objets d'art and to disseminate the whiff of an increasingly influential Buddhism. As incense and in image, "the divinely sweet odour of the sandal expressed to the senses the antidemonic properties concealed within its godlike body" (Schafer 1963:137). A thousand years later, by virtue of powers undreamed of in this philosophy, the properties concealed in sandalwood trees of the New Hebrides, Hawaii, and the Fiji Islands, used to drive out Chinese demons, could thereby be transformed into teas that in turn generated pecuniary returns to American entrepreneurs at whatever the cost to whom it might concern.

In Hawaii the sandalwood trade superseded an earlier commerce in "refreshments" that had already made the Islands "a great caravansary" on the Northwest Coast–Canton fur trade route (Fleurieu, quoted in Bradley 1968:22). The strategic location of the group was one reason for the refreshment trade. Another was the superior ability of Hawaiian chiefs, by comparison to the Northwest Indians, to supply provisions to the shipping (Howay 1930). I say "chiefs" because (as I have elsewhere documented), they took main control of this trade, using traditional privileges such as their tabuing powers to organize it in their own interests (cf. M. Sahlins 1981). Suffice it here to note that the chiefs were able to impose their own demands — at once on Westerners for armaments and on the Hawaiian people for labor and produce, largely unpaid. By 1810, the Hawai'i Island ruler Kamehameha, through a superior access to European trade — grounded in a privileged reaction to the manes of Captain Cook — had unified the group in a conquest kingdom. Hawaiian sandalwood was about to become the staple commercial interest of the Islands. To American merchants it became even more interesting around 1820, as returns declined in the maritime fur trade — whereas, in Hawaii, the sandalwood trade literally enriched the customary conflicts between the king and ranking chiefs, which more and

443

more appeared as demonstrations of indigenous *mana* in the most appropriate forms of foreign wealth. The rivalries became so serious that *Haole* inside-dopesters were predicting a partition of the kingdom among "the grandees" after Kamehameha's death, a kind of decentralization that had also happened before (Whitman 1979:89; Chamisso 1981:431–32; Rocquefeuil 1823, vol. 2:342ff.; cf. M. Sahlins 1972:144ff.). But as it happened now, the king died in 1819, thus bringing the Polynesian political cycle into conjunction with an equally characteristic capitalist economic cycle — and launching the Hawaiian great on their brilliant careers of conspicuous consumption.

America in 1818–1819 was in the grip of a financial crisis. Among New England merchants the shortage of specie put a premium on Hawaiian sandalwood as a means of carrying on a China trade. The Americans thereupon

> descended upon the islands in a swarm, bringing with them everything from pins, scissors, clothing, and kitchen utensils to carriages, billiard tables, house frames, and sailing ships, and doing their utmost to keep the speculating spirit at a fever heat among the Hawaiian chiefs. And the chiefs were not slow about buying; if they had no sandalwood at hand to pay for the goods, they gave promissory notes. (Kuykendall 1968:69)

They were not slow about buying — only about paying. Contemporary documents give the impression of an *opéra bouffe* staged in naive tropical settings richly furnished from an international division of labor: these huge Polynesian notables covered in variegated costumes of fine Chinese silk and English broadcloth, being hauled through the dusty lanes of Honolulu in pony chaises or wheelbarrows by straining menials clad in loincloths, or playing at scenes of European dining in thatched houses at teak tables set with English silver and crystal — with all the good things imported on the never-never. Whereas the common people enter only as supporting characters: arduous work, given the sheer bulk of the ruling chiefs. Although many of the chiefs were now professing Christians, they would never learn to mortify their own

flesh. The family that de facto governed the Islands after Kamehameha's death (the Ka'ahumanu people) included five brothers
and sisters weighing in at contemporary estimates of 250–350
pounds each (Bloxam, "Narrative" 15, 28 May 1825; Dampier
1971:48). Signifying the control of land, food, and people, and the
means of their productivity — all godlike powers — fat was beautiful in the Hawaiian system. But in recompense for the prolonged
labor of working sandalwood, the underlying people were only
poorly fed, or not fed at all; nor did they share in the commercial
returns. Their labor was exacted as a kind of ground rent due to
the chiefly "lord of the land" (haku'āina; cf. Mathison 1825:
384–85).

Meanwhile, the elite consumption fever was being fueled by
two intersecting systems of rivalry: on one side, the American
merchants competing with each other for custom, on the other,
the Hawaiian chiefs with the custom of competing with each
other.[39] And all the while the traders were undercutting one
another — as by advancing ever-more elegant goods while deni-
grating their competitors' — they were appealing to the chiefs'
emulative spirit of self-regard. As a Hawaiian historian says, "The
chiefs were all bent at this time at securing honors for themselves" (Kamakau 1961:265). By the close of 1821, the King and
chiefs are reported to own "Ten large and elegant Brigs, besides a
large number of Sloops & Schooners, all of which they have purchased from Americans" (John C. Jones, United States Consular
Dispatches, Honolulu, 31 Dec. 1821). This includes *Cleopatra's
Barge*, a luxuriously fitted and leaky vessel sent out by a Boston
firm to dazzle the local nobility, which King Liholiho (Kamehameha II) agreed to buy for ninety thousand dollars in sandalwood — which the firm's Honolulu agent Bullard could not
collect (Bullard, "Letterbook"). Still, Bullard reported optimisti-
cally to Boston: "If you want to know how religion stands at the
Islands, I can tell you; all sects are tolerated and the King wor-
ships the Barge" (*ibid*:1 Nov. 1821).

By this time, in fact, the King had formally abolished the old
religion, yet he and the other ruling chiefs continued to testify to
a divinity of ancient memory in their own nature. Hence their

445

appropriation of Western distinctions between "plain" and "fancy" goods, and their appreciation especially for those fineries whose luster, reflecting a celestial brilliance, accorded with their received ideas of aristocratic flash. "Send out articles of a showy kind," the merchant John C. Jones wrote to his suppliers (MaL:9 Mar. 1823); "everything new and elegant will sell at a profit, coarse articles are of no use" (ibid.:31 May 1823); "fine cloth would have commanded any price" (10 Oct. 1822).[40] Trade goods were glorious artificial extensions of sacred chiefly bodies already stretched to their organic limits. Indeed, just as in the case of the chiefs' avoirdupois, all their indulgences seemed designed to magnify their persons, including the expenditures on the large corps of domestic retainers kept to minister to their bodily wants and pleasures (Stewart 1830:138, Corney 1896:105, L.F. Judd 1966:21). The chief's retinue was like a superbeing, its numerous members functioning to sustain the one life with which all were identified. At the same time, given the traditional indeterminacies of chiefly honors, the entropy of the ranking system, each chief was bent on proving in the new medium of commercial prowess that he was equal to and better than, the same as and different from, the others. The elite economy was an arena of differentiation, where invidious distinctions were played out between the powers that be and those which only would-be.

Thus certain other characteristics of this Polynesian market: the endless pursuit of novelty, the rage for the latest Boston fashions, and the hoarding of foreign goods taken as signs and projections of the "civilized" person. Another trader writes to his Boston suppliers that having sold fifteen bedsteads he had exhausted the Honolulu market since "they are all alike." He adds that "your best silks are but little wanted" because stuff of the same kind had come out before in a competitor's ship, "and they [the Hawaiians] want such patterns as they have never seen before" (Hunnewell, Letters:30 Dec. 1829). This pursuit of individual distinction had been running strong since Kamehameha's death — "Everyone that comes brings better and better goods, and such as they have not seen will sell when common ones will not" (Bullard, "Letterbook":4 July 1821). And precisely as the commercial goods contributed to personal distinction, they were not at all destined for general distribution. They were ostentatiously hoarded up, a conspicuous thesaurization: amassed even to the point of waste, as if any depletion of the accumulated foreign goods were the sign of a personal diminishment. The chiefs were disinclined to make any inroads on their stocks in hand, even when needed for some ceremonial purpose. They preferred then to buy more of what they already had in abundance:

> These people have an incurable reluctance to part with anything they have stored away. There is now an immense amount of property stowed away in cases & dirty houses which is rotting away, but which the chiefs will not take out of their repositories even to use themselves. The King [Liholiho] some time ago was in want of duck [cloth] when it was scarce & bought a few bolts at a very high price, when at the same time he had two or three hundred bolts which was stored away rotting. (Hammatt, Journal:18 Aug. 1823)

Related to production by such interests of consumption, the Hawaiian nobility soon showed themselves unable to compete with advancing capitalist modes of exploiting the Islands' resources. As Adam Smith said, "It seldom happens that a great proprietor is a great improver" ([1776] 1991:III.2). The ruling chiefs had a greater ability to accumulate goods than they had to make others pay for them. Even had they been inclined to productive investments, all they had were commercial debts — which the common people lost interest in working off by forced labor perhaps faster than they were losing the population numbers to do so. The chiefs, too, were dying out — a mortality that is usually taken as the reason they gave the authority over to White men. But the explanation reverses matters. The chiefs were obsolete as a ruling class and simply failed to make use of available social means of reproducing themselves as such.[41] In a similar situation of misfortune, the Kwakiutl Indians recruited women and commoner men to noble positions, thereby sustaining the celebrated "potlatch" system for nearly two centuries. And if the Kwakiutl chief had no daughter by whose marriage he could

447

transfer ancestral names and privileges, and thus constitute enduring alliances with other lineages, he could marry off his son's left side or else make someone a wife out of his own left foot (F. Boas 1966a:55).

The Kwakiutl

The early contact histories of British Columbia and the Sandwich Islands are linked by the same European names — Cook and Vancouver, Portlock and Dixon, Meares, Colnett, Ebenezer Townsend, Peter Corney — but the relationship the Kwakiutl fashioned with such Westerners, then and later, was different from the Hawaiian experience. This much was the same: for the Indians, too, wealth and power were traditionally obtained from beyond society, and especially from sea and sky; so in analogous ways certain Western commodities were subsumed as indigenous values. Still, to mention only the most striking difference, the Kwakiutl acquired cosmic powers not by consuming the riches of the market economy, as though to inflate their own persons, but by ostentatiously giving goods away, in a manner that signified the incorporation of other people.

Western commerce had made possible a spectacular process of develop-man on the Northwest Coast, the elaboration of the famous potlatch system (cf. F. Boas 1920, 1921, 1930, 1935, 1966a).[42] Ceremonial and aesthetic as well as political, this was a total cultural development that for over 150 years resisted the equally broad assault of Western imperialism, whether in the form of Christian missionaries, legal sanctions of the Canadian government, or the relations of capitalist production in the lumber, fishing, canning, and prostitution industries. The Kwakiutl could not be faulted for their aptitudes as wage workers, or even as entrepreneurs, but White men often wrung their hands about what the Indians did with their earnings, which was to pile up Hudson's Bay blankets and other bizarre stuff for colossal giveaways.[43] In 1881, the first Indian Agent sent a report of the "apathetic state" of the Kwakiutl, from which he "must endeavour to lift them"; their apathy, as he described it, consisted of being "surrounded with boxes of property all ready for the potlatch"

(Codere 1950:82). Summarizing an extensive study of such official documents, Codere writes:

> Throughout the years, the Kwakiutl are described as industrious but not progressive; as measuring up to almost any standard of enterprise, skillfulness, adaptability and productivity, but as failing to possess these premium qualities in relation to the proper goals, or to be inspired to them by the proper motivations. It is as though Kwakiutl were able to exploit the new culture to their own ends.... (*Ibid.*:8; cf. Fisher 1977)

Potlatches involving Hudson's Bay blankets escalated after the establishment of Fort Rupert in 1849, reaching a high of 33,000 blankets in one affair of 1933, but including such expenditures as 200 silver bracelets, 7,000 brass bracelets, and 240 washbasins in an 1895 distribution, and more recently the likes of sewing machines, gramophones, watches, and pool tables (Codere 1950: 90–91; Codere 1961:464). The blankets replaced the worked skins of various animals and cedar bark robes distributed on analogous occasions (although in smaller quantities) in earlier times. Distinctions of rank formerly made by different types of skins were no longer so signified, a change that seems correlated with the participation of commoners and women in positions traditionally reserved to the nobility. But I draw attention especially to the contrast between this standardization of the main commercial-prestige good, the Hudson's Bay blanket, and the differentiating consumption of the Hawaiian elite, who always demanded "such patterns as they have never seen before" — with no intention either of lavishing their riches on others. Whereas, by giving trade blankets to others, the Kwakiutl testified to different sacred powers.

Hunters on the sea and land, the Indians lived by inflicting death.[44] They reproduced human life by killing sentient beings whom they considered to be, underneath their animal skins or guises, persons like themselves. Animals are of common origin with humanity, part of the same universal society. Indeed, the lives of people and game or fish are interdependent: for if the animals willingly give themselves to the Indians, it is because the

Indians know how to assure the rebirth of their prey through the ritual respects they accord the remains — a cycle of reincarnation that typically passes through a human phase when the animal is consumed as food. Arcane beliefs perhaps, but they were critical to the fur trade and potlatch. As a distribution of worked animal skins donned by the recipients as robes, the potlatch is exactly the same kind of ritual reincarnation staged as a social event.[45] Recall that animals are humans under the skin. Hence, the distribution of skins as blankets re-creates the animal victims in living human form — moreover, in large numbers and in a respectful way, as worked-up and cultural goods. Of course, in the fur trade the animal skins had to be given up; but what other than their own total modes of production and reproduction could compel the Indians to take striped woolen blankets as "economic" equivalents?

Hudson's Bay blankets had yet other powers concealed in their unassuming appearance. In potlatches they were given away by chiefs to validate their privileges and add greatness to their names. The blankets represented the chief's attainments in *nawalak*, a generalized life-giving power that, myth tells, can kill enemies effortlessly, restore the dead to life, and accomplish miracles of hunting and wealth-getting (cf. I. Goldman 1975, Dullabaun 1979). Just so, the gifts are said to "swallow" the recipients who are chiefs of other lineages (*numaym*) and tribes. At issue are certain powers of inclusion: an attempt at hierarchy, which is also the transcending of social boundaries.

Precisely by translation into the common medium of blankets, the unique ancestral privileges (*tlogwe*) of the different Kwakiutl lineages could be matched and compared — that is, as the generic *nawalak* (cf. Dullabaun 1979). Each lineage begins with a distinct and inalienable stock of privileges bestowed by the founder. In the typical narrative, a specific animal descends from the heavens to a particular place on the beach, takes off his animal mask, and becomes the human ancestor. The mask itself is one of these permanent lineage treasures, as are certain totem poles, house posts, carved boxes, feast dishes, and the names that confer given place and precedence in the pan-Kwakiutl potlatch order. Means and signs of the lineage's existence, creators of food and riches, these "precious things," as Marcel Mauss observed, "have in themselves a productive virtue" (1966:220–21). Indeed, the chief who possesses them re-creates himself as the ancestor, and thus crossing the space between present and past, man and spirit, he is able to traverse the paradigmatic boundary of life and death.[46]

This, the heroic overcoming of death, is the Kwakiutl mode of cultural production. Of course it describes hunting, which not only brings life out of death but, as animals are basically human, courts the risks of a *cannibalisme généralisé* (cf. Walens 1981:101). Yet in the same way, Kwakiutl shamanism, warfare, trade, marriages, or the ceremonies of the winter solstice are so many analogous and interrelated projects of derring-do, involving the capture of powerful forces beyond society and their transformation into beneficent sources of human existence.[47] Likewise Kwakiutl politics: the chiefs increased the "weight" of their inherited names by appropriating privileges from other lineages and tribes — external powers they could ultimately validate by potlatch distributions that again subordinated ("swallowed") the names and claims of rival-others. Dullabaun summarizes these homologies in the Kwakiutl negotiations of power:

> Power must be acquired.... The mode of acquisition always involves crossing some kind of categorical boundary. So, for example, one leaves the beach (where the villages are located) and goes deep into the forest to acquire a treasure. Or one travels a long distance over the sea to acquire powers through marriage from these distant fathers-in-law. The most radical kind of boundary crossing (and hence the source of the most valued power) occurs when a person (an initiate in the winter ceremonial) imitates his patron saint and in so doing becomes the spirit (i.e., takes the spirit's name and powers). (1979:49)

Transactions of power involved a second fund of privileges (*tlogwe*), mostly like the original lineage treasures except that they were alienable, as indeed they had been obtained in heroic encounters of the ancestors with spirits of the sea or forest. The most important acquired privileges were rights to the Winter

451

Ceremonial performances in which such ancestral feats were reenacted — in a context where lineage boundaries were also transcended, by the organization of larger communities along the lines of ritual societies. Negotiations of acquired privileges were thus the decisive moves of tribal politics. And family histories were chronicles of the victories thus achieved in marriage and war. The chiefs gained treasures from noble fathers-in-law in marriage — as the so-called payment of the marriage debt, which followed the bride — and in war through the right of the slayer to seize the ceremonial honors of his victim. Once again involving the appropriation of powers across a social boundary, the one and the other are humanized versions of the deeds of legendary heroes in the spiritual outer realms. The son-in-law stands to his father-in-law as the warrior to his victim — or as the hero to his patron spirit.[48] So Kwakiutl say of marriage, "The chiefs make war upon the princesses of the tribes" (F. Boas 1966a:53 and 1935:65n). The object of an ambitious chief was to marry the daughters of all the others. For these others, the alliance with a powerful chief, on whom one bestowed further privileges, was indeed a practical alternative to battle.[49] Whereas for the rising chief, the attendance of numerous relatives at the potlatches following on his marital conquests "showed you were a prominent, you were a big man, and you were related to all the different tribes. That's what it meant" (Spradley 1969:247). And, as a result of the chief's marriages, his descendants could boast in family histories: "Therefore I am full of names and privileges. And therefore I have many chiefs and ancestors all over the world" (F. Boas 1921:844).

Notice the incorporative phrasing: marriage appropriates new ancestors; it includes the powers of other lineages in one's own. It remains only to demonstrate the heritage in potlatch, thereby turning the incorporation of ancestors into the encompassment of contemporaries. And need one demonstrate here that the blankets which will thus transcend the boundaries between groups and combine them in a higher order embody in their own production these same social qualities? Or, better, they incorporate the same qualities in a stronger form, since Hudson's Bay blankets are the product of the successive negotiations of life and death in the hunt, Indian and foreigner in trade.[50] Representing in this way generic powers (*nawalak*), the blankets, counted and distributed, make it possible to compare on a scale of greatness chiefly names and lineage privileges (*tlogwe*) that are otherwise incommensurable. Each lineage has its own unique powers, unrelated in origin to the others: the gift of an independent ancestor, associated with a particular territory. In this respect, the cosmology of Kwakiutl politics is the converse of the Hawaiian. In Hawaii, the sacred ancestral powers are ultimately one, united by common descent in a universal genealogy; accordingly, the political problem to which Hawaiian chiefs devoted herculean efforts of consumption during the sandalwood trade was how to differentiate their sacred claims. If they were obsessed with fashionable differences in Western goods, it was in order to make qualitative distinctions out of their quantitative gradations in standing. The Indians, on the other hand, wanted more and more of the same good, a standardized sign of universal powers, which when publicly distributed made quantitative comparisons of their qualitative differences.[51] The expansion of capitalist trade opened new vistas of social greatness to Kwakiutl chiefs, and withal a spectacular process of local develop-man.[52]

Conclusion: Tea and Other Goods to Think

Things like this had initially happened all around the Pacific because of that god Tea to whom the British were prepared to sacrifice "everything else," especially everything that belonged to other people. Or the historian might have said "the goddess Tea," insofar as its rituals were touted in the eighteenth century as domesticating and its virtues as nonintoxicating, properties that contrasted with its more masculine rivals for popular consumption, beer, ale, and gin.[53] One readily grasps the function of tea as delivering a docile and effective working class into the maws of the developing capitalism. But if the spread of the tea habit were to be studied seriously, one might suppose that here no less than elsewhere the practical function is a situational mode of a native scheme of cosmic proportions. Certainly it involves some peculiar Western ideas of the person as an imperfect creature of need

453

and desire whose whole earthly existence can be reduced to the pursuit of bodily pleasure and the avoidance of pain. A theological tragedy of long standing, this description of the human condition became a philosophical creed in the seventeenth century and then the everyday fare of the eighteenth — as witness the rapid dissemination of what Sidney Mintz has called "drug foods" among the European popular classes (1985). The development of modern Western "civilization" has depended on an enormous soft-drug culture, at least as a condition of tolerability, marked by the daily general consumption of such substances as tea, coffee, chocolate, tobacco, and sugar — a list without much redeeming nutritious value.

If these opiates became rituals of the people — or, indeed, like religion they made bearable the earthly existence of fallen man — was it not because people were condemned to continuous misery by their insatiable bodily needs? Such had been the tragic Western sense of human nature at least since Augustine (below, Chapter Sixteen). Man is fated to a life that is penal not only because it is mortal but because he is alone in a natural world that "does not make good what it promises; it is a liar and deceiveth" (quoted in Deane 1963:45). Its deception consists in the impossibility of satisfying human lusts, notably the avarice for temporal goods. Man therefore never ceases hoping in this world, and never attains what he hopes for. Pursuing one thing after another, he finds "nothing remains permanently... his needs are so multiplied that he cannot find the one thing needful, a single and unchangeable nature" (ibid.). Only the state, law, and morality — imperfect earthly reflections of the heavenly city — have kept this society of self-regarding men from dissolving into a war of each against all: described by Augustine in the same way that Hobbes, more than a thousand years later, will characterize the natural state. But by the seventeenth century, the Augustinian values were on the way to being overthrown. The earthly underside of man, with all its attendant miseries, was about to become a moral virtue. Or at least, in Locke's Whiggish reading of the penalties of the Original Sin, human suffering was the beneficent gift of Providence — as "the great spur to human industry."[54]

So by the time of Adam Smith, every person's permanent misery — that is, scarcity and need — had become the premise of economic wisdom and the source of national welfare. The social and moral sublimation of temporal desires had indeed been dissolved by an oncoming capitalism. What for Augustine was slavery, the human bondage to bodily desires, was in the bourgeois view the essential human freedom. Man became the pleasure-pain machine invented by Hobbes and favored by the Enlightenment philosophes: a creature that moves to those things that do him his own good and away from things that do him evil — motions to-ward and from-ward that were supposed to comprehend the entire universe of human behavior. The new rationality was based on an exquisite sensitivity to pleasure and pain, especially to pain, which is at once more enduring than pleasure and the condition of its possibility. But, then, the capitalist economy had made a supreme fetish of human needs in the sense that needs, which are always social and objective in character, had to be assumed as subjective experiences of bodily affliction.

In the eighteenth century, however, Asia entered into the consciousness of Europe as a cure. Land of spices and drugs, of the preservers of food and life, the Orient, as Dermigny says, presented to Europe not merely a spectacle dazzling to the eye but a presence that insinuated itself into the whole body. "What it procured for a sick and sinful Europe — sick no doubt because it was sinful — were means for restoring health: remedies" (1964, vol. 1:18).[55]

So whatever the pain, "have a cup'a tea, everything'll be all right." Interesting that, like coffee and chocolate, tea was not sweetened in its country of origin, though in the West all these drinks were taken with sugar from the time of their introduction. It is as if the sweetened bitterness of the beverage represented to the taste the kind of transformation it could effect in one's moral existence. And perhaps nothing better demonstrates the social genesis of these magical effects than the fact that in Britain tea soon took on psychological values far removed from its chemical properties. After all, it contains caffeine and was early advertised as a stimulant (Repplier 1932:5–6). Now Englishmen regularly drink tea to calm their nerves. But it would take another essay to catalog all the powers ascribed to this brew by her devotees. Truly, she is a goddess worthy of the sacrifices the world has made for her.

NOTES

1. On Williams's death and various explanations thereof, see G. Turner 1861:490; H.A. Robertson 1902:56–59; Prout 1843:388ff., A.W. Murray 1862: 179, 195–96, 206–208; and Shineberg 1967:205–207. Among the apparent parallels to Cook's death at Hawaii — apart from the manner in which Williams was collectively mobbed after he was drowned in shallow water — was the missionary's reported intrusion in the great annual feast (*nisekar*). From all reports, this was a solstitial event analogous to the Hawaiian Makahiki, also marked by sham battles and an interdiction of war (cf. Humphreys 1926:180–81). As other Europeans, moreover, Williams was locally categorized as *Nobu*, the name of the lost creator-god at Eromanga, again analogous to the Hawaiian Lono, of whom Cook was an avatar (cf. Capell 1938:72–73). It is said that Williams's body was traded to some nearby people in exchange for pigs for the annual feast, although his companion, a certain Harris, was eaten directly. On the ritual dimensions of Cook's death, see M. Sahlins 1985a.

2. Langridge voices the common wisdom of the "martyrdom," to the effect that "the tragic occurrence was due almost entirely to the evil deeds of white men preceding his [Williams's] visit" (1934:15). Shineberg doubts it, noting that the last major violence at Eromanga consisted of attacks by Hawaiians on local people across the island from Dillon's Bay some nine years before Williams's death (cf. Bennett 1832). Shineberg's comments on Eurocentric explanations such as Langridge's are worth repeating in full:

> The retaliation-only theory fits perfectly into the concept of the passive role of the Melanesian in culture contact, for it implies that there must be a white man behind every brown. Only in response to European action is the islander seen to act. He may not take the initiative: he may not have his own independent good reasons for killing Europeans — motives emanating from his own desires and customs — but must wait for the European to offend him. (1967:214)

456

3. "The multiple cultures, the multiple 'traditions' that have flourished within the space-time boundaries of historical capitalism, have been no more primordial than the multiple institutional frameworks. They are largely the creations of the modern world, part of its ideological scaffolding" (Wallerstein, 1983:76; cf. Frank 1966:19).

4. Consider Wallerstein's idea of "cultures" (that is, "ideas, values, science, art, religion, language, passion, and color") as "the ways in which people clothe their politico-economic interests and drives in order to express them, hide them, extend them in space and time, and preserve their memory" (1974/1980: 65).

5. The most striking examples concern the ways Western commodities are indigenized in other cultural logics. Thus Lederman reports from the New Guinea Highlands: "The Mendi we know do not see these objects in the same way as we see them: their purposes supplied for us.... In our objects, they perceive multiple possibilities for satisfying needs the manufacturers never imagined" (1986a:5). The report is echoed in a recent ethnohistory of the Cree: "most technical innovations adopted by Indians were modified to fit their existing perceptions and social system, and many European goods were employed in Indian culture for purposes other than those for which they were produced in Europe" (Thistle 1986:35).

6. See the cogent discussion of the modern development of cultural difference in Bright and Geyer (1988). There is a parallel in the classic World System theory, especially as it applies (or does not apply) to China. The theory holds, on the one hand, that the empire of capital is inconsistent with political hegemony: world empire would impose considerations and interests of other kinds on bourgeois enterprise. Hence the escape of capital from the political framework of the state has been necessary to the development of the modern world economy (Wallerstein 1974/1980:127; cf. Mancall 1984:67). On the other hand, if the World System does not constitute a unified world society, it does suppose a system of autonomous states to bear the costs, as well as a set of complementary local differences in products, demands, and labor-forms. Hence local differentiation is a condition of global integration, and vice versa. Of course, all this would be as true in the era of industrial capitalism as in mercantile capitalism.

7. The "mystique of Western domination" encompasses a whole series of related propositions, ranging in value from absurd to false, and including: first, that before the expansion of the West other peoples had lived and developed "in isolation" — which just means that *we* weren't there; second, that the historic

457

adaptations they were compelled to make to one another do not count as such, for everything then was "pristine" and "indigenous"; third, that their interaction with the West, however, has been a qualitatively different process; since, fourth, European power uniquely destroys the ancient harmonies and coherence of these exotic cultures; and, fifth, in the process of their "acculturation" or assimilation to the West, their own cultural distinctiveness is irreversibly extinguished.

8. In the earlier decades of European contact, Hawaiians called such things as watches and astronomical instruments *akua*, just as Maori called them *atua* or Fijians deemed various European wonders *kalou*. All these Polynesian terms are usually glossed as "god." See note 1, above, on the inclusion of foreign persons in such categories.

9. Cf. Lederman 1986a:12; Codere 1950:81ff. For a number of examples of the develop-man phenomenon, see the volume *Affluence and Cultural Survival* edited by Salisbury and Tooker (1984). Trigger's analysis of the development of the Huron confederacy in the sixteenth and early seventeenth centuries is particularly pertinent. This was a total develop-man process in which the political evolution was complemented by an increase in the extent and volume of trade, growth of craft production, and enrichment of ritual life. "The new social order," Trigger observes, "was based on an expanded application of principles that must already have been present and applied in embryonic form in Huron society in prehistoric times and, in this sense, is traditional" (1984:22). No doubt, the cognate League of the Iroquois could be understood from this vantage (cf. Hunt 1960) — not to forget all the Plains Indian cultures as historically known.

10. Already in the latter sixteenth century, when New World production of silver was booming, "a prime beneficiary of this Potosí-led boom was Ming China" (Axtell 1982:72). As Antónia de Morga "explained in his informative discussion of trade in Manila at this time, the Chinese accepted only silver for their products, 'for they do not like gold, nor any other goods in exchange, nor do they carry any to China'" (*ibid*.: 75–76; cf. Spate 1979). On silver imports to China in the eighteenth century, see Pritchard 1929 and 1936 or Dermigny 1964.

11. The Emperor's edict summarily rejects all the requests Lord Macartney had hoped to "negotiate," reminding the English king that "You, O King, should simply act in conformity with our wishes by strengthening your loyalty and swearing perpetual obedience so as to ensure that your country may share the blessings of peace" (Cranmer-Byng 1962:340). To mark the presentation of

British tributes, the Ch'ien-lung Emperor also composed a poem, which further explicates the theory of his world-constituting virtue:

> Now England is paying homage . . .
> My Ancestors' merit and virtue must have reached their distant shores.
>
> Though their tribute is commonplace, my heart approves sincerely.
> Curios and the boasted ingenuity of their devices I prize not.
> Though what they bring is meagre, yet,
> In my kindness to men from afar I make generous return,
> Wanting to preserve my good health and power.
>
> *(ibid.:* x)

12. The great historian of this trade, H.B. Morse, writes: "as early as 1700, there were experienced the two embarrassments which beset the East India Company during its two centuries of trade to China — the difficulty of providing any English products the Chinese would buy, and the strain of providing the silver the Chinese demanded" (1966, vol. 1:113).

13. Sir George Staunton, secretary of the Macartney embassy, characterized the Canton trade arrangements of the Chinese as "The ancient prejudices against all strangers . . . reduced into a system, supported on the fullest confidence in the perfect state of their own civilization; and the comparative barbarism of every other nation" (1799, vol. 1:8). Besides Morse 1966 and Dermigny 1964, general descriptions of the Canton system in the eighteenth century may be found in the works of Pritchard 1929 and 1936, Greenberg 1951, Fairbank 1969, and Mancall 1984.

14. Nor do these figures accurately chart British consumption, because for some years prior to the Commutation Act of 1784, which drastically reduced import duties on teas, more was being smuggled into the country from the continent than was legally imported by the Company. The Act reduced duties from roughly 119 percent to 12.5 percent — and thereby crippled the trade of all other Western nations at Canton. The American trade, however, was just beginning and soon would have good success. For comparative figures for this period, see Milburn 1813, vol. 2:486. Dermigny gives an indication of the increase in tea exports from China as carried by merchants of all countries: from an average 1,530,275 *livres marc* in 1719–1724, to 44,858,000 *livres marc* in 1827–1833 (1964, vol. 1:74n).

15. Neither opium nor tea, but, rather, woolens were the true drug on the Canton market. In the years 1775–1795, the Company's average annual losses on woolens were calculated at 5.6 percent, but its average annual profit during this period was 28 percent on investment, and for tea alone, 31.4 percent (Pritchard 1936:157, 166).

16. Company records for 1786 indicate that: "The Patterns of Norwich, Manchester & Hallifax Stuffs have been shewn to the [Chinese] Merchants, but it is not their opinion that any of them will answer for this Market: the Cotton Stuffs are too expensive, & the Chinese manufacture a variety of different kinds which tho' not so elegant are better adapted to their modes of dress" (Morse 1966, vol. 2:120).

17. The present account of the Macartney embassy is drawn from Lord Macartney's own journal (Cranmer-Byng 1962) as well as the chronicles of Staunton 1799, Dinwiddie (Proudfoot 1868), Alexander, "Journal," Barrow 1805, and Anderson 1795, the official Chinese correspondence (Cranmer-Byng 1957–58), the East India Company instructions (Pritchard 1938), and pertinent correspondence from missionaries in China (Pritchard 1935). The English journals are not of equal value or probity; that of Barrow is particularly suspect (cf. Proudfoot 1868:44n, 52). An excellent analysis of the Macartney embassy is developed in Hevia's dissertation (1986), to which I am much indebted. On aspects of the Chinese imperium discussed here in connection with the Macartney mission, see especially Fairbank 1942, 1968, and 1971; Fairbank and Têng 1941; Granet 1930 and 1968; Mancall 1984; Franke 1967; de Bary, Chan, and Watson 1960; Spence 1975; and Wakeman 1970.

18. "One fact signals the privileged place that the Chinese give to Politics. For them, the history of the World does not begin before that of Civilization. It does not start with a narrative of creation or cosmological speculations. It is joined from the beginning with the biography of the Sovereign" (Granet 1968: 283).

19. "Sole master of the Calendar and by virtue of this prime mover of the whole Chinese territory, such appears, in the tradition of the Han, the Son of Heaven" (Granet 1930:382). On the Emperor's grand sacrifices in Ch'ing times, see Zito (1984).

20. In 1660, the Russian Tsar, according to official Chinese court records

sent another Embassy to bring a memorial and to present tribute. In the memorial he [the Tsar] did not follow our calendar, but dated it 1165, and called himself a Great Khan with many boastful words. This memorial was sent to the princes and ministers for deliberation.

They argued: "We should expel his embassy and refuse his tribute." (Fu 1966, vol. 1:24)

The Emperor overruled this opinion and said that the Russians should be feasted by the Board of Rites and given presents — as signs of the imperial tolerance — but denied an imperial audience. In 1676, another Russian envoy, although received by the Emperor, was then not recognized and dismissed, according to official records, for failure to ko-tow (*ibid.*:49–50).

21. In granting permission for the Macartney embassy to enter the country, the Ch'ien-lung Emperor observed that in their request the British had properly expressed "the highest reverence (*gong*), obedience (*shun*), earnestness (*gin*) and faithfulness (*zhi*)," as well as "the sincerity of facing toward transformation" (Hevia 1986:265).

22. Previous to the Macartney mission there had been only two Chinese speakers in the Company's service, both now departed from the scene (Pritchard 1938:497n). I would not, however, make too much of the English shows of "ignorance" in regard to the Chinese imperium or Chinese custom. It is clear from Macartney's private and even more from Staunton's published account that they were well aware of the Chinese conception of the Emperor's sovereignty, for, indeed, their intent was to deny it, break it down, and substitute their own. Thus Staunton knew that the Chinese subjects of the Emperor considered he "virtually rules the world," that they "scarcely distinguish the relations or duties of other nations or individuals to him from their own, which are, indeed, unbounded" (1799, vol. 2:25). Staunton also knew the difference between reciprocity and hierarchy in the relations between states and the Chinese view of such matters: "Such were the avowed or affected notions entertained by the Chinese government, of the superiority or independence of the empire, that no transaction with foreigners was admissable to it on the ground of reciprocal benefit, but as a grace and condescension from the former to the latter" (*ibid.*: 72; cf. Pritchard 1935:50).

23. The instructions issued to Lord Macartney by the Home Secretary Henry Dundas remind him that:

The Directors of the East India Company, who have ordered one of their ships to accompany the Embassy, have shipped on board a great variety of articles of British goods not for the purpose of Sale, but to be dispersed and distributed by you in most likely manner to excite a taste for and establish the use of such articles in China. (Morse 1966, vol. 2:240; cf. Pritchard 1935:222)

Moreover, while Macartney was in China, he sent the ship-of-war that also accompanied him, the *Lion* (Sir Erasmus Gower), to Japan, the Philippines, Borneo, and the Celebes, to prepare for a visit from the mission, the instructions to Gower in the case of Borneo saying:

Nothing would be more desirable, or more consistent with the general object of the mission, than any fair and peaceable endeavour to spread the use of British manufactures throughout every part of Asia, from whence any valuable return might be made to Europe, which was eminently the case of Borneo. (Quoted in Staunton 1799, vol. 1:253)

24. And although Macartney was pleased to believe that he had dispelled the Chinese idea of the English as barbarians by the example of his own civilized conduct, his journal suggests that in popular quarters the embassy enjoyed a reputation for cannibalism — the same as attributed to the Portuguese in the early sixteenth century. "A Chinese boy," Macartney writes, "who was appointed to wait upon young George Staunton [son of Sir George] would not for a long time trust himself to sleep in the house with our European servants, being afraid, he said, that they would eat him" (Cranmer-Byng 1962:226; cf. Franke 1967:27ff.).

25. The persistence of Western perspectives on such matters is demonstrated by the mid-twentieth-century echo of Meadows's remarks about the English ship in the comments of Cranmer-Byng, editor of the Macartney journal: "All the scientific apparatus which Macartney took with him, all the obvious superiority of the H.M.S. *Lion*, a 64-gun ship, over the Manchu war junks, was wasted on these men" (Cranmer-Byng 1962:36). But then, in another context, Fairbank cites Meadows's observation in regard to Chinese people who had had no opportunity of knowing Westerners:

I do not recollect conversing with one, and I have conversed with many, whose previous notions of us were not analogous to those we entertain of savages. They were always surprised, not to say astonished, to learn that we have surnames, and understand the family distinctions of father, brother, wife, sister, etc.; in short that we live otherwise than as a herd of cattle. (Quoted in Fairbank 1969:19)

26. On the imperial retreats of Yuan Ming Yuan and Jehol, see Malone 1934, Síren 1949, Hedin 1933, Danby 1950, and M'Ghee 1862:203ff. These retreats are notably located northwest (Yuan Ming Yuan) and north (Jehol) of Peking, thus in more sinister ritual directions (cf. Zito 1984); the European palaces at Yuan Ming Yuan, of which mention is made below, were likewise at the northern border of this summer palace complex.

27. Père Bourgeois goes on to say:

> You ask me if the Emperor has any Venetian and French glass. Thirty years ago he already had so many pieces that, not knowing where to put them, he had a quantity of the first grade broken up to make window panes for his European buildings.... [The] hall which he had made new for the tapestries ... of Gobelins, which the French court sent in 1767 ... 70 feet long and of good width ... is so full of machines that one can hardly move about in it. Some of these machines have cost two or three hundred thousand francs, for the work on them is exquisite and they are enriched with innumerable precious stones. (quoted in Cranmer-Byng 1962: 125–26)

28. For a description of the Emperor Wu's famous Shang-lin garden, which captures all the symbolism in an appropriate poetic form, see the chapter on Ssu-ma Hsiang-na in Ssu-ma Ch'ien's history (Watson, 1961 vol. 2:297–321). The poem "Sir Fantasy" is a political drama in which the wonders of the Son of Heaven's garden encompass the descriptions of the parks of lesser lords, whose own rivalry is likewise represented in competing celebrations of the scale and variety of their pleasure retreats. Cibot records that the successors of the Emperor Wu through the seventh century similarly "attempted to assemble everything that was scarce, dispersed and scattered here and there over the most immense regions ... within their gardens everything was collected, like an abridgement of the universe" (1782b:310).

29. The Ch'ien-lung Emperor recounted how his father, at Yuan Ming Yuan, "to appreciate the hard work of the farmers and mulberry growers ... had fields, and barns, and plots of vegetables, by which he understood the

importance of rain and sunshine for the crops. The wind among the pines and the moon over the water entered his breast, inspiring thoughts of beauty" (quoted in Malone 1934:64).

30. Wakeman draws attention also to the contrast between the "meanders …and carefully chosen grotesqueries" of the Summer Palace and the "formality" of the Forbidden City (1970:8). For him, it is the contrast, as it were, of the king's two bodies, his private and public personae. However, the argument here is that these are complementary aspects of the same imperium, involving also the contrasts of civilization and nature, Chinese and barbarian, passive and active rule, peace and war, expression and acquisition of virtue, and more. The seasonal movements between the palace and the retreats, as well as the different modes of imperial behavior in each, would clearly contribute to a richer elucidation of the theory of rule.

31. Many of Macartney's presents to the Ch'ien-lung Emperor remained at Yuan Ming Yuan until 1860, when an Anglo-French expeditionary force commanded by Lord Elgin — son of the one who took all the marbles — pillaged and burned the priceless summer palace, thus finally proving the "preeminence" of European civilization by one of the greatest acts of vandalism in history.

32. Using H. Watanabe's study (1975) of Ming tributes, one may construct a graphic representation of the decline in foreign-tributary relations in the last half of the dynasty:

Number of tributary missions to China

	Years 1368–1505	Years 1506–1643
by land	611	145
by ocean	355	7

Mutatis mutandis, it is all as in the Sung dynasty's official history: "The *te* of T'ang having declined, the [missions] of distant *hung-fu* areas did not come." Then, with Sung unification, foreign countries came from all directions in response to the dynasty's awe-inspiring majesty and virtue (*wei-te*) (Wang 1968:47).

33. Schafer notes:

The Chinese taste for the exotic permeated every social class and every part of daily life: Iranian, Indian and Turkish figures and decorations appeared on every kind of household object. The vogue for foreign clothes, foreign food and foreign music was especially prevalent in the eighth century, but no part of the T'ang era was free from it. (1963:28)

34. On the efforts of the Hawai'i Island King Kamehameha to "live like King George" in the early 1790s, see M. Sahlins 1981:30. This work and others (M. Sahlins 1985a; Kirch and Sahlins 1992) can be consulted for greater detail in events of Hawaiian history discussed here. Unfortunately, the present necessity of providing comparative materials from Hawaii involves the double academic fault of repeating myself in a too condensed way.

35. Since Cook did not see China and such a present is not mentioned in the chronicles of his voyage, Kamehameha's story seems unlikely, except that fur traders such as Meares and Colnett were perceived by Hawaiians as connected to Cook and perhaps one of these brought the Chinese gown to the Islands.

36. For American participation in the Canton market during the maritime fur trade and subsequent periods, see Latourette 1917, Morse 1966, and Pitkin 1835; and for the particular impact on Hawaii, see Bradley 1968 and Morgan 1948. The British fur traders included local Indian "Country Traders" (cf. Meares 1790). The fact that the Indian Country trade in opium and raw cotton at Canton was well on the way to resolving the problem of British silver expenditures probably made it easier for the Americans to displace the British on the Northwest Coast. In the first decade of the nineteenth century, the Americans also extended their operations to sealing off the California coast and the Falklands. A sense of the shifting presence of British and Americans in the Pacific at this time can be had from a sample of the shipping in the Hawaiian Islands (based on Judd and Lind 1974). In the years 1786–1799, British ships outnumbered Americans in the Islands by a ratio of 6:5; whereas, in the period 1800–1810, Americans took a 19:1 lead (cf. Howay 1930–34).

37. Of all commodities, Latourette writes, specie was "the one which the United States could least spare at that time. They had no silver or gold mines of importance. What came into the country was largely smuggled in from the Spanish colonies and was greatly needed to pay European bills. Specie was consequently hard to obtain for such luxuries as China goods, and when secured, much popular irritation was felt at its use for such a purpose" (1917:28).

38. Americans were in the neutral carrying trade until the Jeffersonian

embargo of 1808–1809; thereafter the European trade was resumed but with an altered set of markets. The War of 1812–1814 also reduced American trade in the Pacific and China (cf. Pitkin 1835:302).

39. "Till now," goes the characteristic complaint of a *Haole* merchant about his competitors' trading practices, "I never knew the rascality of mankind, everyone here is ready to cut his neighbor's throat, truth is never spoken, treachery is the order of the day. I am disgusted with my fellow [White] man" (J.C. Jones, MaL:6 July 1821).

40. The instructions on appropriate Boston cargoes for the Hawaii trade that Jones was sending to the firm of Marshall and Wildes, amounting to a current catalog of Polynesian splendors, are an interesting example of the way the indigenous conception of *mana* shaped the course of capitalist profit. The catalog ranges from "superfine broadcloth & cassimere" or damask tablecloths, writing desks, and trunks covered with red leather, to the steamboat for which "the King and Pitt would give any price." "You'd be surprised how fast these people are advancing toward civilization," Jones writes, telling how just the other day Mr. Pitt asked for three gold-adorned carriages (MaL:31 May 1823). The carriages were of the general type Macartney had brought to China, which had left the Emperor and court unimpressed.

41. Cf. The Minutes of the Hawaiian Council of Nobles during the Session of 1845, where an ennoblement procedure was discussed and adopted (AH/Leg. Journ.).

42. On Kwakiutl potlatching and cosmology, apart from Boas's classical descriptions, I have relied heavily on the interpretive accounts of I. Goldman 1975, Dullabaun 1979, and Walens 1981, as well as the studies of Codere 1950, 1957, and 1961; Drucker and Heizer 1967; and Barnett 1938. An important study of analogous ideas among Nelson Island Eskimo by Fienup-Riordan (1983) has also been most useful.

43. "The Coast Indian demonstrated a comprehension of the economic values of the day. But what did he do when he was paid off after his season of industry? Did he spend his hard-won earnings for things regarded as beneficial and progressive by Victorian standards? Did he invest them sagaciously for future benefit? He did not. He blew the works in a potlatch" (Drucker and Heizer 1967:28).

44. "The Kwakiutl universe," comments Walens, "is predicated on a single, fundamental assumption: that the universe is a place where some beings are eaten by other beings and where it is the role of some beings to die so that other beings may feed on them and live" (1981:12).

45. And perhaps the more necessary inasmuch as certain animals used for skins, among them sea otter and deer, were customarily not eaten by Kwakiutl; cf. Walens 1981:135–36.

46. "To cross what should be an absolute divide and return safely is an exceptional feat confined to the exceptional person who has been chosen or accepted by the spirits" (I. Goldman 1975:100).

47. In the Winter Ceremonial (which was also a time of heightened potlatch activity), the benefits are diffused to the collectivity and the cosmos itself: through the recapture of chiefly initiates who had been abducted and possessed by various spirits of the wild, in ritual dramas that thus recapitulated heroic ancestral feats of mythic time. As the journeys of the initiates endowed them with spiritual powers, so their successful re-incorporation into the community restored the year itself to life, that is, brought it back from the darkness and death of the solstice (*ibid*.:98ff.). Moreover, the principal initiate, the *hamatsa* dancer, victim of a great cannibal spirit, survives and transcends the cannibal proclivities he ritually demonstrates on his return from the wild. Slowly he is reborn and restored into the human community: proof of man's ability to overcome the generalized cannibalism by which he lives. Here it is notable that (impersonated) animal spirits help in the restoration of the *hamatsa* dancer, which thus seems to show the continued willingness of the animals to give their own flesh — on the condition of certain ritual sacrifices of human flesh.

48. Dullabaun explains:

> A man becomes his spirit (takes his name) and obtains the spirit's treasures that enable him to catch game, i.e., obtain food. The son-in-law takes the name of his father-in-law and catches the game (the wife). Marriage and war are parallels in this respect: when a man captures another in war, he takes the captive's name, any dances that he owns, and his body (which is consumed). In marriage, the son-in-law takes names and dances as well as blankets, animal skins and food. These latter are consumed, burned or more typically, given away. (1979:87–88)

49. In his excellent autobiographical account, the Kwakiutl leader James Sewid tells how his father's father was given a daughter in marriage by a certain Bella Coola chief, whose own people had previously attacked Sewid's grandfather's people. So the Bella Coola chief "let him marry his daughter so he [Sewid's grandfather] could get all their masks and songs so he wouldn't

attack their villages" (Spradley 1969:200; for the mythical analog, see F. Boas 1966a:53).

50. Just as marriage negotiations take on the guise of war expeditions, an early notice of trade between a group of Tsimshian and a party of Vancouver's people indicates that the Indians ritually donned war regalia for the purpose of the exchange (Vancouver 1801, vol. 4:133ff.; cf. Gunther 1972).

51. Codere remarks on the traditional disposition of Kwakiutl to produce goods in standardized forms, as it were, a pre-adaptation that allowed them to appreciate certain possibilities of the Industrial Revolution:

> The habituation to standardized and pluralized manufactured objects was carried over into the new economic situation in their acquisition of Euro-pean manufactures. One of the most interesting features of the potlatch was the distribution of great numbers of manufactured goods of the same category. (1950:18)

52. We need not enter the lists of recent debate about whether the protocol of 658 potlatch names among Southern Kwakiutl was put together after the con-struction of Fort Rupert in 1849 or had already existed in 1760. I. Goldman 1975 argues the latter position against Codere 1950 and Drucker and Heizer 1967, who have sought to document the postcontact development of the South-ern Kwakiutl confederation. For present purposes it is enough to note, first, that the expansion of warfare, intertribal marriage alliances, and feasting beginning in the late eighteenth century set the Kwakiutl in a political field that ran far beyond the writ of their own lineage-based potlatch protocol (the 658 names). Second, many of these relations, as manifested in potlatches, aimed at hierarchi-cal inclusions, which cannot be said for the protocol list of 658 names. As I. Goldman shows, the so-called ranking of these names supposed no principle of logic or hierarchical order (1975:27–28). The order was presumed to have been established by fiat in a mythical or an early-human time and consisted merely of a precedence list — which seems to have been used differently on occa-sions of different kinds (cf. Drucker and Heizer 1967). Unlike *nawalak* and the implication of incorporation in the potlatch system, there is nothing here of a rank *principle*.

53. "The tea-pot was a household god, a homely, companionable little god, fitting into every circumstance of life, and always bringing some definite measure of content" (Repplier 1932:40).

54. *Essay Concerning Human Understanding* II.x.6.

55. Nor were the curative powers of the Orient restricted to the physical body alone. Fascinated also by the vision of an immense and well-governed Chinese empire, the philosophers passed easily to exotic prescriptions for the body politic. A country "that furnishes remedies for the health of the body" could also become "the exemplary empire for the order of societies" (Dermigny 1964, vol. 1:18).

CHAPTER FOURTEEN

Goodbye to *Tristes Tropes*:

Ethnography in the

Context of Modern World History*

For Barney Cohn

> The reason an anthropologist studies history is that it is
> only in retrospect, after observing the structure and its
> transformations, that it is possible to know the nature
> of the structure.
>
> — Bernard S. Cohn (1987)

I

In the midst of all the hoopla about the new reflexive anthropology, with its celebration of the impossibility of systematically
understanding the elusive Other, a different kind of ethnographic
prose has been developing more quietly, almost without our
knowing we were speaking it, and certainly without so much
epistemological angst. I mean the numerous works of historical
ethnography whose aim is to synthesize the field experience of a
community with an investigation of its archival past. For decades
now, students of Native America, Indonesia and the Pacific Islands,
South Asia, and Africa have been doing this kind of ethnohistory.
But only a few — notably Barney Cohn, Jean Comaroff, John Comaroff, and Terry Turner — have consciously raised the point that an

* This paper was originally written for and presented as the Nineteenth Annual
Edward and Nora Ryerson Lecture at the University of Chicago, 29 April 1992.
Published in *Journal of Modern History* 65 (March 1993). © 1993 by The Uni-
versity of Chicago Press.

ethnography with time and transformation built into it is a distinct way of knowing the anthropological object, with a possibility of changing the way culture is thought (*ibid.*, Comaroff and Comaroff 1992, T. Turner 1991). This chapter associates itself with this project of historical ethnography as a determinate anthropological genre. In particular, I would like to offer some theoretical justification for a return to certain world areas such as North America and Polynesia, areas that have been too long slighted by ethnographers, ever since it was discovered in the 1930s and 1940s that they were "acculturated." For these peoples have known how to defy their anthropological demotion by taking cultural responsibility for what was afflicting them. The very ways societies change have their own authenticity, so that global modernity is often reproduced as local diversity.

II

When I was a graduate student — back in the Upper Paleolithic period — my teachers were already announcing the death of ethnography. It seemed that Marx's prophecy to the effect that Western hegemony is human destiny was at hand. The bourgeoisie, by the rapid improvement of the instruments of production and communication, proclaimed *Manifesto of the Communist Party*, draws all nations, "even the most barbarian," into "civilization." "The cheap prices of its commodities are the heavy artillery with which it batters down all Chinese walls, with which it forces the barbarians' intensely obstinate hatred of foreigners to capitulate. It compels all nations, on pain of extinction, to adopt the bourgeois mode of production; it compels them to introduce what it calls civilization into their midst, i.e., to become bourgeois themselves. In one word, it creates a world after its own image" (Marx and Engels [1848] 1959:11).

The argument could well convey a sense of inevitability, since its conclusion was already contained in its ethnocentric premise. The effectiveness of this ultimate weapon of cheap commodities already presupposes a universal bourgeois subject, a self-interested creature of desire acting with an eye singular to the main chance. Yet the metaphor is even more ironic inasmuch as the

Chinese wall proves not so vulnerable. On the contrary, as a mark of the limits of "civilization," hence a constraint on demand and the passage of goods, the wall succeeds in its time-honored function, which (according to Lattimore) has been to keep the Chinese in rather than the "barbarians" out (1940). And even when foreign things or barbarian beings do conquer, their local reproduction and meanings are soon sinicized. Western capital and commodities do not easily make their way by demonstration effects. The idea that they will — this same refrain about China — has been playing in Europe for three centuries now: all those hundreds of millions of customers just waiting for British woolens, then cotton textiles, steel cutlery, guns, and ships, and latterly jeeps, perfume, and TV sets. A modern bourgeois version of the quest for El Dorado, the dream of opening China to Western-made products still goes on, undiminished by the perennial failure to make it a reality. Except that now the attempt to discover a northwest passage to Cathay appears as an equally frustrating quest to convert Asian hearts and minds. Consider this recent notice in the *New York Times*:

> "There used to be a missionary aspect to it, with a board of directors having a vision of an enormous consumer market — you know, two billion armpits in need of deodorant," said Matts Engstrom, chairman of California Sunshine Inc., a food company that does extensive business in China. "But since Tiananmen Square, they've realized that it is a long-term prospect, and even then unless you're in the right area you're not going to succeed." (in Kristoff 1990)

Ironic, too, that Western social scientists should be elaborating theories of global integration just when this "new world order" is breaking down into so many small-scale separatist movements marching under the banners of cultural autonomy. Or are these claims of "ethnic identity" merely — to adopt Freud's characterization of Eastern European identities — the narcissism of marginal differences? Presumably, the demands of cultural independence are only temporary. In the long run, the hegemonic forces of the world-capitalist system must prevail. Once again, another science of the future.

473

The cultural self-consciousness developing among imperialism's erstwhile victims is one of the more remarkable phenomena of world history in the later twentieth century. "Culture" — the word itself, or some local equivalent — is on everyone's lips. Tibetans and Hawaiians, Ojibway, Kwakiutl and Eskimo, Kazakhs and Mongols, native Australians, Balinese, Kashmiris, and New Zealand Maori — all discover they have a "culture." For centuries they may have hardly noticed it; but now, as the New Guinea said to the anthropologist, "If we didn't have *kastom*, we would be just like white men." Maurice Godelier tells of *evolués* among another New Guinea people, the Baruya — policemen, teachers, and other town-dwellers — who twenty years earlier had shunned the tribal initiations, only to return in 1979 to the villages to remedy this ritual deficit:

> And it was one of them who ... publicly explained to all the men of the tribe and young initiates that the initiations had to be continued because strength was needed to resist the life of the towns and the lack of work or money; people had to defend themselves. In my presence he shouted, "We must find strength in our customs; we must base ourselves on what the Whites call culture." (1991:395)

It may be true (as Pascal said) that three degrees of latitude make the difference between right and wrong, but with regard to the modern consciousness of "culture," nothing much changes over half the globe (in longitude). Consider Terry Turner's observations on the South American tropical forest: in the late 1980s, even monolingual speakers of Kayapo were using the Portuguese "*cultura*" in reference to traditional customs, including the performances of ceremony, that ought to be followed "in order to preserve the 'life,' 'strength,' and 'happiness' of Kayapo social communities" (1991:304).

Reified notions of cultural differences, as indexed by distinctive customs and traditions, can and have existed apart from any European presence. What distinguishes the current "culturalism" (as it might be called) is the claim to one's own mode of existence as a superior value and a political right, precisely in opposition to a

474

foreign-imperial presence. More than an expression of "ethnic identity" — a normal social-science notion that manages to impoverish the sense of the movement — this cultural consciousness, as Turner again remarks of Kayapo, entails the people's attempt to control their relationships with the dominant society, including control of the technical and political means that up to now have been used to victimize them. The empire strikes back. We are assisting at a spontaneous, worldwide movement of cultural defiance, whose full meanings and historic effects are yet to be determined.

Western intellectuals have been too often disposed to write off the meanings as trivial, on grounds that the claims to cultural continuity are spurious. In the going academic view, the so-called revival is a typical "invention of tradition" — though no slight is intended to Maori or Hawaiian folks, since all traditions are "invented" in and for the purposes of the present. (This functionalist disclaimer, incidentally, while meant to be nice to the peoples, has the effect of erasing the logical and ontological continuities involved in the different ways that societies interpret and respond to the imperialist conjuncture. If culture must be conceived as always and only changing, lest one commit the mortal sin of essentialism, then there can be no such thing as identity, or even sanity, let alone continuity.) In any event, this Maori or Hawaiian "culture" is not historically authentic because it is a reified and interested value, a self-conscious ideology rather than a way of life which, moreover, owes more in content to imperialist forces than to indigenous sources. All unwittingly, ideas of ancient custom are developed out of the colonial experience: an ethnic distinctiveness perceived from the vantage, if not also to the advantage, of the culture-of-dominance. At the Honolulu airport, visitors are welcomed by hula dancers in plastic "grass" skirts, swaying to slack-key Spanish guitars in an expression of the uniquely Hawaiian "aloha spirit." A culture of tourism, of the brand now widely marketed as aboriginal stock in trade. Moreover, it was American Calvinist missionaries — "the mishes," Mark Twain called them — whose obsessions made sexuality emblematic of Hawaiianness. So now Hawaiians have nothing to do but re-create themselves in the image others have made of them.

Alternatively, the indigenous people are said to take their cultural distance only by evolving complementary or inverted forms of the colonial order. An historian can thus find a ready audience for the assertion that Fijians have but recently, since the turn of the twentieth century, elaborated and objectified their well-known customs of generalized reciprocity called *kerekere* — in part by accepting the colonial definition of themselves as "communally organized" and, more important, as a reaction-formation to the even more famous commercial instincts of White men. Reifying their easy give and take of goods, Fijians could represent themselves as generous, in contrast to the self-interest of the colonizers (Thomas 1992a:64–85; cf. Thomas 1992b:213–32). Similarly, an anthropologist argues that the Javanese kingdom of Surakarta was able to survive under Dutch rule by displacing its demonstrations of power from fateful arenas of Realpolitik to innocuous rituals of marriage (Pemberton 1989).

Yet even if these arguments were historically accurate, they would still be culturally insufficient, since under similar colonial circumstances the Samoans did not *kerekere* nor the Balinese merely marry. I return to this point again and again: "tradition" often appears in modern history as a culturally specific mode of change. Fijian exchange or *kerekere* also happens to be a good example of the facile historiography inspired by the principle that "there must be a White man behind every brown," as Dorothy Shineberg put it (1967:214). An "elite historiography," in Ranajit Guha's terms, unmindful of the culture and action of the subalterns (1989). For the journals of missionaries and traders from the earlier nineteenth century not only provide abundant evidence that the *kerekere* custom was self-consciously practiced then in the same way it is described in modern ethnographies — Fijian "begging," as *kerekere* appears in the historical texts and is defined in an 1850 missionary dictionary — but, moreover, the documents also indicate historically what one would expect logically: that the failure of White men to participate in *kerekere* led Fijians to construct them as selfish (for insisting on buying and selling) rather than that the selfishness of White men led Fijians to construct themselves as generous (by inventing *kerekere*). So when the mishes protest to

476

the chief that they have come out of love for Fijians and to save them, the chief objects that it can't be so:

> "You come here and you will only buy and sell, and we hate buying. When we ask you for a thing you say no. If a Feejeean said no, we should kill him, don't you now that. We [of Bau] are a land of Chiefs. We have plenty of riches.... We have them without buying; we hate buying and we hate the lotu [Christianity]." He concluded by begging a knife for one of his friends, which after such a conversation I thought it best to refuse, which I did as respectfully as possible. (Lyth, Tongan and Feejeean Reminiscences [hereafter TFR], vol. 2: 74–76)

"Begging," an early American trader observed, "is the besetting sin of them all & both sexes do not hesitate to Cery Cery fuckabede as they call it." "Cery Cery fuckabede" was Warren Osburn's immortal 1835 transcription of the Fijian *kerekere vakaviti*, meaning "to ask for something in the Fijian manner," a phrase that also proves that Fijians objectified the practice some months before the first missionaries and some decades before the establishment of the Colony, although not before centuries of contact and exchange with people from other island groups of the Pacific — Tonga, Rotuma, Uvea (Osborn, "Journal" 31 Jan. 1835).

There is a certain historiography that is quick to take the agents of imperialism as exclusive players of the only game in town. It is prepared to assume that history is made by the colonial masters, and all that need be known about the people's own social dispositions, or even their "subjectivity," is the external disciplines imposed upon them — the colonial policies of classification, enumeration, taxation, education, and sanitation. The main historical activity remaining to the underlying people is to misconstrue the effects of such imperialism as their own cultural traditions. Worse yet, their cultural false consciousness is normalizing: in the name of ancestral practice, the people construct an essentialized culture — a supposedly unchanging inheritance, sheltered from the contestations of a true social existence. They thus repeat as tragedy the farcical errors about the coherence of symbolic systems supposed to have been committed by an earlier and more naive generation of anthropologists.

Wiser now, we trade in our naiveté for melancholy. Ethnography in the wake of colonialism can only contemplate the sadness of the tropics (*tristes tropiques*). Like the rusting shantytowns in which the people live, here are bits and pieces of cultural structures, old and new, reassembled into corrupt forms of the Western imagination. How convenient for the theorists of the postmodern deconstruction of the Other. Moreover, the new ethnographers can agree with the world systematists, as James Clifford with Eric Wolf, on the incoherence of the so-called cultures — and thus of the anthropologists' culture concept. Both are also critics of imperialism: the postmodernists blaming it for arrogant projects of ethnographic totalization, the world systematists for the empirical impossibility of realizing them. Yet all these *tristes tropes* of Western hegemony and local anarchy, of the contrast between a powerful World System and people's cultural incoherence, do they not mimic on an academic plane the same imperialism they would despise? As an attack on the cultural integrity and historical agency of the peripheral peoples, they do in theory just what imperialism attempts in practice.

Everyone hates the destruction rained upon the peoples by the planetary conquests of capitalism; but to indulge in what Stephen Greenblatt calls the "sentimental pessimism" of collapsing their lives within a global vision of domination in subtle intellectual and ideological ways makes the conquest complete (1991:152). Nor should it be forgotten that the West owes its own sense of cultural superiority to an invention of the past so flagrant it should make European natives blush to call other peoples culturally counterfeit.

III

In the fifteenth and sixteenth centuries, a bunch of indigenous intellectuals and artists in Europe got together and began inventing their traditions and themselves by attempting to revive the learning of an ancient culture which they claimed to be the achievement of their ancestors but which they did not fully understand, as for many centuries this culture had been lost and

478

its languages corrupted or forgotten. For centuries also the Europeans had been converted to Christianity; but this did not prevent them from calling now for the restoration of their pagan heritage. They would once again practice the classical virtues, even invoke the pagan gods. All the same, under the circumstances — the great distance of the acculturated intellectuals from a past that was effectively irrecoverable — nostalgia was not what it used to be. The texts and monuments they constructed were often bowdlerized facsimiles of classical models. They created a self-conscious tradition of fixed and essentialized canons. They wrote history in the style of Livy, verses in a mannered Latin, tragedy according to Seneca, and comedy in the mode of Terence; they decorated Christian churches with the facades of classical temples and generally followed the precepts of Roman architecture as set down by Vitruvius without realizing that the precepts were Greek. All this came to be called the Renaissance in European history, because it gave birth to "modern civilization."

What else can one say about it, except that some people have all the historical luck? When Europeans invent their traditions — with the Turks at the gates — it is a genuine cultural rebirth, the beginnings of a progressive future. When other peoples do it, it is a sign of cultural decadence, a factitious recuperation, which can only bring forth the simulacra of a dead past.

On the other hand, the historical lesson could be that all is not lost.

IV

Hula schools (*halua hula*) have been flourishing in Hawaii since the early 1970s. Many function under the patronage of Laka, the ancient goddess of hula, are led by inspired teachers (*kumu*), and observe various rituals of training and performance. Hula schools are a significant element of what some participants are pleased to call "the Hawaiian renaissance."[1]

Nothing essentialized here. All sorts of differences between schools in styles of music and movement, in rituals, in assertions about what is modern and what is "Hawaiian." Many arguments turn on implications of opposition to the culture of the *Haole*

(White man). Yet the hula as a sign of Hawaiianness, of the indigenous, was not born yesterday nor merely as the construction of the Hawaiian Visitors Bureau and prurient *Haole* interests. The hula has been functioning as a mode of cultural co-optation for more than 150 years — a significance, moreover, that was already inscribed in the meanings of hula performances before the first White men set foot in the islands. For that matter, these first *Haole* visitors, Captain Cook & Co., were entertained by a great deal of lascivious-seeming hula.

"The young women spend most of their time singing and dancing, of which they are very fond," observed David Samwell, minor Welsh poet and surgeon of the *Discovery*, during Cook's stay at Hawai'i Island in early 1779 (in Beaglehole 1967:1181). Cook's stay coincided with the Makahiki, the festival of the annual return of the original god and deposed king Lono, come back at the New Year to renew the earth — or, in another register, to repossess the wife and kingdom taken from him by an upstart rival (cf. M. Sahlins 1985b). The visitation of Lono was ritually mediated and popularly celebrated by hula dancing, especially the sexually arousing dances of young women. Of course, not all Hawaiian hula was of this sort, but Samwell collected two hula chants in 1779 that were sufficiently amorous. The women would thus attract the god — if their performance did not actually signify a Frazerian sacred marriage. But then, toward the end of the Makahiki, the reigning king sacrifices Lono, sending him back to Kahiki, the overseas homeland and ancestral source of life, a removal that captures the benefits of the god's passage for mankind.

Humanizing and appropriating Lono's seminal powers, the women's hula expresses a general function of their sexuality, which is to mediate just such translations between god and man — or, in Polynesian terms, between the states of *tapu* (tabu) and *noa* (free). Hence the essential ambiguity of women from a certain theological point of view: their powers of defiling the god amounted to conditions of the possibility of human existence. Hence also, as the party of humanity, their powers of cultural subversion. Birth itself was a form of this same capacity to bring the divine into the human world, especially the bearing of a royal child. Accordingly, chiefly births were famous occasions for hula, as were the arrivals and entertainments of noble voyagers. And all these hula performances, including the annual seduction of Lono, would have the same broad finality, the domestication of the god. But note that, within this frame, the particular values varied from the restoration of an indigenous and beneficent king, the tragic figure of the dispossessed Lono, to the neutralization of the stranger-king, the classic figure of the usurper — the one who does Lono in.

Thus the historic function of the hula: its recurrent appearance through two centuries of *Haole* domination in defense of the ancien régime, and specifically of a Hawaiian kingship whose powers had been contested early on by a holy alliance of pious chiefly converts and puritanical American missionaries. Adapting the Protestant ethic to Hawaiian projects of authority, the chiefs had learned to forward their commercial interests at the king's expense. Based on traditional conceptions of sacred power, on the establishment of links to Kahiki, this competition among ruling chiefs in the medium of commercial prowess greatly exacerbated the "impact" of the World System on Hawaiian culture. The historic effects of capitalism were not directly proportional to its material force, a simple matter of physics. The huge debt amassed by the chiefs is, rather, a measure of the impetus given by the creative powers of *mana* to the destructive forces of capital. The comprador and foreign agents of the World System played the legendary part of the "sharks who travel inland," rapacious strangers from overseas, and they turned the king into a historic version of Lono.

By the same cultural logic, the period of Lono's return, the Makahiki, was transposed by royal partisans into a festival of rebellion. For decades after it had ceased to be celebrated according to the customary rituals of world renewal, the Makahiki season became the occasion for improvised renewals of Hawaiian custom — expressed in and as the restoration of royal power.[2] Through all this the hula, together with complementary practices of *jouissance*, provided continuities of form and meaning. Indeed, the hula uniquely represented the Makahiki in 1820–1821, the year

481

following the famous "religious revolution" that had in principle abolished all such "idolatry" and ceremony. For many weeks between December and the end of February, the disapproving missionaries were reporting people dancing in the courtyards of Honolulu "in honor of the king," Kamehameha II, and before the image of the hula god (probably Laka). The excitement proved to be the prelude to a series of libertine counterrevolutions in the later 1820s and early 1830s, all of them likewise breaking out at the time of the traditional Makahiki ceremony and enlisting its sentiments and practices in the political cause of the young king, Kamehameha III. Besides the hula, the old games and amusements of the New Year were revived, with effects enhanced by generous libations of *Haole* rum. The king dignified the first rebellion, in 1827, by sleeping with his paternal half-sister; in 1834, he finished off the last by fornicating with his full sister in front of the assembled Christian chiefs. At one time he abolished all the Calvinist interdictions on sexual relations and summoned the prostitutes of Honolulu to pay court to his current mistress. Feminine sexuality was again enlisted in the cause of humanity: in rendering things *noa*, as Hawaiians conceived it, for in the context then existing, the events meant the abolition of the Christian tabus as well as the return of the Hawaiian order. Nor was all this merely symbolic frolic: the king's sexual possession of the earth at times developed into the assertion of his sovereign rights over land, and more than once his carnival opposition to the Christian chiefs came near to armed conflict. But, on each occasion, the king was required to yield. In the denouement, as in other curious historical details, he lived out the destiny of the superseded god.

From 1830 or earlier the Christian chiefs periodically banned the hula, and from 1851 it was curbed by legislation. However, clandestine hula schools kept operating in the countryside, until they were again openly sanctioned — by kings. Excluding foreigners from attending the scene, Kamehameha V in 1866 allowed the people to mourn the death of his sister in the ancient fashion, which included hula dances. Mark Twain managed to gain access to one of the performances:

I lived three blocks from the wooden two-story palace when Victoria was being lamented, and for thirty nights in succession the mourning pow-wow defied sleep. All that time the Christianized but morally unclean Princess lay in state in the palace. I got into the grounds one night and saw hundreds of half naked savages of both sexes beating their dismal tom-toms, and wailing and caterwauling in the weird glare of innumerable torches, and while a great band of women swayed and jiggered their pliant bodies through the intricate movements of a lascivious dance called the hula-hula, they chanted an accompaniment in native words. I asked the son of a missionary what the words meant. He said they celebrated certain admired gifts and physical excellencies of the dead princess. I inquired further, but he said the words were too foul for translation; that the bodily excellencies were unmentionable; that the capabilities so lauded and so glorified had better be left to the imagination. He said the king was doubtless sitting where he could hear these ghastly phrases and enjoy them. (1963:24)

The hula was especially favored with royal patronage during the revivalist reign of King Kalakaua (1871–1891). Kalakaua sponsored spectacular performances at his inauguration and fiftieth birthday celebration. After Hawaii was annexed by the United States, the received functions of the hula were divided between the commercialized domestication of strangers in the tourist sector and the country schools less subject to modernizing innovations. The hula of the current Hawaiian Renaissance is an "invention" evolved particularly from the country schools. But it is not simply a colonial invention — a Western fabrication of Hawaiianness or else a Hawaiian fabrication in response to the West — which a certain colonial historiography, in some haste to make dupes of the ethnographers and victims of the indigenous people, or vice versa, is prematurely inclined to discover.

Not that the purpose of an historical ethnography is just to give salutary lessons in cultural continuity. More important, the purpose is to synthesize form and function, structure and variation, as a meaningful cultural process, sequitur to a specific cultural order rather than an eternal practical logic. The practical

functions of institutions will appear as meaningful relations between constituted forms and historical contexts: the way the hula
and the Makahiki festival — the hula by its translations of *tapu* to
noa, the Makahiki by its reminiscences of sovereignty lost — were
effectively counterposed to a Christianized ruling class.

V

For its own part, the World System, as culture, is no less arbitrary.
But its familiarity allows us to maintain the delusion of a transpar-
ent and disenchanted order, singularly constructed by our material rationality, our human disposition to "rational choice."

However, material forces and circumstances always lead a double
life in human societies; they are at once physical and meaningful.
Without ceasing to be objectively compelling, they are endowed
with the symbolic values of a certain cultural field. Reciprocally,
then, without ceasing to be symbolic, cultural categories and relationships are endowed with materiality. No chemist, Marx once
said, has ever discovered the value of gold in its physical composition. Yet it is by this symbolic value that the objective characteristics of gold, such as its natural geographic distribution in the
earth, become powerful factors of world history. Pardon me for
being so simple, but it is sometimes necessary to remind ourselves
that our pretended rationalist discourse is pronounced in a particular cultural dialect — that "we are one of the others."

Western capitalism in its totality is a truly exotic cultural
scheme, as bizarre as any other, marked by the subsumption of
material rationality in a vast order of symbolic relationships. We
are too much misled by the apparent pragmatism of production
and commerce. The whole cultural organization of our economy
remains invisible, mystified as the pecuniary rationality by which
its arbitrary values are realized. All the idiocies of modern life
from Walkmans and Reeboks to mink coats and seven-million-
dollar-a-year baseball players, and on to McDonald's and Madon-
nas and other weapons of mass destruction — this whole curious
cultural scheme nonetheless appears to economists as the trans-
parent effects of a universal practical wisdom. Yet even the producers who are perpetrating such tastes in the abstract interest of

gain must be informed by the order of cultural values — that is, by what sells. Theirs is a classic fetishism of the commodity: the meaningful values are comprehended as pecuniary values. But then, the market economy, by harnessing an absolute sense of rationality to a relative logic of signs, ushers in a (truly) golden age of symbolic freedom.

So it need not be surprising that when the advanced products of the West are successfully spread abroad, together with its higher attainments in economic rationality, all this practical reason is exposed to some cultural subversion.

VI

As Bakhtin might say, Western commodities become the objects of alien words — or not just words, but a whole alien discourse. In the planetary hinterlands, the powers of capital appear as forces of other universes. Although they may be at the margins of the World System, the people are not (to adopt Marx's image) solitary beings squatting outside the universe. They are social beings, conscious of themselves as persons of certain social sorts. They are fathers, cross-cousins, chiefs, Bear clansmen, elders, married women, Iroquois, or Tibetans: persons functioning in determinate relations of kinship, gender, community, and authority — relations that thus entail specific rights and obligations, amities and enmities; conduct, then, that is materialized in definite modes of exchange and forms of wealth — hence social beings operating on cosmic notions of power, quotidian instincts of morality, selective skills of perception, relative ways of knowing, and, withal, large cultural resources of self-respect. We are not dealing with people who have nothing and are nothing. To put it in the terms of Vološinov's semantics, the capitalist forms in these alien contexts acquire novel local accents. And here at least a synthesis with Saussure proves useful; the novel accents are also positional values whose differential relations to other categories of the indigenous scheme constitute logics of the possible effects of intrusive "forces."

One might suggest an elementary subaltern principle of historiography: that no assertion of an imperialist discipline can be

485

received as an event of colonial history without the ethnographic investigation of its practice. We cannot equate colonial history simply with the history of the colonizers. It remains to be known how the disciplines of the colonial state are culturally sabotaged.

VII

To conceive of a simple opposition between the West and the Rest is in many ways an oversimplification. Colonial history is not well served either by its representation as a Manichaean show-down between the indigenous people and the imperialist forces, to see which one will be able to culturally appropriate the other. A number of anthropologists — among them Bruce Trigger, Ann Stoler, John Comaroff, and Greg Dening — have taught us to re-configure the usual binary opposition as a triadic historical field, including a complicated intercultural zone where the cultural differences are worked through in political and economic prac-tice (Trigger 1975, Stoler 1985, Comaroff 1989, Dening 1980). "The beach," as Dening calls it — though it could as well be the plantation or the town — where "native" and "stranger" play out their working misunderstandings in creolized languages. Here are complex "structures of the conjuncture," such as the alliances that cross ethnic boundaries and correlate oppositions within the colonial society to political differences among the local people. Think of how often the rivalry between Protestants and Catholics has been enlisted by Latin Americans or Pacific Islanders to the service of their own historic disputes. I have already mentioned something of the like in Hawaii. A recurrent conflict between the king and aristocratic chiefs, traditionally waged as the acquisition of foreign-cum-divine powers, was in the nineteenth century joined to the bitter jealousies in the *Haole* community between merchants and missionaries. Believing themselves the true heirs of the Protestant ethic, the commercial men explicitly competed with the clergymen for leadership of the civilizing mission and the control of Hawaiians' devotion (which also entailed control of their labor). The praying chiefs standing with the missionaries and the drinking king with the merchants — the effect was an intercultural chiasmus, a structure that magnified the conflicts among Hawaiians by the differences in interest between *Haole*, and vice versa. The energies of one opposition were superimposed on the enmities of the other. A powerful stimulus was given to the competition for grandeur among Hawaiian notables through the invidious accumulation of foreign luxuries, especially during the flush days of the trade in sandalwood for the Canton market. The chiefly persons could be metonymically extended to the foreign lands in the sky beyond the horizon, extended as far as China and England, by the importation of fancy clothing and swank domestic furnishings. China and England had replaced the old Kahiki, homeland of the gods, and now the flash of the foreign commodities evoked the celestial brilliance of ancient kings (above, Chapter Thirteen). Was this the origin of the aloha shirt?

Of course, there are strictly functional demands to production for the market, adaptations that reach deeply into the indigenous society. And foreign meanings and economic dispositions come across the beach, along with the foreign goods. Yet students of Pacific history are sometimes surprised at how easily the famous "penetration" of capitalism can be effected, with relatively little effort, violence, or threat.

VIII

Disease and destruction have too often followed, but they were not the means of access to the local people's desires or of the deployment of their labor to trade. Not that the islanders (any more than the Chinese) gave Westerners cause to congratulate themselves on the "demonstration effects" of their clearly superior goods, since the demands of the local peoples were soon enough selective rather than eclectic and they involved rather exotic senses of utility. Hence the flourishing nineteenth-century commerce in sperm-whale teeth in Fiji and Hudson's Bay blankets in Northwest America as well as Chinese silks and English broadcloths in Hawaii. Here was a period of indigenous "development," as I shall try to explain in a moment, during which all these foreign commodities were enriching native self-conceptions. It would thus be too easy to conclude from the people's receptivity that "Fijian culture," or "Kwakiutl culture," is an indeterminate

487

concept, inasmuch as the so-called culture appears to lack any boundary, integrity, or totality.

A brief parenthesis only about cultural integrity or coherence, since we are here more concerned with boundaries. Anyhow, we are not soon likely to hear an end to poststructuralist litanies about the contested and unstable character of cultural logics, about categories and perceptions that are different for women and men, chiefs and commoners, rich and poor, this village and that, yesterday and today. All the same, not everything in the contest is contested — which once more proves that we come here to paraphrase Durkheim, not to bury him. As polyphonic or heteroglossic as the monograph may be, one cannot legitimately insert a Japanese "voice" in a Sioux Indian ethnography. In order for categories to be contested at all, there must be a common system of intelligibility, extending to the grounds, means, modes, and issues of disagreement. It would be difficult to understand how a society could function, let alone how any knowledge of it could be constituted, if there were not some meaningful order *in* the differences. If, in regard to some given event or phenomenon, the women of a community say one thing and the men another, is it not because men and women have different positions in, and experience of, the same social universe of discourse? Are not the differences in what men and women say expressions of the social differences in the construction of gender? If so, there is a noncontradictory way — dare one say, a totalizing way? — of describing the contradictions, a system of and in the differences. End parenthesis: return to the boundary dispute.

I mean the currently fashionable idea that there is nothing usefully called "a culture" — no such reified entity — since the limits of the supposed "cultures" are indeterminate and permeable, a lack of closure that again indicates a lack of system. Paradoxically, this argument misreads a cultural power of inclusion as the inability to maintain a boundary. It is based on an underestimate of the scope and systematicity of cultures, which are always universal in compass and thereby able to subsume alien objects and persons in logically coherent relationships. So far as Western imperialism is concerned — the one culture that has not been deconstructed by the changing of the avant-garde, as it retains its essential and monolithic consistency as a system of power — for the local people the European is never altogether a stranger. As Marilyn Strathern says of Melanesia: "It has been something of a surprise for Europeans to realize that their advent was something less than a surprise" (1990:25). Western peoples have no monopoly on practices of cultural encompassment, nor are they playing with amateurs in the game of "constructing the other." Every society known to history is a global society, every culture a cosmological order; and in thus including the universe within its own cultural scheme — as the Maori or native Australians include the order of nature in the order of kinship — the people accord beings and things beyond their immediate community a definite place in its reproduction.

Divinities or enemies, ancestors or affines, the Others are in various ways the necessary conditions of a society's existence. Sources of power and cultural good things, though they may also be dangerous, these beings from the beyond represent a predicament of dependency in which all peoples find themselves. All must construct their own existence in relation to external conditions, natural and social, which they did not create or control, yet cannot avoid. They are constrained in some way, if never the only possible way, by the passage of the seasons, the annual rainfall, the customs and actions of their neighbors. In such respects, no culture is sui generis. And a more or less self-conscious fabrication of culture in response to imperious outside "pressures" is a normal process — dialectic or schismogenic, perhaps, but not pathogenic.

IX

Differences in the modes of cultural invention and reproduction appear with the advent of the colonial state. Interesting that from the perspective of many colonized peoples, it is this moment of domination, the assumption of subaltern status, that is most marked in historical consciousness rather than the first appearance of the White man or the earlier period of "contact." For Europeans, of course, the great rupture in the history of the rest of the world is initiated by their own appearance there — an epiphany that supposedly produces a change in the quality of historical time. In extreme (but not rare) formulations, nothing was happening before the European "discovery" (of places that had been known to mankind for millennia), merely a static reproduction of "traditional" forms; whereas, from the moment the first Western explorer or trader landed, the people's history became evenemential — and adulterated by the foreigners' culture. Still, the Fijians, as many other colonized peoples, figure the historical break differently: "before the flag" and "after the flag," they say, referring to the establishment of British rule. This is the B.C. and A.D. of their world history, "Before Colonization" and "After Domination," and it entails a different sense of the cultural qualities of time and change.

"Before" was the time under their own cultural control. Western commodities and even persons could be encompassed within their own "development" projects. Foreign wealth subsidized native cultural schemes: the kingship in Hawaii, ceremonial feasting in Ponape and the New Guinea Highlands, hunting and warfare on the American Plains, potlatching on the Northwest Coast. This helps to explain why certain things of European provenance — not only horses, tobacco, bush knives, or cloth but even Christianity — are still locally perceived as "traditional" culture. They refer to the kind of indigenous response to the West we have called "develop-man" (Chapter Thirteen). The term captures an indigenous way of coping with capitalism, a passing moment that in some places has managed to survive for over a century. The first commercial impulse of the people is not to become just like us but more like themselves. They turn foreign goods to the service of domestic ideas, to the objectification of their own relations and notions of the good life. Brought into the orbit of the capitalist world system, this global crusade of economic rationality, New Guinea Highlanders indeed prove themselves quick studies in commercial cunning — which they use to stage the most extravagant "traditional" ceremonies anyone could ever remember. More pigs have been eaten and more pearl shells exchanged in these recent festivals than ever was done in the good old days, not to mention the liberal consumption of such novelties as beer and tinned corned beef. Let the neocolonial bureaucrats or the development economists complain as they may, this is neither "waste" nor "backwardness": it is, precisely, *development* from the perspective of the people concerned — their own culture on a bigger and better scale. "You know what *we* mean by development?" says a leader of the Kewa people to the ethnographer. "We mean building up the lineage, the men's house, killing pigs. That's what we have done" (Josephides 1985:44).

X

Of course, under a colonial state that relates to the underlying population by combined techniques of discipline, repression, and persuasion, the conditions of the people's cultural reproduction are radically altered for the worse. It is a period of humiliation, in which the political and economic prose of domination is often improved by a Christian poetry of human degradation. American missionaries used to complain endlessly that the problem with Hawaiians was that they lacked sufficient self-contempt. Eating, laughing, and copulating too much, while never working too long, the islanders simply could not understand how rotten they were. The whole Judeo-Christian cosmology of the human condition, of a human nature inherently corrupted by sin, of life as a punishment, this whole system of self-hatred had to be laid on them — "the furious, vindictive hatred of life," as Nietzsche called it, "life loathing itself." Only then, when they were sufficiently disgusted with themselves, would they be prepared to become like us, "civilized."

Around much of the world, however, the universalizing cultural project of the West does not succeed so well. The subaltern period is a "dominance without hegemony," as Guha puts it (for South Asia), marked by the compromises of the colonial state with the cultural particularism of the local people — who otherwise could not be ruled. In dominance without hegemony, Guha writes, "the life of civil society can never be fully absorbed in the activity of the state" (1989:281). The colonial regime is "doubly alienated" from the indigenous people, at once as foreign and as a state: it is an "absolute externality." The colonized adapt to its impositions by motivated permutations of their cultural traditions. Hence the sublimation of warfare in ceremonial exchange,

491

or the cargo cult that subsumes the colonial experience in a native theory of ancestral powers, to cite well-known Oceanic examples. In the end, the people's humiliation is a double-edged sword, turned back against foreign dominance, as in the current "culturalism" or "the invention of tradition." In the words of Amilcar Cabral:

> Culture has proved to be the very foundation of the liberation movement. Only societies which preserve their cultures are able to mobilize and organize themselves and fight against foreign domination. Whatever ideological or idealistic forms it takes, culture is essential to the historical process.... And since a society that really succeeds in throwing off the foreign yoke reverts to the upward path of its own culture, the struggle for liberation is above all an act of culture. (1973:16)

And how else can the people respond to what has been inflicted on them except by devising on their own heritage, acting according to their own categories, logics, understandings? I say "devising" because the response may be totally improvised, something never seen or imagined before, not just a knee-jerk repetition of ancient custom. "Tradition" here functions as a yardstick by which the people measure the acceptability of change, as Lamont Lindstrom remarks of Tanna islanders (1982:316–29). Cultural continuity thus appears in and as the mode of cultural change. The innovations follow logically — though not spontaneously, and in that sense not necessarily — from the people's own principles of existence. Traditionalism without archaism.

Allan Hanson recounts a conversation with a "mammoth" old Tahitian who "has succeeded rather well in combining indigenous values with French influence." Sinking into a large chair after an excellent dinner and indicating the prominent place that a refrigerator occupied in his living room, he beamed contentedly at Hanson and said, "Le *ma'a* [food] in the refrigerator — voilà la vie tahitienne!" (1970:62).

XI

Notice that for the people concerned syncretism is not a contradiction of their culturalism — of the indigenous claims of authenticity and autonomy — but, rather, its systematic condition. The
first thing, of course, is to survive; this is what the politics is decisively about. Yet the movement almost never envisions a utopian
return to primordial days and ancestral ways. The traditional culture has its superior values, but refrigerators, outboard engines,
and television sets are not among them. Modern culturalism
includes the demand to have these things or, more precisely, to
domesticate them. Defenders of the indigenous order are prepared to make useful compromises with the dominant culture,
even to deploy its techniques and ideals — in the course of distinguishing their own. Hawaiians, Amazonians, or native Australians stake claims to be the world's leading ecologists, the original
friends of the earth (Mother). But then, are they not just acting as
proxy critics of Western society, deceiving and undoing themselves by mystifying Western values as native cultures? This seems
not the correct interpretation, even granted that a peculiar ambiguity attends the modern culture movement — which from the
left can be read as political resistance, if from the right as an
ideological sellout. What I am trying to do here is get above the
mêlée, for it seems to me that the local politics become means or
expressions of a larger process of structural transformation: the
formation of a World System of cultures, a Culture of cultures —
with all the characteristics of a structure of differences.

In the upshot, in any local sector of the global system the
transformation assumes the dual appearance of assimilation and
differentiation. The local people articulate with the dominant
cultural order even as they take their distance from it, jiving to
the world beat while making their own music. Hence Michael
Geyer's argument that similarity and difference develop together
in modern world history, an observation that could be paired with
Terry Turner's notices of the cultural dualism of Kayapo bodies,
villages, and society as a whole — at each level externally Brazilian
and internally Indian. Interesting that earlier scholars of what is
now perceived as "cultural inversion" — this disposition of peoples

493

in contact to elaborate the contrastive features of their respective traditions — saw the cultural inversion as a structural equilibrium. Recall that Gregory Bateson originally defined "complementary schismogenesis" as a phenomenon of acculturation. And in *Naven* he argued that such processes of mutual differentiation are generally limited or counteracted, on pain of total separation and potential destruction (1935:178–83, 1958). Of course, this is the whole idea of how structures travel and are transformed in Lévi-Strauss's *Mythologiques*. Here again the oppositions between peoples in contact are balanced by resemblances as each strives to be as good as and better than — thus the same as and different from — the other. "Everything happens as if, on the plane of beliefs and practices, the Mandan and Hidatsa had succeeded in organizing their differences into a system," Lévi-Strauss wrote in a well-known piece on myths and rites of neighboring peoples (1971b: 163). The myths themselves speak of the wisdom of neighboring tribes staying far enough apart to be independent while remaining close enough together to be interdependent.

Of course, given the current theoretical and moral discourse of domination and subjection, the unearthing of such quaint relics as "structural equilibrium" or "structural complementarity" must appear feckless if not politically perverse. It might be better just to ignore the accumulated anthropological knowledge. This popular tactic is called "poststructuralism."

Alternatively, the old-timers remind us that a politics of culture is a process of structure. Rather than the overthrow of the World System, which is now an irreversible fact of their existence, the local peoples' inventions and inversions of tradition can be understood as attempts to create a differentiated cultural space within it. And actions that are at once indigenizing and modernizing appear structural rather than just hypocritical. Roger Keesing and others make the point that the leaders of modern movements of cultural revival are often the most acculturated people, and most successful in the commercial world whose values they ostensibly repudiate. Not long ago, I spent the better part of a day with one in the mountains of south-central Taiwan, an artist of the Austronesian Paiwan people, the organizer of an aesthetic re-

494

vival that is for him the means of an even larger project of cultural restoration. When I asked him why he wanted to return to Paiwan tradition, he answered with a criticism of modern materialism and individualism of a kind that can be heard in many Third World places: a life of money is inhuman by comparison with Paiwan culture. This he said while eating a steak in a Western restaurant in the Chinese town of Ping Dong, the restaurant being a sort of club to which he belonged and to which he and his young Chinese wife escorted us from the mountains in the Jeep he had recently purchased—from the proceeds of his two stores, where he sells his work and other ethnic products, including textiles from Indonesia and India. Yet there was nothing cynical about the man—on the contrary; and like everything else he did, his movement between cultures was graceful rather than incongruous. But then, who would be in a better position to mediate an intercultural relationship? And, like the Polynesian ecologists or the Amazonian chief who turns a camcorder on the representative of the Brazilian Indian Service, does not the Paiwan artist make an assimilation of the dominant culture the means of sustaining difference?

If all this makes any sense, if the world is becoming a Culture of cultures, then what needs to be studied ethnographically is the indigenization of modernity—through time and in all its dialectical ups and downs, from the earliest develop-man to the latest invention of tradition. Western capitalism is planetary in its scope, but it is not a universal logic of cultural change. In any event, we have been ourselves too dominated, historiographically and ethnographically, by its imperial claims. The agenda now is how it is worked out in other cultural manifolds.

XII

The first fifty years of capitalist develop-man in Fiji, roughly from 1800 to 1850, achieved unprecedented levels of cannibalism, thus confirming a certain totemic nightmare that has haunted the Western imagination at least since Saint Augustine articulated it: that if human venality is unleashed, the big fish will eat the little fish. We have seen that modern academic hawkers of the World System have given too much credit to the trade in European

495

muskets for local sandalwood and bêche de mer as the reason for the interrelated developments in warfare, cannibalism, and state formation in nineteenth-century Fiji (Chapter Twelve).[3] The firepower of the musket and the labor requirements of the bêche de mer trade are said to have made the political fortunes of the kingdoms of Bau, Rewa, and their like; yet these powerful states had already achieved their historic form and much of their dominion before any Europeans came, certainly well before the bêche de mer trade of the 1830s introduced an appreciable number of muskets into Fijian wars. Indeed, the control of Western trade by Bau and Rewa was due to their indigenous dominance, rather than vice versa, as neither of them enjoyed significant resources in sandalwood or bêche de mer within their own territories. Nor were the muskets then obtained by Fijians decisive in their wars. Notoriously subject to misfire in the humid tropics and quickly neutralized by changes in fortifications, muskets were in any event not employed by Fijians with great accuracy or efficiency. Not the muskets or the bêche de mer trade, then, so much as the whale teeth that poured into Fiji in the early nineteenth century – these were the source of the indigenous develop-men. The currency of large-scale politics, the means of making and breaking alliances, the price of an assassination or a cannibal victim – transactions in whale teeth fueled the transcendent schemes of domination, the idea of a universal Fijian order, entertained by ambitious ruling chiefs of that period, especially in Bau (above, Chapter Twelve).

Proof? Lévi-Strauss talks about the chemist who, having carefully synthesized sodium chloride in the laboratory and confirmed its composition with the standard tests, just to make sure it's salt, tastes it. A good proof of the historic value of the whale teeth is that, ethnographically, you can taste it. Not only because whale teeth continue to organize Fijian life – marriage alliances, respects to chiefs, or any "heavy" *kerekere* of goods or persons – and not only because the ritualized formulas of their exchange remain barely altered expressions of a transaction in divine benefits. There is also the extraordinarily high price of whale teeth in the pawnshops of Suva, the capital city. The power of the whale tooth appears in its historic transformations.

Not far from Suva, in the village of Cautâtâ, Poate Matairavula a few years ago showed me a small wooden chest, set in the farthest corner of the rear right-hand bedroom of his "European-style" house. The space was the modern equivalent of the most tabu part of the old Fijian house (the *loqi*), where the head of the family slept with his wife and reproductive forms of wealth were stored, including seed yams and the weapons that procured cannibal victims. The wooden chest, Matairavula explained, was the "basket of the clan" (*kato ni mataqali*), holding the collective treasure in whale teeth. Passing with the leadership of the clan, the chest was a palladium. So long as it is intact, Matairavula said, the *vanua* — the land, including the people — will be preserved. In 1984, Matairavula was showing me an example of an old "basket of state" (*kato ni tu*), the likes of which (so far as I know) have not been anthropologically noticed from this part of Fiji since Hocart's report in 1910 of the reminiscences of an old man from Namata, a village near Cautâtâ.

Matairavula's further explanations continued to echo these ancient memories. As chief of the clan himself, he could not go into the chest and take out whale teeth. That was for the herald, the "face of the land" (*matanivanua*), representative of the collectivity vis-à-vis the chief. A few days later, Matairavula and I and a few other men were on the ceremonial ground of Bau, together with the Cautâtâ herald, who was carrying a large whale tooth concealed in a worn black leather briefcase. We were a delegation from the village to the funeral of a high Bauan, of the ruling war king clan, carrying the whale tooth as our "kissing" (*ai reguregu*) of the corpse. My own presence as a White man on the ceremonial ground of Bau was hardly an historic first. On the contrary, I could be moved beyond telling by the whole entangled history of Whites and Fijians in the nineteenth century which had been played out in this space. History was also palpable in the ceremony: we were obliged to wear "traditional" Fijian costume on the Bau ground. Traditional costume was a cotton cloth sarong in floral print. Christian, yes, but "before the flag." History was present, too, in all the villages that came contributing whale teeth to the store of the Bau war kings' power. The Cautâtâ people were there because they are traditional border warriors of the Bau kingdom. It is a status they do not forget. A recent study indicates that of the villages in the Bau dominions Cautātā has the highest rate of enlistment in the Fiji Military Forces.

As for the Fiji Military Forces, until the two coups d'état they effected in 1987 under Colonel Rabuka, this army was most famous as the mainstay of the United Nations peacekeeping corps in Lebanon and the Sinai. So, after the second coup, when Fiji withdrew from the British Commonwealth and thereby abandoned the queen's birthday celebrations, Colonel Rabuka, an admirer of the Israeli military, proclaimed what day as Fiji's national day? Yom Kippur. I am told that in 1987 T-shirts could be seen in Suva with YOM KIPPUR printed in Hebrew on the front and FIJI NATIONAL DAY in English on the back. In the same year, Colonel Rabuka had himself installed as leader of the Fiji Military Forces — and de facto leader of the nation — in a "traditional" ceremony, the newspaper photos and descriptions of which resemble nothing so much as the installations of ancient war kings. But then, "atonement" would be a fair translation for the appropriate ritual (*i soro*) begging forgiveness from traditional authorities for acts of usurpation — by the presentation of whale teeth.

XIII

In a genial argument of the *Essay Concerning Human Understanding*, John Locke says that we necessarily know things relationally, by their "dependence" on other things (IV.6.11). However absolute and entire the objects of perception may seem to us, they "are but Retainers to other parts of Nature." Their observable qualities, actions, and powers "are owing to something without them; and there is not so complete and perfect a part, that we know, of Nature, that does not owe the Being it has, and the Excellancies of it, to its Neighbours." The observation has capital applications in anthropology — granted that philosophers have never been too happy with these "secondary qualities, mediately perceived." Locke drew the fundamental implication that it is impossible to exhaust the empirical description of any object, since its properties can be known only through interaction with an indefinite number of other objects. It follows that the objectivity of objects is humanly constructed, that is, by an historically relative selection and symbolic valuation of only some of the possible concrete referents. Essentialized descriptions are not the platonic fantasies of anthropologists alone; they are general cultural conditions of human perception and communication.

More directly pertinent here is that Locke is also saying that we know the attributes of things historically. We know things from the changes they make in, or receive from, other things. We know the sun by its powers of melting and bleaching wax, even as we know wax by its melting in the sun and hardening in the cold and being divisible by a knife but unmarked by a feather, impervious to water and indigestible to people — one could wax on. So it is with cultural orders. They reveal their properties by the way they respond to diverse circumstances, organizing those circumstances in specific forms and, in the event, changing their forms in specific ways. Here, then, in an historical ethnography — an ethnography that extends, say, over a couple of centuries — is a method for reconciling form and function in a logic of meaning, for discovering the relatively invariant and mutable dimensions of structures, for testing the historical potentialities and limits of different cultural schemes, for weighing and valuing conflicting contextual variations and thereby allowing a principled description of cultural orders as systems of difference. So far as all kinds of modern and postmodern anthropological problems are concerned, history will decide.

But then, the days are over for an ethnography that was the archaeology of the living, searching under the disturbed topsoil of modernity for the traces of a pristine and "primitive" existence. The cultures thus uncovered were indeed fossilized, but mainly by a way of knowing that abstracted them from life and history. It was a nostalgic calling, this kind of ethnography, inspired by theoretical conceits of progress that turned perceptions of others into glimpses of past time — provided the others were not "acculturated." Now history awakens us from these dogmatic slumbers. The old conceptual oppositions on which scientific ethnography was founded are dissolving: we discover continuity in change, tradition in modernity, even custom in commerce. Still, not all that was solid now melts into air, as a certain postmodernist anthropology has prematurely supposed. There remain the distinctive differences, the cultural differences.

NOTES

1. For a general history of the hula, see Barrère, Pukui, and Kelly 1980.

2. See the accounts of royal revolts in M. Sahlins 1992.

3. On issues of Fijian history raised here, see Clunie 1977 and Routledge 1985.

CHAPTER FIFTEEN

What Is Anthropological Enlightenment? Some Lessons of the Twentieth Century*

Dare to know! But from what intellectual bondage would anthropology need to liberate itself in our times? No doubt from a lot of inherited ideas, including sexism, positivism, geneticism, utilitarianism, and many other such dogmas of the common, average native Western folklore posing as universal understandings of the human condition. I will not presume to talk of all these things, but only to the civilizing theory by which Kant responded to his famous question, "What Is Enlightenment?" ([1784] 1983). For him, the question became, how, by the progressive use of our reason, can we escape from barbarism?

And so it became for us. Modern anthropology still struggles with what had seemed like Enlightenment to the philosophers of the eighteenth century but turned out to be a parochial self-consciousness of European expansion and the *mission civilisatrice*. Indeed, "civilisation" was a word the philosophes invented — to refer to their own society, of course. Following on Condorcet, the perfectibility they thus celebrated became in the nineteenth century a progressive series of stages into which one could fit — or fix — the various non-Western peoples. Nor was the imperialism of the past two centuries, crowned by the recent global victory of capitalism, exactly designed to reduce the enlightened contrasts between the West and the rest. On the contrary, the ideologies of "modernization" and "development" that trailed in the wake of

* Originally published in *Annual Review of Anthropology* 28 (1999). Reprinted with the permission of *Annual Review of Anthropology* © 1999.

Western domination took basic premises from the same old philosophical regime. Even the left-critical arguments of "dependency" and capitalist "hegemony" could come to equally dim views of the historical capacities of indigenous peoples and the vitalities of their cultures. In too many narratives of Western domination, the indigenous victims appear as neo-historyless peoples: their own agency disappears, more or less with their culture, the moment Europeans irrupt on the scene.

What Is Not Too Enlightening

Certain illusions born of the Western self-consciousness of "civilization" have thus proved not too enlightening. Worked up into academic gazes of other peoples, they became the main issues with which modern anthropology has contended, sometimes to no avail. In the interest of examining the contention, I briefly examine this anthropological vision of the Other.

First, the set of defects that make up the "historyless" character of indigenous cultures — in obvious contrast to progressiveness of the West. Indeed, Margaret Jolly notes that when *we* change it's called "progress," but when they do — notably when they adopt some of our progressive things — it's a kind of adulteration, a *loss* of culture (1992). But, then, before we came upon the inhabitants of the Americas, Asia, Australia, or the Pacific islands, they were "pristine" and "aboriginal." It is as if they had no historical relations with other societies, were never forced to adapt their existence the one to the other. As if they had no experience constructing their own mode of existence out of their dependency on peoples — not to mention imperious forces of nature — over which they had no control. Rather, until Europeans appeared, they were "isolated" — which just means that *we* weren't there. They were "remote" and "unknown" — which means they were far from us and we were unaware of them. (My lamented colleague Sharon Stephens used to introduce her lectures on Vico by noting that "though it is often said that Vico lived an obscure life, I'm sure it didn't look that way to him.") Hence, the history of these societies only began when Europeans showed up: an epiphanal moment, qualitatively different from anything that had gone before and culturally devastating. Supposedly, the historical difference with everything precolonial was power. Exposed and subjected to Western domination, the less powerful peoples were destined to lose their cultural coherence — as well as the pristine innocence for which Europeans, incomplete and sinful progeny of Adam, so desired them. Of course, as Renato Rosaldo reminds us, the imperialists have no one to blame for their arcadian nostalgias but themselves (1989). Nor should anything I say here be taken as a denial of the terror that Western imperialism has inflicted on so many peoples, or that so many have gone to the wall.

Accordingly, a main academic consequence of the cultural shock and psychological anomie inflicted by the West was the "despondency theory" that became popular in the mid-twentieth century. Despondency theory was the logical precursor of dependency theory. But as it turned out — when the surviving victims of imperialism began to seize their own modern history — despondency was another not terribly enlightening idea of the power of Western "civilization." Here is a good example from A.L. Kroeber's great 1948 textbook, *Anthropology*:

> With primitive tribes, the shock of culture contact is often sudden and severe. Their hunting lands or pastures may be taken away or broken under the plow, their immemorial customs of blood revenge, head-hunting, sacrifice, marriage by purchase or polygamy be suppressed. Despondency settles over the tribes. Under the blocking-out of all old established ideals and prestiges, without provision for new values and opportunities to take their place, the resulting universal hopelessness will weigh doubly heavy because it seems to reaffirm inescapable frustration in personal life also.[1] (437–38)

A corollary of despondency theory was that the others would now become just like us — if they survived. Of course, the Enlightenment had already prepared this eventuality by insisting on the universality of human reason and progress: a course of development that would be good — in all senses of the term — for the human species as such and as a whole. The "unilinear evolutionism" of the nineteenth century was a logical anthropological sequitur

503

to this enlightened sense of universal rationality. Everyone would have to go through the same sequence of development. In his *Primitive Culture* of 1870, E.B. Tylor showed what doom was in store for the appreciation of cultural diversity by endorsing, as an appropriate procedure for constructing the stages of cultural evolution, Dr. Johnson's immortal observation that "one set of savages is like another" (1903, vol. 1:6). In any case, to get back to other peoples now confronted by Western "civilization," Marx likewise supposed that "the country that is more developed industrially only shows, to the less developed, the image of its own future" (1967:8–9). A late classic of the genre was Walt Rostow's *Stages of Economic Growth* (1960), with its unilinear sequence of five developmental stages from "traditional societies" to "the age of high mass consumption." (Rostow must have been among the first to perceive that the culmination of human social evolution was shopping.) Explicitly argued as an alternative to Marxist stages of progress — the book's subtitle was "A Non-communist Manifesto" — Rostow's thesis had all the character of a mirror image, including the effect of turning left into right. Also shared with many theories of "development" was Rostow's cheerful sense of cultural tragedy: the necessary disintegration of "traditional societies" that functioned, in Rostow's scheme, as a precondition for "economic take-off." A further necessity was the foreign domination that could accomplish this salutary destruction; otherwise, the customary relations of traditional production would set a ceiling on economic growth. By its own providential history, Europe had been able to develop itself, but, according to Rostow, other peoples would have to be "shocked" out of their backwardness by an intrusive alien force — guess who? No revolutionary himself, Rostow could agree with Marx that in order to make an omelette one must first crack the eggs. Interesting that many peoples now explicitly engaged in defending their "culture" against national and international domination — the Maya of Guatemala and the Tukanoans of Colombia, for example (Warren 1992, J. Watanabe 1995, Jean Jackson 1995) — have distanced themselves both from the national-bourgeois Right and the international-proletarian Left, refusing the assimilationist pressures that would sacrifice their ethnicity to either the construction of the nation or the struggle against capitalist imperialism. Contrary to the evolutionary destiny the West had foreseen for them, the so-called savages will be neither all alike nor just like us.

In this vein, and as the century wears on, Max Weber's comparative project on the possibilities for capitalist development afforded by different religious ideologies seems increasingly bizarre. Not that it is bizarre to talk of the cosmological organization of pragmatic action, not by any means. What seems increasingly weird is the way Weberians became fixated on the question of why one society or another failed to achieve this *summmum bonum* of human history, Capitalism as we have known and loved it. When I was in China recently, the topic evoked a lot of Confucian. One American sinologist said China during the Qing dynasty had come oh so close. Yet it all seems like asking why the New Guinea Highlanders failed to develop the spectacular potlatch of the Kwakiutl. This is a question the Kwakiutl social scientist could well ask, since with their elaborate pig exchange ceremonies the New Guineans had come so close. Nearer to the point — or perhaps it is the point — is the Christian missionaries' question of how it could be that Fijians in their natural state failed to recognize the true god. One might as well ask why European Christians did not develop the ritual cannibalism of Fijians — after all, they came so close.

Finally, what has not been too enlightening is the way anthropology in the era of late capitalism is made to serve as a redemptive "cultural critique" — a morally laudable analysis that can amount to using other societies as an alibi for redressing what has been troubling us lately. (There is a deep tradition here: anthropology was also like that when it was "coming of age" in Samoa and elsewhere.) It is as if other peoples had constructed their lives for our purposes, in answer to racism, sexism, imperialism, and the other evils of Western society. The problem with such an anthropology of advocacy is not simply that arguments get judged by their morality but, rather, that as a priori persuasive, morality gets to be the argument. The true and the good become one. Since the moral value is usually an external attribute supplied by (and for) the analyst, however, it is too easy to change the signs, which leads to some curious double-bind arguments of the no-win or no-lose variety.

Take the devastating effects of Western capitalist expansion, on the one hand, and on the other, the autonomous ordering of these effects by local peoples according to their own cultural lights. Opposed as they may be as empirical conclusions, both can be rejected on the *same* moral grounds — and often are. For, to speak of the historical agency of indigenous peoples, true as it may be, is to ignore the tyranny of the Western World System, thus to conspire intellectually in its violence and domination; whereas, to speak of the systematic hegemony of imperialism, true as it may be, is to ignore the peoples' struggles for cultural survival, thus to conspire intellectually in Western violence and domination. Alternatively, we can make both global domination and local autonomy morally persuasive — that is, in favor of the peoples — by calling the latter "resistance." This is a no-lose strategy since the two characterizations, domination and resistance, are contradictory and in some combination will cover any and every historical eventuality. Ever since Gramsci, posing the notion of hegemony has entailed the equal and opposite discovery of the resistance of the oppressed. Just so, the anthropologist who relates the so-called grand narrative of Western domination is also likely to invert it by invoking local discourses of cultural freedom. Cultural differences thrown out the front door by the homogenizing forces of world capitalism creep in the back in the form of an "indigenous counterculture," "subversion of the dominant discourse," or some such politics (or poetics) of indigenous defiance.

Local societies of the Third and Fourth Worlds *do* attempt to organize the irresistible forces of the World System according to their own system of the world: in various forms and with varying success, depending on the nature of the indigenous culture and the mode of external domination. What is not too enlightening is the way that New Guinea pig-feasting, Maori land claims, Zimbabwe medium cults, Brazilian workers' do-it-yourself housing, Fijian exchange custom, and any number of determinate cultural forms are accounted for, to the anthropologist's satisfaction, by their moral-political implications. It is enough to show that they are effects of, or reactions to, imperialist domination, as if their supposed hegemonic or counterhegemonic functions could specify their cultural contents. An acid bath of instrumentality, the procedure dissolves worlds of cultural diversity into the one indeterminate meaning. It is something like the Terror, as Sartre said of a certain crude materialism: an intellectual purge of the cultural forms, marked by "an inflexible refusal to differentiate." It consists in taking the actual cultural content for the "mere appearance" of a more profound and generic function — in this case, "the political" or "power" — and having thus dissolved the historical-substantional in the instrumentally universal, we are pleased to believe we have reduced appearance to truth (Sartre 1963). So nowadays all culture is "power." It used to be that everything "maintains the social solidarity." Then for a while everything was "economic" or "adaptively advantageous." We seem to be on a great spiritual quest for the purposes of cultural things; or perhaps it is that those who do not know their own functionalism are condemned to repeat it.

Up the Indigenous Culture
An end to sentimental pessimism, the subsumption of other people's existence in structures of Western domination. Not that there is no such domination, only that there is also other people's existence. Accordingly, the rest of this chapter is a little more upbeat, being a discussion of how several of the problems bequeathed to us by the Enlightenment have been raised to new levels of perplexity by the advance of anthropology and, more particularly, by recent ethnographic experiences of indigenous modernities. Many of the peoples who were left for dead or dying by dependency theory we now find adapting their dependencies to cultural theories of their own. Confronted by cultural processes and forms undreamed of in an earlier anthropology, such as the integration of industrial technologies in indigenous sociologies and cosmologies, we are not leaving the twentieth century with the same ideas that got us there.

507

One of the surprises of late capitalism, for example, is that hunters and gatherers live — many of them by hunting and gathering. As late as 1966, most people at the famous "Man the Hunter" conference in Chicago thought they were talking about a way of life as obsolete as that title sounds today.[2] Yet just a dozen years later, Richard Lee, one of the original conveners, remarked at another such conference: "Hunting is real. Hunting exists and hunting and gathering economies exist and this is to me a new fact in the modern world, because twelve years ago at the Man the Hunter conference we were writing an obituary on the hunters" (quoted in Asch 1982:347). What Lee realized has not only been true of hunter-gatherers of Africa or Southeast Asia; all across the northern tier of the planet, scattered through the vast arctic and subarctic stretches of Europe, Siberia, and North America, hunting, fishing, and gathering peoples have survived by harnessing industrial technologies to paleolithic purposes.

Nor is the survival of northern hunters a simple function of their isolation, since precisely their subsistence is dependent on modern means of production, transportation, and communication — rifles, snow machines, motorized vessels, and, at least in North America, CB radios and all-terrain vehicles — which means of existence they generally acquire by monetary purchase, which money they have acquired in a variety of ways, ranging from public transfer payments and resource royalties to wage labor and commercial fishing. For upwards of two hundred years, the Eskimo of western and northern Alaska (Yupik and Inupiat) have been engaged with the ever-more powerful economic and political forces of world capitalist domination. You would have thought it was enough to undo them, at least culturally: the commercial whaling, fishing, trapping, and trading; the wage labor in jobs ranging from domestic service to construction of the DEW line and the pipeline; the missionization, education, and migration; the dependence on AFDC and Unemployment Compensation. To all this, the past twenty-five years added the Alaska Native Claims Settlement Act, followed by the formation of regional and local native corporations, followed by the spectacular exploitation of North Slope oil by powerful multinational corporations. If Eski-

mo have proven to be only pseudo-beneficiaries of these developments, it also seems they are only the pseudo-victims. However, I
want to come back later to the Big Theoretical Issues raised by the
apparent successes of native Alaskans and other peoples in dominating the capitalist modes of domination. For now I am simply
making the point that the Eskimo are still there — and still Eskimo. Anthropological enlightenment begins with how wrong we
were about that.

A sense of impending doom attended the concluding chapter
of Charles Hughes's ethnography of Gambell Village on Saint
Lawrence Island in the Bering Sea, a community of Siberian Yupik
speakers he studied in 1954–1955. The chapter was titled "The
Broken Tribe." Indeed, "the time has passed," Hughes said, "when
entire groups or communities of Eskimos can successfully relate
to the mainland economy and social structure" (1960:389). For
Hughes, two movements in opposite directions — of mainland
Western culture to the island, and of islanders to the mainland —
were between them tearing the indigenous society to pieces. The
Gambell villagers who moved to the mainland were "no longer
Eskimos," Hughes believed, "no longer people who retain a cultural tradition of their own." In the 1950s and 60s, when young
men went off to the U.S. military or to mainland schools under
the sponsorship of the missions or the Bureau of Indian Affairs,
when the Bureau of Indian Affairs shipped whole families to
Anchorage, Seattle, or Oakland under "Relocation and Employment Assistance" programs, the understanding was they would
learn to live like White folks of the species *Homo economicus*, sever
their relations to their villages and their cultures — and never go
back. "They perforce have to forsake the overarching structure of
Eskimo belief and practice," said Hughes of the Gambell migrants.
"And the more that people move in that direction the more Gambell, as an Eskimo village, disappears from the human scene"
(*ibid.*).

Yet in the 1980s, Gambell was experiencing spectacular growth
— from 372 people in 1970 to 522 in 1989 — much of it due to returning migrants, come back to resume a "subsistence life style,"
as a new generation of ethnographers explained, the epitomizing

part of what they described as a general cultural "renaissance." Gambell was one of a set of villages, including Wainwright on the North Slope and Unalakleet on the lower Yukon that an anthropological team headed by Joseph Jorgensen got to know in some depth in the 1980s — with a view to determining how these "oil age Eskimos" were dealing with their increasing dependency (Jorgensen 1990, Jorgensen n.d.). Like Richard Nelson, who had first studied Wainwright in the 1960s and mistakenly thought then that the subsistence economy was finished — "subsistence" is a buzzword in Alaskan identity politics, whose meaning in this context would be about equivalent to "traditional custom" — and like many other ethnographers, the Jorgensen team found the Eskimo of the 1980s and 90s had changed very much more and very much less than anyone expected (Jorgensen 1990:5). More, because of the large influx of productive technologies and domestic conveniences; less, because these new techniques were overwhelmingly deployed to the subsistence lifestyle and manipulated through its customary relations of production and distribution. The people's efficiency in hunting, fishing, and gathering was directly proportionate to their dependency on capitalism. But as their own modes of production were kinship-ordered — on Gambell by a still-flourishing patrilineal clan system — the effect was an overall florescence of tradition extending from intensive relations of reciprocity among kinsmen to cosmic relations of reciprocal life-giving between men and animals, passing by way of the revived winter festivals that had classically effected such interchanges. (In the Yukon I have heard these festivals referred to by English-speaking Yupik as "potlatches.") At the same time, instead of the migrant islanders going off to lose their culture, the effect of their stay for longer or shorter periods in Whiteman's Land has been to extend the village of Gambell from its home site in Saint Lawrence Island to clansmen as far away as Oregon and California. Among other reasons: increased "subsistence" at home leads to increased "sharing" abroad. A study of one household's "subsistence sharing" by Lynn Robbins showed it was thus connected to 29 other households in Gambell, 23 in the Saint Lawrence village of Savoonga, 7 in Nome, 2 in Fairbanks, 1 in Sitka, 2 in Oregon, and 6 in California. The network included 315 people in 70 households, with the majority of gifts going to members of the patriclan. Echoing similar reports from all over Alaska, Jorgensen writes, "In short, there is a determination on the part of Eskimos to maintain traditional Eskimo culture and at the same time to adopt a pragmatic acceptance of the benefits of modern technology" (*ibid.*:6).

Still, from the viewpoint of a traditional anthropology — not to mention world systems and dependency theory, development economics and modernization theory, postmodernism and globalization theory — the question is, how did the Eskimo do that?

Moreover, the Eskimo are not alone. In the discussion that follows I evoke the analogous modern experiences of other societies, with a view toward unpacking some of the issues the Eskimo pose — and thus reconstructing a too-traditional anthropology according to the ways the peoples reconstruct their traditional cultures.

The Indigenization of Modernity

This is a modern song of Enga people of New Guinea, about capturing the power-knowledge of Europeans, the "Red Men" in local parlance:

> When the time comes,
> Our youngsters will feed upon their words,
> After the Red Men drift away from this land,
> Our youngsters, like honey birds,
> After the Reds have gone,
> Will suck the flowers,
> While standing back here.
> We will do like them,
> We shall feed upon their deeds
> Like honey-birds sucking flowers.
>
> (Talyaga 1975:n.p.)

Reversing the real relations of exploitation and domination, these verses could easily be mistaken for the wistful fantasies of the powerless. Yet it would be wrong to suppose them motivated by the people's self-contempt or a sense of their impending doom. Everything about the modern ethnography of Highland New Guinea indicates that the sentiment of cultural usurpation — here ambiguously figured as honey-birds feeding on the powers of banished White men — is the guiding principle of the Highlanders' historical action. Rather than despondency, it is a forward action on modernity, guided by the assurance the Enga will be able to harness the good things of Europeans to the development of their own existence. "Develop-man" is the neo-Melanesian term; and it would not be wrong to re-pidginize it back to English as "the development of man," since the project it refers to is the use of foreign wealth in the expansion of feasting, politicking, subsidizing kinship, and other activities that make up the local conception of a human existence (Nihill 1989). This is what the working and warrior youth of Enga are urged to carry on. Rather than the death of tradition, Enga thus express their confidence in a living tradition, a tradition precisely that serves as a means and measure of innovation.

To put the matter anthropologically, which is to say, to perceive great things in little ones, this active appropriation by Enga of the European power imposed upon them is a local manifestation of a new planetary organization of culture. Unified by the expansion of Western capitalism over recent centuries, the world is also being rediversified by indigenous adaptations to the global juggernaut. In some measure, global homogeneity and local differentiation have developed together, the latter as a response to the former in the name of native cultural autonomy. I described this new planetary organization as "a Culture of cultures," a world cultural system made up of diverse forms of life (Chapter Fourteen). As Ulf Hannerz put it: "There is now a world culture, but we had better make sure we understand what this means. It is marked by an organization of diversity rather than a replication of uniformity" (1990:237). Thus, one complement of the new global ecumene is the so-called culturalism of very recent decades: the self-consciousness of their "culture," as a value to be lived and defended, that has broken out all around the Third and Fourth Worlds (see Chapter Fourteen). Everyone now speaks of their "culture," or some near-local equivalent, precisely in the context of national or international threats to its existence. This does not mean a simple and nostalgic desire for teepees and tomahawks or some such fetishized repositories of a pristine identity. A "naive attempt to hold peoples hostage to their own histories," such a supposition, Terence Turner remarks, would thereby deprive them of history. What the self-consciousness of "culture" does signify is the demand of the peoples for their own space within the world cultural order. Rather than a refusal of the commodities and relations of the World System, this more often means what the Enga sang about, a desire to indigenize them. The project is the indigenization of modernity.

So, in certain indigenous respects, their engagement with the international capitalist forces has allowed Enga and other New Guinea Highlanders to "develop" their cultural orders, that is, as they understand develop-man — more and better of what they consider good things. Such is a common ethnographic report from the area since the 1960s. Benefitting from the market returns to migratory labor, coffee production and other cash-cropping, the great interclan ceremonial exchanges — hallmark institution of Highlands culture — have flourished in recent decades as never before. Among Enga, Mendi, Siane, and others, the ceremonies have increased in frequency as well as in the magnitude of people engaged and goods transacted. Accordingly, big-men are more numerous and powerful. Old clan alliances that had lapsed have been revived. Interpersonal kinship networks have been widened and strengthened. Rather than the antithesis of community, money has thus been the means. High-value banknotes replace pearl shells as key exchange valuables, gifts of Toyota land cruisers complement the usual pigs, and large quantities of beer function as initiatory presents (adding certain celebratory dimensions to the customary festivities). Captured in reciprocal obligations and bride wealth payments, "the money which circulates in exchanges is generally not 'consumed' at all," as Andrew Strathern noted of Hageners, "but keeps on *circulating*, through the momentum of *debt and investment*" (1979:546). Rena Lederman reports that among modern Mendi people the exchange obligations between clans and personal kin create "a *demand* for modern currency far greater than the demand generated by existing market outlets" (1986b:332). Hence Mendi say *they* have the true exchange economy, by contrast to the mere "subsistence economy" of White men (*ibid.*: 236). Now there's a howdy-do.

Tradition and Change

The struggle of non-Western peoples to create their own cultural versions of modernity undoes the received Western opposition of tradition versus change, custom versus rationality — and most notably its twentieth-century version of tradition versus development. The antithesis was already old by the time the philosophes undertook to *écrasez l'infâme*, to destroy entrenched superstition by progressive reason. It had been kicking around advanced European thought at least since Sir Francis Bacon proposed to smash the idols of the cave and the tribe by the exercise of rational-empirical wisdom — and thus rescue humanity from the metaphysical consequences of Original Sin. In the redemptive vision (version) of modern Development Economics, as we have seen, so-called tradition, being burdened with "irrationalities," is presented as an obstacle to so-called development. The indigenous people's culture is something the matter with them.

Paradoxically, almost all the "traditional" cultures studied by anthropologists, and so described, were in fact neo-traditional, already changed by Western expansion. In some cases, this happened so long ago that no one, not even anthropologists, now debates their cultural authenticity. The Iroquois confederacy was by most accounts a postcontact develop-man, as were the Plains Indian cultures that flourished through the acquisition of the horse. For all that, were the Iroquois less Iroquoian or the Sioux less Souian? Today in Fiji, Wesleyan Christianity is considered "custom of the land." (I recall a recent man-on-the-street interview in a Suva newspaper, in which a Fijian matron, shocked by the nude bathing at tourist resorts, asked, "how are we going to keep our traditional customs if people go around like that?") Indeed, Margaret Jolly rightly wonders why church hymns and the Christian mass should not be considered "part of Pacific tradition," given that they "have been significantly remade by Pacific peoples, so that Christianity may appear today as more quintessentially a Pacific than a Western faith" (1992:53). If Pacific peoples gloss over the distinction — so critical to our own historical sensibility — between the colonial and the precolonial past, it is because they "are more accepting of both indigenous and exogenous elements as constituting their culture." Since the exogenous elements are culturally indigenized, there is not, for the people concerned, a radical disconformity, let alone an inauthenticity. So-called hybridity is, after all, a genealogical observation, not a structural determination — perhaps appropriate only to the cosmopolitan intellectuals from whose external vantage such cultural theories are fabricated. Anthropologists have known at least since the work of Boas and his students that cultures are generally foreign in origin and local in pattern. Or, if we have forgotten the diffusionists' lessons, we should at least recall the indigenous daily routine of the average American man described some decades ago by Ralph Linton. After breakfast our good man settles down to read the news of the day "imprinted in characters invented by the ancient Semites upon a material invented in China by a process invented in Germany. As he absorbs the accounts of foreign troubles he will, if he is a good conservative citizen, thank a Hebrew deity in an Indo-European tongue that he is 100 percent American" (1936: 329).

Functional Determination by the Basis

As graduate students at the University of Michigan in the 1950s, we used to refer to the technological determinism of our maître, Leslie White, as "the cultural layer cake." Technology was the basis. The middle level, social structure, was determined by the technical base, since it consisted primarily of an organization for putting technology to work. Ideology, the top layer, could only be a reflex of the way people were related socially and of the knowledge of the world to which they were led by their technological activity. I think White really believed that when people ascended to the heavens on rocket ships they would be able to see there was no God — but he was mistaken.

Still, things got even more complicated when Lévi-Strauss, after rendering the homages to Marx that were customary in the 1960s — at that time everyone in France seemed to be a Marxist of some kind; even anti-Marxists would have to excuse themselves by something to the effect, "*je suis peu marxiste*" — things got more complex when Lévi-Strauss argued in effect that practical action is an expression of the meaningful relations of the cultural scheme. In this sense, culture *included* the basis.

Cultural determination by or of the basis: we have seen something very similar in the series of misunderstandings that attended Lord Macartney's ill-fated mission to the Chinese Emperor in 1795 (Chapter Thirteen). What does technology mean? The British not only thought too well of their technical accomplishments, not only that they were irresistible, so that the Chinese would throw away their chopsticks the minute they saw the efficiency of Sheffield cutlery, but also that the demonstration of sophisticated technology would immediately persuade their Chinese hosts of the superiority of British civilization as such. For the Brits, their ships, their scientific apparatuses, their weapons were signs: of good government, good laws, private property, and private enterprise; of superior intelligence and great learning; of an industrious people and an enlightened monarch. Their material things could be the signs of such cultural achievements because the latter were functionally connected to the former; good government and the rest were necessary concomitants of good ships, good guns, and good astronomy. This was the indigenous Western anthropology that time and again was deceived by Chinese reactions. Especially by the reactions of the Chinese court. The British cannon — "these were no novelty in China." The astronomical instruments — "these things are good enough to amuse children." All this elegant machinery — "these are curious things.... But do the Europeans understand the art of government as equally polished?" Clearly, the Chinese had no good (Western) sense of cultural order.

East is East and West is West. Where the twain still have not met is over the Western self-consciousness of culture as a total system erected upon its technological foundations. Here indeed is a native anthropology that has been dominant ever since industrial capitalism and enlightened philosophers combined to install human corporal need as "the onely spur to humane industry" (Locke): the source of our productivity, our sociability, and our empirical sense of reality. By their own theory of culture, the Chinese were always prepared to decouple technique and civilization, infrastructure and superstructure. Even in the late nineteenth century, when Western technology became more interesting to them, they adopted it only on the condition of "Chinese culture, Western skills," or in another celebrated rendering, "Chinese studies as fundamental, Western studies for practical use" (Chou Tse-tsung 1960:13).[3] Still, it would merely remain within the Western structural-functionalism to see this as an inversion of base-superstructure relations. It seems to represent the even more interesting anthropology in which praxis is an expression of a cosmic cultural scheme — by the realization of which matter and form are constituted as empirical and intelligible entities — the realization of a cultural scheme in a pragmatic function. The explication rests on the pertinence of meaningful values rather than mechanical causes. Granet tells the story of a certain duke of the Chou period of whom it was said that he failed to conquer China because at his death human beings were sacrificed to his ghost.

Money and Markets, Moralities and Mentalities

Eskimo culture, Western techniques. Or as the Yukon village leader said to the anthropologist:

> We take whatever technology works and shape it to our purposes and uses.... Apparently that bothers people who want us to remain pristine, or to admit to our contradictions of wanting technology *and* controlling and preserving the resources of our own use.... Why not? We have always accepted and reshaped technology that works for our own purposes. (Jorgensen 1990:69)

I have already mentioned the snow machines, CB radios, all-terrain four-wheelers, rifles, and powered eighteen-foot and thirty-two-foot fishing vessels, but I forgot the Eskimo subsistence airplanes. The anthropologist Steve Langdon tells of five of them owned by the Yupik villagers of Togiak (in Bristol Bay). These planes were used "primarily to 1) extend subsistence range to areas where caribou are located and 2) provide on demand transportation for visiting relatives in nearby villages, objectives totally in congruence with the subsistence-based foundation of the community" (1991:284–85). Such modern modes of paleolithic production bring obvious efficiencies to the subsistence economy — and some not so obvious, such as relief from the necessity of catching, processing, and storing the thousands of chum salmon required to feed a dog team over the winter. But they also make it possible to engage more effectively in the market economy on which wild food-getting depends, affording the mobility or stability to intermittently hunt money also — when and where (and if) the opportunity presents itself. Contrary to the general opinions of the past two centuries, however, Yupik relations to animals have remained altogether distinct from the capitalist relations of production that provided them with the necessary hunting gear. Chase Hensel quotes John Active, a Yupik man who works at the public radio and television station at Bethel — the year of the interview is 1992:

> The animals, birds and plants have an awareness, and we treat them with the same respect we have for ourselves. The non-Natives refer to these animals as "game." Hunting for them is a game. We do not play games with animals. When we bring animals into our houses, we treat them as guests.... We thank them for having been caught and believe their spirits will return to their gods and report about how they are cared for. [The "gods" are apparently species spirit masters, as in the widespread northern cosmology.] If the animals are treated well, then those gods will provide more of the same.... Our ancestors didn't learn that from your book [the Bible]. (Hensel 1996:71)

It is not simply that Eskimo cultures — or other northern groups such as Dené and James Bay Cree, of whom similar recent observations have been made — it is not simply that they have persisted in spite of capitalism or because the people have resisted it. This is not so much the culture of resistance as it is the resistance of culture. Involving the assimilation of the foreign in the logics of the familiar — a change in the contexts of the foreign forms or forces, which also changes their values — cultural subversion is in the nature of intercultural relations. Inherent in meaningful action, such resistance of culture is the more inclusive form of historical differentiation, neither requiring an intentional politics of cultural opposition nor confined to the reactions of the colonially oppressed. Even the subjects of Western domination and dependency-relations act in the world as social-historical beings, so their experience of capitalism is mediated by the habitus of an indigenous form of life. Of course, it is true that their too-classic dependency could do people like the Yupik in. Yet in the meantime, the apparent cultural mystification of dependency produces an empirical critique of the orthodoxy that money, markets, and the relations of commodity production are incompatible with the organizations of the so-called traditional societies.

Marx says that money destroys the archaic community because money becomes the community. As if, Freud complained, a person suddenly got a psyche when he drew his first paycheck. In a book called *Money and the Morality of Exchange*, Maurice Bloch and Jonathan Parry collect a number of examples to the contrary, from a variety of societies. As against the idea that money gives rise to a particular worldview — the unsociable, impersonal, and contractual one we associate with it — they emphasize "how an existing world view gives rise to particular ways of representing money" (1989:19). At issue is the structural position money is accorded in the cultural totality. The famous statements of Marx, Simmel, & Co. about the destructive effects of markets and money on community presuppose a separate "economic" domain, as Bloch and Parry point out, an amoral sphere of transaction separated from the generosities of kith and kin. But where there is no structural opposition between the relationships of economy and sociability, where material transactions are ordered by social relations rather than vice versa, then the amorality we attribute to money need not obtain.

So, in general, one of the Big Surprises of "late capitalism" is that "traditional" cultures are not inevitably incompatible with it nor vulnerable to it. Certainly, the recent ethnographers of the Alaskan and Canadian north have had great academic sport with the classic 1950s and 60s arguments of Service and Murphy and Steward to the effect that commercial trade will be the end of indigenous culture for hunters and trappers. Debt peonage, the breakup of larger communities and collective efforts, disintegration of extended kinship networks, reduction of kinship to nuclearization, the decline of food-sharing and other reciprocities, privatization of property, the development of economic inequalities, and overall individualism, such were the forecasts of hunters' fate. The final phase, according to Murphy and Steward, would be marked by "assimilation of the Indians as a local sub-culture of the national socio-cultural system" and perhaps eventually by a "virtual loss of identity as Indians" (1956:350). To summarily categorize the contrary modern findings among northern hunters, however, their long, intensive, and varied engagements with the international market economy have not fundamentally altered their customary organizations of production, modes of ownership and resource control, division of labor, patterns of distribution and consumption; nor have their extended kinship and community bonds been dissolved or the economic and social obligations thereof fallen off; neither have social (cum "spiritual") relations to nature disappeared; and they have not lost their cultural identities, not even when they live in White folks' towns.

To put it another way, dependency is real, but it is not the internal organization of Cree, Inuit, or Yupik Eskimo existence. The loss of traditional skills — dogsledding, kayak-making, hunting methods, and much, much more — makes their dependency all the more serious. But the real problem this poses for the people is not the unlivable contradiction between the money economy and the traditional way of life. The big problems come when they cannot find enough money to support their traditional life. For if one calculated, as some anthropologists have, how much income from government transfer funds and commercial trade is devoted to subsidizing the indigenous modes of production, then the internal economy clearly subsumes and integrates the external (Langdon 1986). Within the villages, moreover, the greater a person's or family's successes in the money economy, the more they participate in the indigenous order (Lonner 1986; Wolf 1982). Sharing with kinsmen increases with monetary income, typically via the advantages money gives in hunting and gathering. But then, studies also show that the people with the greatest outside experience in education or employment are as much or more engaged as anyone in the local subsistence culture (Kruse 1986). If this helps to explain why seemingly acculturated people are commonly traditional leaders, it also invites the question of why they ever came back to the village — which leads to another area of enlightenment offered by the indigenization of modernity.

Reversing Center and Periphery

Cities are the favored places of *merantu*, the customary journeys of Menangkabau and other Indonesian men beyond the cultural bounds, whence they return with booty and stories worthy of their manhood. The Malay community in Mecca is second in size only to the Arabs. Some remain on the hajj for ten years or more; some are delayed for years returning via Africa or India (Provencher 1976). The Mexican villagers working in Redwood City, California, and the Samoans in San Francisco likewise intend to return, an eventuality for which they prepare by sending money back to relatives, by periodically visiting their native places, by sending their children home for visits or schooling and otherwise maintaining their natal ties and building their local status. But how is it that Oaxacans, Samoans, Africans, Filipinos, Peruvians, Thais — the millions of people now cycling between the "peripherae" and metropolitan centers of the modern World System — are content to return to a bucolic existence "after they've seen Paris"? Is it not true that *Stadt Luft macht Frei*? Or if not free, proletarians forever? Well, apparently not always, however true it may have been in an earlier European history. Today, the huge phenomenon of circular migration is creating a new kind of cultural formation: a determinate community without entity, extending transculturally and often transnationally from a rural center in the Third World to "homes abroad" in the metropolis, the whole united by the to and fro of goods, ideas, and people on the move. "The geographic village is small," writes Uzzell of Oaxacan campesinos, "the social village spreads over thousands of miles" (1979:343).

Taking shape as urban ethnic outposts of rural "tribal" or peasant homelands, these synthetic formations were for a long time unrecognized as such by the Western social scientists studying them. Or, rather, in studying urbanization, migration, remittance dependency, labor recruitment, or ethnic formation, Western researchers presented a spectacle something like the blind men and the elephant, each satisfied to describe the translocal cultural whole in terms of one or another of its aspects. No doubt the Euro-American history of urbanization had a stranglehold on the anthropological imagination. The general presumption was that urbanization must everywhere put an end to "the idiocy of rural life." By the very nature of the city as a complex social and industrial system, relations between people would become impersonal, utilitarian, secular, individualized, and otherwise disenchanted and detribalized. Such was the trend in Robert Redfield's "folk-urban continuum." As the beginning and end of a qualitative change, countryside and city were structurally distinct and opposed ways of life. "After the rise of cities," Redfield wrote, "men became something different to what they had been before" (1953:ix). British social anthropology of the period was hung up on the same dualist a priori. Gluckman was the father of the African version: "The African in the rural area and in town is two different men" (1960:69).

But enlightenment was soon in coming. Explicitly taking on the folk-urban continuum, Edward Bruner demonstrated the continuity of identity, kinship, and custom between Toba Batak villages of highland Sumatra and their urban relatives in Medan. "Examined from the structural point of view, the Toba Batak communities in village and city are part of one social and ceremonial system" (1961:515). Speaking more widely of Southeast Asia, Bruner wrote that "contrary to traditional theory, we find in many Asian cities that society does not become secularized, the individual does not

522

become isolated, kinship organizations do not break down, nor do the social relationships in the urban environment become impersonal, superficial and utilitarian" (*ibid*.: 508). By the mid-1970s such observations had become common in the Latin American homeland of the folk-urban continuum as well as in ethnographies by Gluckman's colleagues and others throughout sub-Saharan Africa. And as the gestalt shifted from the antithesis of the rural-urban to the synthesis of the translocal cultural order, study after study groped for a suitable terminology. The scholars spoke variously of "a bilocal society," "a single social and resource system," a "non-territorial community network," a "common social field" uniting countryside and city, "a social structure that encompasses both donor and host locations," "a single social field in which there is a substantial circulation of members," or some new species of the like (D. Ryan 1993:326, Ross and Weisner 1977:361, Trager 1988:194, Uzzell 1979:343, Bartle 1981:105).

What any and all of these descriptions express is the structural complementarity of the indigenous homeland and the metropolitan "homes abroad," their interdependence as sources of cultural value and means of social reproduction. Symbolically focused on the homeland, whence its members derive their identity and their destiny, the translocal community is strategically dependent on its urban outliers for material wherewithal. The rural order itself extends into the city, inasmuch as the migrant folk are transitively associated with each on the bases of their relationships at home. Kinship, community, and tribal affiliations acquire new functions, and perhaps new forms, as relations of migration: they organize the movements of people and resources, the care of homeland dependents, the provision of urban housing and employment. Since people conceive their social being as well as their future in their native place, the material flows generally favor the homeland people. The indigenous order is sustained by earnings and commodities acquired in the foreign-commercial sector. But should we speak of "remittances" as the foreign economic experts do? This flow of money and goods is better understood by the norms of "reciprocity," Epeli Hau'ofa (1993) argues, since it reflects the migrants' obligations to homeland kin, even as it secures their rights in their native place. "Reciprocity" as opposed to "remittances" appropriately shifts the analytic perspective from a geographic village that is small to a social village spread over thousands of miles, and rather than lament the fate of a village that lives on "remittances," one might with Graeme Hugo commend its success at reversing "the parasitic function traditionally ascribed to cities" (1978:264). In spanning the historic divide between traditional and modern, the developmental distance between center and periphery, and the structural opposition of townsmen and tribesmen, the translocal community deceives a considerable body of enlightened Western social science.

Culture Is Not Disappearing

Of course, it is possible that the translocal community will soon disappear as a cultural form. If the migrants settle permanently abroad, the structure might have a sort of generational half-life, the attachments to the homeland dissolving with each city-born or foreign-born generation. Still in parts of Indonesia, Africa, and elsewhere, circular migration has been going on for many generations. Reports from Nairobi in the 1980s echo observations in Java from 1916: the migrants were not being proletarianized (Elkan 1985, Parkin 1975). From a large review of anthropological literature on culture and development, Michael Kearney recently concluded just that: "migrants have not been proletarianized in any deeply ideological sense" (1986:352). However, the longevity of the form is not the issue I am concerned with here. What is of more interest is the ongoing creation of new forms in the modern world Culture of cultures. No one can deny that the world has seen an overall decrease of cultural diversity in the past five centuries. Indeed, anthropology was born out of the consciousness of the decrease as much as the appreciation of the diversity. There is no special reason now to panic about the death of culture.

Suppose for argument's sake we agree that Malinowski's *Argonauts of the Western Pacific* was the beginning of modern professional ethnography. If so, it is sobering to reflect it opens with these words:

524

Ethnology is in the sadly ludicrous, not to say tragic, position, that at the very moment when it begins to put the workshop in order, to forge its proper tools, to start ready for work on its appointed task, the material of its study melts away with hopeless rapidity. Just now, when the methods and aims of scientific field ethnology have taken shape, when men [N.B.] fully trained for the work have begun to travel into savage countries and study their inhabitants — these die away under our very eyes. (1922:xv)

Past objects? Yes, history studies these. But how many academic disciplines other than high-energy physics originated as the study of disappearing objects? And nowadays the distintegration of the cultural object seems to many anthropologists worse than ever. Confronted by the apparent disappearance of the old anthropol-ogy-cultures, the wreckage of coherent logics and definite bound-aries appreciably effected by the passage of the World System, they are tempted to succumb to a postmodern panic about the possibility that anything like "a culture" actually exists. This panic just when all about them the peoples are talking up their "cul-ture." Now everyone has a culture; only the anthropologists could doubt it. But why lose our nerve? Presented by history with a novel set of cultural structures, practices, and politics, anthropol-ogy should take the opportunity to renew itself. The discipline seems as well off as it ever was, with cultures disappearing just as we were learning how to perceive them, and then reappearing in ways we had never imagined.

The best modern heirs of the Enlightenment philosophes know this. I mean, for example, the West African francophone intellec-tuals who argue, with Paulin Hountondji, that "culture is not only a heritage, it is a project." Yet it is, as Abdou Touré insists, an Afri-can project, or set of projects, and precisely not the universal march of reason proclaimed by the eighteenth century and still worshipped in the development-religions of the twentieth:

That which the minority of [elite] leaders has voluntarily forgotten is Culture as a philosophy of life, and as an inexhaustible reservoir of responses to the world's challenges and it is because they brush aside

this culture that they're able to reason lightly in terms of development while implying a scale of values, norms of conduct or models
of behavior transmissible from one society to another! (1994)

Touré's conclusion is that "Africa is no longer subjected to the
Western model of development for the simple reason that there is
no longer a model of any worth." Finally — enlightenment.

NOTES

1. Another characteristic example:

> A village that is inwardly alive is proof against a government policy as
> well as against natural cataclysms, neither of which affects its spiritual
> energies; but it cannot withstand the disintegrating forces of trade and
> commercial development, the stealthy invasion of money economy, the
> gradual weakening of its agricultural basis, of the tie that binds it to the
> soil — a tie which is but part of the bond that unites man with man, the
> contact with the rest of the world. For these latter are destructive forces
> that kill not only the physical element in the communal bases — agricul-
> ture to supply domestic needs — but also the two spiritual elements
> which underlie the village community — religion and social unity — and
> with these kill the soul of the village. (Boeke 1946:19)

2. The anthropological journal *Man* was recently rechristened the *Journal of
the Royal Anthropological Society*. Perhaps if the above-mentioned conference
were held today, it would be called "The Journal of the Royal Anthropological
Society, the Hunter."

3. Formulas of this kind were popular also in Meiji Japan, for example, *Tōyō
seishin, Seiyō gigei*, "Eastern spirit, Western crafts." Chou Tse-Tsung points out
that a similar cultural theory was expressed in ninth-century Japan by relation to
China: "Japanese spirit, Chinese skill" (1960:13n).

Chapter Sixteen

The Sadness of Sweetness;
or, The Native Anthropology of
Western Cosmology[*]

Sidney Mintz's *Sweetness and Power* (1985) was for me a landmark book because it dared to take on capitalism as a cultural economy. In a double way, it put anthropology at the center of history — not only as a cultural discipline, the academic anthropology we know and love, but in the form of what may be deemed the native anthropology of Western society, the indigenous conceptions of human existence that, at a particular historical juncture, gave sweetness its economic functionality. It is this native Western anthropology I would talk of here, both in relation to Mintz's classic work and in relation to anthropology as a discipline. On the one hand, the aim will be to complement the arguments of *Sweetness and Power* by expanding on certain aspects of the indigenous anthropology. We shall see that it takes some singular ideas of humanity, society, and nature to come up with the *triste trope* that what life is all about is the search for satisfaction, which is to say the melioration of our pains. On the other hand, I will try to make the point that these cosmic notions did not begin or end with the Enlightenment. They are native cultural structures of the long term that still inhabit academic anthropology — as well as other Western social sciences — and bedevil our understandings of other peoples.

Concerned with certain Judeo-Christian dogmas of human imperfection, my argument could be described as an "archaeology" of mainstream social science "discourse." It would be pleasing to

* Originally published in *Current Anthropology* 37.3 (June 1996).

think of it then as the owl of Minerva taking wing at the dusk of
an intellectual era. It has an organization, however, more closely
resembling the flight of the postmodernist wifflebird, moving
in ever-decreasing hermeneutic circles until... Nor should the
mention of Minerva be taken as a claim to profound knowledge.
Although I flit over a vast continent of Western scholarship, it is
only in the capacity of an anthropological tourist, collecting an
intellectual genealogy here and a fragment of academic folklore
there, while making a most superficial inspection of the great
philosophical monuments. Like most tourists, I no doubt consistently make a fool of myself. Not only are the expositions of main
ideas always schematic, usually idiosyncratic, and possibly wrong,
but also insufficient attention has been paid to alternative traditions — without which this essay could not have been written. The
other necessary apologies are as follows: I do not consider all the
premises of the native anthropology that are still in vogue as science, only the four or five that seem most relevant to *Sweetness
and Power*. I do not provide an adequate economic and political
history of the ideas and traditions I discuss, nor do I prove that
they are inadequate — or, as I believe, disastrous — for the study of
non-Western societies. Finally, I am speaking about male writers
who themselves spoke mainly about men and to men. Given what
they had to say about "mankind," you wouldn't want to substitute
"her" for "him" or even speak about "he or she."[1]

Introduction: Flowers of Evil

Paul Ricoeur singles out the biblical story of the Fall as "the anthropological myth *par excellence*, the only one, perhaps, that expressly
makes man the origin (or the co-origin) of evil" (1967:281).[2] A
willful human act, Adam's sin opened the doleful abyss between
"the absolute perfection of God and the radical wickedness of
man." Apart from this unhappy consciousness, Ricoeur means to
distinguish the Genesis tradition from cosmologies in which evil
is primordial rather than historical, preceding or accompanying
the creation rather than the effect of the creature. It is true that in
a fair number of other mythologies the origin of death — and/or
the origin of hunger and toil — is laid to the violation of a divine

528

admonition by a legendary trickster or ancestral hero. Yet even if these faults were due to perversity rather than folly, they did not produce an inherently wicked humanity, banished from the presence of God to a purely natural and antithetical world of thorns and thistles. There is a difference between human evil and regrettable misfortune. And Adam (or "Man") was not only the original agent of evil, but thereby and thenceforth he was corporeally disposed to it. Man cannot not sin, as Augustine said. This kind of self-contempt does not appear to be a general preoccupation of humanity. What makes the Western mythology seem even more singular is the cosmological consequences of Adam's crime: "The whole creation groaneth and travaileth in pain together" (Romans 8:22). Bernard Mandeville voiced a common (Western) complaint when he observed that it was difficult to distinguish the obstacles to human endeavors that were due to man's body from those that came from the condition of the planet "since it has been curs'd." It is impossible to keep these tribulations asunder he said; they "always interfere and mix with one another; and at last make up together a frightful Chaos of Evil" (1988, vol. 1:344). In Adam's fall sinn'd we all: human life became penal and the world hostile.[3] In John Donne's words, "The noblest part, man, felt it first; and then / Both beasts and plants, curst in the curse of man."

As for humanity, pain and death were not the only penalties of Adamic pride. There was also a certain stupidity, the effect of epistemological obstacles. Eating from the tree of knowledge, Adam plunged men into gross ignorance, simultaneously engendering unfortunate consequences for human social relationships. Before the sin, when called upon by God to name the animals, Adam proved himself the world's first and greatest philosopher: he could distinguish the species as they really were, according to their true essences and differences (Aarsleff 1982:25, 59). Adam had then an almost divine knowledge. From the correct names to the confusion of tongues, however, man experienced an all-around fall from intellectual grace. A veil was drawn between one person and another, as well as between humanity and the world.

Mankind was thus subject to a double dissimulation of reality, social as well as natural. Covering themselves in shame, men and women introduced deception into all communication. Relations between societies were marked by the incomprehension and strife of Babel—a fitting sequitur to this second attempt of men "to be as gods." And if within societies people concealed their true (internal) selves from one another, how could their association have been founded on anything *but* this dissimulation, given that mankind had been committed to self-love from the Fall? "It is impossible we could be sociable Creatures without Hypocrisy" (Mandeville 1988, vol. 1:349). Nature too was hidden from us. In a Neoplatonic sense, the truth of the world disguised itself, since it could be known only as the inadequate sensory impressions of defective empirical things. The day was yet to come when Bacon would attempt to reverse the epistemological values by asserting that experiential wisdom was man's great hope for climbing out of the pit into which he had been digg'd by Original Sin. Even so, such empiricism turned out to be an ideological reconciliation with a permanent imperfection. Man had been condemned to an ignorance as profound as his wickedness, a "knowing ignorance," hopelessly separated from God's truth (Cassirer 1963).

Human finitude, the famous "metaphysical evil," was the defect that encompassed all the others. A line of argument running notably from Augustine through Leibniz repudiated the classical pantheistic notion that God made the universe from Himself, on the grounds that "from a god only a god can proceed" (Leibniz 1985:300, Augustine, 1948, Hick 1966). The world, including the creature, was created ex nihilo: nothing divine as such is in it. Not that God was responsible for evil, which, as the absence of good, He did not make. What He made was good. But as created out of nothing, and in contrast to the unchanging and perfect nature of God, man was corruptible (Augustine, *De civitate Dei* 12.1). Free will was the expression of this unfortunate mutability, and the Fall its catastrophic effect. Human finitude was the root of all evil. Both the cause and the crime consisted in the nature of man as an imperfect creature of lack and need. So did the punishment.

The Anthropology of Need

The punishment was the crime, as Augustine said. Man was destined to wear out his body in the vain attempt to satisfy it, because in obeying his own desires he had disobeyed God.[4] By putting this love of self before the love of Him alone who could suffice, man became the slave of his own needs (*De civitate Dei* 13, 14). Or should we not say, Western man, since not many other peoples — except successful Buddhists, perhaps — know "true rest" and "deliverance" as synonyms of death? But then, this life is a "hell on earth," as Augustine said; no wonder babies come into it crying and screaming.[5]

Still, God was merciful. He gave us Economics. By Adam Smith's time, human misery had been transformed into the positive science of how we make the best of our eternal insufficiencies, the most possible satisfaction from means that are always less than our wants. It was the same miserable condition envisioned in Christian cosmology, only bourgeoisified, an elevation of free will into rational choice, which afforded a more cheerful view of the material opportunities afforded by human suffering. The genesis of Economics was the economics of Genesis. Lionel Robbins said as much in his famous determination of what economics is all about:

> We have been turned out of Paradise. We have neither eternal life nor unlimited means of gratification. Everywhere we turn, if we choose one thing we must relinquish others which, in different circumstances, we would wish not to have relinquished. Scarcity of means to satisfy ends of varying importance is an almost ubiquitous condition of human behaviour. Here, then, is the unity of the subject of Economic Science, the forms assumed by human behaviour in disposing of scarce means. (1952:15)

For the moment we will follow Lord Robbins in skipping over much of what happened between the Fall and its Economic Science, such as the advent of capitalism — on the heels of the Renaissance change of heart about the blessings of poverty and the contemptibility of this world. If bourgeois society liberated

531

egoistic man from the prison house of Christian morality and allowed desire to parade shamelessly in the light of day — finessing social justice by the claim that Private Vices were Publick Benefits — still there had been no fundamental change in the Western conception of human nature. Man was ever an imperfect and suffering being, with wants ever beyond his powers. The Economic Man of modern times was still Adam. Indeed, the same scarcity-driven creature of need survived long enough to become the main protagonist of all the human sciences.

I have already rehearsed this argument about "utilitarianism" too many times, so I shall try to be brief.

First, regarding continuity and change in the Adamic concept of man: The change, as I have implied, was rather in the value of human imperfection than in the fact. Originally understood by the Church Fathers as a form of bondage, each man's endless and hopeless attention to his own desires became, in the liberal-bourgeois ideology, the condition of freedom itself.[6] Originally, need had distinguished mankind from God's self-sufficient perfection.[7] After the Fall, as Saint Basil described it, "Nature became corrupted, just as men did, and failed to provide him with his needs" (G. Boas 1948:33). The world "does not make good what it promises," wrote Augustine; "it is a liar and deceiveth." So man is fated "to pursue one thing after another.... [H]is needs are so multiplied that he cannot find the one thing needful, a single and unchangeable nature" (quoted in Deane 1963:45).[8] On becoming a scientific anthropology, however, this self-love changed its moral sign (Dumont 1977, 1986; Hirschman 1977). The original evil and source of vast sadness in Augustine, the needs of the body became simply "natural" in Hobbes or at least a "necessary evil" in Baron d'Holbach to end in Adam Smith or Milton Friedman as the supreme source of social virtue. Following on Hobbes and Locke, the materialist philosophes — Messrs d'Holbach, Helvétius, La Mettrie, Condillac & Co. — found that the rational response to bodily need could provide them with the human parallel to the Newtonian science after which they hankered. Here was a law of motion of human bodies as comprehensive as the law of gravitation.[9] In Hobbes's terms, men move to those things that give them pleasure and from those that cause them pain. In addition to universal motion, pleasure and pain for the philosophes became the general law of cognition. As in the formula made famous by Helvétius, corporeal pleasure and pain, by awakening need and interest, issue in the comparison and judgment of objects.[10] Originally condemned as the author of sin, self-pleasing man turned out to be a good thing and in the end the best thing, since the greatest total good would come of each person's total self-concern. Slavery was thus transformed into liberty, and the human lust that once foretold eternal perdition became the premise of temporal salvation. Over the long run, the native Western anthropology proved to be an extended exercise in the sublimation of evil. Yet through all these happy metamorphoses, the sad figure of needful man remained the invariant.[11] Indeed, human needs came to be the reason for society itself: "Because man is sociable, people have concluded he is good. But they have deceived themselves. Wolves form societies, but they are not good.... All we learn from experience on this head is that in man, as in other animals, sociability is the effect of want" (Helvétius 1795, vol. 7:224–25).

The recurrent attempt to make individual need and greed the basis of sociability, as in this text of Helvétius, has been one of the more interesting projects of the traditional anthropology. Again a long line of academic ancestors — stretching back to Vico and Machiavelli through the Enlightenment philosophes to the English utilitarians and their latest incarnations in the Chicago School of (the) Economics (of Everything) — have all argued that individual self-interest is the fundamental bond of society.[12] So, for d'Holbach, "A nation is nothing more than the union of a great number of individuals, connected to one another by the reciprocity of their wants, or by their mutual desire of pleasure" ([1770] 1989:147). Or Mandeville, who explicitly refers the possibility of society to the fall of man:

> not the Good and Amiable, but the Bad and Hateful Qualities of Man, his Imperfections and the want of Excellencies which other Creatures are endued with, are the first Causes that made Man sociable

beyond other Animals the Moment after he lost Paradise; and ... if he had remain'd in his primitive Innocence, and continued to enjoy the Blessings that attended it, there is no Shadow of Probability that he ever would have become the sociable Creature he is now. (1988, vol. 1:344; see also 4, 67, 369)

O felix culpa! Here was another redeeming paradox of the Fortunate Fault (Lovejoy 1948:ch. 14). Out of the Sin came Society. Men congregate in groups and develop social relations either because it is to their respective advantage to do so or because they discover that other men can serve as means to their own ends. True, the last violates a famous categorical imperative — to which Helvétius countered in turn: "Every writer who, to give us a good opinion of his own heart, founds the sociability of man on any other principle than that of bodily and habitual wants, deceives weak minds and gives a false idea of morality" (1795, vol. 7:228–29). "*Aimer*," said Helvétius, "*c'est avoir besoin*."[13] Pope, in his *Essay on Man*, immortalized the theory: "Thus God and Nature linked the general frame, / And bade Self-love and Social be the same."[14]

Need Among the Indians of New France

According to the Jesuit Joseph Jouvency, one of the two main sources of disease among the Indians of New France was an insatiable desire for objects of a particular kind. Apparently suffering from some form of windigo, the patient, whose affliction was thought to be congenital, was treated by an equal and opposite display of generosity. Without stint or thought of any return, Jouvency reports, his "parents, friends and relatives ... lavish upon him whatever it may be, however expensive." The patient consumes some part of the gift, distributes some to the diviners, "and often on the next day departs from life" (1710:258). This proves that one society's Economics may be another's madness. Or at least that the inevitable insufficiency of means relative to ends does not evoke an innate disposition to truck and barter. Far from such wants serving as the bond of society, the Indian who is beset by them will have a hard time living with others.

534

A certain anthropological functionalism was another legacy of the enlightened Adamic theory, especially as "function" was collapsed into "purpose" and the "purpose" was the satisfaction of need. In this respect, Malinowski's reduction of culture to corporeal needs was a pedantic elaboration of Enlightenment social science. The main advance achieved by Radcliffe-Brown's structural-functionalism was the transposition of the same paradigm to society as a whole, that is, by conceiving the social totality as an organism, a biological individual, whose institutions responded in effect (function) and form (structure) to its life needs. Herbert Spencer was the transitional figure. On the one hand, he adopted the going utilist principle that society was an arrangement that people entered into for the satisfaction of their personal interests. On the other hand, he maintained that society itself was a "life" or a superorganic entity, engaged with other such beings in a struggle for survival (sociological Hobbesianism). Following the lead of Durkheim and Mauss, the British structural-functionalists would sublimate egotistical man in social institutions — which themselves, however, responded to social needs.

Digression: Renaissance Notes

A word might be said about some distinctive contributions of the European Renaissance to the moral promotion of need-driven, self-pleasing man — or to the spirit of capitalism in general — less celebrated perhaps than the Protestant ethic but apparently just as influential. I am not speaking simply of the well-known ideological movements of the fifteenth and sixteenth centuries: the self-affirmation of humanity, the liberation of human will and of the individual generally, the removal of the onus of sensuousness, an end to the contempt of this world, thus the reconciliation of the mind with nature and of the intelligible with the sensible. What gives a real feeling of intellectual vertigo is that certain Italians conceived capitalism as a total order of the universe well before it became a systematic economy. In 1440, Nicholas Cusanus, for example, argued that human will and judgment were God's means of constituting the values of created things. Human preferences are the Deity's way of organizing the world as a *system of values* — as opposed to mere substances, which in and of themselves are nothing:

> For although the human intellect does not give being to the value [i.e., does not create the things valued], there would nevertheless be no distinctions in value without it.... Without the power of judgment and of comparison, every evaluation ceases to exist, and with it value would also cease. Wherewith we see how precious is the mind, for without it, everything in creation would be without value. When God wanted to give value to his work, he had to create, besides the other things, the intellectual nature. (Cusanus, quoted in Cassirer 1963:43–44)

Cusanus thus prefigures the self-regulating market in the form of a cosmological process. By virtue of human preferences, the universe was commoditized — before the commodity was universalized.

Indeed, Lorenzo Valla had already discovered the decisive principle of the economistic plenum: the search for pleasure. "Pleasure," he wrote in 1431, "is not only the highest good, but the good pure and simple, the conserving principle of life, and therefore the basic principle of all value." And insofar as for Valla pleasure was the aim of all sociability, he also anticipated the legion of Western scholars who went on to explicate all variety of sociable relations as personal advantages:

> And what is the aim of friendship? Has it been sought for and so greatly praised by all ages and nations for any other reasons than the satisfactions arising from the performance of mutual services such as giving and receiving whatever men commonly need? ... As for masters and servants, there is no doubt their only aim is one of common advantage. What should I say about teachers and students? ... What finally forms the link between parents and children if it is not advantage and pleasure? (1977:221, 223)

It remained for capitalism, as the material development of this philosophy, to foreground scarcity, and thus privilege pain over

536

pleasure as the prime motive of intellectual judgments, object values, and social relations.

These revolutionary ideas of value and society were the complements of a certain kind of individualism. The individual becomes conscious of himself as the free agent and ultimate end of his own project. As formulated in Giovanni Pico della Mirandola's celebrated *Oration on the Dignity of Man* (1487), it is man's unique privilege "to have what he chooses, to be what he wills to be." Pico thus develops a certain permutation of the Chain of Being which puts nature at humanity's disposition. The last-created in a universe already replete with beings of every kind, man was left without a specific mode of existence or niche of his own. At the same time, unlike the other creatures, who were restricted by the laws of their respective natures, men were free to fashion themselves in whatsoever form they would. "I have placed you at the very center of the world," Pico has God say to man, "so that from that vantage point you may with greater ease glance round about you on all that the world contains" (1956:3). (Speaking of vantage points, it seems relevant that the *Oration* was penned shortly after the development of perspective by Brunelleschi and Alberti, which is to say soon after the artistic technique of opening a window on an indefinitely expanding world from the viewpoint of the individual subject.) Pico's concept of man as endowed with limitless possibilities of self-realization through the appropriation of nature's diversity was destined to run through numerous reincarnations, from the philosophical guises it assumed in Herder or Marx to the crude consciousness of bourgeois consumerism.[15]

Bernardino Telesio's description (1565) of the entire universe as organized by the self-interested actions of all creatures and things makes the vulgar fate of Renaissance philosophy seem inescapable (Van Deusen 1932). Telesio's cosmos was a veritable physics of pleasure and pain, these being the senses all objects possess of the things that respectively sustain and destroy them. As some specific compound of heat and cold in a substratum of matter, every object or creature acts to preserve its own nature — against perpetual opposition and potential destruction by objects

537

of other natures (Fallico and Shapiro 1967:315). Note that Hobbes had studied Telesio, and Sir Francis Bacon called him "the first of the new men" because of his insistence on the principle that human knowledge can come from observation only, limited as it then might be. More recently, Funkenstein sees in Telesio "one of the earliest occurrences of an antiteleological, political, ethical, as well as natural, principle of an 'invisible hand of nature'" (1986: 67). No doubt Funkenstein is referring to passages such as this: "It is quite evident that nature is propelled by self-interest. In fact, nature can tolerate neither a vacuum nor anything without purpose. All things enjoy touching one another, and maintain and conserve themselves by this mutual contact" (quoted in Fallico and Shapiro 1967:304).

May we not conclude that the universe had achieved an ideal state of economic development while Europe was still struggling with premodern relations of production? In one way or another, the philosophers already imagined the cosmos as a capitalist world order.

The Anthropology of Biology
The matter at issue here is the folk wisdom of "human nature." I mean the settled disposition, academic as well as popular, to account for social practices and cultural forms by the innate constitution of *Homo sapiens*. The biological influences are commonly conceived as animal drives and inclinations, which lends them a certain "brute" power. Their supposed effects are either directly expressed in social practices — as, for example, male dominance — or by antithetical customs designed somehow to corral them — as, for example, norms of sexuality. One probably does not need much persuasion that our folk anthropology is disposed to these explanations of culture by nature. Ranging from racism in the streets to sociobiology in the universities and passing by way of numerous expressions of the common tongue, biological determinism is a recurrent ideology of Western society. Its ubiquity, I will argue, is a function of its transmission in anthropological traditions of cosmic dimensions: once again, the concept of man as a willful creature of need, especially as this notion has developed

under the market economy, and, also, the theory of the human constitution inscribed in the Great Chain of Being, especially as linked to the antagonistic dualism of flesh and spirit of the Christian nightmare — the flesh as a brutish, self-regarding animal nature underlying and overcoming the better inclinations of the human soul.

Just as a developed capitalism and the Industrial Revolution were coming upon them, European philosophers consummated centuries of guilt by the discovery that the demands of the flesh increased with the "progress" of the society. Necessarily so, since progress was Reason in the service of needs. Not even Rousseau objected to the premise that desire and want moved the world; his concern was only that the ever-increasing wants of mankind were corrupt and the course of history therefore decadent. Pro or con, the philosophes could agree they were living in an age marked by the unprecedented extent, diversity, and artificiality of human needs. Rousseau again excepted, no one seems to have noticed the contradiction — which we are still living — between a "progress" that supposedly represented the triumph of the human spirit over the body, an escape from our animal nature, on the one hand, and, on the other, the dependence of this happy result on an increasing awareness of bodily affliction — more need.[16]

Even as the philosophes, in speaking of the perfectibility of the species, were revealing new dimensions of human imperfection, the economy was producing unparalleled satisfactions by capitalizing on "the thousand shocks the flesh is heir to." In this regard, the Invisible Hand of the market might well have been the wrathful hand of God, as it would create the wealth of the nation out of the feeling of privation it visited on the person — the aforementioned scarcity of means relative to possible ends of personal gratification. This was the great industrial revelation: that in the world's richest societies, the subjective experience of lack increases in proportion to the objective output of wealth.[17] Encompassed in an international division of labor, individual needs were seemingly inexhaustible. Felt, moreover, as physiological pangs, as deprivations like hunger and thirst, these needs seem to come from within, as dispositions of the body. The bourgeois economy

539

made a fetish of human needs in the sense that needs, which are always social in character and origin and in that way objective, had to be assumed as subjective experiences of pain. Precisely as the individual was taken as the author and the supreme value of his own activity and as the collective economy seemed to be constituted by and for personal satisfactions, so the urgings of the body would appear as the sources of the society.[18]

This peculiarly introverted perception of an enormous system of social values as emanating from individual-corporeal feelings, this consciousness, I submit, helps to account for the persistent popularity among us of biological explanations of culture. In our subjective experience, culture is an epiphenomenon of an economy of the relief of bodily aches. Biological determinism is a mystified perception of the cultural order, especially sustained by the market economy. The market economy makes it seem to the participants that their way of life is precipitated out of the stirrings of their flesh through the rational medium of their wills. Genesis redux.

Actually there is a double mystification at work in the bourgeois fascination with corporeal understandings of culture. The subsumption of use-value in and as exchange-value has something of the same effect. In Marx's classic exposition, the commodity has a double nature: it is a use-value in virtue of the empirical properties of the object which make it suitable to some people's "needs," and it is an exchange-value or price, externally attached to the object by the market, which in the favorable case will put it in people's grasp. In choosing between different goods, therefore, presumably in the interest of maximum satisfaction, one in fact forgoes specific satisfactions that in quality (or use-value) are incommensurable with those chosen, hence the mystification in the idea that economic activity is the rational maximization of satisfactions. It depends on the supposition that things unlike in their objective attributes and human virtues — their different meanings to us as use-values — are indeed comparable as exchange-values. So the economist is able to subtract apples from oranges and convince us that the remainder is all for the best. Yet it remains to haunt us that in choosing between (for example) taking the kids to see their grandparents in California or saving the money to send them to college, either kinship suffers or else education.

This is where biological determinism comes in, for, once again, in people's existential awareness, cultural forms of every description are produced and reproduced as the objects or projects of their corporeal feelings. The system of the society is perceived as the ends of the individual. Not only kinship or college education but also Beethoven concerts or night baseball games, nouvelle cuisine, suburban homes, and the number of children per family, all these and everything else produced by history and the collectivity appear in life as the preferential values of subjective economizing. Their distribution in and as society seems a function of what people want.

Our intuition of culture as dependent on biological nature is compounded by a certain received idea, much older than the capitalist corporeality proper, concerning the stratified architecture of the human body. I mean the body as made up of "higher" and "lower" parts, opposed in composition and function. Below is the material bodily lower stratum, as Bakhtin put it in reference to Rabelais's grotesqueries (1984): that which links man to the earth and to birth and death, expressing his basic bestiality and sexuality. Above is the spirit or soul affiliating man with the angels and heavens, thus expressing his rationality, his morality, and his immortality. One recognizes the legacy of the Great Chain of Being but in its specifically Christianized and tragic version (Lovejoy 1964; Formigari 1973; Augustine, *De civitate Dei* 11.16, 12.21). Half angel and half beast, man is not simply a double and divided being, he is condemned to the perpetual internal warfare of spirit and flesh (a specifically Pauline permutation of classical dualisms). Moreover, the battle is likely to be unequal, given the ontological density of corporeal being and brute force, whose inclinations of avarice and concupiscence are not easily resisted by an intangible and ineffable spirit.[19]

Durkheim, for one, was fully aware that he was drawing on a long philosophical-cum-theological tradition in making the argument that "man is double. There are two beings in him: an individual being which has its foundation in the organism ... and a social being which represents the highest reality in the intellectual and moral order that we can know by observation — I mean society" (1947:16; cf. Lukes 1972:432–33). The human being is, on the one hand, a presocial and sensuous animal, egocentrically given to his own welfare, and, on the other hand, a social creature, able to submit his self-interest to the morality of the society. "As there is no one," said Durkheim, "that does not concurrently lead this double existence, each of us is animated by a double movement. We are carried along in the direction of the social and we tend to follow the inclination of our nature" (1930:360).[20] It deserves emphasis that "our nature" — having sensory appetites as its means and the self as its finality — is not only anterior to the social; it is likewise in the pre-Paleolithic of the conceptual. But in contrast to sensations, which we are unable to transmit as such from one person to another, concepts or symbols are preeminently social. They are collective representations, organizing our private sensory experiences, even doing violence to them, in the form of meaningful values of which we are not the authors (see esp. Durkheim 1960:329).

Now, Durkheim thought that the common reports of body/soul distinctions from all over the world confirmed his arguments about duplex man. Beliefs about a separate existence of these aspects of the human being represented the native apprehension of a universal antagonism between them. But he was mistaken. A difference is not yet a conflict. For all that the distinction between body and soul is universal, what has set the West apart is the notion of the civil war between them. The idea of a war between self and society within every human breast, the eternal conflict of flesh against spirit, is our peculiar Adamic inheritance. "Then began the flesh to lust against the Spirit, in which strife we are born, deriving from the first transgression a seed of death, and bearing in our members, and in our vitiated nature, the contest or even victory of the flesh" (Augustine, *De civitate Dei* 13.13).

If Augustine thus quotes Paul rather one-sidedly — "For the flesh lusteth against the Spirit; and the Spirit against the flesh" (Galatians 5:17) — it is only symptomatic of the agonistic body/soul dualism developed in the Christianity of late antiquity:[21] *Pace*

Durkheim, this schizophrenic struggle of the animal and the social was not even proper to the classical Roman dualism. Peter Brown speaks rather of a "benevolent dualism" or an "unaffected symbiosis of body and soul," which would "make late classical attitudes toward the body seem deeply alien to later, Christian eyes" (1988:27–29). Connected to the fertility and intractability of the wild, the body was inferior to the administering mind; but the Romans had neither anxiety about the city's capacity to domesticate it nor the inclination severely to repress its natural exuberance. Brown quotes Cicero: "Nature itself develops a young man's desire. If these desires break out in such a way that they disrupt no one's life and undermine no household [by adultery], they are generally regarded as unproblematic: we tolerate them" (quoted in *ibid.*:28). Nature spoke through the body "in an ancient, authoritative voice." And if so in Rome, what are we to make of the Durkheimian antithesis between a natural animalism of the body and the morality of the soul in the numerous societies where "nature" itself speaks: that is, societies that know worlds of non-human persons, animals that also have souls, as well as mental and moral qualities as good as or better than people's?

The Human Nature of Animals
This is how Kaluli of the Southern Highlands of New Guinea speak about the beginning of things: There were no trees, animals, streams, or food when the land was first formed. The land was entirely and only covered with people. Having no shelter or food, the people soon began to suffer. But a man arose and commanded the others to gather around him. To one group of people he said, "You be trees," to another, "You be fish"; another became bananas, and so on, until all the animals, plants, and natural features of the world were differentiated and established. The few people left over became the human beings. The name that Kaluli use to refer to this event indicates they conceive it on the model of the way people align themselves into the opposed groups that face each other in revenge battles, marriages, or other ceremonial events. Constituted as complementary and interdependent factions, these groups are eventually involved in reciprocal exchanges that resolve their opposition. In the same way, men and the beings of nature

543

*live in reciprocal social relationships: not only or simply in some eco-
nomic sense but, considering their common origin, in an ontological
sense as beings of equivalent natures. The creatures are also men (Schieffelin 1976:94–95).*

*In the forest, one knows the animals by the sounds they make.
Sounds are the salient percepts of "reality" rather than sight. "Day"
begins when the first birds sing, not when the sun appears. Likewise,
the forms of animals may be discounted, as they are really people, and
their voices are communicating messages of human character and
import. Schieffelin exemplifies:*

> *Out hunting with Wanalugo, we heard the plaintive "juu-juu-juu" of the
> kalo (a small pigeon). Wanalugo turned to me with a wistful expression
> and said, "You hear that? It is a little child who is hungry and calling for
> its mother."... The everyday Kaluli world of gardens, rivers, and forests is
> coextensive with another, invisible side of reality. The remark that the
> voice of the kalo is a little child is not merely a metaphor. The kalo may
> actually be the soul of a child. (1976:96)*

*Accordingly, humans and other creatures live in reversed worlds, mir-
roring each other even in the ways they appear to each other:*

> *"Do you see that huge tree?" another man asked one day on the path. "In
> their [the birds'] world, that is a house. Do you see the birds? To each
> other, they appear as men." Similarly, houses in our world appear as excep-
> tionally big trees or as river pools to them, and we as animals there....
> When asked what the people of the unseen look like, Kaluli will point to a
> reflection in a pool or mirror and say, "They are not like you or me. They
> are like that." In the same way, our human appearance stands as a reflec-
> tion to them. This is not a "supernatural" world, for to the Kaluli it is per-
> fectly natural. (Ibid.: 96–97)*

*In the same general way, the indigenous peoples over a vast area of
what is now Canada knew that men and animals were in the beginning the same kind of cultured beings. Animals were humanoid creatures. They are still in reciprocal life-giving relations with people,
members of the same larger society. And although animals have since*

544

lost some of the external aspects of culture — songs, dances, and deco-rated artifacts are among the things men now provide them — neverthe-less, their mental capacities, including speech, equal those of men, and in some regards they are intellectually superior (Hallowell 1955, 1960; Brightman 1993; Fienup-Riordan 1990; Black 1977).

For that matter, there was a strong tradition of the superiority of animals to men — including moral superiority — in the classical antiq-uity of the West (Lovejoy and Boas 1935:ch. 13). Animal behavior served as a model for humans. Among the virtues of the animals com-monly cited was their restraint in satisfying their needs: their only limited desires, including limited sexuality, without penchants for superfluities, etc.

Of course the (Western) Middle Ages compounded the Paul-ine and Augustinian dualism into paroxysms of fear and hatred of the body.[22] Only death could cure a man of "the leprosy of the body" (Le Goff 1988a:354). The hierarchies of the Chain of Being were also socially manifest in periodic upsurgings of the material bodily lower stratum, as at carnival or in what was in some respects analogous, peasant unrest (Bakhtin 1984, Le Roy Ladurie 1979, Gurevich 1985, P. Sahlins 1994). But then serfdom, Le Goff writes, "was believed in the Middle Ages to have been a consequence of original sin," and, as slaves of the flesh more than others were, serfs deserved to be enslaved themselves (1988b:101).

The flesh was always the formidable foe of the spirit if only because of its materiality. In contrast to the impalpability of spirit, bodies have solidity, mass, weight, and other intuitions of irre-sistibility. And when in the nineteenth century the Chain of Being was transformed into — or at least informed — evolutionary theory, the idea of the temporal precedence of our animal "inheritance" was calqued onto the older fears of its irrepressibility.[23] The com-bined effect was the current common wisdom of human nature as a set of deep-seated genetic compulsions with which human culture must come to terms. The same folk wisdom probably accounts for the relative neglect of the two brilliant pieces Clif-ford Geertz devoted to debunking the phantasm of a determinate and determining human nature (1973:chs. 2 and 3).

545

If anything, it is the other way around: human nature as we know it has been determined by culture. As Geertz observes, the supposed temporal precedence of human biology relative to culture is incorrect. On the contrary, culture antedates anatomically modern man (*Homo sapiens*) by something like two million years or more. Culture was not simply added on to an already completed human nature; it was decisively involved in the constitution of the species, as the salient selective condition. The human body is a cultural body, which also means that the mind is a cultural mind. The great selective pressure in hominid evolution has been the necessity to organize somatic dispositions by symbolic means.[24] It is not that *Homo sapiens* is without bodily "needs" and "drives," but the critical discovery of anthropology has been that human needs and drives are indeterminate as regards their object because bodily satisfactions are specified in and through symbolic values — and variously so in different cultural-symbolic schemes.

Throughout the millions of years of human evolution, the whole emotional economy of survival and selection has been displaced onto a world of meaningful signs, as distinct from the direct reaction to sensory stimuli. Amity and enmity, pleasure and pain, desire and repulsion, security and fear: all these are experienced by humans according to the meanings of things, not simply by their perceptible properties. Otherwise, how could you know that fat is beautiful or that a cross-cousin is marriageable but a parallel cousin is not or remember the Sabbath and keep it holy (as Leslie White used to say)? In the event, the generic determinations of "human nature," the drives and needs, are subject to the specific determinations of local culture. So even if man is inherently violent, still "he wars on the playing fields of Eton, dominates by being nicer to others than he is to himself, hunts with a paintbrush" (above, Chapter One, p. 65).[25]

What happened in the Pleistocene, Geertz observes, was the substitution of a genetics of behavioral flexibility for one that controlled conduct in detail. Thenceforth, insofar as human behavior was to be patterned, the patterns would have to come from the symbolic tradition. These symbols by which people construct their lives "are thus not mere expressions, instrumentalities or correlates of our biological, psychological or social existence; they are prerequisites of it" (Geertz 1973:49). People are not effectively driven by their bodies to act in some given cultural way, for without culture they could not effectively act at all:

> They would be unworkable monstrosities with very few useful instincts, fewer recognizable sentiments, and no intellect: mental basket cases. As our central nervous system — and most particularly its crowning curse and glory, the neocortex — grew up in great part in interaction with culture, it is incapable of directing our behavior or organizing our experience without the guidance provided by systems of significant symbols.[26]

The Anthropology of Power

Why, then, do we have this oppressive sentiment of society as a system of power and constraint, counterposed to our inner desires and secret thoughts? Given that biologically we are human beings only in potentia, indeterminate creatures whose inclinations remain to be culturally specified, society might be better conceived as a means of empowering people rather than subduing them. Socialization in a particular language and culture is the way people who "all begin with the natural equipment to live a thousand kinds of life ... end having lived only one" (Geertz 1973:45). Recall the well-rehearsed parable of Helen Keller's magic moment, when the "mystery of language" was suddenly revealed to her: "I knew then that w-a-t-e-r meant that wonderful cool something that was flowing over my hand. The living word awakened my soul, gave it light, hope, joy, set it free!" (1904:23). And yet in the gloomy fashions of the present day, the scholars speak of "the prison house of language" — such is indeed the current "hegemonic discourse." Society, then, is something "versus the individual," a great beast terrorizing him, whether this leviathan is conceived as a necessary constraint on the self-pleasing person, as in the perspective of Hobbes or Durkheim, or as an unwanted imposition on personal freedom, as in the complementary optics of Adam Smith and Michel Foucault. Either way, society is opposed to the individual as power to libido.

Otherwise there could be anarchy. This was a theory already known to the Church Fathers, who learned it from certain rabbis and perhaps some "anti-primitivist" philosophers such as Cicero (Lovejoy and Boas 1935, G. Boas 1948, Pagels 1988, Markus 1970, Levenson 1988). Irenaeus put the matter succinctly: "Earthly rule has been appointed by God for the benefit of nations, so that, under the fear of human rule, men may not devour one another like fishes..." (quoted in Pagels 1988:47).[27] The most famous exponents of the idea, however, were Augustine and Thomas Hobbes. *The City of God* (413–425) and *Leviathan* (1651) have virtually the same argument about the origin of society or state, based on the same premise of men made vicious and fearful of one another by a restless search for power after power. As Herbert Deane observed, the anthropology is remarkably similar, including the actual or potential war of each against all (1963). In the scarcity that inevitably ensues from the relentless pursuit of self-interest, no one can be sure of securing his own good without subduing the persons and passions of the others. If for Hobbes man became a wolf to other men, for Augustine "not even lions or dragons have ever waged with their kind such wars as we have waged with one another" (*De civitate Dei* 12.22). Or, in the venerable maritime metaphor Augustine also adopted, "How they mutually oppress, and how they that are able do devour! And when one fish hath devoured, the greater the less, itself also is devoured by some greater" (quoted in Deane 1963:47).[28] For Augustine, the postlapsarian human condition was just as nasty and anguished as the life of man in the Hobbesian state of nature. In this earthly existence, the saint lamented, "there is but false pleasure, no security of joy, a tormenting fear, a greedy covetousness, a withering sadness" (quoted in *ibid.* 61).

The remedy was the institution of state. Whether it came about through God's Providence (Augustine) or human reason (Hobbes), men were thus able to suppress their enmity — if not their avidity. The state, law, and morality, pale reflections though they are in Babylon of their perfection in Zion, were conditions of the possibility of human society, which otherwise, given the selfish and violent dispositions of fallen man, would dissolve again into anarchy.[29] But the forms of human rule, to be remedial, had also to be punitive: imposed on naturally wicked men "to keep them all in awe." The state then perpetuated the viciousness it suppressed, since it used men's fear of losing their lives, their property, and their liberty as the legal sanctions of order. The complement of the Western anthropology of self-regarding man has been an equally tenacious notion of society as discipline, culture as coercion. Where self-interest is the nature of the individual, power is the essence of the social.[30]

Motivated by the notion of the social as the control of the individual, Western philosophers have too often conflated the origin of society with the origin of state. Of course the supposition is ethnographically absurd. The great majority of societies known to anthropology, including those of the aeons of prehistory, survived without the benefit of state. Augustine had himself imagined how they managed, for he argued that God was pleased to derive humanity from one individual — as a single cognatic descent group, we could say — in order that "they might be bound together in harmony and peace by the ties of relationship" (*De civitate Dei* 14.1). The Bishop of Hippo also anticipated E.B. Tylor's famous incest theory, noting that the prohibition of sister marriage (in the generations succeeding Adam's progeny) would have the effect of multiplying kinship relations and therewith social concord. Indeed, the social values of exogamy and endogamy are brilliantly expounded in *The City of God* (15.16). The further out the exogamic rule, Augustine observed, the greater and more differentiated will be the kindred group. The process, however, should know a limit, and be counteracted by marriage among cousins or others of the same descent, lest distant kin escape and relationships cease.[31] All the same, kinship among fallen man can be no guarantee of peace. Echoing Cicero and forestalling Rousseau, Augustine sadly concludes that even the bonds of family are broken by "secret treachery," producing an "enmity as bitter as the amity was sweet, or seemed sweet by the most perfect dissimulation" (19.5).

A Symmetrical and Inverse Leviathan

The particular structure by which Augustine represented a kinship or-
der — and presumably, then, by which that order failed to secure hu-
man peace in comparison to the relative success of imperial Rome —
almost perfectly describes the classic Hawaiian system, not only in
the detail of generational or "Hawaiian" terminology but in the com-
plementary workings of exogamy and endogamy in a field of bi-
lateral kinship, the in-marriage among distant kin reversing the nor-
mal tendencies of kindred dissolution (Kirch and Sahlins 1992,vol.
1:196–208). What makes this convergence even more remarkable is the
ideological conclusion, equal and opposite to the Christian-Hobbesian
myth of society, that the Hawaiian intellectual David Malo drew from
the structures in question. Written in the late 1830s or early 1840s as
one of a series of speculations on how Hawaiian chiefs (ali'i) came to
be differentiated from the underlying common people (kānaka), Malo's
story could have been his own invention rather than a received tradi-
tion. Still, the difference may not be important, since in its naturalis-
tic-scientific particulars, much the same can be said about Hobbes's.
Noting that it has never been explained why "in ancient times a cer-
tain class of people were ennobled and made into ali'i [chiefs] and
another into subjects [kānaka]," Malo offers the following as a first
possible explanation:

> *Perhaps in the earliest time all the people [kānaka] were ali'i and it*
> *was only after the lapse of several generations that a division was*
> *made into commoners and chiefs; the reason for this division being that*
> *men in pursuit of their own gratification and pleasure wandered off*
> *in one direction and another until they were lost sight of and forgotten.*
> *([1903]1951:60)*

It only needs to be added that common people were "lost" and "forgot-
ten" insofar as they did not have extensive genealogies — of the sort
that distinguished the Hawaiian aristocracy. As a rule, commoners did
not specifically trace their ancestry beyond their own grandparents.
But the great genealogies of the chiefs connected them at once with the
gods — whom they represented relative to ordinary people — as well as
with one another in complex networks of bilateral kinship. That com-

moners were excluded from such privileges was fitting penalty to their inclination to pursue their own desires.

For Malo, then, and by perfect contrast to Hobbes, the primordial human condition would be peaceable: the people all lived together in a group and as nobles, which meant not only that they were connected by blood (koko) but that they knew how to give things to one another. Hierarchy originated as the differentiation of society from below, when certain people developed a restless self-interest and left the collectivity. This by contrast to the Hobbesian commonwealth: a collectivity that developed out of an antecedent condition of isolated self-interested individuals and was marked by the differentation of a superior ruling stratum. Taking their departures from antithetical beginnings, the two philosophers pass each other in opposite directions on their respective ways to the kingdom. A comment appended by Malo's editor, N.B. Emerson, speaks of the implications for kingship, thus making a connection with the present comparison to Leviathan: *"The development of this thought would have explained the whole mystery of why one became a king and the others remained commoners, kânaka or ma-kaainana" (in ibid. 63).*

The etymological relationships in Western languages between *polis*, *political*, and *police* and between *civility* and *civilization* are best explained by the traditional tale of the bad men and the leviathan. A large amount of scientific anthropology has likewise been constructed from this native ideology, beginning with Durkheim's insistence on the coercive nature of the social fact — corollary to the underlying animal egoism of duplex man. Raymond Aron recognized the critical role of the specifically Hobbesian streak in Durkheim's philosophy:

According to Durkheim, man when left to himself is motivated by unlimited desires. Individual man resembles the creature around whom Hobbes constructed his theory: he always wants more than he has, and he is always disappointed in the satisfactions he finds in a difficult existence. Since individual man is a man of desires, the first necessity of morality and society is discipline. Man needs to be disciplined by a superior force which must have two characteristics: it

in the Foucauldian view an omnipresent power constitutes the subjects. All the same, when Foucault speaks of an incessant war of each against all and in the next breath alludes to a Christian divided self — "and there is always within each of us something that fights something else" (*ibid.* 208) — one is too tempted to believe that he and Hobbes have more in common than the fact that, with the exception of Hobbes, both were bald.

The Anthropology of Providence

> Vous composerez dans ce chaos fatal
> Des malheurs de chaque être un bonheur général.
> — Voltaire

Pleased with the conceit that "this is the best of all possible worlds," the famous optimism of the eighteenth century was nonetheless an unhappy philosophy. Its necessary complement was the received dogma of human suffering, to which it merely added some consolation. So if the shock waves of the great Lisbon earthquake of 1755 also tumbled the belief that nature had been designed for man's benefit, it was because this pious notion of an overarching Providence had already supposed a depressing sense of the human condition. The "fundamental and characteristic premise of the usual proof of optimism," wrote Lovejoy, "was the proposition that the perfection of the whole depends upon, indeed consists in, the existence of every possible degree of imperfection in the parts" (1964:211). Like a celebrated beehive of the time, "every Part was full of Vice, Yet the whole mass a Paradise."

The project of deriving a greater beneficial order from the afflictions of the human lot was an eighteenth-century version of the Augustinian theodicy.[34] For Augustine evil was a privation rather than God's creation. The many and subtle degrees of finitude in sublunary things determine in a contrastive way the perfect goodness of the world — in the well-worn aesthetic metaphor, like the shadows that give form and beauty to a painting. Hence "it is good that there be evil," as a twelfth-century text put it (Hick 1966:97). And it seems fitting that in Alexander Pope's

celebration of the optimist philosophy, the goodness of the providential order is achieved in spite of pride, the original sin. At
the same time, looking forward to the coming Western sciences
of society, this greater harmony is realized in spite of any human
knowledge, will, or reason — but, rather, mysteriously and mechanically, as if by an Invisible Hand:

> All Nature is but Art, unknown to thee:
> All Chance, Direction, which thou canst not see;
> All Discord, Harmony, not understood;
> All partial Evil, universal Good:
> And, spite of Pride, in erring Reason's spite,
> One truth is clear, "WHATEVER IS, IS RIGHT."[35]

Adam Smith's invocation of the Invisible Hand is the best-
known instance, but classical economics is hardly the only intellectual success that can be claimed by this metaphysics of the
imagined totality. The same general sense of the structure of the
world informed medieval and modern natural sciences. And, on
the model of providential theories of the state, the ideology reappears in modern anthropological views of "society" or "culture" as
a transcendent, functional, and objective order. (You will recognize the "superorganic" of Kroeber, White, and Herbert Spencer.)
All these cognate concepts have the double-level structure, the
heavenly and earthly cities of the Neoplatonic, Christian cosmology. They all invoke an unseen, beneficent, and encompassing
system of the whole that mitigates the defects and tribulations to
which empirical matter is subject (cf. Ehrard 1963, vol. 1:11–12),[36]
especially the travails to which man is subject: Providence is the
positive complement of human evil. It turns out that God loves
those who love themselves. Life might be unbearable were it not
for the imagined totality that gives purpose and solace to individual
suffering or, better, makes the partial evils of an alienated existence the means of universal welfare. Thus, each person maximizing his own scarce resources...[37]

So the higher wisdom of Western society has often been just
that — a higher wisdom implied in earthly things. It is often noted

that the Christian Providence is a transformation of the Aristotelian teleology of nature. Just so, from Galileo and Kepler through Newton and Einstein, early modern physicists were convinced that God could not have made the universe as disorderly as it might seem in everyday experience. Indeed, Newton held that the fixed laws of nature were edicts promulgated by God.[38] The kinship between natural law and Divine Providence is part of the theological continuity initiated by the apparently radical changes spoken about as the "humanization" of the Renaissance and the "secularization" of the Enlightenment — ending in the transfer of the attributes of an omnipotent Deity to a Nature at least as worthy of reverence (Becker 1932, Funkenstein 1986:357–58). For a long time despised, Nature nonetheless manifested God's handiwork, and now it appropriated His powers — in ways that are still with us, such as the virtues for human health of whatever can be called "natural." But then, the great medieval symbolics of nature and its providential sciences had been constructed from the same cosmic premises.

Back then, in the Middle Ages, the world was still deceptive, even as man was vile. But for those who knew how to discover them, the sensible traces of God's handiwork could be found in the objects of nature and manipulated for human benefit. Nothing was exactly what — or as bad as — it seemed. In some regard or another, anything could be a sign of the Absolute.[39] Eco cites the affirmation of Johannes Scotus Eriugenia: "In my judgment there is nothing among visible and corporeal things which does not signify something incorporeal and intelligible" (Eco 1986:56–57; cf. Glacken 1967:238). Mediated by the greater Truth and Power that otherwise mendacious things could signify, a system of providential knowledge linked these worldly objects according to certain perceptible resemblances. The walnut looks like the brain, hence it is good for headaches. Yellow and green stones could cure jaundice and liver ailments, whereas red stones were for stopping fluxes and hemorrhages. Resemblances such as those between walnuts and brains now seem arbitrary to us, bringing together things "in reality" or "objectively" quite distinct.[40] Yet it was just these obscure affinities that signified an invisible Providence and —

by amulets or alchemy, just as in curing—synthesized the Adamic opposition of nature and humankind. "Objectionable in itself," the world, Huizinga remarks, "became acceptable by its symbolic purport. For every object, each common trade had a mystical relation with the most holy, which ennobled it" (1954:206).[41]

Jesus and Cosmic Entropy in the New Guinea Highlands
According to Glasse (1965:30), "The Huli [of the Southern Highlands of New Guinea] have little personal interest in the fate of the soul. They have no belief in judgement in the afterlife, and the destination of the soul in no way depends upon a person's character or behaviour prior to death. Their views about the destination or habitation of the soul are in fact hazy and uncertain; they are willing to speculate about the whereabouts of ghosts but the question has no great significance." (The fate of those slain in battle is an exception, as their ghosts go to a desirable resting place in the sky—" about which the Huli again have few concrete notions.") That the Huli seem not to be obsessed with what will happen to them after death has been baffling especially to Christian missionaries, who find themselves frustrated by this indeterminacy of "soul beliefs" in their attempts to peddle the Good News about salvation and, a fortiori, the meaning of Jesus's sacrifice. Of course, what they may be up against is this worldly religion, concerned with people's existence here and now, thus not given to speculation about the afterlife. Conversion to Christianity here requires conversion to a religion of death. In the Huli case, however, the missionaries at least had the advantage of dealing with a people whose ideas about the contemptibility of this world could challenge those of medieval Christianity. The problem was that the indigenous Huli cosmology included nothing like the saving grace of Divine Providence. No higher order of good could be found in earthly circumstances, no greater purpose to human suffering. On the contrary, the world was heading toward chaos and death unless people could establish appropriate exchange relationships with the ever-more numerous and vicious spiritual beings (dama) who were causing the decline. This confirmed pessimism makes it possible to understand the Huli's willingness to adopt Christianity—on the condition that they could take responsibility for Jesus' death. Like many of their own traditional dama, Jesus

was not so much a savior as a source of misery. His death could not make the Huli free, since they had not yet paid the compensation for it (Glasse 1965; Biersack 1995; Allen and Frankel 1991a, b; Frankel 1986; L. Goldman 1993; Ballard 1992a, b).

The Huli live in a dying world. Their Weltanschauung "contains a strong sense of decline, of the deterioration of the physical earth and the decay of their culture into anarchy and immorality" (Allen and Frankel 1991a:95). Already realized in falling yields of crops, diminishing herds of pigs, epidemic diseases, and rebellious youth, the developing entropy is an all-around disaster, eventually threatening to dissolve society in incest, fratricide, and parricide. There is a sense, however, that the fall can be reversed, as has happened before, perhaps more than once — thus a sense of recurrent cycles of destruction and renewal. Apparently evoking the distant memories of a great eighteenth-century volcanic explosion on Long Island (off northeastern New Guinea), the renewal entails the return, effected by ritual means, of a time of darkness (mbingi) marked by the fall of ashlike material from the sky, after which gardens, pigs, and humans would enjoy a remarkable prosperity (cf. Blong 1982, Mai 1981). (Note that such volcanic events are not sufficient in themselves to account for the Huli worldview, since this apocalyptic philosophy is shared only by a few neighboring peoples of southern New Guinea, just a fraction of those affected by the Long Island eruption [Biersack 1995].) The return of the time of darkness is not inevitable, however, nor are its effects necessarily benign. "Huli beliefs do not adequately explain it [mbingi] for them," and much as they desire it they also fear its potential destructiveness (Glasse 1965:46). Everything depends on a potentially fallible human agency. If Huli are unable to accomplish the prescribed rituals or to placate the malicious dama, the result will be world disaster rather than world renewal (Ballard 1992b). Memories remain of two such ritual miscarriages in the twentieth century, one of which was the crucifixion of Jesus Christ about 1925 (Frankel 1986:23–24, Allen and Frankel 1991b:271–72, Glasse 1965:46, Biersack 1995).

As Huli recount it, a "red-skinned" boy named Bayebaye (Perfect), whom they identify also as Jesus, was killed in the course of a ritual devoted to the return of darkness, upon which his body was dismembered and distributed in people's gardens. (Chris Ballard reports that this was a normal ritual procedure, or a normal alternative to the sacrifice of a red-skinned pig [1992b], but other accounts either leave the event unexplained or attribute it to some sort of error, as only the blood from the boy's pricked finger should have been sacrificed [Glasse 1965, Frankel 1986]. "Red-skinned," it might be noted, is the way Huli characterize White people.) Frankel relates that the names of Bayebaye and Jesus "are frequently used interchangeably," and, because many Huli feel responsible for the crucifixion, "a number of attempts to give compensation to missionaries have been made" (1986:23). The boy's mother, a woman of the Duna people (to the West), is identified as the Virgin Mary. Nothing has been reported about her immaculate conception, however, nor has she been any maternal solace to the succeeding generations of suffering mankind. On the contrary, the curse she laid in response to her son's death has brought disaster in every shape and form.

Missionaries of four Christian sects appeared among the Huli in the early 1950s and experienced considerable success. It has been suggested that the parallel between the story of Bayebaye and the killing of Jesus "is a major strand in the explanation of the Huli's enthusiasm for Christianity" (Frankel 1986:23). But one wonders if it is not the other way around, the enthusiasm for Christianity being the reason a certain parallel — with Huli playing the role of Pilate — was devised post factum between the two traditions. Here it is important that the destruction brought by colonization preceded the advent of White men in the Southern Highlands, in the form of epidemic diseases especially. From the turn of the nineteenth century, these misfortunes have also been accompanied by various natural afflictions, such as the prolonged drought that began in the same year as "first contact" with Europeans, 1935. Huli have explained their tribulations as due to the unleashing of malicious dama spirits from the places they were previously confined, and, accordingly, they perceived the first visits of Whites — including the notorious Fox brothers, prospectors whose killings of Huli fully justified the perception — as appearances of evil dama. Only later could they conclude — without much alteration of their original interpretations — that the Whites wreaked havoc among them because compensation for Jesus was still unpaid (Frankel 1986:25). "This is the time for us to die," an old man told the anthropologist: "There is not much time left to us now. The world is dry . . . the earth is old and worn out" (ibid.:24).

Edmund Burke could say something similar about the origins and holiness of the State: "He who gave our nature to be perfected by our virtue willed also the necessary means of perfection: he willed therefore the State" (1959:107). Augustine's idea of the state (or society) as a providential organization of human evil seems to echo across the centuries.[42] The sequitur appears in certain modern academic discourses on the functionality and objectivity of society.[43] Anthropological schools such as structural-functionalism and cultural materialism manifest a kind of naive trust in a beneficial, self-regulating social order that determines some good or utility in each and every customary practice. It is as if in society and culture everything were for the best. For structural-functionalists, the society is designed in such a way that any particular custom or relationship, however baleful or conflictual, mysteriously promotes the general good, that is, maintains the social system as constituted. Explications by class, power, or hegemony are generally more cynical expressions of the same principle. On the other hand, the materialist schools that found Aztec cannibalism supplied people with necessary proteins or that New Guinea pig feasts kept populations from exceeding their ecological carrying capacities returned to a cheerier, if equally credulous, respect for the Invisible Hand.

As Dumont again suggests, however, this greater social wisdom, by its metamorphosis of the grubby subjectivity of human actions into an abstract collective good, has become an academic object in and for itself. In a curious parallel to the development of natural science, the providential quality of society makes it a proper *object* of positive anthropology — and of postmodern scorn.[44] In this connection Dumont refers to Mandeville's "Private Vices, Publick Benefits" argument. Mandeville's formula recognized something not yet explicit in Hobbes: something sui generis, outside and beyond particular human subjects, ordering their particular interests. "This something," Dumont explains,

is the mechanism by which particular interests harmonize: a *mechanism* (as in Hobbes, but on an interpersonal, not a personal, level), that is, not something willed or thought by men, but something that exists independently of them. Society is thus of the same nature as the world of natural objects, a nonhuman thing or, at the most, a thing that is human only insofar as human beings are part of the natural world.[45] (1977:78)

And yet the apparent liberation from theology that could imagine society under the description of a world of natural objects owed a lot to the religion that invented such a world: of pure matter, distinct from God, created by Him out of *nothing*.[46]

The success of the providential principle as a theory of society, however, was no simple Tylorian "survival." It is true that as a structure of the *longue durée*, the idea managed to maintain itself despite the lapse of the Roman imperial authority to which it was initially adapted (Pagels 1988). Dumont's discussion of the dialectics of hierarchy engaging the state and the church through the Middle Ages helps to explain why (1982). Briefly, the church had gambled its ideal superiority by entering into a contest for temporal rule. Therefore, when the state emerged victorious from this conflict, it was graced with the status and functions of its holy adversary, notably including the guardianship of morality. The earthly city absorbed significant aspects of the heavenly city. If Durkheim concluded that "God" was another name for society, was this not because it was already true — that is, of his particular society? It is not that God was society deified but that society was God socialized.

The Anthropology of Reality
The invention of a pure object world occurred long before Descartes distinguished thinking things from extended things. It was also well before the reign of capital in Europe, which Marx thought put an end to "nature idolatry" and for the first time made nature "purely an object for humankind, purely a matter of utility" (1973:409–410). (Note for future reference the conflation of utility with objectivity — or at least objectification — which is indeed the bourgeois ideology.) But it was Christianity and before that Judaism that first disenchanted nature, rendering it merely an object for humankind many centuries before its exploitation

by capital — which religion had thus prepared. Insisting upon an absolute gap between God and His creation, between worldly things and divinity, the Judeo-Christian tradition thus distinguished itself from a "paganism" it understood precisely as nature idolatry. "The deification of nature was seen as the real essence of paganism by both Christians and Jews" (Funkenstein 1986:45; cf. Feuerbach 1967:91 and passim; Berman 1981).[47] The ancient Hebrew religion was absolutely unique, Henri Frankfort was wont to argue, in its insistence on the absolute transcendence of God: a god beyond ontological comparison to any worldly phenomena. God was not in the sun or stars, the rain or wind — nowhere in nature. "In Hebrew religion — and in Hebrew religion alone — the ancient bond between man and nature was destroyed" (Frankfort 1948:343).[48]

If anything, the Christian religion went on to widen the rift between man and nature by its opposition to classical pantheisms — corollary to the contemptibility of the material world that followed upon original sin. Christians had serious doctrinal problems with a God who was everywhere, as this would undermine the whole Christology (Funkenstein 1986:45). Hence the emphasis on a creation ex nihilo, which differentiated the Faith from the emanationist cosmogonies of classical antiquity. But then, in developing this difference, Augustine unwittingly reproaches just about all other religions — including the Polynesian, the basic concepts of which he invents as the reductio ad absurdum of the "irreligious" idea that the world is the body of God. "And if this is so," he says, "who cannot see what impious and irreligious ideas follow, such as that whatever one may trample, he must trample a part of God, and in slaying any living creature, a part of God must be slaughtered?" (De civitate Dei 4.12). Perhaps not coincidentally, given the resemblances between the classical Greek and New Zealand Maori cosmogonies (Schrempp 1992), Augustine most accurately describes the ritual predicament of the Maori who tramples the Earth Mother, Papa, attacks the god Tāne in cutting down trees or killing birds, and consumes Rongo when he eats sweet potatoes (see, for example, Best 1924, vol. 1:128–29). Western people have been spared such blasphemy because God made the world out of nothing. "But what is my God?" Augustine asked. "I put the question to the earth. It answered, 'I am not God, and all things on earth declared the same'" (*Confessions* 10.6). Nature is pure materiality, without redeeming spiritual value.

Relativity of Subject-Object Distinctions

To speak of the "humanized nature" of many other peoples — and also in certain respects of Western peoples — is not to adopt the language of "participation" in the Lévy-Bruhl sense, insofar as that notion involves some mechanism of "projection" of the subject onto the object. Among other prerequisites, "mind" has to be invented, something that seems to be far from universal. The epistemological dynamics may be better exemplified by Lienhardt's discussion of Dinka relations to external "Powers":

> *The Dinka have no conception which at all closely corresponds to our popular modern conception of the "mind" as mediating and, as it were, storing up experiences of the self. There is for them no such interior entity to appear, on reflection, to stand between the experiencing self at any given moment and what is or has been an exterior influence upon the self. So it seems that what we should call in some cases the "memories" of experiences, and regard therefore as in some way interior to the remembering person and modified in their effect upon him by that interiority, appear to Dinka as exteriorly acting upon him, as even the sources from which they derived. (1961:149)*

From this it also seems to follow that:

> *It is not a simple matter to divide the Dinka believer, for analytic purposes, from what he believes in, and to describe the latter then in isolation from him as the "object" of his belief. The Dinka themselves imply this when they speak of the Powers as being "in men's bodies," but also "in the sky" or in other particular places. Their world is not for them an object of study, but an active subject. (Ibid.:155–56)*

Lienhardt's explication thus inverts the usual dogmas of participation — and thus offers a more interesting way of "saving the appearances" (ibid.: 161–62; cf. Barfield 1988): "To use our European type of distinction between nature and Mind, it is rather that some men on occasion incorporate in themselves the ultra-human forces of Nature, than that they endow Nature with qualities they recognize in themselves and in human kind." Without the mediation of mind, subjective experiences of empirical intuitions will appear as attributes or "powers" of the perceived objects. Hence for Dinka the disease catches the man. The philosophy is a kind of anti-Berkeleyism, the elimination of the sensing mind leaving the external object as the essence of all "ideas."

On the possibility of nonexperiential beings, entities, and powers, see also the next box, "The Reality of the Transcendent."

Dare one claim that the determination of nature as pure materiality — absent gods, incarnate spirits, or any such nonhuman persons — is a unique Western invention? True, worldly things could represent or be signs of God, but they are not God. Nor is this differentiation of "natural" from "supernatural" the same as the nature-culture distinctions widely practiced around the world. It is the further argument that nature is only *res extensa*, made of nothing, lacking subjectivity. The idea, moreover, becomes the ontological counterpart of an equally singular epistemology, insofar as knowledge of nature cannot be achieved by communication and the other ways subjects understand subjects. Mediated by Adam's Fall, knowledge of natural things is reduced to sensory experience of the obdurate matter on which humanity was condemned to lay waste its powers. Here was a certain praxis theory of knowledge, appropriate to this-worldly things. "For the Christian theologians," Gurevich writes, "labour was above all educational" (1985:261). He quotes Origen: "God created man as a being who needs work in order that he may fully exercise his cognitive powers" (cf. Glacken 1967:185).[49] For a long time, however, this was hardly the best way of knowing, and the things thus knowable were of no great value. "Scorn all that is visible" was the great medieval injunction. As compared with the experience of the contemptible objects of a contemptible world, the higher Neoplatonic contemplation of intelligible entities could be said to continue in such guises as revelation and the medieval symbology, together with the invidious contrasts of ideal form and empirical token. But even when the embedded empiricist philosophy came out from under in the seventeenth and eighteenth centuries, most of its practitioners still understood its limitations, which were the limitations of human finitude. Some, such as Abbé de Condillac, still knew the terrible reasons why. Before the Fall, he said,

> The soul could absolutely, without the aid of the senses, acquire knowledge. Before the Sin, it was in a system altogether different from that in which it is found today. Free of ignorance and concupiscence, it commanded its senses, suspended their action and modified them at will. It had ideas anterior to the use of the senses. But things changed much by its disobedience. God took from it all that empire: it became as dependent on the senses as if these were the physical cause of that of which they did but occasion; and there were for it only the knowledges that the senses transmitted to it.... Thus when I shall say *that we have no ideas that have not come to us through the senses*, it must be remembered that I speak only of the state we are in since the Sin.[50] ([1798] 1973:109–110)

As if the senses were "the physical cause of that of which they did but occasion." Here was the famous metaphysical evil — in many respects the worst infliction of all. Hobbes, Locke, Hume, and the French *lumières* were fully aware that if knowledge came from the senses alone, we could never know the true essences of things. "We see appearances only ... we are in a dream" (Voltaire). Some even tried to wake us from the dogmatic slumber during which we dreamed that in seeing the appearances we were looking into things-in-themselves. But most Western philosophers — including most of the academy — reconciled themselves to a concept of "reality" that remained burdened with the conjoined imperfections of the postlapsarian epistemology, ignorance, and labor. "Reality" is the sensory impressions we could obtain from the world in the course of practical engagement with it. What there is is the metaphysical complement of our bodily pleasures and pains. Even Descartes, for all his distrust of experience, could be confident of judgments based on perceptions of pleasure and pain, for God would not have deceived us in this but, on the contrary, gave us a decent sensory grip on the world for the sake of our own preservation (*Sixth Meditation*). "As to my self," said Locke, "I think GOD has given me assurance enough of the Existence of Things without me; since by their different application, I can produce in my self both Pleasure and Pain, which is one great concernment of my present state" (*Essay Concerning Human Understanding* 4.11.3). And to the skeptics who would not trust their senses but affirmed that our whole existence is just the "deluding appearances of a long Dream," Locke had this answer:

> That the *certainty of* Things existing *in rerum Natura*, when we have *the testimony of our Senses* for it, is not only *as great* as our frame can attain to, but as *our Condition needs*. For our Faculties being suited not to the full extent of Being, nor to a perfect, clear, comprehensive Knowledge of things free of all doubt and scruple; but to the preservation of us, in whom they are; and accommodated to the use of Life; they serve to our purpose well enough, if they will but give us certain notice of those Things, which are convenient or inconvenient to us. For he that sees a Candle burning, and hath experimented the force of its Flame, by putting his Finger in it, will little doubt, that this is something existing without him.... So that this Evidence is as great, as we can desire, being as certain to us, as our Pleasure or Pain; i.e. Happiness or Misery; beyond which we have no concernment, either of Knowing or Being. Such an assurance of the Existence of Things without us, is sufficient to direct us in attaining the Good and avoiding the Evil, which is caused by them, which is the important concernment we have of being made acquainted with them. (4.11.8)

Locke, it is said, repudiated the doctrine of Original Sin (Cranston 1985:389). Yet his own sensationalist epistemology, yielding far from perfect knowledge and constituting judgments of things through the pleasures and pains they evoke — such being all that God intended for us in "the days of this our pilgrimage" (*Essay* 4.14.2) — this epistemological doctrine surely (pan-) glosses the Adamic condition as a positive philosophy of empiricism.

The Reality of the Transcendent

Kant warned about speculating in the absence of sensible intuitions. Insofar as thought involves the a priori categories — of space, time, substance, quantity, and so on — that constitute intuitions as objective empirical judgments, the extension of thought to transcendental realms or objects entails no metaphysical passage into a domain of unreality. On the contrary, transcendental objects will have all the qualities of objective experiences or empirical intuitions — except that of empirical intuition. Hence "religion" or belief in unperceived "spirits" and also its nonexistence in many societies: the frequent ethnographic report of the nonpertinence of the Western distinction between the "natural" and the "supernatural." It also follows that in the event of a contradiction between the empirical and the transcendental, the reality of the latter is privileged over the perceptible attributes of the former. The nonsensory is the more real — as Hallowell related of Ojibway people:

> *An informant told me that many years before he was sitting in a tent one summer afternoon during a storm, together with an old man and his wife. There was one clap of thunder after another. Suddenly the old man turned to his wife and asked, "Did you hear what was said?" "No," she replied, "I didn't catch it." (1960:34)*

Hallowell goes on to note that "outward appearance is only an incidental attribute of being." As he and other students of Ojibway have discovered, the nonempirical aspects of objects and persons — including in the latter category other-than-human persons such as the Thunderbird — make up a greater and more powerful reality than mere sensory impressions. Indeed, a fundamental dogma of Ojibway epistemology, according to Mary Black, is "the unreliability of outward appearance or the 'face-value' interpretation of sense data" (1977:101).

Hobbes and many others before Locke had the same theory of the mediation of objectivity by utility, as did the French philosophes and many others in Locke's wake.[51] But how many sages then or since have realized the cultural enormities of the proposition that we know the properties of the world in virtue of how they affect our satisfactions? *"Juger est sentir,"* Helvétius said. The arbiter of what there is, the determinant and value of significant empirical properties, is a solipsistic project of adaptation to nature.[52] Thus the long-standing equation in the native Western wisdom between "objectivity" and "rationality" (or, it may be, "practical rationality"). The objectivity of objects — their relevant perceptible features — is factored by corporeal well-being. It is an objectivity *for us*, an objectivity of happiness.

Just so, the initial stages of the Freudian "reality principle," involving the separation of ego from external objects (as from the mother's breast) by differentiated sensations of pleasure and pain, make up a psychoanalytic version of the Hobbesian epistemology. Displacing the sensory economics of objectivity from the state of nature to the state of infancy, certain passages of *Civilization and Its Discontents* seem to rehearse the opening chapters of *Leviathan* — leading up to the same antithesis between this species of individual rationality and the cultural order.[53] Taking the same psychoanalytic premises to a providential anthropological conclusion, Geza Roheim came up with what seems in many respects the quintessential Western characterization of culture: "the sum total of efforts which we make to avoid being unhappy" (quoted in Kroeber and Kluckhohn [1952] 1963:209).

In sum, the historical-cum-logical presupposition of empirical understanding is the lapsed Adam, the limited and suffering individual in need of the object, who thus comes to know it sensually, by the obstacles or advantages it offers to his happiness. Perception and satisfaction are recurrent aspects of an embodied theory of knowledge that seems the appropriate philosophical corollary of the transfer of enchantment from nature to capital.

The Sadness of Sweetness

> Man harbors too much horror; the earth has been a
> lunatic asylum for too long.
> — Nietzsche, *The Genealogy of Morals*

The body, then, has had to bear the structures of society in a particularly intense and notably painful way. This is the point I wanted to make about the archaeology of *Sweetness and Power*. At a certain period in Western history all of human society and behavior came to be perceived, popularly as well as philosophically, through the master trope of individual pleasures and pains. Again, as in *Leviathan*, everything came down to the simple and sad idea of life as movement toward those things that made one feel good and away from those things that hurt. I say "sad" because anyone who defines life as the pursuit of happiness has to be chronically unhappy.

In a recent book called *Sin and Fear*, Jean Delumeau provides an extensive historical catalog of the miseries of the human condition in which European authors have wallowed, especially since the thirteenth century. The dolors Delumeau recounts are too many and varied to repeat here. But somehow the observation of an obscure seventeenth-century moralist, Pierre Nicole, seems best to sum up this history of sadness: "Jesus," he said, "never laughed" (quoted in Delumeau 1990:296). Jesus never laughed. Soon enough, proving that everyone was unhappy would become one of the major satisfactions of French philosophy. Pain, said d'Alembert, is "our most lively sentiment; pleasure hardly ever suffices to make up to us for it":

> In vain did some philosophers assert, while suppressing their groans in the midst of sufferings, that pain was not an evil at all.... All of them would have known our nature better if they had been content to limit their definition of the sovereign good of the present life to the exemption from pain, and to agree that, without hoping to arrive at this sovereign good, we are allowed only to approach it more or less, in proportion to our vigilance and the precautions we take. (1963:10–11)

This sad thought was penned about the time when, as Sidney Mintz has taught, Western people were learning to make the Industrial Revolution tolerable by getting hooked on the "soft drugs" of sugar and tea, coffee, chocolate, and tobacco (Mintz 1985). As was noted in connection with the China trade, none of the beverages in this list were sweetened in their countries of origin (Chapter Thirteen). All, however, were taken with sugar in Europe from the time of their introduction. It is as if the sweetened bitterness of the tea could produce in the register of the senses the kind of moral change people wished for in their earthly existence — "the days of this our pilgrimage."

Yet, as Mintz has remarked of the meliorative consumption that continues into modern times — "retail therapy," as it is sometimes called — all this does not entirely dispel our guilt (or should we not say, our original sin?):

> It is not difficult to contend that contemporary American society, even while consuming material goods at an unprecedented pace, remains noticeably preoccupied by the moral arena in which sin and virtue are inseparable, each finding its reality in the presence of the other. We consume; but we are not, all of us and always, by any means altogether happy about it.... The feeling that in self-denial lies virtue, and in consumption sin, is still powerfully present. (1993:269)

Perhaps we can understand now why Mintz's work on sweetness has produced such a concentrated rush of intellectual energy, especially among anthropologists. At the same time that it epitomizes and synthesizes fundamental cultural themes in Western history, it reveals the historical relativity of our native anthropology.

NOTES

1. It is worth reiterating that I am discussing some common, average mainstream Judeo-Christian ideas of the human condition, to the relative neglect of variant and conflicting positions. In this regard even the "Judeo" in the above phrase could be questioned, since, as a friendly critic has remarked (and Philo of Alexandria notwithstanding), the radical dualisms of Christianity are not so marked in that branch of the tradition. Fair enough, but here I am trying to hit the center of the broad side of a barn, the would-be authoritative discourse.

2. The equivocation ("perhaps") is well taken. The Dinka as described by Lienhardt (1961) come quite close to the Adamic condition singled out by Ricoeur, as may other East African peoples. In Dinka myth, human will and the search for freedom, in opposition to God, likewise brought suffering, hunger,

and death into the world. Certain other dimensions of the Christian anthro-pogeny/theodicy, however, remain distinct (as is argued here).

3. *The Genealogy of Morals* conveys the comparative sense I am trying to evoke: "A single look at the Greek gods will convince us that a belief in gods need not result in morbid imaginations, that there are nobler ways of creating divine figments — ways which do not lead to the kind of self-crucifixion and self-punishment in which Europe, for millennia now, has excelled. The Hellenic gods reflected a race of noble and proud beings, in whom man's animal self had divine status and hence no need to lacerate and rage against itself. For a very long time the Greeks used their gods precisely to keep bad conscience at a distance, in order to enjoy their inner freedom undisturbed; in other words, they made the opposite use of them that Christianity has made of *its* god" (Nietzsche 1956:227).

4. Of course the true fault was Eve's, who as woman represented the flesh, the senses, relative to Adam's intellect (Philo 1929:225–26; Baer 1970; Twain 1904). This proposition — men are to women as the mind is to the senses — has been a long-standing tenet of the native Western folklore (Lloyd 1984, Bordo 1987).

5. A disciple observed that "only pagans cannot understand why Christians delight in the chastisement and discipline which their loving Father justly sends as a necessary means to a blessed end" (Löwith 1949:176, paraphrasing Orosius). Augustine's line about babes born crying into the world would be cheerfully repeated for centuries. "We are all born wailing," wrote Pope Innocent III, "that we might express the misery of our nature" (Marchand 1966:8).

6. "That which in a slave is effected by bonds and constraint in us is effected by passions, whose violence is sweet, but none the less pernicious" (Leibniz 1985:289).

7. "Thus it [the spiritual body] is a wholly miraculous body, the fulfillment of man's supernatural wish to have a body that is free of sickness and suffering, invulnerable and immortal, and hence without needs. For the manifold needs of our body are the source of its manifold ailments.... But the heavenly, spiritual body needs neither air, food or drink; it is a divine body without needs" (Feuer-bach 1967:260–61).

8. Augustine had his predecessors, of course, such as Philo of Alexandria: "when...men have poured themselves out wildly into their passions and guilty yearnings of which it is not right to speak, fitting punishment is decreed, vengeance for impious practices. And the punishment is the difficulty of satisfy-

ing our needs" (quoted in G. Boas 1948:12). And there were many medieval successors to the same philosophy, such as Pope Innocent III: "Desires are like a consuming fire which cannot be extinguished.... Who was ever content after his desire has been fulfilled? When man achieves what he desired he wants more and never stops longing for something else" (Marchand 1966:35). Another continuity from the Augustinian tradition seems so simpleminded and vertiginous that I am inclined to bury it here, in a footnote. It concerns the so-called triple libido Augustine spoke about (after I John 2:16, and others): the human lusts for temporal goods, for domination, and for carnal pleasures (see Deane 1963:ch. 2). Is it too crude to point out that the three main Western theories of human social behavior, or of the formation of society, would invoke the same desires: gain (Marx), sex (Freud), and power (Nietzsche, Foucault)? — not to mention the syntheses that have been made of these, which is also to say, the difficulties of keeping them apart.

9. *"Par le seul mouvement il [Dieu] conduit la matière: Mais c'est par le plaisir qu'il conduit les humains"* (Voltaire, quoted in Hampson 1968:103).

10. In Helvétius's words: "all judgments occasioned by the comparison of objects one with another suppose in us an interest in comparing them. And this interest, necessarily founded on our love of happiness, can only be the effect of physical sensibility, whence all our troubles and pleasures take their source.... I thus conclude that physical pleasure and pain is the unknown principle of all actions of men" (1795:204).

11. So Europeans never shook off a certain theological guilt. In "'Pride' in Eighteenth-Century Thought," Lovejoy documents the continuing castigation of this original frailty, the source of the sin. The eighteenth-century denunciations of pride, Lovejoy observes, "are often, at bottom, expressions of a certain disillusionment of man about himself — a phase in that long and deepening disillusionment which is the tragedy of a great part of modern thought" (1948:165).

12. Nor should old Aquinas be forgot. The idea that society originates to meet individual needs of course goes behind early modern times. Schumpeter notes that for Aquinas, apart from the Church, society "was treated as a thoroughly human affair, and moreover, as a mere aggregation of individuals brought together by their mundane needs. Government, too, was thought of as arising from and existing for nothing but those utilitarian purposes that individuals cannot realize without such an organization" (1954:91–92).

13. This aphorism occurs in Helvétius's *De l'esprit*, of which work Halevy points out, "However much this book may be forgotten today, it is impossible to

exaggerate the extent of its influence throughout Europe at the time of its appearance" (1949:18). The influence was especially marked in England. Among the first to submit to it was Jeremy Bentham.

14. "Self-love, which an earlier generation would have attributed to man's turning away from the service of God, is treated by Pope as a necessary force of nature, without which reason would remain inactive" (Hampson 1968:101). This is also the Hobbesian relation between self-love and reason. It seems to have become common in the eighteenth century, even in the perverse forms in which Rousseau cast it.

15. "In creating an *objective world* by his practical activity, in *working-up* inorganic nature, man proves himself a conscious species being.... Admittedly animals also produce.... But an animal only produces what it immediately needs for itself or its young. It produces one-sidedly, while man produces universally.... An animal produces only itself, whilst man reproduces the whole of nature.... An animal forms things in accordance with the standard and the need of the species to which it belongs, whilst man knows how to produce in accordance with the standards of other species" (Marx 1961:75–76).

16. The notion that human progress was a movement from bodily to intellectual control, a liberation of humanity from the constraints of matter and animal nature, was very general through the mid-twentieth century in European anthropological thought. Condorcet, Comte, J.S. Mill, and E.B. Tylor might be cited as prominent exponents, as also Friedrich Engels: "Friedrich Engels calls the final victory of the socialist proletariat a stride by humankind from the animal kingdom to the kingdom of liberty" (Luxemburg 1970:168). The notion in question, typically expressed as a threefold sequence of development from savagery through barbarism to civilization, has specific precedents in the Middle Ages, for example, in Joachim of Florus: "Now there was one period in which men lived according to the flesh, that is, up to the time of Christ. It was initiated by Adam. There was a second period in which men lived between the flesh and the spirit, which was initiated by Elisha, the prophet, or by Uzziah, King of Judah. There is a third, in which men live according to the spirit, which will last until the end of the world. It was initiated by the blessed Benedict" (quoted in G. Boas 1948:210). Alternatively, of course, the three stages were *before Christ*, when men lived in sin, *from Christ to Judgment*, when men lived in hope of redemption, and *kingdom come*.

17. Hume thus reflected on the tragic human condition: "Of all the animals, with which this globe is peopled, there is none towards whom nature seems, at

first sight, to have excercis'd more cruelty than towards man, in the numberless wants and necessities, with which she has loaded him, and in the slender means which she affords of relieving these necessities. In other creatures these two particulars generally compensate each other.... In man alone, this unnatural conjunction of infirmity, and of necessity, may be observed in its greatest perfection" (*Treatise on Human Nature* 3.2.2). Indeed, since needs are endlessly expandable, the effective "unnatural conjunction" in the Western viewpoint is between infirmity and infinity, a fair definition of hopelessness.

18. This point has been excellently made for anthropologists by Dumont: "In modern society...the Human Being is regarded as the indivisible, 'elementary' man, both a biological being and a thinking subject. Each particular man in a sense incarnates the whole of mankind. He is the measure of all things (in a full and novel sense). The kingdom of ends coincides with each man's legitimate ends, and so the values are turned upside down. What is still called 'society' is the means, the life of each man is the end. Ontologically, the society no longer exists, it is no more than an irreducible datum, which must in no way thwart the demands of liberty and equality. Of course, the above is a description of values, a view of mind.... A society as conceived by individualism has never existed anywhere for the reason...that the individual lives on social ideas" (1970:9–10).

19. The same hierarchical structure is repeated in relation to the human brain itself, conceived in much biological literature as made up of "higher" and "lower" centers, the notion being that it was only our "higher" (and perhaps fragile) intellectual centers that held back the animal propensities of the "lower" (Sacks 1995:61).

20. Perhaps the most developed of Durkheim's expositions of duplex man is his 1914 article "The Dualism of Human Nature and Its Social Conditions," where it is said, "Our intelligence, like our activity, presents two very different forms: on the one hand, are sensations and sensory tendencies; on the other, conceptual thought and moral activity. Each of these two parts of ourselves represents a separate pole of our being, and these two poles are not only distinct from one another but are opposed to one another. Our sensory appetites are necessarily egoistic: they have our individuality and it alone as their object. When we satisfy our hunger, our thirst, and so on, without bringing any other tendency into play, it is ourselves, and ourselves alone, that we satisfy. [Conceptual thought] and moral activity are, on the contrary, distinguished by the fact that the rules of conduct to which they conform can be universalized. Therefore, by definition, they pursue impersonal ends. Morality begins with disinterest,

574

with attachment to something other than ourselves" (1960:327).

21. Betz's exegesis of Galatians 5:17 has a triadic form perhaps familiar to psychoanalysis: "In v. 17a the dualism is set up in a rather simple form: flesh and Spirit are named as opposite forces, both agitating against each other. The flesh and its 'desiring'... are human agents of evil, while the Spirit is the divine agent of the good. Verse 17b spells out the anthropological consequences of this dualism.... Man is the battlefield of these forces within him, preventing him from carrying out his will. The human 'I' wills, but it is prevented from carrying out its will... because it is paralyzed through these dualistic forces within. As a result, the human 'I' is no longer the subject in control of the body" (Betz 1979:279–80). As mediated by the Durkheimian opposition of egocentric and social, "flesh," "spirit," and "human I" could easily pass for id, superego, and ego.

22. For summary statements of the medieval regard of the body, see Delumeau 1990; Le Goff 1988a:354–55, 1988b:83–103; G. Boas 1948; Peter Brown 1988:428–47; Gurevich 1985.

23. Starobinski observes that the sentiment of an underlying savagery has repeatedly subverted Western notions of "civility" and "politesse" by making them mere outward forms rather than something inherent in the individual or society. "Reduced to mere appearances, politeness and civility give free reign, inwardly, in depth, to their opposites, malevolence and wickedness — in short, to violence, which was never truly forsaken" (1993:11).

24. This is another way of putting the argument that has been made at least since Rousseau and Herder: that people differ from animals by their relative lack of instinctual governance, their freedom from somatic control, which is the complement to the variety of their cultures and their adaptability to a great variety of environments.

25. For an example of this paradigm of the relation between culture and biological "human nature," see Chapter Four in this volume.

26. One of the few fully to appreciate Geertz's conceptions of "human nature" has been Sidney Mintz — specifically in relation to the question of the desire for sugar (1988). Commenting on the same passage from Geertz, Mintz notes that the usual attempts to define human nature "as some pre-cultural bill of particulars" are most likely to express the specific cultural premises of the interpreters. Human nature turns out to be "a distinctive but somewhat skewed projection of the values of the inventor's society." It is not such "human nature" that is universal, Mintz continues, "but our capacity to create cultural realities, and then to act in terms of them." Precisely this capacity is involved in the ways

we are pleased to describe ourselves "before culture," that is, our cultural constructions of the so-called human nature (*ibid.*: 14). The conscious invention of human nature is its ultimate cultural specification.

27. Compare John Chrysostom: "If you deprive the city of its rulers, we would have to live a life less rational than that of the animals, biting and devouring one another" (quoted in Pagels 1988:101).

28. The fish metaphor, which Irenaeus had taken from a rabbinical tradition, was repeated not only by Augustine but again throughout the Middle Ages. Huizinga says it was proverbial: "*Les grans poissons mangent les plus petits*" (1954: 229). It still lives, interestingly enough, as a one-line definition of capitalism: big fish eating little fish.

29. Augustine on the functionality of coercion: "Surely it is not without purpose that we have the institution of the power of kings, the death penalty of the judge, the barbed hooks of the executioner, the weapons of the soldier, the right of punishment of the overlord, even the severity of the good father. All those things have their methods, their causes, their reasons, their practical benefits. *While these are feared, the wicked are kept within bounds and the good live more peacefully among the wicked*" (quoted in Deane 1963:138–39).

30. It is true that Augustine and Hobbes — as also Machiavelli and Edmund Burke — were apologists for the forms of absolutism of their day (see Pagels 1988 on Augustine). But they share the idea of state or society as counterposed to antisocial man with the likes of Vico, Hume, Freud, Durkheim, and Foucault, to name a few who cannot so easily be typed as ideologues of the totalitarian state. Particular functional uses of the idea of society as power would seem to be situational versions of the same generic anthropology (-cum-cosmology) rather than vice versa. Hume provides exemplary statements of the generic theory: "This avidity alone, of acquiring goods and possessions for ourselves and our nearest friends, is insatiable, perpetual, universal, and directly destructive of society. There is scarce any one, who is not actuated by it; and there is no one, who has not reason to fear from it, when it acts without any restraint, and gives way to its first and most natural movements, so that upon the whole, we are to esteem the difficulties in the establishment of society, to be greater or less, according to those we encounter in regulating and restraining this passion" (*Treatise on Human Nature* 3.2.2).

31. Augustine noted that cousin marriage was infrequent though not prohibited by divine or human law. People shrank from it "because it lay so close to what was illegitimate, and in marrying a cousin seemed almost to marry a sister

— for cousins are so closely related that they are called brothers and sisters, and are almost really so. But the ancient fathers, fearing that near relationship might gradually in the course of generations diverge, and become distant relationship, or cease to be relationship at all, religiously endeavoured to limit it by the bond of marriage before it became distant, and thus, as it were, to call it back when it was escaping them. And on this account, even when the world was full of people, though they did not choose wives among their sisters or half-sisters, yet they preferred them to be of the same stock as themselves" (*De civitate Dei* 15.16).

32. The duality of command and lovability in the overlying social order is a version of the anthropology of Providence, discussed in the next section.

33. For the assertions about the history of "culture" and "civilization" in these paragraphs, see Elias 1978, Bénéton 1975, Benveniste 1971:ch. 28, Berlin 1976 and 1982:1–24, Bunzl 1996, Meyer [1952] 1963, M. Sahlins 1995.

34. And before Augustine the tradition goes back to Plotinus especially, whose formulation of the Chain of Being as a hierarchy of perfection entails both the Augustinian theodicy and, with certain assumptions, the optimists' notion of the best possible world (Lovejoy 1964:61–66, Hick 1966).

35. By "partial Evil" is meant the evil in or suffered by individuals (cf. Pope 1970:133n).

36. Berkeley's version of the Invisible Hand theory is particularly striking for the way it necessarily counterposes a systematic abstract whole to the pains of our finite and imperfect experiences: "As to the mixture of pain or uneasiness which is in the World, pursuant to the general laws of Nature, and actions of finite imperfect spirits: this, in the state we are in at present, is indispensably necessary to our well-being. But our prospects are too narrow: we take, for instance, the idea of some one particular pain into our thoughts, and account it *evil*; whereas if we enlarge our view, so as to comprehend the various ends, connexions, and dependencies of things, on what occasions and in what proportions we are affected with pain and pleasure, the nature of human freedom, and the design with which we are put into the world; we shall be forced to acknowledge that those particular things, which considered in themselves appear to be *evil*, have the nature of *good*, when linked to the whole system of beings" (*Treatise Concerning the Principles of Human Knowledge* par. 153). But then, the philosophy that requires God in order to guarantee the reality of things when we aren't looking at them is about as good an expression of the providential theory as one might find.

37. Again, this Christian anthropology of Providence has classical antecedents, as in Stoic philosophy: "Those things which you call hardships, which you call adversities and accursed, are, in the first place, for the good of the persons themselves to whom they come; in the second place ... they are for the good of the whole human family, for which the gods have a greater concern than for single persons" (Seneca, *On Providences* 3.1). But, on the other hand, "The Greeks did not see the Homeric gods above them as masters and themselves below them as servants, as did the Jews. They saw, as it were, only the reflection of the most successful specimens of their own caste, that is, an ideal, not a contrast to their own nature. They felt related to them, there was a reciprocal interest, a kind of *symmachia* [alliance]. Man thinks of himself as noble when he gives himself such gods, and puts himself into a relationship similar to that of the lesser nobility to the higher....

"Christianity, on the other hand, crushed and shattered man completely, and submerged him as if in deep mire. Then, all at once, into his feeling of deep confusion, it allowed the light of divine compassion to shine, so that the surprised man, stunned by mercy, let out a cry of rapture, and thought for a moment that he carried all of heaven within him" (Nietzsche 1984:85).

38. Obviously, the transformation of divine to natural law meant the end of transcendent being (Cassirer 1951:45), but for all that, and even beyond the theological dispositions of Newton, Galileo, et al. (*ibid.*: 42), a certain transcendence of mean experience by higher (intellectual) order, the Christian edition of Platonism, inhabits the new natural science: "Thus the new conception of nature, seen in the perspective of the history of thought, owes its origin to a double motive and is shaped and determined by apparently opposing forces. It contains both the impulse toward the particular, the concrete, and the factual, and the impulse toward the absolutely universal; thus it harbors the elemental impulse to hold fast to the things of this world as well as the impulse to rise above them in order to see them in their proper perspective. The desire and joy of the senses unite here with the power of the intellect to break away from all the objects of concrete experience and to risk flight into the land of possibilities" (*ibid.*: 38).

39. For Augustine, God's Providence was the explicit guarantee of the absolute readings of earthly things. These allegorical interpretations could be likened to digging up truths "from certain mines of Divine Providence, which is everywhere infused" (quoted in D.W. Robertson 1958:xiv; cf. On *Christian Doctrine* 2.40.60). Augustine's methods of scriptural exegesis, moreover, proved to have a

578

certain compatibility with medieval art as well as its symbolic science – all alike in their appeal to an abstract pattern beneath the surface of things. D.W. Robertson further notes the difference between this intellectual relation to objects, words, or images and what might be called the bourgeois mode of apprehension in and as personal-bodily feeling. Referring to the figurative disposition in medieval writing and much of the symbolism in medieval art, he writes, "The function of figurative expression was not to arouse spontaneous emotional attitudes based on the personal experience of the observer, but to encourage the observer to seek an abstract pattern of philosophical significance beneath the symbolic configuration. In this respect, as in other respects, medieval art is considerably more objective than modern art, even in those instances where it is least 'realistic'" (1958:xv).

40. Thus Foucault highlighted the Cartesian critique of what was a fading science of resemblances: "'It is a frequent habit,' says Descartes in the first lines of his *Regulae*, 'when we discover several resemblances between two things, to attribute to both equally, even on points in which they are in reality different, that which we have recognized to be true of only one of them'" (1973:51).

41. "To escape from this vain, deceiving and ungenerous world is, from the bottom to the top of medieval society, the incessant project. To find the other side of the mendacious terrestrial reality – *integumenta*, veils, fill medieval literature and art, and the intellectual or aesthetic technique of the Middle Ages is above all an unveiling – to find the hidden truth ... that is the main preoccupation of men of the Middle Ages" (Le Goff 1964:420).

42. Chadwick writes of Augustine: "Government was for him an exemplification of the providential principle of order imposed on the disruptive forces let loose by the Fall.... The domination of one man over another may be abused, but it is the lesser of two evils where the alternative is anarchy and every man for himself" (1986:102).

43. Vico spoke of the "eternal property that when men fail to see reason in human institutions, and much more if they see it opposed, they take refuge in the inscrutable counsels hidden in the abyss of divine providence" (*New Science* par. 948). Vico's own recurrent response to Providence to account for human institutions – notwithstanding the *verum factum* principle – seems itself a case in point.

44. An ethnographic confirmation of Dumont's insight comes in a recent article by Verdery (1995), which capitalizes brilliantly (if one may say so) on recent economic events in Romania by documenting the developing conscious-

ness of an abstract total order that accompanies a novel obsession with private interests. Here the sentiment of such an impersonal social object is heightened by the contrast between a modern, moneymaking pyramid scheme and the ideology of agency associated with the ancien (socialist) régime.

45. Burke provides a characteristic example of the naturalization of the providential social process, in speaking of the ancien régime as having "that variety of parts... all that combination, and all that opposition of interests... that action and counteraction which, *in the natural and in the political world*, from the reciprocal struggle of discordant powers, draws out the harmony of the universe" (1959:40; emphasis added).

46. Vico's *New Science* repeatedly describes how private self-interested vices are turned into social virtues by the guidance of divine Providence. For example, the military, merchant, and governing classes were created out of "the three vices which run throughout the human race," ferocity, avarice, and ambition, from which have thus resulted "the strength, riches, and wisdom of commonwealths" (1984:62, par. 132–33). In the conclusion, Vico summarizes the principle:

> It is true that men have themselves made this world of nations... but this world without doubt has issued from a mind often diverse, at times quite contrary, and always superior to the particular ends that men had proposed to themselves; which narrow ends, made means to serve under ends, it has always employed to preserve the human race upon this earth....
>
> The evidence clearly confirms the... position of the political philosophers, whose prince is the divine Plato, who shows that providence directs human institutions. (*Ibid.*: 425, par. 1108–109).

The whole cosmology of the Invisible Hand was announced in the first paragraph of the first edition of the *New Science*, where it is said, "We wish there to be a force superior to nature... which is to be found solely in a God who is not that very nature itself" (quoted in Momigliano 1977:253–54).

47. Glacken makes the general point in a discussion of Augustine: "In the Judeo-Christian doctrine, the distinction between the Creator and the created... is unequivocal, as it must be: there can never be any question of the inferiority of the natural order, lovely as it is, to God. It is a distinction that lies at the root of Christian belief and in the Christian attitude toward nature: one

should never become so entranced with the beauties of nature that he mistakes them for anything other than creations like himself.... Augustine protests that the pagan ideas of the gods start with the conception of earth as mother of the gods. The earth is no mother; it itself is a work of God. Augustine expresses contempt of and disgust with the effeminate and emasculated men consecrated to the worship of the Great Mother Earth" (1967:196–97; see also 151, 160).

48. Frankfort and Frankfort express the point even more generally in another work:

> The dominant trend of Hebrew thought is the absolute transcendence of God. Yahweh is not in nature. Neither earth nor sun nor heaven is divine; even the most potent natural phenomena are but reflections of God's greatness....
>
> The God of the Hebrews is pure being, unqualified, ineffable. He is *holy*. This means he is *sui generis*.... It means that all values are ultimately attributes of God alone. Hence all concrete phenomena are devalued....
>
> Nowhere else do we meet this fanatical devaluation of the phenomena of nature and the achievements of man: art, virtue, social order — in view of the unique significance of the divine. (1946:367 and 369)

49. On the praxis theory, G. Boas also quotes Philo of Alexandria:

> For, to tell the truth, God has appointed toil for men as the source of all good and all virtue, apart from which you will find nothing fair established for the human race. For just as without light it is impossible to see, since neither colors nor eyes are sufficient for visual perception — for nature created light as a link for the two by which the eye is connected and joined to color, but in darkness the power of each is useless — in the same way also the eye of the soul cannot apprehend virtuous practices unless it makes use of toil, like light, as a co-worker. (1948:12)

The current dualism of the symbolic and the pragmatic would thus be a development on the two modes of medieval knowledge, that is, by signs of things and by work on things. However, these are not dissociated in other epistemologies, as seems to be implied by Tambiah (1990), following the venerable Western intellectual tradition (see M. Sahlins 1995:ch. 4).

50. In a compendium famous in its day titled *The Fall of Man; or the Corrup-*

tion of Nature (1616), Godfrey Goodman had already argued that "any skill that today requires study and labor to acquire, 'must' have been possessed by man, innately, before the Fall, and required no laborious process of learning. Goodman's instances range from abilities like swimming to intellectual activity and human communication in general.... Today 'we (that is, our souls) doe not receive the things themselves, but the *species* or images of things'" (p. 46). "'Were it not, that man is falne,' we should be able to reason infallibly; the soul dealing 'directly' with 'intelligible objects' themselves" (Hepburn 1973:507).

51. Funkenstein calls this an "ergetic sense of knowing," knowing by doing, and associates it with Vico, Descartes, and Hobbes, by contrast to the contemplative ideal of many medieval and ancient philosophers (1986:290–93). For Berman, "the equation of truth with utility, the purposive manipulation of the environment, is the Cartesian or technological paradigm" (1981:46). See also Schmidt 1971:110–11, Lenin 1972.

52. Nidditch writes: "The empiricism of Hobbes (1588–1679), Locke (1632–1704), and Hume (1711–1776) should be seen as a compound of several doctrines, not all of them exclusively epistemological. Among these are, as a first approximation: that our natural powers operate in a social and physical environment that we seek to adapt ourselves to, and that the variable functioning of these powers in that environment is the agency by which we get and retain all our ideas, knowledge, and habits of mind; that our capacities of conscious sense-experience and of feeling pleasure or discomfort are primary natural powers ..." (1975:viii).

53. An infant, wrote Freud,

> must be very strongly impressed by the fact that some sources of excitation, which he will later recognize as his own bodily organs, can provide him with sensations at any moment, whereas other sources evade him from time to time — among them what he desires most of all, his mother's breast — and only reappear as a result of his screaming for help. In this way there is for the first time set over against the ego an "object," in the form of something which exists "outside" and which is only forced to appear by a special action. A further incentive to a disengagement of the ego from the general mass of sensations — that is, to the recognition of an "outside," an external world — is provided by the frequent, manifold and unavoidable sensations of pain and unpleasure the removal and avoidance of which is enjoined by the pleasure principle, in the exercise of its unre-

stricted domination. A tendency arises to separate from the ego everything that can become a source of such unpleasure, to throw it outside
and to create a pure pleasure-ego which is confronted by a strange and
threatening outside.... In this way one makes the first step towards the
introduction of the reality principle which is to dominate development.
([1930] 1961:14)

*————. "The Fire Next Time: British Petroleum, the Book of Revelation, and Huli Ritual." Paper presented for the First European Colloguium on Pacific Studies, Nijmagen, Holland, 17–19 December, 1992b.

Barfield, Owen. *Saving the Appearances: A Study in Idolatry*. 2d ed. Middletown, CT: Wesleyan University Press, 1988.

Barnes, John Arundel. "African Models in the New Guinea Highlands." *Man* 62 (1962). Pp. 5–9.

Barnett, Homer Garner. "The Nature of the Potlatch." *American Anthropologist* 40 (1938). Pp. 349–58.

Barrère, Dorthy B., Mary Kawena Pukui, and Marion Kelly. *Hula: Historical Perspectives*. Bishop Museum, Pacific Anthropological Records 30. Honolulu, 1980.

Barrow, John. *Travels in China. . . .* Philadelphia: W.F. McLaughlin, 1805.

Barthes, Roland. "Pour une psycho-sociologie de l'alimentation contemporaine." *Annales* (1961). Pp. 977–86.

————. *Système de la mode*. Paris: Seuil, 1967.

————. "The Death of the Author." In *The Rustle of Language*. Trans. Richard Howard. Berkeley: University of California Press, 1989. Pp. 49–55.

Bartle, Philip F.V. "Cyclical Migration and the Extended Community: A West African Example." In R.B. Mandal, ed., *Frontiers in Migration Analysis*. New Delhi: Concept Publishing, 1981. Pp. 107–39.

Bartley, S. Howard. *Principles of Perception*. New York: Harper, 1958.

Basedow, Herbert. *The Australian Aboriginal*. Adelaide, Australia: Preece, 1925.

Bastide, Roger. "Evénement." *Encylcopaedia Universalis* 6 (1980). Pp. 822–24.

Bateson, Gregory. "Cultural Contact and Schismogenesis." *Man* 35 (1935). Pp. 178–83.

————. *Naven*. 2d ed. Stanford, CA: Stanford University Press, 1958.

Baudrillard, Jean. *Le Système des objets*. Paris: Denoël-Gonthier, 1968.

————. *Le Société de consommation*. Paris: S.G.P.P., 1970.

————. *Pour une critique de l'economie politique du signe*. Paris: Gallimard, 1972.

Beaglehole, John Cawte, ed. *The Journals of Captain James Cook on His Voyages of Discovery*. Vol. 1: *The Voyage of the Endeavour, 1768–71*. Cambridge, UK: Hakluyt Society, 1955.

————. *The Journals of Captain James Cook on His Voyages of Discovery: The Voyage of the "Resolution" and "Discovery," 1776–80*. Part 2. Cambridge, UK: Hakluyt Society, 1967.

Becker, Carl. *The Heavenly City of the Eighteenth-Century Philosophers.* New Haven, CT: Yale University Press, 1932.

Bell, Edward. "Log of the Chatham." *Honolulu Mercury* 1.4, pp. 7–26; 1.5, pp. 55–69; 1.6, pp. 76–96; 2.1, pp. 80–91; 2.2, pp. 119–29. (1929–30).

Bénéton, Philippe. *Histoire de mots: Culture et civilisation.* Travcuix et Recherches de Science Politique, no. 35. Paris: Fondation Nationale des Sciences Politiques, 1975.

Bennett, G. "Account of the Islands Erromanga and Tanna, New Hebrides Group." *Asiatic Journal* 3, n.s. (1832). Pp. 119–31.

Benveniste, Emile. *Le Vocabulaire des institutions indo-européenes.* Vol. 1: *Economie, parenté, societé.* 2 vols. Paris: Editions de Minuit, 1969.

—————. *Problems in General Linguistics.* Trans. Mary Elizabeth Meek. Coral Gables, FL.: University of Miami Press, 1971.

Berlin, Brent, and Paul Kay. *Basic Color Terms: Their Universality and Evolution.* Berkeley: University of California Press, 1969.

Berlin, Isaiah. *Vico and Herder: Two Studies in the History of Ideas.* New York: Vintage, 1976.

—————. *Against the Current: Essays in the History of Ideas.* Harmondsworth, UK: Penguin, 1982.

Berman, Morris. *The Reenchantment of the World.* Ithaca, NY: Cornell University Press, 1981.

Best, Elsdon. *The Maori.* 2 vols. Wellington, NZ: Harry H. Tombs, 1924.

Betz, Hans Dieter. *Galatians: A Commentary on Paul's Letter to the Churches in Galatia.* Philadelphia: Fortress Press, 1979.

Biard, Père Pierre. "Relation of New France, of Its Lands, Nature of the Country, and of Its Inhabitants…." In R.G. Thwaites, ed., *The Jesuit Relations and Allied Documents.* Vol. 3. Cleveland: Burrows, 1897. (First French ed., 1616.) Pp. 431–60

Bidwell, Sheldon. *Curiosities of Light and Sight.* London: Swan Sonnenschein, 1899.

Biersack, Aletta, ed. Introduction to *Papuan Borderlands: Huli, Duna, and Ipili Perspectives on the Papua New Guinea Highlands.* Ann Arbor: University of Michigan Press, 1995. Pp. 1–56.

Birren, Faber. *Selling Color to People.* New York: University Books, 1956.

—————. *Color Psychology and Color Therapy.* New York: University Books, 1961.

Black, Mary. "Ojibwa Power-Belief Systems." In Raymond D. Fogelson and Richard N. Adams, eds., *The Anthropology of Power.* New York: Academic Press, 1977. Pp. 141–51.

Blackwood, Beatrice. *Both Sides of Buka Passage*. Oxford, UK: Clarendon Press, 1935.

Bloch, Marc. *The Historian's Craft*. Trans. Peter Dutnam. New York: Vintage, 1953.

Bloch, Maurice, and Jonathan Parry, eds. *Money and the Morality of Exchange*. Cambridge, UK: Cambridge University Press, 1989.

Blong, Russell J. *The Time of Darkness*. Seattle: University of Washington Press, 1982.

*Bloxam, Richard Roland. "A Narrative of a Voyage to the Sandwich Islands in H.M.S. *Blonde*. 1824–1825–1826." (MS 4255). National Library of Australia.

Boas, Franz. "The Social Organization of the Kwakiutl." *American Anthropologist* 22 (1920). Pp. 111–26.

———. *Ethnology of the Kwakiutl*, parts I and II. Bureau of American Ethnology. Report no. 35 (1921).

———. *The Religion of the Kwakiutl Indians*, part II. Columbia University Contributions to Anthropology, vol. 10 (1930).

———. *Kwakiutl Culture as Reflected in Mythology*. Memoirs of the American Folklore Society, vol. 28 (1935).

———. *Race, Language, and Culture*. New York: Free Press, 1940.

———. *The Mind of Primitive Man*. 1938. New York: Free Press, 1965.

———. *Kwakiutl Ethnography*. 1896. Ed. Helen Codere. Chicago: University of Chicago Press, 1966a.

———. *Introduction to the Handbook of American Indian Languages* published with J.W. Powell, *Indian Linguistic Families of America North of Mexico*. 1911. Ed. P. Holder. Lincoln: University of Nebraska Press, 1966b.

———. "The Study of Geography." 1887. In *Race, Language, and Culture*. New York: Free Press, 1968. Pp. 639–47.

Boas George. *Essays of Primitivism and Related Ideas in the Middles Ages*. Baltimore: Johns Hopkins Press, 1948.

Boeke, Julius Herman. *The Evolution of the Netherlands Indies Economy*. New York: Institute of Pacific Relations, 1946.

Bogatyrev, Peter. *The Functions of Folk Costume in Moravian Slovakia*. 1937. Trans. Richard G. Crum. The Hague: Mouton, 1971.

Bonwick, James. *Daily Life and Origin of the Tasmanians*. London: Low and Merston, 1870.

Bordo, Susan. *The Flight to Objectivity: Essays on Cartesianism and Culture*. Albany: State University of New York Press, 1987.

Bornstein, Marc H. "Color Vision and Color Naming: A Psycho-Physiological Hypothesis of Cultural Difference." *Psychological Bulletin* 80 (1973). Pp. 257–85.

Bourdieu, P. "La Maison Kabyle ou le monde renversé." In P. Maranda and J. Pouillon, eds., *Echanges et communications: Mélange offerts à Claude Lévi-Strauss*. Vol. 2. Paris: Mouton, 1971. Pp. 739–58.

Boynton, Robert M. "Color Vision." In J.A. Kling and Lorrin A. Riggs, eds., *Woodworth and Schlosberg's Experimental Psychology*. 3d ed. New York: Holt, Rinehart and Winston, 1971. Pp. 315–68.

Bradley, Harold Whitman. *The American Frontier in Hawaii*. 1943. Gloucester, MA: Peter Smith, 1968. Reissue.

Braidwood, Robert J. *The Near East and the Foundations for Civilization*. Eugene: Oregon State System of Higher Education, 1952.

———. *Prehistoric Men*. 3d ed. Chicago Natural History Museum Popular Series, Anthropology 37 (1957).

Braidwood, Robert J., and Gordon R. Wiley, eds. *Courses Toward Urban Life*. Chicago: Aldine, 1962.

Braudel, Fernand. *The Mediterranean and the Mediterranean World in the Age of Philip II*. Trans. Sian Reynolds. 2 vols. New York: Harper and Row, 1972.

———. *On History*. Trans. Sarah Matthews. Chicago: University of Chicago Press, 1980.

Bright, C., and M. Geyer. "For a Unified History of the World in the 20th Century." *Radical History Review* 39 (1988). Pp. 69–91.

Brightman, Robert A. *Grateful Prey: Rock Cree Human-Animal Relationships*. Berkeley: University of California Press, 1993.

Bromley, M. "A Preliminary Report on Law Among the Grand Valley Dani of Netherlands New Guinea." *Nieuw Guinea Studien* 4 (1960). Pp. 235–59.

Brown, Paula. "Chimbu Tribes: Political Organization in the Eastern Highlands of New Guinea." *Southwestern Journal of Anthropology* 16 (1960). Pp. 22–35.

Brown, Peter. *The Body and Society: Men, Women, and Sexual Renunciation in Early Christianity*. New York: Columbia University Press, 1988.

Bruner, Edward M. "Urbanization and Ethnic Identity in North Sumatra." *American Anthropologist* 63 (1961). Pp. 508–21.

Buck, Sir Peter H. *Ethnology of Mangareva*. Bernice P. Bishop Museum Bulletin 157. Honolulu: Bernice P. Bishop Museum, 1938.

Bukharin, N. *La Théorie du matérialisme historique*. 1921 [Russia]. Paris: Editions Anthropos, 1967.

*Bullard, Charles B. "Letterbook of Charles B. Bullard, Supercargo for Bryant and Sturgis at the Hawaiian Islands and Canton, March 20, 1821–July 11, 1823." Typescript copy at the Hawaiian Mission Children's Society Library, Honolulu.

Bulmer, Ralph. "Political Aspects of the Moka Exchange System Among the Kyaka People of the Western Highlands of New Guinea." *Oceania* 31 (1960–61). Pp. 1–13.

———. "Why Is the Cassowary Not a Bird? A Problem of Zoological Taxonomy Among the Karam of the New Guinea Highlands." *Man*, n.s., 2 (1967). Pp. 5–25.

Bunzl, Matti. "Franz Boas and the Humboldtian Tradition: From *Volksgeist* and *Nationalcharakter* to an Anthropological Concept of Culture." In George Stocking, ed., *Volksgeist as Method and Ethic*. Madison: University of Wisconsin Press, 1996. Pp. 17–78.

Burguière, Andre. "L'Anthropologie historique." In Jacques Le Goff, ed., *La Nouvelle histoire*. Paris: Editions Complexe, 1988. Pp. 137–66.

Burke, Edmund. *Reflections on the Revolution in France*. New York: Holt, Rinehart and Winston, 1959.

Burnham, Robert W., Randall M. Hanes, and C. James Bartleson. *Color: A Guide to Basic Facts and Concepts*. New York: Wiley, 1963.

Burridge, Kenelm. *Mambu: A Melanesian Millennium*. London: Methuen, 1960.

Cabral, Amilcar. "The Role of Culture in the Battle for Independence." *UNESCO Courier*, Nov. 1973. Pp. 12–16.

*Calvert, James. Journals. Methodist Missionary Society, School of Oriental and African Studies, University of London (South Seas Box 1), London.

*———. Vewa Record, Notebooks and Miscellaneous Papers, James Calvert Papers, Box 2, Methodist Missionary Society Archives, School of Oriental and African Studies Library, University of London.

*———. Personal Papers and Correspondence, James Calvert Papers, Box 2, Methodist Missionary Society Archives, School of Oriental and African Studies Library, University of London.

Cameron, Nigel. *Barbarians and Mandarins*. New York: Weatherhill, 1970.

Campbell, Ian Christopher. "The Historiography of Charles Savage." *Journal of Polynesian Society* 89 (1980). Pp. 143–66.

Capell, Arthur. "The Stratification of Afterworld Beliefs in the New Hebrides." *Folklore* 49 (1938). Pp. 51–84.

———. *A New Fijian Dictionary*. 4th ed. Suva, Fiji: Government Printer, 1973.

591

Carbonell, Charles-Olivier. *Histoire et historiens: Une Mutation ideologique des historiens français, 1865–85.* Toulouse: Privat, 1976.

Cargill, David, ed. *Memoirs of Mrs. Margaret Cargill.* 2d ed. London: J. Mason, 1855.

———. *The Diaries and Correspondence of David Cargill, 1832–43.* Ed. Albert J. Schutz. Canberra: Australian National University Press, 1977.

Cary, William S. *Wrecked on the Feejees.* 1887. Fairfield, WA: Ye Galleon Press, 1987.

Cassirer, Ernst. "Le Language et la construction de monde des objets." *Journal de Psychologie Normale et Pathologique* 30 (1933). Pp. 18–44.

———. *The Philosophy of the Enlightenment.* Trans. Fritz C. A. Koelln and James P. Pettegrove. Princeton, NJ: Princeton University Press, 1951.

———. *The Individual and the Cosmos in Renaissance Philosophy.* Trans. Mario Domandi. Philadelphia: University of Pennsylvania Press, 1963.

Certeau, Michel de. "Travel Narratives of the French to Brazil: Sixteenth to Eighteenth Centuries." *Representations* 33 (1991). Pp. 221–26.

Chadwick, Henry. *Augustine.* Oxford, UK: Oxford University Press, 1986.

Chamisso, Adelbert von. *Voyage autour du monde.* Paris: Le Sycomore, 1981.

*Cheever, G.N. Journal of the Schooner Warwick (G.N. Cheever). 31 Dec. 1842–12 Aug. 1845. PMB 210.

Chou Tse-tsung. *The May Fourth Movement.* Cambridge, MA: Harvard University Press, 1960.

Cibot, Pierre Martial. "Notice sur les objets de commerce à importer en Chine." *Memoires concernant l'histoire, les sciences, les arts, les moeurs, les usages, etc. des Chinois par les missionaires de Pe-kin.* Vol. 8. Paris: Nejon, 1782a. Pp. 267–70.

———. "Essai sur les jardins de plaisance des Chinois." *Memoires concernant l'histoire, les sciences, les arts, les moeurs, les usages, etc. des Chinois par les missionaires de Pe-kin.* Vol. 8. Paris: Nejon, 1782b. Pp. 301–36.

Clark, Colin, and Margaret Haswell. *The Economics of Subsistence Agriculture.* London: Macmillan, 1964.

Clark, Graham. *From Savagery to Civilization.* New York: Schuman, 1953.

Clunie, Fergus. *Fijian Weapons and Warfare.* Bulletin of the Museum of Fiji 2. Suva, Fiji: Fiji Museum, 1977.

———. "The Fijian Flintlock." *Domodomo: Fiji Museum Quarterly* 1 (1983). Pp. 102–22.

———. "The Manila Brig." *Domodomo: Fiji Museum Quarterly* 2 (1984). Pp. 42–86.

———. *Yalo i Viti: Shades of Fiji — A Museum Catalogue*. Suva, Fiji: Fiji Museum, 1986.

Codere, Helen. *Fighting with Property: A Study of Kwakiutl Potlatching and Warfare, 1792–1930*. Monographs of the American Ethnological Society 18. New York: J.J. Augustin, 1950.

———. "Kwakiutl Society: Rank Without Class." *American Anthropologist* 59 (1957). Pp. 473–86.

———. "Kwakiutl." In E.H. Spicer, ed., *Perspectives in American Indian Culture Change*. Chicago: University of Chicago Press, 1961. Pp. 431–516.

———. "Money-Exchange Systems and a Theory of Money." *Man*, n.s., 3 (1968). Pp. 557–77.

Cohn, Bernard S. *An Anthropologist Among the Historians and Other Essays*. Delhi and New York: Oxford University Press, 1987.

Collingwood, R.G. *The Idea of History*. Oxford, UK: Clarendon Press, 1946.

Comaroff, Jean, and John Comaroff. *Ethnography and the Historical Imagination*. Boulder, CO: Westview Press, 1992.

Comaroff, John. "Images of Empire, Contests of Conscience: Models of Colonial Domination in South Africa." *American Ethnologist* 16 (1989). Pp. 661–85.

Committee on the Judiciary United States Senate. *The Anti-Vietnam Agitation and the Teach-In Movement: The Problem of Communist Infiltration and Exploitation*. Washington: U.S. Government Printing Office, 1965.

Condillac, Etienne Bonnot de. *Essai sur l'origine des connaissances humaines*. 1798. Paris: Galilée, 1973.

Conklin, Harold C. "Hanunóo Color Categories." *Southwestern Journal of Anthropology* 4 (1955). Pp. 339–44.

———. *Hanunóo Agriculture*. FAO Forestry Development Paper 12. Rome: Food and Agricultural Organization of the United Nations, 1957.

———. "Color Categorization." Review of *Basic Color Terms*, by Brent Berlin and Paul Kay. *American Anthropologist* 75 (1973). Pp. 931–42.

Cook, Captain James, and Captain James King. *A Voyage to the Pacific Ocean . . . in His Majesty's Ships* Resolution *and* Discovery. 3 vols. Dublin: H. Chamberlaine et al., 1784.

Corney, Peter. *Voyages in the Northern Pacific: Narrative of Several Trading Voyages from 1813–18*. 1821. Honolulu: Thos. G. Thrum, 1896.

Cornsweet, Tom W. *Visual Perception*. New York: Academic Press, 1970.

Council of Chiefs. *Proceedings of the Native Council, or Council of Chiefs, from 1875 to 1910*. Suva, Fiji: National Archives of Fiji.

Cox, Ross. *Adventures on the Columbia River*. New York: Harper, 1832.

Cranmer-Byng, John L. "Lord Macartney's Embassy to Peking in 1793 (from Official Chinese Documents)." *Journal of Oriental Studies* 1 (1957–58). Pp. 117–86.

————. An Embassy to China: Being the Journal Kept by Lord Macartney During His Embassy to the Emperor Ch'ien-lung, 1793–94. London: Longmans, 1962.

Cranston, Maurice. *John Locke: A Biography*. Oxford, UK: Oxford University Press, 1985.

Crawley, Ernest. *Dress, Drinks, and Drums*. London: Methuen, 1931.

*Cross, Reverend William. Diary of Reverend William Cross, 28 Dec. 1837–1 Oct. 1842. MOM/ML.

*————. Extracts from Letters and Diary, 1839–42. ML (B686).

*CSO-MP 7259/1910, 14 May 1910.

*CSO-MP 5947/1917, 11 July 1917. National Archives of Fiji.

Curr, Edward Micklethwaite. *Recollections of Squatting in Victoria, then Called the Port Phillip District, from 1841–51*. 1883. Melbourne: University Press, 1965.

The Cyclopedia of Fiji. 1907. Suva Fiji Museum, 1984.

Dalton, George. "Economic Theory and Primitive Society." *American Anthropologist* 63 (1961). Pp. 1–25.

Dampier, Robert. *To the Sandwich Islands on H.M.S.* Blonde. Ed. P.K. Joerger. Honolulu: University of Hawaii Press, 1971.

Danby, Hope. *The Garden of Perfect Brightness*. Chicago: Regnery, 1950.

Deacon, A. Bernard. *Malekula: A Vanishing People in the New Hebrides*. Ed. C.H. Wedgewood. London: Geo. Routledge and Sons, 1934.

Deane, Herbert Andrew. *The Political and Social Ideas of St. Augustine*. New York: Columbia University Press, 1963.

de Bary, William Theodore, W.-T. Chan, and Burton Watson, eds. *Sources of Chinese Tradition*. New York: Columbia University Press, 1960.

Delumeau, Jean. *Sin and Fear: The Emergence of a Western Guilt Culture, 13th–19th Centuries*. Trans. Eric Nicholson. New York: St. Martin's, 1990.

Dening, Greg. *Islands and Beaches: Discourse on a Silent Land, Marquesas 1774–1880*. Carlton: Melbourne University Press, 1980.

————. *Mr. Bligh's Bad Language: Passion, Power, and Theatre on the* Bounty. Cambridge, UK: Cambridge University Press, 1992.

Dermigny, Louis. *La Chine et l'Occident: Le Commerce à Canton au XVIII siècle*. 3 vols. Paris: S.E.V.P.E.N., 1964.

594

Derrick, Ronald Albert. *A History of Fiji.* 2d rev. ed. Suva, Fiji: Printing and Stationery Department, 1950.

Dichter, Ernst. *The Strategy of Desire.* Garden City, NJ: Doubleday, 1960.

Dillon, (Chevalier Capt.) Peter. *Narrative and Successful Result of a Voyage in the South Seas...* 2 vols. London: Hurst, Chance, and Co., 1829.

Douglas, Mary. *Purity and Danger.* London: Routledge and Kegan Paul, 1966.

————. "Deciphering a Meal." In Clifford Geertz, ed., *Myth, Symbol, and Culture.* New York: Norton, 1971. Pp. 61–82.

————. "Self-Evidence." *Proceedings of the Royal Anthropological Institute of Great Britain and Ireland, 1972* (1973a). Pp. 27–42.

————. *Rules and Meanings.* Harmondsworth, UK: Penguin, 1973b.

Drucker, Philip, and Robert Fleming Heizer. *To Make My Name Good: A Reexamination of the Southern Kwakiutl Potlatch.* Berkeley: University of California Press, 1967.

Duby, Georges. *The Legend of Bouvines: Religion and Culture in the Middle Ages.* 1973. Trans. Catherine Tihanyi. Berkeley: University of California Press, 1990.

*Dullabaun, M. A. "Being, Value and Supernatural Power: A Reinterpretation of Kwakiutl Exchange." Master's thesis, University of Chicago, 1979.

Dumont, Louis. *Homo-hierarchicus.* Trans. Mark Sainsbury. Chicago: University of Chicago Press, 1970.

————. *From Mandeville to Marx.* Chicago: University of Chicago Press, 1977.

————. "A Modified View of Our Origins: The Christian Beginnings of Modern Individualism." *Religion* 12 (1982). Pp. 1–27.

————. *Essays on Individualism.* Chicago: University of Chicago Press, 1986.

Dumont d'Urville, Jules Sébastien César. *Voyages de découvertes autour du monde et à la recherche de la Pérouse... sur la corvette l'Astrolabe pendent les années 1826–29.* Paris: Tastu, 1832–34.

Durbin, Marshall. "Basic Terms — Off Color?" *Semiotica* 6 (1972). Pp. 257–78.

Durkheim, Emile. *Le Suicide.* Paris: Quadrige/Presses Universitaires de France, 1930.

————. *The Elementary Forms of the Religious Life.* 1914. Trans. Joseph Ward Swain. Glencoe, NY: Free Press, 1947.

————. "The Dualism of Human Nature and Its Social Conditions." 1914. In Kurt Wolff, ed., *Emile Durkheim.* Columbus: Ohio State University Press, 1960. Pp. 325–40.

Duyvendak, Jan Julius Lodewijk. "The Last Dutch Embassy to the Chinese Court (1794–1795)." *T'oung Pao Archives* 34 (1938). Pp. 1–137.

595

Dyen, Isidore. Review of *The Position of the Polynesian Languages Within the Austronesian (Malayo-Polynesian) Language Family*, by George W. Grace. *Journal of the Polynesian Society* 69 (1960). Pp. 180–84.

*Eagleston, John H. "Ups and Downs Through Life." Photocopy of a typescript. Essex Institute, Salem, MA.

Eco, Umberto. *Art and Beauty in the Middle Ages*. Trans. Hugh Bredin New Haven, CT: Yale University Press, 1986.

Ehrard, Jean. *L'Idée de nature en France dans la première moitié du XVIIIᵉ siècle*. 2 vols. Paris: S.E.V.P.E.N., 1963.

Elias, Norbert. *The Civilizing Process: History of Manners*. Trans. Edmund Jephcott. New York: Urizen Books, 1978.

Elkan, Walter. "Is a Proletariat Emerging in Nairobi?" In R. Mansell Prothero and Murray Chapman, eds., *Circulation in Third World Countries*. London: Routledge and Kegan Paul, 1985. Pp. 369–79.

Ellis, Havelock. "The Psychology of Red." *Popular Science Monthly* 57 (1900). Pp. 365–75, 517–26.

*Emmons, George Foster. Journals of George Foster Emmons on U.S. Exploring Expedition, 1838–1842, in the Pacific. Beinecke Library, Yale University (Western Americana 166; microfilm copy).

*Endicott, William. "Journal of a Voyage from Salem to the South Seas in the Ship Glide Commanded by Henry Archer, Jr, Began May 20th 1828 & terminated [Blank]." PMB 218.

Erskine, John Elphinstone. *Journal of a Cruise Among the Islands of the Western Pacific*. 1853. London: Dawson's of Pall Mall, 1967.

Escobar, Arturo. *Encountering Development: The Making and Unmaking of the Third World*. Princeton, NJ: Princeton University Press, 1995.

Evans, Ralph M. *Introduction to Color*. New York: Wiley, 1948.

Evans-Pritchard, Edward Evan. *Witchcraft, Oracles, and Magic Among the Azande*. Oxford, UK: Clarendon Press, 1937.

*Evans Collection, National Archives of Fiji, Suva.

Eyre, Edward John. *Journals of Expeditions of Discovery into Central Australia, and Overland from Adelaide to King George's Sound, in the Years 1840–1*. 2 vols. London: Boone, 1845.

Fairbank, John King. "Tributary Trade and China's Relations with the West." *Far Eastern Quarterly* 1 (1942). Pp. 129–49.

———. *Trade and Diplomacy on the China Coast*. Stanford, CA: Stanford University Press, 1969.

596

———. *The United States and China*, 3d ed. Cambridge, MA: Harvard University Press, 1971.

———. ed. *The Chinese World Order*. Cambridge, MA: Harvard University Press, 1968.

Fairbank, John King, and Suu-Yü Têng. "On the Ch'ing Tributary System." *Harvard Journal of Asian Studies* 6 (1941). Pp. 135–246.

Fallico, Arturo B., and Herman Shapiro. *Renaissance Philosophy*. Vol. 1: *The Italian Philosophers*. New York: Modern Library, 1967.

Feuerbach, Ludwig. *The Essence of Christianity*. Trans. George Eliot. New York: Harper Torchbooks, 1957.

———. *Lectures on the Essence of Religion*. Trans. Ralph Mannheim. New York: Harper and Row, 1967.

Fienup-Riordan, Ann. *The Nelson Island Eskimo*. Anchorage: Alaska Pacific University Press, 1983.

———. *Eskimo Essays*. New Brunswick, NJ: Rutgers University Press, 1990.

Firth, Raymond. *Primitive Economics of the New Zealand Maori*. London: G. Routledge, 1929.

———. *Primitive Polynesian Economy*. 1939. New York: Humanities Press, 1950.

———. *We, the Tikopia*. 2d ed. London: Allen and Unwin, 1957.

Fisher, Robin. *Contact and Conflict: Indian-European Relations in British Columbia, 1774–1890*. Vancouver: University of British Columbia Press, 1977.

*Fison, Lorimer. Miscellaneous Papers on Fiji, 1865–68. 5 Jan. 1868. PMB 28.

———. *Tales from Old Fiji*. London: A. Moring, Ltd., De La More Press, 1904.

Fletcher, J.F. "China and Central Asia, 1368–1884." In John King Fairbank, ed., *The Chinese World Order*. Cambridge, MA: Harvard University Press, 1968. Pp. 206–24.

Formigari, Lia. "Chain of Being." In I. Berlin et al., eds., *Dictionary of the History of Ideas*. New York: Scribner, 1973. Pp. 325–35.

Fornander, Abraham. *An Account of the Polynesian Race*. Vol. 2. London: Trübner, 1880.

Foucault, Michel. *The Order of Things: An Archaeology of the Human Sciences*. Trans. Alan Sheridan. New York: Vintage, 1973.

———. *Power/Knowledge*. Trans. and ed. Colin Gordon. New York: Pantheon, 1980.

———. "What Is an Author?" In *The Foucault Reader*. Trans. Josué V. Harari. Ed. Paul Rabinow. New York: Pantheon, 1984. Pp. 101–20.

France, Peter. *The Charter of the Land*. Melbourne: Oxford University Press, 1969.

Frank, Andre Gunder. "The Development of Underdevelopment." *Monthly Review* 18 (1966). Pp. 17–31.

Franke, Wolfgang. *China and the West*. Trans. R. A. Wilson. Columbia, SC: University of South Carolina Press, 1967.

Frankel, Stephen. *The Huli Response to Illness*. Cambridge, UK: Cambridge University Press, 1986.

Frankfort, Henri. *Kinship and the Gods*. Chicago: University of Chicago Press, 1948.

Frankfort, Henri, and Henrichte A. Frankfort. "Conclusion: The Emancipation of Thought from Myth." In Henri Frankfort and Henrichte A. Frankfort, eds., *The Intellectual Adventure of Ancient Man*. Chicago: University of Chicago Press, 1946. Pp. 363–88.

Freeman, Derek. *Iban Agriculture*. Colonial Research Studies 18. London: Her Majesty's Stationery Office, 1955.

Freud, Sigmund. *Civilization and Its Discontents*. 1930. Trans. and ed., James Strachey. New York: W.W. Norton, 1961.

Fried, Morton H. "The Classification of Corporate Unilineal Descent Groups." *Journal of the Royal Anthropological Institute* 87 (1957). Pp. 1–29.

Friedrich, Paul. "Shape in Grammar." *Language* 46 (1970). Pp. 379–407.

Fu, Lo-shu. *A Documentary Chronicle of Sino-Western Relations (1644–1820)*. 2 vols. Tucson: University of Arizona Press, 1966.

Funkenstein, Amos. *Theology and the Scientific Imagination*. Princeton, NJ: Princeton University Press, 1986.

Furet, François. *L'Atelier de l'histoire*. Paris: Flammarion, 1982.

Gallagher, Catherine. "The History of Literary Criticism." *Daedalus* 126.1 (1997). Pp. 133–53.

Gallie, W.B. *Philosophy and the Historical Understanding*. 2d ed. New York: Schocken, 1968.

Geertz, Clifford. *The Interpretation of Cultures*. New York: Basic, 1973.

———. *After The Fact*. Cambridge, MA: Harvard University Press, 1995.

Gernet, Jacques. *China and the Christian Impact: A Conflict of Cultures*. Trans. Janet Lloyd. Cambridge, UK: Cambridge University Press, 1985.

Giddens, Anthony. *New Rules of Sociological Method*. London: Hutchinson, 1976.

———. *Profiles and Critiques in Social Theory*. Berkeley and Los Angeles: University of California Press, 1982.

———. *The Constitution of Society*. Berkeley and Los Angeles: University of California Press, 1984.

Gifford, Edward Winslow. *Tongan Society*. Bernice P. Bishop Museum Bulletin 61. Honolulu, 1929.

Glacken, Clarence J. *Traces on the Rhodian Shore: Nature and Culture in Western Thought from Ancient Times to the End of the Eighteenth Century*. Berkeley: University of California Press, 1967.

Glasse, Robert R.M. "The Huli of the Southern Highlands." In P. Lawrence and M.J. Meggitt, eds., *Gods, Ghosts, and Men in Melanesia*. Melbourne: Oxford University Press, 1965. Pp. 27–49.

Gluckman, Max. "Tribalism in Modern British Central Africa." *Cahiers d'Etudes Africaines* 1 (1960). Pp. 55–70.

Godelier, Maurice. "Is the West the Model for Humankind? The Baruya of New Guinea Between Change and Decay." *International Social Science Journal* 128 (1991). Pp. 387–99.

Goldman, Irving. "Status Rivalry and Cultural Evolution in Polynesia." *American Anthropologist* 57 (1955). Pp. 680–97.

———. "Variations in Polynesian Social Organization." *Journal of the Polynesian Society* 66 (1957). Pp. 374–90.

———. "The Evolution of Polynesian Societies." *Culture in History*. Ed. Stanley Diamond. New York: Columbia University Press, 1960. Pp. 687–712.

———. *The Mouth of Heaven*. New York: John Wiley, 1975.

Goldman, Laurence. *The Culture of Coincidence: Accident and Absolute Liability in Huli*. Oxford, UK: Clarendon Press, 1993.

Golson, Jack. "Polynesian Culture History." *Journal of the Polynesian Society* 70 (1961). Pp. 498–508.

Goodenough, Ward. "Oceania and the Problem of Controls in the Study of Cultural and Human Evolution." *Journal of the Polynesian Society* 66 (1957). Pp. 146–55.

Gordon-Cumming, C.F. *At Home in Fiji*. Edinburgh: William Blackwood and Sons, 1882.

Gorz, André. *Le Socialisme difficile*. Paris: Seuil, 1967.

*Graeber, David. "The Generalization of Avoidance: Manners and Money in Early Modern Europe." Master's thesis, University of Chicago, 1987.

Grace, George. "Subgroupings of Malayo-Polynesian: A Report of Tentative Findings." *American Anthropologist* 557 (1955). Pp. 337–39.

———. *The Position of the Polynesian Languages within the Austronesian (Malayo-Polynesian) Language Family*. Indiana University Publications in Anthropological Linguistics 16. Baltimore: Waverly Press, 1959.

Graff, Gerald. "The Pseudo-Politics of Interpretation." *Critical Inquiry* 9 (1983). Pp. 597–610.

Granet, Marcel. *Chinese Civilization*. London: Kegan Paul, Trench, Trübner, and Co., 1930.

———. *La Pensée chinoise*. 1934. Paris: Editions Albin Michel, 1968.

Graves, Maitland. *The Art of Color and Design*. New York: McGraw-Hill, 1951.

Greenberg, Michael. *British Trade and the Opening of China, 1800–1842*. 1951. New York: Monthly Review Press, 1979.

Greenblatt, Stephen. *Marvelous Possessions: The Wonder of the New World*. Chicago: University of Chicago Press, 1991.

Gregory, Chris A. *Gifts and Commodities*. New York: Academic Press, 1982.

Grey, Sir George. *Journals of Two Expeditions of Discovery in North-West and Western Australia, During the Years 1837, 38, and 39. . . .* 2 vols. London: T. and W. Boone, 1841.

Gruner, Rolf. *The Notion of an Historical Event*. Aristotelian Society supplementary vol. 43 (1969). Pp. 141–52.

Guha, Ranajit. "Dominance Without Hegemony and Its Historiography." In Ranajit Guha, ed., *Subaltern Studies*. Delhi and Oxford, UK: Oxford University Press, 1989. Pp. 210–309.

Gunson, Niel. "Pomare II of Tahiti and Polynesian Imperialism." *Journal of Pacific History* 4 (1969). Pp. 65–82.

Gunther, Erna. *Indian Life on the Northwest Coast of North America: As Seen by the Early Explorers and Fur Traders During the Last Decades of the Eighteenth Century*. Chicago: University of Chicago Press, 1972.

Gurevich, A.J. *Categories of Medieval Culture*. Trans. G.L. Campbell. London: Routledge and Kegan Paul, 1985.

Gusinde, Martin. *The Yamana*. 5 vols. New Haven, CT: Human Relations Area Files, 1961. (German ed., 1931.)

Guy, R. Kent. *The Emperor's Four Treasuries: Scholars and the State in the Late Ch'ien-lung Era*. Cambridge, MA: Council on East Asian Studies, Harvard University, 1987.

Haber, Ralph Norman, and Maurice Hershenson. *The Psychology of Visual Perception*. New York: Holt, Rinehart, and Winston, 1973.

Halevy, Elie. *The Growth of Philosophical Radicalism*. New York: Augustus M. Kelly, 1949.

Hallowell, A. Irving. *Culture and Experience*. Philadelphia: University of Pennsylvania Press, 1955.

————. "Objibwa Ontology, Behavior, and World View." In Stanley Diamond, ed., *Culture in History: Essays in Honor of Paul Radin*. New York: Columbia University Press, 1960. Pp. 19–52.

*Hammatt, Charles H. Journal, Sandwich Islands, 6 May 1823–9 Sept. 1825. Baker Library, Harvard University.

Hampshire, Stuart. *Thought and Action*. Notre Dame, IN: University of Notre Dame Press, 1983.

Hampson, Norman. *The Enlightenment*. Harmondsworth, UK: Penguin, 1968.

Handy, Edward Smith Craighill. *The Native Culture in the Marquesas*. Bernice P. Bishop Museum Bulletin 9. Honolulu, 1923.

————. *History and Culture in the Society Islands*. Bernice P. Bishop Museum Bulletin 79. Honolulu, 1930.

Hannerz, Ulf. "Cosmopolitans and Locals in World Culture." In Mike Featherstone, ed., *Global Culture*. London: Sage, 1990. Pp. 237–51.

Hanson, Allan. *Rapan Lifeways*. Boston: Little, Brown, 1970.

Harris, Marvin. *The Rise of Anthropological Theory*. New York: Thomas Y. Crowell, 1968.

*Hartwell, Joseph (attrib.). Brig Gambia (Joseph Hartwell) of Salem, Voyage from 15–19 Dec. 1844 to 19 Aug., 1845. PMB 218.

Hau'ofa, Epeli. *A New Oceania: Rediscovering Our Sea of Islands*. Suva: School of Social and Economic Development, University of the South Pacific, 1993.

Haury, Emil W. "The Greater American Southwest." In R.J. Braidwood and G.R. Willey, eds., *Courses Toward Urban Life*. New York: Wenner-Gren Foundation 1962. Pp. 106–31.

Hedin, Sven Anders. *Jehol: City of Emperors*. Trans. E. G. Nash. New York: Dutton, 1933.

Heider, E.R. "Probabilities, Sampling, and Ethnographic Methods: The Case of the Dani." *Man*, n.s., 7 (1972). Pp. 448–66.

Held, Gerrit Jan. *The Papuas of Waropen*. The Hague: Koninklijk Institut Voor Taal-, Land- en Volkerkunde, 1957.

Helvétius. *Oeuvres complétes*. Vol. 7. Paris: Garnery, 1795.

Henry, Teuira. *Ancient Tahiti*. Bernice P. Bishop Museum Bulletin 48. Honolulu, 1928.

Hensel, Chase. *Telling Our Selves: Ethnicity and Discourse in Southwestern Alaska*. New York: Oxford University Press, 1996.

Hepburn, R.W. "Cosmic Fall." In Isaiah Berlin et al., eds., *Dictionary of the History of Ideas*. New York: Scribner's, 1973. Pp. 504–13.

Hering, Ewald. *Outlines of a Theory of the Light Sense.* 1920. Cambridge, MA: Harvard University Press, 1964.

Herskovits, Melville J. *Economic Anthropology: The Economic Life of Primitive Peoples.* 1940. New York: Norton, 1958.

*Hevia, James. "Guest Ritual and Interdomainal Relations in the Late Qing." Ph. D. diss., University of Chicago, 1986.

Hexter, J.H. *On Historians.* Cambridge, MA: Harvard University Press, 1979.

Hiatt, Lester Richard. *Kinship and Conflict.* Canberra: Australian National University, 1965.

Hick, John. *Evil and the God of Love.* London: Macmillan, 1966.

Hirschman, Albert O. *The Passions and the Interests: Political Arguments for Capitalism Before Its Triumph.* Princeton: Princeton University Press, 1977.

*Hocart, Arthur Maurice. Fijian Field Notes [FFN]. Turnbull Library, Wellington.

*————. The Heart of Fiji [HF]. Turnbull Library, Wellington.

————. "On the Meaning of Kalou and the Origins of Fijian Temples." *Journal of the Royal Anthropological Institute* 42 (1912). Pp. 437–49.

————. "Chieftainship and the Sister's Son in the Pacific." *American Anthropologist* 17 (1915). Pp. 631–46.

————. "The Uterine Nephew." *Man* 4 (1923). Pp. 11–13.

————. *Lau Islands. Fiji.* Bernice P. Bishop Museum Bulletin 62. Honolulu, 1929.

————. *Caste.* New York: Russell and Russell, 1950.

————. *The Northern States of Fiji.* Royal Anthropological Institute of Great Britain and Ireland, Occasional Publication no. 11 (1952).

————. *Kingship.* 1927. Oxford: Oxford University Press, 1969.

————. *Kings and Councillors.* 1936. Chicago: University of Chicago Press, 1970a.

————. *The Life-Giving Myth and Other Essays.* London: Tavistock, 1970b.

Hodgkinson, Clement. *Australia, from Port Macquarie to Moreton Bay, with Descriptions of the Natives.* London: Boone, 1845.

Hoebel, Edward Adamson. *Man in the Primitive World.* 2d ed. New York: McGraw-Hill, 1958.

Hogbin, Herbert Ian. "Culture Change in the Solomon Islands: Report of Field Work in Guadalcanal and Malaita." *Oceania* 4 (1933–34). Pp. 233–67.

————. "The Hill People of North-Eastern Guadalcanal." *Oceania* 8 (1937–38a). Pp. 62–89.

———. "Social Advancement in Guadalcanal, Solomon Islands." Oceania 8 (1937–38b). Pp. 289–305.

———. Experiments in Civilization. London: G. Routledge, 1939.

———. "Native Councils and Courts in the Solomon Islands." Oceania 14 (1943–44). Pp. 258–83.

———. Transformation Scene: The Changing Culture of a New Guinea Village. London: Routledge and Kegan Paul, 1951.

Hogbin, Herbert Ian, and Camilla H. Wedgwood. "Local Groupings in Melanesia." Oceania 23 (1952–53), pp. 241–76, and Oceania 24 (1953–54), pp. 58–76.

Holbach, Paul Henri Thiery, Baron d'. The System of Nature. 1770. Boston: J.P. Mendum, 1989.

*Hooper, Steven. "A Study of Valuables in the Chiefdom of Lau, Fiji." Ph.D. diss. Cambridge University, 1982.

Horn, Marilyn J. The Second Skin: An Interdisciplinary Study of Clothing. Boston: Houghton Mifflin, 1968.

*Hountondji, Paulin. "Culture and Development in Africa: Lifestyles, Modes of Thought, and Forms of Organization." Manuscript of paper prepared for the World Commission on Culture and Development. UNESCO, CCD-IV/94/REG/INF.9. Paris, 8 June 1994.

Howay, Frederic William. "Early Relations Between the Hawaiian Islands and the Northwest Coast." In A.P. Taylor and R.S. Kuykendall, eds., The Hawaiian Islands...Captain Cook Sesquicentennial Celebration. Honolulu: Archives of Hawaii, 1930. Pp. 11–38.

———. "A List of Trading Vessels in the Maritime Fur Trade, 1795 ... to ... 1825." Transactions of the Royal Society of Canada. 3d ser., section 2, 24 (1930–34), pp. 111–34; 25, pp. 117–49; 26, pp. 43–86; 27, pp. 119–47; 28, pp. 11–49.

Howe, K.R. "Firearms and Indigenous Warfare: A Case Study." Journal of Pacific History 9 (1974). Pp. 21–38.

Hughes, Charles Campbell. An Eskimo Village in the Modern World. Ithaca, NY: Cornell University Press, 1960.

Hugo, Graeme J. Population Mobility in West Java. Yogyakarta, Indonesia: Gadjah Mada University Press, 1978.

Huizinga, Johan The Waning of the Middle Ages. Garden City, NY: Doubleday Anchor, 1954.

Hume, David. Treatise on Human Nature. 1740. Oxford, UK: Clarendon, 1941.

Humphreys, Clarence Blake. *The Southern New Hebrides*. Cambridge, UK: Cambridge University Press, 1926.

*Hunnewell, James. Letters. "Papers of James Hunnewell." Vol. 29a, Baker Library, Harvard School of Business.

Hunt, George T. *The Wars of the Iroquois*. Madison: University of Wisconsin Press, 1960.

*Hunt, John. "Fiji Journals of Rev. John Hunt." MMS. (South Seas Box 5B), London.

Hurvich, Leo Maurice. "The Opponent-Process Scheme." In Y. Galifret, ed., *Mechanisms of Color Discrimination*. New York: Pergamon Press, 1960. Pp. 199–212.

Hurvich, Leo Maurice, and Dorothea Jameson. "An Opponent-Process Theory of Color Vision." *Psychological Review* 4 (1957). Pp. 384–404.

Im Thurn, Sir Everard, and Leonard C. Wharton, eds. *The Journal of William Lockerby . . . & Other Papers Connected with the Earliest European Visitors to the Islands*. London: Printed for the Hakluyt Society, 1925.

Ivens, Walter George. *Melanesians of the Southeast Solomon Islands*. London: Kegan Paul, Trench, Trübner, and Co., 1927.

Jackson, Jean. "Culture Genuine and Spurious: The Politics of Indianness in the Vaupés Colombia." *American Ethnologist* 22 (1995). Pp. 3–27.

Jackson, John. "Jackson's Narrative." In John E. Erskine, ed., *Journal of a Cruise Among the Islands of the Western Pacific*. 1853. London: Dawsons of Pall Mall, 1967. Pp. 412–77.

*Jaggar, Thomas. Diaries of Thomas James Jaggar, 1837–43. Microfilm. Pacific Collection, Adelaide University Library. Original in National Archives of Fiji.

————. *Unto the Perfect Day: The Journal of Thomas James Jaggar, Feejee 1838–45*. Ed. Esther Keesing-Styles and William Keesing-Styles. Avondale, Auckland: Solent Publishers, 1988.

Jayawardena, Chandra. "Analysis of a Social Situation in Aceh Basur: An Exploration in Micro-History." *Social Analysis* 22 (1987). Pp. 30–41.

Johansen, J. Prytz. *The Maori and His Religion in its Non-ritualistic Aspects*. Copenhagen: Munksgaard, 1954.

Jolly, Margaret. "Specters of Inauthenticity." *Contemporary Pacific* 4 (1992). Pp. 3–27.

Jorgensen, Joseph G. *Oil Age Eskimos*. Berkeley: University of California Press, 1990.

*————. "Effects of Renewable Resource Harvest Disruptions on Socieoeconomic and Sociocultural Systems on St. Lawrence Islands." Technical Report 89. Social and Economic Studies Program Sponsor. Mineral Management Services, n.d. (Manuscript courtesy of author.)

Josephides, Lisette. *The Production of Inequality: Gender and Exchange Among the Kewa*. London and New York: Tavistock, 1985.

Jouvency, Joseph. "Concerning the Country and Manners of the Canadians, or the Savages of New France." In Reuben Gold Thwaites, ed., *The Jesuit Relations and Allied Documents*. Vol. 1. Cleveland: Burrows Brothers, 1710. Pp. 240–91.

Judd, Bernice, and Helen Yonge Lind. *Voyages to Hawaii Before 1860*. Honolulu: University Press of Hawaii for Hawaiian Mission Children's Society, 1974.

Judd, Deane B. "Basic Correlates of the Visual Stimulus." In S.S. Stevens, ed., *Handbook of Experimental Psychology*. New York: Wiley, 1951. Pp. 811–67.

Judd, Laura Fish. *Honolulu: Sketches of Life in the Hawaiian Islands from 1828 to 1861*. Chicago: Lakeside Press, 1966.

Kaberry, Phyllis M. "The Abelam Tribe, Sepik District, New Guinea: A Preliminary Report." *Oceania* 11 (1940–41). Pp. 233–58, 345–67.

————. "Law and Political Organization in the Abelam Tribe." *Oceania* 12 (1941–42). Pp. 79–95, 209–25, 331–63.

Kamakau, Samuel M. *Ruling Chiefs of Hawaii*. Honolulu: Kamehameha Schools Press, 1961.

Kant, Immanuel. "An Answer to the Question, What Is Enlightenment?" 1784. In *Perpetual Peace and Other Essays*. Trans. Ted Humphreys. Indianapolis, IN: Hackett, 1983. Pp. 41–48.

Kearney, Michael. "From the Invisible Hand to Visible Feet." *Annual Review of Anthropology* 15 (1986). Pp. 331–61.

Keller, Helen. *The Story of My Life*. Garden City, NY: Doubleday, Page and Co., 1904.

*Kelly, John Dunham. "Bhakti and the Spirit of Captalism in Fiji." Ph.D. diss., University of Chicago, 1988.

*Kintner, Minnie. "Color Trends in Daytime Dresses, 1935–39." Master's thesis, University of Chicago, 1940.

Kirch, Patrick V., and Marshall Sahlins. *Anahulu: The Anthropology of History in the Kingdom of Hawaii*. 2 vols. Chicago: University of Chicago Press, 1992.

Kirchhoff, Paul. "The Principles of Clanship in Human Society." *Davidson Anthropological Journal* 1 (1955). Pp. 1–11.

*Knights, John B. Journal of the Brig "Spry" (John B. Knights, Master), Salem, 8 Aug. 1832–Dec. 1833, Peabody Museum, Salem, MA.

*Koto, Seteriki. Ko Viti (Fiji). Typescript in possession of D.A. Scarr.

Kristoff, Nicholas D. "Suddenly China Looks Smaller in the World." *New York Times*, 27 Mar. 1990.

Kroeber, Alfred L. *Anthropology*. New York: Harcourt, Brace, 1948.

Kroeber, Alfred L., and Clyde Kluckhohn. *Culture: A Critical Review of Concepts and Definitions*. 1952. New York: Vintage, 1963.

Kruse, John A. "Subsistence and the North Slope Inuit." In Steve Langdon, ed., *Contemporary Alaskan Native Economics*. Lanham, MD: University Press of America, 1986. Pp. 121–52.

Kuykendall, Ralph Simpson. *The Hawaiian Kingdom*. Vol. 1: *1778–1854*. Honolulu: University of Hawaii Press, 1968.

Lafargue, Paul. *The Right to Be Lazy*. 1883. Chicago: Kerr, 1909.

Landtman, Gunnar. *The Kiwai Papuans of British New Guinea*. London: Macmillan, 1927.

Langdon, Stephen J. "Contradictions in Alaskan Native Economy and Society." In Steve Langdon, ed., *Contemporary Alaskan Native Economics*. Lanham, MD: University Press of America, 1986. Pp. 121–52.

———. "The Integration of Cash and Subsistence in Southwest Alaskan Yup'ik Eskimo Communities." In Toshio Matsuyama and Nicolas Peterson, eds., *Cash, Commoditisation, and Changing Foragers*. Senri Studies 30. Osaka: National Museum of Ethnology, 1991. Pp. 269–91.

Langridge, Albert Kent. *The Conquest of Cannibal Tanna*. London: Hodder and Stoughton, 1934.

Latourette, Kenneth Scott. "The History of Early Relations Between the United States and China, 1784–1844." *Transactions of the Connecticut Academy of Arts and Sciences* 22 (1917). Pp. 1–209.

Lattimore, Owen. *Inner Asian Frontiers of China*. New York: American Geographical Society, 1940.

Lawry, Rev. Walter. *Friendly and Feejee Islands: A Missionary Visit in the South Seas, in the Year MDCCCXLVII*. 2d ed. London: J. Mason, 1850.

Leach, Edmund Ronald. *Political Systems of Highland Burma*. London: G. Bell and Sons, 1954.

———. "Anthropological Aspects of Language: Animal Categories and Verbal Abuse." In Eric H. Lenneberg, ed., *New Directions in the Study of Language*. Cambridge, MA: MIT Press, 1964. Pp. 23–63.

——. *Claude Lévi-Strauss*. New York: Viking, 1970.

Lederman, Rena. "Changing Times in Mendi: Notes Towards Writing Highland New Guinea History." *Ethnohistory* 33 (1986a). Pp. 1–30.

——. *What Gifts Engender: Social Relations and Politics in Mendi, Highland Papua New Guinea*. Cambridge, UK: Cambridge University Press, 1986b.

Lee, Richard. "What Hunters Do for a Living, or, How to Make Out on Scarce Resources." In Richard Lee and Irven DeVore, eds., *Man the Hunter*. Chicago: Aldine, 1968. Pp. 30–48.

——. "!Kung Bushman Subsistence: An Input-Output Analysis." In A. Vayda, ed., *Environment and Cultural Behavior*. Garden City, NY: Natural History Press, 1969. Pp. 47–79.

Lee, Richard, and Irven DeVore, eds. *Man the Hunter*. Chicago: Aldine, 1968.

Le Goff, Jacques. *La Civilisation de l'Occident mediéval*. Paris: B. Arthaud, 1964.

——. "Is Politics Still the Backbone of History?" In Felix Gilbert and Stephen R. Graubard, eds., *Historical Studies Today*. Trans. Barbara Bray. New York: Norton, 1972. Pp. 337–55.

——. *Medieval Civilization*. Trans. Julie Barrow. Oxford: Basil Blackwell, 1988a.

——. *The Medieval Imagination*. Trans. Arthur Goldhammer. Chicago: University of Chicago Press, 1988b.

——. *La Nouvelle histoire*. Paris: Editions Complexe, 1988c.

Leibniz, G.W. *Theodicy*. Trans. E. M. Hubbard. La Salle, IL: Open Court, 1985.

LeJeune, le Père Paul. "Relation of What Occurred in New France in the Year 1634." 1635. In R.G. Thwaites, ed., *The Jesuit Relations and Allied Documents*. Vol. 6. Cleveland: Burrows, 1897. Pp. 91–317.

Lenin, V.I. *Materialism and Empirio-Criticism: Critical Comments on a Reactionary Philosophy*. Peking: Foreign Language Press, 1972.

Lenneberg, Eric H., and John M. Roberts. "The Language of Experience, a Study in Methodology." Supplement to *International Journal of American Linguistics* 22 (1956). Memoir 13.

Le Roy Ladurie, Emmanuel. "Evénement et longue durée dans l'histoire sociale: L'Exemple chouan." *Communications* 18 (1972). Pp. 72–84.

——. *The Territory of the Historian*. Trans. Benal Siān Reynolds. Chicago: University of Chicago Press, 1979.

Lester, R.H. "Kava Drinking in Viti Levu, Fiji." *Oceania* 12 (1941–42). Pp. 97–121, 226–54.

Levenson, Jon D. Creation and the Persistence of Evil. San Francisco: Harper and Row, 1988.

Lévi-Strauss, Claude. Race and History. Paris: UNESCO, 1968.

————. Structural Anthropology. Trans. Claire Jacobson and Brooke Grundfest Schoepf. New York: Basic Books, 1963a.

————. Totemism. Trans. Rodney Needham. Boston: Beacon Press, 1963b.

————. The Savage Mind. Chicago: University of Chicago Press, 1966.

————. L'Homme nu. Paris: Plon, 1971a.

————. "Rapports de symétrie entre rites et mythes de peuples voisins." In Thomas O. Beidelman, ed., The Translation of Culture. London: Tavistock, 1971b. Pp. 161–78.

————. "Structuralism and Ecology." Barnard Alumnae (spring 1972). Pp. 6–14.

Levy, Sidney. "Symbols by Which We Buy." In James F. Engel, ed., Consumer Behavior. Homewood, IL: Irwin, 1968.

Lienhardt, Godfrey. Divinity and Experience: The Religion of the Dinka. Oxford, UK: Clarendon, 1961.

Lindstrom, Lamont. "Kastom: The Political History of Tradition on Tanna, Vanuatu." Mankind 13 (1982). Pp. 316–29.

Linksz, Arthur. Physiology of the Eye. Vol. 2: Vision. New York: Grune and Stratten, 1952.

————. An Essay on Color Vision and Clinical Color-Vision Tests. New York: Grune and Stratten, 1964.

Linton, Ralph. The Study of Man. New York: D. Appleton–Century, 1936.

————. "Marquesan Culture." In Ralph Linton and A. Kardiner, eds., The Individual and His Society. New York: Columbia University Press, 1939. Pp. 137–96.

Lloyd, Genevieve. The Man of Reason: "Male" and "Female" in Western Philosophy. Minneapolis: University of Minnesota Press, 1984.

Lo, J.-P. "The Decline of the Early Ming Navy." Oriens Extremus 5 (1958). Pp. 149–68.

Lockerby, William. The Journal of William Lockerby Sandalwood Trader in the Fijian Islands During the Years 1808–1809. Ed. Sir Everard Im Thurn. London: The Hakluyt Society, 1925.

Lonner, Thomas D. "Subsistence as an Economic System in Alaska: Theoretical Observations and Management Implications." In Steve Langdon, ed., Contemporary Alaskan Native Economics. Lanham, MD: University Press of America, 1986. Pp. 15–28.

Lothrup, Samuel K. *The Indians of Tierra del Fuego*. New York: Museum of the American Indian, Heye Foundation, 1928.

Lovejoy, Arthur O. *Essays in the History of Ideas*. Baltimore: Johns Hopkins Press, 1948.

————. *The Great Chain of Being*. Cambridge, MA: Harvard University Press, 1964.

Lovejoy, Arthur O., and George Boas. *Primitivism and Related Ideas in Antiquity*. Baltimore: Johns Hopkins Press, 1935.

Lowie, Robert H. "Subsistence." In Franz Boas, ed., *General Anthropology*. Boston: Heath, 1938. Pp. 282–326.

————. *An Introduction to Cultural Anthropology*. 2d ed. New York: Rinehart, 1946.

Löwith, Karl. *Meaning in History*. Chicago: University of Chicago Press, 1949.

Lukes, Steven. *Emile Durkheim: His Life and Works*. New York: Harper and Row, 1972.

Luxemburg, Rosa. *Rosa Luxemburg Speaks*. Ed. Mary Alice Waters. New York: Pathfinder, 1970.

Lynes, Russell. *A Surfeit of Honey*. New York: Harper, 1957.

*Lyth, Richard Birdsall. "Daybook and Journal, 11 Aug. 1850–31 Dec. 1851." ML B539.

*————. "Journal 1836–42." ML B533; 1842–44, ML B534; 1845–48, ML B535; 1848–50, ML B536; 1852, ML B540; 1853, ML B541; 1853–60, ML B548.

*————. "Letters to and from Rev. Dr. R.B. Lyth, 1836–54." ML A836.

*————. "Reminiscences 1851–53." ML B548.

*————. Tongan and Feejean Reminiscences 2 vols. ML B533.

*MaL Firm of Marshall and Wildes. Copies of Letters from the Sandwich Islands and Canton, 1820–1832. Houghton Library, Harvard University.

MMS. "History of Fiji." Special Collections, University of Santa Cruz–Santa Cruz Library.

M'Ghee, Robert James Leslie. *How We Got to Pekin: A Narrative of the Campaign in China of 1860*. London: Bentley, 1862.

Mai, Paul. "The 'Time of Darkness' or *Yuu Kuia*." In Donald Denoon and Roderic Lacey, eds., *Oral Tradition in Melanesia*. Port Moresby: University of Papua New Guinea and Institute of Papua New Guinea Studies, 1981. Pp. 125–40.

Malinowski, Bronislaw. *Argonauts of the Western Pacific*. London: Routledge and Kegan Paul, 1922.

Malo, David. *Hawaiian Antiquities,* 1903. Honolulu: Bernice P. Bishop Museum, 1951.

Malone, Carroll Brown. *History of the Peking Summer Palaces Under the Ch'ing Dynasty.* Illinois Studies in the Social Sciences, vol. 21, nos. 1–2, 1934.

Manby, Thomas. "Journal of Vancouver's Voyage to the Pacific Ocean (1791–93)." *Honolulu Mercury* 1.2 (1929). Pp. 33–45.

Mancall, Mark. *China at the Center.* New York: Free Press, 1984.

Mandel, Ernest. *Traite d'économie marxiste.* 2 vols. Paris: Julliard, 1962.

Mandeville, Bernard. *The Fable of the Bees; or, Private Vices, Publick Benefits.* 2 vols. Indianapolis, IN: Liberty Classics, 1988.

Marchand, Bernard, ed. *Two Views of Man: Pope Innocent III "On the Misery of Man," Gianozzo Manetti "On the Dignity of Man."* New York: Ungar, 1966.

Mariner, William. *An Account of the Natives of the Tonga Islands in the South Pacific Ocean.* 2 vols. 3d ed. Compiler John Martin. Edinburgh: Constable and Co., 1827.

Markus, R.A. *Saeculum: History and Society in the Theology of St. Augustine.* Cambridge, UK: Cambridge University Press, 1970.

Marshall, Lorna. "Sharing, Talking, and Giving: Relief of Social Tensions Among !Kung Bushmen." *Africa* 31 (1961). Pp. 231–49.

Marx, Karl. *Economic and Philosophic Manuscripts of 1844.* Moscow: Foreign Languages Publishing House, 1961.

———. *Capital: A Critique of Political Economy.* Vol. 2. New York: International Publishers, 1967.

———. *Grundrisse.* Trans. Martin Nicolaus. Harmondsworth, UK: Penguin, 1973.

Marx, Karl, and Friedrich Engels. *Manifesto of the Communist Party.* 1848. In Marx and Engels, *Basic Writings on Politics and Philosophy.* Ed. Lewis S. Feuer. Garden City, NY: Doubleday, 1959. Pp. 1–41.

———. *The German Ideology.* London: Lawrence and Wishart, 1970.

Mathew, John. *Two Representative Tribes of Queensland.* London: Unwin, 1910.

Mathison, Gilbert Farquhar. *Narrative of a Visit to Brazil, Chile, Peru, and the Sandwich Islands During the Years 1821 and 1822.* London: Knight, 1825.

Maude, H.E. *Of Islands and Men: Studies in Pacific History.* Melbourne: Oxford University Press, 1968.

Mauss, Marcel. *Sociologie et anthropologie.* Paris: Presses Universitaires de France, 1966.

———. *A General Theory of Magic.* 1902–1903. Trans. Robert Brain. New York: W.W. Norton, 1972.

Maxwell, James Clerk. "On Color Vision." In David L. MacAdam, ed., *Sources of Color Science*. 1872. Cambridge, MA: MIT Press, 1970. Pp. 75–83.

McArthur, Margaret. "Food Consumption and Dietary Levels of Groups of Aborigines Living on Naturally Occurring Foods." In C.P. Mountford, ed., *Records of the Australian-American Scientific Expedition to Arnhem Land*. Vol. 2: *Anthropology and Nutrition*. Melbourne: Melbourne University Press, 1960. Pp. 90–135.

McCarthy, Frederick D., and Margaret McArthur. "The Food Quest and the Time Factor in Aboriginal Economic Life." In C. P. Mountford, ed., *Records of the Australian-American Scientific Expedition to Arnhem Land*. Vol. 2: *Anthropology and Nutrition*. Melbourne: Melbourne University Press, 1960. Pp. 145–95.

Mead, Margaret. *Coming of Age in Samoa: A Psychological Study of Primitive Youth for Western Civilization*. New York: Morrow, 1928.

———. "Kinship in the Admiralty Islands." *American Museum of Natural History Anthropology Papers* 34 (1934). Pp. 181–358.

———. "The Manus of the Admiralty Islands." In Margaret Mead, ed., *Cooperation and Competition Among Primitive Peoples*. New York: McGraw-Hill, 1937a. Pp. 210–39.

———. "The Arapesh of New Guinea." In Margaret Mead, ed., *Cooperation and Competition Among Primitive Peoples*. New York: McGraw-Hill, 1937b. Pp. 20–50.

———. "The Mountain Arapesh I. An Importing Culture." *American Museum of Natural History Anthropology Papers* 36 (1938). Pp. 139–349.

———. "The Mountain Arapesh III. Socio-Economic Life." *American Museum of Natural History Anthropology Papers* 40 (1947). Pp. 159–232.

Meadows, Thomas Taylor. *Desultory Notes on the Government and People of China...* London: W.H. Allen, 1847.

Meares, John. *Voyages Made in the Years 1788 and 1789, from China to the North-west Coast of America, to Which Are Prefixed an Introductory Narrative of a Voyage Performed in 1786, from Bengal, in the Ship* Nootka. London: Logographic Press, 1790.

Meggitt, Mervyn. "Enga Political Organization: A Preliminary Description." *Mankind* 5 (1957). Pp. 133–57.

———. "The Enga of the New Guinea Highlands: Some Preliminary Observations." *Oceania* 28 (1957–58). Pp. 253–330.

———. "Indigenous Forms of Government Among the Australian Aborigines."

Bildragen tot de Taal- Land- en Volkerkunde 120 (1964). Pp. 163–80.

Merleau-Ponty, Maurice. *Phenomenology of Light and Colour.* New York: Academic Press, 1962.

*Methodist Missionary Society. "History of Fiji." Special Collections, University of Santa Cruz-Santa Cruz Library.

*————. In-Letters. 1835–57. Library of the School of Oceanic and Oriental Studies (SOAS), University of London, Box 533.

Meyer, Alfred. "Historical Notes on the Ideological Aspects of the Culture in Germany and Russia." In Alfred L. Kroeber and Clyde Kluckhohn, eds., *Culture: A Critical Review of Concepts and Definitions.* 1952. New York: Vintage, 1963. Pp. 403–13.

Milburn, William. *Oriental Commerce . . .* 2 vols. London: Black, Parry and Co., 1813.

Mintz, Sidney. *Sweetness and Power: The Place of Sugar in Modern History.* New York: Viking Penguin, 1985.

————. *The Power of Sweetness and the Sweetness of Power.* The Eighth Duijker Lecture. Amsterdam: Van Loghum Slaterus, 1988.

————. "The Changing Roles of Food in the Study of Consumption." In John Brewer and Roy Porter, eds., *Consumption and the World of Goods.* London: Routledge, 1993. Pp. 261–73.

Moles, Abraham A. "Notes pour une typologie des événements." *Communications* 18 (1972). Pp. 90–96.

Molino, Jean "L'Evénement: De la logique à la semiologie." In *L'Evénement.* Actes du colloque organisé à Aix-en-Provence par le Centre Méridional d'Histoire Sociale . . . 1983. Aix-en-Provence: Université de Provence, 1986. Pp. 251–70.

Momigliano, Arnold. *Essays in Ancient and Modern Historiography.* Middletown, CT: Wesleyan University Press, 1977.

Moretti, Mauro "Fragments d'une analyse historiographique: Origines et premiers developpements d'un 'discours sur l'événement' dans l'experience des 'Annales.'" In *L'Evénement.* Actes du colloque organisé à Aix-en-Provence par le Centre Méridional d'Histoire Sociale . . . 1983. Aix-en-Provence: Université de Provence, 1986. Pp. 183–202.

Morgan, Theodore. *Hawaii: A Century of Economic Change, 1778–1876.* Cambridge, MA: Harvard University Press, 1948.

Morin, Edgar. "Le Retour de l'événement." *Communications* 18 (1972a). Pp. 6–20.

————. "L'Evénement-sphinx." *Communications* 18 (1972b). Pp. 173–92.

Morison, Samuel Eliot. *The Maritime History of Massachusetts, 1783–1860.* Boston: Houghton Mifflin (Sentry), 1961.

Morse, Hosea Ballou. *The Chronicles of the East India Company Trading to China, 1635–1834.* 4 vols. Taipei: Ch'eng-Wen Publishing Company, 1966.

Murphy, Robert, and Julian Steward. "Tappers and Trappers: Parallel Processes in Acculturation." *Economic and Cultural Change* 4 (1956). Pp. 393–408.

Murray, Archibald Wright. *Missions in Western Polynesia.* London: John Snow, 1862.

Murray, David C., and Herdis L. Deabler. "Colors and Mood-Tones." *Journal of Applied Psychology* 41 (1957). Pp. 279–83.

Needham, Joseph. *Science and Civilisation in China.* Vol. 3. Cambridge, UK: Cambridge University Press, 1959.

————. *Science and Civilisation in China.* Vol. 5. Cambridge, UK: Cambridge University Press, 1971.

Needham, Rodney. "Siriono and Penan: A Test of Some Hypotheses." *Southwestern Journal of Anthropology* 10 (1954). Pp. 228–32.

Nidditch, Peter H. Introduction to *An Essay Concerning Human Understanding,* by John Locke. Oxford, UK: Clarendon, 1975.

Nietzsche, Friedrich. *The Birth of Tragedy and the Genealogy of Morals.* Trans. Francis Golffing. Garden City, NJ: Doubleday Anchor, 1956.

————. *Human, All Too Human: A Book for Free Spirits.* Trans. Marion Faber with Stephen Lehmann. Lincoln: University of Nebraska Press, 1984.

Nihill, Michael. "The New Pearlshells: Aspects of Money and Meaning in Anganen Exchange." *Canberra Anthropology* 12 (1989). Pp. 144–60.

*NLC/EB/L: Native Lands Commission, Evidence Books and Records: Lomaviti. Suva, Fiji.

*NLC/EB/T: Native Lands Commission, Evidence Books and Records: Tailevu, vol. 2. Suva.

*NLC/Final Reports: Native Lands Commission, Final Reports: Tailevu North, Rewa, Naitasiri and Colo East. Suva, Fiji, 1959.

*NLC/TR: Native Lands Commission, Tukutuku Raraba; Tailevu South, Tikini ko Bau: Yavusa Kubuna. Suva, Fiji.

*NLC/TR: Native Lands Commission, Tukutuku Raraba: Tailevu North, Namalato. Suva, Fiji.

*NLC/TR: Native Lands Commission, Tukutuku Raraba: Nairai. Suva, Fiji.

Nora, Pierre. "Le Retour de l'événement." In Jacques Le Goff and Pierre Nora, eds., *Faire de l'histoire*. Vol. 1: *Nouveaux problèmes*. Paris: Gallimard, 1974. Pp. 210–28.

Oliver, Douglas, *A Solomon Islands Society*. Cambridge, MA: Harvard University Press, 1955.

*Osborn, Joseph Warren. "Journal of a Voyage in the Ship *Emerald*... During the Years 1833.4.5 & 6." Pacific Manuscripts Bureau, Research School of Pacific Studies, Australian National University, Canberra, Microfilm 223. Original in Peabody Museum, Salem, MA.

Padgham, C.A., and John E. Saunders. *The Perceptions of Light and Colour*. New York: Academic Press, 1975.

Pagels, Elaine. *Adam, Eve, and the Serpent*. New York: Random House, 1988.

Parkin, David. "Migration, Settlement, and the Politics of Unemployment: A Nairobi Case Study." In David Parkin, ed., *Town and Country in Central and Eastern Africa*. London: Oxford University Press for the International African Institute, 1975. Pp. 145–55.

Parry, John T. *Ring-Ditch Fortifications of the Rewa Delta*. Bulletin of the Fiji Museum, no. 3. Suva, Fiji: Fiji Museum, 1977.

*Pemberton, John. "The Appearance of Order: A Politics of Culture in Colonial and Post-colonial Java." Ph.D. diss., Cornell University, 1989.

Percy, Walker. "Symbol, Consciousness, and Intersubjectivity." *Journal of Philosophy* 55 (1958). Pp. 631–41.

Perrin, Noel. *Giving Up the Gun: Japan's Reversion to the Sword, 1543–1879*. Boston: G.K. Hall, 1979.

Philo of Alexandria. *Philo*. Vol. 1. Loeb Classical Library. Cambridge, MA: Harvard University Press, 1929.

Pico della Mirandola, Giovanni. *Oration on the Dignity of Man*. 1487. Trans. A. Robert Caponigri. Los Angeles: Gateway Editions, 1956.

Pitkin, Timothy. *A Statistical View of the Commerce of the United States of America*. New Haven, CT: Durrie and Peck, 1835.

Poffenberger, A.T., and B. Barrows. "The Feeling Value of Lines." *Journal of Applied Psychology* 8 (1924). Pp. 187–205.

Pokorny, Joel, and Vivienne C. Smith. "Color Vision of Normal Observers." In A.M. Potts, ed., *The Assessment of Visual Function*. St. Louis: Mosby, 1972. Pp. 105–35.

Polanyi, Karl. *The Great Transformation*. New York: Farrar and Rinehart, 1944.

————. "Our Obsolete Market Mentality." *Commentary* 3 (1947). Pp. 109–17.

———. "The Economy as Instituted Process." In K. Polanyi, C. Arensberg, and H. Pearson, eds., *Trade and Market in the Early Empires*. Glencoe, NY: Free Press, 1957. Pp. 243–69.

———. "Anthropology and Economic Theory." In Morton Fried, ed., *Readings in Anthropology*. Vol. 2. New York: Crowell, 1959. Pp. 215–38.

Polanyi, Karl, Conrad Maynardier Arensberg, and Harry W. Pearson, eds. *Trade and Market in the Early Empires*. Glencoe, NY: Free Press, 1957.

Pomian, Krzysztof. "L'Histoire des structures." In Jacques Le Goff, ed., *La Nouvelle histoire*. Paris: Editions Complexe, 1988. Pp. 109–36.

Pope, Alexander. *The Selected Poetry of Pope*. Ed. Martin Price. New York: Signet Classic, New American Library, 1970.

Pospisil, Leopold. *Kapauku Papuans and Their Law*. Yale University Publications in Anthropology 54. New Haven, CT: Yale University Press, 1958.

———. "The Kapauku Papuans and Their Kinship Organization." *Oceania* 30 (1958–59). Pp. 188–205.

Powdermaker, Hortense. *Life in Lesu*. New York: W.W. Norton, 1933.

Powell, H.A. "Competitive Leadership in Trobiand Political Organization." *Journal of the Royal Anthropological Institute* 90 (1960). Pp. 118–45.

Pritchard, Earl Hampton. *Anglo-Chinese Relations During the Seventeenth and Eighteenth Centuries*. University of Illinois Studies in the Social Sciences 17, nos. 1–2, 1929.

———. "Letters from Missionaries at Peking Relating to the Macartney Embassy (1793–1803)." *T'oung Pao* 31 (1935). Pp. 1–57.

———. "The Crucial Years of Early Anglo-Chinese Relations." *Research Studies of the State College of Washington* 4.3–4 (1936). Pp. 95–442.

———. "Instructions of the East India Company to Lord Macartney on His Embassy to China and His Reports to the Company, 1792–94." *Journal of the Royal Asiatic Society for 1938* (1938). Pp. 201–30, 374–96, 493–509.

———. "The Kotow in the Macartney Embassy to China in 1793." *Far Eastern Quarterly* 2 (1943). Pp. 163–201.

Proudfoot, William Jardine. *Biographical Memoir of James Dinwiddie, L.L.D., Astronomer in the British Embassy to China, 1792, '3, '4* ... Liverpool, UK: Edward Howell, 1868.

Prout, E. *Memoir of the Life of the Rev. John Williams*. New York: Allen, Morrill, and Wardwell, 1843.

Provencher, Ronald. "Shifts in the Cycle of Experience: Malay Perceptions of Migration." In David Guillet and Douglas Uzzell, eds., *New Approaches to the*

Study of Migration. Rice University Studies 62.3. Houston: William Marsh, Rice University, 1976. Pp. 63–71.

Purdy, D.McL. "On the Saturations and Chromatic Thresholds of the Spectral Colours." *British Journal of Pyschology* 21 (1930–31). Pp. 283–313.

———. "Spectral Hue as a Function of Intensity." *American Journal of Psychology* 43 (1931). Pp. 541–59.

Quain, Buell. *Fijian Village*. Chicago: University of Chicago Press, 1948.

Quimby, George I. "A Year with a Chippewa Family, 1763–64." *Ethnohistory* 9 (1962). Pp. 217–39.

Quine, Willard Van Orman. *From a Logical Point of View*. 2d ed. New York: Harper and Row, 1963.

Rabuku, Niko. "Ai Sau ni Taro me Kilai." *Na Mata* (1911). Pp. 154–58, 172–76.

Radcliffe-Brown, Alfred Reginald. "The Social Organization of the Australian Tribes." *Oceania* 1 (1930–31). Pp. 34–63, 206–56, 322–41, 426–56.

———. "On Social Structure." *Journal of the Royal Anthropological Institute* 70 (1940).

———. *The Andaman Islanders*. 1922. Glencoe, NY: Free Press, 1948.

———. *Structure and Function in Primitive Society*. London: Cohen and West, 1952.

———. *A Natural Science of Society*. Glencoe, NY: Free Press, 1957.

Rapapport, Roy A. *Pigs for Ancestors*. New Haven, CT: Yale University Press, 1967.

Read, Kenneth E. "Social Organization in the Markham Valley, New Guinea." *Oceania* 17 (1946–47). Pp. 93–118.

———. "The Political System of the Ngarawapum." *Oceania* 20 (1949–50). Pp. 185–223.

———. "The Nama Cult of the Central Highlands, New Guinea." *Oceania* 23 (1952–53). Pp. 1–25.

———. "Leadership and Consensus in a New Guinea Society." *American Anthropologist* 61 (1959). Pp. 425–36.

Reay, Marie. *The Kuma*. Melbourne: Melbourne University Press, 1959.

Redfield, Robert. *The Primitive World and Its Transformation*. Ithaca, NY: Cornell University Press, 1953.

Reid, A.C. *Tovata I and II*. Suva, Fiji: Fiji Museum, 1990.

Repplier, Agnes. *To Think of Tea!* Boston: Houghton Mifflin, 1932.

Richardson, Jane, and Alfred L. Kroeber. "Three Centuries of Women's Dress

———. "Forum on Theory in Anthropology." *Current Anthropology* 38 (1997). Pp. 272–76.

———. "Two or Three Things That I Know About Culture." *Journal of the Anthropological Institute* 5 (1999). Pp. 399–421.

Sahlins, Peter. *Forest Rites*. Cambridge, MA: Harvard University Press, 1994.

Salisbury, Richard Frank. *From Stone to Steel*. Cambridge, UK: Cambridge University Press, 1962.

Salisbury, Richard Frank, and Elisabeth Tooker, eds. *Affluence and Cultural Survival*. 1981 Proceedings of the American Ethnological Society. Washington, DC: American Ethnological Society, 1984.

Samwell, David. "Some Account of a Voyage to the South Seas." In John Cawte Beaglehole, ed., *The Journals of Captain James Cook on His Voyages of Discovery: The Voyage of the "Resolution" and "Discovery," 1776–80*. Part 2. Cambridge, UK: Hakluyt Society, 1967. Pp. 987–1300.

Sargent, Walter. *The Enjoyment and Use of Colors*. New York: Scribners, 1923.

Sartre, Jean-Paul. *Search for a Method*. Trans. Hazel E. Barnes. New York: Vintage, 1968.

Saussure, Ferdinand de. *Course in General Liguisitics*. 1915. Trans. Wade Baskin. New York: Philosophical Library, 1959.

*Sayes, Shelley Ann. "Cakaudrove: Ideology and Reality in a Fijian Confederation." Ph.D. diss., Australian National University, 1982.

———. "The Paths of the Land: Early Political Hierarchies in Cakaudrove, Fiji." *Journal of Pacific History* 19 (1984). Pp. 3–20.

Scarr, Deryck A. "Cakobau and Ma'afu: Contenders for Pre-eminence in Fiji." In J.W. Davidson and Deryck A. Scarr, eds., *Pacific Island Portraits*. Wellington: A.H. and A.W. Reed, 1970. Pp. 95–126.

———. *Fiji: A Short History*. Sydney: George Allen and Unwin, 1984.

Schafer, Edward H. *The Golden Peaches of Samarkand*. Berkeley: University of California Press, 1963.

Schieffelin, Edward L. *The Sorrow of the Lonely and the Burning of the Dancers*. New York: St. Martin's, 1976.

Schmidt, Alfred. *The Concept of Nature in Marx*. Trans. Ben Fowkes. London: NLB, 1971.

Schneider, David M. *American Kinship: A Cultural Account*. Englewood Cliffs, NJ: Prentice Hall, 1968.

———. "What Is Kinship All About?" In P. Reining, ed., *Kinship Studies in the Morgan Centennial Year*. Anthropological Society of Washington, 1972. Pp. 32–63.

Schrempp, Gregory Allen. *Magical Arrows: The Maori, the Greeks, and the Folklore of the Universe*. Madison: University of Wisconsin Press, 1992.

Schumpeter, Joesph A. *History of Economic Analysis*. New York: Oxford University Press, 1954.

Schurmann, Franz, and Orville Edward Schell, eds. *Imperial China*. New York: Vintage, 1967.

*Schwartz, Jack. "Men's Clothing and the Negro." Master's thesis, University of Chicago, 1958.

Seneca, Lucius Annaeus. *Treatises on Providence, on Tranquility, on Shortness of Life, on Happy Life*... Rev. ed. New York: Harper and Bros., 1877.

Service, Elman R. *Primitive Social Organization: An Evolutionary Perspective*. New York: Random House, 1962.

————. *Profiles in Ethnology*. New York: Harper and Row, 1963.

Sewell, William. *Toward a Theory of Structure: Duality, Agency, and Transformation*. Working Paper no. 392. Center for the Comparative Study of Social Transformations at the University of Michigan, 1989.

Sharp, Lauriston. "Ritual Life and Economics of the Yir-Yiront of Cape York Peninsula." *Oceania* 5 (1934–35). Pp. 19–42.

————. "People Without Politics." In V.F. Ray, ed., *Systems of Political Control and Bureaucracy in Human Societies*. American Ethnological Society. Seattle: University of Washington Press, 1958. Pp. 1–8.

Shineberg, Dorothy. *They Came for Sandalwood: A Study of the Sandalwood Trade in the South-West Pacific, 1830–65*. Melbourne: Melbourne University Press, 1967.

————. "Guns and Men in Melanesia." *Journal of Pacific History* 6 (1971). Pp. 61–82.

Simiand, François. "Méthode historique et science sociale: Etude critique d'après les ouvrages récents de M. Lacombe et de M. Seignobos." *Revue de Synthèse Historique* 6 (1903). Pp. 1–22, 129–57.

Simmel, George. "Fashion." *International Quarterly* 10 (1904). Pp. 130–55.

Simmons, W.S. "Culture Theory in Contemporary Ethnohistory." *Ethnohistory* 35 (1988). Pp. 1–14.

Síren, Osvald. *Gardens of China*. New York: Ronald Press, 1949.

Smith, Adam. *The Wealth of Nations*. 1776. New York: Knopf, 1991.

Smyth, R. Brough. *The Aborigines of Victoria*. 2 vols. Melbourne: Government Printer, 1878.

Southall, James P.C. *Introduction to Physiological Optics*. London: Oxford University Press, 1937.

Spate, Oskar Hermann Khristian. *The Spanish Lake*. Minneapolis: University of Minnesota Press, 1979.

Spence, Jonathan D. *Emperor of China: Self-Portrait of K'ang-hsi*. New York: Vintage, 1975.

———. *To Change China: Western Advisors in China, 1620–1960*. Harmondsworth, UK: Penguin, 1980.

Spencer, Sir Baldwin, and Francis James Gillen. *The Native Tribes of Central Australia*. London: Macmillan, 1899.

Spencer, Robert F. *The North Alaskan Eskimo: A Study in Ecology and Society*. Smithsonian Institution Bureau of American Ethnology Bulletin 171. Washington, DC: U. S. Government Printing Office, 1959.

Spengler, Oswald. *The Decline of the West*. Vol. 1. 1918. Trans. Charles Francis Atkinson. New York: Knopf, 1956.

Sperber, Dan. *Rethinking Symbolism*. Cambridge Studies in Social Anthropology. Cambridge, UK: Cambridge University Press, 1975.

Spradley, James P., ed. *Guests Never Leave Hungry: The Autobiography of James Sewid, a Kwakiutl Indian*. New Haven, CT: Yale University Press, 1969.

Starobinski, Jean. *Blessings in Disguise, or, The Morality of Evil*. Trans. Arthur Goldhammer. Cambridge, MA: Harvard University Press, 1993.

Staunton, Sir George. *An Authentic Account of an Embassy from the King of Great Britain to the Emperor of China*. 2 vols. Philadelphia: Campbell, 1799.

Steward, Julian. *Basin-Plateau Aboriginal Sociopolitical Groups*. Smithsonian Institution Bureau of American Ethnology Bulletin 120. Washington: U.S. Government Printing Office, 1938.

Steward, Julian H., and Louis C. Faron. *Native Peoples of South America*. New York: McGraw-Hill, 1959.

Stewart, Charles Samuel. *Journal of a Residence in the Sandwich Islands, During the Years 1823, 1824, and 1825...* 3d ed. London: H. Fisher, Son, and P. Jackson, 1830.

Stocking, George W., Jr. *Race, Culture, and Evolution*. New York: Basic Books, 1968.

———. *The Shaping of American Anthropology, 1883–1911: A Franz Boas Reader*. New York: Basic Books, 1974.

Stoler, Ann. *Capitalism and Confrontation in Sumatra's Plantation Belt, 1870–1979*. New Haven, CT: Yale University Press, 1985.

*Stone, Gregory P. "Clothing and Social Relations: A Study of Appearance in the Context of Community Life." Ph.D. diss., University of Chicago, 1959.

Stone, Lawrence. *The Past and the Present*. Boston: Routledge and Kegan Paul, 1981.

Strathern, Andrew. "Gender, Ideology, and Money in Mount Hagen." *Man* 14 (1979). Pp. 530–48.

Strathern, Marilyn. "Artifacts of History: Events and the Interpretation of Images." In Jukka Siikala, ed., *Culture and History in the Pacific*. Helsinki: Finnish Anthropological Society, 1990. Pp. 25–44.

Suggs, Robert C. *Ancient Civilizations of Polynesia*. New York: Mento, 1960.

Swinhoe, Robert. *Narrative of the North China Campaign of 1860*. London: Smith, Elder and Co., 1861.

Talyaga, Kundapen. *Modern Enga Songs*. Port Moresby: Institute of Papua New Guinea Studies, 1975.

Tambiah, Stanley Jeyaraja. "Animals Are Good to Think and Good to Prohibit." *Ethnology* 8 (1969). Pp. 423–59.

———. *Magic, Science, Religion, and the Scope of Rationality*. Cambridge, UK: Cambridge University Press, 1990.

Tatawaqa, Emosi. "Ai Tukutuku kei Charlie Savage mai na gauna ka voca kina na Josephine [*sic*] e na Cakau ko Mocea mai Nairai 1809 [*sic*] ka Yacova na Nona Mate." *Na Mata* (1913).

Taussig, Michael. *Shamanism, Colonialism, and the Wild Man*. Chicago: University of Chicago Press, 1987.

Teggart, Frederick John. *Theory and Processes of History*. Berkeley: University of California Press, 1960.

Thistle, Paul Clifford. *Indian-European Trade Relations in the Lower Saskatchewan River Region to 1840*. Manitoba Studies in Native History, no. 11. Winnipeg: University of Manitoba Press, 1986.

Thomas, Nicholas. *Entangled Objects: Exchange, Material Culture, and Colonialism in the Pacific*. Cambridge, MA: Harvard University Press, 1991.

———. "Substantivization and Anthropological Discourse." In James G. Courier, ed., *History and Tradition in Melanesian Anthropology*. Berkeley: University of California Press, 1992a. Pp. 64–85.

———. "The Inversion of Tradition." *American Ethnologist* 19 (1992b). Pp. 213–32.

Thomson, Sir Basil H. *The Diversions of a Prime Minister*. Edinburgh and London: William Blackwood and Sons, 1894a.

———. *South Sea Yarns*. London: 1894b.

———. *The Fijians: A Study of the Decay of Custom*. London: William Heinemann, 1908.

Thomson, Donald F. *Economic Structure and the Ceremonial Exchange Cycle in Arnhem Land*. Melbourne: Macmillan, 1949a.

———. "Arnhem Land: Explorations Among an Unknown People." *Geographical Journal* 113 (1949b). Pp. 1–8, 114, 54–67.

Tippett. Alan Richard. *Fijian Material Culture*. Bernice P. Bishop Museum Bulletin 232. Honolulu, 1968.

———. *Aspects of Pacific Ethnohistory*. Pasadena, CA: William Carey Library, 1973.

*Toganivalu, Ratu Deve. "Ai Tukuluku kei Bau" (A history of Bau), manuscript, National Archives at Fiji (F 62/247).

———. "The Customs of Bau before the Advent of Christianity." *Transactions of the Fijian Society for the Year 1911* (1912).

*Touré, Abdou. "Minority Culture, Majority Development." Manuscript of paper prepared for the World Commission on Culture and Development. UNESCO, CCD-IV/94/REG/INF.11. Paris, 3 June 1994.

Townsend, Ebenezer, Jr. "The Diary of Mr. Ebenezer Townsend, Jr." *Papers of the New Haven Colony Historical Society* 4 (1888). Pp. 1–115.

Trager, Lillian. *The City Connection: Migration and Family Interdependence in the Philippines*. Ann Arbor: University of Michigan Press, 1988.

Trigger, Bruce G. "Brecht and Ethnohistory." *Ethnohistory* 22 (1975). Pp. 12–25.

———. "The Road to Affluence: A Reassessment of Early Huron Response to European Contact." In Richard Frank Salisbury and E. Tooker, eds., *Affluence and Cultural Survival*. Washington, DC: American Ethnological Society, 1984. Pp. 12–25.

Trubetskoy, Prince Nikolaj Sergejevic. *Principles of Phonology*. 1939. Trans. C.A.M. Baltaxe. Los Angeles: University of California Press, 1968.

Turnbull, Colin. *Wayward Servants*. Garden City, NY: Natural History Press, 1965.

Turner, George. *Nineteen Years in Polynesia*. London: Snow, 1861.

Turner, Terence. "Representing, Resisting, Rethinking: Historical Transformations of Kayapo Culture and Anthropological Consciousness." In George W. Stocking, Jr., ed., *Colonial Situations*. Madison: University of Wisconsin Press, 1991. Pp. 285–313.

Turner, Victor. *The Forest of Symbols*. Ithaca, NY: Cornell University Press, 1967.

*Turpin. Edwin J. Diary and Narratives of Edward J. Turpin. National Archives of Fiji, MS 1.

Twain, Mark. "Extracts from Adam's Diary." In Mark Twain, *The Man That Corrupted Hadleyburg and Other Essays and Stories*. New York: Harper and Brothers, Hillcrest ed., 1904. Pp. 260–75.

———. "The Sandwich Islands." In *The Complete Essays of Mark Twain*. Ed. Charles Neider. Garden City, NY: Doubleday, 1963. Pp. 14–27.

Tylor, E.B. *Primitive Culture*. 1870. 2 vols. 4th ed. London: John Murray, 1903.

Ukers, William Harrison. *All About Tea*. 2 vols. New York: Tea and Coffee Trade Journal Co., 1935.

Uzzell, Douglas. "Conceptual Fallacies in the Rural-Urban Dichotomy." *Urban Anthrpology* 8 (1979). Pp. 333–50.

Valeri, Renee. "Study of Traditional Food Supply in the Southwest of France." *Ethnologia Scandinavica* (1971). Pp. 86–95.

Valeri, Valerio. "Le Fonctionnement du système des rangs à Hawai'i." *L'Homme* 12 (1972). Pp. 29–66.

———. "Pouvoir des dieux, rire des hommes." *Anthropologie et Société* 5.3 (1981). Pp. 11–34.

———. *Kingship and Sacrifice: Ritual and Society in Ancient Hawaii*. Trans. Paula Wissing. Chicago: University of Chicago Press, 1985.

———. "Diarchy and History in Hawaii and Tonga." In Jukka Siikala, ed., *Culture and History in the Pacific*. Transactions 27. Helsinki: Finnish Anthropological Society, 1990. Pp. 45–79.

Valla, Lorenzo. *On Pleasure*. Trans. A. Kent Hieatt and Maristella Lorch. New York: Abaris Books, 1977.

Vancouver, Capt. Goerge. *A Voyage of Discovery in the North Pacific Ocean . . . in the Years 1790, 1791, 1792, 1793, 1794, and 1795*. Vol. 3. 5 vols. London: Stockdale, 1801.

van der Post, Laurens. *The Lost World of the Kalahari*. New York: Morrow, 1958.

*Van Deusen, Neil C. "Telesio: The First of the Moderns." Ph.D. diss., Columbia University, 1932.

Vayda, Andrew Peter. "Polynesian Cultural Distributions in New Perspective." *American Anthropologist* 61 (1959). Pp. 817–28.

Veblen, Thorstein. *The Theory of the Leisure Class*. 1899. New York: Modern Library, 1934.

*"Veitarogi ni Qoliqoli. Inquiry into Fishing Rights in Viti Levu, 1947." Suva, Fiji: Native Lands Commission, 1947.

Verdery, Katherine. "'Caritas' and the Reconceptualization of Money in Roumania." *Anthropology Today* 11 (1995). Pp. 3–7.

Veyne, Paul. *Writing History*. Trans. Mina Moore-Rinvolucri. Middletown, CT: Wesleyan University Press, 1984.

Vico, Giambattista. *The New Science of Giambattista Vico*. Trans. and ed. Thomas Goddard Bergin and Max Harold Fisch. Ithaca, NY: Cornell University Press, 1984.

Von Hügel, Anatole, Baron. *The Fiji Journals of Baron Anatole Von Hügel, 1875–77*. Eds. Jane Roth and Steven Hooper. Suva, Fiji: Fiji Museum, 1990.

Vovelle, Michel. "L'Histoire et la longue durée." In Jacques Le Goff, ed., *La Nouvelle histoire*. Paris: Editions Complexe, 1988. Pp. 77–108.

*Wainiu Etuate. Wainiu Papers, Tippett Collection. St. Marks College, Canberra. (J2⅓)

Wakeman, Frederic, Jr. "High Ch'ing: 1683–1839." In J.B. Crowley, ed., *Modern East Asia*. New York: Harcourt, Brace and World, 1970. Pp. 1–28.

Walens, Stanley. *Feasting with Cannibals*. Princeton, NJ: Princeton University Press, 1981.

Walker, Richard Louis. *China and the West: Cultural Collision*. Sinological Series, no. 5. New Haven, CT: Far Eastern Publications, Yale University, 1956.

Wall, Colman. "Beachcombing." *Transactions of the Fijian Society* (1911).

———. "Sketches in Fijian History." *Transactions of the Fijian Society* (1919).

Wallerstein, Immanuel. *The Modern World System*. 2 vols. New York: Academic Press, 1974/1980.

———. *Historical Capitalism*. Thetford, Norfolk: Thetford Press, 1983.

Wallis, Mary D. *Life in Feejee . . . or . . . Five Years Among the Cannibals (by a Lady)*. Suva: Fiji Museum; facsimile of 1851 ed. Boston: William Heath, 1983.

Walters, Michael A.H.B. "A $40,000 Question, or: Some Remarks on the Veracity of Certain Ancient Mariners, Beachcombers, and Castaways." *Journal of the Polynesian Society* 83 (1974). Pp. 58–83.

Wang, G.-W. "Early Ming Relations with Southeast Asia: A Background Essay." In J.K. Fairbank, ed., *The Chinese World Order*. Cambridge, MA: Harvard University Press, 1968. Pp. 34–62.

Ward, Ralph Gerard. "The Pacific Bêche-de-mer Trade with Special Reference to Fiji." In Ralph Gerard Ward, ed., *Man in the Pacific Islands*. Oxford: Clarendon, 1972. Pp. 91–123.

Warner, W. Lloyd. *A Black Civilization*. 1937. New York: Harper and Row, 1964.

Warren, Kay B. "Transforming Memories and Histories: The Meanings of Ethnic Resurgence for Mayan Indians." In Alfred C. Stepan, ed., *Americas: New Interpretive Essays*. New York: Oxford University Press, 1992. Pp. 89–219.

Watanabe, H. "An Index of the Embassies and Tribute Missions from Islamic Countries to Ming China (1368–1466) as Recorded in the *Ming Shih-lu* Classified According to Geographic Area." *Memoirs of the Research Department of the Tajo Bunko* 33 (1975). Pp. 285–374.

Watanabe, John M. "Unimagining the Maya: Anthropologists, Others, and the Inescapable Hubris of Authorship." *Bulletin of Latin American Research* 14 (1995). Pp. 25–45.

Waterhouse, Joseph. *The King and People of Fiji.* Facsimile of the original 1866 ed. London: Wesleyan Conference/AMS Press, 1978.

Watsford, John. *Glorious Gospel Triumphs as Seen in My Life and Work in Fiji and Australasia.* London: C.H. Kelly, 1900.

Watson, Burton, ed. and trans. *Records of the Grand Historian of China* [Ssu-ma Ch'ien]. 2 vols. New York: Columbia University Press, 1961.

Weber, Max. *The Protestant Ethic and the Spirit of Capitalism.* Trans. Talcott Parsons. Foreword by R.H. Tawney. New York: Scribner, 1930.

Wedgwood, Camilla H. "Report on Research in Manam Island, Mandated Territory of New Guinea." *Oceania* 4 (1933–34). Pp. 373–403.

———. "Manam Kinship." *Oceania* 29 (1958–59). Pp. 239–56.

Wexner, Lois B. "The Degree to Which Colors (Hues) Are Associated with Mood-Tones." *Journal of Applied Psychology* 38 (1954). Pp. 432–35.

White, Leslie A. *The Science of Culture.* New York: Farrar, Straus, 1949.

———. *The Evolution of Culture.* New York: McGraw-Hill, 1959.

Whitman, John B. *An Account of the Sandwich Islands: The Hawaiian Journal of John B. Whitman, 1813–35.* Ed. John Dominis Holt. Honolulu and Salem, MA: Topgallant and Peabody Museum of Salem, 1979.

Wilkes, Charles. *Atlas. Narrative of the United States Exploring Expedition During the Years 1838, 1839, 1840, 1841, 1842.* Philadelphia: C. Sherman, 1844.

———. *Narrative of the United States Exploring Expedition During the Years 1838, 1839, 1840, 1841, and 1842.* 5 vols. Philadelphia: Lea and Blanchard, 1845.

Williams, Francis Edgar. *Orokaiva Society.* London: Oxford University Press, Humphrey Milford, 1930.

———. *Drama of Orokolo.* Oxford, UK: Clarendon, 1940.

Williams, Raymond. *Keywords.* New York: Oxford University Press, 1983.

Williams, Thomas. *The Journal of Thomas Williams, Missionary in Fiji, 1840–1853.* Ed. G.C. Henderson. 2 vols. Sydney: Angus, Robertson, 1931.

Williams, Thomas, and James Calvert. *Fiji and the Fijians.* 2 vols. New York: Appleton, 1859.

Williamson, Robert W. *The Mafulu: Mountain People of British New Guinea*. London: Macmillan, 1912.

Wills, John E., Jr. "Maritime China from Wang Chih to Shih Lang: Themes in Peripheral History." In Jonathan D. Spence and John E. Wills, Jr., eds., *From Ming to Ch'ing*. New Haven, CT: Yale University Press, 1979. Pp. 204–38.

Wittgenstein, Ludwig. *Philosophical Investigations*. 3d ed. Trans. G.E.M. Anscombe. New York: Macmillan, 1973.

Wolf, Eric R. *Europe and the People Without History*. Berkeley: University of California Press, 1982.

Woodburn, James, director. *The Hadza*. 1966. (Film available from the anthropological director, Department of Anthropology, London School of Economics.)

Woodburn, James. "An Introduction to Hadza Ecology." In Richard Lee and Irven DeVore, eds., *Man the Hunter*. Chicago: Aldine, 1968. Pp. 49–55.

Worsley, Peter M. *The Trumpet Shall Sound*. London: Macgibbon and Kee, 1957.
———. "The Utilization of Food Resources by an Australian Aboriginal Tribe." *Acta Ethnographica* 10 (1961). Pp. 153–90.

Worth, Henry J. "Voyage of H.M.S. 'Calypso,' Captain Worth, to the Pacific," *Nautical Magazine and Naval Chronicle* 22 (1853). Pp. 361–67.

Yang, H.-Y., and G. Yang, eds. *Records of the Historian, Written by Szuma Chien*. Trans. Yang Hsien-yi and Gladys Young. Hong Kong: Commercial Press, 1974.

Yang, L.-S. "Historical Notes on the Chinese World Order." In John King Fairbank, ed., *The Chinese World Order*. Cambridge, MA: Harvard University Press, 1968. Pp. 20–33.

Young, Robert J.C. *Colonial Desire: Hybridity in Theory, Culture, and Race*. London: Routledge, 1995.

Zito, A.R. "Re-presenting Sacrifice: Cosmology and the Editing of Texts." *Ch'ing-shi Wen-ti* 5.2 (1984). Pp. 47–78

Index

Aquinas, St. Thomas: and utilitarianism, 572n.12.

Affluence, 95–96, 128; among Aboriginals, 101–102, 118–23; among Bushmen, 103–104; among Fijians, 349nn.21, 22; among Hadza, 121–22; among Hawaiians, 444–47 and n.40. *See also* Materialism; Prodigality; Scarcity; Subsistence.

Africa: culture as project, 525–26. *See also* Asia; China; Culture; Fiji; World System theory.

African Americans: dress habits, 180. *See also* Racism.

Agriculture: grain, 168; primitive, 129–30; and progress, 132; rejected in favor of hunting, 122–23 and n.20. *See also* Hunter/gatherers.

American-Australian Scientific Expedition to Arnhem Land (1948), 109ff.; data compared with studies of !Kung Bushmen, 116.

Animals: in Eskimo culture, 518; humans compared with (Marx), 13, 32n.5, 537n.15, 543–45, 546 and n.24; in Kwakiutl culture, 450–51; naming of, 529. *See also* Cattle; Food; Horses; Meat; Pigs; *other individual categories.*

Annales historians, 294, 295, 296, 297. *See also* History.

Anthropology: Bernard Cohn on, 471; and biology (of human needs), 538–47, 551; contamination of, 214, 268, 416; and culture, 12, 505–507; defined, 29, 30–31, 268, 354–55, 527–28; and history, 28, 293–351, 353, 361–63, 406–407n.6, 418, 499; Marx as originator of, 167, 524; material vs. symbolic within (1960s), 17; methods of, 278, 527–28; native, 527–83; of need, 531–35; of power, 547–54; of Providence, 554–62; relation to Third World, 263. *See also* Culture; Ethnocentrism; Ethnography; Ethnohistory; Ethnology; History; Language; Society; Structuralism; *individual place-names and peoples.*

Apes: human evolution from, 51–52, 56, 58–59, 60–61, 62. *See also* Animals; Human being.

Ardrey, Robert, 35–36, 43–44; parodied, 43–70.

Aron, Raymond: on Hobbes/Durkheim, 551–52.

Art, 579n.39, 580n.41; nature as (Pope), 555; perspective(s), 537. *See also* Color; Culture.

Asia: as curer of societies, 455–56 and n.55. *See also* China; Trade.

Attiret, le Père: description of Yuan

sanction of, 395; George Duby on, 344–45; (Fijian) theory of, 329–36; Union Jack as emblem of (Tahiti), 405.

Spencer, Herbert: on society, 535.

Status (social): related to eating habits, 173–74; — clothing, 177.

Steffens, Lincoln, 55.

Storehouse, psychology of (Malo), 83–84.

Strathern, Marilyn, 489.

Structuralism: applied toward Bau (Fiji), 380–99; — clothing fabric, 199n.14; — Fijian "schismogenesis," 340–41 and fig. 11.4; — gardens in China, 433–34; — history, 293–351; — money and worldview, 519; — U.S. eating habits, 172 and n.7, 173; — U.S. naming habits, 196–97n.6; Augustine and, 579n.39; confrontation between structures, 272–73 and n.1, 336, 340–41 and fig. 11.4, 341–42, 343–44; force vs. lineage (Fijian), 373–80, 391–92, 394–95, 399, 400; inner-outer separation (of Chinese emperor), 435–36 and n.30 and figs. 13.2, 13.3; intercultural chiasmus, 486–87; marked/unmarked clothing indicators, 183–85 and fig. 5.3 and n.19; movement of structures, 494; politics of culture and, 494–95; in scholarship, 17–19 and n.6, 22; of sign within systems, 285–91; "system" vs. "event," 298–301; technology and, 517; and Vietnam War, 24; L. White's "cultural layer cake," 515–17. See also Anthropology; "Anti-symmetry"; Culture; History; Language; Lévi-Strauss, Claude; Nature; Saussure, Ferdinand de.

Subsistence: among hunter/gatherers, 108–27, 508–10; threat of diminishing returns, 128–29. See also

Affluence; Economics; Scarcity.

Supply-demand-price, 168.

Suva (Fiji), 497; destruction of, 312–15; genealogy of rulers, fig. 11.2; location of, 338–39 and map 11.2; pig (war catalyst,1841), 308, 312, 314, 321, 324, 326, 332, 333, 338, 340, 342; war casualties, 314–15. See also Fiji; Ratu Qara.

Symbolic discourse, 31n.3, 281–85, 299, 342–43, 361, 379, 484–85, 546–47; and art (Robertson), 579n.39; Chinese garden as universe, 432–33 and n.29; and technology (L. White), 13–14; and translocal community village, 521–24. See also Binary coding; Culture; Language.

Synthesis: "of the heterogeneous," 304, 327; religious, 559–60; Ricoeur on, 303; between structure and event, 26, 295–304, 342, 483; of translocal cultural order, 522–24; of "triple libido" (Augustine), 572n.8. See also Culture; Hegel; Marx, Karl; Structuralism.

Tabu: exemption from, 391, 394; in Fiji, 497; in Hawaii, 289–90, 480, 482; among Kwakiutl, 467n.45; in Polynesia, 83; in United States (food-related), 169, 279; *Vasu*, 333. See also Incest; Ritual.

Taylor, E. B., 504.

Taylor, General Maxwell, 221.

Tea: British addiction to, 274, 420, 424 (history of) and n.15, 455–56 and nn. 53, 55. See also British, the; Trade.

Teach-in: as protest form, 23–24. See also National Teach-In; Vietnam War.

Technology: basis of modern society, 515–17; technological determinism (L. White), 11, 515. See also Science.

British, the; Capitalism; Culture;
Economics. History; Men; Trade;
Women.
White, Leslie A., 11, 12, 13–14; conflicts in 1960s, 17; on individual in
culture, 15–16, 23, 280; on
neolithic vs. paleolithic, 100; on
technological determinism, 11,
515.
Williams, Reverend John: martyrdom
of, 415–16 and nn.1, 2.
Williams, Thomas, 374.
Witchcraft: in Azande culture,
299–300.
Wittgenstein, Ludwig: on ostension,
149.
Wolf, Eric: ethnocentric view of
White presence in Pacific, 416–17;
on rise of Bau, 359 and n.6.
Women: clothing and fabric preferences, 179–80 and n.14; — upper-
class, 200n.16; control of, by
(Fijian) chiefs, 329–30; as gifts,
336–38; seduction of as usurpation (Fiji), 318, 330–31, 384,
412n.30, 441–42; in society, 50.
See also Gender; Marriage; Men;
Sexuality.
World System theory, 416–21 and
n.6, 473, 477, 481, 484–85,
490–91, 506–507, 512–14, 555–56
and n.36; Chinese and, 435–38 and
figs. 13.2, 13.3; passage of, 525;
question of circular migration,
521–24. *See also* Capitalism;
Colonialism; Culture; Economics;
History.

Yuan Ming Yuan (Chinese
Versailles), 432, 433–35 and
fig. 13.1 and n.31, 463n.26.